The International Survey of Family Law

2011 Edition

Published on behalf of the International
Society of Family Law

The International Survey of Family Law

2011 Edition

General Editor
Bill Atkin
Faculty of Law
Victoria University of Wellington
PO Box 600
Wellington
New Zealand

Associate Editor (Africa)
Fareda Banda
Reader in the Laws of Africa
School of Oriental and African Studies
London

Family Law

Published by Family Law
a publishing imprint of
Jordan Publishing Limited
21 St Thomas Street
Bristol BS1 6JS

British Library Cataloguing-in-Publication Data

A catalogue record for this book is available from the British Library.

ISBN 978 1 84661 284 8

Typeset by Letterpart Ltd, Reigate, Surrey

Printed in Great Britain by CPI Antony Rowe, Chippenham, Wiltshire

MEMBERS OF THE INTERNATIONAL SOCIETY OF FAMILY LAW

ASSOCIATION INTERNATIONALE DE DROIT DE LA FAMILLE

INTERNATIONALE GESELLSCHAFT FÜR FAMILIENRECHT

Website: www.law2.byu.edu/ISFL

Officers and Council Members 2008–2011

PRESIDENT
Professor Bea Verschraegen
Universität Wien
Institut für Rechtsvergleichung Juridicum
Schottenbastei 10–16
A-1010 Wien
AUSTRIA
Tel: +43 1 4277 3510
Fax: +43 1 4277 9351
E-mail: bea.verschraegen@univie.ac.at

EDITOR OF THE INTERNATIONAL SURVEY
Professor Bill Atkin
Faculty of Law
Victoria University of Wellington
PO Box 600
Wellington, 6140
NEW ZEALAND
Tel: +64 4 463 6343
Fax: +64 4 463 6366
E-mail: bill.atkin@vuw.ac.nz

TREASURER
Professor Adriaan van der Linden
Beetslaan 2
3818 VH Aersfoort
THE NETHERLANDS
Tel: +31 33 461 90 97
Fax: +31 33 465 94 29
E-mail: a.vanderlinden@law.uu.nl

SECRETARY-GENERAL
Professor Marsha Garrison
Brooklyn Law School
250 Joralemon Street
Brooklyn, NY 11201
USA
Tel: +1 718 780 7947
Fax: +1 718 780 0375
E-mail: marsha.garrison@brooklaw.edu

EDITOR OF THE NEWSLETTER
Professor Margaret F Brinig
Associate Dean for Faculty Development & Fritz Duda Family Chair in Law
Notre Dame Law School
Notre Dame, IN 46556
USA
Tel: +1 574 631 2303
Fax: +1 574 631 8078
E-mail: mbrinig@nd.edu

Immediate past president

Professor Paul Vlaardingerbroek
Faculty of Law
Tilburg University
PO Box 90153
5000 LE Tilburg
THE NETHERLANDS
Tel: +31 13 466 2032/2281
Fax: +31 13 466 2323
E-mail: p.vlaardingerbroek@uvt.nl

Vice-presidents

Professor Olga Dyuzheva
Law Faculty
Moscow State University
Leninskie Gory
119991 Moscow
RUSSIA
Tel: +7 95 690 1697
Fax: +7 95 939 5195
E-mail: odyuzheva@mtu-net.ru

Professor Dominique Goubau
Faculté de droit de l'Université Laval
Pavillon De Koninck
1030, av des Sciences-Humaines
Québec (Québec)
CANADA
G1V 0A6
Tel: +1 418 656 2131 (poste 2384)
Fax: +1 418 656 7230
E-mail: Dominique.goubau@fd.ulaval.ca

Professor Satoshi Minimakata
Faculty of Law
Niigata University
8050 Ikarashi-ninocho
Nishi-ku
Niigata
JAPAN 950-2181
Tel/Fax: +81 25 262 6478
E-mail: satoshi@jura.niigata-u.ac.jp

Professor Hugues Fulchiron
Faculté de Droit
Université Jean Moulin
Lyon 3, 15 quai Claude-Bernard
F-69007 Lyon
FRANCE
Tel: +33 4 72 41 05 54
Fax: +33 4 78 78 71 31
E-mail: hugues.fulchiron@online.fr

Professor Giselle Groeninga de Almeida
Rua das Jaboticabeiras
420 Cida de Jardim
Sao Paolo – SP 05674-010
BRAZIL
E-mail: giselle@att.net

Professor June D Sinclair
Special Adviser to the Rectorate
University of Pretoria
Lynnwood Road
Pretoria 0002
SOUTH AFRICA
Tel: +27 11 883 2969
Fax: +27 82 900 869
E-mail: june.sinclair@up.ac.za

Executive council

Professor Penelope Agallopoulou
University of Piraeus
4 Kyprou Str
154 52 P Psychico
Athens
GREECE
Tel/Fax: +30 210 67 75 404
E-mail: agal@otenet.gr

Professor Dr MV Antokolskaia
Vrije Universiteit
Faculty of Law
De Boelelaan 1105
1081 HV Amsterdam
THE NETHERLANDS
Tel: +31 20 5986294
Fax: +31 20 5986280
E-mail: m.v.antokolskaia@rechten.vu.nl

Associate Professor Datin Noor Aziah Mohd Awal
Faculty of Law
Universiti Kebangsaan Malaysia
43600 Bangi
Selangor
MALAYSIA
Tel: +60 603 8921 5921
Fax: +60 603 8921 5117

The Rt Hon the Baroness Ruth Deech
St. Anne's College
Oxford OX2 6HS
UK
Tel: +44 207 219 3000
Fax: +44 186 579 3405
E-mail: ruth.deech@st-annes.ox.ac.uk

Professor Sanford N Katz
Boston College Law School
885 Centre Street
Newton Centre, Mass 02459
USA
Tel: 1-617-552-437
Fax: 1-617-552-2615
E-mail: sanford.katz@bc.edu

Professor Whasook Lee
Yonsei University College of Law
262 Seongsanno, Seodaemun-gu
Seoul 120-749
KOREA
Tel: +82 2 2123 6002
Fax: +82 2 2313 0822
E-mail:lws@yonsei.ac.kr

Professor Dr Miquel Martin-Casals
Facultat de Dret
Universitat de Girona
Campus de Montilivi 17071
Girona
SPAIN
Tel: +34 972 41 81 39
Fax: +34 972 41 81 46
E-mail: martin@elaw.udg.edu

Professor David Bradley
Law Department
London School of Economics and Political Science
Houghton Street
London WC2A 2AE
UK
Tel: +44 207 955 7239
E-mail: d.bradley@lse.ac.uk

Professor Dr Nina Dethloff, LLM
Institut für Deutsches, Europäisches und Internationales Familienrecht
Universität Bonn
Adenauerallee 8a
D 53113 Bonn
GERMANY
Tel: +49 228 739290
Fax: +49 228 733909
E-mail: dethloff@uni-bonn.de

Professor Olga A Khazova
Institute of State and Law
Russian Academy of Sciences
Znamenka Str 10
119992 Moscow
RUSSIA
Tel: +7 495 691 1709
Fax: +7 495 691 8574
E-mail: oak25@mail.ru

Professor Nigel Lowe
Cardiff Law School
University of Wales
PO Box 427
Cardiff CF10 3XJ
UK
Tel: +44 029 208 74365
Fax: +44 029 208 74097
E-mail: lowe@cardiff.ac.uk

Professor Marie-Therese Meulders
29, Chaussee de la verte voie
1300 Wavre
BELGIUM
Tel: +32 10 24 78 92
Fax: +32 10 22 91 60
E-mail: meulders@cfap.ucl.ac.be

Professor Linda Nielsen
Copenhagen University
Faculty of Law
Studiegården, Studiestræde 6
1455 Copenhagen K
DENMARK
Tel: +45 35 32 31 23
Fax: +45 35 32 32 06
E-mail: Linda.Nielsen@jur.ku.dk

Professor Patrick Parkinson
Faculty of Law
University of Sydney
SYDNEY 2006
AUSTRALIA
Tel: +61 2 9351 0309
Fax: +61 2 9351 0200
E-mail: patrickp@law.usyd.edu.au

Professor Anna Singer
Uppsala University
Faculty of Law
PO Box 512
SE-751 20 Uppsala
SWEDEN
Tel: +46 18 471 20 35
Fax: +46 18 15 27 14
E-mail: anna.singer@jur.uu.se

Professor Hazel Thompson-Ahye
Eugene Dupuch Law School
Farrington Road
PO Box SS-6394
Nassau, NP
THE BAHAMAS
Tel: +242 326 8507/8
Fax: +242 326 8504
E-mail: thomahye2000@yahoo.com

Professor Barbara Bennett Woodhouse
LQC Lamar Chair in Law
Co-Director of the Barton Child Law and
Policy Clinic
Emory University
Gambrell Hall
1301 Clifton Road
Atlanta, Georgia 30322
USA
Tel: +1 404 727 4934
Fax: +1 404 727 6820
E-mail: barbara.woodhouse@emory.edu

Professor Avv Maria Donata Panforti
Dipartimento di Scienze del linguaggio e
della cultura
Largo Sant'Eufemia 19
I-41100 Modena
ITALY
Tel: +39 059 205 5916
Fax: +39 059 205 5933
E-mail: panforti.mariadonata@unimore.it

Professor JA Robinson
Faculty of Law
Potchefstroom Campus of the North West
University
North West University
Potchefstroom 2520
SOUTH AFRICA
Tel: +27 18 299 1940
Fax: +27 18 299 1933
E-mail: robbie.robinson@nwu.ac.za

Professor dr juris Tone Sverdrup
Department of Private Law
Faculty of Law, University of Oslo
PO Box 6706 St Olavs plass
NO-0130 Oslo
NORWAY
Tel: +47 228 59781
Fax: +47 228 59620
E-mail: tone.sverdrup@jus.uio.no

Professor Lynn D Wardle
Bruce C Hafen Professor of Law
518 J Reuben Clark Law School
Brigham Young University
Provo, UT 84602
USA
Tel: +1 801 422 2617
Fax: +1 801 422 0391
E-mail: Wardlel@law.byu.edu

Professor Xia Yinlan
Dean of School of International Studies
China University of Political Science &
Law
No 25 Xitucheng Road
Beijing
PR CHINA 100088
Tel: +86 10 82650072
Fax: +86 10 82650072
E-mail: yinlan112@sina.com

HISTORY OF THE INTERNATIONAL SOCIETY OF FAMILY LAW

A THE HISTORY OF THE SOCIETY

On the initiative of Professor Zeev Falk, the Society was launched at the University of Birmingham, UK, in April 1973. The Society's first international conference was held in West Berlin in April 1975 on the theme *The Child and the Law*. There were over 200 participants, including representatives of governments and international organisations. The second international conference was held in Montreal in June 1977 on the subject *Violence in the Family*. There were over 300 participants from over 20 countries. A third world conference on the theme *Family Living in a Changing Society* was held in Uppsala, Sweden in June 1979. There were over 270 participants from 26 countries. The fourth world conference was held in June 1982 at Harvard Law School, USA. There were over 180 participants from 23 countries. The fifth world conference was held in July 1985 in Brussels, Belgium on the theme *The Family, The State and Individual Security*, under the patronage of Her Majesty Queen Fabiola of Belgium, the Director-General of UNESCO, the Secretary-General of the Council of Europe and the President of the Commission of the European Communities. The sixth world conference on *Issues of the Ageing in Modern Society* was held in 1988 in Tokyo, Japan, under the patronage of HIH Takahito Mikasa. There were over 450 participants. The seventh world conference was held in May 1991 in Croatia on the theme, *Parenthood: The Legal Significance of Motherhood and Fatherhood in a Changing Society*. There were 187 participants from 37 countries. The eighth world conference took place in Cardiff, Wales in June/July 1994 on the theme *Families Across Frontiers*. The ninth world conference of the Society was held in July 1997 in Durban, South Africa on the theme *Changing Family Forms: World Themes and African Issues*. The Society's tenth world conference was held in July 2000 in Queensland, Australia on the theme *Family Law: Processes, Practices and Pressures*. The eleventh world conference was held in August 2002 in Copenhagen and Oslo on the theme *Family Life and Human Rights*. The Society's twelfth world conference was held in Salt Lake City, Utah in July 2005 on the theme *Family Law: Balancing Interests and Pursuing Priorities*. The Society's thirteenth world conference was held in Vienna in September 2008. The Society has also increasingly held regional conferences including those in Lyon, France (1995); Quebec City, Canada (1996); Seoul, South Korea (1996); Prague, Czech Republic (1998); Albuquerque, New Mexico, USA (June 1999); Oxford, UK (August 1999); and Kingston, Ontario (2001). In 2003, regional conferences took place in Oregon, USA; Tossa de

Mar, Spain; and Lyon, France and, in July 2004, in Beijing, China, on the theme *Divorce and its Consequences*. In 2005, a regional conference took place in Amsterdam (the Netherlands) and dealt with the centennial anniversary of the establishment of legislation on child protection and the juvenile courts. In 2007 there were regional conferences in Chester (England), entitled *Family Justice: For Whom and How?* and Vancouver (Canada), entitled *Making Family Law: Facts, Values and Practicalities*. In 2009 there were conferences in Tel Aviv (Israel), Porto (Portugal) and Sao Paolo (Brazil), and in 2010 Kansas City (USA), Tsukuba University (Japan), the University of Ulster (Northern Ireland) and the Caribbean. A World Conference takes place in Lyon (France) in July 2011.

B   ITS NATURE AND OBJECTIVES

The following principles were adopted at the first Annual General Meeting of the Society held in the Kongresshalle of West Berlin on the afternoon of Saturday 12 April 1975.

(1)   The Society's objectives are the study and discussion of problems of family law. To this end the Society sponsors and promotes:

    (a)   International co-operation in research on family law subjects of world-wide interest.

    (b)   Periodic international conferences on family law subjects of world-wide interest.

    (c)   Collection and dissemination of information in the field of family law by the publication of a survey concerning developments in family law throughout the world, and by publication of relevant materials in family law, including papers presented at conferences of the Society.

    (d)   Co-operation with other international, regional or national associations having the same or similar objectives.

    (e)   Interdisciplinary contact and research.

    (f)   The advancement of legal education in family law by all practical means including furtherance of exchanges of teachers, students, judges and practising lawyers.

    (g)   Other objectives in furtherance of or connected with the above objectives.

C   MEMBERSHIP AND DUES

In 2010, the Society had approximately 630 members.

(a)   Membership:

- Ordinary Membership, which is open to any member of the legal or a related profession. The Council may defer or decline any application for membership.

- Institutional Membership, which is open to interested organisations at the discretion of, and on terms approved by, the Council.

- Student Membership, which is open to interested students of law and related disciplines at the discretion of, and on terms approved by, the Council.

- Honorary Membership, which may be offered to distinguished persons by decision of the Executive Council.

(b) Each member shall pay such annual dues as may be established from time to time by the Council. At present, dues for ordinary membership are €50 (or equivalent) for 1 year, €120 (or equivalent) for 3 years and €180 (or equivalent) for 5 years, plus €12.50 (or equivalent) if cheque is in another currency.

D   DIRECTORY OF MEMBERS

A Directory of Members of the Society is available to all members.

E   BOOKS

The proceedings of the first world conference were published as *The Child and the Law* (F Bates, ed, Oceana, 1976); the proceedings of the second as *Family Violence* (J Eekelaar and S Katz, eds, Butterworths, Canada, 1978); the proceedings of the third as *Marriage and Cohabitation* (J Eekelaar and S Katz, eds, Butterworths, Canada, 1980); the fourth, *The Resolution of Family Conflict* (J Eekelaar and S Katz, eds, Butterworths, Canada, 1984); the fifth, *Family, State and Individual Economic Security (Vols I & II)* (MT Meulders-Klein and J Eekelaar, eds, Story Scientia and Kluwer, 1988); the sixth, *An Ageing World: Dilemmas and Challenges for Law and Social Policy* (J Eekelaar and D Pearl, eds, Clarendon Press, 1989); the seventh *Parenthood in Modern Society* (J Eekelaar and P Sarcevic, eds, Martinus Nijhoff, 1993); the eighth *Families Across Frontiers* (N Lowe and G Douglas, eds, Martinus Nijhoff, 1996) and the ninth *The Changing Family: Family Forms and Family Law* (J Eekelaar and T Nhlapo, eds, Hart Publishing, 1998). The proceedings of the tenth world conference in Australia were published as *Family Law, Processes, Practices and Pressures* (J Dewar and S Parker, eds, Hart Publishing, 2003). The proceedings of the eleventh world conference in Denmark and Norway were published as *Family Life and Human Rights* (P Lødrup and E Modvar, eds, Gyldendal Akademisk, 2004). The proceedings of the twelfth world conference held in Salt Lake City, Utah have been published as *Family Law: Balancing Interests and Pursuing Priorities* (L Wardle and C Williams, eds, Wm S Hein & Co, 2007). The proceedings of the thirteenth world conference held in Vienna in 2008 have been published as *Family Finances* (B Verschraegen, ed, Jan Sramek Verlag, 2009). These proceedings are commercially marketed but are available to Society members at reduced prices.

F   THE SOCIETY'S PUBLICATIONS

The Society regularly publishes a newsletter, *The Family Letter*, which appears twice a year and which is circulated to the members of the Society and reports on its activities and other matters of interest. *The International Survey of Family Law* provides information on current developments in family law throughout the world and is received free of charge by members of the Society. The editor is currently Bill Atkin, Faculty of Law, Victoria University of Wellington, PO Box 600, Wellington, New Zealand 6140. The Survey is circulated to members or may be obtained on application to the Editor.

PREFACE

Family law is no longer the simple study of the rules relating to marriage and divorce, with a few issues relating to children thrown in. That model is now long gone, if it ever really existed. In its place, the word 'diversity' rings much more truly, perhaps even more so if we say 'cultural diversity'. Family forms have changed and, for the most part, no longer is there the stigma that used to attach to non-marital relationships and same-sex couples.

Previous editions of the International Survey have explored these issues. This edition does so even more, especially as countries, most notably in the Western world, grapple with changing social phenomena. In some instances we find that marriage has been extended to same-sex couples. However, this is sometimes the beginning rather than the end of the matter, for this may raise other legal questions which have not properly been addressed. In some countries changes have been made to the law relating to unmarried couples without extending it to same-sex couples. Another major area of debate is how all of this affects parenting. This is especially acute where a same-sex couple intends to do the nurturing of a child.

The latter touches on another legal problem, viz surrogacy. How should the law treat two gay men who have used a surrogate in order to have a child of 'their own'? There are questions of status, immigration, and financing, not to mention the law on surrogacy itself. In short, as we scan developments in different parts of the world, we find very little international consensus. Caught in the middle is the child. As family lawyers how do we react? Let the market decide? Enforce bans on surrogacy especially if it is used for profit? Put the welfare of the child first? How do we decide what the welfare of the child is?

This edition covers many other important family law topics and I trust that it will prove valuable for all readers.

One regular contributor to the Survey, for very many editions, has been Frank Bates. He has faithfully produced his chapter on Australia on schedule every year. He has decided to make the 2011 edition his last contribution. His sterling efforts can only be admired and we are all extremely grateful to him.

Occasionally chapters are submitted in a non-English language. In the past Peter Schofield has freely and willingly done translations for us but following a severe stroke he is regrettably no longer able to assist. Our special thanks go to him and we wish him well. I must acknowledge the translation work done on the chapter from Argentina by Raquel Direnzo and Joss Opie. Life would have been very difficult without their help. The French chapter was translated by my research assistant, David Neild, and his sister, Susannah. Again, I am very thankful for this. David has been a wonderful research assistant, helping me with other chapters and other projects. We have worked very well together and share other interests such as music: David is a first rate pianist, which is a great counterpoint to the study of law.

Each chapter is headed by a French résumé. Dominique Goubau, assisted by Hugues Fulchiron and his team in Lyon, has borne the responsibility for producing the French versions. Thanks are due to them, and also to our publishers especially Greg Woodgate and Cheryl Prophett who does the copy editing. Finally, I thank all the authors who have written such excellent pieces for this edition.

Bill Atkin

General Editor

Wellington

June 2011

CONTENTS

SUBSCRIPTION FORM

INTERNATIONAL SOCIETY OF FAMILY LAW
SUBSCRIPTION FORM

[ ] I prefer to communicate in   [ ] English   [ ] French

[ ] Please charge my credit card   [ ] **MASTERCARD or EUROCARD**   [ ] **VISA or JCB**

[ ]   Subscription for 1 year   €50

[ ]   Subscription for 3 years   €120

[ ]   Subscription for 5 years   €180

Name of Card Holder: _____

Card no. | | | | | | | | | | | | | | | | | | | |

CVC-code (three figures at the back of your card behind the 16 figures): | | | |

Expiry date: ——— / ———

Address of Card Holder: _____

_____

[ ] I pay by *postgiro* to **63.18.019** €180[1] for 5 years, €120 for 3 years or €50 for one year, *plus €12.50* **if cheque in another currency** (from)

The International Society of Family Law,
Beetslaan 2
3818 VH Amersfoort
The Netherlands

(We have a bank account at the Postbank, Amsterdam, The Netherlands. The IBAN code is: NL22 PSTB 0006 3180 19; BIC: PSTBNL21)

[ ] Payment enclosed *by cheque* to the amount of €180[1] for 5 years, €120 for 3 years or €50 for one year, *plus €12.50* **if cheque in another currency**.

Date: _____   Signature: _____

[ ] *New member, or*

[ ] *(Change of) name/address:* _____

_____

Tel: _____

Fax: _____

E-mail: _____

Comments: _____

_____

To be sent to the treasurer of the ISFL:
Dr Adriaan van der Linden, International Society of Family Law
Beetslaan 2, 3818 VH Amersfoort
THE NETHERLANDS (or by fax: +31-33-4659429;
E-mail address: a.p.vanderlinden@uu.nl)
Website ISFL: http://www.law2.byu.edu/ISFL

[1] Or its *counter*value in US dollars.

ASSOCIATION INTERNATIONALE DE DROIT DE LA FAMILLE FORMULAIRE DE COTISATION

☐ Je désire de communiquer ☐ en français ☐ en anglais

☐ Je vous prie de charger ma carte de crédit: ☐ **MASTERCARD/EUROCARD** ☐ **VISA/JCB**

☐
☐ Souscription pour une année €50

Souscription pour trois années €120

☐ Souscription pour cinq années €180

Le nom du possesseur de la carte de crédit: _____

Carte no ☐☐☐☐☐ ☐☐☐☐☐ ☐☐☐☐☐ ☐☐☐☐☐

CVC-code (trois numéros sur l'arrière-coté de votre carte) ☐☐☐☐

Date d'expiration: ____ / ____

L'adresse du possesseur de la carte de crédit: _____

_____

☐ Je payerai par postgiro à **_63.18.019_** €180[1] pour 5 ans ou €120 pour 3 ans ou €50 pour 1 an, ***plus €12.50* surcharge si paiement est un autre cours**,

(du) International Society of Family Law
Beetslaan 2
3818 VH Amersfoort
Les Pays-Bas
(Nous avons un crédit au Postbank, Amsterdam, les Pays-Bas. Le *code IBAN* est: *NL22 PSTB 0006 3180 19; BIC: PSTBNL21*)

☐ Paiement est inclus avec un chèque de €180[1] pour 5 ans ou €120 pour 3 ans ou €50 pour 1 an, ***plus €12.50* surcharge si paiement est un autre cours**.

La date: _____ Souscription: _____

☐
☐ *Nouveau membre, ou*

(Changement de) nom/adresse: _____

_____

Tel: _____
Fax: _____
E-mail: _____

Remarques: _____

_____

Veuillez envoyer ce formulaire au trésorier de l'Association:
Dr Adriaan van der Linden, International Society of Family Law
Beetslaan 2, 3818 VH Amersfoort
LES PAYS BAS (ou par fax: +31-33-4659429;
E-mail address: a.p.vanderlinden@uu.nl)
Website ISFL: http://www.law2.byu.edu/ISFL

[1] Ou la *contre*valeur en US dollars.

ANNUAL REVIEW OF INTERNATIONAL FAMILY LAW 2009

*Elaine O'Callaghan**

Résumé

En 2009, les principales réformes ont eu lieu aux niveaux internationaux et régionaux. En droit international privé, de nombreuses conventions adoptées par la Conférence de la Haye ont été ratifiées par les Etats membres. En outre, des avancées importantes ont eu lieu en ce qui concerne les discussions ayant trait aux instruments internationaux relatifs au recouvrement des aliments envers les enfants et d'autres membres de la famille. Les Nations unies ont célébré le 20ème anniversaire de l'adoption de la Convention sur les Droits de l'Enfant (CRC). Il a également été procédé aux signatures des deux Protocoles Facultatifs au CRC. Quant au conseil de l'Europe, trois jugements significatifs de la Cour européenne des droits de l'homme mérite d'être cités, le premier intéresse les droits des pères à la garde d'un adultérin d'enfant, l'éloignement des étrangers et le droit de respecter pour la vie familiale et la violence familiale.

I INTRODUCTION

In 2009, a number of significant developments took place in many different legal fora at international and regional levels. The Hague Conference on Private International Law saw a great number of ratifications and signatures across its wide range of conventions. The value of direct judicial communications in international child protection cases was a core issue for the Hague Conference in 2009 and a number of conclusions and recommendations were reached in this regard. There was also substantial progress in relation to the Convention on the International Recovery of Child Support and Other Forms of Family Maintenance. A Special Commission was convened to discuss the operation of the Convention and a number of conclusions and recommendations were also reached in this regard. Further, an Explanatory Report was also published in relation to the Convention.

In the United Nations, 2009 marked the twentieth anniversary of the adoption of the Convention on the Rights of the Child (CRC) by the United Nations General Assembly. There were a number of ratifications and signatures of the two Optional Protocols to the CRC. The Committee on the Rights of the Child also published the much anticipated General Comment on the Right of the

---

* Post-doctoral Researcher, Dublin, Ireland.

Child to be Heard following on from the Day of General Discussion on the Right of the Child to be Heard in 2006.

As regards the Council of Europe, this year's review has concentrated on three significant judgments of the European Court of Human Rights which concern fathers' rights to custody of a child born out of wedlock, the deportation of non-nationals and the right to respect for family life, and domestic violence. Of particular note this year is the Court's reference to and reliance on international and comparative law. For example, the Court referred to international instruments, case-law of the Inter-American Court of Human Rights and research reports by various domestic and international bodies. In doing this, the Court sought to interpret the European Convention on Human Rights in the light of best practice and experience gained in other jurisdictions.

II THE HAGUE CONFERENCE ON PRIVATE INTERNATIONAL LAW

In 2009, the Hague Conference on Private International Law focused, in particular, on emerging topics in areas such as international child abduction, intercountry adoption, unpaid child support and the resolution of disputes across borders.[1] While doing this, it also concentrated on monitoring and reviewing the operation of existing Hague Conventions to ensure their proper implementation and effectiveness in dealing with the emerging issues.

It is evident that the Hague Conference is consistently cementing its reputation through its work in developing and implementing conventions, so much so that it is now at the forefront of a great number of areas within family and child law on the global level. The Hague Conference comprised of 68 member states and one member organisation, that is, the European Community, by the year end of 2009.[2] Further, some 66 member states and 66 non-member states were parties to one or more Hague Conventions adopted since 1951. There were also a number of ratifications and signatures in 2009. For example, both the United States and the European Union (EU) signed the 2005 Choice of Court Convention.

Further, Switzerland, Uruguay and the Dominican Republic ratified the 1996 Child Protection Convention, while Greece, Cape Verde, Liechtenstein, the Republic of Togo and Nepal all either ratified or signed the 1993 Intercountry Adoption Convention. Switzerland and the Republic of Mauritius ratified the 2006 Securities Convention while Cape Verde acceded to the 1961 Apostille Convention. Belize acceded to the 1965 Service Convention while Croatia and the Republic of Korea acceded to the 1970 Evidence Convention.

---

[1]   HCCH Annual Report 2009, Foreword, p 5. This report is available at www.hcch.net/upload/annualreport2009.pdf (accessed 30 March 2011).
[2]   Ibid, p 11.

(a) Direct judicial communications

The year 2009 marked the tenth anniversary of the International Hague Network of Judges.[3] This Network, which aims to secure the international protection of children, facilitates communication and co-operation between judges, from all regions of the world and different legal traditions, at the international level. Judges can liaise with their national Central Authorities, other judges within their jurisdictions and judges in other states. In 2009, there were 40 members from 26 states around the world.

The Judges' Newsletter, which provides information concerning judicial co-operation in matters of international child protection, also marked its tenth anniversary in 2009.[4] The Newsletter is an important source for developing direct judicial communications as it updates judges as to any changes in personal contact details of other judges, outlines examples of successful practice in international judicial co-operation as well as any significant national developments, such as case-law, procedural or organisational changes and judicial conferences. The Newsletter is distributed to some 900 judges in more that 115 countries as well as being available on the HCCH website.

In January 2009, judges and experts from more than 50 countries and leading international judges' associations met, under the auspices of the European Commission and the Hague Conference, to discuss direct judicial communications on family law matters and the development of judicial networks.[5] The judicial conference reached 17 recommendations and conclusions. In particular, it emphasised the value of direct judicial communications in international child protection cases, especially given the broad range of international instruments in relation to which direct judicial communications can play a valuable role.

The Conference encouraged those states which do not yet have designated Network judges to do so. As regards the designated Network judges, it was concluded that they should be sitting judges with appropriate authority and experience in that area. It was also recommended that efforts should be made within states to promote the appropriate use of direct judicial communications in the international protection of children and to increase awareness of the existence and role of Network judges. Adequate resources, including administrative and legal resources, were viewed as necessary to support the work of Network judges.

---

[3] See: www.hcch.net/index_en.php?act=events.details&year=2009&varevent=159 (accessed 30 March 2011).
[4] See N Sauvage 'The ten years of *The Judges' Newsletter*', available at www.hcch.net/index_en.php?act=publications.details&pid=4823 (accessed 30 March 2011).
[5] See: www.hcch.net/upload/judcomm_concl2009e.pdf (accessed 30 March 2011).

(b) Convention on the International Recovery of Child Support and Other Forms of Family Maintenance

The increasing mobility of individuals and families has meant that the breakdown of relationships and indeed, families, creates great social and legal dilemmas. As a result, the importance of sound structures for the governance of cross-border child support and family maintenance is profoundly evident. In 2009, representatives from over 50 states and the European Community agreed on a number of practical measures and principles to promote and implement the Hague Convention on the International Recovery of Child Support and Other Forms of Family Maintenance. The Convention was adopted in November 2007, by the Twenty-First Diplomatic Session of the Hague Conference on Private International Law.[6] Its central object is to ensure the effective international recovery of child support and other forms of family maintenance.[7] A Protocol on the Law Applicable to Maintenance Obligations was also adopted at that time which sets out the applicable rules to be used.[8] Both the Convention and the Protocol are of particular use as they recognise the urgency of the situation of dependent persons and they purport to provide a simplified means to solve the problem by overcoming serious, legal and practical difficulties. The Convention has yet to come into force; to date, it has been signed by the United States (23 November 2007), Burkina Faso (7 January 2009), Norway (8 June 2010) and Ukraine (7 July 2010).[9]

Professor William Duncan, Deputy Secretary General of the Permanent Bureau of the Hague Conference on Private International Law, discussed the background to the adoption of this Hague Convention and the initial steps which sought to demonstrate whether there was a need to establish a new international instrument to govern the recovery of maintenance abroad.[10] Prior to the publication of this Convention, there was an abundance of multilateral, bilateral and regional instruments already available which could merely be improved upon.[11] For example, the Hague Conference itself has a number of conventions governing the issue of child and family maintenance including the Hague Convention of 24 October 1956, on the Law Applicable to Maintenance Obligations towards Children, the Hague Convention of the 15 April 1958, concerning the Recognition and Enforcement of Decisions relating to Maintenance Obligations towards Children and the Hague Convention of the 2 October 1973, on the Recognition and Enforcement of Decisions Relating to Maintenance Obligations.

---

[6]   Convention of 23 November 2007 on the International Recovery of Child Support and Other Forms of Family Maintenance, available at www.hcch.net.

[7]   Article 1 of the Convention. For discussion of this Convention, see E O'Callaghan and U Kilkelly 'Annual Review of International Family Law 2007' in B Atkin (ed) *The International Survey of Family Law 2009 Edition* (Jordan Publishing Limited, 2009).

[8]   Protocol of 23 November 2007, on the Law Applicable to Maintenance Obligations, available at www.hcch.net/index_en.php?act=conventions.text&cid=133 (accessed 1 April 2011).

[9]   See: www.hcch.net/index_en.php?act=conventions.status&cid=131 (accessed 1 April 2011).

[10] W Duncan 'The Developments of the New Hague Convention on the Internal Recovery of Child Support and Other Forms of Maintenance' (2004) 38 Fam LQ 663.

[11] Ibid.

This array of conventions has led to confusion as to their applicability in individual cases and in this sense the Hague Conference reached the conclusion that a completely distinct instrument was essential. This was particularly so because, as Duncan observes, there was 'an acceptance of the need to take account of the many changes that have occurred in national (especially child support) systems for determining and collecting maintenance payments, as well as the opportunities presented by advances in information technology'.[12] Duncan further noted that there was 'a realisation that the proliferation of instruments (multilateral, regional and bilateral), with their varying provisions and different degrees of formality, were complicating the tasks of national authorities, as well as legal advisers'.[13]

In 2009, the Special Commission published Conclusions and Recommendations of the Special Commission on the Implementation of the 2007 Child Support Convention and of the 2007 Protocol on the Law applicable to Maintenance Obligations.[14] In particular, the Special Commission agreed that a number of practical tools to assist implementation of the Convention, such as a handbook for case workers, profiles of states parties and the development of an implementation checklist are necessary. The increasingly important and useful role of information technology in managing international child support payments was also discussed as regards to its ability to speed up transactions and enhance the operation of the Convention.

An Explanatory Report on the Convention on the International Recovery of Child Support and Other Forms of Family Maintenance was also published in 2009.[15] In essence, this Explanatory Report outlines and describes the general framework for the Convention as well as an article–by-article analysis. The detail which it provides, as well as the emphasis which it places on the context for the Convention, means that this Explanatory Report should be at hand for any person or body who is subject to the Convention.

It is worth noting, in particular, the emphasis and explanations which the Explanatory Report offers as regards information technology. In demonstrating the Hague Conference's commitment to the use of information technology in supporting the effective use and implementation of the Convention, it is explained that 'the Drafting Committee has taken great care to develop a text that would allow the implementation of technologies without endangering due process principles'. What this means in practice is that the Convention 'avoids as much as possible the use of terms such as "signature" (where what is usually needed is a simple identification), "writing", "original", "sworn"', and "certified"'. Indeed, the Convention seeks the use of electronic funds transfers

---

[12] Ibid, pp 665–666.
[13] Ibid.
[14] Available at www.hcch.net/upload/wop/maint2009concl_e.pdf (accessed 30 March 2011).
[15] See: www.hcch.net/upload/expl38e.pdf (accessed 30 March 2011).

under Art 35. It also seeks the use of cross-border electronic case management and communications systems such as the iSupport software which the Hague Conference is continually developing.[16]

III UNITED NATIONS

The 20 November 2009, marked the twentieth anniversary of the adoption of the Convention on the Rights of the Child (CRC) by the United Nations General Assembly.[17] To mark this anniversary, the Committee on the Rights of the Child, the Office of the High Commissioner (OHCHR) and other partners organised a 2-day conference and celebration in Geneva, Switzerland. The focus of this event centred on the broad themes of dignity, development and dialogue which were viewed as the three main challenges facing the CRC. More specifically, the importance of ensuring the dignity of the child, providing the child with full possibilities for development and facilitating dialogue between adults and children in accordance with the participatory approach of the CRC were discussed. The status and implementation of the CRC was also evaluated in the light of its 193 ratifications and 17 years of reporting. Finally, the Conference focused on identifying priorities for the future taking into consideration the two Optional Protocols to the CRC.

In 2009, there were no further ratifications of the CRC, but states continued to ratify the Optional Protocols to the Convention. For example, the Optional Protocol on the Involvement of Children in Armed Conflict was acceded to by Algeria and the Solomon Islands while Bhutan, Mauritius and the Netherlands ratified the Optional Protocol.[18] There are now 139 parties to the Protocol.[19] In relation to the Optional Protocol on the Sale of Children, Child Prostitution and Child Pornography, this instrument was acceded to by Congo and the Solomon Islands and ratified by Bhutan, Germany, Malawi and the United Kingdom.[20] This brings the total number of state parties to 142.[21]

The Committee on the Rights of the Child published a General Comment on the Right of the Child to be Heard and this is discussed in the following section, in the light of the Committee's preceding work as regards the implementation of this right.[22]

---

[16] See p 16 of the Report.

[17] See: www2.ohchr.org/english/bodies/crc/20thAnnivCRC.htm (accessed 30 March 2011).

[18] For full details, see: http://treaties.un.org/Pages/ViewDetails.aspx?src=TREATY&mtdsg_no=IV-11-b&chapter=4&lang=en (accessed 30 March 2011).

[19] As of March 2011.

[20] See: http://treaties.un.org/Pages/ViewDetails.aspx?src=TREATY&mtdsg_no=IV-11-c&chapter= 4&lang=en (accessed 30 March 2011).

[21] As of March 2011.

[22] See: www2.ohchr.org/english/bodies/crc/comments.htm (accessed 30 March 2011).

(a) The right of the child to be heard

In 2009, the Committee on the Rights of the Child published its General Comment on the Right of the Child to be Heard, thereby focusing on the implementation of Art 12 of the CRC in order to provide states and other actors with more comprehensive guidance as to their obligations to promote and protect the right to be heard.[23] Article 12 forms the cornerstone of the child's procedural rights in the CRC and 'constitutes one of the fundamental values of the Convention'.[24] Indeed, the Committee on the Rights of the Child identified Art 12 as one of four general principles which must guide the implementation of every provision of the CRC.[25] It provides that:

'(1) State Parties shall assure to the child who is capable of forming his or her own views the right to express those views freely in all matters affecting the child, the views of the child being given due weight in accordance with the age and maturity of the child.

(2) For this purpose the child shall in particular be provided the opportunity to be heard in any judicial and administrative proceedings affecting the child, either directly, or through a representative or an appropriate body, in a manner consistent with the procedural rules of national law.'

Article 12(1) acknowledges that the views of the child of sufficient age and maturity must be given due weight in all matters affecting him or her. Article 12(2) meanwhile specifically sets out the child's right to be heard directly or indirectly in any judicial and administrative proceedings affecting his or her interests.

States parties reaffirmed their commitment to the realisation of Art 12 at the twenty-seventh special session of the General Assembly on children in 2002.[26] The child's right to be heard is a well-established right within the CRC. The text of the Convention itself, as well as the General Comments and the Days of General Discussion of the Committee on the Rights of the Child, point to

---

[23] The overall objectives of the General Comment are to: (1) strengthen understanding of the meaning of Art 12 and its implications for governments, stakeholders, NGOs and society at large; (2) elaborate the scope of legislation, policy and practice necessary to achieve full implementation of Art 12; (3) highlight the positive approaches in implementing Art 12, benefiting from the monitoring experience of the Committee; (4) propose basic requirements for appropriate ways to give due weight to children's views in all matters that affect them. See: General Comment No 12 *The Right of the Child to be Heard* CRC/C/GC/12, para 8.

[24] General Comment No 12 *The Right of the Child to be Heard* CRC/C/GC/12, para 2.

[25] The other principles are: the principle of non-discrimination under Art 2, the best interests principle as set out in Art 3 and the right of the child to life, survival and development under Art 6. UN Committee on the Rights of the Child, *General Guidelines regarding the Form and Content of Initial Reports to be submitted by States Parties under Article 44(1)(a) of the Convention*, UN Doc CRC/C/5, paras 13–14, 30 October 1991. See further, General Comment No 12 *The Right of the Child to be Heard* CRC/C/GC/12.

[26] Resolution S-27/2 'A world fit for children', adopted by the General Assembly in 2002. See CRC/C/GC/12, para 4.

this.[27] For example, the Committee held a Day of General Discussion on the Right of the Child to be Heard in 2006 and it is largely from this that the General Comment of the same name arises in 2009.[28]

As to what Art 12 means in practice for children's lives, it is evident that all children who are capable of forming views have the right to be heard in all decisions affecting them. The General Comment on the Right of the Child to be Heard presents a literal analysis of the text of Art 12 and this is worthy of consideration by any person or body who is concerned with the implementation of this right.[29] For example, as regards determining whether a child is 'capable of forming his or her own views', states parties are advised that they should view these words as an obligation to assess the capacity of the child to form an autonomous opinion to the greatest extent possible.[30] This means that states parties cannot begin with the assumption that a child is incapable of expressing his or her own views. Instead, states parties should presume that a child has the capacity to form his or her own views. The Committee emphasises that Art 12 does not impose an age limit on the right of the child to express his or her views, and discourages states parties from introducing age limits either in law or in practice which would restrict the child's right to be heard in all matters affecting him or her. Indeed, in the General Comment on Implementing Child Rights in Early Childhood,[31] the Committee emphasised that:[32]

> ' . . . article 12 applies both to younger and to older children. As holders of rights, even the youngest children are entitled to express their views, which should be "given due weight in accordance with the age and maturity of the child" (art. 12.1). Young children are acutely sensitive to their surroundings and very rapidly acquire understanding of the people, places and routines in their lives, along with awareness of their own unique identity.'

While Art 12 does not set out how exactly a child's views can be ascertained, it does establish that children can be heard either directly or indirectly.[33] The Committee recommends that, wherever possible, the child must be given the

---

27 See, eg, General Comment No 5 *General Measures of Implementation of the Convention on the Rights of the Child* CRC/GC/2003/5; General Comment No 7 *Implementing Child Rights in Early Childhood* CRC/C/GC/7/Rev 1; General Comment No 9 *Children's Rights in Juvenile Justice* CRC/C/GC/10; General Comment No 12 *The Right of the Child to be Heard* CRC/C/GC/12; *Day of General Discussion on the Right of the Child to be Heard* 29 September 2006, as well as the *Role of the Family in the Promotion of the Rights of the Child* 10 October 1994, all available at: www.ohchr.org (accessed 31 March 2011).

28 See General Comment No 12 *The Right of the Child to be Heard* CRC/C/GC/12, para 5.

29 Ibid, paras 19–39.

30 Ibid, paras 20–21.

31 See also UN Committee on the Rights of the Child, General Comment No 4 *Adolescent Health and Development in the Context of the Convention on the Rights of the Child* (2003) HRI/GEN/1/Rev 7, p 321 which also stresses the importance of the family life for the adolescent, pp 324–325.

32 General Comment No 7 *Implementing Child Rights in Early Childhood* CRC/C/GC/7/Rev 1, para 14.

33 Article 12(2).

opportunity to be directly heard in any proceedings.[34] Furthermore, the child must be heard 'in a manner consistent with the procedural rules of national law'.[35] This grants a great deal of discretion to states parties, including the courts, as to how the voice of the child can be heard. As regards hearing the child directly, the most common example is the use of judicial interviews of children in chambers. As regards hearing the child indirectly, courts commonly appoint experts such as child psychologists, psychiatrists or social workers to interview or ascertain the views of children or appoint a separate representative such as a guardian ad litem or a legal professional to convey the child's views. The Committee stresses that: 'States parties are urged to make provisions for young children to be represented independently in all legal proceedings by someone who acts for the child's interests and for children to be heard in all cases where they are capable of expressing their opinions or preferences.'[36] The Committee also calls on states to establish legal aid support systems to provide children with qualified support and assistance.[37]

The Committee emphasises that the representative must be aware that he or she exclusively represents the interests of the child and not the interests of other persons such as parents or institutions or bodies such as residential homes, for example.[38] Further, the Committee recommends that codes of conduct should be developed for representatives who are appointed to represent the child's views.[39] It is evident that specially trained professionals, with both legal and non-legal experience, are required in order to ensure that this right is safeguarded.

The General Comment on the Child's Right to be Heard points out that the child's right to be heard has many links with other Articles in the Convention.[40] In particular, for example, as a general principle, it is linked to the other general principles of the Convention including Arts 2 (the right to non-discrimination) and 3 (best interests principle). There is also a connection with Art 5 (evolving capacities of the child) as well as Art 13 (the right to freedom of expression) and Art 17 (the right to information).

Article 2, which enshrines the right to non-discrimination, is an essential consideration. Along with Art 12, this right clearly demands that all children have the right to be heard in decisions affecting them. Indeed, the Committee expressly outlined that discrimination includes restricting the right to 'free expression of feelings and views'.[41] According to the Committee, children 'are

---

[34] General Comment No 12 *The Right of the Child to be Heard* CRC/C/GC/12, para 35.

[35] Article 12(2).

[36] General Comment No 7 *Implementing Child Rights in Early Childhood* CRC/C/GC/7/Rev 1, para 13(a).

[37] See *Day of General Discussion on the Right of the Child to be Heard*, 29 September 2006, para 43. See www.ohchr.org (accessed 31 March 2011).

[38] General Comment No 12 *The Right of the Child to be Heard* CRC/C/GC/12, para 37.

[39] Ibid, para 37.

[40] Ibid, paras 68–69.

[41] General Comment No 7 *Implementing Child Rights in Early Childhood* CRC/C/GC/7/Rev 1, para 11(a).

relatively powerless and depend on others for the realisation of their rights'.[42] This clearly emphasises the obligation on states to ensure the effective implementation of Art 12 for all children in practice.

Article 3 establishes that the 'best interests' of the child must be considered in all actions concerning him or her.[43] While the CRC does not offer a definition as to what the concept of 'best interests' encompasses, it is clear that the views of the child must be heard in determining this.[44] As the Committee on the Rights of the Child noted, 'children are reliant on responsible authorities to assess and represent their rights and best interests in relation to decisions and actions that affect their well-being, while taking account of their views and evolving capacities'.[45] It is therefore clear that the Convention requires that the child has the opportunity to be heard in any decision concerning the child's best interests.

The importance of the 'evolving capacities' of the child, which is set out in Art 5 of the CRC, in relation to Art 12, must also be considered.[46] Article 5 requires that the child be involved in the decision-making process affecting his or her upbringing, subject to the child's age and maturity.[47] Crucially, Art 5 recognises children's development as an ongoing process, unique to each individual child, and in this regard can be read in the light of Art 12 when determining the weight to be afforded to the child's views.

Furthermore, at the Day of General Discussion on the Right of the Child to be Heard,[48] the Committee, referring specifically to the child's right to be heard in judicial and administrative proceedings, detailed the child's right to be informed 'in a child friendly manner' about the right to be heard and how this may be carried out.[49] In this regard, the Committee also reaffirmed the links

---

[42]   Ibid.
[43]   Article 3(1): 'In all actions concerning children, whether undertaken by public or private welfare institutions, courts of law, administrative authorities or legislative bodies, the best interests of the child shall be a primary consideration.'
[44]   Article 3 should be read in conjunction with Art 2 as regards any decision making in relation to a child's life: this is because the Convention is to be read holistically and the articles strengthen each other. See Preamble to the CRC, at www2.ohchr.org/english/law/crc. htm#preamble (accessed 1 April 2011). See further R Hodgkin and P Newell *Implementation Handbook for the Convention on the Rights of the Child* (UNICEF, 2007).
[45]   General Comment No 7 *Implementing Child Rights in Early Childhood* CRC/C/GC/7/Rev 1, para 13.
[46]   See Preamble to the document, *Day of General Discussion on the Right of the Child to be Heard*, 29 September 2006. See www.ohchr.org (accessed 31 March 2011).
[47]   The Committee on the Rights of the Child discussed the concept of the 'evolving capacities' of the child in its General Comment No 7 *Implementing Child Rights in Early Childhood* CRC/C/GC/7/Rev 1, para 17. The Committee outlined the concept as referring to: 'processes of maturation and learning whereby children progressively acquire knowledge, competencies and understanding, including acquiring understanding about their rights and about how they can best be realized'.
[48]   *Day of General Discussion on the Right of the Child to be Heard*, 29 September 2006. See www.ohchr.org (accessed 31 March 2011).
[49]   Ibid, para 40. See also General Comment No 12 *The Right of the Child to be Heard* CRC/C/GC/12, paras 80–83.

between Arts 12, 13 and 17, which set out that children have the right to freedom of expression including the right 'to seek, receive and impart information and ideas of all kinds'.[50] According to the Committee, 'the right to receive and impart information is an important pre-requisite to realise participation of children' and it urged states parties to consider developing child-friendly information in relation to all matters affecting children.[51] To this end, Arts 13 and 17, read in conjunction with Art 12, clearly demand that children are given all the relevant information so as to ensure that they can reach a properly informed decision.

The importance of mandatory training on the implications of Art 12 of the Convention for all professionals involved in judicial and administrative proceedings was emphasised by the Committee.[52] In particular, the Committee sought to strengthen this obligation by outlining that '(j)udges and other decision makers should, as a rule, explicitly state and explain the outcome of the proceedings, especially if the views of the child could not be accommodated'.[53] This would ensure that children are adequately involved in the decision-making process.

Overall, Art 12 makes clear that involving the child in the decision-making process does not necessarily mean that his or her wishes will be adhered to. Instead, the child's views are another important factor to be taken into account by the court. The crucial point is, however, that these views are heard and considered in the decision-making process.[54]

---

[50] Article 13(1): 'The child shall have the right to freedom of expression; this right shall include freedom to seek, receive and impart information and ideas of all kinds, regardless of frontiers, either orally, in writing or in print, in the form of art, or through any other media of the child's choice.' Article 17: 'States Parties recognise the important function performed by the mass media and shall ensure that the child has access to information and material from a diversity of national and international sources, especially those aimed at the promotion of his or her social, spiritual and moral well-being and physical and mental health. To this end, States Parties shall:
(a) Encourage the mass media to disseminate information and material of social and cultural benefit to the child and in accordance with the spirit of article 29;
(b) Encourage international co-operation in the production, exchange and dissemination of such information and material from a diversity of cultural, national and international sources;
(c) Encourage the production and dissemination of children's books;
(d) Encourage the mass media to have particular regard to the linguistic needs of the child who belongs to a minority group or who is indigenous;
(e) Encourage the development of appropriate guidelines for the protection of the child from information and material injurious to his or her well-being, bearing in mind the provisions of articles 13 and 18.'
[51] *Day of General Discussion on the Right of the Child to be Heard*, 29 September 2006. See www.ohchr.org (accessed 31 March 2011).
[52] Ibid, para 41. See also *General Measures of Implementation of the Convention on the Rights of the Child* CRC/GC/2003/5, paras 53–55; General Comment No7 *Implementing Child Rights in Early Childhood* CRC/C/GC/7/Rev 1, para 41.
[53] See *Day of General Discussion on the Right of the Child to be Heard*, 29 September 2006, para 41. See www.ohchr.org (accessed 31 March 2011).
[54] See further General Comment No 12 *The Right of the Child to be Heard* CRC/C/GC/12.

Conclusions

Overall, it is evident that the text of the CRC is certain as regards the legal obligations on states parties to ensure that children have the right to be heard in all proceedings affecting them. The Committee advocates that state parties must ensure that the child's rights under Art 12 be 'implemented from the earliest stage in ways appropriate to the child's capacities, best interests, and rights to protection from harmful experiences'.[55] In order to ensure the worldwide implementation of Art 12, the Committee recommends that states parties widely disseminate the General Comment on the Right of the Child to be Heard within government and administrative structures as well as to children and civil society.[56] This will necessitate translating it into the relevant languages, making child-friendly versions available, holding workshops and seminars to discuss its implications and how best to implement it, and incorporating it into the training of all professionals working for and with children. The combination of these measures will help to ensure reflection on as well as assessment of the implementation of the child's right to be heard.

IV COUNCIL OF EUROPE: CASE-LAW OF THE EUROPEAN COURT OF HUMAN RIGHTS

This year's discussion of the case-law of the European Court of Human Rights focuses on three individual cases which respectively concern fathers' rights to custody of a child born out of wedlock, the deportation of non-nationals and the right to respect for family life, and domestic violence. Article 8 of the European Convention on Human Rights, which concerns the right to respect for private and family life, is the focal point of the former two of these cases and the Court discusses the extent to which member states are required to realise this right in practice.[57]

Particular attention is focused on the latter case in this section, which concerns the issue of domestic violence, as the Court provided important jurisprudence as regards the treatment of this issue. In particular, the Court drew on both international and comparative law material in reaching a decision as to what the precise obligations are for member states.

---

55 General Comment No 7 *Implementing Child Rights in Early Childhood* CRC/C/GC/7/Rev 1, para 14(a). Specific reference is made to 'legal proceedings' in para 14(b).
56 General Comment No 12 *The Right of the Child to be Heard* CRC/C/GC/12, para 7.
57 Article 8 of the European Convention on Human Rights (ECHR): '(1) Everyone has the right to respect for his private and family life . . . (2) There shall be no interference by a public authority with the exercise of this right except such as is in accordance with the law and is necessary in a democratic society in the interests of national security, public safety or the economic well-being of the country, for the prevention of disorder or crime, for the protection of health or morals, or for the protection of the rights and freedoms of others.'

(a)   Fathers' rights to custody of a child born out of wedlock

Every year sees a significant number of cases concerning child custody and contact disputes in the European Court of Human Rights. These rights are well established within the jurisprudence of the Court. 2009 saw a number of particularly interesting cases in this regard and the case of *Zaunegger v Germany* is a good example.[58]

In this case, the applicant complained under Art 8 of the Convention that the German court decisions refusing joint custody had infringed his right to respect for family life, and under Art 14 read in conjunction with Art 8 of the Convention that the application of s 1626a(2) of the German Civil Code amounted to unjustified discrimination against unmarried fathers on the grounds of sex and in comparison with divorced fathers.[59] The Court held that there had been a violation of Art 14 of the Convention, taken together with Art 8.[60] It was not necessary, in the Court's view, to determine whether there has also been a breach of Art 8 of the Convention taken alone.[61]

As to the facts of this case, the applicant is the father of a daughter born out of wedlock in 1995. The applicant and the mother of the child separated in August 1998; their relationship had lasted 5 years. Until January 2001, the daughter lived with the applicant. The mother moved to another flat which was located in the same building. The parents did not make a joint custody declaration and so the mother obtained sole custody pursuant to s 1626a(2) of the German Civil Code.

In January 2001, the child moved to the mother's flat. Subsequently, the parents started to argue about the applicant's contact with the child. In June 2001, they agreed on contact arrangements amounting to approximately 4 months per year, with the assistance of the Cologne-Nippes Youth Welfare Office. In 2001, the applicant applied for a joint custody order, as the mother was unwilling to agree on a joint custody declaration, although otherwise both parents were co-operative and on good terms.

In June 2003, the Cologne District Court dismissed the applicant's application. It found that there was no basis for a joint custody order. Under German law, joint custody for parents of children born out of wedlock could only be obtained through a joint declaration, marriage or a court order under s 1672(1) of the German Civil Code which required the consent of the other parent. The Cologne District Court considered s 1626a of the German Civil Code to be constitutional and referred to a leading judgment of the Federal Constitutional

---

58   *Zaunegger v Germany* [2009] App no 22028/04, 3 December 2009.
59   Article 14 of the ECHR: 'The enjoyment of the rights and freedoms set forth in [the] Convention shall be secured without discrimination on any ground such as sex, race, colour, language, religion, political or other opinion, national or social origin, association with a national minority, property, birth or other status.'
60   *Zaunegger v Germany* [2009] App no 22028/04, 3 December 2009, para 64.
61   Ibid, para 65.

Court of 29 January 2003.[62] Having regard to the fact that the pertinent legal provisions did not allow for a different decision, the District Court did not consider it necessary to hear the concerned parties in person.

The applicant appealed and in October 2003,the Cologne Court of Appeal dismissed the appeal. It held that, as the applicant and the mother were unmarried, the applicant's participation in the exercise of custody was only possible in accordance with s 1626a of the Civil Code. The applicant and the mother had, however, not submitted the required joint custody declaration. In its judgment of 29 January 2003, the Federal Constitutional Court had found that s 1626a of the Civil Code was constitutional with regard to the situation of parents of children born out of wedlock who had separated after 1 July 1998.[63] The Cologne Court of Appeal noted that the applicant and the mother of the child had separated in August 1998. Thus, they had had a period of one-and-a-half months before they separated in which they could have made a joint custody declaration. The Cologne Court of Appeal further noted that the new legislation, which had entered into force on 1 July 1998, had received public attention for a considerable period. Unmarried parents might have been expected therefore to have shown an interest in the matter and to have noticed the new legislation. In December 2003, the Federal Constitutional Court, referring to the pertinent provisions of its Rules of Procedure, declined to consider the applicant's constitutional complaint, without giving further reasons.

In determining this issue, the Court reiterated that the notion of 'the family' under Art 8 is not confined to marriage-based relationships and may encompass other de facto family ties where the parties are living together out of wedlock.[64] A child born out of such a relationship is ipso jure part of that family unit from the moment and by the very fact of his or her birth.[65] The existence or non-existence of 'family life' within the meaning of Art 8 is essentially a question of fact depending upon the real existence in practice of close personal ties, in particular the demonstrable interest in and commitment by the father to the child both before and after the birth.[66]

The Court observed that the applicant's paternity was established from the beginning and that he lived together with the mother and the child until the child reached the age of $3^{1}/_{2}$.[67] Following the parents' separation in 1998, the child continued to live for more than 2 years with the applicant. Since 2001, the child has lived with her mother, while the father has enjoyed extensive contact rights and during which time he has provided for the child's daily needs.

---

[62]   Ibid, paras 18–21.
[63]   Ibid.
[64]   Ibid, para 37.
[65]   *Keegan v Ireland*, Series A, App no 290, 26 May 1994, para 44.
[66]   *Lebbink v the Netherlands*, App no 45582/99, ECHR 2004-IV, para 36.
[67]   *Zaunegger v Germany* [2009] App no 22028/04, 3 December 2009, para 39.

In the light of the facts of the case, the Court held that the decisions which dismissed the applicant's request for joint custody, the right to exercise joint parental authority as regards, inter alia, his daughter's education, care and the determination of where she should live, amounted to interference with the applicant's right to respect for his family life as guaranteed by Art 8(1) of the Convention.[68] The Court found that the facts of the case fell within the scope of Art 8 of the Convention and that, accordingly, Art 14 was applicable.[69]

The Court reiterated that in the enjoyment of the rights and freedoms guaranteed by the Convention, Art 14 affords protection against different treatment, without an objective and reasonable justification of persons in similar situations.[70] Under German law, joint custody against the will of the mother of a child born out of wedlock is prima facie considered as not being in the child's interest.[71] The Court held that there was discrimination as German law does not provide for judicial examination as to whether the attribution of joint parental authority to both parents would be in the child's best interests. The Court held that in respect of this discrimination, there was not a reasonable relationship of proportionality between the general exclusion of judicial review of the initial attribution of sole custody to the mother and the aim pursued, namely the protection of the best interests of a child born out of wedlock.[72] The Court held that 'very weighty reasons need to be put forward before a difference in treatment of the father of a child born of a relationship where the parties were living together out of wedlock as compared with the father of a child born of a marriage-based relationship' can be regarded as compatible with the Convention.[73]

(b) Deportation of non-nationals and the right to respect for family life

The case of *Omojudi v United Kingdom* concerns the deportation of a non-national who had committed a number of criminal offences in the United Kingdom.[74] The Court held that there has been a violation of Art 8 of the Convention, having regard to the strength of the applicant's family ties to the UK, his length of residence, and the difficulty that his children would face if they were to relocate to Nigeria.

---

[68] Ibid, para 40.

[69] Ibid, para 41.

[70] Ibid, paras 42 and 49. See the cases of *Hoffmann v Austria*, Series A, App no 255-C, 23 June 1993, para 31; *Inze v Austria*, Series A, App no 12628, October 1987, para 41; *Mazurek v France*, App no 34406/97, ECHR 2000-II, para 48.

[71] *Zaunegger v Germany* [2009] App no 22028/04, 3 December 2009, para 49.

[72] Ibid, para 63.

[73] See *Sommerfeld v Germany [GC]* App no 31871/96, ECHR 2003-VIII, para 93; *Karlheinz Schmidt v Germany*, Series A, App no 291-B, 18 July 1994, para 24; *Mazurek v France* App no 34406/97, ECHR 2000-II, para 49.

[74] *Omojudi v United Kingdom* [2009] App no 1820/08, 24 November 2009.

As to the facts of the case, the applicant was born in Nigeria and lived there until 1982. He was educated in Nigeria and for a period he was employed by a Nigerian aviation handling company. In September 1982, when he was 22 years old, he was granted 2 months leave to enter the UK as a student. His leave was subsequently extended to January 1986. In 1983, the applicant was joined by his partner, who was also a national of Nigeria. The applicant married his partner in the UK in 1987. They had three children, all of whom are British citizens. The oldest child has a daughter, who is now 2 years old.

Prior to the expiry of his leave in January 1986, the applicant applied for a further extension. The following day, however, he was caught returning from the Netherlands with a British visitor's passport obtained by deception. Although he was not prosecuted for the offence, the application to extend his leave was refused. In March 1987, the applicant was informed of his liability for deportation. He was served with a deportation order in July 1987. He attempted to appeal against the order and a second deportation order was served in December 1990. The applicant appealed against the second order, but the appeal was subsequently withdrawn.

The applicant was convicted of theft and conspiracy to defraud in March 1989. He was sentenced to 4 years' imprisonment. Other convictions on the same day resulted in five terms of 12 months' imprisonment to run concurrently. In October 1995, the applicant claimed asylum by post, but in January 1998, the application was refused for non-compliance. In September 2000, the applicant and his wife applied for leave to remain under an overstayer's regularisation scheme. In April 2005, they both were granted indefinite leave to remain.

In November 2006, the applicant was convicted of sexual assault. He was sentenced to 15 months' imprisonment, with half to be spent in custody and half on licence, and he was registered as a sex offender. The Secretary of State for the Home Department made a deportation order in March 2007, on the basis that deportation was necessary for the prevention of disorder and crime and for the protection of health and morals. The applicant appealed against that decision but the appeal was dismissed in July 2007. Although the judge accepted that the applicant had established a family life in the UK, and that deportation would interfere with that family life, he concluded that the measure was proportionate because the applicant remained a potential offender who posed a threat to society. The applicant sought permission to apply for judicial review, which was refused in August 2007, and again in November 2007.

The applicant was subsequently served with removal directions set for January 2008. On 18 January 2008, he introduced his case with the Court and on 24 January 2008, the Court ordered that the case be notified urgently to the government under rule 40 of the Rules of Court. On the same day the applicant again sought permission to apply for judicial review. Permission was refused and in April 2008, the appeal against this decision was dismissed at an oral hearing. The applicant was served with new removal directions and he was deported to Nigeria.

The Court held that the measures complained of interfered with both the applicant's 'private life' and his 'family life'. Of note is the Court's finding that the applicant's private life was interfered with.[75] In doing this, the Court observed that Art 8 also protects the right to establish and develop relationships with other human beings and the outside world and can sometimes embrace aspects of an individual's social identity. In this regard, the Court held that it must be accepted that the totality of social ties between settled migrants and the community in which they are living constitutes part of the concept of 'private life' within the meaning of Art 8. In the Court's view, regardless of the existence or otherwise of a 'family life', the expulsion of a settled migrant therefore constitutes an interference with his or her right to respect for private life. It will, however, depend on the circumstances of the particular case whether it is appropriate for the Court to focus on the 'family life' rather than the 'private life' aspect.[76]

The Court observed, however, that such interference will only be in breach of Art 8 of the Convention in circumstances where it is not 'in accordance with the law', it does not pursue one or more of the legitimate aims listed therein, or is not 'necessary in a democratic society', as provided for in Art 8(2). The Court found that the principal issue which had to be determined was whether the interference was 'necessary in a democratic society'.[77] The relevant criteria that the Court uses to assess whether an expulsion measure is necessary in a democratic society were summarised in the case of *Üner v the Netherlands*:[78]

'57. Even if Article 8 of the Convention does not therefore contain an absolute right for any category of alien not to be expelled, the Court's case-law amply demonstrates that there are circumstances where the expulsion of an alien will give rise to a violation of that provision (see, for example, the judgments in *Moustaquim v. Belgium, Beldjoudi v. France* and *Boultif v. Switzerland*, [cited above]; see also *Amrollahi v. Denmark*, no. 56811/00, 11 July 2002; *Yılmaz v. Germany*, no. 52853/99, 17 April 2003; and *Keles v. Germany*, 32231/02, 27 October 2005). In the case of *Boultif* the Court elaborated the relevant criteria which it would use in order to assess whether an expulsion measure was necessary in a democratic society and proportionate to the legitimate aim pursued. These criteria, as reproduced in paragraph 40 of the Chamber judgment in the present case, are the following:

–   the nature and seriousness of the offence committed by the applicant;
–   the length of the applicant's stay in the country from which he or she is to be expelled;
–   the time elapsed since the offence was committed and the applicant's conduct during that period;
–   the nationalities of the various persons concerned;
–   the applicant's family situation, such as the length of the marriage, and other factors expressing the effectiveness of a couple's family life;

---

[75]   Ibid, para 37.
[76]   *Maslov v Austria [GC]* App no 1638/03, ECHR 2008, para 63.
[77]   *Omojudi v United Kingdom* [2009] App no 1820/08, 24 November 2009, para 41.
[78]   *Üner v the Netherlands [GC]* App no 46410/99, ECHR 2006, paras 57–58.

–   whether the spouse knew about the offence at the time when he or she entered into a family relationship;

–   whether there are children of the marriage, and if so, their age; and

-     the seriousness of the difficulties which the spouse is likely to encounter in the country to which the applicant is to be expelled.

58.   The Court would wish to make explicit two criteria which may already be implicit in those identified in the *Boultif* judgment:

–   the best interests and well-being of the children, in particular the seriousness of the difficulties which any children of the applicant are likely to encounter in the country to which the applicant is to be expelled; and

–   the solidity of social, cultural and family ties with the host country and with the country of destination.'

The Court observed that the applicant's most serious offences were committed in 1989 and 2005.[79] During the 16 years between these offences, the applicant largely stayed out of trouble. Further, the applicant's offences were of a completely different nature and there was no indication that they were the result of any 'underlying problem'. In particular, there was no evidence of any pattern of sexual offending. The Court also noted that it attached 'considerable weight to the fact that the Secretary of State for the Home Department, who was fully aware of his offending history, granted the applicant Indefinite Leave to Remain in the United Kingdom in 2005'.[80] Indeed, because of this, the Court found that for the purposes of assessing whether the interference with the applicant's family and private life was necessary in a democratic society, the only relevant offences were those committed after the applicant was granted indefinite leave to remain.[81]

The Court attached considerable weight to the solidity of the applicant's family ties in the UK and the difficulties that his family would face were they to return to Nigeria.[82] In particular, it was the Court's view that the two youngest children, who were born in the UK and have lived there their whole lives, were not of an adaptable age and would likely encounter significant difficulties if they were to relocate to Nigeria. It was further observed that it would be virtually impossible for the oldest child to relocate to Nigeria as he has a young daughter who was born in the UK. By way of conclusion, the Court held that having regard to the circumstances of the present case, in particular the strength of the applicant's family ties to the UK, his length of residence, and the difficulty that his youngest children would face if they were to relocate to Nigeria, the Court found that the applicant's deportation was not proportionate to the legitimate aim pursued.[83] It was held that there has been a violation of Art 8 of the Convention.[84]

---

[79]   *Omojudi v United Kingdom* [2009] App no 1820/08, 24 November 2009, para 42.
[80]   Ibid, para 42.
[81]   Ibid, para 43.
[82]   Ibid, para 46.
[83]   Ibid, para 48.
[84]   Ibid, para 49.

(c) Domestic violence

The case of *Opuz v Turkey* concerns the issue of domestic violence carried out on the applicant and her mother, which resulted in the murder of the applicant's mother and persistent threats on the life of the applicant.[85] As to the facts of the case, the applicant's mother married AO and the applicant married HO, AO's son. There were seven distinct instances of domestic violence perpetrated by HO, including one instance by HO with AO, which came to the attention of the public authorities. All of these rendered the applicant and her mother unfit to work for a number of days and some involved life-threatening injuries. The applicant and her mother made complaints to the Diyarbakir Public Prosecutor's Office on a number of occasions but subsequently withdrew their complaints. This meant that the basis for the proceedings was removed under art 456(4) of the Criminal Code.

In March 1998, the applicant brought divorce proceedings against HO on the ground that he was mistreating her, as proved by medical reports. The applicant moved in with her mother and in April of that year, they sought protective measures from the authorities as they stated that HO had attempted to kill them with his car and had threatened to kill them if the applicant did not return to HO. The Diyarbakir Chief Public Prosecutor's Office indicted HO and AO and charged them with issuing death threats against the applicant and her mother, contrary to art 188(1) of the Criminal Code. In May 1998, the Assize Court classified the offence involving an incident with HO's car as attempted murder. During the hearing in July 1998, HO said that the incident with the car had been an accident. The applicant and her mother confirmed HO's statement and maintained that they no longer wished to continue the proceedings. In June 1998, the Diyarbakir Assize Court acquitted HO and his father of the charges of issuing death threats for lack of sufficient evidence. In November 1998, the Diyarbakir Assize Court decided that, although the applicant's mother had withdrawn her complaint in respect of the incident with the car, HO should still be convicted of that offence, since the injuries were serious. Subsequently, the court sentenced HO to 3 months' imprisonment and a fine; the sentence of imprisonment was later commuted to a fine.

In October of that year, HO stabbed the applicant to the extent that she had seven knife injuries on different parts of her body. However, the injuries were not classified as life-threatening. HO handed himself in at a police station but was released after his statement had been taken. In November 2001, both the applicant and her mother lodged a criminal complaint with the Diyarbakir Public Prosecutor's Office, alleging that HO had been threatening them. The police took statements from HO and in March, 2002, the public prosecutor decided that there was no concrete evidence to prosecute HO apart from the allegations made by the applicant and her mother. In March 2002, HO shot and killed the applicant's mother. In May of that year, the Diyarbakir 2nd Magistrates' Court imposed a fine on HO for the knife assault on the applicant.

---

[85] *Opuz v Turkey* [2009] App no 33401/02, 9 September 2009.

In March 2008, the Diyarbakir Assize Court convicted HO of murder and illegal possession of a firearm. It sentenced him to life imprisonment. However, taking into account the fact that the accused had committed the offence as a result of provocation by the deceased and his good conduct during the trial, the court mitigated the original sentence, changing it to 15 years and 10 months' imprisonment and a fine. In view of the time spent by the convict in pretrial detention and the fact that the judgment would be examined on appeal, the court ordered the release of HO.

In April 2008, the applicant sought measures to protect her life from the authorities. She alleged that HO threatened her boyfriend and told him that he would kill him and the applicant. She also said that she had been changing her address constantly so that HO could not find her. In May 2008, the applicant's representative asked the European Court of Human Rights to request the government to provide sufficient protection.

The European Court held that there had been a violation of Art 2 of the Convention in respect of the death of the applicant's mother, a violation of Art 3 of the Convention in respect of the authorities' failure to protect the applicant against domestic violence perpetrated by HO and that there has been a violation of Art 14 read in conjunction with Arts 2 and 3 of the Convention. Of particular note is the Court's comment that, 'in domestic violence cases perpetrators' rights cannot supersede victims' human rights to life and to physical and mental integrity'.[86]

In reaching a decision in this case, the Court drew on relevant international and comparative law material. In particular, the Court drew on the Convention on the Elimination of All Forms of Discrimination against Women (CEDAW) which was adopted by the UN General Assembly in 1979 and ratified by Turkey in 1986.[87] The Court referred to the CEDAW Committee's General Recommendation No 19 on 'Violence Against Women' which found that 'gender-based violence is a form of discrimination that seriously inhibits women's ability to enjoy rights and freedoms on a basis of equality with men' which is prohibited under Art 1 of CEDAW.[88] Within the general category of gender-based violence, the Committee includes violence by 'private act' and 'family violence'.[89] Crucially, CEDAW observed that gender-based violence triggers duties in states, including a duty on states to 'take all legal and other measures that are necessary to provide effective protection of women against

---

[86]   Ibid, para 147.

[87]   Ibid, para 73.

[88]   Ibid, para 74. See CEDAW, General Recommendation No 19 on 'Violence Against Women' (1992) UN Doc CEDAW/C/1992/L 1/Add 15.

[89]   *Opuz v Turkey* [2009] App no 33401/02, 9 September 2009, para 74. See CEDAW, General Recommendation No 19 on 'Violence Against Women' (1992) UN Doc CEDAW/C/1992/L 1/Add 15 at para 24(a) and para 24(b). See also, para 24(r).

gender based violence including penal sanctions, civil remedies and compensatory provisions to protect women against all kinds of violence'.[90]

The Court also drew on the Council of Europe's Recommendation Rec(2002)5 of 30 April 2002, on the Protection of Women against Violence which noted that member states should introduce, develop and/or improve where necessary national policies against violence based on maximum safety and protection of victims, support and assistance, adjustment of the criminal and civil law, raising of public awareness, training for professionals confronted with violence against women and prevention.[91] The Council of Europe also recommended that member states should penalise serious violence against women such as sexual violence and rape, abuse of the vulnerability of pregnant, defenceless, ill, disabled or dependent victims, as well as penalising abuse of position by the perpetrator.[92] The Recommendation also stated that member states should ensure that all victims of violence are able to institute proceedings, make provisions to ensure that criminal proceedings can be initiated by the public prosecutor, encourage prosecutors to regard violence against women as an aggravating or decisive factor in deciding whether or not to prosecute in the public interest, ensure where necessary that measures are taken to protect victims effectively against threats and possible acts of revenge and take specific measures to ensure that children's rights are protected during proceedings.[93]

With regard to violence within the family, the Council of Europe recommended that member states should classify all forms of violence within the family as criminal offences and envisage the possibility of taking measures in order, inter alia, to enable the judiciary to adopt interim measures aimed at protecting victims, to ban the perpetrator from contacting, communicating with or approaching the victim, or residing in or entering defined areas, to penalise all breaches of the measures imposed on the perpetrator and to establish a compulsory protocol for operation by the police, medical and social services.[94]

The Court also examined the Inter-American Court's approach to violence against women.[95] In particular, its case-law holds that states must act with due diligence to prevent human rights violations, investigate and sanction perpetrators and provide appropriate reparations to their families.[96] The Court also referred to reports concerning domestic violence in Turkey which detailed,

---

[90] *Opuz v Turkey* [2009] App no 33401/02, 9 September 2009, para 74. See CEDAW, General Recommendation No 19 on 'Violence Against Women' (1992) UN Doc CEDAW/C/1992/L 1/Add 15 at para 24(t)(i).

[91] *Opuz v Turkey* [2009] App no 33401/02, 9 September 2009, para 80. This Recommendation is available at: https://wcd.coe.int/wcd/ViewDoc.jsp?id=280915 (accessed 24 May 2011).

[92] *Opuz v Turkey* [2009] App no 33401/02, 9 September 2009, para 81.

[93] Ibid.

[94] Ibid, para 82.

[95] Ibid, para 84.

[96] American Convention on Human Rights, signed at the Inter-American Specialized Conference on Human Rights, San Jose, Costa Rica, 22 November 1969. See, eg, the case of *Maria Da Penha v Brazil*, Case 12.051, Report No 54/01, Inter-Am CHR, Annual Report 2000, OEA/Ser L/V.II.111 Doc 20 rev (2000).

inter alia, delays in fixing hearing dates, failure to implement injunctions and tolerance of domestic violence in many areas.[97]

The Court noted that Art 2(1) requires states to take appropriate steps to safeguard the lives of those within its jurisdiction.[98] This involves putting in place effective criminal law provisions and law enforcement machinery for deterrence, punishment and the protection of individuals whose life is at risk from the criminal acts of another individual.[99] For a positive obligation to arise, it must be established that the authorities knew or ought to have known of the existence of a real and immediate risk to the life of an identified individual from the criminal acts of a third party and that they failed to take measures within the scope of their powers which, judged reasonably, might have been expected to avoid that risk.[100] The due process rights of parties, including the guarantees contained in Arts 5 and 8 of the Convention, must also be adhered to.[101]

On the facts of the case, the Court observed that there was escalating violence against the applicant and her mother by HO and there was a significant risk of further violence.[102] Further, the crimes committed by HO were sufficiently serious to warrant preventive measures. The authorities' reaction to the applicant's and her mother's petitions was limited to taking statements from HO. The Court held that the authorities could have foreseen a lethal attack by HO and that they failed to take reasonable measures which could have had a real prospect of altering the outcome or mitigating the harm.[103]

The Court noted that there seems to be no general consensus among states parties regarding the pursuance of the criminal prosecution against perpetrators of domestic violence when the victim withdraws complaints.[104] It drew on comparative material and noted, for example, that in 11 member states

---

[97] The Court considered the following: *The opinion of Purple Roof Women's Shelter Foundation (Mor Cati Kadin Siginagi Vakfi) on the implementation of Law no. 4320* (7 July 2007); Women's Rights Information and Implementation Centre of the Diyarbakir Bar Association (KA-MER) *Implementation of Law no. 4320* (25 November 2005); *Diyarbakir KA-MER Emergency helpline statistics regarding the period between 1 August 1997 and 30 June 2007*; Amnesty International's 2004 Report *Turkey: Women Confronting Family Violence*; Diyarbakir Bar Association's Justice For All Project and the Women's Rights Information and Implementation Centre *Research Report on Honour Crimes* (cited in para 192 of *Opuz v Turkey*).

[98] Article 2(1): 'Everyone's right to life shall be protected by law. No one shall be deprived of his life intentionally save in the execution of a sentence of a court following his conviction of a crime for which this penalty is provided by law'. *Opuz v Turkey* [2009] App no 33401/02, 9 September 2009, para 128. See the case of *LCB v the United Kingdom*, 9 June 1998, para 36, Reports 1998-III.

[99] See *Osman v the United Kingdom*, 28 October 1998, para 115, Reports 1998-VIII, cited in *Kontrová v Slovakia* App no 7510/04, ECHR 2007, para 49.

[100] *Opuz v Turkey* [2009] App no 33401/02, 9 September 2009, para 129.

[101] *Osman v the United Kingdom*, 28 October 1998, para 115, Reports 1998-VIII.

[102] *Opuz v Turkey* [2009] App no 33401/02, 9 September 2009, para 134.

[103] Ibid, para 136. See also *E and Others v the United Kingdom* [2002] App no 33218/96, 26 November 2002, para 99.

[104] *Opuz v Turkey* [2009] App no 33401/02, 9 September 2009, para 138.

of the Council of Europe, namely in Albania, Austria, Bosnia and Herzegovina, Estonia, Greece, Italy, Poland, Portugal, San Marino, Spain and Switzerland, the authorities are required to continue criminal proceedings despite the victim's withdrawal of complaint in cases of domestic violence.[105] The Court observed that states should strike a balance between a victim's Art 2, Art 3 and Art 8 rights in deciding on a course of action and held that the following factors should be taken into account:[106]

> '–   the seriousness of the offence;
> –   whether the victim's injuries are physical or psychological;
> –   if the defendant used a weapon;
> –   if the defendant has made any threats since the attack;
> –   if the defendant planned the attack;
> –   the effect (including psychological) on any children living in the household;
> –   the chances of the defendant offending again;
> –   the continuing threat to the health and safety of the victim or anyone else who was, or could become, involved;
> –   the current state of the victim's relationship with the defendant;
> –   the effect on that relationship of continuing with the prosecution against the victim's wishes;
> –   the history of the relationship, particularly if there had been any other violence in the past;
> –   and the defendant's criminal history, particularly any previous violence.'

The Court further observed that the more serious the offence or the greater the risk of further offences, the more likely that the prosecution should continue in the public interest, even if victims withdraw their complaints.[107] In the Court's opinion, the authorities in Turkey did not sufficiently consider the above factors when repeatedly deciding to discontinue the criminal proceedings against HO. Instead, they seemed to have given exclusive weight to the need to refrain from interfering in what they perceived to be a 'family matter'.[108] The Court reiterated that, in some instances, the national authorities' interference with the private or family life of the individuals might be necessary in order to protect the health and rights of others or to prevent commission of criminal acts.[109] The Court held that the legislative framework in Turkey fell short of the requirements inherent in the state's positive obligations to establish and apply effectively a system punishing all forms of domestic violence and providing sufficient safeguards for the victims. Further, the Court observed that the local public prosecutor or the judge at the Magistrates' Court could have ordered a protective measure, such as an injunction.[110] The Court concluded that the national authorities cannot be considered to have displayed due diligence and

---

[105]   Ibid, para 87.
[106]   Ibid, para 138.
[107]   Ibid, para 139.
[108]   Ibid, para 143.
[109]   See *KA and AD v Belgium* App no 42758/98 and 45558/99, 17 February 2005, para 81.
[110]   *Opuz v Turkey* [2009] App no 33401/02, 9 September 2009, para 148.

failed in their positive obligation to protect the right to life of the applicant's mother within the meaning of Art 2 of the Convention.[111]

The Court also held that states are required, under Arts 1 and 3 of the Convention, to take measures designed to ensure that individuals within their jurisdiction are not subjected to torture or inhuman or degrading treatment or punishment, including such ill-treatment administered by private individuals.[112] Children and other vulnerable individuals, in particular, are entitled to state protection, in the form of effective deterrence, against such serious breaches of personal integrity.[113] The Court noted that the applicant may be considered to fall within the group of 'vulnerable individuals' entitled to state protection and that the violence suffered by the applicant was sufficiently serious to amount to ill-treatment.[114] The Court held that the authorities did not display the required diligence to prevent the recurrence of violent attacks against the applicant.[115] It further held that the judicial decisions in this case revealed a lack of efficacy and a certain degree of tolerance, and had no noticeable preventive or deterrent effect on the conduct of HO.[116]

V CONCLUSIONS

This year's survey has highlighted the many developments which have taken place in the field of international family law. There were a great number of ratifications and signatures of various international instruments, including instruments of the Hague Conference and the UN. Further, the issue of children's rights, for example, was a frequently discussed issue by the Hague Conference in the context of child support and also in the context of the need for direct judicial communications in international child protection cases. Further, the UN Committee on the Rights of the Child published its General Comment on the Right of the Child to be Heard, a document which will undoubtedly be most useful for all those seeking to implement this right across a wide range of areas.

In relation to the Council of Europe, the issue of discrimination arose in two of the European Court of Human Rights cases discussed in this chapter, first in

---

[111] Ibid.

[112] Article 3 of the Convention: 'No one shall be subjected to torture or to inhuman or degrading treatment of punishment.' See *Opuz v Turkey* [2009] App no 33401/02, 9 September 2009, para 159. See also *HLR v France*, 29 April 1997, para 40, Reports 1997-III.

[113] *A v the United Kingdom*, 23 September 1998, para 22, Reports 1998-VI.

[114] *Opuz v Turkey* [2009] App no 33401/02, 9 September 2009, paras 160–161. The Court reiterated that ill-treatment must attain a minimum level of severity if it is to fall within the scope of Art 3; para 158. The assessment of this minimum is relative: it depends on all the circumstances of the case, such as the nature and context of the treatment, its duration, its physical and mental effects and, in some instances, the sex, age and state of health of the victim; *Costello-Roberts v the United Kingdom*, Series A, App no 247-C, 25 March 1993, para 30.

[115] *Opuz v Turkey* [2009] App no 33401/02, 9 September 2009, para 169.

[116] Ibid, para 170.

the context of a father's right to custody of his child and second in the context of domestic violence and its impact on women. Both cases are instructive as regards the boundaries which the Court will accept as regards discrimination. The other case discussed in this section highlights the importance which the Court attaches to the strength of a non-national's ties to a country through length of residence and potential difficulties for the non-national and his or her family if they were required to relocate elsewhere. Indeed this case offers important jurisprudence as regards non-nationals' rights under Art 8 of the Convention, in relation to both the right to family life as well as the right to private life.

Argentina

FAMILY, PLURALISM AND EQUALITY: MARRIAGE AND SEXUAL ORIENTATION IN ARGENTINE LAW

*Cecilia P Grosman and Marisa Herrera**

'Reality is too rich and its contours too complex to be fully seen by the light of a single lamp'

Ilya Prigogine

Résumé

La grande diversité des modèles familiaux est désormais une réalité sociale. En légalisant le mariage entre personnes de même sexe, l'Argentine a fait un grand pas dans la reconnaissance de cette diversité et elle devint ainsi, en juillet 2010, le premier pays d'Amérique latine à emprunter cette voie. Toutefois, cette réforme demeure inachevée. L'encadrement légal complet de la reproduction assistée fait encore défaut, en matière de nom de famille, c'est encore la primauté du père qui domine et les lois persistent à accorder la priorité à la mère dans les disputes concernant la garde des enfants. Ce texte aborde également la question complexe de la filiation légale.

I INTRODUCTION

Reality clearly demonstrates that the family takes multiple forms. It shows that besides the nuclear family – which is the principal determinant of civil or family legislation throughout the world and particularly in Latin America – there other modalities of living together which are available to couples, all based on affection. For example, there are persons who do not wish to formalise their

---

*   Cecilia P Grosman, Doctor in Law, UBA (University of Buenos Aires). Professor and Director of the Family and Inheritance Law Centre, Faculty of Law, University of Buenos Aires; Senior researcher of CONICET (National Council of Scientific and Technical Research); Director of the Specialization in Family Law and the Master in Family Law, Childhood and Adolescence of the Faculty of Law, University of Buenos Aires. Director of the Interdisciplinary Journal of Doctrine and Jurisprudence, Director of Family Law edited by Abeledo Perrot, Buenos Aires, Argentina.
   Marisa Herrera, Doctor in Law, UBA (University of Buenos Aires). Specialist in Family Law, University of Buenos Aires. Researcher of CONICET; Sub-Director of the Specialization in Family Law and the Master in Family Law, Childhood and Adolescence of the Faculty of Law, University of Buenos Aires. Lecturer of the Faculty of Law, University of Buenos Aires and the University of Palermo.

relationship and live together informally for many years, and there are also longstanding relationships made up of people of the same sex. Is it the case that only matrimonial heterosexual relationships deserve express legal recognition? Should not the law concern itself with – and consequently regulate – what actually occurs at the factual or emotional level, totally independent from its members' beliefs and morphology? What forms of familial organisation should be included in the sociological concept of the family, important to the law in light of the obligatory international doctrine of human rights?

In other words, the concept of the family based on matrimony and two people of different sexes, and the plainly erroneous idea of procreation or 'propagation of the species' as an element or basic requirement for the existence of the family, in fact shares the stage with other familial configurations, still rendered invisible in so many countries.

For exactly this reason, and with the aim of reducing the gap between the law and reality in relation to the regulation of the family, Law 26.618 was enacted in Argentina on 15 July 2010. This law extends the institution of civil marriage to same-sex couples; in other words, it allows every person, regardless of his or her sexual orientation, to marry. Argentina was the first country in Latin America to pass a law of this nature.[1]

Law 26.618 has become known as the law of *matrimonio igualitario* on the understanding that, in light of the basic human rights principles of equality and non-discrimination, the institution of marriage must be accessible to same-sex couples, and that sexual orientation may not be relied upon to exclude certain people from a social institution open to others. A clear-cut constitutional-international analysis (the principle of equality and non-discrimination) was one of the central foundations, or indeed the backbone, of this legal reform.

---

[1] It should be noted that another jurisdiction in the region which permits same-sex marriage is the Federal District of Mexico. However, Argentina remains the first country in Latin America to legislate to this effect, as the Federal District's legislation only applies to that one state within Mexico. In Argentina civil legislation is the same for all the provinces, while in the Mexican legal system, each state has the freedom to legislate for itself in respect of substantive as well as procedural civil law matters. On 21 December 2009, the Federal District introduced several reforms to its Civil Code and Civil Practice Code, including the legal recognition of marriage regardless of the sexual orientation of the couple. Essentially, art 146 of the Civil Code was amended to state: 'Marriage is the free union of two people for the realisation of a life in common, in which both seek respect, equality and mutual assistance . . . It must be celebrated before the Judge of the Civil Registry and comply with the formalities stipulated in the present code'. As this amendment follows several pieces of legislation which also extend the institution of marriage to same-sex couples, not only does it modify every reference to the notions of 'man' and 'woman', but it also removes every reference to the 'procreation of children in a free, responsible and informed way' as a proper outcome of marriage (according to Andrés Gil Domínguez, María Victoria Famá and Marisa Herrera *Matrimonio Igualitario. Derecho Constitucional de Familia* (Buenos Aires: Ediar, 2010) p 149ff).

As we will see, Law 26.618 follows, albeit with certain differences, the basic structure adopted in Spain's Law 13/2005 and in other norms dealing with the same subject matter, which permit all couples to marry regardless of their sexual orientation. Accordingly, of the ten[2] countries which allow same-sex marriage in this broad fashion, none undertook a substantial modification of all the aspects of family law affected by this egalitarian law. One of the fears of the reformist movements (ie those in favour of the legal recognition of same-sex marriage) was that such recognition may not be achieved if a comprehensive reform were attempted. It is for this reason that none of the laws passed in the still scarce number of countries around the globe that permit same-sex marriage introduced substantial or radical legislative modifications in each one of the civil law institutions which would have been affected by such laws. Instead, more general reforms were carried out.

As we will see in the course of this chapter, the Argentine reform could be classified as having gone half way. Not only did it produce modifications of a terminological nature, but Law 26.618 also expresses something else in relation to certain family law concepts, albeit with some problems or errors.

In addition, it may be noted that Law 26.618 exists in a highly complex normative context. In Argentina, there is no comprehensive regulation of the use of assisted reproduction techniques; the legal regime concerning children's surnames remains centred around the father, and there are still laws which provide a preference to mothers in custody cases, on the basis that a priori and in the abstract, mothers 'naturally' are better equipped to be entrusted with the care of their children. It was within this context, characterised by certain silences and inequalities, that Law 26.618 came into being. As a result, and as will be analysed briefly below, it brings with it a series of interpretative problems.[3]

Generally speaking, the Law – as is the case in all the foreign legislation regarding this issue – emphasises the recognition of the right of every person to marry, whatever his or her sexual orientation. To this end, it introduced terminological modifications, replacing a number of texts centred on the difference of gender with others that contain neutral principles. In this way, it

---

[2]   The countries which permit marriage on an equal rights basis are, in chronological order, Holland (2001), Belgium (2003), Canada (2005), Spain (2005), South Africa (2006), Norway (2009), Sweden (2009), Portugal (2010), Iceland (2010) and Argentina (2010). Likewise, some states in the United States permit same-sex marriage, namely: Massachusetts (2004), Connecticut (2008), Iowa (2009), District of Columbia (2009), Vermont (2009), New Hampshire (2010) and Washington DC (2010), as well as the Federal District of Mexico (2009), referred to above.

[3]   For more information on the reform of the civil marriage regime in Argentina, we recommend, besides the work already cited and along with so many others, Martin Aldao and Laura Clérico (eds), *Matrimonio Igualitario* (Eudeba, Buenos Aires, 2010) ; Bruno Bimbi *Matrimonio igualitario. Intrigas, tensiones y secretos en el camino hacia la ley* (Buenos Aires: Planeta, 2010) and Nora Lloveras and Olga Orlandi and Fabian Faraoni *Régimen jurídico del matrimonio civil. Ley 26.618* (Córdoba: Enfoque Jurídico, 2010); AAVV Nuevo régimen legal del matrimonio civil. Ley 26.618 (Santa Fe: Rubinzal Culzoni, 2010) and Alejandro Ossola *Modificación al régimen del matrimonio. Ley 26.618* (Córdoba: Advocatus, 2010).

avoided the words 'man' and 'woman', and replaced them with 'spouse'. Also, and expressly, it modified art 172 of the Civil Code, in which the requirements for a legal marriage are specified. Following the entry into force of Law 26.618, the relevant part of art 172 reads:

> 'An indispensible requirement for marriage is full and free consent, personally expressed by the betrothed before the competent authority. Each marriage will give rise to the same obligations and effects, whether the betrothed are of the same sex or of a different sex . . .'[4]

In addition, as well as introducing terminological modifications and other, more significant amendments to various articles of the Civil Code, Law 26.618 reformed a number of the provisions of Law 18.248, concerning people's names, and Law 26.413, which regulates Civil Registry 26.413.[5] How was this cutting-edge legislative recognition achieved? This question is tackled in a very succinct way in the next section.

II SOME REFLECTIONS ON THE BACKGROUND TO LAW 26.618

(a) The concept of the family in constitutional texts: the broad approach as an incentive for the recognition of rights

The law exists within an extensive constitutional context and is therefore able to generate debate in democratic fora, such as the Argentine Congress or Parliament. Unlike so many countries, which in their constitutional texts restrict the recognition of the family to opposite-sex couples,[6] the National Constitution of Argentina has nothing to say about the matter; referring instead, and in an extensive way, to 'the integral protection of the family' in its

---

4   The former text provided: 'An indispensable requirement for marriage is full and free consent, personally expressed by the man and the woman before the competent authority. An act which lacks any of these requirements will be of no legal effect . . .'.

5   Aída Kemelmajer de Carlucci, Marisa Herrera and Eleonora Lamm 'Filiación y homoparentalidad. Luces y sombras de un debate incómodo y actual', Revista La Ley, Buenos Aires, 2010-E-977.

6   To cite a number of examples from Latin America, the reform of the 2005 Constitution of Honduras amended art 112 to read as follows: 'The right of men and women to marry is recognised, where each has that status naturally, as is the legal equality of the spouses . . . De facto unions between persons equally capable of marriage are recognised. The law will establish the conditions upon which such a marriage may have effect. Marriage and de facto unions between people of the same sex are prohibited. Same-sex marriages or de facto unions celebrated or recognised under the laws of other countries law will not be valid in Honduras'. Or more recently, the 2010 Constitution of the Dominican Republic provides in art 55, regarding 'The Rights of the Family' that 'The State will promote and will protect the organisation of the family founded on the institution of marriage between a man and a woman. The law will establish the requirements in relation to contracting for it, the formalities for its celebration, its personal and patrimonial effects . . . The singular and stable union between a man and a woman, free from marital impediments, who form a home, gives rise to rights and obligations in respect of their personal and patrimonial relations, as provided in law' (subsection 5).

art 14 bis. In this way, the definition of what is understood by 'family' is left to be determined by democratic debate (that which occurs within the framework of the legislature or Parliament).

In this sense, it is relevant to recall that, in a judgment dated 20 November 2005, Argentina's Supreme Court of Justice of the Nation stated: 'Since 1853 [the date in which the National Constitution was enacted] we have been required to make the Republic of Argentina into a Constitutional State of Law'.[7] On a number of occasions, an issue has been raised about the nature of a state model based on these characteristics, and the response has been that it is a state principally founded upon the concepts of pluralism, tolerance and participation. It has been argued, along these lines, that:[8]

'The legislators and judges, as representatives of the duly constituted state powers, should, in creating and applying laws, comply with supreme law norms, and, therefore, may not make decisions on the basis of their own discretionary criteria, even if that represents the thinking or absolute desire of the majority. Any belief or conviction – even, we insist, a predominant one – is subject to the same absolute limit: the essential cores of the fundamental, universal and inalienable rights, which tend toward the development of interpretations which reflect the plurality of an open society.'

Therefore, such a state has no official religion, is secular or disestablished and free of any ecclesiastical influence, and the concepts of the state, the law and religion are clearly differentiated. Accordingly, it would not be possible to construct a normative system for such a state on the basis of moral/Christian rules. Instead, such a system must be based on legal rules derived from the Constitution and the international treaties which complement it. These are the key legal tools, and they play a fundamental role for all subordinate law.[9]

It is precisely from this constitutional-international perspective that it has been argued in academic writings that:[10]

'The variety of the forms in which the family may be constituted represents a significant split from the standard family model based on marriage . . . [O]ther

---

[7]   Paragraph 14 from the summarised findings of the judgment of Judges Petracchi, Maqueda, Zaffaroni and Lorenzetti (CSJN, 20 September 2005, 'Casal, Matías E. and other', LL, 2005-F, 110, with a commentary by Augusto M Morello and Germán González Campaña 'Reformulación de la casación penal').

[8]   Andrés Gil Domínguez, María Victoria Famá and Marisa Herrera *Derecho Constitucional de Familia* (Buenos Aires: Ediar, 2006) vol II, pp 21 and 22.

[9]   For further discussion of the secularisation of family law, we recommend 'A Secularização do Direito de Família' in Belmiro Pedro Welter and Rolf Hanssen Madaleno (eds) *Direitos Fundamentais do Direito de Família* (Porto Alegre: Livraria do Adrogado, 2004) pp 87ff and Rodrigo Da Cunhna Pereira *Direito de Família. Uma abordagem psicoanalítica* (Belo Horizonte: Del Rey, 3rd edn, updated and enlarged, 2003) chapters I and II.

[10]   María Claudia Crespo Brauner 'O pluralismo no Direito de Família brasileiro: realidade social e reinvenção da família' in Belmiro Pedro Welter and Rolf Hanssen Madaleno (eds), ibid p 259.

forms of relationships are equally deserving of legal protection, in recognition of the principle of pluralism and liberty that personifies postmodern society.'

One of main challenges of contemporary family law is to define and to regulate the concept of the family with the understanding that 'essentially, it has moved from being a nucleus of finances and reproduction to being a place of affection and love'.[11] This is so much the case that a Brazilian author, María Berenice Dias, talks about the right of 'families' in the plural, confirming by the use of this expression that there is no single definition of the family – such as the traditional or nuclear family based on marriage between people of the opposite sex – but rather that there are multiple types of family structures.[12]

Undoubtedly, Law 26.618 has profoundly disturbed the concept of the family in Argentine law, modifying the notion of marriage, the most entrenched institution in Argentine legislation and around the world. In other words, this reform requires the revision of deeply rooted ideas, such as that marriage is 'naturally' between a man and a woman. With reference, once again, to the doctrine of international human rights, and, particularly, the principle of equality and non-discrimination, it may be understood that the error lies in considering certain social facts as something 'natural', forgetting that everything that occurs between human beings has a history, a context and, therefore, a particular interpretation. Following this line of argument, it should be recalled that, for centuries, the expression 'natural' was used 'to justify' restricting the right to vote to men and denying it to women; a distinction which for a long period now has been unsustainable.[13] Has the time not now arrived in which this revisionist perspective should be applied to the denial of access to certain rights or institutions, such as marriage, based on a person's sexual orientation? In Argentina, this question has been answered affirmatively, through the enactment of Law 26.618.

(b)   The force of jurisprudence, 'judicial activism' and the system of diffuse constitutional control

Before the enactment of the law, a number of judgments were handed down regarding the constitutionality of art 172 of the Civil Code (referred to above). That article stipulated that marriage could only be between people of the opposite sex.

---

11   Rodrigo Da Cunha Pereira 'Da união estável' in Maria Berenice Dias and Rodrigo Da Cunha Pereira (eds) *Direito de Família e o Novo Código Civil* (Belo Horizonte: Del Rey, IBDFAM, 4th edn, 2006) p 220.

12   According to Dias, the constitutional foundation of the legal recognition of other forms of family organisation revolves around the 'pluralism' already referred to, on the understanding that family entities founded on the basis of affection and which give rise to mutual commitments should not be foreign to the law: Maria Berenice Dias *Manual de Direito das Famílias* (Porto Alegre: Livraria do Adrogado, 2005) pp 62 and 63.

13   See Aída Kemelmajer de Carlucci and Marisa Herrera 'El principio de no discriminación en una reciente sentencia del Tribunal Europeo de Derechos Humanos. Una cuestión en movimiento desde el ámbito regional y una responsabilidad desde el ámbito estatal' *Revista La Ley*, 6 July 2010, pp 3ff.

Argentina has a diffuse system of constitutional control, which is to say that all judges have the power to decree the unconstitutionality of a norm as it applies to a particular case and not erga omnes, as is the case in those jurisdictions which restrict constitutional control to a court or a specialised organ. On this basis, a number of judicial proceedings were commenced by same-sex couples with the intention of obtaining authorisation to marry by means of a declaration of unconstitutionality of the relevant norm (ie art 172) and a consequential judicial order to the civil registry to perform the marriage.

The first case, before the Federal Capital's National Family Court, was dismissed.[14] However, in other cases brought in different jurisdictions (the City of Buenos Aires's Disputes, Administrative and Tax jurisdictions), it was considered that the refusal of a local administrative organ, as the Civil Registry is, to authorise the marriage of same-sex couples violated a series of principles and rights deeply rooted in Argentine constitutional tradition, such as equality and non-discrimination.

In the judgments which found that art 172 was unconstitutional, and which enabled the couples who brought the proceedings legally to marry, a series of different and complementary arguments were made. We highlight the following:

(1) 'The application for amparo [similar to judicial review] brought against the Government of the City of Buenos Aires, with the aim of requiring the authorities of the Civil and Legal Capacity Registry to celebrate a marriage between two people of the same sex, is upheld as the exclusion of the litigants from the right to marry is based on their sexual orientation, which constitutes a category susceptible to discrimination . . . and the State has failed to show that discrimination on the basis of that category is strictly necessary to achieve a legitimate aim';

(2) 'It follows that articles 172 and 188 of the Civil Code should be declared unconstitutional to the extent that they prevent two people of the same sex from marrying, as these norms constitute discrimination by the State

---

[14] We refer to the case *Rachid Maria de la Cruz and Another v the National Registry of the State and Capacity of People (precautionary measures)* of 22 June 2007 by the National Civil Court, No 88 of the Federal Capital, the finding in which was confirmed by Tribunal F of the National Civil Appeals Court on 26 September 2007 (published in LL, 2007-F, 487). In the first judgment, it was stated that 'The non-authorization of marriage between people of the same sex is based in positive law and in the very nature of the institution, given that not only a literal reading but also the spirit of article 172 of the Civil Code support this principle' and that 'There is no illegality in denying the right to marry to those who cannot, due to their nature, meet its objectives. This institution is legislated for persons of the opposite sex who engender and educate their children to achieve humanity's continuation, and the objective and reasonable justification for this difference is that the State privileges those unions which provide the basis for a family, which in turn provides the basis for Argentine society'.

based on sexual orientation, and therefore they violate articles 16 and 19 of the National Constitution, and article 11 of the Constitution of the City of Buenos Aires';[15]

(3) 'on the face of it, nowadays articles 172 and 188 of the Civil Code must be contrasted with the constitutional rules which prohibit discriminatory treatment on the basis of sexual orientation (articles 16 and 19, National Constitution; article 11, Constitution of the City of Buenos Aires; article 26 of the International Covenant of Civil and Political Rights; and amongst others, article 2(2) of the International Covenant of Economic, Social and Cultural Rights; in relation to the Covenant, see in particular General Comment No. 20, by the Committee on Economic, Social and Cultural Rights, dated 22/05/09 which states in relevant part: '"Other status' as recognized in article 2, paragraph 2, includes sexual orientation. States parties should ensure that a person's sexual orientation is not a barrier to realizing Covenant rights . . ."')'; and

(4) 'If the rights of minorities only extend far enough to ensure that their members are tolerated, then little progress has been in relation to achieving sincere and full respect for peoples' way of life. From the perspective of the constitutional regime of the City of Buenos Aires, it is clear that there are no good or bad sexual orientations or genders: sexual preference and gender are extra-moral matters. There is no legal framework according to which normal and pathological genders may be established. The point is to accept that liberty and recognition are very important for human dignity'.[16]

The result of this contradictory jurisprudence was that, while some couples were unable to marry as a result of unfavourable judicial determinations, others could. In addition, some judgments sought to overturn those which had authorised same-sex marriage.[17] A situation of jurisprudential 'chaos' arose, with completely contradictory judgments being given in relation to similar situations. It was in this context that the debate about the bill to reform the legal regime relating to civil marriage took place; with the result of the reform being that the right to marry was extended to all people, regardless of their sexual orientation.

---

[15] The Court of Contentious Administrative and Tax Proceedings, No 15, Ciudad Autónoma de Buenos Aires, 10 November 2009, F A c GCBA, LL, 2009-F, 796.

[16] The Court of Contentious Administrative and Tax Proceedings, No 4, Ciudad Autónoma de Buenos Aires, 22 February 2010, B, D A y Otros c Gcba, La Ley Online.

[17] A judgment given by the National Civil Court no 85 on 8 March 2010 held the following: 'a marriage celebrated between two people of the same sex before the Register of Civil Status and the Capacity of People is absolutely null and void, it being an act the object of which is contrary to public order, under which the institution of marriage is established, as it does not meet the requirements that art. 172 of the Civil Code imposes for a valid marriage, and it is detrimental to the right of men and women to marry and to found a family' (JNac Civ, No 85, 8 March 2010, L, E R, La Ley Online).

There is no doubt that invoking this jurisprudential uncertainty constituted a tool followed by various organisations which defend homosexual rights, in that it served as a means of exerting pressure to achieve a final decision for all the nation's inhabitants. And such a decision was made through the passing of Law 26.618. Therefore, the debate was concluded in the most democratic manner possible, through a law which expressly permits people of the same sex to marry. Is it a good law? Does it resolve all the conflicts and questions that may be perceived from a neutral perspective on sexual orientation matters? What does it regulate and how does it regulate? In the following section, we briefly analyse these questions.

III THE REFORM OF THE LEGAL REGIME FOR CIVIL MARRIAGE: LAW 26.618

(a) General considerations

Without referring to all the substantial changes that would have had to be have been made to achieve the standard of an egalitarian legal regime in family law and the effects or consequences in other areas of law, it is the case that, in relation to a number of issues, there have been certain, albeit deficient, amendments. This has led to national doctrine (at this stage, jurisprudence has not been extended or committed in this respect) being required to devise interpretative positions generating deep and antagonistic debates which continue to this day.

The objective of this chapter is not to go into great detail in relation to all of the amendments – whether substantive, formal or terminological – which Law 26.618 introduced, but rather to discuss a number of them, emphasising the new issues which the reform has generated. Accordingly, we have selected the following issues affected by Law 26.618: filiation, adoption, custody of children after a breakdown of a relationship and children's surnames, with the aim of presenting a more general perspective about this very important reform.

Of course, these are not the only issues which the reform has created. By way of a quick review, we note for example that the extension of the right to marry to same-sex couples requires a rethinking of impotence as causal of the 'relative nullity' of a marriage, as established by the Civil Code (art 220(3)) or the issue of adultery as one of the faults or subjective grounds for separation and binding divorce (art 202(1ro) of the Civil Code). At least until Law 26.618, both concepts were linked to the notion of intercourse. Consequently, Argentine doctrine argued that the maintenance of sexual relations with a person other than one's spouse was adulterous on the basis that the duty of fidelity had been materially violated, while, on the contrary, sexual relations with someone of the same sex was classified as 'grave slander' (art 202(4) of the Civil Code) because of the factual impossibility of intercourse between two people of the same sex. Can different grounds and rules be applied when a spouse maintains sexual relations with another person, despite there being no intercourse? Through the application of the egalitarian principle that inspires all of the reform that Law 26.618 introduced, it follows that these 'notions', which are of a 'heteronomic' character, based as they are on the differentiation between the sexes, should be revised.[18]

Another revisionist perspective could also be observed in the family violence laws and, in particular, those which give special protection to women. In 2009, Argentina passed Law 26.485, which provides comprehensive protection to women, and its regulatory decree is 1011/2010. The issue that doctrine raises, in this area, is whether it is possible to extend the application of this law to couples of the same sex, to couples comprised of two women or to those made up of two men if situations arise in which, as generally occurs in cases of gender violence, the weaker partner – the woman – is subordinated by the stronger – the man. Is it not the case that this clear inequality, which should attract special protection for the weaker party, could not also occur in same-sex relationships?[19]

Clearly, as it may be observed, the introduction of an egalitarian or equal rights perspective in relation to gender in civil law is not a simple task, as it affects or impacts upon a large number of laws, many of which the reform did not expressly amend. A series of issues have arisen as a result, to which doctrine and jurisprudence should attempt to respond.

(b) Determining the matrimonial filiation of two people of the same sex

In Argentina, there is no comprehensive regulation of assisted reproduction, despite the frequent use of such techniques and despite the fact that, in accordance with numerous judgments, they are covered by medical insurance. Recently the province of Buenos Aires approved a law that will allow members of any public medical insurance scheme or private prepaid scheme to receive, for free, cover for assisted fertility treatments. In addition, the law authorises social welfare offices to provide assistance in this regard to people without medical insurance.[20] Accordingly, there is a need for a national law which deals with all of the possible variables regarding filiation, rather than simply the issue of cover for assisted reproduction treatment.

The first and most important question to which the reform gave rise is if the presumption of paternity of a mother's husband, as set out in art 243 of the Civil Code, may be extended to the spouse of a woman who gives birth. The fact is that in Argentina, despite the lack of legislation on the use of assisted reproduction treatments alluded to above, the notion that surrogate maternity is prohibited by art 953 of the Civil Code has always been defended. That

---

[18] Andrés Gil Domínguez and María Victoria Famá and Marisa Herrera, above n 1, p 531ff.
[19] Ibid, p 549ff.
[20] We refer to provincial law 14.208 enacted on 2 December 2010 and regulated by Decree 2980/2010, of 20 December 2010.

article deems null and void any agreement which has as its object 'acts which [are] impossible, illicit, contrary to good customs or prohibited by law, or which are against freedom of action or conscience, or that prejudice the rights of a third party'. On that basis, a determination regarding filiation of children of married couples of the same sex could only occur in a marriage comprised of two women.

In relation to this issue, the reform did not introduce any express amendment to the norms regarding filiation, as set out in the Civil Code. It only modified an aspect of art 36 of Law 26.413, which regulates the role and operation of the Civil Registry. That amendment was as follows:

> 'The first name and surname of the father and the mother or, in the case of children from marriages between people of the same sex, the name and surname of the mother and her spouse, and the type and number of the respective identity documents.' (art 36 of Law 26.618)

Therefore, it appears that if a married woman gives birth to a child, and her maternity of that child is established through the act of giving birth (as provided for in art 242 of the Civil Code), filiation would also be determined in this way in the case of a same-sex (female) couple. This interpretation would be reinforced by the application of the latest regulation issued in relation to Law 26.618 that, by way of an 'interpretative keystone', stipulates in its last paragraph that:

> 'No norm of the Argentine legal system may be interpreted or applied in a way which limits, restricts, excludes or suppresses the exercise or enjoyment of the same rights and obligations, whether in relation to a marriage constituted by people of the same sex or to a marriage comprised of two (2) people of different sex.' (art 42 of Law 26.618)

Moreover, this interpretation is based on one of the basic principles of filiation by the use of assisted reproduction techniques, namely, the will to procreate. It is this will from which the filial link or designation of filiation, and the consequential parental[21] responsibility, are derived. In this way, recognition of the right to identity is encouraged in a dynamic fashion, that is, the sociological-emotional identity determined by the will to assume actively the duties and rights inherent in parental responsibility[22] by the couple that has decided to care for a child, whether that couple be heterosexual or homosexual. In the case of the presumption of filiation (in a broad sense, without considering in a rigid or binary manner that a person should have a mother in the female form and a father with a man's body, but should have two points of reference, regardless of the sex of each), the will to procreate as referred to

---

21 Luz María Pagano 'El apellido de los cónyuges y de los hijos a partir de la ley 26.618' (2011) 48 *Revista Interdisciplinaria de Doctrina y Jurisprudencia. Revista de Derecho de Familia* (Abeledo Perrot, Buenos Aires).

22 María Victoria Famá 'Filiación y homoparentalidad en la ley 26.618 del matrimonio igualitario' (2011) 48 *Revista Interdisciplinaria de Doctrina y Jurisprudencia. Revista Derecho de Familia* (Abeledo Perrot, Buenos Aires).

above would also be present, through marriage. This would particularly be so when through the development of medical science, a woman may engender or gestate a child with genetic material of her spouse, thereby making it possible for the child to be genetically linked with that spouse. Nevertheless, this interpretation cannot be considered as settled in Argentine doctrine and in practice, at least up until now.

In Argentina, the first case of two married women who have used assisted reproduction techniques has already occurred. During the pregnancy of one of the women, they were married. Upon the birth of their child, Vicente, both went to register him. The understanding of the Civil Registry was that art 36 (of Law 26.618, referred to above) only recognised the filiation of Vicente with the woman who gave birth to him but not with her spouse. This was on the basis that the presumption of paternity that arises in the case of the husband of a mother only applied to a man. Consequently, while it was recorded in the birth certificate that the mother who gave birth was married to another woman, it was not recorded that the child was related to this other woman. Further, the child could not take the surname of the other woman, but rather only the surname of the woman who gave birth to him, she being the only one to whom he would be legally related.[23]

The issue becomes even more complicated in the case of a marriage between two married women in which one conceives a child naturally through sexual relations with a man, who then asserts paternity in relation to the child and an intention to exercise the rights and duties that flow from this voluntary act. In such a case, would the presumption of filiation in favour of the mother's spouse apply, or should priority be given to the man's rights, or should the law allow a person to be legally related to three people, and in this way move beyond the traditional binary system?

Further, it must be recalled that the reform was restricted to the institution of marriage and therefore did not introduce any amendments in relation to unmarried same-sex couples or in relation to the issue of extramarital filiation. The result is an incomplete and unequal system, in that the laws relating to matrimonial filiation must be revised due to Law 26.618, but this is not the case in relation to extramarital filiation. This is another concerning gap in the current legal regime.

All of these issues which have arisen as a result of this reform have not been considered in case-law, only in academic debate. In this debate, the civil registries have adopted the most traditional position, namely, that the presumption of paternity in favour of the husband can only be applied in relation to a heterosexual marriage; and in the case of two women, the spouse should not be recognised as another mother, but rather that she should apply to adopt the child of her partner.

---

[23]   Andrés Gil Domínguez and María Victoria Famá and Marisa Herrera *Matrimonio Igualitario. Ley 26.618. Derecho Constitucional de Familia*, above n 1, pp 225ff.

We have a number of reservations in relation to these arguments. First, in the case of two married women where a child is born to one but also possesses genetic material from the other, is it reasonable for the woman who did not give birth to have to adopt her own biological child? On the other hand, the principle of the best interests of the child is relevant. A child born into a same-sex female marriage would have a definite legal connection to the spouse of the mother only after a process of adoption, when this could have been achieved earlier through acceptance of an extension of the presumption of filiation (ie so that the presumption would apply not only to paternity but rather to filiation in a neutral and wider sense).

To conclude this section, we refer to a judgment which highlights the new conflicts arising from the use of assisted reproduction techniques, and the traditional binary position, which considers that a person may only have two parents.

In this judgment, handed down by the Family Court of Córdoba, 4th Division, on 28 June 2010,[24] a visitation rights regime was established in favour of the former lesbian partner of the biological mother of a child, conceived through artificial insemination with semen from a man in a homosexual relationship. It should be clarified that all four people involved had wanted and consented to the insemination and the applicant had lived with the child performing her role as a mother, together with the biological mother. The judge stated:

> '[In t]he life history of the child from his conception to his birth . . . the applicant has played a relevant part . . . The desire to be mothers was determinative in the formation of the relationship between S and M, in relation to both the mutual choice the consolidation of the relationship . . . Moreover, the applicant had very close, intimate and affectionate contact with the child in the first years of his life, all of which both parties to the relationship had agreed to.'

Against this factual background, it was highlighted that:

> ' . . . it cannot be validly argued that a human being is only able to develop him or herself within the family, excluded from other affectionate or social ties, which are also essential for the achievement of a fulfilled adult life. Mrs [S] cannot be considered as unconnected to or a stranger to the child's emotional world and, as a result, to deny her the possibility of making contact with V would not only be prejudicial to the child, as it would impede him from maintaining a relationship with an important person in his life, but there is also no justification for it, especially when the biological mother agreed to and consented to this type of family arrangement from the outset, of which the applicant forms an indivisible part. Considering and respecting the child as a legal subject also means that the behaviour of his role models, who are both necessary and responsible for him, must be coherent and clear, as these persons cannot any longer be considered as

---

[24] Family Court no 4, Córdoba, 28 June 2010, 'A. S. G. v M. V. S. and Another (urgent measures)' (2011) I *Derecho de la Familia. Revista Interdisciplinaria de Doctrina y Jurisprudencia* (Abeledo Perrot, Buenos Aires) pp 137ff with a commentary by Nora Lloveras 'Una madre invisibilizada y una madre biológica "visible": dos madres y la filiación del niño'.

self-contained individuals, but rather have projected themselves onto a third party, the son, permanently marking and incorporating themselves into his life history . . . It follows from this that when V. was born, *in the historical-emotional-individual context that his biological parents chose for him, the decision that they made was not one that concerned only them, as the child was a legal subject with that history and no other.'*[25]

However, in addition to setting a broad regime of visitation rights (twice a week and Friday and Saturday in between), the judgment referred to this regime as 'a maternal or familial contact regime'. In that sense, it was considered necessary to 'distinguish the blood or legal relationship, from that established through the force of circumstance (or affection) and which enjoys a level of social acceptance, which in turn legitimates it, even though it is unrecognised by law'. The judgment also stated that:

' . . . all the parties to this dispute agreed upon the roles that each would fulfil in the family that was to be formed . . . in the case of M and S, a "dual maternity" was agreed upon . . .. The applicant took on this role in day to day life, in relation to the care and attention of the child . . . this type of quasi-kinship does not originate from nature but rather as a result of functions performed. In parallel, for some time psychology has defined paternity and maternity in terms of functions performed rather than in relation to the mere fact of nature.'

And the basis of this decision is set out in the ruling, in the following passage:

'It is because of this that the concept of "socio-affectiveness" is so strong, defined as the necessary element of family relations based on people's will and desire to maintain emotional bonds that go beyond the law, gradually converting itself, together with the legal and biological criteria into a new criterion for establishing the existence of the parental link. From this point of view, there can be no doubt that Mrs [S] possesses all the qualities that undeniably make her a relative of V, and also that this kinship, connected with the idea of family relationships, is related to a socio-affective motherhood, created by strong and dynamic parental bonds that are reciprocally taken on and accepted by her and the child, but also and simultaneously agreed with his progenitors prior to his birth.'

Consequently, it was concluded that '[t]he right of V to have and to receive affection from the person who acted as a "foster mother" in his early years cannot be denied'.

(c) Joint adoption by married same-sex couples

One of the issues that provoked considerable debate prior to, during and even after the enactment of Law 26.618 was whether same-sex couples should be able to adopt.[26] The prominence and importance of the debate which occurs in

---

[25] Our emphasis.
[26] For more information on this issue, see Marisa Herrera 'Adopción y "Homo-parentalidad u Homo-fobia" Cuando el principio de igualdad manda' (2010) *Revista Jurisprudencia Argentina*, fascículo 12, 2010-III, 22 September 2010, Buenos Aires, pp 3ff.

some countries about the access of same-sex couples to maternity/paternity depends upon the breadth or narrowness of the notion of family, as defined by law.

The issue of adoption and sexual orientation arises in a series of different cases, such as: (1) an adoption by an individual, where the person who intends to adopt is homosexual; (2) an integrative adoption, that is, the adoption by a person of the biological or adopted child or children of his or her same-sex partner and (3) joint adoption by two people of the same sex, whether married or in a de facto partnership. In all such cases, to a greater or lesser extent, the persons wishing to adopt have been subject to discriminatory treatment because of their sexual orientation.

From the legislative point of view, the vast majority of states allow single person or individual adoption. Accordingly, in theory, sexual orientation cannot be a valid reason to deny authorisation for adoption. However, in practice there is a clear disapproval of single person adoption in general and particularly in relation to homosexual people (men more than women, because of that still deeply rooted notion of 'maternal instinct').

Of all the legislation around the world which extends the institution of civil marriage to all persons, regardless of sexual orientation, all but Portugal allow for joint adoption by same-sex married couples. In some legislation, that recognition is also extended to unmarried couples, whether hetero or homosexual. This is not the case in Argentina. The most recent reform of the institution of adoption, through Law 24.779 of 1997, restricts this legal right to married couples, denying unmarried couples the possibility of adopting (in conformity with arts 312 and 320 of the Civil Code). However, a number of judicial precedents have declared the unconstitutionality of these laws, finding that they violate various rights and principles of human rights, and in particular, the right to equality and non-discrimination, on the basis that what really matters in making the final decision about whether to authorise an adoption or not is the suitability of the petitioners as adoptive parents, and not the formal link which connects them; that is, whether they are or are not married. Would it not be possible to extend this jurisprudential view, in favour of adoption by unmarried opposite-sex couples, to unmarried same-sex couples, through application of the principle of equality which has inspired Law 26.618?

Returning to the analysis of the countries which allow marriage on an equal-rights basis, amongst all of them, initially the relevant Belgian legislation, passed in 2003, specifically excluded adoption by same-sex couples. However, in 2006 this law was substantially amended to allow adoption, on the basis of the principle of equality and the perception that there was a lack of convincing and non-discriminatory arguments in favour of the notion that a child should not be raised and cared for by two people of the same sex.

As was clearly stated in a judgment dated 16 August 2010 of the Mexican Supreme Court of Justice, in which the constitutionality of not permitting married same-sex couples to adopt was debated:

'There is no basis for affirming that homoparental homes or families possess some anomalous factor the result of which will inevitably be a poor upbringing. Whoever believes the opposite, must provide evidence for their view. Neither the Attorney-General of the Republic, nor anybody else in the world, has presented such empirical evidence, supported by serious and methodologically well-founded research. The burden of proof falls on those who argue, discriminatorily, that a homosexual couple is not equal to or is worse for the health and well-being of minors than a heterosexual couple. In reality, those who hold this belief make a flawed generalisation, on the basis of some anecdotal or limited information, which they elevate to a characteristic of a whole social group. These flawed generalisations are called stereotypes and these constitute, in turn, the erroneous cognitive foundation of social prejudices and intolerance.'

Therefore, if there are no objective and solid arguments against a child being raised by two people of the same sex, or nothing to show that a child will suffer harm as a result of such an upbringing, legislation which restricts this possibility would lead to discriminatory treatment based only on sexual orientation; and this should be regarded with suspicion.

The only country in which same-sex marriage is permitted, but in which these arguments have been disregarded, is Portugal. The relevant law was passed in 2010. In relation to adoption, art 3 of the law provides: 'The amendments introduced by the present law do not imply that adoption in any of its forms by people married to same-sex partners is legal.' With the aim of reinforcing this prohibition, the following article affirms: 'No legal provision regarding adoption may be interpreted in a contrary sense to that set out in the preceding article.'

The second category mentioned above relates to integrative adoption, whether of the biological or the adopted child of one member of a same-sex couple. This issue was considered and resolved favourably in the summarised sentence of the Brazilian Superior Court of Justice on 27 April 2010. The case concerned a woman who had adopted two girls, and who over time had formed a very strong intimate relationship with another woman. That woman became fond of and cared for her partner's daughters, and wished to adopt them. The judgment found in favour of allowing the adoption, giving priority to the dynamic notion of identity (in the construction of the emotional link developed between the applicant and the girls), and holding on that basis that 'studies do not indicate any problems arising from the adoption of children by homosexual couples. What is more important is the level of unity and affection in the family environment into which they will be placed'.[27]

---

[27] 'Estudos não indicam qualquer inconveniência em que crianças sejam adotadas por casais homossexuais, importando mais a qualidade do vínculo e do afeto no meio familiar em que serão inseridas' (author's translation).

Is sexual orientation a sine qua non to exclude a person from paternity/maternity through adoption? If a negative answer to that question is required as a result of the application of the principle of equality and non-discrimination, all legislation which imposes this restriction would be clearly discriminatory.

This is what was highlighted in a report signed by a number of Argentine researchers who work from distinctive viewpoints and professions in topics related to the notion of 'homoparentality', and which was presented in the Senate in the course of the debate on the bill in favour of same-sex marriage:

> 'The possibility that a boy or girl may suffer in the future because society is discriminatory cannot be raised as an objection to marriage. This objection is truly fallacious and senseless. All of us may or may not experience suffering. Nobody says to blacks or to Jews that they should not reproduce in certain contexts because their children are going to suffer. That argument . . . is associated with the ideal of the pure race, concealed by the invocation of future suffering. The problem belongs to the society that discriminates and not to the person who is discriminated against.'

The report added that:

> 'For decades, research has been carried out on the impact on children of family arrangements which vary from the standards set by law as being the most desirable: studies on children of "single mothers", of divorced parents, of widows and widowers, brought up by grandmothers and grandfathers . . . The results invariably showed that the fundamental variables relevant to the development of one's personality are influenced by other factors: emotional support and affection, by the atmosphere at home, by respect and responsibility.'

The law analysed in this chapter has followed the permissive stance in favour of joint adoption by same-sex married couples. From the perspective of human rights and particularly the principle of non-discrimination, this is the correct position to adopt.

(d) Child custody in homoparental families

One of the conflicts that arises with greater frequency in judicial practice and which directly implicates the rights of boys, girls and adolescents, is the issue of their custody after the break-up of their parents, whether those parents are married or unmarried (due to the principle of equality between children of married and unmarried couples). Now, following the reform which is the subject of this chapter, the scope of the conflict has been expanded, bringing within it potential break-ups of same-sex couples.

In Argentine law, as in so many other Latin American countries – even with no age restrictions as is the case in Chile, art 225 of the Civil Code – there is an ongoing preference in favour of the mother in relation to awarding custody of children of a certain age (in Argentina, up to 5 years of age) following the break-up of a couple. Therefore, in the current legal system, there exists an abstract priority in favour of one of the progenitors: the mother. From the constitutional-international perspective, and for some time now, the validity of this preference has been the subject of considerable doubt. This is on the basis that it violates or at a minimum contradicts a basic and inviolable principle of a democratic state: equality between men and women. This preference hides or is drawn from the deeply rooted idea of the woman-mother as the principal caregiver of children, by virtue of an assumed and natural 'maternal instinct'. Is it not the case that maternity, as all other roles and functions, is a social construction?

In relation to this, it is useful to refer to an article of the most important international instrument in relation to boys, girls and adolescents, in both international and national jurisdictions. Article 18(1) of the United Nations Convention on the Rights of the Child states that:

> 'States Parties shall use their best efforts to ensure recognition of the principle that both parents *have common responsibilities for the upbringing and development of the child*. Parents or, as the case may be, legal guardians, have the primary responsibility for the upbringing and development of the child. The best interests of the child will be their basic concern.'[28]

On the other hand, one should not lose sight of another and also especially significant international instrument concerned with the rights of women, the Convention on the Elimination of All Forms of Discrimination against Women. Article 16 of the Convention states that:

> 'States Parties shall take all appropriate measures to eliminate discrimination against women in all matters relating to marriage and family relations and in particular shall ensure, on a basis of equality of men and women: . . . (d) The same rights and responsibilities as parents, irrespective of their marital status, in matters relating to their children; in all cases the interests of the children shall be paramount.'

In this context, for some time we have been asking ourselves if the preference in favour of mothers is consistent or inconsistent with the aforementioned principle of equality and if the reform introduced by Law 26.618 has introduced a change or improved upon this position, or if, on the contrary, it has reinforced it. The current text of art 206 of the Civil Code (following the reform introduced by Law 26.618) related to the preference in favour of mothers, reads:

> 'Following confirmation of separation by a definitive judicial decision, each spouse may freely determine his or her domicile or residence. If there are children which are the responsibility of each, the following provisions relating to the parental responsibility regime will apply. Children of less than five (5) years of age will remain under the mother's care, unless there are serious reasons to the contrary relating to the minor's interests. In cases of same-sex marriages, if there is

---

[28] The emphasis is ours.

no agreement, the judge will resolve the issue taking into account the minor's interests. Where older children are concerned, and there is no agreement between the relevant spouses, custody will be awarded to the spouse who in the opinion of the judge is most suitable. The progenitors will continue to be subject to all the applicable responsibilities and obligations in respect of their children.'

As we can see, this norm maintains the maternal preference in relation to heterosexual spouses, but where the married couple is comprised of two women, no such preference applies: the parties may agree on who will take custody and if there is no agreement, it is for the judge to decide who is the person most suitable to assume that function. Accordingly, it is a simple matter to understand that the reform has not only wasted the opportunity to revoke the preference in favour of mothers that is inconsistent with fundamental principles of human rights, but that it has also established a type of 'inverse discrimination' in favour of opposite-sex progenitors. Thus, where same-sex parents are involved, there is no specified age limit while, on the contrary, heterosexual parents continue to be bound to this inflexible – and in our opinion, unconstitutional – variable concerning age. As a result of this rule, a father/man who wishes to be awarded custody of a child of his who is younger than 5 must irrefutably prove that he is better equipped to be in charge of the upbringing of his child in order to reverse the legal presumption in favour of the mother/woman (which applies due to the maternal preference already discussed).

In our opinion, there should not be any specified age limit or preference in favour of either parent. Instead, the general rule should be as art 206 provides in the case of same-sex couples: any controversy must be resolved by application of the best interests of the child principle.[29]

Although we do not wish in this chapter to consider in detail the ways in which disputes in relation to the care or upbringing of children may be avoided (whether in hetero or homosexuals couples), we do want to mention that many of these disputes would be done away with if – as is already the case in many countries around the world – the institution of shared upbringing or custody were recognised, this being the system that best aligns with the human rights principles referred to above, which recognise the importance of both parents and that each have an active role in the upbringing of their children. This is what may be deduced from the concept referred to as 'coparentality', promoted by the Convention on the Rights of the Child in a number of its articles.

(e) Children's surnames

(i) Introduction

In today's society the existence of a person without an identifier that differentiates him or her from everybody else is inconceivable. The equality of

---

[29] Aída Kemelmajer de Carlucci and Marisa Herrera 'Matrimonio, orientación sexual y familias. Un aporte colaborativo desde la dogmática jurídica' *Revista La Ley*, 4 June 2010, pp 1ff.

human nature is linked to the right of every person to affirm his or her identity, to be different, something which is consolidated in the development of a person's personality and the resulting social projection. An essential element of this identity is expressed through one's name, the protection of which has been recognised internationally.[30]

In this section, we will be concerned with summarising the position that the law which regulates same-sex marriage has adopted in respect of the spouses' surname and the children who originate from these unions, whether biologically, as the result of assisted reproduction techniques, or through adoption.

In order to comprehend the reform which Law 26.618 introduced in relation to children's surnames more easily, we note that in Argentine law the issue of people's names is governed in general by Law 18.248, which entered into force in 1948. Law 26.618 brought with it a number of express changes to precisely this law.

(ii)   Children of married couples

Law 26.618 retains different sets of rules in respect of the surname of children of married couples depending on whether the spouses are of the same sex or the opposite sex, and treats the first group in a discriminatory fashion. In relation to children of a married opposite-sex couple, the rule set out in art 4 of Law 18.248 applies. That is to say, the children will take the first surname of the father, and only at the progenitors' request will they be given the full surname of the father (both his maternal and paternal surnames) or have the mother's surname added. In other words, the addition of the mother's surname is not obligatory and requires the consent of both spouses. In addition, a child may choose to take his mother's surname upon reaching 18 years of age. This means that if there is no agreement between the spouses, the patriarchal rule remains and the child is registered with the father's surname.

On the other hand, it is provided that children of same-sex married couples will take the first surname of one or other of the parents. At the spouses' request,

---

[30]   Article 18 of the American Convention on Human Rights (more commonly referred to as the Pact of San José, Costa Rica, signed on 21 November 1969), states that 'Every person has the right to a given name and to the surnames of his parents or that of one of them. The law shall regulate the manner in which this right shall be ensured for all . . .'. On the other hand, in relation to childhood and adolescence, Art 8(1) of the Convention on the Rights of the Child provides: 'States Parties undertake to respect the right of the child to preserve his or her identity, including nationality, name and family relations as recognized by law without unlawful interference.' Further, as cited above, Art 16(d) of the Convention on the Elimination of All Forms of Discrimination against Women, obliges states parties to 'ensure, on a basis of equality of men and women . . . the same rights and responsibilities as parents . . .'. In Argentina, these articles have a constitutional status, as provided for in art 75(22) of the National Constitution. Therefore, the name as a human right has a superior status that must be respected in the domestic legal order. In addition, it is an element of the right to identity, both in its static and dynamic aspect.

the full surname of the spouse whose first surname the child has been given may be registered, or the surname of the other spouse may be added. If there is no agreement about which surname the child will take, about whether the child's surname should be the full surname of one of the spouse's, or the order of the surnames where the child is to take the surname of both, priority will be given according to alphabetical order. As is the case with children of married opposite-sex couples, the child has the right upon reaching 18 years of age to apply to the Civil Registry to take the full surname of the spouse whose surname the child has, or to take the surname of the other spouse (art 37 of Law 26.618, which amends art 4 of Law 18.248).

Although the possibility which this Law has given rise to only applies to adopted children, doctrine has interpreted it as extending to biological as well as adopted children, taking into account the equal rights principle that governs the condition of children.[31] Applying the principle of the immutability of the name, the norm provides that once a surname has been added it cannot be replaced. On the other hand, the law states that all the children of the same family must carry the same surname; and that surname must be the name given to the oldest child.

(iii)   Adopted children

In contrast to the legal regime in force in a number of countries, Argentine law continues to maintain a dual regime in relation to adoption. This means that full adoption (that which extinguishes all legal linkages with the birth family, except with regard to matrimonial impediments as set out in art 323 of the Civil Code) co-exists with the institution of simple adoption, in which the legal linkage with the original family subsists and the only legal linkage created is that between the adoptee and the adopter or adopters (depending on whether the adoption is individual or joint, as provided for in art 329 of the Civil Code). These differences have an impact or effect on the issue of the surname of adopted children. Basically, although in both full and simple adoptions the adoptee takes the surname of the adopter or the adopters, it is only in the case of a simple adoption that the adoptee can add his or her own surname when he or she reaches the age of majority (which in Argentina has been 18 years of age since 2009, when Law 26.579 decreased the age of majority from 21 to 18).

In a second paragraph, a surviving spouse of a couple which has adopted a child is authorised to request that the adopted child take the surname of his or her previously deceased spouse, provided that he or she can show good reasons for this (art 332 of the Civil Code). If the recognition were subsequent, the same rule applies; that is, once the adopted child reaches 18 years of age, he or she may make an application to the Civil Registry that his or her original surname be added.

---

[31] Andres Gil Domínguez, María Victoria Famá and Marisa Herrera *Matrimonio igualitario y Derecho Constitucional de Familia* (Buenos Aires: Ediar, 2010) pp 491ff.

Another law applies to situations in which one member of a married couple has individually adopted a child or children. In the case of a woman married to a man, where the man has not adopted the minor, the minor will take the maiden name of the woman, unless the male spouse expressly authorises the giving of his surname to the minor. In the case of a woman or a man married to a person of the same sex whose spouse has not adopted the minor, the minor will take the maiden name of the spouse who adopted him, unless the other spouse expressly authorises the giving of his or her surname to the minor (art 41 of Law 26.618, which amends art 12 of Law 18.248).

In relation to the simple adoption of the son or daughter of one spouse by the other – also referred to as an integrative adoption – the same rule applies to heterosexual and homosexual marriages (arts 313 and 331 of the Civil Code, which have not been amended by the law under analysis).

In the case of a full adoption, the same rule which applies in relation to children born to married couples applies to the adopted child. Article 326 of the Civil Code is substituted in the following way: the adopted child takes the adopter's first surname or full surname if the adopter so requests. If the adopting spouses are of the opposite sex, at their request the adopted child may take the full surname of the adoptive father or add the first surname of the adoptive mother to that of the adoptive father. Where the spouses are of the same sex, at their request the adopted child may take the full surname of the spouse from whom the first surname comes or may add the first surname of the other spouse to that surname. If there is no consensus between the spouses regarding the surname the adopted child will take, in relation to whether the child should take the full surname of one of them or how the surnames should be ordered, priority will be given according to alphabetical order. In either case, once the adopted child has reached 18 years of age he or she may request this addition (art 326 of the Civil Code, amended by art 16 of Law 26.618).

As this makes clear, the same rule that applies to children of married spouses applies to adopted children, including the different rules which apply to same-sex and opposite-sex marriages. In the case of opposite-sex marriages, the spouses are free to decide whether the child will take the full surname of the adoptive father or that the adopted mother's first surname will be added to that of the father.

Accordingly, the consent of both parents is required, and where there is a lack of agreement, the child will be registered with his or her father's surname. In the case of same-sex marriages, at both spouses' request the adopted child may take the full surname of the spouse from whom the first surname came, or may add the other spouse's first surname to that name. If there is no consensus about the surname the adoptee will take, whether it should be the full surname of one of the spouses, or in relation to the ordering of the surnames, the names will be given priority according to alphabetical order (art 326 of the Civil Code). Put another way, the man's surname is no longer given any priority; instead, the neutral rule of alphabetical order applies. This method of resolving disagreement between progenitors is a matter of debate, as it reduces the possibility of reaching a decision on the basis of consensus. This is because the parent whose name appears first in the alphabet will not be interested in reaching an agreement, comfortable in the knowledge that his or her name will prevail if there is a lack of consensus. As a result, it has been argued that a more impartial system would be drawing lots, in which the resolution of the conflict is left to chance. Such a system would provide stronger motivation for spouses to reach a mutual decision.

IV BRIEF COMMENTS IN CLOSING

As Enrique Marí, a recognised and well-remembered philosopher of Argentine law, brilliantly stated:

> 'Legal discourse must, therefore, be understood and evaluated not only by that which it excludes, but also by what it implies through such exclusion.'[32]

The following statement is eloquent and indisputable: social reality demonstrates that there is a great diversity of family forms. The Argentine state has taken a momentous step along the path of pluralism and diversity. In light of the reform introduced by Law 26.618, it appears that Argentine law is willing to narrow the gap between law and reality in relation to the family. The recognition of the right of same-sex couples to marry is a clear indication of this approach, guided by the concepts of equality and pluralism.

This debate has been well promoted, as has been the case with all the great normative changes of recent periods, by the international doctrine of human rights. In this sense, and as the writer, historian and journalist Michael Ignatieff has strongly argued:

> 'Human rights language exists to remind us that there are some abuses that are genuinely intolerable, and some excuses for these abuses that are genuinely unbearable.'[33]

Fortunately, for some time now in the law, the 'traditional' concept of the family has been questioned. The backdrop to the expansion of the institution of civil marriage to all people, regardless of their sexual orientation, is this reformist and vital viewpoint on the concept of the family, a concept which has always been heavily influenced by extra-legal perspectives such as religion.

---

[32] As cited by Carlos M Cárcova 'Notas acerca de la Teoría Crítica del Derecho' in Christian Courtis *Desde otra mirada. Textos de Teoría Crítica del Derecho* (Buenos Aires: Eudeba, 2001) p 31.
[33] Cited by Emilio García Méndez 'Origen, sentido y futuro de los derechos humanos: Reflexiones para una nueva agenda' (2010) 1 *Revista Internacional de Derechos Humanos* primer semestre 2004 available at www.surjournal.org/esp/index1.php (accessed 13 June 2011).

In summary, decisions to move forward and transform or to hide and silence are political and can be the result of action or omission. Law 26.618 has been a positive and clear step by the legislature (and through it and the public debate generated by the reform, of society in general); that is, a political decision in the best sense of that term. In this way, a necessary policy of inclusion (in relation to all the ways of living as a family) continues to be strengthened and prioritised over and above a policy of exclusion (of only some of those ways). The reform analysed in the course of this chapter had a lot to say in relation to this tension, and tipped the balance in favour of inclusion.

Australia

'REALITY IS THE BEGINNING …' AUSTRALIAN FAMILY LAW IN 2009

*Frank Bates**

Résumé

Dans plusieurs communications publiées dans la Revue de l'Association internationale de droit de la famille, des auteurs soulignent les difficultés d'envisager les changements du droit de la famille ou la manière selon laquelle ces mutations auront lieu ou encore de prévoir la nature de tels changements. Pourtant, 2009 constitue une année importante dans les mutations du droit de la famille en Australie car la jurisprudence a été novatrice, notamment dans son interprétation de la Loi de 1975 sur le droit de la famille en soutenant des modifications importantes de certaines dispositions de cette Loi. En même temps, 2009 une jurisprudence substantielle intéresse d'autres domaines dans lesquels la loi der 1975 est en cause et présent un intérêt majeur. En outre, en 2009 ont été rendues des décisions jurisprudentielles importantes en ce qui concerne le droit de propriété et les obligations alimentaires tant à propos des couples hétérosexuels que des couples homosexuels. En cas de conflits dans les relations hétérosexuelles, la jurisprudence a traité la situation en appliquant les a été traitée conformément aux dispositions de la loi de 1975 sur le droit de la famille. La mise en ouvre de la loi de 1975 à ces nouveaux modes conjugaux est l'objet du présent article.

I   INTRODUCTORY

In various other commentaries in *The International Survey of Family Law*, I have sought to point out the dangers of attempting to predict either the possibility of change or the manner in which that change will be effected or, indeed, the nature of such potential change. The year 2009, however, does seem to represent an exception in that jurisdictional changes have been effected to

---

*   'Reality is the beginning not the end,
   Naked Alpha, not the hierophant Omega,
   Of dense investiture, with luminous vassals.
    It is the infant A standing on infant legs,
   Not twisted, stooping, polymathic Z,
   He that kneels always on the edge of space
    In the pallid perceptions of its distances,
   Alpha fears men or else Omega's men
   Or else his prolongations of the human.'
    Wallace Stevens 'An Ordinary Evening in New Haven' in *The Auroras of Autumn* (1950).
    Frank Bates is Professor of Law, University of Newcastle (NSW), Australia.

the Family Law Act 1975,[1] as continuously amended, and there is the possibility of radical change to one, at any rate, of its less than totally successful amendments, as well as that amendment's being one of the most, apparently, radical in the substantive law.[2]

At the same time, 2009 has also seen not insignificant case-law in various areas of activity with which the Act has traditionally been concerned and which are of continuing interest. Also, 2009 has seen a major jurisdictional change in relation to property and maintenance as they affect the majority of heterosexual and same-sex unformalised couples. These matters will, on the breakdown of such relationships, be dealt with under the provisions of the Family Law Act 1975. These new provisions will be considered in more detail later in this chapter.[3]

All in all, as will be observed, 2009 has been an intriguing year in the development, in many planes, of Australian family law.

II   INTERNATIONAL ISSUES

(a)   Immigration

It is so well known by now as not specifically to need documentation that Australia is an immigrant and, consequently, multicultural society. However, strangely perhaps, case-law on family law aspects of immigration and its consequences is sporadic and haphazard in its development. However, in 2009, the High Court of Australia was finally faced with its implications in the case of *Minister for Immigration and Citizenship and Amit Kumar and Another*.[4] *Kumar* involved an appeal by the Minister against a decision of the Full Court of the Federal Court of Australia which had allowed an appeal by the first respondent against the dismissal by the Federal Magistrates' Court of his application to quash a decision of the second respondent, the Migration Review Tribunal.

The application for review by the tribunal was the decision of a delegate of the Minister, that the first respondent was not entitled to the grant of a temporary or residence partner visa.[5] The delegate had to be satisfied that the parties were in a continuing and genuine marriage relationship, or had a mutual commitment to a shared life as husband and wife.[6] The first respondent was born in Fiji and had gone through a form of marriage, as specified in the provisions of the Marriage Act 1961, with an Australian citizen and had

---

[1]   Below text at n 58ff.
[2]   Below text at n 220.
[3]   Below text at n 58.
[4]   (2009) FLC 93–398.
[5]   As provided in the Migration Regulations 1994, made under the Migration Act 1961 (Cth).
[6]   See ibid, r 1.15A(1A).

applied for permanent residence on the grounds of his marriage shortly after the ceremony. The High Court of Australia[7] allowed the Minister's appeal.

First, the Court held[8] that the Tribunal had complied with the requirements of the Migration Act 1961[9] by notifying the first respondent that it had received, in confidence, information which stated that the marriage had been contrived for the sole purpose of the first respondent's immigration into Australia. The purpose of the relevant provision, the High Court stated,[10] was to accommodate the concerns which had been expressed in the earlier decision of that Court in *Applicant VEAL of 2002 v Minister for Immigration and Multicultural and Indigenous Affairs*.[11] In that case, the court[12] had emphasised, initially, the fundamental requirements of the Act that those who were entitled to a visa should be granted it and that those who were not so entitled should be refused. At the same time, the court had emphasised that information which was supplied by an informer should not be denied to the executive in its administration of the legislation. Accordingly, the High Court said, in *Kumar*, that the legislation 'affords to visa applicants a measure of procedural fairness and protection to informants, lest, without that protection, information be withheld and the Tribunal be denied material which assists the performance of its functions'.

As regards the substantive issue in *Kumar*, the High Court noted[13] that the tribunal had found that there was insufficient evidence upon which it could satisfy itself that, at the time of the decision, the first respondent and his wife were holding themselves out to the world as being in a genuine spousal relationship. The court said:

> 'If that conclusion were, as it was expressed to be, independent of the non-disclosable information relied upon by the Tribunal then even in the absence of that information, Mr Kumar could not have succeeded.'

The difficulty which all of the parties faced in *Kumar* is readily apparent: the first respondent had argued that knowledge of the identity of the informant and the content of the information would assist in understanding and, thus, testing the cogency of the case against him. On the other hand, as the High Court pointed out *VEAL*,[14] 'there should be no impediment to the giving of information to authorities about claims that are made for visas'. However, *Kumar* does seem to be a less serious instance, in some respects at least, than other cases which have come before Australian courts in that no element of fraud appeared to have been perpetrated on the other party to the ceremony.[15]

---

7   French CJ, Gummow, Hayne, Kiefel and Bell JJ.
8   (2009) FLC 93–398 at 83,350.
9   Migration Act 1961, s 359A(1).
10 (2009) FLC 93–398 at 83,350.
11 (2005) 225 CLR 88 at 98.
12 Gleeson CJ, Gummow, Kirby, Hayne and Heydon JJ.
13 (2009) FLC 93–398 at 83,352.
14 (2005) 225 CLR 88 at 100.
15 Unlike, for instance, *In the Marriage of Deniz* (1977) FLC 90–252.

(b) The Hague Convention on Civil Aspects of International Child Abduction

There have been two cases in 2009 dealing with the Australian response to the Hague Convention on Civil Aspects of International Child Abduction,[16] one, a decision of the High Court of Australia, being of especial note and both being concerned with the issue of *habitual residence* as it arises under that Convention.

LK and Director-General, Department of Community Services[17] involved an appeal by a mother against orders[18] providing that the children of the marriage be returned to Israel. The facts were not typical of those in cases which I have elsewhere[19] documented: the mother and father, who were married and living in Israel, separated in 2005. The four children of the marriage had been born in Israel, though were entitled to Australian citizenship by descent from their mother. Following the separation, the children of the marriage continued to live with their mother in the matrimonial home. In May 2006, the mother and children, holding return tickets to Israel for August of that year, travelled by air to Australia.

Before they left Israel, the father knew and accepted their intention and, also, that the mother would return were the parents to be reconciled. However, prior to leaving Israel, and immediately on reaching Australia, the mother prepared to establish a home for herself and her children in Australia. Some 2 months later, the father informed the mother that he wanted the children to return to Israel, but that he wished to divorce the mother. The major focus of the appeal, which the High Court[20] allowed, was whether the children were habitually resident in Israel.

The first issue which the court considered was the existence of a *settled purpose* in abandoning habitual residence in Israel. In that regard, the High Court noted[21] that the Full Court of the Family Court of Australia had treated the finding that the mother did not have such a *settled purpose* or intention to abandon habitual residence in Israel as dispositive. The High Court straightaway stated that it found such a view to be in error and, in order to substantiate their opinion examined the notion of habitual residence in some detail.

In that context, the court sought to emphasise that habitual residence, although frequently used in international conventions, was a term more directly referable

---

16   Decided 2 days apart in March 2009.
17   (2009) FLC 93–397.
18   Made pursuant to the Family Law (Child Abduction Convention) Regulations 1986 (Cth).
19   F Bates '"Escaping Mothers" and the Hague Convention – The Australian Experience' (2008) 41 CILSA 245.
20   French CJ, Gummow, Hayne, Heydon and Kiefel JJ.
21   (2009) FLC 93–397 at 83,337.

to *fact* rather than to *law,* per se. Thus, in the words of McClean,[22] the phrase has, 'repeatedly been presented as a notion of fact rather than law, as something to which no technical legal definition I attached so that judges from any legal system can address themselves to the facts'. However, the High Court in *LK* could not wholly accept that view and stated that, if habitual residence were to be given meaning, 'some criteria must be engaged at some point in the inquiry and they are to be found in the ordinary meaning of the composite expression'. Nevertheless, the High Court declined to attempt a universal description, although they did seek to devise general points. The first of those was that the application of the phrase 'permits consideration of a wide variety of circumstances that bear upon where a person is said to reside and whether that residence is to be described as habitual'. Second, the court considered that 'the past and present intentions of the person under consideration will often bear upon the significance that is to be attached to particular circumstances like duration of a person's connections with a particular place of residence'.

It followed that use of the phrase for the purposes of identifying a necessary connection between a person and particular legal system amounted to a rejection of other possible connecting factors, such as domicile[23] or nationality. The High Court regarded that as crucial when they stated that the deliberate use of the phrase entailed discarding domicile which gave questions of intent a decisive importance in determining whether a domicile of choice had been acquired.

Having made that point, the court went on[24] to discuss problems which might be inherent in the application of the phrase 'habitual residence' to particular factual circumstances. In so doing, they accepted the view of Scoles, Hay, Borchers and Symeonides[25] that 'habitual residence, consistent with the purpose of its use, identifies the centre of a person's personal and family life as disclosed by the facts of the individual's activities'. Accordingly, the High Court stated that it was unlikely (though not necessary) to exclude the possibility that a person could be found to be habitually resident in more than one place at the same time. They continued:

> 'But, even if a place of habitual residence is necessarily singular, that does not entail that a person must always be so connected with one place that it is to be identified as that person's place of habitual residence. So, for example, a person may abandon a place as the place of that person's habitual residence without at once becoming habitually resident in some other place: a person may lead such a nomadic life as not to have a place of habitual residence.'

---

[22] JD McClean *Recognition of Family Judgments in the Commonwealth* (London: Butterworths, 1983) p 28.

[23] Indeed, the distinguished United States commentators EF Scoles, P Hay, P Borchers and S Symeonides *Conflict of Laws* (St Paul: West Group, 4th edn, 2004) at p 247 stated that the phrase had been used in the Convention so as 'to avoid the distasteful English concept [of domicile] and the uncertainties of meaning and proof of subjective intent'.

[24] (2009) FLC 93–397 at 83,339.

[25] Above n 23 at p 247.

Of course, the case itself was not concerned with the movements of a *sui generis* individual but with a child and, in such cases, the High Court considered that it was necessary to consider the context[26] in which the inquiry was required. In *LK* itself, that context was provided by the aims of the Hague Convention on Civil Aspects of International Child Abduction, particularly as manifested in the Australian regulations giving effect to them. The purpose of those regulations[27] was 'to facilitate resolution of disputes between parents relating to a child's welfare and development in one forum – the child's country of habitual residence – rather than any other forum'. Whilst, the court stated, that may have the effect of suggesting that a child did have a place of habitual residence, neither the Convention nor the Regulations provided for a particular verification or enforcement of rights in relation to the child. That, in turn, was a decision to be made by the courts of the forum to which both Convention and Regulations pointed: those of the child's place of habitual residence.

To a degree, of course, that dictum begs the very question which it is seeking to answer. The child is not, of necessity, sui generis and, hence, as the High Court did, indeed, point out, it will normally 'be very important to examine where the person or persons who are caring for the child live – where those persons have their habitual residence. The younger the child, the less sensible it is to speak of the place of habitual residence of the child as distinct from the place of habitual residence of the person or persons upon whom the child is dependent for care and housing'. At the same time, though, as relevant commentators[28] point out, if the issue of habitual residence is one of fact, it is important 'not to elevate the observation that a child looks to others for care and housing to some principle of law like the (former) law of dependent domicile of a married woman'.

Having made those central observations, the High Court of Australia in *LK* went on[29] to discuss the relevance of *purpose and intention*, which they considered to be relevant to the issue of determining where a person was *habitually resident*, just as it was in the determination of a domicile of choice. However, unlike *domicile*, considerations relevant to deciding where a person has *habitually resident* were not necessarily confined to physical presence and intention and, hence, *intention* was not to be given controlling weight.

On that issue, the High Court especially noted, first, that 'individuals do not always act with a clearly formed and singular view of what is intended (or hoped) that the future will hold. Their intentions may be ambiguous'. *LK*, itself, provided an interesting instance of those circumstances – it was not possible to say that the mother had a settled intention to reside permanently in either Australia or Israel and, more particularly, neither suggestion properly acknowledges the significance to be attached to the possibility of the parties'

---

[26] Author's emphasis.
[27] See Family Law (Child Abduction Convention) Regulations 1986 (Cth), r 1A(2)(b).
[28] See, for instance, n 22.
[29] (2009) FLC 93–397 at 83,339.

reconciliation. Because, the High Court continued,[30] that possibility had not been excluded when the mother left Israel, it might legitimately be said that her intentions, at that time, were ambiguous, at least to that extent. The court said:

> 'Even accepting that to be so, because the notion of habitual residence does not require that it be possible to say of a person at any and every time that he or she has a place of habitual residence, it is important to recognise that a person may cease to reside habitually in one place without acquiring a new place of habitual residence.'

Secondly, the court pointed out because a person's intentions may be ambiguous, that if one were to ask whether a person had *'abandoned'*[31] residence in a place, it is necessary to recognise the possibility that that person may not have formed a singular and irrevocable intention not to return, yet properly be described as no longer being habitually resident in that place. In other words, in the ipsissima verba of the High Court:[32]

> 'Absence of a final decision positively rejecting the possibility of returning to Israel in the foreseeable future is not necessarily inconsistent with ceasing to reside their habitually.'

Thirdly, the court considered that, when seeking to determine where a child was habitually resident, attention could not be confined to the intentions of the parent who, in fact, has the day-to-day care of the child. The High Court suggested that:

> 'It will usually be necessary to consider what each parent intends for the child. When parents are living together, young children will have the same habitual residence as their parents. No less importantly, it may generally be accepted that the general rule is that neither parent can unilaterality change that place of habitual residence. The assent of the other parent (or a court order) would be necessary.'

By way of conclusion to that part of their judgment, the High Court of Australia commented[33] that it followed from each of those three matters that:

> ' . . . to seek to identify a set list of criteria that bear upon where a child is habitually resident or to attempt to organise the list of possible matters that might bear upon the question according to some predetermined hierarchy of importance, would deny the simple observation that the question of habitual residence will fall for decision in a very wide range of circumstances.'

Having reached that interim conclusion and having noted the observation made in the earlier decision of the same court in *Povey v Qantas Airways Ltd*[34] to the effect that international treaties should be uniformly interpreted by contracting

---

[30]   Ibid at 83,340.
[31]   The High Court of Australia's emphasis.
[32]   (2009) FLC 93–397 at 83,340.
[33]   Ibid at 83,340.
[34]   (2005) 223 CLR 189 at 202, per Gleeson CJ, Gummow, Hayne and Heydon JJ.

states, the High Court of Australia then sought to analyse prior, and divided, authority. Although detailed comment on this analysis is beyond the scope of a commentary of this nature, it is necessary to draw attention to some notable salient matters. First, after considering the well-known English decisions of *R v Barnet London Borough Council; Ex parte Shah*[35] and *Re B (Minors) (Abduction) (No 2)*,[36] which considered the application of the phrase 'settled purpose'[37] to the issue, the High Court stated[38] that:

> ' . . . if references to settled intention were to be understood as requiring inquiries about intention like those that are necessary to the application of the law of domicile, such an understanding would be sharply at odds with the use of the expression "habitually resident" in the Regulations and the Abduction Convention in preference to domicile.'

In the event, the High Court found support in the majority judgment in the New Zealand Court of Appeal's decision in *Punter v Secretary for Justice*.[39] There, having decided that the inquiry into *'habitual residence'* was a broad factual inquiry,[40] the majority went on to say that:

> ' . . . such an inquiry should take into account all relevant factors, including settled purpose, the actual and intended length of stay in a state, the purpose of the stay, the strength of ties to the state and to any other state (both in the past and currently), the degree of assimilation into the state, including living and schooling arrangements and cultural, social and economic integration.'

In particular, attention was paid to the comment of McGrath J in the earlier decision of the same court in *SK v KP*[41] who had referred to the underlying relating of the connection between the child and the particular state.

The High Court of Australia agreed[42] with that view as expressed in the New Zealand cases and commented that the majority view in *Punter* regarding settled purpose was to be interpreted as referring to the intentions of the parents, though, as they had earlier explained,[43] the relevant criterion was 'a shared intention that the children live in a particular place with a sufficient degree of continuity to be properly described as settled'. In addition, the court was of the view that the approach to be found in *Punter* accords with the

---

[35]   [1983] 2 AC 309, especially at 402, per Lord Scarman. See also *IRC v Lysaght* [1928] AC 234 at 243, per Lord Summer.
[36]   [1993] 1 FLR 993 at 995, per Waite J.
[37]   See also, *A v A (Child Abduction)* [1993] 2 FLR 225 at 235, per Rattee J. For comment see also the Australian decisions in *D W v Director-General, Department of Child Safety* (2006) FLC 93–255; *Cooper v Casey* (1995) FLC 92–575; *Panayotides v Panayotides* (1997) FLC 92–733.
[38]   (2009) FLC 93–397 at 83,342.
[39]   [2007] 1 NZLR 40 at 61, per Anderson P, Glazebrook, William Young and O'Regan JJ.
[40]   Author's emphasis.
[41]   [2005] 3 NZLR 590 at 595.
[42]   (2009) FLC 93–397 at 83,342.
[43]   Above text at n 33ff.

general tenor of United States' decisions[44] where the common thread was the need to look at *all the circumstances of the case.* That was the approach, as described in *Punter,* which should be followed.

The High Court then sought to apply[45] the principle which they had attempted to distill to the facts of *LK* itself. They considered that if the parents' intentions at the time of the wife and children's departure from Israel were expressed conditionally and the mother had taken the steps to establish a new and apparently permanent home in Australia, then it ought to have been found that the children were not habitually resident in Israel. The possibility that they might take up residence in Israel once again[46] did not mean that they had ceased to be permanently resident in Israel. What the High Court regarded as being decisive was that 'the children left Israel with both parents agreed that unless there was a reconciliation they would stay in Australia, and their mother, both before and after departure, set about effecting that shared intention'.

LK is a most interesting and valuable case and of global importance: it seeks to deal comparatively with the meaning of the phrase habitual residence and consider its practical application to the Hague Convention on Civil Aspects of International Child Abduction. The discussion and application to the facts of *LK* are worthy of consideration in all of the jurisdictions to which reference was made in the High Court of Australia's judgment. In Australia, its explication is likely to remain the ultimate comment for quite some time.

Despite the wide-ranging discussion of the notion of habitual residence, it did not deal with every aspect of its application. Two day after *LK* was decided in the High Court, the Full Court of the Family Court of Australia decided *Sharmain and Director-General, Department of Community Services.*[47] That case was concerned with an appeal by a mother against an order which required the return of the child to the United States, pursuant to the provisions of the Family Law (Child Abduction Convention) Regulations 1986. The child, who was a dual citizen of Australia and the United States, had been born in Australia in 2004 and had begun living with his parents in the United States in 2005. The parents separated in 2007 and the mother left the United States with the child and went to Australia where they continued to live. Thereupon, the father instituted proceedings in the American State of Colorado under the Hague Child Abduction Convention for the return of the child. On appeal, the issue was whether the trial judge had made an error in his findings regarding the exercise of jurisdiction by a court in the United States.

The mother argued that the child had not been resident in the State of Colorado for a period of 6 months at the time of removal and that, therefore,

---

[44]   See, for example, *Feder v Evans-Feder* 63 F 2d 217 (3rd Cir 1995); *Mozes v Mozes* 239 F 3d 1067 (9th Cir 2001); *Karkainnen v Kovalcuk* 445 F 3d 280 (3rd Cir 2006); *Robert v Tesson* 507 F 3d 918 (6th Cir 2007).
[45]   (2007) FLC 93–397 at 83,343.
[46]   Should the parents be reconciled.
[47]   (2009) FLC 93–96.

there was no court in that state which could exercise jurisdiction over the child. In consequence of that want of jurisdiction, the father could not, at the present time, enforce his rights of custody. The Full Court of the Family Court of Australia[48] dismissed the mother's appeal.

First, the Court took the view[49] that the respondent Director-General had demonstrated, by reference to the relevant statute law, that there was a basis upon which the father could invoke jurisdiction in the United States to enforce his rights of custody immediately prior to the time of removal and, further, that courts in the United States had jurisdiction to hear and determine proceedings if the child were to be returned.[50] Hence, the Full Court did not accept that the trial judge was in error regarding his findings as to the exercise of jurisdiction by the courts of Colorado.

That, of itself, would have justified the dismissal of the appeal. However, the jurisdiction issue apart, another issue arose which would also justify the appeal's dismissal. The Full Court held[51] that it was not incumbent on an applicant seeking the return of a child also to establish that, in a Convention country, a court would have jurisdiction to enforce rights of custody. The court stated that they did not propose to analyse previous case-law dealing with the meaning of rights of custody or allied notions.[52] However, note should be taken of the joint judgment of Gaudron, Gummow and Hayne JJ of the High Court of Australia in *DP v Commonwealth Central Authority; Department of Community Services*[53] where it was said that:

> 'Nothing in the definitions of "removal" or "retention" or of "rights of custody" requires that, before removal or retention, there shall have been any judicial decision about rights of custody and nothing in those definitions requires that at some later time there be any application to a court to determine who shall have future rights of custody in relation to the child. All that the definitions require is that by the law of the place of habitual residence immediately before removal or retention, the child's removal to Australia or the child's retention in Australia is in breach of the rights of custody of some person, institution or body. Often enough, that will be so where, by operation of the law of the place of habitual residence, both parents have joint rights of custody of children of their union.'

---

48   Boland, O'Ryan and Ryan JJ.
49   (2009) FLC 93–396 at 83,331.
50   The court, ibid at 83,325, noted that the trial judge had 'identified the law of the United States as comprising annotations to legislation in the State of Colorado; similar material in relation to the State of Montana; annotated United States Federal Law being the *Uniform Child Custody Jurisdiction and Enforcement Act* (1997) and two affidavits of Ms D, an attorney who was a member of the Colorado State Bar'.
51   (2009) FLC 93–396 at 83,332.
52   Such as the provisions of s 111B of the Family Law Act 1976 (Cth) which specify when a person has custody of, or access to, a child for the purposes of the Convention, given that the expressions, per se, are no longer part of Australian law.
53   (2001) 206 CLR 401 at 421. For English authority to like effect, see *Re F (Child Abduction: Custody Rights Abroad)* [1995] 2 FLR 31.

In *Sharmain*, the court stated[54] that there was nothing in the Regulations which spoke of the need for an applicant to establish that, as a threshold requirement, he or she had a right to approach a court in the Convention country. Such a view had likewise been earlier emphasised by Gaudron, Gummow and Hayne JJ in *DP*, when they stated[55] that:

> ' . . . the construction of the Regulations cannot proceed from a premise that they are designed to achieve return of children to the place of their habitual residence for the purpose of the courts of that jurisdiction conducting some kind of hearing as to what will be in that child's best interests. As the regulations recognise, questions of rights of custody in the country to which return is sought are regulated in some cases by operation of law, by administrative decisions or by agreement. There may be neither occasion nor opportunity for any engagement of the judicial processes of that country.'

In *Sharmain*, the court noted[56] that both parents had rights of custody by operation of law which they were exercising until the time of the removal of child. Taking all of that into account, *Sharmain* is a useful decision which elucidates what is, as the court itself said,[57] a 'narrow issue'. Narrow though it might be, it is one which, mutatis mutandis, may very well recur and it should also be borne in mind that one area of public dissatisfaction with the operation of the Convention is the manner in which countries of habitual residence may deal with the future welfare of the child.

III UNFORMALISED RELATIONSHIPS AND THE NEW LAW

(a) Introductory

The Family Law Amendment (De Facto Financial Matters and Other Measures) Act 2008 came into force on 1 March 2009. This legislation, as already noted,[58] provides for the majority of heterosexual and same-sex de facto couples to have matters relating to finance and property dealt with under the Family Law Act 1975 on the breakdown of any such relationship.[59] That basic goal is achieved by four essential measures: first, a new Part VIIIAB is inserted into the Act, and there is a close resemblance to the existing Part VIII which deals with property and maintenance. Secondly, Part VIIIB, which deals with superannuation, is amended so as to include de facto couples. Thirdly, a new s 90TA is inserted into the Act which replicates, by means of a schedule,[60]

---

54   (2009) FLC 93–396 at 83,331.
55   (2001) 206 CLR 401 at 414.
56   (2009) FLC 93–396 at 83,332.
57   Ibid at 83,331.
58   Above text at n 3.
59   For a detailed commentary, see Family Law Section of the Law Council of Australia *The New De Facto Regime: A Handbook* (Canberra: Family Law Section, 2009).
60   This is done so as to avoid the creation of an entirely new additional Part VIIIAA for de facto couples.

Part VIIIAA, which deals with orders and injunctions affecting third parties and fourthly, transitional provisions are enacted in a schedule to the amending Act.[61] It should also be noted that all states, apart from South Australia and Western Australia, have referred power to the Commonwealth legislature.[62]

After the commencement date, any de facto partner governed by the new law will be able to bring proceedings only in relation to appropriate matters under it.[63] Courts having jurisdiction under the legislation are: the Family Court of Australia, the Federal Magistrates Court of Australia, the Supreme Courts of Australian Capital Territory and the Northern Territory[64] and courts of summary jurisdiction in the referring jurisdictions.

(b) The nature of the relationship

'De Facto relationship' is defined in s 4AA of the Family Law Act 1975. This provides that a person is in a de facto relationship with another person if: first, the persons are not legally married to each other and, secondly, the persons are not related by family and, thirdly, 'having regard to all the circumstances of the relationship, they have a relationship as a couple of living together on a genuine domestic basis'. It is, of course, the last part of the third criterion which will, at the outset, give rise to difficulty as it, inevitably, becomes necessary for courts and, more problematically, administrative agencies to determine whether the 'genuine domestic basis' actually exists. In turn, this has, perhaps unfortunately, led to a statutory list of criteria needed to satisfy the requirement of the new s 4AA(2). The criteria now found in s 4AA(2) were derived, according to the major commentary on the new regime,[65] from the decision of Powell J of the New South Wales Supreme Court, in *Roy v Sturgeon*.[66] The list contained in s 4AA(2) is as follows:

(a)   the duration of the relationship;

(b)   the nature and extent of common residence;

(c)   whether a sexual relationship exists;

(d)   the degree of financial dependence or interdependence, and any arrangements for financial support between the parties;

(e)   the ownership, use and acquisition of their property;

---

61   These transitional provisions also included provisions for opting in, for couples whose relationship has broken down prior to the commencement date. See below text at n 99.
62   See Constitution of Australia, s 51 (xxxvii). For comment on the situation in South Australia and Western Australia, see below text at n 86-90.
63   Family Law Act 1975, s 39A (5).
64   See Constitution of Australia, s 122.
65   Above n 59 at 52.
66   (1986) 11 Fam LR 271 at 274.

(f)   the degree of mutual commitment to a shared life;

(g)   whether the relationship is or was registered under a prescribed law;

(h)   the care and support of children; and

(i)   the reputation and public aspects of the relationship.

It is regrettable, at least to this commentator, that this formulation, redolent as it is of social security legislation which was aimed at denying women benefits if they were living in such a relationship should have been so uncritically adopted. The only changes from Powell J's initial formulation was the deletion of the reference to 'the procreation of children', though performance of household duties is not mentioned and there is an additional provision relating to registration.[67] But, more fundamentally, since the regime is effectively concerned with property and finance, one might legitimately ask as to whether there is any need to include the criterion relating to the existence of a sexual relationship.[68] Its relevance to the operation of s 4AA(2)(d) relating to financial interdependence and support is, at the very best, tenuous whilst it will readily be apparent that that latter provision must be central to the operation of the entire regime.

To a degree, it must be said that the other provisions may operate in mitigation of the criticisms which I have made. Thus, it is clear[69] that no particular finding in relation to any particular matter is regarded as determinative as to whether a de facto relationship exists. The court is likewise required to attach such weight to any particular matter as is appropriate in the circumstances of each individual case.[70] The new law, it is specified,[71] encompasses both heterosexual and same-sex relationships. It also takes into account[72] that a de facto relationship may exist notwithstanding that one of the parties is legally married to someone else or is in another de facto relationship.

It will be remembered that s 4AA(2)(g) refers to the registration of relationships. It should be borne in mind that, for the purposes of the legislation, registration will not be determinative of the fact that a relationship exists – it is but one factor, though possibly a powerful one, which is to be taken into account in making the ultimate determination. However, it would seem, from s 4AA at large, that other circumstances would have to exist in addition to the fact of registration for a conclusion to be drawn that a relevant relationship

---

67   Family Law Act 1975, s 4AAA(2)(g).
68   Ibid, s 4AAA(2)(c).
69   Ibid, s 4AA(3).
70   Ibid, s 4AA(4).
71   Ibid, s 4AA(5).
72   Ibid, s 4AA(5)(b).

exists. However, it seems[73] as though the federal legislature was not intending that registration of relationships, notably same-sex relationships, be the equivalent of marriage.[74]

In addition to satisfying the courts that de facto relationships exist in particular circumstances, applicants must satisfy the courts that one of four gateway requirements is satisfied. These are set out in s 90SB of the new legislation: first, that the period, or total periods, of the relationship is at least two years or; secondly, that there is a child of the de facto relationship or; thirdly, that the party to the relationship who applies for an order or declaration made substantial contributions[75] and a failure to make an order or declaration would result in a serious injustice to the applicant or; fourthly, that the relationship is, or was, registered under a prescribed law of a state or territory.

Prescription is important because the Act[76] permits the federal prescription of state and territory registration laws. The effect[77] of this provision is that, if a de facto relationship exists, the registration of relationships that are not marriages may lead to the creation of rights and obligations which are very similar to those arising from formal marriage. Thus, same-sex couples who register their relationship in a state or territory will be in very much the same situation as married couples should their relationship break down and orders are required to be made in relation to property or finance.[78] In this context, the prohibition on same-sex marriages begins, if it already did not do so, to appear distinctly futile and foolishly discriminatory!

Section 90SB, it will be remembered, includes the existence of a child of the de facto relationship as a gateway requirement. In a somewhat circular manner, s 90RB(1) of the Family Law Act states that a child will be a child of the de facto relationship if the child is a child of both parties to the relationship. However, it then becomes necessary to determine whether a person will be regarded as a parent of a child. In order to avoid some of the problems which have occurred in the past,[79] significant amendments have been made to the definitions which existed hitherto in Part VII of the Family Law Act.

The effect of these changes is that both parties to a marriage or a de facto relationship will be regarded as parents of: first, a child of whom each of the

---

73   Above n 59 at 9.
74   Although s 90SB(d), see below text at n 76, may be to that effect.
75   Of a kind mentioned in s 90SM(a), (b) or (c) of the legislation.
76   Family Law Act 1975, s 90SB(d).
77   Above n 59 at 12.
78   Thus, to utilise an example postulated by the Family Law Section of the Law Council of Australia, above n 59 at 12: 'For example, a rich and a poor man meet, commence to live together on a genuine domestic basis and register their relationship on a Relationships Register. A month later the men separate. The poor man makes a property claim relying on prospective factors and a maintenance claim based on his needs. In this example, the registration of the relationship creates rights and obligations in the same way as a marriage does.'
79   See, for example, the decision of Guest J in the sad case of *Re Patrick* (2002) FLC 93–096.

parties is the biological parent,[80] secondly, a child adopted by the parties or either of them with the consent of the other;[81] thirdly, a child born by means of an artificial conception procedure when one of the parties is the birth mother and the donor of the genetic material has consented to its use;[82] fourthly, a child born as part of a surrogacy arrangement where a court has made an order under a law of a state or territory regarding a child's parentage.[83] Finally, it should be noted that, as of 1 July 2009, a parent of a child in a same-sex relationship which has broken down may claim child support from the other parent.[84]

One other matter to which reference has already been briefly made[85] is the position of people living in South Australia and Western Australia, or who may have lived substantially there during their relationship. In order to attract jurisdiction in matters relating to property[86] and maintenance[87] a geographical requirement is established. This may be achieved in three ways: first, the parties need to be ordinarily resident in a referring state during at least one-third of their de facto relationship or; secondly, the applicant must have made substantial contributions[88] in a referring state or; thirdly, the parties were ordinarily resident in a participating jurisdiction when the relationship broke down. It must be noted that the Act[89] does not seek to apply these amendments so as to exclude the law of a non-referring state if the geographical connection does not exist.[90]

It is also provided[91] that financial applications may be brought only if the application is brought within 2 years of the breakdown of the de facto relationship. However, the Act provides[92] for two exceptions – first, where hardship would be caused to the party or to a child[93] were leave to apply out of time not granted. Secondly, in the case of maintenance applications, the parties' circumstances were, at the end of the prescribed period, such that the applicant would not have been able to support him or herself without an

---

[80]   Family Law Act 1975, s 60HA(1)(a).

[81]   Ibid, s 60HA(1)(b).

[82]   Ibid, s 60HA(1). That change, ipso facto, gives the status of parent to the non-birth mother in a lesbian relationship.

[83]   At present, the Australian Capital Territory is the only jurisdiction in Australia which allows same-sex couples to enter into such agreements. The effect of its provision is, potentially, to provide for a child born under a surrogacy agreement involving a same-sex couple. See Family Law Act 1975, s 60HB.

[84]   It should also be noted that the Family Law Act 1975, s 60EA provides for the relationship of step-parent to be immediately created if a relationship is registered under relevant legislation.

[85]   Above text at n 62.

[86]   Family Law Act 1975, s 90SK.

[87]   Ibid, s 90SD.

[88]   Above n 75.

[89]   Family Law Act 1975, s 90RC(3).

[90]   For examples see above n 59 at 65. Also those contained in s 90RC(3) itself, above n 59 at 16.

[91]   Family Law Act 1975, s 44(5).

[92]   Ibid, s 44(6).

[93]   It should be noted that child, in this context, is not confined to a child of a de facto relationship, above text at n 79.

income tested pension, benefit or allowance. It must be emphasised[94] that, should the limitation period expire, rights under the new legislation may not be revived. Property matters would, thus, be dealt with in state courts according to general law. Hence, issues relating to resulting and constructive trusts would still continue to be relevant.

A particular problem which has attached to the consequences of the breakdown of a de facto relationship is the ascertainment of the date of that breakdown.[95] A new s 90RD is introduced into the Family Law Act which provides for declarations. It is specified[96] that declarations may be made in relation to five matters: first, the period, or periods, during which the de facto relationship subsisted; secondly, whether there is a child of the de factor relationship;[97] thirdly, whether one of the parties to a de facto relationship has made substantial contributions; fourthly, when the de facto relationship ended and, fifthly, where each of the parties to the de facto relationship was ordinarily resident.

On the question of declarations at large two points should be made: first, it is apparently envisaged[98] that there would be bifurcated hearings. This is derived from the experience of the Family Court of Western Australia, which has long been dealing with the law relating to de facto relationships, including same-sex relationships. In that jurisdiction, it seems as though there are preliminary hearings, often strongly contested, dealing with the issues to which reference is made in the provisions of the new legislation. Secondly, there must be some substantive relief sought for which a declaration is sought to establish jurisdiction.

Finally, on the question of the nature and juridical structure of de facto relationships as envisaged by the new legislation, the question arises whether couples who might otherwise be ineligible may choose to take advantage of the new law. In the First Schedule to the amending legislation, it is specified[99] that couples whose relationship has broken down before 1 March 2009 may opt in and have their dispute determined by the new law. However, that choice is, once made, unconditional and irrevocable.[100] Couples may not take advantage of that provision either if their dispute has been determined by final orders of a state or territory court or by written and unrevoked financial agreement. The choice to opt in must be in writing and signed by *both* parties, each party having obtained independent legal advice regarding the relative advantages and

---

[94] Above n 59 at 17.
[95] See F Bates 'Violence, Money and Informal Families in Australia and New Zealand' (1999) 7(1) Asia Pacific LR 1 at 18.
[96] Family Law Act 1975, s 90RD(2).
[97] In this context, the parentage testing provisions, already existing in Part VII of the Family Law Act 1975 apply to all proceedings under the new legislation. Hence, such procedures could be ordered in connection with an application for a declaration under s 90RD(2).
[98] Above n 59 at 17.
[99] Schedule 1, Part 2, item 86A.
[100] Ibid, item 86A(2).

disadvantage of the course of action.[101] In these respects, the processes are redolent of those attaching to financial agreements under the Act, as amended in 2000.[102] Courts may set aside a choice[103] if satisfied that it would be unjust and inequitable not to do so having regard to the circumstances under which the choice was made and may make orders which restore a party to the position prior to signing the document. It seems unlikely, given that there may be not inconsiderable differences between rights provided by the new laws and some others, that opting in will not be very frequent, especially given the mutuality requirement as well as other perceived safeguards.

(c)   Finance and property: the new developments

(i)   Introductory

Most new provisions relating to de facto relationships mirror those already found in the Family Law Act referring to disputes between married people. Hence, this commentary will be confined to especially novel areas. Initially, the definition of property as found in s 4(1) is extended so that the original definition applies now to de facto relationships.

(ii)   Financial agreements

First of all, it must be said that the original law relating to financial agreements, as found in Part VIIIA of the Family Law Act as amended in 2000, has not gone uncriticised, not least by the present writer.[104] Hence, it is a little disquieting to find the formal requirements, already found in s 90G(1) reiterated in relation to de facto relationships in the new s 90UJ(1). However, an additional ground for setting aside financial agreements in de facto relationships may be found in s 90K(1)(aa). This provision aims, in the words of the Family Law Section of the Law Council of Australia[105] 'to stop a married person from defrauding or defeating a claim of a de facto partner by a sweetheart deal with a new or old spouse'. In order to set aside an agreement under that provision, the de facto partner has to show that the married person either had a purpose to defraud or had a purpose to defeat the de facto's interest or had a reckless disregard for the de facto's interest. It is, thus, apparent that the test to be found in s 90K(1)(aa) is more stringent than that already found in s 106B, which applies to married couples. This, given the subsection's aims, is probably as it ought to be.[106]

---

[101]   Schedule 1, Part 2, item 86A(5). The legal practitioner who provides the independent legal advice must provide a signed statement that the necessary advice was given.

[102]   See below text at n 104.

[103]   Schedule 1, Part 2, item 86A(7).

[104]   See F Bates 'What Change is for the Better? Australian Family Law in 2000' in A Bainham (ed) *International Survey of Family Law* (Jordan Publishing Limited, 2002) p 35.

[105]   Above n 59 at 19.

[106]   There is an obverse provision contained in s 90UM(1)(d) where a de facto couple enters into an agreement with the intent of defrauding or defeating a claim of a party who was once married to one of the parties to the de facto relationship.

In addition to those provisions, Part 2 Division 3 and 4 (Transitional Provisions) provide that the new laws will recognise prior valid state agreements as being effective to exclude jurisdiction to enforce prior valid state agreements and, if there are grounds, set aside prior valid state agreements.[107] The effect of these provisions is that prior state agreements which do not meet the formal requirements of a binding financial agreement under the new law but which do meet the requirements under the old state law will be recognised as being able to exclude jurisdiction and may be enforced or set aside under the new law.[108]

Related to those provisions is an addition to the grounds on which old state agreements may be set aside. The purpose of this addition is to permit a retrospective challenge to the effect of otherwise valid agreements in Queensland, the Northern Territory and, probably South Australia, where the requirements as to independent legal advice are not as strict as elsewhere, and injustice and inequity are found present.

It is provided in ss 90UM(1)(k) and 90UM(5) of the Family Law Act that state agreements may be set aside if, first, at least one of the parties to the agreement was not provided with independent legal advice from a legal practitioner, prior to signing the agreement, regarding the effect of the agreement and the rights of the parties and the advantages and disadvantages at the time the advice was given to the party making the agreement or, secondly, if such advice had been provided, but no certificate signed by the legal practitioner had been included or attached to the agreement or given to the party; and, thirdly, it would be unjust or inequitable not to set the agreement aside.

It is hard to prejudge the likely effect of the totality of these provisions, but, as matters presently stand, the original provisions introduced in 2000 do not appear to be greatly used. This may be because they have worked reasonably well but, anecdotal evidence, at least, suggests that their complexity and disorganisation have caused them to be avoided. These provisions, in that event, will probably reinforce that position.

(iii)   Superannuation

Inevitably, if only because of the amounts of money involved, issues relating to division of superannuation funds are necessarily complex. The object section of Part VIIIB of the Family Law Act 1975 now permits superannuation interests of de facto parties to be split. Thus, s 90MC(2) provides that a superannuation interest of a party is to be treated as property. This is expressed in exactly the

---

[107]   To qualify, the prior state agreement must, first, deal with how property financial resources are to be distributed and deal with maintenance or matters which are incidental or ancillary. Secondly, the agreements must have been validly made under state law so that a state court – ignoring any power to vary or set aside the agreement – could not make an order inconsistent with the terms of the agreement.

[108]   Above n 59 at 20.

same terms as the pre-existing s 90C.[109] This means that the problems represented by the case-law[110] are just as applicable to the new law as to the earlier.

Further, it is not provided, in an amended s 90MS, that the courts, in making orders for alteration of property interests of de facto couples,[111] may make orders in accordance with Part VIIIB in relation to a de facto couple's superannuation interests. The court, though, will not be able to make an order under that section in relation to the superannuation interests of a de facto couple, except in accordance with the new law.[112]

(iv)   Additional s 75(2) matters

There are certain s 75(2) issues – s 75(2) of the original Act deals with criteria for the award of maintenance and is taken into account in s 79, which deals with alteration of property interests – which are replicated in the new s 90SF(3)(naa). The latter provides that one matter which must be taken into account is the terms of any order or declaration made, or proposed to be made, under the new Part VIIIAB in relation to a person who is a party to a de facto relationship, or a party to a marriage, or the priority of a person covered by such an order or declaration. The new s 90SF(3)(o) mirrors s 75(2)(naa).

Secondly, a new s 75(2)(q) provides that the terms of any de facto financial agreement that is binding on a party to a marriage should also be taken into account. Like s 75(2)(q), the new s 90SF(3)(s) requires courts, when dealing with the alteration of property interests between a de facto couple, to take into account the terms of any binding financial agreement that one of the de facto parties has with a current or former marriage partner.

In addition to these specific provisions, the new law deals with matters such as multiple relationships in relation to superannuation,[113] s 75(2) matters and consolidation of claims.[114] Injunctive powers are also included, albeit in a rather convoluted manner,[115] which may be made in support of orders for substantial financial relief. In addition, injunctions may be made in respect of exclusive occupancy by one party to a de facto relationship of property held by either or both.[116]

Perhaps most intriguing is the effect of the foregoing on s 43(a) of the Family Law Act. Since the very commencement of the Act, s 43 set out the principles which courts exercising jurisdiction under the Act must observe, the first of

---

[109] Which now becomes s 90MC(1) in respect of married couples.
[110] See, for example, *Coghlan and Coghlan* (2005) FLC 93–220.
[111] Family Law Act 1975, s 90SM.
[112] Above n 59 at 23.
[113] Family Law Act 1975, s 90MX(3).
[114] Ibid, ss 79(10)(aa), 90SM(10)(d), (e).
[115] Ibid, ss 90SS(1)(k), 90SS(5)(b).
[116] Ibid, s 114(2A).

which enjoined those courts to have regard to the 'need to preserve and protect
the institution of marriage as the union of a man and a woman to the exclusion
of all others voluntarily entered into for life'. I have long considered this
enactment both of questionable anthropological validity[117] and of scant effect
on the mundane operation of the legislation at large;[118] however, s 43 is
amended so that s 43(a) does not apply in relation to de facto financial causes.
It would be more than paradoxical were it to apply. Courts are not now
required to protect the institution of marriage when the parties have elected not
to enter into it. Given the whole context of the new legislation,[119] the utility of
it, at least that part of s 43, must surely be more in question, especially in
response to multiple relationships, both chronologically and spatially.

IV   FINANCE AND PROPERTY

In 2009, issues relating to bankruptcy appear to have dominated curial activity.
An especially interesting instance is provided by the decision of the Full Court
of the Family Court of Australia in *Rand and Rand (No 2)*[120] where the
husband had appealed against a number of orders made in proceedings
between the husband, wife and various other entities. The husband submitted
that certain intellectual property rights were, on the trial judge's finding of
facts, property, which vested in the husband's trustee in bankruptcy, pursuant
to the provisions of the Bankruptcy Act 1966 (Cth) and, hence, no order could
be made personally against the husband in relation to those rights. Conversely,
the wife argued that, notwithstanding that the husband had been discharged
from bankruptcy and that the intellectual property rights were vested in the
former trustee in bankruptcy, the trustee had, either formally or informally,
disclaimed any such property. Thus, the intellectual property rights were
submitted to have been vested in the husband at the date of the orders at first
instance. The Full Court of the Family Court[121] dismissed the husband's
appeal, though for rather different reasons.

First, Coleman and Crisford JJ found,[122] though the matter was not without
uncertainty, the husband's trustee in bankruptcy had neither disclaimed, nor
purported to disclaim, any interest in the technology, or any other divisible
property which the husband might be found to have had. In reaching that
decision, the judges were required to consider[123] the application of s 133 of the
Bankruptcy Act 1966. They reached that conclusion even though there seemed
to be some evidence that the trustee in bankruptcy might have done so.

---

[117] See F Bates *An Introduction to Family Law* (Melbourne: Law Book Co, 1987) p 14.
[118] See F Bates 'Principle and the Family Law Act: The Uses and Abuses of Section 43' (1981) 55
       Aust LJ 181.
[119] See, particularly, above text at n 77.
[120] (2009) FLC 93–410.
[121] Coleman, Warnick and Crisford JJ.
[122] (2009) FLC 93–410 at 83,593.
[123] Ibid at 83,589.

Secondly, Coleman and Crisford JJ were of the view[124] that, though the failure of the husband's former trustee in bankruptcy to appear before the appellate court might have obviated some of the problems, nothing persuaded Coleman and Crisford JJ that 'the trial judge's orders would defeat attempts by the wife to enforce them against the husband's former trustee in bankruptcy if he does not disclaim the technology, or against the husband if he does'. However, the judges noted that it was hard to predict how successful any such attempts might prove.[125]

Warnick J considered[126] that the appeal failed on two major grounds. The first was that the trial judge had not found that the husband did, in fact, have proprietary interest in the relevant technology – even though he had access to and control in respect of the invention and of the technology, which was continuing. Secondly, Warnick J was of the view[127] that there was nothing to be found in the trial judge's reasons, or the orders which had been appealed, which demonstrated that a finding that the husband did have such a proprietary interest necessarily underpinned those orders. Warnick J agreed that the trustee had not disclaimed any interest.

Thus, it will be apparent that *Rand (No 2)* is a case of more than local interest in that it raises, even though it does not necessarily solve, matters relating to the relevance of intellectual property, which, after all, Warnick J found[128] to be worth, to the husband, something in the order of at least $1 million! In other words, even though the case may not have solved those problems, it could profitably be borne in mind by people likely to be faced with them.

The immediate relevance of principles of bankruptcy law to issues relating to distribution of family property is starkly illustrated by the decision of the Full Court of the Family Court of Australia[129] in *Trustee of the Property of G Lemnos, a Bankrupt and Lemnos and Anor*.[130] That case concerned an appeal by the trustee of the bankrupt estate of the husband against orders for property settlement which provided that the matrimonial home vested in the trustee be sold and the net proceeds be equally divided between the trustee and the wife. The key fact was that a debt lodged by the Deputy Commissioner of Taxation in the husband's bankrupt estate, in consequence of his improper tax deductions over the years, significantly exceeded the net equity in the matrimonial home, which was the parties' only worthwhile asset.

It was argued by the trustee that, first, the trial judge ought to have considered all of the relevant factors and circumstances and, having regard to the bankruptcy of the husband, to treat the wife and the creditors of the husband

---

124 Ibid at 83,594.
125 But that issue did not require determination in the case at hand.
126 (2009) FLC 93–410 at 83,595.
127 Ibid at 83,597.
128 Ibid at 83,596.
129 Coleman, Thackray and Ryan JJ.
130 (2009) FLC 93–394.

equally. Secondly, the trial judge had failed to follow the procedure enunciated in *Biltoft and Biltoft*[131] for identification of the property of the parties, their assets and financial resources net of their liabilities. In that case, the Full Court of the Family Court of Australia had stated[132] that:

> 'Where the assets are not encumbered and moneys are owed by the parties or one of them to unsecured creditors, the Court ascertains the value of their property by deducting from the value of their assets the value of their total liabilities, including the unsecured liabilities.'

Thirdly, if the trial judge had properly taken into account the husband's liabilities, there would have been no property of his available so as to alter property interests under s 79(1) of the Family Law Act 1975. The Full Court allowed the appeal, although, once more, for differing reasons.

Coleman J, first of all,[133] discussed the legislative history of the relevant statutory provision[134] and stated that, prior to that paragraph's insertion, the position was that the creditors in bankruptcy had effective priority over spouses.[135] The result of legislative change, Coleman J emphasised,[136] was that the 'interests of creditors do not automatically trump the interests of the spouse and children. Rather the FLA now requires the Court to balance the interests of family members and of creditors in the exercise of its discretion'. It was, though, as Coleman J sought further to emphasise,[137] in the exercise of the wide discretion that the trial judge had fallen into error. More particularly, Coleman J considered the relevance of s 75(2)(ha) of the Family Law Act. That paragraph provides that, when considering issues relating to maintenance, which is essentially needs based, the court must consider 'the effect of any proposed orders on the ability of a party to recover the creditor's debt, so far as that effect is relevant'. Coleman J was of the view[138] that the trial judge's discretion had miscarried, especially because of his 'focus on the absence of complicity or culpability on the part of the wife [which had] diverted him from the discretionary exercise which the statute required him to undertake'.

Thackray and Ryan JJ, although agreeing with Coleman J on most of the significant issues, disagreed on others. First, and most fundamentally, they took the view[139] that the trial judge had acted outside the range of discretion which

---

[131] (1995) FLC 92–614.
[132] Ibid at 82,124, per Nicholson CJ, Ellis and Buckley JJ.
[133] (2009) FLC 93–394 at 83,271.
[134] Family Law Act 1975, s 79(1)(b).
[135] Coleman J continued by saying that: 'Once a sequestration order was made against a party to a marriage, his or her property vested in the trustee in bankruptcy. The result was that the vested property ceased, automatically and irretrievably, to be available to claims by the spouse or susceptible to orders of this Court. Some saw this as harsh.'
[136] (2009) FLC 93–394 at 83,271, derived, on the judge's own admission from the submission on behalf of the trustee in bankruptcy.
[137] Ibid at 83,283.
[138] Ibid at 83,287.
[139] Ibid at 83,304.

was permitted by the legislation. A major reason[140] was that the trial judge was in error in determining that the non-bankrupt spouse – the wife, that is – ought to be excused from any burdens of the primary taxation liabilities. In so doing, the judges specifically declined to comment on the application of general principles[141] to cases involving proceedings between a non-bankrupt spouse and a trustee in bankruptcy in circumstances where liabilities to unsecured creditors could only be met by resort to property *'already'*[142] owned by the non-bankrupt spouse.[143] Yet, as will have been clear from the statement of the facts in *Lemnos*, the role of the Deputy Commissioner of Taxation appears crucial. The judges found[144] that there had been no challenge to the finding that the husband had been 'reckless and negligent' in the way in which he had completed his income tax returns. Likewise, there had not been any challenge to the fact that the wife had not been, in any way, complicit in their preparation. Nonetheless, as the judges pointed out, there could be little in the way of escape from the dictum of Baker J in *Kowaliw and Kowaliw*[145] that 'financial losses incurred by the parties or either of them in the course of a marriage whether such losses result from a joint or several liability, should be shared by them (although not necessarily equally)'. Thackray and Ryan JJ concluded that the conduct of the husband could not be subsumed into any of the exceptions to this broad statement.[146] Thackray and Ryan JJ emphasised[147] that they could not accept that the husband's conduct was designed other than to maximise the assets, which his tax deductions had enabled him to do. The judges said that:[148]

'Having had the benefit of the funds flowing from the husband's conduct, it would seem to us to be neither just nor equitable for the wife to escape all responsibility for payment of the primary tax that would otherwise have been paid.'

The issue of taxation arose once more in the decision of the Full Court of the Family Court of Australia in *Commissioner of Taxation and Warsnap and Another*[149] which concerned an appeal by the Commissioner as intervener in property proceedings between husband and wife. In those proceedings, the only significant asset was the former matrimonial home which was valued at $475,000; however, the husband had a tax liability of $12,031,124 and a company, of which the husband was the sole director and shareholder, had a tax liability of $421,756. The trial judge ordered that the former matrimonial

---

[140] Ibid at 83,296.

[141] As represented by the decision of the Full Court of the Family Court of Australia (Ellis, Kay and Dessau JJ) in *Johnson and Johnson* [1999] Fam CA 369.

[142] Thackray and Ryan JJ's emphasis.

[143] That, of course, would raise basal issues of the nature of matrimonial property as described in s 4(1) of the Family Law Act 1975.

[144] (2009) FLC 93–394 at 83,295.

[145] (1981) FLC 91–092 at 76,644.

[146] These were, first, where one of the parties had embarked on a course of conduct designed to reduce or minimise the effective value or worth of matrimonial assets. Or, second, where one of parties has acted negligently or wantonly with matrimonial assets, the overall effect of which had reduced or minimised their value.

[147] (2009) FLC 93–394 at 83,295.

[148] Ibid.

[149] (2009) FLC 93–392.

home be sold and that, after costs of sale, the proceeds should be divided equally between the Commissioner and the wife, both of whom appealed.

The Commissioner argued that, first, the trial judge was in error in not making a finding that the source of the funds of the spouses' acquisition of property[150] was income on which tax had not been paid. It was also claimed, secondly, that the judge had erred in the exercise of his discretion and, thirdly, that he had failed to provide adequate reasons. The cross-appeal by the wife alleged that the trial judge had fallen into error by failing to add back, as a notional asset, substantial legal fees which the husband had paid.[151] The Full Court of the Family Court of Australia[152] dismissed both appeals.

A major difficulty, the Full Court found,[153] was that, despite the husband's business acumen,[154] there had been a flow in the manner in which the husband had controlled his business activities due to his failure to disclose taxable income over several years. In making that comment, the Full Court had adopted the views expressed by the trial judge that the wife had 'unwittingly continued to have the benefits of a lifestyle which for some years was enhanced by the failure of the husband to disclose taxable income to the intervener'. All of that meant, the Full Court stated,[155] that the degree to which the source of funds for the purchase of real estate was either unpaid tax, or at least income tax on which tax ought to have been paid, was one which, according to the available evidence, no precise findings could have been made. Hence, the issue of the source of funds for the purchase of the real estate was one which could have been disposed by recognition of the *broad* facts which related to it, rather than a detailed analysis of the evidence relating to it.[156] The trial judge had done that and, in addition, the Full Court found that the trial judge had not, in principle, erred in his application of the legislation,[157] nor had he erred in principle in the manner in which he had generally exercised his discretion under the legislation.[158]

Yet, inevitably, there has been more to matters relating to finance and property in Australia family law: quite some time ago, I warned[159] about problems which might attach to the manner in which the various kinds of financial agreement entered into by parties to a marriage might be recognised. So, by reason of

---

[150] Which included the former matrimonial home.
[151] Amounting to $1,040,943.
[152] Boland CJ, Warnick and Cronin JJ.
[153] (2009) FLC 93–392 at 83,217.
[154] As the court described the situation, ibid: 'As a result of the business success enjoyed by the husband, the husband and wife were able to lead a luxurious lifestyle both in England and Australia featuring *high priced real estates*, exotic motor vehicles, first class travel and a general lifestyle befitting the "Tales from the Arabian nights"!'
[155] (2009) FLC 93–392 at 83,222.
[156] (2009) FLC 93–392 at 83,223.
[157] Ibid at 83,225.
[158] Ibid at 83,227.
[159] Above n 104.

amendments to the Family Law Act 1975,[160] as effected in 2000, much of what I had presaged has come to pass – unfortunately! In 2009, the decision of Murphy J of the Family Court of Australia in *Fevia and Carmel-Fevia*[161] obviously demonstrates the difficulties involved, both to parties who are unwise enough to involve themselves in them and to lawyers who advise them.

In that case, the parties had entered into a financial agreement pursuant to s 90B of the Family Law Act in contemplation of their marriage. At that time, the wife argued she had signed a document which did not include an annexure which set out the husband's financial situation. However, the husband did then sign an agreement which did include the relevant annexure, but a copy of that agreement was not given to the wife until the proceedings in the Family Court, some 7 years later. The wife submitted that the agreement which she had signed was not binding within the meaning of s 90G of the Family Law Act.[162] The husband, consequently and predictably, argued that the Family Court was precluded from making orders under Part VIII of the Act, at least to the extent that the financial agreement dealt with relevant and appropriate matters. The husband objected unsuccessfully to the wife's applications for property settlement and maintenance orders under the Act when the marriage broke down.

First, Murphy J found[163] that no financial agreement, whether binding or otherwise, was in existence between the parties. The husband, in other words, had signed a document which was materially different from that signed by the wife. Secondly, it followed that the judge was required to inquire as to how the requirements of s 90G of the Act could be fulfilled. In so doing, Murphy J commented[164] that the *overriding* purpose of the provision was 'to remove the necessity for court intervention in order to make binding an agreement otherwise arrived at between contracting marriage partners (or prospective marriage partners)'. Therein lies one of the major weaknesses of the 2000 amendments:[165] the personal and financial situations and aspirations of people, however well intentioned, may not be even remotely similar. In addition, the judge continued by saying that:

> 'In keeping with that intention, there is also evident a further intention to introduce notions of ordinary contractual or commercial interaction between marriage partners (or prospective marriage partners) who wish to avail themselves of a contract to determine their financial matters in the event of the marriage breaking down, albeit that those usual contractual or commercial interactions have as their end point the creation of a contract that is a creature of statute and has, additionally, a purpose circumscribed by statute.'

---

[160] Ibid.
[161] (2009) FLC 93–411.
[162] That is, as Murphy J put the matter, ibid at 83,599, it was intended by the parties that the agreement would be in substitution for their rights to financial relief under the Family Law Act at large were the marriage to break down.
[163] (2009) FLC 93–411 at 83,617.
[164] Ibid at 83,620.
[165] See above n 159.

This, though an accurate statement of the policy behind the law, must surely help demonstrate how thoroughly bad this part of the Family Law Act is: agreements entered into before the marriage (as in *Fevia*), during the subsistence of the marriage and after its breakdown are all treated by these amendments in the same way. There can be few couples, including those in *Fevia*, who would contemplate basic contractual notions, such as misrepresentation, mistake and so on, as being directly relevant to their present or, indeed, future situations.

Murphy J then went on[166] to emphasise that the requirements of the receipt of independent legal advice to each party, as well as its formalisation, were 'the *cornerstone* of the protection for the contracting parties'. Indeed, the legislation had the receipt of that advice and its formalisation as its centrepiece. It followed, the judge continued, that, with such a centrepiece, its purpose was to provide protection for the contracting parties and to operate, in effect, in lieu of the role that the court had played, both under the previous version of the Family Law Act and the Act, and 'it is to be expected that a court would require that the terms of s 90G be attended with solemnity, and that strict compliance with its items would be insisted on'.

It inevitably followed that the next issue which arose was the manner in which the statutory requirements were to be implemented. After a very detailed discussion, the judge stated[167] that compliance with s 90G could be achieved by each party receiving an originally signed document, one clearly being marked 'original' and the other clearly marked 'copy'. Further, compliance might be achieved by one party receiving an originally signed document and the other receiving a photocopy of the originally signed document. However, Murphy J emphasised, that the copy must be identical to the original. This requirement meant that, for an agreement to comply with the legislation, it could not comprise signed counterparts. In addition, s 90KA of the Family Law Act made it clear, Murphy J said, that ordinary contractual and equitable principles did have a role to play in the operation of financial agreements under the Act. But, because of the generally expressed aims of Part VIIIA, they had no application to the possible grant of relief under s 90G from compliance with its requirements. Thus, for instance,[168] estoppel could not be raised in relation to non-compliance with the requirements of s 90G. All of that meant, especially in the context of the case at large, that the wife was not precluded from pursuing her claim for relief under Part VIII of the legislation.

Quite apart from the important explanation of some of the technicalities involved in the mundane operation of Part VIIIA, *Fevia* ought to suggest to readers of this commentary that the Australian legislation can provide a useful template for what should be avoided in legislation relating to financial agreements.

---

[166] (2009) FLC 93–411 at 83,620.
[167] Ibid at 83,633.
[168] Ibid at 83,634.

Prior to leaving the area of finance and property, another issue which has continually arisen is the matter of superannuation. An interesting illustration of the problems which can arise is provided by the decision of the Full Court of the Family Court of Australia in *Edwards and Edwards*.[169] At the date of the hearing, in that case, the parties had been separated for some 15 years and had divided, apart from their superannuation benefits, on a generally equal basis. The central issue, therefore, was the wife's application for a share in two superannuation funds.[170] The trial judge had made orders, pursuant to legislation,[171] that a base amount of $84,000 be awarded to the wife in a First State fund. The wife appealed, unsuccessfully, to the Full Court. In that appeal, she claimed that, in addition to the initial order, an order be made under the same provision[172] that she be awarded a 50% interest in the husband's DFRDB[173] interest. Alternatively, she sought that the order with regard to the First State fund be increased to $150,000.

In so doing, she claimed that the trial judge was in error, first, because, the determination of the proceedings was directed to a determination of the wife's entitlement to the husband's superannuation or pension entitlements; secondly, in relation to her approach and findings in relation to the DFRDB entitlements; thirdly, effectively inevitably,[174] that she had erred in relation to the assessment of the parties' contributions and, especially, in relation to the application of s 75(2); and finally, in failing to consider the effect of the proposed orders.

In dismissing the appeal, the Full Court[175] was dismissive[176] of the first ground and noted that the real issue was whether the trial judge's determination of the issue fell beyond the exercise of a reasonable discretion. As regards the second ground, the Full Court noted[177] that the judge at first instance had clearly indicated that 'the payment of the entitlement, which was in the payment phase as a pension could not be converted to a lump sum and would thus forever remain a pension'. Thus, the Full Court concluded, on that issue, that the first instance approach was flawed – though the consequences of such an approach might be differently viewed.[178] On the third issue, the court concluded[179] that the trial judge had considered, in an appropriate manner, the real value and impact of the husband's DFRDB entitlement and the orders which she had made in respect of it.

---

[169] (2009) FLC 93–409.
[170] These were, First State Superannuation Fund and the Defence Force Retirement and Death Benefits Scheme (DFRDB).
[171] Family Law Act 1975, s 90MT1(a).
[172] Ibid.
[173] Above n 170.
[174] See, for example, F Bates 'Discretion, Contributions and Needs – Family Property in Australia' [2005] Int Fam L 218.
[175] Coleman and Cronin JJ, with whom Finn J agreed.
[176] (2009) FLC 93–409 at 83,568.
[177] Ibid at 83,569.
[178] Ibid.
[179] (2009) FLC 93–409 at 83,570.

The point which *Edwards* represents is that the amendments to the Family Law Act 1975 in relation to relative superannuation entitlements do not effectively represent the end of the reform process – but, in reality, only the beginning.

V   PARENTING AND PARENTAGE

To begin at the beginning, as Dylan Thomas urged,[180] one should instantly consider the decision of the Full Court of the Family Court of Australia in *Tryon and Clutterbuck (No 2)*[181] which concerned an appeal by both husband and wife against a declaration made pursuant to a declaration made at first instance, under s 69VA of the Family Law Act 1975, as amended, that the respondent was the father of two children.

The husband and the wife had, prima facie, five children, two of whom were the subject of the proceedings. The proceedings in the Family Court of Australia had begun when the respondent to the instant appeal filed an application to spend time with the two relevant children. He claimed that he was their father since he had had a sexual relationship with the wife for some 10 years, during which time the children were born, and that the wife had actually told him that he was their father. The wife, however, sought the dismissal of the application on the grounds that the children were those of herself and her husband, to whom she had been married for over 20 years.

At first instance, orders were made pursuant to legislation[182] that parentage tests be carried out on the claimant, the husband and the wife, as well as the two children in question. The husband and wife failed to comply with those orders in respect of both themselves and the children. Ultimately, the trial judge made a declaration, under the legislation,[183] that the claimant was the father of the two children. The husband and wife appealed, unsuccessfully, to the Full Court of the Family Court of Australia.[184]

In so doing, they argued that, at first instance, error had been made, first, that judgment had miscarried in that the transcript demonstrated prejudgment of issues which were also represented in the judgment's structure. Secondly, no, or inadequate, weight had been given at first instance to the burden which was cast on the claimant to prove his case and that findings of fact had not properly been made in the context of statutory presumptions relating to the paternity. Thirdly, incorrect inferences had been drawn from the husband and wife's failure to take part in the testing and, also, from the wife's failure to give evidence. Before seeking to explicate the Full Court's reasons for rejecting the appeal, it should be said that there were two judgments – one by Finn J and another by Warnick and Strickland JJ – which were extremely detailed. These

---

[180]   Dylan Thomas, *Under Milk Wood*, Act I.
[181]   (2009) FLC 93–412.
[182]   Family Law Act 1975, s 69W.
[183]   Ibid, s 69VA.
[184]   Finn, Warnick and Strickland JJ.

long and detailed judgments have become a notable feature of decisions of the Full Court of the Family Court of Australia in recent times.

In so dismissing the appeal, the judges, first, rejected any argument that there was anything in the structure of the judgment at first instance which indicated prejudgment of the issues. In particular, Warnick and Strickland JJ set out a detailed analysis of the processes which had been adopted at first instance. Warnick and Strickland JJ rejected[185] any such submission and, in so doing, usefully pointed out that:

> 'While in some cases reasons for judgment might well discuss the evidence of an applicant first, often findings as to disputed facts will only be made after consideration of all of the evidence. In this case one of the two expected "primary" witnesses gave no evidence. The husband's evidence was restricted in scope. We see no reason why it should have been assessed "first".'[186]

Secondly, the court could see no foundation for any argument that findings of fact had been made, at first instance, which were out of the context of relevant statutory presumptions. Further, the Full Court found[187] no basis for any argument that there was a failure at first instance to appreciate that the applicant was obliged to prove his case and the standard of proof which was cast upon him.

Thirdly, the court also found that inferences had not been wrongly made at trial regarding the husband and wife's failure to attend DNA testing. In so doing, Warnick and Strickland JJ referred[188] to the judgment of Fogarty J in *Re C (No 2)*,[189] where it had been said that 'parentage is a medical rather than a legal issue. The procedures now adopted are well recognised and legislatively approved. They are likely to be determinant of the issue either way and in a manner which takes it out of the area of challenged evidence about past events, credibility and presumptions'. Warnick and Strickland JJ emphasised[190] that s 70NDA of the Family Law Act[191] made it plain that the onus of establishing reasonable excuse for not so attending falls on the respondent, in the present instance, the husband and wife, to a contravention application. Although these proceedings were not a formal contravention application, the judges thought it 'clear that in any event the evidentiary onus in respect of excuse fell upon the husband'.

Finally, and of more than passing significance, Warnick and Strickland JJ considered[192] the effect which making the declaration of paternity might have

---

[185] (2009) FLC 93–412 at 83,645.
[186] In any event, the judges considered, ibid, much of the applicant father's case was set out under the headings of 'uncontested evidence' and 'The Children's Names'.
[187] (2009) FLC 93–412 at 83,647 per Warnick and Strickland JJ.
[188] Ibid at 83,651.
[189] (1992) FLC 92–284 at 79,104.
[190] (2009) FLC 93–412 at 83,653.
[191] Especially by reason of s 70NDA(c).
[192] (2009) FLC 93–412 at 83,657.

on the various relationships involved. In so doing, the judges assumed that the decision whether to make a declaration was one in which the best interests of the children were paramount – accordingly, an assessment of the factors set out in s 60CC of the Family Law Act was necessary – but they could see no error in the first instance findings. Those, in essence, were that, as the children had had a continuing relationship with the applicant, the declaration was unlikely to have any deleterious effect. Similarly, the declaration would be unlikely to affect their relationship with the respondents adversely. Indeed, it was suggested, at first instance that, were the order not made, the children might be denied the benefit of an ongoing relationship with their biological father.

All in all, *Tryon and Clutterbuck (No 2)* provides an interesting example of the operation of the law relating to parentage declarations, but it also shows the complications of family forms and interactions – even though they might, at times, not appear especially edifying.

On the issue of parenting (as opposed to parentage) itself, the Full Court of the Family Court of Australia was, once again, forced to consider the effect of international relocation in the case of *McCall and Clark*,[193] which involved an appeal by a father against parenting orders involving international relocation which had initially been made by a Federal Magistrate. In October 2005, the mother and child had left Australia for Dubai, where it was planned that the parties would marry and, return to Australia. The marriage never took place as the parties' relationship had collapsed. The mother and child continued to live in Dubai, while the father argued that the child should be returned to Australia. The Federal Magistrate, inter alia, ordered that the parties have equal shared responsibility for the child and that the child continue living with the mother in Dubai. His orders also provided for arrangements relating to the child's residence if the father himself relocated to Dubai and also restrained the mother from changing the child's residence from Dubai without the father's permission.[194] The Full Court of the Family Court of Australia[195] allowed the father's appeal.

The court's first reason for so doing was that the magistrate, although he had discussed various aspects of the relocation proposals under s 60CC of the Family Law Act 1975, as amended in 2006, appeared only to have seriously considered two of those proposals. In so doing, the court took the view[196] that, in dealing with a parenting application involving a relocation where the presumption of shared parenting applies, and an order for equal shared parental responsibility is made, the court must consider three matters: first, whether equal time (or substantial and significant time) with both parents would be in the child's best interests. Secondly, the court should consider and weigh up an equal time (or substantial and significant time) regime against all

---

[193] (2009) FLC 93–405.
[194] It should be noted that the United Arab Republics was not a party to the Hague Convention on Civil Aspects of International Child Abduction.
[195] Bryant CJ, Faulks DCJ and Boland J.
[196] (2009) FLC 93–405 at 83,467.

the factors having advantages for the child in the relocation proposal. Thirdly, the court should consider whether an order should be made for equal time (or substantial and significant time) in one location or for the child to reside with one parent in a distant location, with such other orders as would maintain the benefit of a meaningful relationship for the child if appropriate to do so. In other words,[197] the issue of the Full Court's determination was whether the Federal Magistrate had properly considered and weighed 'all'.[198]

The second ground on which the appeal was allowed was that the magistrate had failed to give appropriate consideration to the matters contained in s 65DAA of the Act. The court noted[199] that the asserted errors fell into three categories: first, there was a failure to deal with the need to consider an equal time and a substantial time arrangement when weighing up the advantages and disadvantages of the relocation proposal. Secondly, there had been a failure properly to analyse and address the primary consideration of the promotion of the meaningful relationship with the child and there had been a failure to consider the reasonable practicality of each of the possible arrangements. Most particularly, the court considered[200] that the magistrate had not considered whether the orders which were ultimately made 'would enable the child to develop a meaningful relationship with the father other than a brief reference that the father could develop a meaningful relationship with the child if he relocated to Dubai without any real consideration of practical difficulties inherent with such a proposal'.

Finally, the court was of the view[201] that the Federal Magistrate had not considered how the mother's proposals could provide the child with a meaningful relationship with both parents, and whether her proposal was appropriate – the mother had proposed, in the event that the child was ordered to be returned to Australia, that she would return as well.

McCall and Clark illustrates the very significant problems which arise when the 2006 amendments to the Family Law Act 1975 and the problem of international relocation collide. If *McCall and Clark* does nothing more than suggest the need for further revision of the statutory process, then it will surely have been of value.

Some parts of the 2006 amendments are altogether less happy than others[202] and one of the most confusing is that relating to the relevance of Aboriginal culture.[203] A problematic and graphic instance is provided by the decision of

---

[197]   Ibid at 83,468.
[198]   The Full Court's emphasis.
[199]   (2009) FLC 93–405 at 83,463.
[200]   Ibid at 83,478.
[201]   Ibid at 83,479.
[202]   See F Bates 'Blunting the Sword of Solomon – Australian Family Law in 2006' in B Atkin (ed) *International Survey of Family Law* (Jordan Publishing Limited, 2008) p 21.
[203]   Family Law Act 1975, s 60CC(6).

the Full Court of the Family Court of Australia in *Hart and Verran*.[204] That case involved an appeal against orders which had been made by a Federal Magistrate by the mother in proceedings between her, the child's father and paternal grandparents. Inter alia, the orders provided that the children reside primarily with their paternal grandmother and that she should be the sole decision maker as to when the father could spend time with the children in the absence of compliance with conditions that he undertake drug and alcohol counselling.

The mother argued, on appeal, that the Federal Magistrate had not given sufficient weight to the children's right to enjoy and maintain a connection with their Aboriginal Tiwi culture.[205] Conversely, the children's parental grandmother asserted that that consideration had been given sufficient weight. The mother further argued that the magistrate was in error in awarding the grandmother sole decision-making power with respect to the children's spending unsupervised time with their father, particularly in the light of the magistrate's own findings regarding the father's record of violence and alcohol abuse. The mother's appeal was resisted by the father and the paternal grandmother as well as the independent children's lawyer.[206] The Full Court of the Family Court[207] allowed the appeal in part.

On the issue of the children's Aboriginal heritage, the court took the view[208] that it was clear from his judgment that the Federal Magistrate had been acutely aware of the need for the children to maintain a *'real connection'*[209] with their Tiwi culture. The central issue, as the magistrate had pointed out, was 'balancing the entitlement of the children to a real connection with their Tiwi culture against other issues in the case, and particularly those relating to the stability of the children's living arrangements'. Although there was no anthropological evidence before the Federal Magistrate, the Full Court noted[210] that there was evidence from the children's maternal grandmother, a Tiwi elder, who was able to present 'extensive evidence with respect to what was broadly described . . . as "Aboriginality"'. The court continued[211] that there was no suggestion that the absence of any anthropological evidence had impeded the magistrate in determining the best interests of the children nor did he accept the maternal grandmother's view that it was only by living in a Tiwi community that the children could properly pursue their cultural heritage or identity. The court further emphasised,[212] indeed, that it was 'somewhat disingenuous' to suggest that the proceedings were, in some unspecified way, deficient without anthropological evidence. Even were it to be provided, any such witness would be reliant on information of the kind which had been

---

[204] (2009) FLC 93–418.
[205] Family Law Act 1975, s 60CC(3)(h).
[206] Ibid, ss 69L, 68LA.
[207] Coleman, O'Ryan and Strickland JJ.
[208] (2009) FLC 93–418 at 83,771.
[209] Author's emphasis.
[210] (2009) FLC 9–418 at 83,771.
[211] Ibid at 83,773.
[212] Ibid at 83,774.

provided by the maternal grandmother. On that issue, the court found[213] that it had not been demonstrated that the Federal Magistrate had reached a conclusion that was not reasonably open to him or had unreasonably given inadequate or excessive weight to any relevant fact or circumstance.

However, that was not the end of the story, the court took a different view[214] of the magistrate's order which placed the paternal grandmother in a situation potentially unfair to her and would not be in the children's best interests. Accordingly, the Federal Magistrate's discretion had miscarried.

Hort and Verran is a difficult decision to evaluate, as it clearly depended on its particular facts and on the relative behaviour and interpersonal relationships of the adults involved in the case. However, both the Federal Magistrate and the Full Court seem to have taken an open-minded, as well as straightforward, approach to the continuing issue of the relevance of Aboriginality. The other finding is more dependent on the particularities of the case, including the magistrate's assessment of the parties.

Yet it is clear that disentangling these issues, particularly in the context of the 2006 amendments, may very well prove no easy task as the decision of the Full Court in *Partington and Cade (No 2)*[215] demonstrates. *Partington and Cade* involved an appeal by a mother against parenting orders requiring her to return to Tasmania from New South Wales with the children and for time to be spent between the children and their father. However, the trial judge's findings included that there was an unacceptable level of risk to the children if they were to spend unsupervised time with their father, even though there were significant and meaningful relationships between the children and their father. The judge had also found that the mother had actively discouraged any relationship between the children and the father and was also of the view that the relationship between the children could only be maintained by direct physical contact. Accordingly, the trial judge ordered that the mother's application to live in New South Wales be dismissed; that she return with the children to Tasmania; that the children live with their mother and that she have sole parental responsibility for them and that the father spend supervised time with the children. The Full Court[216] allowed the mother's appeal.

In so doing, the court specifically noted[217] the trial judge's 'attention to and careful weighing of the many other relevant features' but nonetheless found that the judge had given no regard to findings of unacceptable risk. Accordingly, the mother's appeal had merit. The court found that the findings which underlay the findings of unacceptable risk were very relevant to both the issue of the father's parenting capacity and also to the possible nature of the longer term relationship between the father and the children. Notably, the court

---

[213] Ibid at 83,775.
[214] Ibid at 83,777.
[215] (2009) FLC 93–422.
[216] Bryant CJ, Warnick and Boland JJ.
[217] (2009) FLC 93–422 at 83,852.

pointed out the degree of uncertainty which surrounded any future time the father might spend with the children. Those factors were not simply relevant to the questions of the orders which might serve to obviate that risk. In addition, they were relevant to the parenting capacity of the father in the future and, thus, ultimately, the matter of whether the mother should be required to relocate to Tasmania.

There are, as will be readily apparent, many facets to the decision in *Partington and Chard (No 2)*: first, it demonstrates the problems involved in predicting the manner in which children will develop,[218] a matter which has long been recognised, as well as the factors which may influence that development. Secondly, it also illustrates another long-standing view that making one decision in one matter may very well affect others matters – thus, deciding with which parent a child will live may very well lead, albeit indirectly, to decisions regarding the location of the child's residence, the nature of the child's education and many other like, or unlike, matters. All in all *Partington* is a most illustrative case!

VI CONCLUSIONS

It will have been apparent that 2009 has been a most interesting, if turbulent, year in Australia family law. As well as in the areas of parentage and parenting and finance and property, where change through the medium of case-law can be reasonably expected, there have been developments in international aspects of family law. In particular, the decisions of *LK*[219] and *Sharmain*[220] on the Child Abduction Convention are of immediate and global interest. If a single lesson is to be drawn from the cases on finance and property it is that the law must be sufficiently flexible to permit people to be able to organise their affairs in the various ways which appropriately serve their needs, wants, contributions and ultimate aspirations. Where direct legislative intervention seems to be required is the area of parentage and, more especially, parenting. It is, thus, not altogether surprising that the Commonwealth of Australia's Attorney-General has appointed a former judge of the Family Court of Australia to inquire into the operation of the 2006 amendments to the Family Law Act. Although this commentator has long regarded those amendments as being, at the very best, unfortunate, it is uncertain as to what the investigation will ultimately reveal. However, as *Partington*[221] shows, the amendments did not abolish central problems. Finally, the changes wrought by the important Family Law Amendment (De Facto Financial Matters and Other Matters) Act seems to shift the emphasis from state to Commonwealth.

---

[218] See, for instance, SR Okpaku 'Psychology: Aid or Impediment in Child Custody Cases' (1976) 29 Rutgers LR 1117.

[219] Above n 17.

[220] Above n 47.

[221] Above n 215.

These are all instances of change, but, since 1976, that process has been, and will continue to be, maintained.

Belgium

LEVERING THE FUNCTIONING OF FAMILIES WITH FAMILY (SELF-) GOVERNANCE?

*Frederik Swennen**

Résumé

Des conseillers familiaux dans des domaines différents prennent de plus en plus un intérêt dans un nouveau secteur de pratique(cabinet) : gouvernance familiale. La gouvernance familiale consiste dans l'utilisation d'instruments légaux privés, comme des contrats, en vue d'organiser l'adhésion d'une famille, les droits et obligations des membres de la famille et la gestion de conflit dans la famille. Ainsi, on considère la famille comme une organisation privée soumise à la bonne gouvernance. La gouvernance familiale ressemble ainsi fortement aux lois de maison prémodernes (Hausgesetze, Lois domestiques) de familles royales, nobles ou en vue. La gouvernance de familles dans des temps modernes a traditionnellement été une compétence des autorités publiques et exercé par des règles légales familiales considérées pour appartenir à la politique publique. La question est donc de savoir si l'auto-gouvernance familiale est compatible avec la politique publique, particulièrement en ce qui concerne l'application possible de l'état de droit. L'auteur illustre cette question en se demandant brièvement dans quelle mesure ces nouvelles pratiques peuvent se référer aux droits de l'homme.

Ce chapitre interroge la question du point de vue belge. L'auteur explore premièrement l'apparition de la gouvernance familiale, en vue de définir le concept. Dans une deuxième partie de cette contribution, il explique les formes différentes de gouvernance familiale. Dans la partie trois, il démontre qu'une structure théorique suffisante manque actuellement. L'auteur illustre cette conclusion à un quart, sur la l'application horizontale de droits de l'homme dans la famille comme 'l'organisation'. Une structure théorique plus élaborée peut promouvoir la gouvernance comme un levier de soutien pour le fonctionnement de la famille dans l'ensemble, plutôt qu'être un fardeau pour les membres de la famille.

---

* Associate Professor of Law, University of Antwerp Law Research School; Attorney-at-law, Brussels Bar (Greenille).The author would like to thank Matthias E Storme for sharing his thoughts. This is a revisited version of my articles in (2011) 19(2) *European Review of Private Law* and (2011) 33(1) *Tijdschrift voor Familie- en Jeugdrecht* 4–11.

I THE CONCEPT OF FAMILY GOVERNANCE

(a) Governance

Every organisation needs management. Therefore governance, and particularly good governance, have been developed as theories regarding all the substantive and procedural guidelines that allow for the development and implementation of a policy in organisations. Originating in the management of public organisations, the concept was subsequently applied to the private sphere of governing, particularly to corporate governance. One justification therefore is that the impact on public life of private corporations resembles that of public authorities so that they should be committed to comparable governance values.

In line with the established theories of corporate governance, family governance initially found an application with a view to governing the (large) families behind family businesses to secure the latter's future.[1] The objective of corporate governance is flavoured here with 'governance' techniques aimed at the controlled transfer of family assets and family values to future generations, thus creating a transcendent dynasty. Imaginative examples are the Mulliez family in France[2] and the Piëch family in Austria.

(b) Family governance

One further step is to consider any family as an organisation subject to good governance, even in the absence of a family business. The object of family governance will then solely be the controlled committed ownership[3] by the current generation, and transfer to future generations, of patrimonial assets in dividends or capital and/or non-patrimonial values.[4] Governance regarding the family estate, for example, finds application in premarital agreements or conditions to a gift from parents to children, excluding the partners of the children as beneficiaries. Governance regarding family values can be found in contracts between elderly parents and their adult children regarding their care. Both forms of governance will be based upon a set of basic values, as reflected in the family governance instruments.

---

[1] M Bruel, JR Geerlings and JA Van Hamel *Uitblinken als familiebedrijf. Over de inrichting en werking van goed bestuur* (Assen: Van Gorcum, 2008); J Lievens *Governance in het familiebedrijf* (Tielt: Lannoo, 2004); J Lievens 'Familiale governance, een verkenning' (2009) 9 *Journal of Estate Planning*; J Lievens 'Opvolging in familiebedrijven Juridische en fiscale aspecten' in *Familierecht. Vormingsprogramma 2009* (Orde van Advocaten van de balie van Kortrijk) (Brussels: Larcier, 2010), p 111; H Paridaens *It's all in the Family* (Roeselare: Roularta Books, 2008).

[2] B Gobin *Le secret des Mulliez. Révélations sur le premier empire familial français* (Editions La borne seize, 2006), also see www.leblogmulliez.com.

[3] J Lievens 'Familiale governance, een verkenning' (2009) 9 *Journal of Estate Planning* 48.

[4] P Laleman 'Private governance & privacy: (on)verzoenbaar?' (2010) 7 *Journal of Estate Planning* 2; J Lievens 'Familiale governance, een verkenning' (2009) 9 *Journal of Estate Planning* 4.

Family governance is applicable to every family. Until now, the literature has been focused particularly on governance for families whose family, or even personal, estates' net-worth is equal to or higher than those of listed companies, though lacking the latter's organisational structure.[5] Other families have a long-standing tradition of acting upon values they want to pass on to future generations.

Family governance is not new. From a historical perspective, it strongly resembles pre-modern house laws (*Hausgesetze, lois domestiques*) of royal, noble or prominent families. Such house laws on the one hand organised transfer of hereditary titles and the coat of arms. More importantly on the other hand, they regulate(d) family membership through birth or marriage,[6] rights and duties of the family members, and enforcement through disciplinary proceedings before the chieftain (*Oberhaupt*) or an arbitration board.[7] They also organised the inheritance of the entailed family estate (*Hausvermogen*), for example through agnatic primogeniture whereby the eldest son became temporary owner of the estate and was under a duty to provide living allowances for the other family members.[8]

Family laws seemed to have no legal authority under common law.[9] The French *lois domestiques* only survived the Revolutionary legislation and the Civil Code under transitional dispositions,[10] private autonomy being firmly restricted afterwards.[11] By contrast, the German house laws of the principalities still apply, as contracts or as appointment of heirs and remaindermen, insofar as they are compatible with the German Basic Law (*Grundgesetz*) and Civil Code. The Federal Constitutional Court of Germany (*Bundesverfassungsgericht* (BVerfG)) indeed has found the house law of the House of Leiningen compatible,[12] and the house law of the House of Hohenzollern (Prussian branch) partly incompatible[13] therewith.[14] Finally, house laws still apply in

---

[5] Ibid.

[6] See, eg, art 1, 5 and 7 of the Hausgesetz des Fürstlichen Hauses Liechtenstein (Constitution of the Princely House of Liechtenstein) published in *Liechtensteinisches Landesgesetzblatt* (Liechtenstein's Legal Gazette) 100, 6 December 1993, available at www.gesetze.li.

[7] See, eg, art 8 of the Hausgesetz des Fürstlichen Hauses Liechtenstein (1993) *Liechtensteinisches Landesgesetzblatt* 100, 6 December 1993, available at www.gesetze.li.

[8] See, eg, § 3 of the Testamentary Contract of 1938 between Prince Royal Wilhelm von Preußen and Louis Ferdinand von Preußen, cited in BVerfG, 1 BvR 2248/01 of 22 March 2004, para 1, www.bverfg.de.

[9] BA Garner (ed) *Black's Law Dictionary* (St Paul, Minn: West Publishing, 9th edn, 2009) definition of *House law* at 808.

[10] Cass fr 13 thermidor an 13, *Sirey* VI, 1806, I, 114–118 and Court of Appeal of Toulouse 18 May 1832, *Sirey* XXXII, 1832, II, 510, case note. Cf the disciplinary nature of house laws, regulating the consequences of being caught in adultery by a slave: Montesqieu *De l'esprit des lois* (Paris: Ed Garnier, 1949) Book XXVI, Chapter XIX.

[11] See, in general, J-M Augustin *Les substitutions fidéicommissaires à Toulouse et en Haut-Languedoc au XVIIIe siècle* (Paris: PUF, 1980).

[12] BVerfG, 1 BvR 1937/97 of 21 February 2000, www.bverfg.de.

[13] BVerfG, 1 BvR 2248/01 of 22 March 2004, www.bverfg.de; BVerfG, 1 BvR 2723/06 of 19 December 2006, www.bverfg.de.

Liechtenstein; the house law of the Princely House of Liechtenstein[15] in particular is referred to in art 3 of the Liechtenstein Constitution,[16] with a view to determining the succession to the throne, coming-of-age and guardianship.

Today, family governance experiences a 'rebirth'. First, an extensive practice of legal and tax advice on family estate planning already exists. Such planning is increasingly preceded by strategic consultations in the extended family, to which also non-legal or tax experts such as psychologists or organisational experts collaborate. Such a participatory process with attention to the family dynamics serves as a 'lubricant' for actual legal and tax planning. It can also help to prevent and manage family conflicts.

Secondly, the governance of non-pecuniary issues of families is emerging as a new field of practice. It originated in the United States, partly as a result of the management approach to motherhood ('working mom time management'), and partly by the religiously inspired movement that promotes the strengthening of family values.

(c)   Personal governance

The theme of good governance can also be applied at the individual level of personal governance – albeit with less emphasis on the organisational aspects, but rather more on the person's estate and values, and the elaboration and implementation of objectives in this regard.[17] Lawmakers have created various sorts of advance directives regarding self-determination, for example, on powers of attorney, guardianship, medical treatment, euthanasia, funerals, organ transplants, etc.[18] A general framework on personal self-governance is however lacking. Personal advisers, including lawyers, should be aware of the value of general charters that reflect a person's values and objectives. Such a life charter at the very least facilitates substituted decisions in the case of (mental) incompetence. In the United States the personal life charters of betrothed couples are even compared with a view to drafting a family charter.[19]

---

[14]   See, in general, A Horsch 'Familiensolidarität als Begriff und Rechtsprinzip in der Rechtsprechung des BVerfG zur Erbrechtsgarantie' (2010) 4 *Neue Zeitschrift für Verwaltungsrecht* 232, 235.

[15]   (1993) *Liechtensteinisches Landesgesetzblatt* 100, 6 December 1993, available at www.gesetze.li.

[16]   Available at www.gesetze.li.

[17]   P Laleman 'Private governance & privacy: (on)verzoenbaar?' (2010) 7 *Journal of Estate Planning* 1.

[18]   A Vandewiele 'Levenstestament' (2008) *Tijdschrift voor notarissen* 521.

[19]   Cf L McClain 'Family Constitutions and the (New) Constitution of the Family' (2006–2007) 75 *Fordham Law Review* 833 at 855.

II FORMS OF FAMILY GOVERNANCE[20]

(a) Value-oriented family governance

Families are concerned with social reproduction on the one hand and protection of individual family members on the other. The legal framework for supporting families in those functions has in recent decades largely been reduced in Western countries. I consider value-oriented, family governance as being installed with a view to filling the gap thus left by the public lawmakers.[21] Instruments of family governance may also be useful for those families who want to strengthen the existing legal framework[22] as their 'family privacy'.

On the one side of the continuum of value-oriented family governance are the traditionalist families. Many states have systematically abolished statutory provisions evidencing a substantive ethical position in favour of pluralist legislation. Such pluralist legislation is rather procedural than substantive. Family governance would then reflect the moral choices of the family concerned.

The following two clear examples can be found in marriage law.

(a) The current marital rights and duties are based on equality between the two spouses. Article 213 of the Civil Code formerly stipulated that a woman had a duty of obedience to her husband. Apparently, some interest exists in letting religious opinions inspire family governance instruments, with a view to stipulating on the basis of Ephesians 5, 22–24 that wives should submit to their husbands.[23]

(b) Divorce is currently organised as a no-fault system. Again, some interest exists in excluding certain no-fault grounds for divorce, thereby reinstalling fault-based divorce, as some states already allow in their public family governance rules as 'covenant marriage'.[24]

Other initiatives aim at legally empowering families in light of the growing number of divorces. Proposals have thus been made with a view to formulating an 'Education Pledge' by the parents at the time of the birth of their child, and that will be upheld in case of a separation of the couple.[25] Some legislators, for example in the Netherlands,[26] even require a 'Parenting Plan' for separation

---

[20] Ibid, at 846 et seq describes five contexts in which family governance might be useful.

[21] Ibid, at 835, 837 and 841.

[22] M Garrison 'Toward a Contractarian Account of Family Governance' (1998) *Utah Law Review* 241 at 258.

[23] L McClain 'Family Constitutions and the (New) Constitution of the Family' (2006–2007) 75 Fordham L Rev 833 at 858.

[24] KB Rosier and SL Feld 'Covenant Marriage: A New Alternative for Traditional Families' (2000) 31 *Journal of Comparative Family Studies* 385.

[25] H Van Crombrugge et al *Van huwelijkscontract naar opvoedingsbelofte* (Brussels: Hoger Instituut voor de Gezinswetenschappen, 2006).

[26] Article 815 of the Dutch Code of Civil Proceedings.

proceedings to be admissible.[27] Some parents might want to include such a plan in a general agreement on family governance.[28] Furthermore, some families apply techniques of governance under current legislation, for example, with a view to organising the personal and financial care by children of their elderly parents.[29]

On the other side of the continuum are families that use family governance as an instrument for household management, for practical reasons, for example time management, family rituals (eg bedtime stories), written contracts on pocket money, etc.[30] Each family applies such agreements; they are usually informal and do not include rules of enforcement. To consider this practice as family governance allows more awareness and a more focused approach to it.

(b)   Asset-oriented family governance

More up to date and frequently applied is family governance with a view to controlling ownership and distribution of the family's assets over the generations. A first aspect of asset-oriented family governance is to organise committed ownership of the estate within generation n and to transfer (the economic value of) the assets to generations n+x at the lowest possible (tax) cost. The preceding generations then 'govern from the grave'. A second aspect is, more importantly, not to transfer 'dominion', in other words to organise who will be in control of the assets (after one's death) and how. The ultimate objective thereof is to stick to the estate's 'mission' and to keep it, and therefore its economic impact, intact.

Many examples of embryonic asset-oriented family governance can currently be found in the jurisprudence on, and practice of, estate planning. Planning instruments concern every stage in life, as shown in the following examples.

(a)   The administration of the estate of underage children is controlled by different means, such as the exclusion of usufruct and/or administration by the in-laws or even both parents, deviations from the legal age of majority, increasing it to 30, etc.

---

[27]   M Antokolskaia and L Coenraad 'Het verplicht ouderschapsplan bij beeindiging van formele en informele relaties in rechtsvergelijkend perspectief' (2007) 29 *Tijdschrift voor Familie- en Jeugdrecht* 309.

[28]   F Schonewille 'Kunnen huwelijkse voorwaarden en samenlevingscontract een ouderschapsplan bevatten?' (2008) 138 *Weekblad voor Privaatrecht, Notariaat en Registr a tie* 6717, 604.

[29]   A Vandewiele 'Het (notarieel) zorgcontract. Zal het u een zorg wezen? Bespreking en modellen' (2008) *Tijdschrift voor notarissen* 364.

[30]   L McClain 'Family Constitutions and the (New) Constitution of the Family' (2006–2007) 75 Fordham L Rev 833, at 835 and 850.

(b)   Restrictions on alienation, exclusion of ownership by in-laws in the next generations, exclusion of the divorced spouse of the pater or mater familias, premarital and mid-marriage agreements, etc[31] often characterise ownership by adults.

(c)   Different techniques of in extremis estate planning have finally been developed for end-of-life decisions.[32]

Estate planning, however, is not synonymous with asset-oriented family governance. Family governance is the general strategy behind the implementing instruments of estate planning and mirrors the family's values.[33] It will therefore always be connected to values on wealth-education and stewardship that should be internalised, on which financial incentives might subsequently depend.[34] We will see in Part III that the validity of such provisions much depends on the *causa*. Grandparents may, for example, make a donation to their grandchildren and grant usufruct to the parents only on certain conditions regarding the education of the grandchildren, such as school choice.[35] Societal commitment will, for example, result in philanthropic efforts.[36] Such long-term strategy is not always present, though it should be.[37]

(c)   Constitutional and corporate family governance

Family governance thus consists of a general strategy, based on a set of basic values, implemented in different instruments. Many families apply such strategy in unwritten family laws, which generally are culturally determined. The phenomenon of arranged marriages in non-Western cultures is one example thereof – although this can hardly be described as an expression of good governance as accepted in Western culture. For the formulation in writing of the family strategy based on good governance, and of executive instruments, we rely in Western cultures on known models of public governance, of corporate governance, or on a combination thereof.[38]

---

[31]   Ibid, at 845.

[32]   N Geelhand, et al '(Fiscale) successieplanning "in extremis" in Vlaanderen: naar een nieuw concept inzake fiscale successieplanning' in *Handboek Estate Planning, bijzonder deel 1* (Brussels: Larcier, 2008).

[33]   R Williams *For Love & Money. A Comprehensive Guide to the Successful Generational Transfer of Wealth* (Bandon (Oregon): Robert D Reed Publishers, 1997).

[34]   L McClain 'Family Constitutions and the (New) Constitution of the Family' (2006–2007) 75 Fordham L Rev 833, at 862–864 on so-called 'incentive trusts'. Cf E Dirix 'Grondrechten en overeenkomsten' in K Rimanque *De toepasselijkheid van de grondrechten in private verhoudingen* (Antwerpen: Kluwer, 1982) 35, at p 20.

[35]   Article 387 of the Belgian Civil Code.

[36]   R Williams and V Preisser *Philanthropy, Heirs & Values. How Successful Families are using Philanthropy to Prepare their Heirs for Post-Transition Responsibilities* (Bandon (Oregon): Robert D Reed Publishers, 2005).

[37]   PA Angus 'The Family Governance Pyramid: From Principles to Practice' (2005) *The Journal of Wealth Management* Summer 2005, 7 at 9 and 10; BR Hauser 'Family Governance: Who, What, and How' (2002) *The Journal of Wealth Management* Fall 2002, 10 at 11.

[38]   L McClain, 'Family Constitutions and the (New) Constitution of the Family' (2006–2007) 75 Fordham L Rev 833, at 835.

Constitutional family governance is eventually based on the drafting of a family constitution[39] or charter,[40] consisting of a preamble and a rights and duties section. The family constitution is drafted by a constituent assembly so as to safeguard its legitimacy. Such assembly, based on a representative system per family branch and generation, but with hearing rights for non-members,[41] sometimes only comes into existence in the third generation. The first generation (parents) is then characterised as dictatorial, the second (brothers and sisters) as communist/collectivist. Such a structure is not workable from the third generation (nieces and nephews) on.[42] Some families however opt for a participatory model from the first phase on (parents and children). Such a democratic approach is recommended in scholarly literature.[43]

Corporate family governance consists of applying the instruments of corporate governance to families.[44] The articles of incorporation are drafted on the basis of a mission (and visions) statement. They are implemented in family by-laws.

III   FAMILY GOVERNANCE AND THE LAW

(a)   Family governance versus family law

As mentioned before, family governance builds on pre-modern models of self-governance. In modern times, families of course still need to be governed. Since the codifications, it has however been the responsibility of civil authorities to determine the family structure and the distribution of assets and values. Such rules were considered to belong to public policy, with no derogation by contract allowed. There was a strong focus on the family group, to the detriment of individual family members.[45]

Ever since the enactment of the Civil Code, we have witnessed a gradual shift from a collective, family-oriented, perspective in family law, towards the current paradigmatic individualistic approach. The abovementioned advance directives as tools of self-determination have emerged from that approach. Paradoxically, family governance is both in line with and contrary to that evolution. On the one hand, the privatisation of family governance reflects increasing party autonomy. On the other, family governance aims at reinstalling (reimposing) a

---

[39]   See the reference to the Hohenzollern *Hausverfassung* in § 1 of the Testamentary Contract of 1938 between Prince Royal Wilhelm von Preußen and Louis Ferdinand von Preußen, cited in BVerfG, 1 BvR 2248/01 of 22 March 2004, para 1, www.bverfg.de.

[40]   J Lievens *Governance in het familiebedrijf* (Tielt: Lannoo, 2004) p 130.

[41]   Cf art 931 of the Belgian Judicial Code regarding minors.

[42]   BR Hauser 'Family Governance: Who, What, and How' (2002) *The Journal of Wealth Management* Fall 2002, 10, at 14–15.

[43]   L McClain 'Family Constitutions and the (New) Constitution of the Family' (2006–2007) 75 Fordham L Rev 833, at 836, 849 and 863–864.

[44]   See principle 9.5 of the Code Buysse II Corporate Governance Recommendations for non-listed companies available at www.codebuysse.be.

[45]   M Garrison 'Toward a Contractarian Account of Family Governance' (1998) Utah L Rev 241, at 242.

collective perspective.[46] Families in this regard refer to their right to privacy as a family, whose intrafamily relationships, such as education of children, should be free from state intervention.[47]

(b)   Tools of family governance and the law

In the above paragraphs, I have defined family governance as the use of private legal instruments with a view to governing collective committed ownership of assets and values by current generations and distribution thereof to future generations of a family, according to rules that reflect the family values. Its basic instrument is the family constitution/charter or articles of incorporation.

Some jurisprudence and case-law exists regarding the assessment of instruments that implement family governance. Discontented family members will indeed attack implementing instruments rather than the family constitution/charter or the articles of incorporation as such.

A first example concerns a shareholder who judicially forces his resignation by reason that his brothers did not respect an 'operating agreement' and its preamble. The agreement however contained an arbitration clause that was not applied.[48] A second category of example concerns the (in)validity of premarital, mid-marital and pre-divorce agreements on alimony in which behaviour regarding the stability of the marriage is rewarded or penalised. The value of family governance behind such agreements may not aim at restricting one's right to (re)marry or to divorce.[49] A third category of example concerns the nullity of conditions to a gift, or even of the gift as such, in cases where the underlying cause of the condition or the gift, contrary to public policy, aims at influencing family behaviour.[50]

(c)   Family governance *as such* and the law

By contrast, no scientific knowledge or practice exists regarding the legal status of family constitutions/charters or family articles of incorporation as such.

---

[46]   BR Hauser 'Family Governance: Who, What, and How' (2002) *The Journal of Wealth Management* Fall 2002, 10 at 13; L McClain 'Family Constitutions and the (New) Constitution of the Family' (2006–2007) 75 Fordham L Rev 833, at 845.

[47]   See in general L McClain 'Family Constitutions and the (New) Constitution of the Family' (2006–2007) 75 Fordham L Rev 833, p 869 regarding the 'liberty interest' under the US Constitution; N Molfessis 'Les lois domestiques' (2009) 130 *Pouvoirs* 3, at 81, 83 regarding parental authority.

[48]   Court of Appeal Brussels 20 April 1999, *TRV* 1999, 431.

[49]   F Swennen 'Over alimentatieovereenkomsten en echtscheiding (en ook een beetje over Odysseus)' (2008) 45 *Tijdschrift voor Privaatrecht* 1287, at 33–35.

[50]   With regard to testamentary contracts: BVerfG, 1 BvR 1937/97 of 21 February 2000, www.bverfg.de; BVerfG, 1 BvR 2248/01 of 22 March 2004, www.bverfg.de.

The Belgian Code Buysse II[51] in its principle 9.5 limits itself to stating that it 'is advisable for the [family charter] to have a legally binding character'.[52] How then?

McClain recommends compliance for corporate family governance, but admits that the uncertainty of internal and external legal enforceability might be an obstacle.[53] State-defined powers of enforcement within a family, for example through penalty clauses, are indeed lacking.[54] To approach the charter as a pure (accession) contract[55] would be denying its complexity. The legal enforceability of the family charter is therefore mainly assessed through its different operative parts or implementing instruments. Research into the legal status of the family charter would be relevant with a view to assessing its binding character and enforceability for the family's board and the governed family members. I will illustrate this with the example of the rule of law.

IV   FAMILY GOVERNANCE AND THE RULE OF LAW

(a)   The problem

Family governance may thus become a means of deviating from the default legal family system laid down in non-mandatory rules. Examples thereof are the exclusion of family members by alliance from the family capital or from the usufruct of the property that the child received from the other parent's line. More interesting, however, is the use of family governance as a means to indirectly deviate from imperative family law rules, for example by interposition of a private foundation or a private partnership. Some techniques may thus result in the exclusion, from the 'contractual' family, of 'default legal family members'. The family as designed in private legal instruments may thus deviate significantly from the public legal family instruments (of the Civil Code, in the Continental systems). In case such course of action is not voidable, the question arises how the private legal status of the 'governed' family members is protected.

Continuing the line of reasoning to consider family governance as an application of models of constitutional or corporate governance would imply the application of the rule of law. This is all the more so since the implementation of family governance may influence the legal position of the governed family members to a large extent. The rule of law should apply as the relationship of the governed family more strictly members vis-à-vis the

---

[51]   www.codebuysse.be.

[52]   Cf J Lievens 'Familiale governance, een verkenning' (2009) 9 *Journal of Estate Planning* 17, where the moral nature of the charter is stressed.

[53]   L McClain 'Family Constitutions and the (New) Constitution of the Family' (2006–2007) 75 Fordham L Rev 833, at 839–840 and 844–845.

[54]   M Garrison 'Toward a Contractarian Account of Family Governance' (1998) Utah L Rev 241, at 242.

[55]   J Lievens 'Familiale governance, een verkenning' (2009) 9 *Journal of Estate Planning* 21.

governing family members resembles that of citizens vis-à-vis the public authority.[56] This would be the case for non-founding family members who did not 'contract' into the 'terms and conditions' of the family governance but acceded to it later.

The application of the rule of law amounts particularly to the question of what judicial relief exists for governed family members with regard to family constitutions, charters, by-laws, etc. Judicial remedies exist in public family law, where, for example, a guardian may be removed from office if he does not respect the values to which the parents had subscribed regarding the education of the children.[57] But which remedies are there, for example, for a female heiress in a case where the pater familias transfers his full estate to a private foundation, giving the board discretionary power to grant only benefits in kind, only to the male descendants of the founder, and finally excludes from any benefit anyone who brings judicial proceedings against the foundation?

The balancing of the conflicting legal positions in this regard is virgin territory in legal science.[58] Likewise, the economic or sociological approaches towards family governance do not include a legal perspective[59] – which might influence the assessment of family governance in the long run.

(b)   Human rights protection

The governing family members could oppose the application of the rule of law by reference to their private autonomy.[60] Private, and particularly family, relations are pre-eminently considered a 'purely private matter'[61] in the modelling of which the state may not intervene,[62] for example with a view to protecting the interests of other parties concerned. The private autonomy of the governing family members is protected under Art 8 of the European Convention of Human Rights (ECHR) and Art 1 of the First Protocol to the Convention. Since the landmark case of *Pretty*, the right to respect for private life is broadly defined as including a right to personal autonomy and personal development. It can embrace aspects of one's social identity and protects 'the right to establish and develop relationships with other human beings and the outside world'.[63] With regard to the disposable portion of their estate, private individuals may 'discriminat[e] by drawing distinctions when disposing of their

---

[56]   A Clapham *Human Rights Obligations of Non-State Actors* (Oxford University Press, 2006) p 528; E Dirix 'Grondrechten en overeenkomsten' in K Rimanque *De toepasselijkheid van de grondrechten in private verhoudingen* (Antwerpen: Kluwer, 1982) 35, at p 10.

[57]   See arts 405, § 1, 1st section and 398–399 of the Belgian Civil Code. Cf M Garrison 'Toward a Contractarian Account of Family Governance' (1998) Utah L Rev 241, at 243.

[58]   J Lievens 'Familiale governance, een verkenning' (2009) 9 *Journal of Estate Planning* 2.

[59]   L McClain 'Family Constitutions and the (New) Constitution of the Family' (2006–2007) 75 Fordham L Rev 833, at 845.

[60]   E Dirix 'Grondrechten en overeenkomsten' in K Rimanque *De toepasselijkheid van de grondrechten in private verhoudingen* (Antwerpen: Kluwer, 1982) 35, at p 14.

[61]   N Van Leuven *Contracten en mensenrechten* (Antwerpen: Intersentia, 2009) p 227 et seq.

[62]   N Molfessis 'Les lois domestiques' (2009) 130 *Pouvoirs* 3, 81–95.

[63]   *Pretty v United Kingdom* App no 2346/02, 29 April 2002, para 61.

property', 'even if there may appear to be no objective and reasonable justification for the distinction'.[64] The same principle was accepted by the German Constitutional Court with regard to testamentary contracts: a testator is not required to treat equally all descendants, even if he would dispose contrary to general societal beliefs or the views of a majority.[65]

The same right to respect for private and family life, however, applies to the governed family members.[66] Article 14 of the ECHR (prohibition of discrimination regarding the rights guaranteed in the Convention) and the 12th Protocol to the Convention (general prohibition of discrimination) will also be relevant in this regard. Both 'traditional' and 'non-traditional' family relations are indeed protected as family life. Noteworthy landmark cases concern the protection of children born out-of-wedlock in *Marckx*,[67] of children conceived during an adulterous relationship in *Merger and Cros*[68] and protection of the emotional and sexual relationship of a cohabiting same-sex couple in a stable de facto partnership in *Schalk and Kopf*.[69]

Moreover, horizontal application of human rights is generally accepted in Belgium,[70] both indirectly with a view to flavouring general private law notions such as public policy and bona mores and directly[71] which latter opinion is preferred.[72] The state is thus under a positive obligation to prevent private parties from interfering in each other's human rights interests.[73]

(c)   Balancing of conflicting legal positions?

Horizontal applicability of human rights, however, does not mean that private parties have (positive) human rights obligations towards each other equal to those of public authorities towards citizens.[74] Public authorities indeed cannot

---

[64]   *Pla & Puncernau v Andorra* App no 69498/01, 13 July 2004, Partly Dissenting Opinion of Judge Bratza, para 4 and Dissenting Opinion of Judge Garlicki, para 2.

[65]   BVerfG, 1 BvR 1937/97 of 21 February 2000, para 9, www.bverfg.de (*Leiningen* case).

[66]   BR Hauser 'Family Governance: Who, What, and How' (2002) *The Journal of Wealth Management* Fall 2002, 10, at 13.

[67]   *Marckx v Belgium* App no 6833/74 13 June 1979, 2 EHRR 330 PC, para 31.

[68]   *Merger and Cros* App no 69498/01, 22 December 2004, para 46. Cf *Mazurek v France* App no 34406/97, 1 February 2000, where the violation of Art 8 was not examined.

[69]   *Schalk and Kopf v Austria* App no 30141/04, 24 June 2010, para 94.

[70]   Critically: BJ De Vos *Horizontale werking van grondrechten: een kritiek* (Apeldoorn: Maklu, 2010).

[71]   A Clapham *Human Rights Obligations of Non-State Actors* (Oxford University Press, 2006) pp 521–523; E Dirix 'Grondrechten en overeenkomsten' in K Rimanque *De toepasselijkheid van de grondrechten in private verhoudingen* (Antwerpen: Kluwer, 1982) 35, pp 4 et seq; N Van Leuven *Contracten en mensenrechten* (Antwerpen: Intersentia, 2009) pp 363–366.

[72]   E Dirix 'Grondrechten en overeenkomsten' in K Rimanque *De toepasselijkheid van de grondrechten in private verhoudingen* (Antwerpen, Kluwer, 1982) 35, pp 5, 10, 14 and 38.

[73]   A Clapham *Human Rights Obligations of Non-State Actors* (Oxford University Press, 2006) pp 523 et seq; KS Kay 'The European Convention on Human Rights and the Control of Private Law' (2005) EHRLR 5, 466, at 466 and 475 et seq.

[74]   A Clapham *Human Rights Obligations of Non-State Actors* (Oxford University Press, 2006) p 526.

rely on human rights of their own, whereas citizens and organisations can. The European Court of Human Rights (ECtHR) brought this to mind in the *Obst* and *Schüth* cases, that concerned the dismissal of the Mormon director of public relations for Europe and a Catholic organist and choirmaster, for having an adulterous relationship – and the latter: for bigamy too. The Court reminded that the Convention rights of both Churches should be weighed against, and may even outweigh, the Convention rights of the Church employees, at least insofar as the organisational principles do not conflict with the fundamental principles of the legal order of the state.[75]

The same applies to family governance which, by contrast to public governance, is a 'purely private matter'.[76] Only exceptionally, to the extent that it cannot be considered a private matter (any more),[77] would a balancing of conflicting legal positions be allowed. Such is the case in the following three hypotheses.

(1) A so-called *Notstandsfest* (non-derogable) human right of the governed is violated, for example if corporal punishment of the partner or children is provided as a sanction for not respecting the Family Constitution (Art 3 of the ECHR).[78] This restriction applies even in a case where the governed family member would consent to the violation of his rights; *volenti non fit iniuria* is no defence in this regard.[79]

(2) A human right that cannot be considered *Notstandsfest* is violated in a way that is blatantly inconsistent with the Convention, or under circumstances that provide the state a particularly serious reason to intervene. In other words: more discretion is left to private parties than to public authorities.

According to the two dissenting opinions in the *Pla and Puncernau* judgment, the freedom to dispose of one's property in private instruments must be given effect 'save in exceptional circumstances where [it] may be said to be repugnant to the fundamental ideas of the Convention or to aim at the destruction of the rights and freedoms set forth therein'.[80] The judgment concerned the interpretation of a testament by a national judge, which was overruled because the ECtHR found it 'blatantly inconsistent with the prohibition of discrimination and more broadly with the principles underlying the

[75] *Obst v Germany* App no 425/03, Judgment and *Schüth v Germany* App no 1620/03, Judgment, both of 23 September 2010.

[76] E Dirix 'Grondrechten en overeenkomsten' in K Rimanque *De toepasselijkheid van de grondrechten in private verhoudingen* (Antwerpen: Kluwer, 1982) 35, at p 10.

[77] A Clapham *Human Rights Obligations of Non-State Actors* (Oxford University Press, 2006) pp 530–531: the answer to such a question of course is not easy.

[78] Cf *A v United Kingdom* App no 25599/94, Judgment 23 September 1998, para 22. Regarding the prevention of intrafamily violence: N Molfessis 'Les lois domestiques' (2009) 130(3) *Pouvoirs* 81, at 85 and 92.

[79] Cf dwarf tossing and human dignity: UN Human Rights Committee, *Wackenheim* Communication No 854/1999 of 26 July 2002.

[80] *Pla and Puncernau v Andorra* App no 69498/01, Judgment of 13 July 2004, Partly Dissenting Opinion of Judge Bratza, para 4 and Dissenting Opinion of Judge Garlicki, para 2.

Convention'.[81] Such was the case because the national judge had interpreted a *fideicommis* in favour of 'a son or grandson of a lawful and canonical marriage' as excluding adoptive children. The Court reminded that 'very weighty reasons need to be put forward before a difference in treatment on the ground of birth out of wedlock can be regarded as compatible with the Convention'.[82]

A comparable way of reasoning was followed by the German Constitutional Court in the *Hohenzollern* case. A provision in a testamentary contract was found incompatible with the right to marry protected by art 6 of the Basic Law because it constituted a serious interference (*einem schweren Eingriff*) with that right. That was the case because the provision excluded as remainderman any descendant who would enter into a morganatic marriage that is a marriage with a woman of uneven social rank. Such indirect discrimination on the basis of birth was considered contra bona mores.[83]

It is not clear what makes an inconsistency 'blatant' or which reasons might be 'weighty' enough to justify a difference in treatment on the basis of birth status.

Would a limitation of the right to marry and found a family, be 'blatantly inconsistent' with the Convention only if it restricts or reduces 'the right in such a way or to such an extent that the very essence of the right is impaired'?[84] This seemed to be the opinion of the German Constitutional Court, when accepting the provision of a testamentary contract under which a descendant was excluded as remainderman where the chieftain would not consent to his marriage. The refusal of his consent could only be based on family traditions and could be assessed by an arbitration board. It was therefore not considered contra bona mores.[85] Some authors, however, consider any restriction unacceptable.[86]

To what extent would the prohibition of discrimination apply to the granting of, for example, habitation rights in real estate of a private foundation to married couples only?[87] What about financial incentives or penalties which only indirectly try to influence the behaviour of the governed family members?[88] It becomes clear that the family constitution or the family's articles of

---

81   Judgment of 13 July 2004, paras 46–59.
82   Judgment of 13 July 2004, para 61.
83   BVerfG, 1 BvR 2248/01 of 22 March 2004, para 42, www.bverfg.de (*Hohenzollern* case) and A Staudinger 'Case note' (2004) 10 *Zeitschrift für das gesamte Familienrecht* 768, 769.
84   *Schalk and Kopf v Austria* App no 30141/04, Judgment of 24 June 2010, para 49. Cf Art 17 of the ECHR.
85   BVerfG, 1 BvR 1937/97 of 21 February 2000, paras 13–14, www.bverfg.de (*Leiningen* case). See generally with regard to the parents' right to consent: BJ De Vos *Horizontale werking van grondrechten: een kritiek* (Apeldoorn, Maklu, 2010) p 166.
86   E Dirix 'Grondrechten en overeenkomsten' in K Rimanque *De toepasselijkheid van de grondrechten in private verhoudingen* (Antwerpen: Kluwer, 1982) 35, at p 27.
87   Cf Belgian Cour d'Arbitrage (Constitutional Court) nr 54/2004, 24 March 2004, *Echtscheidingsjournaal* 2005, 2, case note N Van Leuven.
88   E Dirix 'Grondrechten en overeenkomsten' in K Rimanque *De toepasselijkheid van de grondrechten in private verhoudingen* (Antwerpen: Kluwer, 1982) 35, at p 20.

incorporation becomes highly relevant with a view to assessing the validity of implementing instruments, for example with regard to the causa.[89]

In the *KA and AD* judgment, the ECtHR dealt with boundaries of the right to respect private life. Since (the nature of) sexual relationships concern 'a most intimate part of an individual's private life, there must exist particularly serious reasons' for state interference to be acceptable under Art 8(2) of the ECHR. Such was the case in the *KA and AD* judgment, where a sadomasochist sexual relationship had escalated beyond the control of the parties concerned.[90]

(3) When family governance enters the public sphere,[91] the same human rights obligations should apply to the private governance system as to public governance systems.[92] One may think of a Private Foundation publicly offering support to traditional families only. Much will depend on the answer to the question of whether the offer is 'public', for example when the statutes of a foundation state that the board may, at its discretion, decide to award benefits in kind to family members as further defined.

Such an approach also underlies the Belgian antidiscrimination legislation. Regarding private law, the Act of 10 May 2007 on the Criminalizing of certain Acts of Racism or Xenophobia applies to art 5(1) the access to and offering of products and services available to the public and (8) the access to and participation in, as well as any other exercise of, economic, social, cultural and political activity accessible to the public. The Act of 10 May 2007 on the Combating of Discrimination between Women and Men and the Act of 10 May 2007 on the Combating of Discrimination on Certain Grounds have the same scope. The latter Act applies to discrimination on the grounds of age, sexual orientation, civil status, birth, property, religion or ideological or political opinions, trade union beliefs, language, current or future health, impairment, physical or genetic properties and social origin.

Reference may also be made to *Roberts v United States Jaycees*,[93] which found that the Jaycees' exclusion of women from full membership was not acceptable under the prohibition of discrimination. It was decisive that the Jaycees were a

---

[89] M Coene 'Erfrecht en testeervrijheid' in K Rimanque *De toepasselijkheid van de grondrechten in private verhoudingen* (Antwerpen: Kluwer, 1982) p 311. Cf A Horsch 'Familiensolidarität als Begriff und Rechtsprinzip in der Rechtsprechung des BVerfG zur Erbrechtsgarantie' (2010) 4 *Neue Zeitschrift für Verwaltungsrecht* 232, 235 with regard to the *Leiningen* and *Hohenzollern* cases.

[90] *KA & AD v Belgium* App nos 42758/98 and 45558/99, Judgment of 17 February 2005, para 85, with reference to the *Smith & Grady* App nos 33985/96 and 33986/96, Judgment of 27 September 1999, para 89.

[91] A Clapham *Human Rights Obligations of Non-State Actors* (Oxford University Press, 2006) p 528; N Van Leuven (Summary of ECtHR 24 June 2010) (2005–06) 69 *Rechtskundig Weekblad* 1159.

[92] E Dirix 'Grondrechten en overeenkomsten' in K Rimanque *De toepasselijkheid van de grondrechten in private verhoudingen* (Antwerpen: Kluwer, 1982) 35, at pp 10, 15 and 17.

[93] 468 *US* 609 (1984).

very large organisation, with no selective membership acceptance – except for the exclusion of women and certain age groups, and focused exclusively on providing tangible benefits.

V   CONCLUSIONS

Families and professional family advisers of all kinds take an increasing interest in perpetuating structures of committed ownership, and transfer to future generations, of both family assets and values. A practice of family governance is emerging from that interest.

The formulation of the basic values for a family, and developing a strategy on that basis, can serve as a lubricant for healthy family relationships. Conflicts can be prevented and, even if they do arise, family governance may serve to resolve such conflicts in a transparent manner within the family and out of court. Again, this is not new from an historical perspective. The French Revolutionary Act of 20–25 September 1792 for example obliged spouses to submit their dispute to a family council before the divorce by mutual consent could be sought before a court.[94]

Nevertheless, it is also clear that, with family governance, the impact of the family on the status of the individual family members is strengthened, whereas we have witnessed a shift from a collective towards an individualistic approach in public family law. Family governance can therefore also be a threat. To avoid that flaw, all principles of good governance should be applied when designing structures of family governance. In particular, attention should be paid to the protection of individual family members by the rule of law.

It would be dangerous for a practice of family governance to emerge outside any scholarly legal framework on the boundaries of private family laws on the one hand and the relationship between private and public family law on the other. I have tried to illustrate this danger with the example of the horizontal applicability of human rights.

---

[94]   Act of 20–25 September 1792, § II, art 1 et seq.

HOMOAFFECTIVE PARENTAGE IN RELATION TO MEDICALLY ASSISTED REPRODUCTION: A PARALLEL BETWEEN BRAZIL AND PORTUGAL

*Marianna Chaves**

Résumé

La question du droit des homosexuels à la paternité ou à la maternité, que ce soit biologiquement ou par adoption, est excessivement controversée. Et celle de leur accès à la procréation techniquement assistée, l'est plus encore. À cet égard, l'analyse de la législation et de la doctrine, démontre que le Brésil et le Portugal ont adopté des approches diamétralement opposées. Alors que le Brésil s'est abstenu de légiférer en la matière, le Portugal n'a pas hésité à le faire. La question se pose de savoir quelle voie est la meilleure: une législation très restreinte et, au surplus, discriminatoire, ou une totale abstention législative?

Plusieurs questions se posent dans ce contexte. La première est celle de savoir s'il existe réellement un droit d'être parent. Et que dire de la gestation pour le compte d'autrui? Dans ces domaines, tient-on suffisamment compte de l'intérêt de l'enfant qui demeure tout de même le facteur primordial?

Il y aura toujours des divergences d'opinion dans un secteur aussi sensible que le droit de la famille. Mais il reste que toute solution doit tenir compte du meilleur intérêt de l'enfant, né ou à naître, et qu'elle doit respecter les droits fondamentaux tels le droit à l'égalité, à la liberté, à la non-discrimination et à la dignité humaine. Les préjugés ancrés dans la société et les jugements homophobes n'ont pas leur place ici.

---

* PhD student at Coimbra University, Portugal. Masters degree in Juridical Sciences at Lisbon University, Portugal; Specialist in Juridical Sciences from Lisbon University; Post-graduate course in Filiation, Adoption and Infants Protection from Lisbon University; Post-graduate in Bioethics and Medicine Law from Lisbon University and APDI – Portuguese Association of Intellectual Property Law; Director of the division of International Relations from IBDFAM-PB (Brazilian Institute of Family Law – Estate of Paraíba); Member of International Society of Family Law; Member of the American Bar Association; Member of the International Bar Association; Assistant Researcher of the Instituto de Investigación Científica de la Universidad de Lima, Peru; Lawyer. A version of this contribution is to be published in the journal *Medicine and Law*.

I IS THERE A RIGHT TO PARENTAGE *AND* A RIGHT TO REPRODUCTION?

Homoparentality (same-sex parenting) may be considered one of the most 'tortuous' issues in the field of homoaffectivity.[1] In this context, several heterogeneities and divergences are found in the doctrine.[2] There are those who believe that in fact there is a right to be a father and a mother, constitutionally guaranteed. For others, there is no such right, on the argument that we would be reducing the child to a 'thing', treating him or her like a mere object of desire.

It is imperative to emphasise that not all human beings have the capacity or vocation for parenthood, but, undoubtedly, it should not be the individual's sexual orientation that defines whether he or she is able to carry out, with dedication, affection and effectiveness, the parental function.

Very often, the infant's best interest is invoked to deny same-sex couples the right to carry out parenting.[3] Observing judicial practice, it is noticed that the infant's interest depends mainly on the opinion of those who have the decision-making power – the judge – an opinion based on his culture, education and the preconceptions of his generation.[4] It is realised, though, that the child's best interest is an undetermined juridical concept, that is always moving, and it

---

[1]   The terms 'homoaffectivity' and 'homoaffective unions' were created by the Brazilian jurist Maria Berenice Dias in the late 1990s and published in the first edition of her book: *União homoafetiva: o preconceito & a justiça* (Sao Paulo: Editora Revista dos Tribunais, 4th edn, 2009). Today this terminology is widely accepted in the doctrine and jurisprudence of Brazil and other countries.

[2]   On this subject, Maria Berenice Dias makes the point that among all the discrimination and bias homosexuals are victims of, 'the refusal to acknowledge the right to have children – either through adoption or medically assisted reproduction – is the cruellest. It makes impossible an accomplishment which is part of being human, to have family and children, whom parents can love and teach the lessons they have learned throughout life'. DIAS, Maria Berenice. *União homoafetiva: o preconceito & a justiça* (Sao Paulo: Editora Revista dos Tribunais, 4th edn, 2009) p 210.

[3]   Regarding this, namely on the techniques of medically assisted reproduction, Roger Raupp Rios states that 'the defence of children's rights may work as a pretence to promote the opposite thing, which is the exclusive and excluding privilege of a specific form of family, not respecting the Constitution and the democratic values consecrated in the fundamental juridical principles here mentioned. In response to the issue of the extent of access to assisted reproduction, therefore, we cannot forget the reality and the constitutional framework: discrimination which only takes into account one kind of family community is illegitimate from both points of view. This is consistent with the concretization, through a wider view of family community, of the norms from the constitutional principles of the Democratic State of Law, of equality, of liberty, of autonomy, of respect for diversity and pluralism': Roger Raupp Rios 'Acesso às tecnologias reprodutivas e princípios constitucionais: igualdade, pluralismo, Direito Constitucional de Família e orientação sexual no debate bioético brasileiro' in Débora Diniz and Samantha Buglione *Quem pode ter acesso às tecnologias reprodutivas? Diferentes perspectivas do Direito brasileiro* (Brasília: Letras Livres, 2002) pp 51–72 at p 61.

[4]   As discussed by Caroline Mécary 'La protection juridique des enfants élevés par deux personnes de même sexe' in Martine Gross (ed) *Homoparentalités, état des lieux* (Toulouse: Éditions Érès, 2005) pp 83–100 at p 83.

should be given material effect after the analysis of the case before the court, with a properly based decision and without prejudice.

In October 2000, the thesis of a young psychiatrist specialising in infants[5] showed that the psychological development of children raised by homosexual couples is similar to those raised by heterosexual parents. There are many similar studies in this field in the United States. The American Academy of Pediatrics has spoken publicly in favour of adoption by an individual or homosexual couples.[6]

The Universal Declaration of Human Rights may contain the solution for the questions discussed here. In Art 16, it is expressed that:

> 'Men and women of full age, without any limitation due to race, nationality or religion, have the right to marry and to found a family. They are entitled to equal rights as to marriage, during marriage and at its dissolution.'[7]

It is understood, therefore, that the right to parentage is acknowledged, that it should be seen as a personal right, not transferable, not unavailable and protected by the state.[8]

The right to have a child is not like a right of property over the infant and it is not developed through 'acquiring' a human life. Instead, it promotes responsibility, encouraging adults to carry out the right to paternity in a responsible and conscious form.[9] Besides, this right to parenthood must be guaranteed by the state, consistent with the constitutional principles of liberty, equality, autonomy, non-discrimination and, obviously, the dignity of the human being, along with the principle of full protection of the child.[10]

In Brazil, with the acknowledgement of single parent families and the appearance of the new Constitution in 1988, the tie between legal marriage and stable unions with filiation has been broken. Therefore, the Constitution recognised that all human beings can accomplish their parental aim, no matter whether a marital link or a permanent quasi-marital bond exists. They can, as a

---

[5]   PhD thesis in Medicine at University of Bordeaux, S Naudau *Approche psychologique et comportamentale des enfants vivant en milieu homoparental* cited by Caroline Mécary 'La protection juridique des enfants élevés par deux personnes de même sexe', ibid at p 84.

[6]   See Committee on Psychosocial Aspects of Child and Family Health 'Coparent or Second-Parent Adoption by Same-Sex Parents' (2002) 109(2) *Pediatrics* (the official journal of the American Academy of Pediatrics, Elk Grove Village: American Academy of Pediatrics) 339–340 at 339.

[7]   There is an analogous norm in the European Convention of Human Rights. Cf Art 12 of the European Convention of Human Rights.

[8]   See Maria Cláudia Crespo Brauner *Direito, sexualidade e reprodução humana: conquistas médicas e o debate bioético* (Rio de Janeiro: Renovar, 2003) p 52.

[9]   See Vera Lucia da Silva Sapko *Do direito à paternidade e maternidade dos homossexuais: sua viabilização pela adoção e reprodução assistida* (Curitiba: Juruá, 2005) p 80.

[10] See the Constitution of the Portuguese Republic, art 1; art 13(1) and (2); art 26(1); art 36(1); art 68(2); art 69(1) and (2). See the Constitution of the Federative Republic of Brazil, art 1(III); art 3(IV); art 5(I), (XLI); art 227.

matter of fact, have a unilateral parental aim, since the single parent family has the same dignity as other forms of family, according to the Brazilian *Lex Fundamentalis.*

The Brazilian Magna Carta provides that family planning must be based on the dignity of the human being and on responsible parentage. The state is forbidden to control or interfere with this right. Therefore, there is a fundamental right to reproduction and, as a consequence, a fundamental right to form a family.[11] Speaking of paternity and responsible parentage, one of the biggest differences between heterosexual and homosexual couples is that for gays and lesbians parentage is, as a rule, a conscious decision.[12]

Anything which denies the right to parenthood to a certain group of individuals (homosexuals), ignoring their personal accomplishments, violates their fundamental rights to equality and to non-discrimination, obstructs the process of citizenship and puts democracy itself and the people's dignity in check by not positively promoting the fundamental liberties and equality of all its citizens.[13]

Taking into account that family rights are typically subjective, and that those connected with filiation can enhance human personality, it is possible to defend the idea of a subjective right belonging to homosexuals, to become progenitors, which would include the possibility of adopting children and adolescents, as well as access to medically assisted procreation (MAP).

In the field of MAP techniques and surrogate maternity, the only viable basis for opposing its application to homosexuals would be any possible harm to the best interest of the child who is about to be born. Arguments such as possible psychological disturbance that the child might suffer from finding out about the way he or she was generated have been canvassed. Such allegations are fallacious. As Vera Lúcia Raposo correctly states, children generated by MAP techniques can be sure they were desired.[14] Moreover, they will never suffer from the possible psychological traumas of 'accidental children'.

---

[11]   On this subject, Viviane Girardi asserts that 'from the systematic interpretation of §§ 4° and 7° of art. 226 of the Brazilian Constitution, it is possible to defend the existence of a right to personality connected to the idea of a juridically protected interest in paternity that has its root in an essentially subjective right because it is connected to the particular concept of happiness, understood and deriving from the major principle of the dignity of the human being': Viviane Girardi *Famílias contemporâneas, filiação e afeto: possibilidade jurídica de adoção por homossexuais* (Porto Alegre: Livraria do Advogado Editora, 2007) p 92.

[12]   As is asserted in North American doctrine, there is a tendency – almost invalid – of non-planned pregnancies or adoptions by homosexuals. On this, see Shana Priwer and Cynthia Philips *Gay Parenting: Complete Guide to Same-Sex Families* (Far Hills: New Horizon Press, 2006) p 3.

[13]   See Vera Lucia da Silva Sapko *Do direito à paternidade e maternidade dos homossexuais* (Curitiba: Juruá, 2005) pp 101–102.

[14]   The author warns of the dangerous fact seen in such situations in which the child is used as a means to reach an end. If this were so, the rights to reproduction could be denied to a considerable part of the population. Eg, couples who have children in order to save their

Couples of the same sex are not able to have children naturally. Having a child who has the genetic background of both parents is, at the moment, impossible practically. The child can have, at the most, one of the fathers' or mothers' DNA even with all the existing genetic engineering resources these days.[15] Denying parentage to couples due to their sexual preferences should not be acceptable. It is discriminatory and unreasonable: it punishes those who opt into a relationship in which procreation is not possible, as if this 'infertility' were the individual's choice.

It is possible to affirm that homosexuals do have a right to parentage. But does this right extend to a right to reproduction? Due to the references to equality and liberty, constitutionally guaranteed in Brazil and Portugal, impeding gay couples from access to MAP techniques while this access is guaranteed to heterosexual couples requires a powerful reason to justify the discrimination; this does not seem to exist, and is therefore considered arbitrary.

The right to parentage, extending to the right to reproduce and generate a child, emphasises the right to intimacy and to self-determination, which should not be limited. A country that imposes an arbitrary human reproduction policy hinders the inalienable right people have to bear children.

Besides, it is important to point out that the decision about this matter must not be taken in isolation from the surrogate motherhood issue, which is the only method available to male homosexual couples to procreate. Thus, a system which allows lesbians the resources of MAP techniques must admit surrogate motherhood for the procreation of male homosexuals. Otherwise, the principle of equality is not fully effected.[16]

II NATURAL PROCREATION AND SELF-INSEMINATION

It is imperative to highlight that nothing can stop homosexuals from making use of the natural reproduction method. Homosexual couples are naturally infertile, but the individuals, themselves, are not. For instance, a lesbian can

---

marriage: would this not be the use of a child as an instrument? Vera Lúcia Raposo *De mãe para mãe: questões legais e éticas suscitadas pela maternidade de substituição* (Coimbra: Coimbra Editora, 2005) p 48.

[15] Which does not prevent parentage from being carried on equally by both members of the couple, since affectivity must prevail in relation to biology. And being a genetic father/mother, surrogate mother or social father, both will always be affective parents.

[16] In the same way, Vera Lúcia Raposo asserts that the obstacle to surrogate maternity constitutes discriminatory treatment, comparing the situation of a man with the situation of a single woman who wishes to be a mother, since the latter can make use of a sperm donor without medical intervention. Speaking of two men, it is necessary that a woman carry this baby as a surrogate. She finishes her opinion by saying that 'the prohibition of surrogate maternity ends up being different treatment of men who want to be single parents and male homosexual couples compared to women who want to be single mothers and female homosexual couples': Vera Lúcia Raposo *De mãe para mãe* (Coimbra: Coimbra Editora, 2005) pp 17–18.

inseminate herself without looking for a medical centre.[17] If she were single
there is no problem at all and filiation is established in relation to her, and if the
sperm donor is known (for example, a friend) and, if she wishes, paternity can
also be established in relation to him.

The problem arises when the same woman who inseminated herself has a
female partner. In this case, they may know who the sperm donor was, but the
intention is that filiation be established with both women because, although
only one of them is the genetic and natural mother, they planned to be parents
together.

The matter is even more complex when there is an 'arrangement' between two
couples: one gay and one lesbian, where one of the women conceives a baby
with one of the men. Notice that although there is no doubt about the juridical
paternity of this child, the parenting plan was thought up by four people.
Probably the child will live with the women and spend periods of time with the
men.[18] The questions that may rise from this situation are: if the genetic and
legal mother passes away, will the child start to live automatically with the
biological father (who is the living progenitor) without taking into account that
this child always lived with the mother and her partner? If the infant's father
passes away, would his partner be without any rights or obligations towards the
child? Would he be forbidden to visit and be on familiar terms towards this
child? These are practical situations that go beyond judicial thinking and what
the legislature has so far provided for.

III   MEDICALLY ASSISTED PROCREATION

Before moving to the possibility (or not) of using techniques of assisted
reproduction (AR) for homosexual couples, it is necessary to make some
general points about the development of this area in Brazil and Portugal.

Although many countries already have special legislation on MAP, as is the
case of Portugal, in Brazil there is only one resolution (no 1.957/2010) of the
CFM (the Federal Council of Medicine) which complements the legal system,
filling the gap where legislation is silent.[19]

In Portugal, the Law 32/2006 of 26 July, called 'the MAP Law', fills a huge gap
that existed in this area. However, as Jorge Duarte Pinheiro states, this Act is

---

[17]   An example brought up by Carlos Pamplona Corte-Real 'Homoafectividade: a respectiva
        situação jurídico-familiar em Portugal' in Maria Berenice Dias and Jorge Duarte Pinheiro
        (eds) *Escritos de direito das famílias: uma perspectiva luso-brasileira* (Porto Alegre: Magister,
        2008) pp 24–38 at p 35, where the author asserts that such a situation is not legally controllable
        and it is not within the applicable fields of art 34 of the Medically Assisted Procreation Law
        (which discusses punishment for those who make use of MAP outside authorised centres) since
        it is not a medical situation.
[18]   Like holidays, vacations, etc.
[19]   See Eduardo Dantas and Marcos Coltri *Comentários ao Código de Ética Médica* (Rio de
        Janeiro: Editora GZ, 2010) p 99.

not sufficient to resolve all issues relating to the matter, since this is an area that is constantly evolving. In the words of the eminent jurist, 'there is and always will be gaps in the field of assisted reproduction'. He adds that 'within such a sui generis field, it is especially important that someone interpreting the law fills any gaps with norms based on the spirit of the system'.[20]

In relation to the beneficiaries of MAP, the resolution of the CFM is limited to defining those who are allowed to use AR techniques:[21]

> ' . . . all capable people, who have requested the procedure and whose profile does not deviate from limits in this resolution can be recipients of the techniques of AR provided that the participants are in full agreement and fully informed about the same, in accordance with current legislation.'

In Portugal, the MAP Law, in art 6, limits access to MAP to married people (legally capable) who are not legally separated from each other or, in fact, separated, and to those, of different sex, who have lived in similar conditions to spouses for at least 2 years.

With these points in mind, the question is to what extent the resolution of the CFM regulates the matter and to what extent the MAP Law in Portugal is in accordance with the constitutional principles that guide the Portuguese juridical system.[22]

(a)   Is it possible for both partners in a lesbian relationship to be biological parents of the same child?

Where a couple want a child biologically related to both partners, the current legislation on MAP techniques is limited to situations where there is a man (husband or partner) and a woman (wife or partner).[23] However, this section

---

[20]   Jorge Duarte Pinheiro *O Direito da Família Contemporâneo* (Lisboa: AAFDL, 2008) pp 218–219.

[21]   The revoked resolution no 1.358/92 merely provided that the users of the techniques of AR could be 'every woman, capable under the law, who has requested and whose treatment does not deviate from the limits of this resolution. They may receive the AR techniques, since they have agreed freely and consciously in an informed consent document'. Note that with the new resolution, there was an opening up of access to assisted reproduction techniques to homosexuals.

[22]   Some Portuguese experts consider it to be unconstitutional. Thus, Carlos Pamplona Corte-Real asserts that MAP techniques must be guaranteed to all citizens respecting the principle of non-discrimination by sexual orientation. He adds that 'LAW 32/2006 goes against such a principle, being, therefore, unconstitutional by virtue of the fundamental right to constitute a family (art 36, n 1, first part of CRP) in which the right to procreate in accordance with the sexual orientation is accepted. Similarly, also art 18, n.1 (direct linkage of public and private departments to the fundamental right,) and art 26, n.1 and n.3 (respect for personal identity, personality development, private and family life, intimacy from any kind of discrimination, and the guarantee over the human dignity)': Carlos Pamplona Corte-Real 'Homoafectividade: a respectiva situação jurídico-familiar em Portugal' in *Escritos de direito das famílias*, above n 17, p 35.

[23]   Namely Portugal and Brazil.

looks at potential AR techniques where the baby could have the genetic material of both members of the relationship, even where both partners are women.

Recent research has raised the possibility of an infant being the biological child of both his lesbian mothers. There are two possibilities, both concerning in vitro fertilisation. In the first case the fecundation of an egg by another egg would happen. Lesbians who wished to generate a child with the genetic material from both partners would proceed in the following way: a mature egg would be collected from both mothers and these two gametes would be fertilised in vitro, the same way an egg attaches to a sperm. The male progenitor in this process of procreation would be removed since, according to this study, the egg has the necessary reservoir and the metabolic 'equipment' to begin life. The egg, fecundated by the confluence of two eggs, would be transplanted into the uterus of one of the partners.[24]

A second possible method concerns nuclear transference, a revolutionary technique performed by the North-American physician Jamie Grifo, the director of the New York University Fertility Center. The nucleus of an egg is collected which is then transported to an egg donated by the partner and from which the primitive nucleus was removed. As the cytoplasm and the nuclei of the mixed egg come from different women, the child will have two genetic mothers.[25] The technique was brought to public attention in 1998 and succeeded. It has been prohibited, however, since 2001 in the United States.[26]

Note that, for the purpose of establishing paternity, the legal mother is still the one to carry the child in accordance with the laws of Brazil and Portugal. In addition, the first is an experimental technique, which has not even been tested on humans. The second has had some success, but for reasons unrelated to this work it is no longer in use.

There has been one real case with a lesbian couple in Rio de Janeiro where the genetic material of both women can be found in their child. A lesbian couple wanted to have a child together and, after examination, found that one of them was the best person to carry the child. The donation of semen came from the *univitelin* twin brother of the gestational mother's partner. Thus, the child, a girl, happened to have the genetic makeup of the two mothers. This phenomenon is known as pseudo-homologous.

---

24 This kind of fecundation, until now, has been done with success in female mice. Its study was started in 1977 by P Soupart. See Maria Helena Machado *Reprodução humana assistida: aspectos éticos e jurídicos* (Curitiba: Juruá, 6th edn, 2008) p 60.

25 See ibid, p 61.

26 See 'What's Next – The Future of IVF: Human Nuclear Transfer and Oocyte Reconstruction' available at: http://miniivf.com/whats-next-future-of-ivf_cytoplasmic-nuclear-transfer.shtml (accessed May 2011).

(b) Partially heterologous in the case of an unmarried woman or a single gay man

A single homosexual man or woman may wish to be a parent, commonly called 'independent production'. In the man's case, when it comes to non-natural reproduction, he would have to look for the services of a surrogate mother.

In Brazil, resolution no 1.358/92 issued by the CFM, as described above, simply stated that 'every capable woman under the law' may use AR techniques. Thus, it is clear that, in accordance with the provisions of the revoked resolution, MAP techniques were already available to unmarried homosexual women who want to generate a child. With the emergence of resolution no 1.957/2010, the implicit has become explicit, since AR is now open to any capable person, regardless of their marital status.

In Portugal, the MAP Law limits access of the techniques to couples united by marriage and heterosexual couples living together for at least 2 years, creating an obstacle for single women – homosexual or heterosexual – wishing to utilise such techniques.

In the case of a gay man who wants to beget a child without any sexual contact, the only option is surrogate maternity. The CFM's new resolution – like the revoked one – makes surrogacy available only for women who cannot naturally conceive. However, due to the principle of equality, it is arguable that men should be able to access the same resources as women.[27]

The resolution also states that 'the temporary uterus donor must be a family member of the genetic donor, up to second degree, with the other cases to be submitted for authorization by the CFM'. In these specific cases, for genetic reasons, it is not advisable that the surrogate mother belong to the family, unless the semen of another man is used, which is not allowed. However, the fact must always be taken into account that 'the temporary uterus donation must not be with profitable or commercial ends', which makes it more likely that the man will rely on a friend or a distant relative to be a surrogate mother.

The legal issue is establishing filiation. It is impossible for a man, nowadays, to go to a Registry Office and establish his own paternity without the mother also becoming a legal parent. Thus, filiation would be established with both the surrogate mother and the man, a situation which does not reflect the parental plan in which the gestational mother is only 'lending' her uterus and not intending to take part in this plan.

---

[27] Even the Medical Ethics Code (resolution no 1.897/2009 of the CFM), in its explanatory memorandum states that 'we live in a democratic state of law obedient to constitutional principles, firstly, and other legal devices that follow the hierarchy of Kelsen's Classic Pyramid, which is defined as 1) the Federal Constitution, 2) Supplementary laws, 3) ordinary laws, 4) Decrees and Precedents and 5) Ordinances and other pieces of legislation'. Thus, it is understood that, in addition to conforming to constitutional dictates, the Medical Ethics Code is subjugated to the principles that emanate from the Constitution, among them, equality.

In Portugal, the matter seems to be even stricter for single gay men who become parents since art 8(1) of the MAP Law states that 'any legal arrangement, for free or for charge, that comes from surrogate motherhood is not valid'. Article 8(3) determines that 'a woman who becomes a surrogate mother for another woman, for legal purposes, will be the mother of this infant'. Thus, in an arrangement between a gay man and a woman in order to have a child, whether or not by natural means, maternity will always be established with the woman who bore the infant. Is this solution suitable for a woman who has never wanted that infant, but only made use of her body in order that the child could come into this world? Is 'punishing' this woman, forcing her to assume a maternity she had never wanted, a fair end for both woman and infant?[28] Would the child's best interest be promoted, which is the only criterion that should prevail in matters concerning infants (including unborn children)?

Artifices and manipulations can always be used, hoping that the law adapts itself to social reality, regulating, in an appropriate way, the situations which occur in the real world but are put aside in the juridical world.[29]

(c)   Heterologous or partially heterologous

(i)   In the case of a lesbian couple

In the case of a lesbian couple who decide to have a baby, one of the main decisions – not to say the most important – is choosing which partner is going to carry the child. If one of the women undergoes artificial insemination or in vitro fertilisation, making use of her own genetic material, together with the semen of an anonymous donor, the infant would have filiation established only in relation to the mother who gave birth to the child, who would also be the genetic mother.

Unlike heterosexual families who have made use of MAP techniques, lesbian families using a donor replace the male progenitor with the second woman (affective mother, social mother or socioaffective mother).

There is also the unusual option of choosing a donor who would recognise the child as his. An example of this situation is the case of Nancy (biological mother) and Amy (affective mother), both 'mothers' of Sarah. Nancy

---

[28]   Besides this sanction, the MAP Law in its art 39 establishes that 'those who sign surrogacy contracts charging money are to be punished with 2 years in jail or a fine up to 240 days, and for those who promote, by any means, by a direct invitation or by sending a person, or through a public announcement, paid surrogate maternity contracts are to be punished with 2 years in prison or a fine up to 240 days'. Note that each day of a fine corresponds to an amount of between €5 and €500, which the court decides on the basis of the economic and financial situation of the offender.

[29]   In Portuguese doctrine it is stated that 'nobody cares, in the end, about realising a gay man's natural right to procreation. But caution in the legal regulation of the availability of a uterus and surrogate motherhood is justified'. Carlos Pamplona Corte-Real 'Homoafectividade: a respectiva situação jurídico-familiar em Portugal' in *Escritos de direito das famílias*, above n 17, p 36.

interviewed many men (gay and straight) until they met Doug and his boyfriend at that time. Contrary to the idea that lesbian couples are opposed to the argument that infants need parents of both sexes, they wanted a man in their story so that they could point to him if Sarah asked about her father. Instead of a couple getting together, falling in love and having a child, four people got together, had a child and became good friends. In fact, their lives became interlaced. Although it was not part of the deal, Doug insisted on financially contributing to Sarah's expenses. Even though she calls her biological mother by 'Mummy', and her socioaffective mother 'Amy', Sarah says she is the daughter of both. And Doug is 'Daddy'. A family constituted by a daughter, a father and two mothers.[30]

However, in this case, filiation would be established between the birth mother and the donor, leaving the socioaffective mother outside the scope of legal protection, which could lead to future problems for filiation under the Portuguese and the Brazilian systems, which determine that motherhood lies with the woman who 'gave birth'. It should be recalled, however, that 'the definition of motherhood from birth is scientifically fallible'.[31]

In the case of homosexual female couples, reproduction could be carried further as follows: one member of the pair would give birth to the child, whose embryo had been fertilised with the egg from the other woman of the pair and sperm from a donor. Some countries have clinics and hospitals that will do this. The University Hospital of the Vrije Universiteit Brussel; the Center for Reproductive Medicine is one of the best in the world.[32] In this case, the mother who gives birth and the genetic mother are not the same.

In one recent and famous case in Brazil, a lesbian couple underwent this type of procedure and they are currently fighting in court for the name of both mothers to appear on the birth certificates of their twins. Note that the legal mother is not the genetic one. A lawsuit for recognition of parentage was filed on behalf of the children, whose application for injunctive relief was denied. Neither succeeded on appeal.[33]

---

[30]   See Lindsay Van Gelder 'A Lesbian Family' in Robert M Baird and Stuart E Rosebaum (eds) *Same-Sex Marriage: The Moral and Legal Debate* (New York: Prometheus Books, 2nd edn, 2004) pp 117–121.

[31]   This is pointed out by Rafael Luís Vale e Reis *O Direito ao Conhecimento das Origens Genéticas* (Coimbra: Coimbra Editora, 2008) p 482.

[32]   On the philosophy of the Centre about opening the doors to MAP techniques, the doctrine from Belgium affirms that '*ce centre adhère au principe que le désir d'être parent est un désir universel et qu'être homosexuel n'exclut pas le droit d'avoir un enfant*': Tom Lenie, Patricia Baetens and Ingrid Ponjaert-Kristoffersen 'Une étude sur les demandes d'insémination artificielle avec sperme de donneur (IAD) chez des couples homosexuels féminins' in Martine Gross (ed) *Homoparentalités, état des lieux* (Toulouse: Éditions Érès, 2005) pp 231–240 at p 231.

[33]   For a detailed analysis of this case, consult Maria Berenice Dias 'Milagre da ciência' available at: www.ibdfam.org.br/?artigos&artigo=507 (accessed 15 May 2009).

However, there is a precedent of a lesbian couple who underwent the same type of artificial insemination, in the state of Santa Catarina, who managed to establish parentage for both women. The decision of a judge of the 8th Family Court of Porto Alegre, declared it possible for the infants to receive the surname – and all rights therein – of both mothers.[34]

This solution is not usually possible – as a rule, it is always appropriate for the partner's male partner to seek legal adoption of her child – who, after all, is also her son – on the basis of art 1626 of the Brazilian Civil Code.[35] As Maria Berenice Dias stated, any response that does not recognise double motherhood – and of course, the paternity of two men – 'is prejudiced'. The renowned jurist adds that allowing only one of the mothers or only one of the fathers to have a legal relationship with the child 'ignores everything that justice points to in the light of a wider view of the family structure'.[36]

In Portugal, such a situation is far from becoming a possibility, since the use of MAP techniques, as mentioned before, is restricted to married couples and the members of a heterosexual union, according to art 6 of the MAP Law. This is, to reiterate, in conflict with the principle of non-discrimination on the basis of the sexual orientation stated in the Constitution of Portugal.

Although the traditional family has been replaced by other forms of family, such as single parent and reconstituted families, lesbian parenthood is still a controversial issue. One of the recurrent criticisms argues that factors such as the absence of a father, the mothers' homosexual orientation and the involvement of an anonymous donor would have negative consequences for the infant's psychosocial development. This opinion is, however, contradicted by an increasing number of studies that indicate that they are not legitimate arguments to justify the refusal of giving access to AR techniques to lesbian couples.[37]

It is also noted that research conducted into lesbian families and the biological offspring of either parent (as a result of MAP) leads to the conclusion that the role of both mothers (the biological and the social parent) have the same

---

[34] See 'Casal homossexual registra filhos com duas mães' available at: www.direitohomoafetivo. com.br/NoticiaView.php?idNoticia=29 (accessed 26 October 2010).

[35] Art 1.626: Adoption attributes the situation of being a son to the adopted child, disconnecting him from his biological parents or relatives, except when there are impediments for marriage. If one of the partners adopts the son of the other, the link of filiation between the adopted child and the adopter's partner and their relatives is kept.

[36] Maria Berenice Dias *Manual de Direito das Famílias* (São Paulo: Editora Revista dos Tribunais, 5th edn revised, 2009) p 340.

[37] See Tom Lenie, Patricia Baetens and Ingrid Ponjaert-Kristoffersen 'Une étude sur les demandes d'insémination artificielle avec sperme de donneur (IAD) chez des couples homosexuels féminins', above n 32, p 231. Cf similarly, Katrien Vanfraussen, Ingrid Ponjaert-Kristoffersen and Anne Brewaeys 'L'insemination artificielle dans les familles lesbiennes: grandir dans une famille non traditionnelle' in Martine Gross (ed) *Homoparentalités, état des lieux* (Toulouse: Éditions Érès, 2005) pp 241–250 at p 245, that refers to a study that indicates that children originating from homoaffective families have the same adapting problems as those originating from heterosexual families.

intensity in the infant's life. Children answered questionnaires discussing what they felt about their biological and affective mothers concerning sensibility, affection and tenderness towards them, as well as their authority over the infants. Disparities were not found. In addition to this, the social mothers are as involved as the biological mothers in the children's education.[38] Moreover, researchers found that the traditional nuclear family is not the only kind in which the children can grow up and become healthy teenagers, psychologically speaking.

The studies evidenced that the infants have an equally healthy relationship with their biological and socioaffective progenitors. The fact that they only know half of their genetic origin and are potentially curious about the donor does not seem to interfere in the children's behaviour.[39]

If the lesbian parents' relationship ends, other problems may arise. What will happen to the child's relationship with the socioaffective mother?[40] Does she have to pay alimony for the child? Are there any visitation rights? The answer should be yes because, regardless of the fact that filiation was established for only one of the women, the plan to be parents was conceived by both of them. A slightly different problem may occur once a stable union between two women has been recognised in Brazil, because the offspring remain linked to the biological mother's partner by 'kinship by affinity', since the partner would fit into the structure established by art 1595 of the Civil Code.[41]

On the last issue, Brazilian jurisprudence has favoured guaranteeing the legal mother's former partner the 'right and duty of conviviality'[42] with the child.[43]

---

[38] 'Les résultats suggèrent que l'absence ou la présence d'un lien biologique ne se reflète pas dans les mesures qui ont été utilisées pour examiner le comportement parental d'education. Un lien biologique entre le coparent et l'enfant n'est pas un prérequis pour une relation d'acceptation ouverte dans laquelle l'autorité est bien établie. Contrairement à la première partie de cette étude, les enfants ne mentionnent plus de sentiments davantage positifs à l'égard de la mère biologique': Katrien Vanfraussen, Ingrid Ponjaert-Kristoffersen and Anne Brewaeys 'L'insemination artificielle dans les familles lesbiennes: grandir dans une famille non traditionnelle', above n 37, p 244.

[39] See ibid, p 249.

[40] Where the socioaffective mother is denied the possibility of adopting her partner's biological children.

[41] Article 1.595: Each spouse or partner is linked to the other's relatives by affinity. (1) Kinship by affinity is limited to the ascendants, descendents and brothers or sisters of the spouse. (2) Next, affinity does not end with the dissolution of the marriage or the stable union.

[42] Terminology often used in most modern Brazilian writing.

[43] HOMOPARENTAL FILIATION. RIGHT TO VISIT. Incontrovertible that they lived in a homoaffective union for more than 12 years. Although there is only the biological mother's name on the child's birth certificate, filiation was planned by both, with the socioaffective mother rearing the child since he was born, performing all the maternity functions. Nobody questions any more that affectiveness is a matter that deserves injunctive relief, the judiciary not being about to get far away from the facts. Being clear of the filiation status between the appellant and the infant, it is important that the right to be on familiar terms with the infant be guaranteed, which is more the child's right than the mother's right. Thus, the previous decision that established visits must be kept. Motion denied. (TJRS, 7.ª C.Cív., AC 70018249631, Rel. Desa. Maria Berenice Dias, judgment 11 April 2007).

Similarly, on the North American continent, a justice of Pennsylvania granted visiting rights to the former partner of the biological mother of a 7-year-old girl.[44] In both cases, the presence of love and affection was important.

(ii)   Heterology or partial heterology in the case of gay couples – with the aid of surrogate motherhood

It is necessary first to consider some issues about surrogate maternity. Later, the doctrinal position in Brazil and in Portugal about subrogate maternity will be discussed. Note that, in the field of adoption, men and women have equal rights to be parents. In the case of assisted reproduction, women are given prevalence, for biological reasons.[45]

Surrogate motherhood can be understood as an agreement in which a woman contracts to bear an infant, and later to give him to a third party, abdicating all her rights over the infant, including the juridical classification of 'mother'.[46]

Normally, when a gay couple look for the aid of a surrogate, it is the couple who choose the donor of the semen. If possible, they may choose to mix their genetic material so that they do not know who the biological father is. However, the egg will only be fertilised with the sperm of one father.

Fertility experts think that this procedure reduces the chances of conception because the sperm of the two men would 'compete'. Others say such a practice can reduce the chances of success due to antibodies that could cause problems for the normal functioning of sperm. In any case, the majority of the experts in the area think it is preferable to choose just one to be the sperm donor.[47] The question then arises: is surrogate motherhood a viable alternative in Portugal or Brazil?

As mentioned before, surrogate motherhood is completely banned in Portugal, under the provisions of art 8 of the Law 32/2006. Despite the apparent position of legislative prohibition, differences are found among commentators.[48] The

---

44   See 'Custody battle finally ends for lesbian moms in Pennsylvania' available at: www.proudparenting.com/node/2720 (accessed 24 February 2009).

45   See Emmanuel Gratton 'Les déclinaisons de la paternité gaye' in Martine Gross (ed) *Homoparentalités, etát des lieux* (Toulouse: Éditions Érès, 2005) pp 281–290 at p 283.

46   It is basically the concept advanced by Vera Lúcia Raposo *De mãe para mãe: questões legais e éticas suscitadas pela maternidade de substituição* (Coimbra: Coimbra Editora, 2005) p 13.

47   See Shana Priwer and Cynthia Philips *Gay Parenting: Complete Guide to Same-Sex Families* (Far Hills: New Horizon Press, 2006) pp 5 and 47.

48   Vera Lúcia Raposo takes a position in favour of surrogate maternity, extending the right to homosexual couples. Vera Lúcia Raposo *De mãe para mãe: questões legais e éticas suscitadas pela maternidade de substituição* (Coimbra: Coimbra Editora, 2005) pp 70–71, asserting that 'the restrictions imposed by the State to one's right of reproduction must not be based in any kind of moral values linked to prejudices to the sexual, family and social behaviors and their refractions in the society's moral consciousness'. The jurist adds that psycho sociological studies do not show that 'this kind of family formations obstruct the healthy growing of a child. The presented argument, though based in legal reasons (the well-being of a new being)

MAP Law patently affronts art 13(2) of the Portuguese Constitution, which prohibits any discrimination based on the individual's sexual orientation.

In Brazil, the scope of resolution no 1.957/2010 is limited to surrogate maternity 'when there is a medical condition that prevents or makes it difficult to attain pregnancy with the genetic donor'. And, as already mentioned, that the 'temporary uterus donor must be linked to the genetic donor by kinship up to the second degree, with other cases subject to authorisation by the Federal Council of Medicine'. The expression 'other cases' opens up the possibility that gay couples could have access to AR techniques with the help of surrogate motherhood. If it were not for such an expression, it would be out of respect for the equality and non-discrimination principles, elevated in the Constitution of the Federal Republic of Brazil.

However, the same problem that arises in the case of lesbian couples rears its head: the establishment of paternity.[49] Who is the father? Even if the semen of both men is mixed, as already mentioned, only one will be the genetic father. Do we attribute fatherhood to him? It does not seem a fair decision, taking into account the value of the socioaffective father. The parental plan originated from the will and the affections of both men, and therefore, it is arguable that the child can be registered in the name of both fathers, on behalf of the interests of the child, effecting a legal link with both men, carrying the rights and duties of parenthood.[50]

Finally on surrogate motherhood, particular attention should be paid to the words of Vera Lucia Raposo in order to understand that the fact that a woman can 'offer a child to those who want it, but who cannot by themselves have one, is a priceless offer, because it is a gift of life'. The same jurist ends by wondering how the right to life as one of the most basic human rights should be taken into account, understanding thus that 'all actions that encourage or support [the right to life] will have to be legally allowed'.[51]

---

start from a petition of principles: the definition of what is the interest and the well-being of a child emerges in a moralist concept connotation.'

[49] Surrogate motherhood is simply a legal gap in the Brazilian legal system in both the establishment of filiation and also in relation to the prohibition or permission of it. The doctrine and jurisprudence consider a mother, for registering and succession matters, the woman who delivered a baby after gestating it in her body.

[50] As Maria Berenice Dias alerts, 'denying the possibility of registering the child under both names subtracts the right the child has to gain benefits with reference to whom she equally considers to be – or it is in fact – the father. The child who was conceived by the wish of more than one person must be registered in the name of both': *União homoafetiva: o preconceito & a justiça* (Sao Paulo: Editora Revista dos Tribunais, 4th edn, 2009) p 226.

[51] Vera Lúcia Raposo *De mãe para mãe: questões legais e éticas suscitadas pela maternidade de substituição* (Coimbra: Coimbra Editora, 2005) pp 87–88.

IV   THE MATTER OF SURPLUS EMBRYOS

Finally, we have the matter of surplus embryos, which has special importance in Portugal, since as already mentioned, MAP techniques are restricted to heterosexual married couples and those who live together. In Brazil, as stated before, there is an opening, even if it is not explicit, for AR techniques to be used by same-sex couples.

Collecting an egg is a surgical procedure with the use of anesthesia, which is a risk for the mother and therefore cannot be done frequently. There is the potential for some physical and, sometimes, psychological suffering. In order to minimise the number of times the woman must go through the procedure, 'hyper induction' is used, leading to 'embryonic leftovers'.[52]

There is not, so far, a safe way to conserve and freeze eggs at a low temperature, which must be collected and fertilised immediately due to the impossibility of their conservation. Moreover, due to the possibility of not obtaining success in the development of the implanted embryos, simultaneous preparation of several unimplanted embryos is necessary, which will be used if the initial attempt at implanting and developing fails.[53]

The questions that may arise, following Jorge Duarte Pinheiro's arguments, are: What should we do with surplus embryos? Should they be conserved to be used by the same couple or by another one? Should they be destroyed, preserved ad infinitum or used for scientific investigation purposes? As the Portuguese jurist warns, 'the solution is still open because it depends on the status recognized and given to the human embryo'.[54]

In order to answer the questions above, a further question is involved: when does a combination of molecules change from a simple chemical mixture to a living organism?

There are two major streams of opinion on the issue. On one side, some argue that life begins with fecundation. There are authors who state that choosing a point when a 'combination of molecules' becomes a human being and begins to exist would be a scientific lie, a fiction.[55]

The opposing stream is the pre-embryo theory, which began with the renowned Warnock Report about Fertilization and Embryology, published in 1984 in the United Kingdom, which suggested that before the fourteenth development day,

---

[52]   See Olga Jubert Gouveia Krell *Reprodução Humana Assistida e Filiação Civil: Princípios Éticos e Jurídicos* (Curitiba: Juruá, 2006) p 127.
[53]   See Maria Helena Machado *Reprodução humana assistida*: aspectos éticos e jurídicos, above n 24, p 126.
[54]   Jorge Duarte Pinheiro *O Direito da Família Contemporâneo*, above n 20, p 250.
[55]   See Marília de Siqueira 'O início da vida e a Medicina atual' in Ricardo Henry Marques Dip (ed) *A vida dos direitos humanos: Bioética médica e jurídica* (Porto Alegre: Sergio Fabris, 1998) pp 335–353 at pp 338 et seq.

the zygote still does not have a central nervous system and would be only a 'combination of cells'. Such an approach is followed in several countries, among them Brazil, which issued resolution no 1.358/98 from the CFM, and subscribed to such a theory.[56]

The spirit of the Brazilian Magna Carta, as well as the Constitution of the Portuguese Republic, is undoubtedly in favour of the right to life, which is the first, the most fundamental and important of all the fundamental rights which humans possess.[57] The Brazilian Constitution protects the life of any human being, though with 'imperfections' and 'limitations'. In other words, quality of life is not guaranteed.[58]

This approach supports the idea of the *in dubio pro embryo* (give the embryo the benefit of the doubt). Thus, consistently with Jorge Duarte Pinheiro's argument, we may affirm that, in the case of surplus embryos, a door should be opened to single people and lesbian couples, leading to a solution that most dignifies and protects the embryo.[59]

Note that the solution stated here is not designed to stimulate embryo production so that they can be 'adopted'. Scientists and doctors must be cautious in deciding the quantity of eggs obtained, avoiding more embryos than necessary to gain reasonable success in implantation. The ideal is that all the embryos produced are transferred to the patient. In the case of surplus

---

[56] See Olga Jubert Gouveia Krell *Reprodução Humana Assistida e Filiação Civil: Princípios Éticos e Jurídicos,* above n 52, p 125.

[57] We have to state that the Portuguese Civil Code, in art 66, determines the beginning of personality to be birth. However, the majority of the Portuguese commentary admits juridical personality at conception, based on the inviolability of human life. For Paulo Otero, it is possible to talk about the 'human embryos' fundamental rights'. He also asserts that 'even before birth, the law can and must interfere in the protection of the human being, being that a circumstance independent of the acknowledgement of juridical personality, at least, as it emerges in the Portuguese Civil Code': Paulo Otero *Personalidade e identidade pessoal e genética do ser humano: um perfil constitucional da bioética* (Coimbra: Almedina, 1999) pp 32 et seq and 61-62. The Brazilian Civil Code stipulates, in art 2, that 'civil personality begins with a live birth; but the law guarantees, from conception, the rights of the future child'. The scope of the matter is in conception. The Brazilian Civil Code seems to be based on the Conceptionist Theory, which considers the beginning of life to be the mere joining of the egg and the sperm (fecundation), in opposition to the theory adopted by the Resolution of the CFM.

[58] Similarly see Ives Granda da Silva Martins 'O Direito Constitucional comparado e a inviolabilidade da vida humana' in Ricardo Henry Marques Dip (ed) *A vida dos direitos humanos: Bioética médica e jurídica* (Porto Alegre: Sergio Fabris, 1998) pp 127–144 at p 137.

[59] It is essential to emphasise, however, that the author creates a kind of hierarchy of possible receivers of surplus embryos. In his opinion, first, we should accept 'its implantation *post mortem,* using the survivor where one party has already died. This would legally bypass the biparenthood principle in contrast to the view that it should be used for artificial insemination of a woman or in vitro fertilisation. And, in the absence of a desire to carry out the original couple's plan to become parents, the embryo could be implanted in a member of a heterosexual couple, so long as the possibility of "embryonic adoption" does not stimulate the tendency to create surplus embryos. Where no heterosexual couples are interested in receiving the embryo, it could be implanted in one person alone or in a member of a lesbian couple'. Jorge Duarte Pinheiro *O Direito da Família Contemporâneo* (Lisboa: AAFDL, 2008) pp 251–252.

ones, it is preferable, however, that they be used for single mothers or homosexual couples, rather than cryopreservation, experimental or commercial ends.

In early 2011, resolution no 1.957/2010 of the CFM in Brazil determined that 'surplus viable embryos will be cryopreserved'. In addition, it stated that:

> '. . . at the time of cryopreservation, spouses or partners should express their willingness, in writing, about the fate of the pre-cryopreserved embryos in case of divorce, serious illness or death, and when they wish to donate them.'

In Brazil, the matter seems to have been handled by the resolution. However, despite the freedom and autonomy of the parties, it is to be understood that donation for the purpose of implementation in other couples should be the first option. Where there are no candidates to 'adopt' the embryos, an alternative may be appropriate. The right to life should have prevalence over the techniques of scientific investigation.

V   CONCLUSION

In Portugal, MAP techniques are restricted to heterosexual couples united by marriage or living in de facto unions, making it hard for single people as well as homosexual couples to utilise this resource to become parents. Such a legislative solution seems to suffer from a strong taint of unconstitutionality. Being from a one-parent family or homoparental family does not make a child more or less adjusted, or more or less happy, as indicated by numerous scientific and psychosocial studies.

Only in the case of surplus embryos can a way out for celibate women or lesbian couples be glimpsed, in reliance on the prevalence of the right to life.

Analysing the Brazilian situation, in some cases legislative silence is less perverse than the presence of discriminatory laws. In the absence of a specific law on the subject in Brazil, the situation is saved by resolution no 1.957/2010 of the CFM. MAP techniques have been used widely in Brazil by homosexuals.

The biggest problem that arises is the establishment of filiation. Despite reproductive techniques being open to same-sex couples, only one partner is legally recognised as the parent. Even if a lesbian has taken part in a pregnancy whose embryo has genetic material from her partner, the pregnant partner will be the legal mother while the other woman is left without rights or duties over the child. At the moment, while other solutions are not available, socioaffective paternity or maternity should be recognised. Both partners are 'authors' of the plan to be parents. The parenthood of the woman who was not the gestational mother must be recognised; a legal role in the life of that child must be created.

The same formula should apply to gay couples using surrogacy. If paternity cannot be established for both, the man who is not the legal father should be treated as the socioaffective parent, it being sufficient in these cases that there is evidence of the existence of possession of the child.

This remains the position until justice matches social reality and moves to allow the registration of a child's same-sex parents or, potentially, beyond that to two or three parents.

Canada

POLYGAMY AND UNMARRIED COHABITATION

*Martha Bailey**

Résumé

L'interdiction et la criminalisation de la polygamie, définie comme le fait de vivre dans une relation conjugale, font l'objet de discussions dans la province canadienne de la Colombie-Britannique. Le gouvernement provincial a saisi les tribunaux de la question de la constitutionnalité de l'article du Code criminel qui interdit la ploygamie, après que ses experts juridiques eurent exprimé des doutes à ce sujet. La Colombie-Britannique est la terre d'accueil du groupe fondamentaliste mormon le plus connu au Canada et dont les membres pratiquent le «mariage» multiple, en conformité avec leurs croyances religieuses. Des préoccupations relatives à des abus et à l'exploitation au sein de ce groupe, ont provoqué des appels pour une application plus rigoureuse de la loi. Le résultat de cette contestation constitutionnelle, pavera la voie soit à des poursuites criminelles soit à la mise en place de stratégies différentes visant à répondre aux problèmes rencontrés au sein de cette communauté fondamentaliste.

La Cour suprême du Canada a rendu deux décisions importantes en matière d'union de fait. La première est un arrêt portant sur le droit des fiduciesrésultoireset par interprétation. Ces mécanismes sont particulièrement intéressantes pour les conjoints de fait qui, dans la plupart des provinces canadiennes, ne bénéficient pas des droits patrimoniaux découlant du mariage. La deuxième décision est l'autorisation de pourvoi accordée par la Cour dans une affaire provenant du Québec et concernant l'obligation alimentaire entre conjoints de fait. Pour l'heure, le Québec est la seule province canadienne à ne pas reconnaître une telle obligation.

I INTRODUCTION

Canada's criminal prohibition against polygamy, defined as living in a conjugal relationship with multiple parties, came under scrutiny in the province of British Columbia. The government of that province asked its courts to rule on the constitutionality of the Criminal Code provision after its legal experts expressed doubt on that issue.[1] British Columbia is home to Canada's most notorious group of fundamentalist Mormons, who practice plural 'marriage' in

---

* Professor of Law, Queen's University, Canada.
[1] Criminal Code, RSC 1985, c C-46.

accordance with their professed religious beliefs. Concerns about abuse and exploitation within the fundamentalist group have led to calls for more assertive enforcement of the law. The ruling on the constitutionality of the criminal prohibition against polygamy will either clear the way for prosecutions under that law or lead to formulation of a different strategy to address the problems.

In early 2011, the Supreme Court of Canada made two important decisions in relation to unmarried cohabitation. In *Kerr v Baranow*,[2] the law relating to resulting and constructive trusts was determined. These trust doctrines are significant for unmarried parties, who do not enjoy statutory marital property rights in most provinces. In addition, the Supreme Court of Canada granted leave to appeal in a case from Quebec dealing with the support for parties who are not either married or a member of a civil union. Quebec is the only province in Canada that does not extend support rights and obligations to unmarried parties.

II POLYGAMY

The Canadian province of British Columbia is home to a community of fundamentalist Mormons that practice plural marriage. This community has attracted extensive negative media coverage, and there have been calls to address identified problems in the community in part by enforcing the criminal law prohibition of polygamy.[3] Charges eventually were laid against two patriarchs of the fundamentalist group. However, after the appointment of a special prosecutor to pursue the charges were quashed because of irregularities, these charges were stayed.[4] Rather than attempting again to lay criminal charges, the British Columbia government instead sought an advisory opinion from its Supreme Court,[5] a trial court that also has jurisdiction to hear and consider questions referred to it by the provincial government.[6]

Two questions have been put to British Columbia's Supreme Court:

(1) Is s 293 of the Criminal Code of Canada consistent with the Canadian Charter of Rights and Freedoms?[7] If not, what particular or particulars and to what extent?

---

2   2011 SCC 10.
3   In particular, Daphne Bramham, a columnist for the *Vancouver Sun*, has written extensively about the fundamentalist community and published *The Secret Lives of Saints: Child Brides and Lost Boys in a Polygamous Mormon Sect* (Random House Canada, 2008).
4   *Blackmore v British Columbia (Attorney General)* (2009), 247 CCC (3d) 544.
5   *Reference re: Criminal Code*, s 293, 2009 BCSC 1668.
6   See British Columbia's Constitutional Question Act, RSBC 1996, c 68.
7   Canadian Charter of Rights and Freedoms, Part I of the Constitution Act, 1982, being Sch B of the Canada Act 1982 (UK), 1982, c 11, s 15.

(2) What are the necessary elements of the offence in s 293 of the Criminal Code of Canada? Without limiting this question, does s 293 require that the polygamy or conjugal union in question involved a minor, or occurred in a context of dependence, exploitation, abuse of authority, a gross imbalance of power or undue influence?

The hearing began on 22 November 2010 and closing arguments were scheduled to begin at the end of March 2011. It is likely that the decision of the British Columbia Supreme Court will be appealed, ultimately to the Supreme Court of Canada.

To put this constitutional reference in context, it should be emphasised that Canada is a monogamous country and will remain so regardless of the outcome. Only monogamous marriages may take place in Canada. The Civil Marriage Act defines marriage as between two people.[8] A married person cannot marry again unless the existing marriage is dissolved by death or divorce. Any marriage by a person who has a prior subsisting marriage is void. Bigamy is a crime. Canada's 'cultural commitment to monogamous marriage' is protected by the civil laws of marriage and the criminal prohibition of bigamy.[9] In the extensive media debate, supporters of Canada's criminal provision on polygamy have suggested that without this provision Canada would become a polygamous country or would somehow be endorsing polygamy.

Canada's criminal provision on polygamy is broadly worded and not clearly consistent with the general approach in Canada to moral offences. Canada has never had much appetite for criminalising private sexual activity.[10] Neither adultery nor fornication was criminalised here,[11] except insofar as such activity harms children.[12] And back in 1968, Parliament, agreeing with Pierre Trudeau

---

[8]   Civil Marriage Act 2005, c 33, C-31.5, s 2 provides: 'Marriage, for civil purposes, is the lawful union of two persons to the exclusion of all others.'

[9]   Benjamin L Berger describes the criminalisation of polygamy as 'a use of the criminal law to protect a cultural commitment to monogamous marriage' in 'Moral Judgment, Criminal Law and the Constitutional Protection of Religion' (2008) 40 SCLR (2d) 513 at 549.

[10] This is in contrast to at least some US states – for a thorough review of the many sexual offences in the USA, see Harriet F Pilpel and Theodora Zavin 'Sex and the Criminal Law' (1952) 14 *Marriage and Family Living* 238.

[11] On the failed attempt in 1882 by John Charlton, a Liberal Member of Parliament, to have adultery criminalised, see Patrick Brode *Courted and Abandoned: Seduction Law in Canada* (Toronto: The Osgoode Society and U of Toronto P, 2002) pp 81 et seq. On adultery as an 'ecclesiastical' but not criminal law offence, see *Smith v Smith* [1952] 2 SCR 312, where Locke J said: 'In Fairman's case Lord Merriman's expression is that adultery is a "quasi-criminal" offence. It is true that in many of the proceedings before the ecclesiastical courts reference is made to the "crime" of adultery, this, I must assume to be, due to the fact that adultery was an ecclesiastical offence but, as pointed out by Lindley LJ, it was not an offence at common law and it was not a criminal offence in England and is not in the Province of British Columbia.'

[12] Canada's Criminal Code, RSC 1985, c C-46 ('Criminal Code'), s 172 (1) provides: 'Every one who, in the home of a child, participates in adultery or sexual immorality or indulges in habitual drunkenness or any other form of vice, and thereby endangers the morals of the child or renders the home an unfit place for the child to be in, is guilty of an indictable offence and liable to imprisonment for a term not exceeding two years.' When first enacted in 1918 this provision, titled 'Corrupting Children', did not include the term 'adultery' but only 'indulgence

that 'There's no place for the state in the bedrooms of the nation',[13] repealed the old criminal prohibition of sodomy.[14] For the most part, Canada does not criminalise non-commercial sexual activities carried out between two consenting adults in private.[15]

As for non-commercial private sexual activities involving *more* than two consenting adults, the only explicit prohibition is in regard to anal intercourse, which must involve the presence of only two people to avoid sanction under s 159 of the Criminal Code. Even this limitation must be viewed in light of the Supreme Court of Canada ruling that group sex (perhaps involving anal intercourse?) among consenting adults who had joined a private swingers club for the purpose of exchanging partners and participating in group sex was not 'indecent' and therefore the operator of the club was not guilty of keeping a 'common bawdy-house'.[16] The Chief Justice described the club activities as follows:[17]

---

in sexual immorality, in habitual drunkenness or in any other form of vice': SC 1918, c 16, s 1. The specific reference to adultery was added by SC 1932–33, c 53, s 3. Debates in the House of Commons indicate that the provision was originally taken from Ontario's Juvenile Delinquents Act, that it was considered ultra vires Ontario and therefore required parliamentary adoption if it were to be valid law, and that it was aimed at protecting and 'forming the character of' children: Canada, Parliament, House of Commons, *Debates,* 13th Parliament, 1st Session, 1918, vol 2 (10 May 1918) (Ottawa: J de Labroquerie Taché, 1918) at 1704–1710. In *R v E (L)* 1997 Carswell Ont 5530, the court provided an extensive review of the history and case-law relating to s 172, it commented at para 12: 'The jurisprudence has clearly established that mere acts of the enumerated offences are not sufficient in and of themselves. The Crown must prove that these acts, in the home of the child, endanger the morals of children or that they render the home of the child unfit.'

13 CBC Television (21 December 1967), online: CBC Archive available at http://archives.cbc.ca/ politics/rights_freedoms/clips/2671 (accessed May 2011).

14 Criminal Law Amendment Act 1968–69 (SC 1968–69, c 38). The Criminal Code, s 159 now provides:
'159. (1) Every person who engages in an act of anal intercourse is guilty of an indictable offence and liable to imprisonment for a term not exceeding ten years or is guilty of an offence punishable on summary conviction.
(2) Subsection (1) does not apply to any act engaged in, in private, between
(a) husband and wife, or
(b) any two persons, each of whom is eighteen years of age or more, both of whom consent to the act.
(3) For the purposes of subsection (2),
(a) an act shall be deemed not to have been engaged in in private if it is engaged in in a public place or if more than two persons take part or are present; and
(b) a person shall be deemed not to consent to an act
(i) if the consent is extorted by force, threats or fear of bodily harm or is obtained by false and fraudulent misrepresentations respecting the nature and quality of the act, or
(ii) if the court is satisfied beyond a reasonable doubt that the person could not have consented to the act by reason of mental disability.'

15 By the phrase 'non-commercial sexual activities carried out between two consenting adults in private', I am intending to exclude sexual activities that are commercial, public, or non-consensual, or that involve animals or minors. And my use of the term 'sexual activity' is meant to refer to the activity itself not to the making of images or records of such.

16 *R v Labaye* 2005 SCC 80, [2005] 3 SCR 728 ('*Labaye*'); *R v Kouri* [2005] 3 SCR 789, 2005 SCC 81. The Criminal Code, s 197 defines a 'common bawdy-house' as 'a place that is (a) kept or

'A number of mattresses were scattered about the floor of the apartment. There people engaged in acts of cunnilingus, masturbation, fellatio and penetration. On several occasions observed by the police, a single woman engaged in sex with several men, while other men watched and masturbated.

Entry to the club and participation in the activities were voluntary. No one was forced to do anything or watch anything. No one was paid for sex. While men considerably outnumbered women on the occasions when the police visited, there is no suggestion that any of the women were there involuntarily or that they did not willingly engage in the acts of group sex.'

However unsavoury, the swingers' club activities did not amount to 'indecency' within the meaning of the Criminal Code. The Chief Justice concluded that: 'Consensual conduct behind code-locked doors can hardly be supposed to jeopardize a society as vigorous and tolerant as Canadian society.'[18]

Clearly then, Canada is tolerant of private non-commercial sexual activities among consenting adults. The major exception to this general rule of tolerance is incest. The Criminal Code provides:[19]

'Every one commits incest who, knowing that another person is by blood relationship his or her parent, child, brother, sister, grandparent or grandchild, as the case may be, has sexual intercourse with that person.'

Incest is a crime even when the act takes place in private between consenting adults.[20]

At first blush, the Criminal Code provision on incest seems to mirror the law governing capacity to marry. If it did so, it would support extending to Canada the following description of American regulation of sexual activity:[21]

'Historically, criminal law and family law have worked in tandem to produce a binary view of intimate life that categorizes intimate acts and choices as either legitimate marital behavior or illegitimate criminal behavior.'

But this statement, however applicable to the American states, has never been true of Canada, where the space for sexual activities that are 'neither marital nor criminal' has always been larger than in some US states.[22] For example, adultery is not a crime, but adulterers by definition are not married to one

---

occupied, or (b) resorted to by one or more persons for the purpose of prostitution or the practice of acts of indecency', and under s 210 keeping a common bawdy-house is an indictable offence.

[17] *Labaye*, paras 7 and 8.

[18] *Labaye*, para 71.

[19] Criminal Code, s 155(1). Section 155(4) provides: 'In this section, "brother" and "sister", respectively, include half-brother and half-sister.'

[20] *R v RP* (1996), 149 NSR (2d) 91, 105 CCC (3d) 435 (CA).

[21] Melissa Murray 'Strange Bedfellows: Criminal Law, Family Law, and the Legal Construction of Intimate Life' (2009) 94 Iowa L Rev 1253 at 1256.

[22] Murray, ibid at 1257. Murray argues that, in light of cases such as *Lawrence v Texas*, the US is

another and are not free to marry because of the prior existing marriage. Even in regard to incest, there is space for sexual activities that are neither criminal nor marital.

In order to identify the 'law-free' zone of incestuous relationships, it is necessary to turn to the Marriage (Prohibited Degrees) Act, which provides an exhaustive list of the relatives one may not marry: 'No person shall marry another person if they are related lineally, or as brother or sister or half-brother or half-sister, including by adoption.'[23] This statute substantially reduced the restrictions on marrying relatives. Today, stepfathers and adult stepdaughters (or stepsons), aunts and adult nephews (or nieces), etc are not subject to any criminal sanctions for engaging in sexual activity, and their family relationship is not an impediment to marriage. But there remains a law-free zone of relationships that are neither sanctioned as marriages nor criminalised. The current restrictions on marriage include adoptive relationships, whereas the Criminal Code provision applies only to blood relationships. Therefore adoptive parents or grandparents and their (adult) children or grandchildren, or adoptive siblings are not subject to criminal sanctions for having sexual intercourse, but they are not able to marry.

In summary, Canada, for the most part, does not intrude into the bedrooms of the nation by imposing criminal sanctions for private, non-commercial sexual activity among consenting adults. Behaviours such as adultery, group sex, and sexual relations between adoptive fathers and their adult children may be considered immoral or repugnant to many or most Canadians, but these activities are not crimes. That sexual activity is not criminalised does *not* mean that the activity is necessarily legalised in the sense of governed by marriage law or otherwise deemed acceptable or in any way endorsed. In Canada, it is *not* the case that 'sexual acts and choices are categorized as either legitimate (marriage) or illegitimate (crime)'.[24] There is a law-free space within which parties may engage in sexual activity without criminal sanction but are not permitted to marry.

Canada's criminal provision on polygamy is included with but different from the other Criminal Code offences that are grouped under the heading 'Offences Against Conjugal Rights'. These five offences are bigamy (s 290), procuring a feigned marriage (s 292), polygamy (s 293), pretending to solemnise marriages without legal authority (s 294) and solemnising a marriage that contravenes the law (s 295).

Putting aside the provision on polygamy, these 'offences against conjugal rights' have long historical roots, stemming from a time in English history when the legal and social significance of marriage was far greater than it is today. The rules regarding creation of legal marriages were uncertain and in flux. Families,

---

now developing a larger 'law-free' zone of sexual activity that is not criminal and not marital. This would move the US closer to the situation in Canada.

23   SC 1990, c 46, s 2(2).
24   Murray (above n 21) at 1302.

the state and the church were accorded far greater control over marriages. Divorce was largely unavailable. In this context, clandestine marriages and irregular marriages (bigamous, incestuous or involving minors) were a problem.[25] Drawing on criminal provisions first enacted in Britain from the early seventeenth century, Canada first enacted its own criminal law on bigamy in 1869,[26] shortly after confederation, on procuring or assisting in procuring a feigned marriage in 1886,[27] on solemnising a marriage without legal authority in 1886,[28] and on solemnising a marriage that contravenes the law in 1886.[29]

Canada's bigamy law now provides:

'290. (1) Every one commits bigamy who

(a)   in Canada,
      (i)   being married, goes through a form of marriage with another person,
      (ii)   knowing that another person is married, goes through a form of marriage with that person, or
      (iii) on the same day or simultaneously, goes through a form of marriage with more than one person; or
(b)   being a Canadian citizen resident in Canada leaves Canada with intent to do anything mentioned in subparagraphs (a)(i) to (iii) and, pursuant thereto, does outside Canada anything mentioned in those subparagraphs in circumstances mentioned therein.

(2) No person commits bigamy by going through a form of marriage if

(a)   that person in good faith and on reasonable grounds believes that his spouse is dead;
(b)   the spouse of that person has been continuously absent from him for seven years immediately preceding the time when he goes through the form of marriage, unless he knew that his spouse was alive at any time during those seven years;
(c)   that person has been divorced from the bond of the first marriage; or
(d)   the former marriage has been declared void by a court of competent jurisdiction.

---

[25]   Lawrence Stone *Uncertain Unions and Broken Lives* (Oxford University Press, 1995); Law Reform Commission of Canada *Bigamy* Working Paper 42 (Ottawa: Law Reform Commission of Canada, 1985) at 7–8; David Lemmings 'Marriage and the Law in the Eighteenth Century: Hardwicke's Marriage Act of 1753' (1996) 39(2) The Historical J 339; RB Outhwaite *Clandestine Marriage in England, 1500–1850* (London: The Hambledon Press, 1995).
[26]   Offences against the Person, SC 1869 (32–33 Vict), c 20, s 58 (this provision was based on existing provisions enacted in provinces).
[27]   An Act to punish seduction, and like offences, and to make further provision for the Protection of Women and Girls, SC 1886 (49 Vict), s 52, s 3 (this provision was based on existing provisions enacted in provinces).
[28]   An Act respecting Offences relating to the Law of Marriage, RSC 1886 (49 Vict), c 161, s 1 (this provision was based on existing provisions enacted in provinces).
[29]   Ibid, s 3 (again, this provision was based on existing provisions enacted in provinces).

(3) Where a person is alleged to have committed bigamy, it is not a defence that the parties would, if unmarried, have been incompetent to contract marriage under the law of the place where the offence is alleged to have been committed.

(4) Every marriage or form of marriage shall, for the purpose of this section, be deemed to be valid unless the accused establishes that it was invalid.

(5) No act or omission on the part of an accused who is charged with bigamy invalidates a marriage or form of marriage that is otherwise valid.'

Bigamy had first been made a criminal offence in England in 1603.[30] Prior to this it was an ecclesiastical offence. England's criminal provision on bigamy law was aimed at deceptive conduct. It punished those who bigamously married an innocent victim and also couples who sought social acceptance or some other advantage by entering into a bigamous marriage. The existence of a prior marriage was kept secret from the innocent spouse or society at large or both.[31] The bigamy law did not address open polygamy, although polygamy was practised and discussed in Europe at the time.[32] England did not then and has not since criminalised polygamy, in the sense of open, ongoing cohabitation of multiple parties, only bigamy.

Canada's criminal provision on polygamy was not imported from England (or France, Canada's other 'mother country'). It was first enacted in 1890 in response to the criminalisation of polygamy in the US, the renunciation of polygamy by American Mormons and the potential move to Canada of fundamentalist Mormons who wished to continue to practise polygamy.[33] Parliamentary debates and the wording of the provision itself indicate that the law was aimed at the Mormons. Indeed one early unreported case apparently ruled that it applied only to Mormons.[34] However, since 1890 there has only

---

[30] 1 Jac 1, c 11.

[31] The deceptive nature of bigamy, which is misuse of a ceremony that would otherwise be valid to create a state-sanctioned union, was emphasised in *R v Friar* (Ont Co Ct, 1983), unreported, Borins J, as cited in *R v Sauve* [1997] AJ No 525 (Prov Ct) at para 3, put it: 'The essential gravity of the offence remains the deception which the bigamist exhibits, in some cases, where he has said nothing about the original marriage to the new partner; but, perhaps, more importantly which he exhibits in all cases by the falsification of state records in the application for the marriage licence.'

[32] Samuel Chapman *Polygamy, Bigamy and Human Rights Law* (Xlibris, 2001) pp 26–27.

[33] An Act further to amend the Criminal Law, SC 1890, c 37, s 11 (1890). The provision read: 'Every one who practises, or, by the rites, ceremonies, forms, rules or customs of any denomination, sect or society, religious or secular, or by any form of contract, or by mere mutual consent, or by any other method whatsoever, and whether in a manner recognized by law as a binding form of marriage or not, agrees or consents to practise or enter into (a) any form of polygamy; or (b) any kind of conjugal union with more than one person at the same time; or (c) what among the persons commonly called Mormons is known as spiritual or plural marriage; or (d) who lives, cohabits, or agrees or consent to live or cohabit, in any kind of conjugal union with a person who is married to another or others in any kind of conjugal union . . . is guilty of a misdemeanor, and liable to imprisonment for five years and to a fine of five hundred dollars ....'

[34] *R v Liston* (1893) (Toronto assizes, unreported).

ever been one conviction under the polygamy provision, and that was of a native Canadian who had two wives in accordance with tribal customary law.[35]

The references to religion have been expunged, and the current Canadian polygamy provision states:

'293. (1) Every one who

(a) practises or enters into or in any manner agrees or consents to practise or enter into
  (i) any form of polygamy, or
  (ii) any kind of conjugal union with more than one person at the same time,
  whether or not it is by law recognized as a binding form of marriage, or
(b) celebrates, assists or is a party to a rite, ceremony, contract or consent that purports to sanction a relationship mentioned in subparagraph (a)(i) or (ii), is guilty of an indictable offence and liable to imprisonment for a term not exceeding five years.

(2) Where an accused is charged with an offence under this section, no averment or proof of the method by which the alleged relationship was entered into, agreed to or consented to is necessary in the indictment or on the trial of the accused, nor is it necessary on the trial to prove that the persons who are alleged to have entered into the relationship had or intended to have sexual intercourse.'

This broad provision does not contain the limitation included in the US Uniform Model Penal Code provision on polygamy, which provides:[36]

'A person is guilty of polygamy, a felony of the third degree, if he marries or cohabits with more than one spouse at a time in purported exercise of the right of plural marriage. The offense is a continuing one until all cohabitation and claim of marriage with more than one spouse terminates. *This section does not apply to parties to a polygamous marriage, lawful in the country of which they are residents or nationals, while they are in transit through or temporarily visiting this State.*'

On its face, the Canadian provision applies to visitors to Canada who have a valid foreign polygamous marriage. Canada is a monogamous country, but its public policy against polygamy may not require exposing such visitors to the risk of criminal prosecution. There is no obvious state interest in prosecuting transient parties to a polygamous marriage.[37]

The provision applies to all parties to the relationship. It is not limited to blameworthy patriarchs who use their position of authority to acquire multiple

---

[35] *The Queen v Bear's Shin Bone* (1899) 4 Terr LR 173, 3 CCC 329.
[36] American Law Institute, Model Penal Code, art 230.1(2). Author's emphasis.
[37] On this issue it may be useful to consider the fact that most countries do not permit same-sex marriage and many impose criminal penalties on same-sex relations. Canada may be more successful in persuading the latter to be tolerant, at least to the point of not criminalising same-sex married couples visiting from Canada, if we refrain from criminalising their visiting polygamous families.

'wives'. It applies to the women as well. Although law enforcement officers may adopt a policy of not charging the women, casting them as outlaws may in itself be problematic. There is reason to believe that some polygamous families may be isolated and suspicious of government intervention. Casting all members, including the 'victims', as criminals may exacerbate the isolation and suspicion and thereby impede efforts to provide assistance to vulnerable members.

The provision applies to cases involving adults who freely choose to carry on conjugal relationships with multiple parties. It is not limited to cases involving minors or where any of the parties lacked the capacity to consent for any reason. It appears to criminalise consensual egalitarian 'polyamorous' relationships.[38] In light of the fact that state has largely withdrawn from the bedrooms of the nation, it is difficult to see the rationale for intervening in cases of polygamy involving only consenting adults. Such intervention is particularly hard to justify because the crime described in s 293 is difficult to distinguish from adultery, which is not a crime. Because Canadians can carry on adulterous relationships or join swingers clubs without criminal penalty, it cannot credibly be claimed that carrying on conjugal relationships with multiple parties is so violative of our social norms that, like incest, it must be criminalised even when it involves only consenting adults.[39]

Supporters of the polygamy provision argue that it is needed to deal with the harms in closed communities such as Bountiful. Such communities, isolated from mainstream society, particularly those led by patriarchs who control the resources and sexuality of the members and sustained by religious or cult beliefs, have a sorry history.[40] Whether or not polygamy is a feature of such

---

[38]   In the reference case now before the British Columbia Supreme Court, the Attorney-General of British Columbia is arguing that s 293, properly interpreted, is constitutional, and has submitted that: 'on its face and when interpreted in light of its purpose, legislative history, social context, and Canadian and international human rights norms, the prohibition in s. 293 should be interpreted as follows: "Section 293 prohibits marriages or marriage-like relationships involving more than two persons that purport to be (a) sanctioned by an authority having power or influence over the participants and (b) binding on any of the participants."' The Attorney-General has further submitted that: 'The Criminal Code prohibition was and is addressed to the overwhelmingly dominant form of polygamy, and the one most closely associated with demonstrable and apprehended social harms: that is, a patriarchal polygyny that is intergenerationally normalized and enforced through more or less coercive rules and norms of non-state social institutions. Section 293 leaves the balance of multi-partner human sexual behaviour, that which is unrelated to the harms the prohibition seeks to address, unaffected': *Reference re: Criminal Code*, s 293, 2010 BCSC 1308 at para 8. Whatever may be the submissions of the Attorney-General on the proper interpretation of s 293, the provision on its face does not carry the limitations that are suggested. The Attorney-General appears to be inviting the court to effectively rewrite the provision in order that it pass constitutional muster.

[39]   Justices Bastarache and LeBel in *Labaye* at para 109 said that: 'According to contemporary Canadian social morality, acts such as child pornography, incest, polygamy and bestiality are unacceptable regardless of whether or not they cause social harm. The community considers these acts to be harmful in themselves.' Insofar as this statement suggests that polygamy as defined in the Criminal Code is so violative of social norms that criminalisation is justified, I respectfully disagree.

[40]   See, eg, Kate Barlow *Abode of Love: Growing Up in a Messianic Cult* (Goose Lane Editions,

closed communities, there may be concerns about abuse of vulnerable people, particularly children, trapped in such communities and fragile souls who may be drawn to such groups. Governments wanting to address apparent abuses in such communities are greatly challenged. Efforts to rescue vulnerable people from closed communities may have the effect of drawing the group closer together. Some ham-fisted government interventions have been self-defeating or of questionable effect.[41] Even those within the group who perceive problems and would like outside assistance may be distressed by what they perceive as overly zealous or unfair targeting of the community.

The reactions of closed communities that practise polygamy to aggressive criminal enforcement efforts are referred to in the handbook for law enforcement officials published jointly by the Utah and Arizona Attorney-Generals:[42]

> 'The fundamentalists adapted to a secret, underground lifestyle to avoid prosecution and what they perceived as persecution from the "world". Mass arrests were made in some polygamous communities in 1935 and 1944, culminating in the largest raid of that era occurring in 1953, when more than 100 officers descended upon Short Creek (now Hildale, Utah and Colorado City, Arizona) in an aggressive crusade to stamp out polygamy. The husbands were arrested, while the panicked women and children were bussed to southern Arizona. Images of crying children being torn from the arms of polygamous mothers triggered a public relations backlash.
>
> Recently, a community-wide raid took place in the FLDS community near Eldorado, Texas, in April of 2008. Although this raid did not occur in Utah or Arizona, many of the families involved had recently relocated to Texas expressly to distance themselves from perceived persecution. These events have resulted in deep scars among Fundamentalist Mormons and helped to foster a fear of government agencies and a distrust of "outsiders".'

The current strategy outlined in the Utah/Arizona handbook is to increase efforts to enforce laws when child abuse, domestic violence or fraud is alleged, rather than prosecuting for bigamy, or polygamy, per se.[43] Instead of focusing on the polygamous 'lifestyle', the states are working to reduce the fear and distrust of government so that they can provide needed services and education to those remaining in or making the transition out of the polygamous community. The advantage of this strategy is that it may help to decrease the secrecy and isolation that can shield abusers and prevent victims from seeking help.

2006) about the nineteenth-century English group Agapemone formed by a defrocked clergyman who claimed to be guided by the Holy Ghost.

[41]   In the extreme case of the 1993 FBI assault on David Koresh's Branch Davidians in Waco Texas, well-meaning but clumsy government efforts ended in tragedy. See Dick Reavis *The Ashes of Waco: An Investigation* (New York: Simon and Schuster, 1995).

[42]   Utah Attorney-General's Office and Arizona Attorney-General's Office *The Primer: A Handbook for Law Enforcement and Human Services Agencies Who Offer Assistance to Fundamentalist Mormon Families* (updated August 2009) at 8.

[43]   Ibid at 9.

The question in Canada is whether the polygamy provision is a useful tool to deal with potential problems in closed polygamous communities. Because living in a conjugal relationship with more than one person seems no worse than adultery, which is not a crime, those who consider polygamy consistent with their religious beliefs are likely to perceive the provision as evidence of public hostility to their religion. The history of the criminal offence and its terms support the narrative of religious persecution among polygamous groups. Prosecuting for polygamy, rather than dealing directly with child abuse, domestic violence, fraud or other crimes, is likely to appear as persecution and may increase secrecy and isolation.

Supporters of the polygamy provision also argue that it is needed to protect children who might be harmed by polygamy as a result of growing up in a polygamous household and being exposed to polygamy or by becoming a 'child bride' in a polygamous union or by becoming a superfluous 'lost boy' who is ejected from a polygamous community.[44] Preventing such harms would be a justification for criminalisation. Canada's polygamy provision, however, does not target any of these potential harms directly. There is no reference to children in the provision. There is no requirement that there be any children involved for there to be a conviction. The current provision applies whether children are present or not and whether children are harmed or not. The provision is overly broad because it applies to cases involving no children and only consenting adults.

There are provisions in the Criminal Code that directly target harms to children and that might apply to children in polygamous communities. Section 172 of the Criminal Code criminalises adultery, sexual immorality, habitual drunkenness and other forms of vice carried on in the home of a child if the effect is to endanger the morals of the child. These behaviours generally carry no criminal penalty but do so when it can be shown that they endanger children. As for cases of minors becoming 'wives' in polygamous unions, the Criminal Code imposes sanctions for sexual activity with children and, in particular, for sexual touching of minors by those in a position of trust or authority towards the child, or who is someone with whom the young person is in a relationship of dependency, or who is in a relationship with a young person that is exploitive of that young person.[45]

In addition to the Criminal Code provisions, there is also child protection legislation, which allows authorities to apprehend children who are in need of protection.[46] It should also be noted that the laws of each province restrict the marriage of minors. In British Columbia, for example, parties under the age of 19 (the age of majority in that province[47]) may not marry without the consent

---

[44] The terms are borrowed from Daphne Bramham *The Secret Lives of Saints: Child Brides and Lost Boys in a Polygamous Mormon Sect* (Random House Canada, 2008).

[45] Criminal Code, s 153.

[46] See, eg, Child, Family and Community Service Act, RSBC 1996, c 46.

[47] Age of Majority Act, RSBC 1996, c 7, s 1.

of their parents (or parent substitutes) or a court order, and parties under the age of 16 cannot be married without a court order.[48]

Canada's polygamy provision at best offers an indirect way of preventing possible harms to children. The criminal provisions that directly deal with harms to children and current child protection legislation and marriage laws (and other laws, including education laws and child labour laws) appear to address potential harms to children in polygamous families.

Supporters of the polygamy provision also argue that it is needed to address the harms to women involved in polygamous relationships. Polygamy is associated with gender inequality, and Canada is committed to eliminating discrimination against women. Canada has obligations under the Canadian Charter of Rights and Freedoms and the Convention on Civil and Political Rights and the Convention on the Elimination of All Forms of Discrimination Against Women to ensure gender equality and eliminate discrimination against women. The Committee on the Elimination of Discrimination Against Women issued a General Recommendation 1994, stating:[49]

> '14. States parties' reports also disclose that polygamy is practised in a number of countries. Polygamous marriage contravenes a woman's right to equality with men, and can have such serious emotional and financial consequences for her and her dependents that such marriages ought to be discouraged and prohibited. The Committee notes with concern that some States parties, whose constitutions guarantee equal rights, permit polygamous marriage in accordance with personal or customary law. This violates the constitutional rights of women, and breaches the provisions of article 5 (a) of the Convention'.

Rebecca Cook and Lisa Kelly noted that:[50]

> 'Beyond international human rights treaty law, it is clear that customary international law requires the prohibition or at the least restriction of polygyny. Surveying state practice, it is evident that the majority of states prohibit the practice.'

Supporters of the polygamy provision argue that it is needed to comply with international human rights treaties and the Canadian Charter of Rights and Freedoms. However, a distinction must be drawn between giving state sanction to polygamous marriages on one hand, and criminalising the practice of living in a conjugal relationship with more than one person on the other. Canada, like most Western countries, does not permit polygamous marriages under its marriage laws. Furthermore Canada, like many Western countries, criminalises bigamy. It is not at all clear that, in addition, a criminal prohibition against living in a conjugal relationship with more than one person is necessary, and many monogamous countries have not enacted such a law. If polygamous

---

48 Marriage Act, RSBC 1996, c 282, ss 28 and 29.
49 General Recommendation No 21 (13th session, 1994).
50 Rebecca Cook and Lisa Kelly 'Polygyny and Canada's Obligations under International Human Rights Law' (September 2006), research report for Department of Justice Canada, in part VA.

marriages are not permitted under a country's civil marriage laws and if bigamy is a crime, the country has established that it is a monogamous country that 'prohibits' polygamy and in compliance with human rights norms. There are no reports of international human rights bodies suggesting that monogamous countries that do not permit polygamous marriages and criminalise bigamy must also criminalise the practice of carrying on a conjugal relationship with more than one person in order to comply with their human rights obligations. Nor is it at all clear that carrying on a conjugal relationship with more than one person, in and of itself, violates the guarantee of gender equality.

In polygamous countries, polygamy is legal and endorsed by the state, which extends the status of marriage and incidents of marriage to those who enter into this unequal form of marriage. Legalised polygamy is part of a package of laws, policies and practices that maintain gender inequality in polygamous countries. The package often includes one-sided divorce laws, and unequal access to education and economic opportunities for women. The obligation under the United Nations human rights conventions is to get rid of or at the very least restrict state-sanctioned legal polygamy. This obligation does not require that carrying on a conjugal relationship with more than one person be criminalised.

Supporters of the provision also argue that it is needed to protect Canada from immigration by polygamous families. Canada's immigration laws protect Canada's monogamous character by excluding multiple spouses from the family reunification programme and from the list of family members who can immigrate with a successful applicant.[51] In addition, applicants who qualify independently may be deemed 'inadmissible' for 'criminality' – applications will be turned down if there are reasonable grounds for an immigration officer to believe that an applicant will commit an offence under the polygamy provision.[52] The polygamy provision, then, provides a basis for determining

---

[51]   The Immigration and Refugee Protection Regulations (SOR/2002–227), s 117(9)(c), provides: '(9) A foreign national shall not be considered a member of the family class by virtue of their relationship to a sponsor if . . . (b) the foreign national is the sponsor's spouse, common-law partner or conjugal partner, the sponsor has an existing sponsorship undertaking in respect of a spouse, common-law partner or conjugal partner and the period referred to in subsection 132(1) in respect of that undertaking has not ended; (c) the foreign national is the sponsor's spouse and (i) the sponsor or the foreign national was, at the time of their marriage, the spouse of another person, or (ii) the sponsor has lived separate and apart from the foreign national for at least one year and (a) the sponsor is the common-law partner of another person or the conjugal partner of another foreign national, or (b) the foreign national is the common-law partner of another person or the conjugal partner of another sponsor ....'

[52]   Immigration and Refugee Protection Act, SC 2001, c 27, I-2.5, s 36(2)(d), which provides: 'A foreign national is inadmissible on grounds of criminality for committing, on entering Canada, an offence under an Act of Parliament prescribed by regulations.' This must be read in light of s 33, which provides: 'The facts that constitute inadmissibility under sections 34 to 37 include facts arising from omissions and, unless otherwise provided, include facts for which there are reasonable grounds to believe that they have occurred, are occurring or may occur.' See, eg, *Ali v Canada (Minister of Citizenship and Immigration)* [1998] FCJ No 1640 (TD); *Awwad v Canada (Minister of Citizenship and Immigration)* [1999] FCJ No 103; [1999] ACF no 103; 162 FTR 209; 85 ACWS (3d) 892.

that an applicant is inadmissible for criminality. Canada could more directly carry out its policy of not permitting immigration of polygamists by including in the list of those who are inadmissible to Canada anyone who is coming to Canada to practise polygamy. This direct approach is used in other countries, for example, the United States.[53]

If it were not a crime to carry on a conjugal relationship with more than one person at a time, it would not follow that there would be a constitutional right to marry more than one person at a time or that more than one person could be sponsored for immigration as a 'conjugal partner'. A person with standing could bring a constitutional challenge to Canada's marriage law, which permits only monogamous marriages, or to the exclusion of polygamous parties from the category of eligible family members under the immigration law. It is highly unlikely that any such challenge would be successful, but this issue is distinct from the issue of retaining criminal prohibition of polygamy. Protecting Canada's monogamous marriage law and immigration policy from constitutional challenges does not depend on making the practice of living in a conjugal relationship with more than one person a criminal offence.

As the constitutional reference proceeds through the courts, it is to be hoped that the confusion relating to the issues will be cleared away. This confusion is in part based on confusion between 'decriminalisation' and 'legalisation'. 'Decriminalisation' refers to repealing the criminal offence of polygamy. Some people use the term 'legalisation' as a synonym for 'decriminalisation,' in other words, to mean repeal of the polygamy provision. Others use 'legalisation' to mean changing the marriage laws to allow polygamous marriages to take place. It is important to clarify that decriminalisation does *not* mean changing the marriage laws to allow polygamous marriages to take place. Eliminating the criminal prohibition against polygamy would not change the civil laws, which do not permit polygamous marriages to take place in Canada.

There is also confusion in the use of the terms 'prohibit,' 'ban' and 'criminalise'. Sometimes the terms 'prohibit' or 'ban' are used as synonyms for 'criminalise', but other times these terms are used to describe the effect of civil marriage laws that do not permit polygamy. This can lead to misunderstandings. For example, a Canadian government report says that 'In the United Kingdom, polygamy is also prohibited'.[54] This may lead readers to think that polygamy is a crime. But Britain does not have a criminal offence of polygamy, only bigamy. This is also an instance of the confusion in the use of the terms 'polygamy' and 'bigamy'.

The Law Reform Commission of Canada noted that:[55]

---

[53] See, eg, Immigration and Nationality Act, 8 USC 1182, s 212(15)(A): 'Any immigrant who is coming to the United States to practice polygamy is inadmissible.'

[54] Rebecca Cook and Lisa Kelly 'Polygyny and Canada's Obligations under International Human Rights Law' (September 2006), research report for Department of Justice Canada, in part V4.

[55] Law Reform Commission of Canada *Bigamy* Working Paper 42 (Ottawa: Law Reform Commission of Canada, 1985) at 13.

' . . . polygamy consists in the maintaining of conjugal relations by more than two persons. When the result of such relations is to form a single matrimonial or family entity with the spouses, this is regarded as polygamous marriage . . . The maintaining of more than one monogamous union by the same person corresponds with the popular notion of bigamy . . . In legal terms, however, [polygamy and bigamy] have a more specific meaning. In particular bigamy, which is defined in relation to the legal institution of marriage, is distinguished from polygamy by the requirement of formal marital ties.'

As the terms are used in Canada's Criminal Code, 'bigamy' is going through a form of marriage while married to someone else. 'Polygamy' is the practice of living in a conjugal relationship with more than one person at the same time. Some use the term 'polygamy' to mean 'bigamy'. For example, a reporter wrote that 'polygamy' is illegal in Britain and punishable by imprisonment for up to 7 years,[56] but, as already noted, polygamy is not a criminal offence in Britain, and it is bigamy that is punishable by imprisonment for up to 7 years.

It is particularly important to be specific as to what is meant by 'ban,' 'prohibit' and 'criminalise' and by 'polygamy' and 'bigamy' in the comparative law context. Policy makers may well look to what other jurisdictions have done in relation to polygamy. The material cited above may well give the impression that Britain has a criminal offence of polygamy, when in fact it does not. Many countries maintain their monogamous character without creating a criminal offence of polygamy, and it is helpful to know that.

Confusion has also arisen in regard to use of the term 'recognition'. Canada does not 'recognise' polygamous unions by extending status to such unions under its domestic laws, but it does 'recognise' valid foreign polygamous marriages, as do most Western countries. The recognition of valid foreign polygamous marriages does not vitiate Canada's character as a monogamous country or suggest endorsement of polygamy. Incidents of marriage – the rights and obligations, benefits and burdens that flow from marital status – are extended to valid foreign polygamous marriages only to the extent that doing so does not violate Canada's public policy. Canada's commitment to monogamy does not require a blanket refusal to extend the incidents of marriage to those validly married in polygamous countries. Any such blanket refusal would disproportionately affect the women, because it would effectively strip them of the marital rights that they reasonably expected to enjoy as the result of entering into a legally valid marriage in their home country.

---

[56] Susan Martiuk 'Polygamous marriages drain taxpayer dollars' *Calgary Herald*, 15 February 2008. See also Christina Hall 'Bay City Wife Charged With Polygamy' *Detroit Free Press*, 5 September 2009. See also 4 Am & Eng Enc L (2d ed) 39: 'Bigamy, or polygamy, therefore consists in the making of the unlawful contract and the abuse of the formality which the law has enjoined as requisite to the creation of the marital relation. And it is the abuse of this formal and solemn contract, by entering into it a second time when a former husband or wife is still living, which the law forbids because of its outrage upon public decency, its violation of the public economy, as well as its tendency to cheat one into a surrender of the person under the appearance of right.'

III PROPERTY RIGHTS OF UNMARRIED COHABITANTS

Some Canadian provinces and territories have extended statutory family property rights and obligations to unmarried couples who have cohabited for a defined period.[57] Most jurisdictions in Canada, however, do not include unmarried couples in their family property regimes. An argument that this exclusion violates the Canadian Charter of Rights and Freedoms by discriminating on the basis of marital status was rejected by the Supreme Court of Canada in 2002.[58] Therefore, most unmarried parties must look outside of family law to claim a share of the property accumulated during cohabitation.

Courts in common law Canada have a long history of using trust doctrines to remedy inequitable divisions of family property. These doctrines were initially used for married couples. After the doctrine of coverture was modified by the introduction of Married Women's Property Acts, women no longer ceded ownership of their property to their husbands on marriage. Under the new system of separate property each spouse owned his or her own property, and on dissolution of a marriage, each spouse was entitled to his or her own property.[59] Because of the sexual division of labour within families, however, most often men acquired more assets during marriage than did women. Property claims were based on title, not on rights and obligations arising from the marital relationship. Women without their own means could be left propertyless under the separate property regime. Unless they held title to property acquired during the marriage, they had no claim to share in it. So applying a system of separate property on dissolution of marriage meant that men often left marriage with all or most of the assets that the family had accumulated. Courts used trust doctrine to remedy this situation.

The primary doctrine used to give women a share of marital property was the resulting trust. If a wife contributed to the purchase price of property taken in the name of the husband, the court would apply the presumption that a beneficial interest in the property resulted back to the wife.[60] The resulting trust device was expanded to apply to cases where the contribution of the wife to the acquisition of property was indirect. This indirect contribution could take the form of such actions as providing labour during construction of the matrimonial home or paying household costs while the husband acquired title

---

[57] Family Property Act, CCSM, c F25, s 1, 2.1 (Manitoba, 2 years cohabitation); Family Law Act, SNWT 1997, s 18, ss 1, 36 (Northwest Territories, 2 years cohabitation or less if child); Family Law Act, SNWT (Nu), ss 1, 36 (Nunavut, 2 years cohabitation or less if child); Family Property Act, SS 1997, c F-6.3, ss 2, 21 (Saskatchewan, 2 years cohabitation).

[58] *Attorney-General of Nova Scotia v Walsh* [2002] 4 SCR 325.

[59] Lori Chambers *Married Women and Property Law in Victorian Ontario* (Toronto: University of Toronto Press, 1997); Berend Hovius and Timothy G Youdan *The Law of Family Property* (Scarborough: Carswell, 1991).

[60] *Re Whitely* (1974) 4 OR (2d) 293 (CA).

to the matrimonial home.[61] The doctrine of resulting trust was also applied where the contribution of the non-titled spouse was to the improvement, rather than the acquisition, of property.[62]

Under the traditional doctrine of resulting trust, the presumed intention of the contributor is that a beneficial interest in the property proportionate to the contribution should result back to the contributor. But the expansion of the doctrine to apply to indirect financial contributions or non-financial contributions created challenges in determining whether a presumption arose and the extent of the interest of the contributor. Courts focused increasingly on the 'common intention' of the parties to resolve these challenges. In the infamous case of *Murdoch v Murdoch*, the evidence was that during her 25-year marriage the wife had made substantial contributions of physical labour not only doing household work but as a rancher.[63] She was responsible for 'haying, raking, swathing, moving, driving trucks and tractors and teams, quietening horses, taking cattle back and forth to the reserve, dehorning, vaccinating, branding, anything that was to be done'.[64] Her claim for an equal share of the family property that was acquired during the marriage but held in the name of the husband was dismissed. The majority found that there was no common intention that ownership of the property was to be shared, and therefore her trust-based claim was dismissed.[65]

The doctrine of resulting trust did not provide an adequate tool to deal with family property division, and Canadian courts after the *Murdoch* case turned the unjust enrichment and the 'remedial constructive trust' to divide family property.[66] At the same time, provincial and territorial marital property legislation created a statutory right to a division of marital property. While married parties now rely on the family property statutes, most unmarried cohabitants continue to assert claims based on unjust enrichment or resulting trust in order to claim a share of property.

Remedial constructive trusts provide a proprietary remedy in situations of unjust enrichment. In a series of cases decided by the Supreme Court of Canada in the 1970s and 1980s, women who had contributed substantially in money and labour to the acquisition and improvement of property owned by their husband or unmarried intimate partner were awarded a beneficial interest in the property by way of a constructive trust.[67] Claimants to ownership by way of constructive trust must prove four things:

---

61 *Madisso v Madisso* (1975) 21 RFL 51 (Ont CA); *Trueman v Trueman* 5 RFL 54 (Alta CA).
62 *Rathwell v Rathwell* [1978] 2 SCR 436.
63 [1975] 1 SCR 423.
64 Ibid at para 47.
65 *Murdoch v Murdoch* [1975] 1 SCR 423.
66 *Pettkus v Becker* [1980] 2 SCR 834.
67 *Rathwell v Rathwell* [1978] SCR 436; *Pettkus v Becker*, ibid; *Sorochan v Sorochan* [1986] 2 SCR 38.

(1)   that by their contributions of money or labour they have enriched the legal title holder of the property in question;

(2)   that the enrichment of the other has resulted in a corresponding deprivation of the contributor;

(3)   that there is no juristic reason for the enrichment, such as a contract or legal obligation to make the contribution; and

(4)   that there is a nexus (or 'causal connection') between the deprivation of the plaintiff and the property in question.

The first three elements are the elements of unjust enrichment. If unjust enrichment can be proven, but there is no nexus between the plaintiff's deprivation and the property in question, the court can award monetary compensation.

Courts have sometimes been willing to find a causal connection and to award a property interest even without direct contribution to the property itself. For example, where the claimant, by taking almost complete responsibility for childcare and household management, has freed the title holder to acquire property, the Supreme Court has granted the claimant a proprietary remedy by way of constructive trust. This was the case in *Peter v Beblow*, a major decision of the Supreme Court of Canada on unjust enrichment and remedial constructive trusts in the context of unmarried cohabitation.[68] In *Peter v Beblow*, the court ruled that if the claimant is entitled to the proprietary remedy of a constructive trust, the value of the trust is to be determined on the basis of the 'value survived' approach, in other words, according to the portion of the actual value of the property in question that is attributable to the claimant's services. The court suggested in obiter dicta that if the claimant is entitled only to monetary compensation, the amount should be assessed on a quantum meruit basis, balancing the benefits and detriments to the claimant from the relationship.

With the development of the doctrine of unjust enrichment and the remedial constructive trust, there has been uncertainty about the continuing role of the resulting trust, and, in particular, the doctrinally questionable development of the resulting trust based on the common intention of the parties that was developed in an effort to provide relief on breakdown of relationships. In regard to claims based on unjust enrichment, there has been a division among Canadian courts in cases where money damages, rather than a remedial constructive trust, is the appropriate remedy. Some courts have ruled that the 'value survived' approach may be used when quantifying a monetary award,[69] while others have ruled that the 'value received' approach must be used for

---

[68]   [1993] 1 SCR 980.
[69]   See, eg, *Panara v Di Ascenzo* (2005) 16 RFL (6th) 177 (Alta CA).

monetary awards.[70] This issue is of great practical significance, because the 'value survived' approach inevitably results in a higher amount than does the 'value received' approach, which is simply a quantum meruit calculation. The former would result in a percentage share of the property acquired by the couple during the relationship, whereas the latter would result in payment for the services of the claimant, taking into account the benefits received by the claimant.

These continuing problems in relation to resulting trusts and unjust enrichment were addressed by the Supreme Court of Canada in two cases that were heard together, *Kerr v Baranow* and *Vanasse v Seguin*.[71] The Court ruled that the resulting trust arising solely from the common intention of the parties is no longer good law in Canada. The Court rejected the doctrinally questionable modifications of the traditional doctrine and clarified that the proper role for the doctrine of resulting trusts in domestic cases is to address gratuitous transfers of property from one party to the other, or cases where both parties contributed to the acquisition of property but title was taken in the name of only one.

As for claims of unjust enrichment, the Court addressed three issues that have given rise to difficulties: (1) assessment of monetary awards; (2) balancing benefits and detriments when calculating a monetary award; and (3) the parties' reasonable or legitimate expectations.

On the issue of assessing monetary awards, the courts rejected the notion that there is a 'remedial dichotomy', that is, the 'view that there are only two choices of remedy for an unjust enrichment: a monetary award, assessed on a fee-for-services basis; or a proprietary one (generally taking the form of a remedial constructive trust), where the claimant can show that the benefit conferred contributed to the acquisition, preservation, maintenance, or improvement of specific property'.[72] The Court ruled that there should be flexibility in the approach taken to monetary awards, and that limiting the power of courts to a 'fee-for-services' calculation is inappropriate. The Court reasoned that inevitably using a quantum meruit approach: (1) 'fails to reflect the reality of the lives of many domestic partners'; (2) 'is inconsistent with the inherent flexibility of unjust enrichment'; and (3) 'ignores the historical basis of *quantum meruit* claims'.[73]

In some cases a quantum meruit award is appropriate for unjust enrichment. But '[w]here the unjust enrichment is best characterized as an unjust retention of a disproportionate share of assets accumulated during the course of . . . a "joint family venture" to which both partners have contributed, the monetary remedy should reflect that fact'.[74] In such cases, the monetary award for unjust

---

[70]	See, eg, *Bell v Bailey* (2001) 203 DLR (4th) 589, (Ont CA).
[71]	2011 SCC 10.
[72]	Ibid at para 57.
[73]	Ibid at para 58.
[74]	Ibid at para 80.

enrichment should be assessed, not on a quantum meruit basis, but 'by determining the proportionate contribution of the claimant to the accumulation of the wealth'.[75]

The Court noted that unmarried couples form a diverse group, and that not all such couples could be described as engaging in a 'joint family venture' sufficient to attract the deviation from a quantum meruit assessment. The Court outlined factors that should be considered in determining whether parties were engaged in a joint family venture. The first of these factors was 'whether the parties worked collaboratively towards common goals'. The Court noted that '[i]ndicators such as the pooling of effort and team work, the decision to have and raise children together, and the length of the relationship may all point towards the extent, if any, to which the parties have formed a true partnership and jointly worked towards important mutual goals'.[76] The second factor was the existence of economic interdependence and integration. The Court commented that '[t]he more extensive the integration of the couple's finances, economic interests and economic well-being, the more likely it is that they should be considered as having been engaged in a joint family venture'.[77] Evidence that the parties prioritised the welfare of the family unit over their individual interests will be relevant in regard to this factor. The third factor was the intention of the parties, either express or inferred. The final factor is the extent to which the parties gave priority to the family in their decision making.

The Court went on to address the difficult question of balancing benefits and detriments when calculating monetary awards for unjust enrichment. The Court first addressed cases where such balancing will not be required. Those are the joint family venture cases where the remedy will be a share of the wealth proportionate to the claimant's contributions. The Court commented that:[78]

'Once the claimant has established his or her contribution to a joint family venture, and a link between that contribution and the accumulation of wealth, the respective contributions of the parties are taken into account in determining the claimant's proportionate share. While determining the proportionate contributions of the parties is not an exact science, it generally does not call for a minute examination of the give and take of daily life. It calls, rather, for the reasoned exercise of judgment in light of all of the evidence.'

Where a quantum meruit award is the appropriate remedy for unjust enrichment, it will be appropriate to carry out a balancing of benefits and detriments. For those cases, the Court ruled that 'mutual benefit conferral' can be taken into account at two stages. It can be considered when determining whether unjust enrichment has been proven, specifically in regard to whether or not there was any juristic reason for the enrichment of the defendant. At that point mutual benefit conferral can be considered if it provides relevant evidence

---

[75]   Ibid at para 81.
[76]   Ibid at para 90.
[77]   Ibid at para 92.
[78]   Ibid at para 102.

of the existence of a juristic reason for the enrichment. Mutual benefit conferral should also be considered at the remedy stage in accordance with established principles of quantum meruit claims, where any benefits that flowed from the defendant to the claimant are taken into account by reducing the claimant's recovery.

Finally, the Court expressly reduced the role of the reasonable expectations of the parties in claims of unjust enrichment. The Court noted that these expectations have been significant in regard to whether there was a juristic reason for the enrichment, and acknowledged that they may continue to play a minor role in that determination.

The decision of the Court in *Kerr v Baranow* and *Vanasse v Seguin* has provided much needed clarity to the doctrines of resulting trust and unjust enrichment in the context of unmarried cohabitation. Most important was the Court's ruling that monetary awards for unjust enrichment are not necessarily limited to quantum meruit assessments and do not always require a balancing of benefit and detriments. The availability of monetary awards that are calculated as a proportionate share of the wealth acquired during cohabitation for couples who engaged in a joint family venture is a significant increase in the rights of claimants.

IV   SUPPORT FOR UNMARRIED COHABITANTS

On 24 March 2011, the Supreme Court of Canada granted leave to appeal in an important case from Quebec relating to the support rights of unmarried cohabitants.[79] Quebec is the only province in Canada that does not extend support rights and obligations to parties who are not either married or a party to a civil union. This regime affects a large percentage of the population – according to the 2006 census, in 28.8% of all families in Quebec the couples were unmarried.[80] Quebec accommodates couples who do not wish to marry by maintaining a civil union scheme that is available to parties of the same or opposite sex and that carries with it the rights and obligations available to married couples under Quebec law. But parties who are not married or in a civil union are not included in Quebec's family laws. This exclusion is for a principled reason. Quebec has taken the view that thrusting the private law rights and obligations of marriage on those who have not chosen to marry violates autonomy rights.[81]

---

[79] *Attorney-General of Quebec, et al v A et al* (SCC) docket number 33990, 24 March 2011.

[80] Statistics Canada 'Census families by number of children at home, by province and territory (2006 Census)(Quebec)' available at www40.statcan.gc.ca/l01/cst01/famil50f-eng.htm (accessed May 2011).

[81] Back in 1998, then Minister of Justice Serge Ménard stated: 'Lorsque le législateur a révisé le droit de la famille, tant en 1980 qu'en 1991, il s'est interrogé sur l'opportunité de prévoir des conséquences civiles aux unions de fait. S'il s'est abstenu de le faire, c'est par respect pour la volonté des conjoints: quand ils ne se marient pas, c'est qu'ils ne veulent pas se soumettre au régime légal du mariage.': Quebec, Debates of the National Assembly, 18 June 1998.

Because the Quebec court does not permit the parties to be identified by name, the media has dubbed it the 'Lola' and 'Eric' case. Eric is well-know billionaire, who met Lola in her native Brazil in 1992, when he was 32 and she was just 17. Their 10-year relationship produced three children, who receive substantial child support. Lola challenged the exclusion of unmarried parties from Quebec's support scheme. She was unsuccessful at trial, but her appeal was granted. The Quebec Court of Appeal ruled that the law was discriminatory. Now the Supreme Court of Canada will make a final ruling on the issue.

In 2002, the Supreme Court of Canada ruled that family property statutes that extend only to married persons the presumptive right to an equal share of a couple's property in the event of separation or death were constitutional.[82] In that ruling, the Court emphasised the importance of respecting the personal autonomy and dignity of individuals by not imposing on them rights and benefits that they did not choose. Exclusion of unmarried couples was not considered by the Court to be based on stereotype or presumed characteristics that perpetuate the notion that such couples are less worthy of respect or less valued members of society.

Whether the same emphasis on personal autonomy will prevail in the Lola and Eric case is doubtful. In the 2002 case, the distinction between support on one hand and marital property on the other was explicitly addressed. Justice Gonthier, in a concurring opinion, stated that family property division is aimed at dividing assets according to the regime chosen by parties, either explicitly or implicitly by getting married. In contrast, stated Gonthier J, the purpose of support laws, which generally apply to both marriage and cohabitation, is to meet the needs of spouses and children. Family property schemes are contractual in nature, while support laws are not contractual but rather responsive to situations of dependency. Most commentators expect that this distinction will be reiterated in the Lola and Eric case, and that the decision of the Quebec Court of Appeal that the Quebec law is unconstitutional will be upheld.

---

[82]   *Attorney-General of Nova Scotia v Walsh* [2002] 4 SCR 325.

China

GENDER MAINSTREAMING IN THE FAMILY LAW OF THE PEOPLE'S REPUBLIC OF CHINA

*Wang Wei**

Résumé

L'égalité entre hommes et femmes est l'égalité non seulement littérale ou formelle, mais aussi, de manière plus importante encore, l'égalité réelle, dans l'essence et dans le résultat. La loi familiale en République Populaire de Chine, basée sur le principe d'égalité entre hommes et femmes, promouvant l'intégration du genre et augmentant l'égalité des sexes, a une grande valeur. Cependant, du point de vue du genre, la loi actuelle n'est pas parfaite. Pour protéger les droits de la femme dans la pratique juridique, nous devrions présenter le concept de genre, prendre raisonnablement en considération les femmes dans la législation et poursuivre l'effort d'intégration du genre.

I INTRODUCTION

Equality between men and women is a symbol of civilisation and progress of a society. But what do we mean by equality? The theory of gender is an improvement on the traditional theory on the issue of equality between men and women. The theory of gender aims at eliminating real inequality between men and women and realising the essential equality between them. Gender mainstreaming, as a global strategy to promote gender equality, has been embodied in the public policy of the People's Republic of China. This chapter studies family law in the People's Republic of China, examines the progress of gender mainstreaming in China, and raises questions about relevant legislation and practice from the perspective of the theory of gender, advocating further advancement of gender mainstreaming and equality between men and women.

*   Institute of Administration in Dongguan, Guangdong 523083, China.

II   EQUALITY BETWEEN MEN AND WOMEN AND GENDER MAINSTREAMING

Men and women are not only discriminated against in the sense of sex, but also and more importantly, there is discrimination in the sense of gender. The latter concept embraces how a society's culture views the differences and similarities between men and women.[1] The concept of 'gender' was first advanced by American anthropologist Gagle Rubin in 1975.[2] Expanded by feminists, it spawned 'the theory of gender'. According to this theory, the culture in society defines women's and men's personalities or characteristics, as well as their different functions and opportunities in the economy and culture. The theory of gender attempts to construct a kind of equal and mutual companionate relationship based on mutual respect, namely the dynamic equality of gender. To achieve gender equality, different conduct, different expectations and different requirements of men and women should be considered, evaluated and treated equally. All persons, whether male or female, free from the restriction of diversified prejudice, rigid views on the role of gender, and various forms of discrimination, should be able to develop their personal abilities and to make choices freely.[3]

Gender mainstreaming, also known as gender equality mainstreaming or bringing a gender perspective into mainstreaming, has been developing since the United Nation's Third World's Conference on Women in 1985. The Platform for Action adopted by the United Nation's Fourth World Conference on Women in 1995 points out that a gender perspective should be brought into mainstreaming in all fields of society. In 1997, the United Nations Economic and Social Council defined the concept of gender mainstreaming as follows:[4]

> 'Mainstreaming a gender perspective is the process of assessing the implications for women and men of any planned action, including legislation, policies or programmes, in any area and at all levels. It is a strategy for making the concerns and experiences of women as well as of men an integral part of the design, implementation, monitoring and evaluation of policies and programmes in all political, economic and societal spheres, so that women and men benefit equally, and inequality is not perpetuated. The ultimate goal of mainstreaming is to achieve gender equality.'

---

[1]   Tan Jingchan and Xin Chunyin (eds) *English-Chinese Legal Dictionary on Women and Law* (Beijing: CTPC, UNESCO, 1995) p 145.
[2]   Gagle Rubin *The Traffic in Women* (Master's thesis, University of Michigan, 1974).
[3]   Wang Liping 'Equality Between Man and Woman and Woman's Human Rights Protection' in Chen Wei (ed) *Study on Family Law* (Beijing: the Mass Press, 2006) p 36.
[4]   See www.ilo.org/public/english/bureau/gender/newsite2002/about/defin.htm.

III THE COURSE OF GENDER MAINSTREAMING IN FAMILY LAW IN THE PEOPLE'S REPUBLIC OF CHINA

The Chinese government has all along paid much attention to equality between men and women, as well as the protection of women's rights. At present, China has constructed a legal system based on the Constitution, taking the Law of Woman's Rights Protection as a main part, and including relevant laws and regulations, so as to promote women's development and protect women's rights. As far as family law is concerned, the Family Law 1950, the Family Law 1980, and the amended Family Law 2001 greatly reflect the course of gender mainstreaming in the family law of the People's Republic of China.

The Family Law 1950, the first family law code since the founding of the People's Republic of China, declared at the very beginning that the feudal marriage system (such as marriage upon the arbitrary decision of a third party), mercenary marriage, and disregard of women's rights, were abrogated. A modern Western marriage system based on the free choice of partners, on monogamy, on equality between men and women, and on the protection of the lawful rights and interests of women and children was applied. Two-thirds of this Act aimed to protect women who had been subject to exploitation and oppression which had been in place for centuries. Articles on matrimonial property and custody of children after divorce in this Law fundamentally embodied the idea of the protection of women's rights. At this stage, the protection of women's lawful rights and interests was mainly implemented by way of protective policies; women's social status was increased though it was constrained. Anyway, the Family Law 1950 changed the role of women remarkably at the time. Consciously or not, it was the first step in the course of gender mainstreaming in the family law of the People's Republic of China.

The Family Law 1980, which carries over the spirit of the Family Law 1950, reiterates its basic principle of equality between men and women, and makes some necessary amendments to the content. On the issue of the relationship between husband and wife, the Family Law 1980 explicitly provides for the equal status of husband and wife within the family; on the issue of matrimonial property, the Family Law 1980 abandons provisions in the Family Law 1950 that the property that belonged to the wife before marriage was to belong to the wife after marriage; on the issue of divorce, the Family Law 1980 adds a provision that divorce shall be granted if mediation fails because mutual affection no longer exists; on issues such as matrimonial domicile, children's surname and given name, the Family Law 1980 pays much attention to carrying out the basic principle of equality between man and woman. The Family Law 1980 also tries to achieve equality between man and woman by way of protective policies for women. It relies more on the government to protect women's lawful rights and interests, but embraces less practical gender mainstreaming. It is difficult to change women's weak status in respect of family violence, housework and cohabitation in this way. Although the Family Law 1980 strengthens and refines the principle of equality between man and woman, the gender perspective was not mainstreamed.

When the Family Law of the People's Republic of China was amended in 2001, gender mainstreaming was regarded by the United Nations as a global strategy to promote gender equality, and thus became an international trend. Using the theory of gender more or less, legislators recognised the actual differences between men and women, and did not try to adapt women to society but to alter the social system and social structure to accommodate differences between men and women.[5] The amended Family Law, with respect to rural women's vulnerability in the matter of property disposition and debt payment at the time of divorce, prescribes that the rights and interests enjoyed by the husband or the wife in contracting land management on a household basis[6] shall be protected in accordance with the law; with respect to women's domestic role, it stipulates the right to request compensation for housework at the time of divorce.[7] Gender analysis is also embodied in related articles on economic assistance at the time of divorce, the innocent party's right to claim compensation at the time of divorce and family violence. Conflict between women's awareness and women's dependence on the family has been emphasised, and gender inequality within the family has been addressed. The amended Family Law of the People's Republic of China made notable progress in promoting gender mainstreaming.

IV   GENDER ANALYSIS OF CURRENT FAMILY LAW OF THE PEOPLE'S REPUBLIC OF CHINA

Since the foundation of the People's Republic of China, its family law has been committed to realising equality between men and women; the current Family Law contains no obvious provisions discriminating against women, but it includes a few protective provisions for women. However, if we examine specific provisions from the gender perspective, we might find that neutral legislation ignores the essential diversity between men and women, still lacking an awareness of gender.

---

[5]   Teresa Rees 'Model of Equal Opportunities: Reparative Policy, Adaptive Policy and Reformative Policy' (2002) 2 *Collection of woman's studies* 4.

[6]   This is something special in China. Land in China is owned by the state in urban areas, and by the community in rural areas. Since 1978, the government affirmed a kind of contract made between a family (household) and its community in rural areas. According to the contract, the family promises to use the land owned by the community for agriculture planting, aquaculture, pasturage, etc. Proceeds from the land then belong to the family, after paying an amount of money to the community.

[7]   According to art 40 of the amended Family Law, where the husband and the wife agree in writing that the property acquired by them during the period in which they are under contract of marriage is in their separate possession, if one party has performed more duties in respect of bringing up the child, taking care of the old and assisting the other party in work, that party shall, at the time of divorce, have the right to request the other party to make compensation for the above, and the other party shall do so accordingly.

(a)   Gender analysis of marriage contract law

Article 6 of the current Family Law concerns the age at which marriage may be contracted. It provides that no marriage may be contracted before the man has reached 22 years of age and the woman 20 years of age. This kind of regulation affirms the traditional convention of old husband and young wife, and takes the woman's physiological characteristics into account. However, in practice it confirms the traditional marriage and family structure, in which the man is respected and the woman is ignored. It also leads to inequality of available people when men and women are seeking partners. On the one hand, a man may marry a woman who is younger than him, but a woman, especially a divorced woman, usually can only choose a man who is older than her; on the other hand, a woman may get married to a man older than her, but if a man married a woman who is older than him, the marriage deviates from the norm. Different age requirements between men and women for when a marriage may be entered contravenes the principle of equality between men and women.[8]

'Non-marital cohabitation', the relationship between two unmarried persons who live together like husband and wife publicly and lastingly without getting married, was not mentioned in the amended Marriage Law 2001. Judicial interpretations afterwards ignored de facto marriage, and disallowed lawsuits arising from non-marital cohabitation. The current laws and regulations of China endorse a policy of no protection and no intervention in non-marital relationships. This attitude goes against the protection of the vulnerable party in non-marital relationships, usually associated with the female partner. Consistent with the growing strength of the right which people have to choose their lifestyles independently, the weaker party's rights should be better protected. At present, China does not regulate non-marital cohabitation through its family law as some Western countries do, but we can set up a special non-marital cohabitation law, for the purpose of promptly preventing and solving the disputes which non-marital cohabitation may trigger, protecting the rights and interests of the partners and their children.[9]

Furthermore, the current Family Law of the People's Republic of China defines the parties to be married as a man and a woman. But if two men or two women establish an interdependent living unit in terms of love, economy and sex, so long as it complies with monogamy and other imperative rules of law, it is essentially the same as marriage or cohabitation (a living unit between a man and a woman similar to marriage). Some countries like the Netherlands and Belgium have now recognised same-sex marriage. Chinese social conditions make that impossible at present but non-marital cohabitation law may be applied equally to same-sex partners and opposite-sex partners. Thus the rights and interests of parties in lifestyles different than marriage could be protected, although not by the Family Law as such.

---

8   Chen Wei and Ran Qiyu 'Gender in Public Policies – Gender Analysis of Marriage Law and Its Improvement' (2005) 1 *Journal of Gansu College of Political Science and Law* 43.
9   Chen Wei and Wang Wei 'Social Basis and Legislative Suggestion on Non-marital Cohabitation Law of P. R. C' (2008) 1 *Gansu Social Science* 28.

(b)   Gender analysis of husband and wife relationship law

With regard to the law of the relationship between husband and wife, there are two outstanding and contentious issues, which are family violence and the right of giving birth. The 2001 amended Family Law not only provides generally that family violence be prohibited, but also prescribes family violence as one of the cases in which divorce shall be granted if mediation fails. The innocent party has the right to claim compensation and the right to advance a request to persuade the person to cease violence and enter mediation. However, some scholars have pointed out that in the face of frequent family violence towards women, provisions in the Family Law become a kind of propaganda, lacking practicality.[10] There are several issues to be considered from the perspective of gender in laws relating to family violence. First, sexual violence between husband and wife is included in the concept of family violence; the wife is not a sexual object with obligations to the husband as she was in traditional society. Secondly, torts between husband and wife are recognised; the victim in family violence has the right to claim compensation whether divorced or not. Thirdly, a 'protection order' may be granted in order to prevent family violence. Fourthly, the responsibility to take action is on the side of the person committing family violence, lessening or avoiding the harm to the victim, protecting the victim's body and mental health, so as to avoid increasing violence.

Provisions relating to the right to give birth are very simple in the current Family Law. Neither the Law of Woman's Rights Protection nor the Law of Population and Family Planning solved the problem of conflicting rights between husband and wife on the issue of giving birth. According to the theory of gender, there are three arguments in favour of preferring the woman's rights. First, the man's right to reproduce is actualised through the woman. If man has the right to decide on giving birth or not, it will certainly reinforce the man's power and legitimise coercive sexual activity, leading to the deprivation of the woman's freedom and doing harm to woman's body and mental health. Secondly, the woman suffers a lot in pregnancy, giving birth and child-bearing, and usually contributes more in respect of children's care and education. So, the law should give more care and special protection to the woman. Last, but not least, so long as the woman has the decisive right on birth, the man might choose someone else after divorce to actualise his right. The cost in this way is obviously less than in giving the decision-making power to the man. Therefore, if the husband and wife have different opinions on giving birth, the wife should have the right to decide.

(c)   Gender analysis of illegitimacy

Laws in the People's Republic of China have always attached importance to protecting children born out of wedlock, whose rights and duties are as the

---

[10]   Zhou Anping 'Jurisprudence on Principles of Chinese Family Law' (2001) 1 *China Law Science* 170–171.

same as those of children born in wedlock. However, there are two problems with this area of the law. First, different titles are inclined to cause children feelings of inferiority and discrimination, as well as discriminating between married and unmarried parents. The best solution is to abandon the titles 'born in wedlock' and 'born out of wedlock', to use neutral titles such as 'natural children' and 'children', and to apply uniformly relevant provisions of the Marriage Law governing the relationship between parents and children.[11] The second problem is that a sound system of presuming that children are born in wedlock should be established in China. Instead of setting up a system for claiming that children are born out of wedlock, we should learn from the provisions in the Civil Code of Ethiopia, extending the application of the presumptions about children born in wedlock to non-marital cohabitation relationships.[12]

(d) Gender analysis of divorce law

There are three main questions in divorce law from the perspective of gender analysis: first, the parents' duty to bring up minor children after divorce; secondly, rights and interests enjoyed by divorced women in contracting land management; and thirdly, women's status in lawsuits claiming compensation in divorce cases.

With regard to the parents' duty to bring up minor children after divorce, art 36 of the current Marriage Law provides that:

> 'In principle, the mother shall have the custody of a breast-fed infant after divorce. If a dispute arises between the two parents over the custody of their child who has been weaned and they fail to reach an agreement, the People's Court shall make a judgment in accordance with the rights and interests of the child and the actual conditions of both parents.'

In practice, most minor children are under the custody of their mother by the time of the judgment, for the reason that the mother is more appropriate as a custodian than the father. That reflects the traditional idea of gender and family roles, and it supports the obsolete idea that women's activities should be confined to the household. As a result, it makes it even harder for divorced women to remarry, and does not realise the best interests of children. In the trend of gender mainstreaming, this practice is out-dated.

On the question of rights and interests enjoyed by divorced women in contracting land management (see above), art 39 of the current Marriage Law prescribes that: 'The rights and interests enjoyed by the husband or the wife in contracting land management on a household basis shall be protected in

---

[11]   Chen Wei *Legislative Study on Chinese Family Law* (The Mass Press, Beijing, 2000) pp 315 and 356–357.

[12]   Chen Wei and Lie Yuxin 'On the Establishment of the Presumption and Disavowal System on Children and Parents Relationship in China' in Liang Huixing (ed) *Civil and Commercial Law Forum* (Beijing: Law Press, 2003) vol 27 at pp 245–279.

accordance with law.' This is just a principle and declaration, and is not practical. The Rural Land Contract Law, which is more practical, explicitly protects women's rights and interests in contracting land management. But some provisions in it result in emphasising women's dependent status, through its special protection for women. For example, art 30 of the Rural Land Contract Law stipulates that:

> 'If a woman gets married in the period of the contract, and she does not get contracting land in the new residence, the contract-issuing party shall not draw back her original contracting land; if a divorced woman or widow still lives in her original residence, or does not get contracting land in her new residence, the contract-issuing party shall not draw back her original contracting land.'

This provision aims to protect women's rights and interests, but actually its probable result is that a woman who remarried in another country could not get contracting land in her new residence because of this provision, and neither could she care about her original contracting land. What is more, why does this provision emphasise women especially? It is either unfair to the man, or emphasises the wife's dependent status in her husband's family. Both go against its original aim.

Claiming compensation in cases of divorce was added to the amended Marriage Law 2001 in order to protect woman. According to art 46 of the Marriage Law, where one of the following circumstances leads to divorce, the innocent party has the right to claim compensation: bigamy is committed; one spouse cohabits with another person of the opposite sex; family violence is committed; or a family member is maltreated or abandoned. But in practice, few women succeed in claiming compensation, because of the difficulty in producing evidence. The court cannot recognise disputed facts.[13] Bigamy and cohabitation are committed secretly. The innocent party, especially the wife, finds it hard to collect enough direct evidence by herself. Family violence, maltreatment and abandonment must be recognised by evidence such as case recording initiated by the victim and diagnoses by the doctor. In fact, laymen are not aware of the law and the burden of proof. If one party disavows, the other party falls into a dilemma. When neighbours are asked to attend a court as a witness, they often refuse out of consideration for their own self-interest. The difficulty in producing evidence throws the woman into a helpless dilemma in the divorce lawsuit claiming compensation.[14]

---

[13] Civil Court II, the People's Court of Haidian District, Beijing 'Analysis and Strategy on New Categories Family Cases Since Enforcement of Amended Family Law' (2004) 10 *Legal Application* 21–22.

[14] Ye Yingping 'Study on the Legislation and application of Chinese Family Law from the Gender View' in Long Yifei and Xia Yinnan *Legal Reconstruction of Family Relationships in Harmonious Society – 5th Anniversary of Amended Family Law* (Political and Law Press of China, 2007) p 41.

V   CONCLUSION

In summary, under the trend of gender mainstreaming, the Family Law of the People's Republic of China has been constantly trying to pursue equality between men and women. But we still find some problems when we do a gender analysis of the current Chinese Family Law. Some provisions confirm the traditional female status which goes against women's development; some provisions though emphasise equality literally, ignoring diversities between men and women, and resulting in disadvantage to women; some provisions are too protective, failing to consider the self-determination and independence of women. Therefore, on the one hand, we should, through the law, protect the woman as the weak party; on the other hand, we should avoid enhancing woman's weak role by the using the language of 'protecting'. As far as women's rights and interests are concerned in judicial practice, we should introduce a gender perspective, take women reasonably into account in legislation, and further advance the course of gender mainstreaming.

Denmark

REGISTERED AND UNMARRIED PARTNERS IN DENMARK – RECENT LEGAL DEVELOPMENTS

*Ingrid Lund-Andersen**

Résumé

Les dispositions sur l'adoption et sur le droit garde qui, dans la loi danoise concernant le partenariat enregistré prévoyaient des exceptions en regard des couples de même sexe, ont été abolies en 2010. La voie est ainsi ouverte à une éventuelle reconnaissance du mariage entre personnes de même sexe, même si la majorité parlementaire s'y oppose. Un débat a eu lieu au sein des cercles ecclésiastiques danois sur la question de savoir si les couples de même sexe devraient avoir le droit d'enregistrer leur partenariat auprès de l'Église nationale et si une nouvelle liturgie devrait être créée pour de telles célébrations. En septembre 2010, cette deuxième possibilité fit l'objet d'une recommandation par le comité ecclésiastique sur les partenariats enregistrés.

La loi sur les successions fut amendée en 2007 afin d'accorder aux conjoints de fait, hétérosexuels ou de même sexe, le droit de se désigner mutuellement héritiers comme s'ils étaient mariés. Cependant, la nouvelle loi ne contient pas de droits automatiques en faveur des cohabitants alors qu'un comité législatif avait pourtant recommandé de leur accorder de tels droits.

I INTRODUCTION

In Scandinavia there has been a long tradition for trying to harmonise family law and succession law.[1] In 1989, Denmark was the most progressive of the Scandinavian countries when, as the first of them, it introduced a law on Registered Partnerships for same-sex couples. Denmark has since been overtaken by developments in Norway and Sweden as these two countries introduced gender-neutral marriage in 2008 and 2009 respectively.[2]

---

* Associate Professor Dr, Faculty of Law, University of Copenhagen, Denmark.
[1] See in more detail Ingrid Lund-Andersen 'Approximation of Nordic Family Law within the Framework of Nordic Cooperation' in Masha Antokolskaia (ed) *Convergence and Divergence of Family Law in Europe* (Intersentia, 2007) pp 51–61; and Peter Lødrup 'The Reharmonisation of Nordic Family law' in Katharina Boele-Woelki and Tone Sverdrup (eds) *European Challenges in Contemporary Family Law* (Intersentia, 2008) pp 17–26.
[2] See John Aslan and Peter Hambro 'New Developments and Expansion of Relationships

In Danish ecclesiastical circles it has been debated whether same-sex couples should have the right to register their partnerships in the National Church and whether a new authorised liturgy for blessing registered partnerships should be introduced. In September 2010, an ecclesiastical committee recommended introducing a new authorised liturgy for blessing civil registered partnerships. However, many have pointed out that this would only represent a modest step forward, and that Denmark should also introduce a law on gender-neutral marriage. A proposal to this effect has been voted on several times in the Danish Parliament, but so far without being able to secure a majority.[3]

In one respect Denmark has gone further than Norway and Sweden with regard to the legal situation of unmarried cohabitants. A reform of the Inheritance Act in 2007 gave unmarried cohabitants, whether of the same or different sex, the right to make an 'expanded cohabitation will', in which certain groups of cohabitants can decide to inherit from each other in the same way as if they were married and had separate property.[4]

In my view, it is likely that within the next few years there will be a majority in Parliament in favour of allowing the marriage of same-sex couples. The repeal, in 2010, of the exception to the rules on adoption and custody in the Registered Partnership Act has prepared the way for this.

II   REGISTERED PARTNERS

(a)   The newest development

With a few exceptions, the Danish Act on Registered Partnership for same-sex couples[5] copied the institution of marriage. These exceptions were: the right to adopt a child, the right to joint custody, and the right to be married in a church.[6] In 2010, these three exceptions were on the agenda in Denmark.

Covered by Norwegian Law' in Bill Atkin (ed) *The International Survey of Family Law* (Jordan Publishing Limited, 2009) pp 377–378; and Anna Singer 'Equal Treatment of Same-Sex Couples in Sweden' in Bill Atkin (ed) *The International Survey of Family Law* (Jordan Publishing Limited, 2010) pp 397–399.

[3]   In June 2010, Parliament once again debated a bill on gender-neutral marriage (B 122) proposed by the opposition parties. It was rejected by all the governing parties as well as the Danish Peoples' Party on a 51–57 vote. 71 were absent.

[4]   Law No 515 of 6 June 2007.

[5]   Law No 372 of 7 June 1989. The Act is described by Ingrid Lund-Andersen 'The Danish Registered Partnership Act' in Katharina Boele-Woelki and Angelika Fuchs (eds) *Legal Recognition of Same-Sex Couples in Europe* (Intersentia, 2003) pp 15–23; and by Christina G Jeppesen de Boer and Annette Kronborg 'National Report on Registered Partnership in Denmark' in *XVIIIth Congress of the International Academy of Comparative Law* (Washington, 2010).

[6]   Further, the provisions in Danish legislation with gender-specific rules on marriage do not apply to registered partnerships, nor do provisions on marriage in international treaties, unless special agreements are made.

First, in May 2010 the exception with respect to children was repealed.[7] The intention was to put registered partners on the same footing as spouses. Like married couples, registered partners can now only adopt jointly. A couple has to be approved as adopters and, at the time of applying to adopt, they must have lived together for at least 2½ years, except under special circumstances. It is a condition for registered couples who want to adopt a child from abroad that the foreign country agrees to the adoption of children by registered partners of the same sex.

Under the change in the adoption rules, it is permitted to transfer custody to a registered couple by an agreement approved by a regional authority. This possibility may be relevant as a less far-reaching alternative to family or stepchild adoption, as the ties between a child and its biological parent or parents remain as for inheritance, the duty to maintain the child and the right to have contact with the child.

These amendments are the result of the softening of the view of homosexual partners as parents which started in 1999, when it became possible for a registered partner to adopt the child of the other partner provided the child had not been adopted from abroad.[8] Further, in 2006, s 3 of the Act on Artificial Procreation was repealed, so that lesbians and single women were given access to publicly financed reproductive treatment.[9] In Parliament, the members were given a free vote and the bill was adopted with reference to the principle of equality.

Secondly, on 15 September 2010, a committee on the National Church and Registered Partnership published its report.[10] The committee was asked to consider the following questions:

> 'Should marriages still take place in the National Church, or should all partnerships be entered into before the civil authorities, after which it would be possible for a marriage to be blessed in church, and, if so, what form of liturgy should be used?

> In what form should it be possible to enter into a registered partnership in the National Church, so that two persons of the same sex have the same possibilities as married couples to enter into their partnership in a religious ceremony, and, if so, what form of liturgy should be used?

---

[7] See Law No 537 of 25 May 2010. During the preceding years, the possibility of allowing registered partners to adopt together had been discussed several times in Parliament. On 17 March 2009 a majority voted in favour of a resolution ordering the government to introduce a bill on foreign adoption by registered partners.

[8] See Law No 360 of 2 June 1999. In 2009 it became permissible to adopt a stepchild before the usual minimum of 3 months from the date of birth of the child, provided the registered partners live together and the reproduction has been by use of anonymous donor sperm: see Law No 105 of 28 May 2009.

[9] See Law No 535 of 8 June 2006.

[10] The Minister for Ecclesiastical Affairs set up the committee. The chairman was the Bishop of Copenhagen and most of the members of the committee had church backgrounds.

How can it be ensured that clergy who, on grounds of conscience, cannot officiate in proceedings for the entry into a registered partnership in church have the right to refuse?'

On the first question, the majority of the committee recommended that the current system of freedom of choice between civil and church weddings should be maintained. On the second question, the majority stated that marriage and registered partnership must be considered as two *different* arrangements, and the church wedding ceremony of a man and a woman should not be extended to same-sex couples. However, most members of the committee found that an authorised ceremony should be introduced for the church blessing of registered partnerships. With regard to the third question, the committee unanimously recommended that the right to refuse to bless a registered partnership ought to be laid down by law. A minority of the committee was in favour of moving the legal part of a wedding out of the church, implying that a church wedding would be a blessing of a civil marriage.

The report has been criticised for not being in line with the predominant opinion in society and in the church. According to a poll in September 2010, of 813 clergy who responded, 46% were in favour of marrying homosexual couples and 43% were against.[11]

(b) Statistics on registered partnerships

It is assumed that about 5% of people are homosexual; in Denmark this corresponds to about 250,000 people. From this perspective, only a limited proportion of homosexuals have registered their partnerships.

Statistics for Denmark

	Registered Partnerships		Dissolved Partnerships		Surviving Partner		Total
	Men	Women	Men	Women	Men	Women	
1990	518	122	1	–	1	3	645
1994	1,777	704	105	79	130	14	2,809
1998	2,275	1,266	322	218	225	31	4,337
2002	2,895	2,061	519	389	266	56	6,186
2007	3,541	4,096	798	722	307	88	9,552
2009	3,943	3,955	874	870	325	106	10,073

[11] Article by Marie Sæhl and Emil Bergløv on 'Homosexual weddings divide the National Church', in the newspaper *Politiken* 20 September 2010.

From 1 January 1990 to 1 January 2009, a total of 10,073 people registered their partnerships, 1,744 people dissolved their partnerships, and 431 people living in a registered partnership died. In the first years far more men than women registered their partnerships, but this trend has changed and today more women than men register their partnerships.

Statistics for Denmark, Statistikbanken, at 1 January 2009

Age	Registered Partnerships		Dissolved Partnership		Surviving Partner		Total
	Men	Women	Men	Women	Men	Women	
<25	31	54	2	10	–	–	97
25–34	545	912	126	157	7	1	1,748
35–44	1,203	1,343	347	360	34	8	3,295
45–54	990	925	226	214	70	14	2,439
55–64	783	533	120	109	108	33	1,686
65–74	319	155	42	16	76	33	641
75<	72	71	11	4	30	17	205

The majority of the people who have contracted partnerships have been between 25 and 54 years of age, but the 55–64 age group is also well represented. Very few people under the age of 25 have registered partnerships. The number of registered partners with children has increased significantly, from 266 partnerships at the beginning of 2002[12] to 702 on 1 January 2009.[13]

III PROVISIONS ON COHABITANTS IN THE INHERITANCE ACT

(a) The committee's proposal

In 2000, a committee was appointed to consider, among other things, the legal rights of inheritance for unmarried cohabitants. In the terms of reference it was stated that:

> 'Changes in family structures mean that there can be grounds for considering whether there is a need to change the law on inheritance in order to strengthen the legal position of surviving spouses and unmarried cohabitants . . . among other things the committee is requested to consider . . . whether a legal right of inheritance should be introduced for cohabitants whose relationship has not been formalised.' (translation)

---

[12] News from Statistics for Denmark No 57, 12 February 2002.
[13] Statistics for Denmark, Befolkning og valg, 2009:7.

The committee submitted its report in 2006.[14] The committee recommended that unmarried cohabitants should be given rights of inheritance, as there was found to be a large number of cohabitants[15] and many unmarried couples do not make a will. However, the committee also pointed out that the group of cohabitants is very heterogeneous, for which reason it is difficult to legislate in this field. In the committee's opinion, cohabitants should not be put on the same footing as married couples, but rules should be introduced for longer-lasting relationships, especially if a couple has a child in common.[16]

The committee suggested three different ways in which cohabitants could inherit from each other without being entitled to an indefeasible portion of the deceased's estate:

- *inheritance under the intestacy rules* should give entitlement to a quarter of the entire estate, up to DKK 500,000, provided the cohabitant had lived together with the deceased for the last 2 years before the date of the death, and they had, have had or expected a child in common;[17]

- *inheritance based on social needs,* so that in special cases the probate court could decide that a cohabitant who has lived in a marriage-like relationship with the deceased should be entitled to inherit an amount;[18] and

- *inheritance under a will of the cohabiting couple.* In a will a couple can decide to inherit from each other as if they were married and had separate property. It is possible to lay down some limits so that it is not necessary to give the partner all the benefits that a spouse is normally given. The partners would have to fulfil the conditions for being married or being registered partners. Furthermore, the will would only be valid if they lived together at the time of the death of the first deceased partner and if at the time of the death they had, have had or expect a child in common *or* had lived together for the last 2 years.[19]

(b) The Ministry of Justice's proposal

Most of the comments from the public consultation supported the idea of strengthening the legal position of a surviving cohabitant.[20] Thus, it was surprising that the bill for a new Inheritance Act, which was introduced on 6

---

14 See Report No 1473 on revision of the Inheritance Act (revision af arvelovgivningen mv) 2006.
15 On 1 January 2009, 587,720 people lived in unmarried cohabitation, see Statistics for Denmark, Befolkning og valg 2009:7. On 1 January 2009, the number of cohabiting couples with children in common was 94,297.
16 See Report No 1473 p 27.
17 The committee's draft of s 40 of the Inheritance Act.
18 The committee's draft of s 41 of the Inheritance Act.
19 The committee's draft of s 92 of the Inheritance Act.
20 The comments from the public enquiry can be found in Ministry of Justice's 'Hvidbog om lov nr. 515 af 6. juni 2007 Arvelov'.

December 2006, departed from the view of the committee.[21] Although the Ministry of Justice had great understanding for the reasons behind the committee's proposals, it found that there were weighty reasons for dismissing the proposals to give legal rights to cohabitants. The Ministry referred to three grounds. First, there is a difference, in principle, between marriage and unmarried cohabitation. In particular, cohabitants do not have a mutual duty obligation to maintain each other; cohabitants have separate property; and cohabitants are free to dissolve their relationship. Secondly, the Ministry stressed that the parties' choice not to marry must be respected, and it referred to the parties' autonomy. Thirdly, the Ministry emphasised that the provisions in the Inheritance Act must be as simple as possible, so that conflicts about proving the character of the relationship of cohabitants could be avoided. My comment on this last argument is that it is a technicality, and it can be used whenever there is a proposal to legislate for cohabitants.

Consequently, the Ministry of Justice did not propose that there should be inheritance under the intestacy rules or inheritance based on social needs, but only submitted a proposal for inheritance under the will of a cohabitant.[22] The position of the Ministry of Justice expresses liberal thinking and attaches importance to the parties' choice not to marry. Therefore, the parties have to make a will to demonstrate their wish to favour each other.

In spite of severe criticisms from legal experts[23] and from several political parties in Parliament,[24] the provisions adopted in the new Inheritance Act are in line with the Ministry of Justice's proposal. Critics have pointed out that, every year, surviving cohabitants will be left in the lurch in very many cases.

In my view, the present legal situation is only a half solution. The overall objective of family law – to protect the weaker party in the family and to resolve conflicts in families – is not fulfilled. Further, I do not agree with the assumption that most cohabitants have deliberately chosen a relationship without any legal rules.[25] This impression is confirmed by the fact that a great

---

[21] See Bill No 100 Folketinget 2006–07. See Folketingstidende 2006–07, Tillæg A, pp 3286–3413.

[22] Compared with the committee's draft of s 92, s 88 of the Inheritance Act had been changed so that the requirements of the relationship had to be met at the time the cohabitant died and not at the time when the will was drawn up.

[23] See Professor Rasmus Kristian Feldthusen's minute of 22 January 2007 for the Legal Affairs Committee of Parliament, and Professor Finn Taksøe-Jensen's minute of 26 April 2007 for the Legal Affairs Committee of Parliament. The minutes can be found in Ministry of Justice's 'Hvidbog om lov nr. 515 of 6. juni 2007 Arvelov'.

[24] All the opposition parties – the Social Democrats, the Social-Liberal Party, the Social National Party and the Red-Green Alliance – were more in line with the proposals of the committee on the Inheritance Act than the bill submitted by the Ministry of Justice; see the official report of parliamentary proceedings from 11 January and 1 June 2007, Folketingstidende 2006–07, Forhandlinger, pp 2811–2822 and pp 7864–7869.

[25] See also the statement of the Norwegian Department of Justice when introducing a bill for a legal right to inherit and 'uskifte'- right for cohabitants: 'In the Department's view it can no longer be presupposed that most cohabitants deliberately choose to avoid the legal effects of marriage'; see Ot prp No 73 (2007–2008) p 14 col 1. The Norwegian rules were enacted by Law No 112 of 19 December 2008. See John Aslan and Peter Hambro 'New Developments and

number of cohabitants have made wills according to the rule on *inheritance under a will of the cohabiting couple*.[26] It is possible to buy standard forms for such wills on the internet.

IV CLOSING CONSIDERATIONS

Since 2001, centre-right parties have had a majority in the Danish Parliament. An election for a new Parliament has to be held this year. The opinion polls point towards a shift in political power, and it is very likely that the new prime minister will be a Social Democrat. If this happens, the odds are that homosexuals will be given a right to contract a civil marriage without regard for the position of the National Church as regards an authorised ceremony for same-sex marriage.

Likewise, it is probable that the Inheritance Act will be amended in line with the proposals of the Inheritance Act committee (described above). Thus, on 1 June 2007, during the reading of the bill on a new Inheritance Act the spokesman for the Social Democrats declared that the committee's two proposals with regards to cohabitants, *inheritance under the intestacy rules* and *inheritance based on social needs*, would be part of Social Democrat policy if they came to power. The fact that legal inheritance rules for some groups of cohabitants were introduced in Norway in 2008 may also encourage a Danish reform.[27]

Expansion of Relationships Covered by Norwegian Law' in Bill Atkin (ed) *The International Survey of Family Law* (Jordan Publishing Limited, 2009) pp 380–384.

26 I am unable to refer to any official statistics. My statement is based on informal interviews with several family lawyers.

27 See John Aslan and Peter Hambro 'New Developments and Expansion of Relationships Covered by Norwegian Law' in Bill Atkin (ed) *The International Survey of Family Law* (Jordan Publishing Limited, 2009) pp 380–384.

England and Wales

THIS CHILD IS MY CHILD; THIS CHILD IS YOUR CHILD; THIS CHILD WAS MADE FOR YOU AND ME – SURROGACY IN ENGLAND AND WALES

Mary Welstead[*]

Résumé

Depuis que la question des mères porteuses a été discutée devant les comités Warnock (1984) et Brazier (1989), plusieurs décisions ont été rendues dans les juridictions de l'Angleterre et du pays de Galles en rapport avec la gestation pour le compte d'autrui, qu'elle soit nationale ou internationale. Ces décisions ont mis en lumière de sérieuses lacunes dans la réglementation actuelle. Certains tribunaux ont insisté pour que soient repensées tant la pratique elle-même que les quelques normes qui l'encadrent actuellement.

Le présent texte fait état du droit relatif à la gestation pour autrui et analyse les décisions les plus importantes en la matière. Il suggère que les fondements éthiques de cette pratique devraient être revus par une instance normative, tel la HFEA (Human Fertilisation and Embryology Authority) ou l'institution qui pourrait la remplacer, et que de nouvelles lois soient adoptées afin d'intégrer les principes éthiques que privilégiera cette instance.

I INTRODUCTION

Since 1984, when surrogacy was first discussed by the Warnock Committee, a committee fiercely divided on the topic, there has been an increase in its use in England and Wales. There are several reasons for this. First, infertility is a growing problem; women are attempting reproduction at an age when they are less fertile, and surrogacy is seen as the only means of having a child genetically connected to them. Secondly, there are very limited numbers of domestic babies available for adoption, and the international adoption route has been closed down in many countries. Thirdly, IVF and other forms of reproductive treatment in fertility clinics, which are licensed by the Human Fertilisation and Embryology Authority (HFEA),[1] have become readily available both in the

---

[*]   Fellow CAP Harvard Law School, Visiting Professor, University of Buckingham.
[1]   See ss 9–22 of the Human Fertilisation and Embryology Act 1990; the Human Fertilisation and Embryology Authority (HFEA) came into existence in 1990 as a quasi-autonomous

jurisdiction and overseas. This has made it possible for surrogacy to take place other than by self-insemination at home. Fourthly, gay couples are now able to form civil partnerships, and transsexuals able to marry. Many of them are seeking surrogacy as a solution to having children who are genetically linked to them.

In spite of the increase in the practice of surrogacy, it remains controversial. A number of recent decisions have highlighted the failure of successive Parliaments to address the problems inherent in surrogacy and regulate it in any other than a minimalist way. Judicial calls for reform have triggered a debate about surrogacy and its future in the jurisdiction of England and Wales. The media has added its voice to that of the judiciary; whilst its attention has concentrated primarily on the more sensational aspects of surrogacy, and on those surrogate births which have involved high profile celebrity couples, it has also provided evidence of the problematic nature of the practice in situations which never reach the courts.

In this year's *International Survey*, I propose examining the legislation relating to surrogacy and a number of the important decisions in this field which have fuelled the demands for legislative reform, and draw from them those issues which urgently need to be considered for reform.

II THE NATURE OF SURROGACY

Surrogacy may be full or partial. Full surrogacy occurs when the surrogate, or gestational mother, who gives birth has no genetic relationship to the child. The parents for whom the child is intended provide their own eggs and sperm, or donated eggs and donated sperm, or a combination of these to create the embryo. The process whereby the embryo is created and its implantation, if it takes place in the jurisdiction, must be in a licensed clinic.

Partial surrogacy occurs where the sperm of the intended father, or donated sperm, is used to fertilise the egg of the surrogate mother. It is often undertaken by the surrogate mother and the intended father at home, usually by artificial means rather than by a sexual relationship. Where partial surrogacy involves medical intervention, it too must take place in a clinic licensed by the HFEA.

Surrogacy, of course, is not a new solution to reproductive problems. It has a long history dating back to biblical times where it was seen as an altruistic activity which often took place within the extended family. Men were exhorted to impregnate their widowed sisters-in-law to secure heirs for their dead

---

non-governmental organisation to license and monitor all UK fertility clinics and all UK research involving human embryos, and to provide information to the public about such matters. The government threatens it with extinction and it remains uncertain how clinics will be controlled if that happens.

brothers. It was regarded as their familial duty.[2] There are recorded instances of husbands, whose wives were infertile, engaging in a sexual relationship with a family servant to provide a child for them.[3]

Today, this altruistic practice of familial, or friendship, surrogacy continues. Newspaper reports abound with stories of family members, or friends, who conceive babies for their desperate childless relatives. One woman became a surrogate mother for her daughter who had searched unsuccessfully for an unrelated surrogate mother for 4 years. Embryos were created from the daughter's eggs and her husband's sperm and implanted in the surrogate mother. She gave birth to twins, and simultaneously acquired the dual status of mother and grandmother to them.[4]

In 2009, a woman agreed to become a surrogate mother for her gay brother and his partner using her eggs and the partner's sperm.[5] More unusually, a 29-year-old woman offered to act as a surrogate mother for her mother and stepfather. Using the latter's sperm she impregnated herself at home. She subsequently gave birth to a baby, and so became his mother and his stepsister at the same time. Her own three older children acquired a half-brother and stepuncle.[6]

Familial surrogacy has the attraction that the surrogate mother is unlikely to refuse to hand over the child. Indeed, the altruism of these women extends in some cases to ensuring that the baby bonds with the intended parent at the moment of birth. One surrogate mother gave birth to a baby for her daughter who had a rare lung condition which prevented her from carrying a child. The surrogate mother requested that the baby be born by Caesarean section under a general anaesthetic so that her daughter would hold the baby first.[7]

In a similar case, a woman had a rare blood disorder which made pregnancy impossible. Her sister offered to become a surrogate mother for her, using her own eggs and her brother-in-law's sperm. At birth the baby was delivered straight into the intended mother's arms.[8]

---

[2]   See Deuteronomy 25:5ff; see also Genesis 38, where Onan was punished by God for his refusal to act in this way, and Mark 12:19.

[3]   In Ruth 4:7, Ruth became a surrogate mother and gave birth to a child, named Obed, for Naomi. The father of the child was Naomi's husband Boaz. In Genesis 16, the story is told of Sarah, Abraham's wife who was unable to have children, so she gave her servant, Hagar, to Abraham to bear a child for her. Jacob and Zipah, his wife Leah's maid, had a child together for Leah (Genesis 30:9ff). He also had a child with Bilhah, his other wife Rachel's maid, on behalf of Rachel (Genesis 30:3ff).

[4]   *The Times*, 30 January 2004.

[5]   *Daily Telegraph*, 27 July 2009.

[6]   *Daily Mail*, 12 February 2004.

[7]   *The Times*, 1 October 2005.

[8]   *Daily Mail*, 3 March 2003; see also the case of two sisters who joined forces to give two children to a third sister left infertile because of cancer treatment. One donated her eggs to the other who acted as the surrogate mother on two separate occasions, *Daily Mail*, 13 August 2008.

In spite of journalistic accounts of celebrities who do not wish to go through pregnancy for fear of losing their well-honed bodies, the majority of couples do not fit that description. Rather, they seek surrogacy because they cannot conceive,[9] or carry a baby to full term, or the mother's life would be endangered by pregnancy.[10] Gay men, or couples where the female is a male to female transsexual, have little choice other than to find a surrogate mother if they wish to have a child who has a genetic link to one of them.

The social and economic consequences of infertility are clearly very significant both for the couple concerned and for the state. Many infertile couples experience emotional distress, depression, a sense of exclusion from society (where it is assumed that children are an essential component of a relationship) and relationship breakdown.

III SURROGACY FIGURES

It is difficult to assess how many surrogate births take place within the jurisdiction. In the case of partial surrogacy and the fertilisation taking place at home, it will remain a private matter for those involved. Even where the surrogacy takes place in a licensed clinic, it is not easy to estimate numbers. The HFEA has been collecting information on surrogacy only since 1999. Between that date and 2008, 221 babies have been recorded as born to surrogate mothers as a consequence of treatment in a licensed clinic. It is, of course, possible for a patient to be treated who does not admit that she is acting as a surrogate mother. The voluntary agencies involved in the provision of surrogacy advice do keep records. One of these agencies, Childlessness Overcome Through Surrogacy (COTS), recorded 600 surrogate births between 1988 and 2007; in 98% of those cases the surrogate mother handed over the baby to the intended parents.[11]

IV THE LAW RELATING TO SURROGACY

The law relating to surrogacy is decidedly ambivalent; it reflects the divided ethical views expressed by the Warnock Commission in 1984, and to a lesser extent those of the Brazier Surrogacy Review in 1997.[12] Parliament decided that it should not enact any form of legislation which might encourage surrogacy but, at the same time, accepted that it would be impossible to outlaw

---

9   It is impossible to estimate how many couples are actually infertile. However, in 2005, the British Fertility Society estimated that 25% of couples who wish to conceive experience problems in doing so.
10 See www.britishfertilitysociety.org.uk/public/factsheets/keyfacts.html (accessed 24 May 2011).
11 See www.surrogacy.org.uk; see also www.surrogacyuk.org.
12 See M Brazier, S Golombok and A Campbell *Surrogacy: Review for the UK Health Ministers of current arrangements for payments and regulation*: Consultation Document (London: Department of Health, 1997). See also M Freeman 'Does Surrogacy Have A Future After Brazier?' (1999) 7(1) Med Law Rev 1.

it. It, therefore, chose to regulate it in a minimalist manner, first, by way of the Surrogacy Arrangements Act 1985 (SAA 1985) and, second, by way of the Human Fertilisation and Embryology Act 1990 (HFEA 1990), both of which have been amended recently by the Human Fertilisation and Embryology Act 2008 (HFEA 2008).[13] In spite of the amendments, the legislation remains complex, confusing and highly unsatisfactory from the point of view of both those who favour surrogacy and those who would prefer to see it outlawed.

The SAA 1985 prohibits any commercial surrogacy arrangement. However, no offence will be committed if the intended parents pay reasonable expenses to a surrogate. There is no fixed figure as to what is considered reasonable; it is left to the judiciary to determine the matter.[14] Furthermore, a commercial surrogacy arrangement may, in effect, be legalised judicially because the court may retrospectively authorise payments which it judges to be unreasonable.[15] It is illegal for any one to advertise for surrogate mothers, or intended parents, on a commercial basis. In spite of this prohibition, surrogacy agencies, which operate as voluntary non-profit organisations, are not illegal.[16] These agencies, which unlike the fertility clinics are not licensed, and therefore not regulated by the HFEA, are financed by the membership fees of intended parents and potential surrogate mothers, and to a lesser extent by donations. They may provide information to their members to enable them to achieve a successful surrogacy.

One agency, COTS, is run on very limited resources by a group of volunteers. It describes its role as advisory and supportive. COTS arranges medical examinations for its members and undertakes criminal record checks. Once the checks have been completed, COTS passes the details of those offering to be surrogate mothers and the intended parents on to a splinter group of COTS, 'Triangle'. It is the splinter group which actually puts intended couples in touch with surrogate parents.

Anyone may set up a surrogacy agency; no qualifications are required in spite of the legal and psychological complexities surrounding the practice. Former surrogate mothers or intended parents tend to be those who set up and run surrogacy agencies.

---

[13] The significant change in the HFEA 2008 with respect to surrogacy, other than enlarging the categories of couples who may apply for a parental order, has been brought about by the 2010 Regulations (the Human Fertilisation and Embryology (Parental Orders) (Consequential, Transitional and Saving Provisions) Order 2010, SI 2010/986). The Regulations import into s 54 of the Act the provisions of s 1 of the Adoption and Children Act 2002 which makes the welfare of the child paramount rather than only the first consideration, see *Re L (A Minor)* [2010] EWHC 3146.

[14] See the words of Hedley J in *X and Y (Foreign Surrogacy)* [2008] EWHC 3030 (Fam) relating to the generally held view that there is a standard guideline figure of £10,000 for reasonable expenses: 'Such figures may have utility but, in my opinion, prospective commissioning couples should be cautious about relying on them without satisfying themselves that they are realistic in their case; an obvious example would be whether the surrogate mother was or was not going to sustain an ascertainable loss of earnings by reason of the surrogacy.'

[15] See HFEA 2008, s 54(8).

[16] See SSA 1985, ss 1–3.

The Brazier Report in 2004 recommended the regulation of all surrogacy agencies, and in *Re P (Surrogacy: Residence)*,[17] Coleridge J expressed his concern that the recommendations had not been acted upon:

> 'The court's understanding is that surrogacy agencies such as COTS are not covered by any statutory or regulatory umbrella and are therefore not required to perform to any recognised standard of competence. I am sufficiently concerned . . . to question whether some form of inspection or authorisation should be required in order to improve the quality of advice that is given to individuals who seek to achieve the birth of a child through surrogacy. Given the importance of the issues involved when the life of a child is created in this manner, it is questionable whether the role of facilitating surrogacy arrangements should be left to groups of well-meaning amateurs. To this end, a copy of this judgment is being sent to the Minister of State for Children, Young People and Families for her consideration.'

By contrast all fertility clinics must be licensed and must comply with the HFEA's code of practice and, of course, the legislation in this field. It is not illegal for a licensed clinic to charge a fee for the impregnation of, or the implantation of an embryo, in a surrogate mother. However, the clinic may not offer a commercial matching service. This means that the intended parents must find a surrogate mother for themselves. The code of practice states clearly that surrogacy may only be used where the commissioning mother is unable to undergo pregnancy for physical or medical reasons or her health would be damaged were she to do so. It may not be undertaken for personal convenience.

(a) Legal parentage

The question of legal parentage in cases of surrogacy is complex. The surrogate mother (regardless of whether conception has been achieved using her eggs, the eggs of the intended mother, or donor eggs) is always the mother of the child.[18] If she is married, her husband will be the father of the child, unless he did not consent to the surrogacy. If he did not consent, and the intended male parent's sperm was used to create the child, the latter will be the child's legal father.[19] If the surrogate mother is a civil partner, her partner, unless she did not consent to the surrogacy, will also be the parent of the child. If the surrogate mother is unmarried, and she was impregnated using the intended male parent's sperm, according to common law, he will be the legal father of the child. In order to accommodate gay and lesbian intended parents, if the unmarried surrogate mother was treated in a licensed clinic with donor sperm (other than that of the

---

17 *Re P (Surrogacy: Residence)* [2008] 1 FLR 177.
18 See HFEA 2008, s 33.
19 Ibid, ss 35.

intended parent), and had agreed that the intended parent was to be the parent of the child, the latter will be the legal father or, in the case of a lesbian couple, the legal second parent of the child.[20]

Legal parentage does not necessarily determine the important issue of parental rights. It is the persons who have actual parental rights who may make the everyday decisions about the child's life to be made. To obtain those parental rights, the intended parents must make an application for a parental order or an order under the Children Act 1989 or the Adoption Act 2002.[21] Any intended parents, if they are a couple (a single person may not apply) who are spouses, civil partners, or other partners living in an enduring familial relationship and are not within the prohibited degrees of relationship with respect to each other, may apply to the court for a parental order. This order terminates the parental rights of the surrogate mother and her husband, or civil partner, or any other person with parental rights over the child. Once an order has been granted, the child will receive a new birth certificate which names the intended parents as his or her parents. An order under the Adoption Act 2002 has a similar effect but an order under the Children Act 1989 does not.

Applicants for parental orders must fulfil certain conditions:

- one of them must have provided the gametes for the creation of the embryo carried by the surrogate mother, and any insemination must have been by artificial means and not by means of a sexual relationship;

- both must be over the age of 18 and be applying as husband and wife, civil partners of each other, or living together in an enduring family relationship and are not within the prohibited degrees of kindred with respect to each other;

- they must apply within 6 months of the child's birth;

- at least one of the applicants must be domiciled in the jurisdiction;

- the child must be in their care at the time of the application;

- the surrogate mother and any other person who is a parent of the child but is not one of the applicants (including any man who is the father by virtue of ss 35 or 36 or any woman who is a parent by virtue of ss 42 or 43), her husband, or civil partner must give their full and free consent to the order being made (unless they cannot be found or are incapable of giving their consent);

---

[20]　Ibid, ss 36, 37 with respect to an agreement with an intended male parent (the agreed fatherhood conditions) and ss 43, 44 with respect to a female intended parent (the agreed female parenthood conditions).

[21]　HFEA 2008, s 54 (prior to the 2008 Act see HFEA 1990, s 30).

- the surrogate mother may not give her consent until 6 weeks after the birth of the child; and

- the surrogate mother must not have been paid more than reasonable expenses for her pregnancy, or the court must have agreed to authorise any additional payments which have been made.

If the conditions are met, the court will look at the welfare reports and decide whether to grant the parental order on the basis of the paramountcy of the child's welfare.[22] If the conditions are not met, the court may not grant the parental order regardless of the child's welfare, but the intended parents may be eligible to apply for an order under the Children Act 1989,[23] or an adoption order.[24] The child's welfare will once again be the paramount consideration.[25]

V   SURROGACY PROBLEMS

(a)   The surrogate wishes to keep the child

The fear of most intended parents is that the surrogate mother will refuse to relinquish the child. This is more likely to happen where the surrogate mother has used her own eggs and therefore has a genetic connection with the child. There has been only one case where the surrogate mother refused to hand over the twin babies who were not genetically connected to her. In 2007, the intended parents, whose own eggs and sperm had been used to create the embryo, went to court to seek a residency order for the twins under the Children Act 1989. However, before the final hearing to decide the children's future, the surrogate mother gave up her battle to keep the babies and they went to live with the intended parents.[26]

In the majority of the surrogacy disputes where the surrogate mother has decided to keep the child, the court has normally refused to grant any order, under the Children Act 1989 or the Adoption Act 2002, in favour of the intended parents. It is the rare judge who has been prepared to destroy what is perceived to be the unbreakable maternal bond between the surrogate mother and the child; gestation combined with her biological link to the child tends to triumph.[27]

---

[22]   Prior to the enactment of HFEA 2008 and the effect of the 2010 Regulations (S1 2010/986), applications for parental orders were made under HFEA 1990, s 30 and the child's welfare was not the paramount consideration but the first consideration of the court.

[23]   See s 8.

[24]   See Adoption Act 2002, ss 42, 49, 50 and 51.

[25]   See Children Act 1989, s 1(1) and Adoption Act 2002, s 1(2).

[26]   *Daily Mail*, 1 March 2008.

[27]   See, eg, *A v C* [1985] FLR 445; *Re T (a child) (surrogacy: residence order)* [2011] All ER (D) 171 (Jan).

One of the rare cases in which the surrogate mother's rights did not prevail is that of *Re P (Surrogacy: Residence)*.[28] One can have nothing but sympathy for Coleridge J, when faced with the decision about a child's future against the background of the extremely dysfunctional behaviour of the surrogate mother, Mrs P, and her husband.

Mrs P was a 38-year-old woman and addicted to procreation. After working as a prostitute, she gave birth to three children with three different fathers none of whom was Mr P; he had had a vasectomy before the couple began to live together. Three children were not enough for Mrs P; she decided to approach the surrogacy agency, COTS, and agreed to act as a surrogate mother for Mr and Mrs R. She rapidly became pregnant after insemination with Mr R's sperm. Early on in the pregnancy, she lied to Mr and Mrs R when she claimed to have had a miscarriage. Mrs P's pregnancy continued and she gave birth to a baby girl, C.

Three years after C's birth, Mrs P began the search for her next child. After an abortive attempt to foster a Down's Syndrome child, she returned to COTS. She told the agency that she had become pregnant with C very soon after the purported miscarriage, and that Mr P was C's father. In the light of Mr P's vasectomy, this was hardly possible. However, COTS believed her, and Mrs P signed another surrogacy agreement with Mr and Mrs J. She soon became pregnant after insemination with Mr J's sperm. Once again she lied to Mr and Mrs J, and maintained that she had miscarried early in the pregnancy. A few months later, she gave birth to a baby boy N. A family dispute took place and Mrs P's eldest daughter decided to blow the whistle on her mother.

When Mr R learned of the existence of his biological daughter, who was then aged 4, he immediately applied to the court for orders under the Children Act 1989.[29] He wanted C to be told about her paternity and to be allowed contact with him and his wife. At first, Mr and Mrs P tried to deny the truth about C but were forced to change their minds after DNA tests showed otherwise. They agreed that they would tell C of her true paternity and would allow Mr R to have an ongoing visiting relationship with her. Somewhat surprisingly, given past history, Mr R believed them, and withdrew his application for contact. Nonetheless, the court decided that C should be made a ward of court which would allow it to be involved in all important future decisions about her life. The court also decided that all future contact between Mr and Mrs R and C should be monitored by social services.

Mr and Mrs J took a very different stance; 10 days after N's birth, they obtained leave to apply to the court for a residence order for N to come and live with them.[30] Their application and the DNA tests to establish N's paternity took some time to be resolved, and by the date of the final court hearing N was

---

[28] [2008] 1 FLR 177.
[29] See ss 1, 8 and 10.
[30] Because the insemination of Mrs P took place with the consent of her husband, he was treated under the HFEA 2002, s 28(2) (now see HFEA 2008, s 35) as N's father and, in law, no other

18 months old. He had had contact with Mr and Mrs J since his first birthday but had clearly bonded with Mr and Mrs P and his siblings. Coleridge J explained the difficult task of deciding with which of the two families, the Ps or the Js, N should live. He found the test under the Children Act 1989, s1(1) to be:

> '... a simpler one to formulate, though not necessarily to answer; namely, as between the two competing residential care regimes on offer from the two parents (with their respective spouses) and available for his upbringing, which, after considering all aspects of the two options, is the one most likely to deliver the best outcome for him over the course of his childhood and in the end be most beneficial. Put very simply, in which home is he most likely to mature into a happy and balanced adult and to achieve his fullest potential as a human? The fact that both families constitute one of the child's natural parents means that both sides start from the same position, neither side being able to claim that the blood tie should favour their claim.'

Coleridge J recognised that it was both understandable and natural for a surrogate mother to change her mind about giving up the child, which had been in her womb for 9 months, and to whom she had given birth. However, Mrs P had deliberately embarked on a cruel and inhuman plan to trick both the intended fathers, each desperate to have a child, into parting with their sperm. Their expectations and that of their wives had been falsely raised. The police had at one point considered referring the case for criminal prosecution.

In the light of factual information about Mr and Mrs P's lifestyle, the expert evidence given to the court about their parenting skills was surprisingly positive. One health visitor expressed shock that there was any problem with this 'lovely' family. It was acknowledged that N would be devastated to leave Mr and Mrs P and his siblings, the only family he had ever known, and go to live with Mr and Mrs J, 200 miles away. It would be impractical to expect them to travel to visit him; they lived on welfare benefits. Coleridge J emphasised that he did not wish to penalise Mr and Mrs P for breaking the surrogacy agreement and deceiving Mr and Mrs J. However, he acknowledged that their lies and unreliability were inappropriate skills for parenting. He found that Mr and Mrs P:

> '... were often incapable of distinguishing fact from fiction and that they did indeed take grains of truth and amplify and distort them into unrecognisable factual conclusions. In the end I think they are prepared to make it up as they go along ... on occasions they were hardly conscious of the extent to which they were fabricating.'

He was convinced that, if N remained with Mr and Mrs P, they would be grudging about contact with Mr and Mrs J and would be likely to sabotage it. He saw no hope of a change in Mrs P in the near future; he regarded her

---

person, not even Mr J as N's biological father could be treated as the father. This meant that Mr and Mrs J required leave of the court to apply for the residence order; this was readily given.

problems as deep rooted and probably stemmed from her early life experiences which only extensive psychotherapy could possibly resolve.

In deciding to hand N over to the intended parents, Mr and Mrs J, Coleridge J explained that he had found them to be quiet, intelligent, decent, honest professional people. They already had an older child born of a successful surrogacy agreement. Mrs J had given up her career to become a full-time mother. They were prepared for N to remain in contact with Mr and Mrs P and his siblings to ensure that he developed in a balanced way. They accepted that counselling would be necessary to help them and N cope with what had happened.

Coleridge J reserved his final words for surrogacy agencies and suggested that some surrogate mothers might have psychological difficulties relating to their own unacknowledged and unmet needs. Background checks on all potential surrogates and commissioning parents should be a priority for surrogacy organisations to avoid the muddle and emotional pain which had occurred in *Re P*. An immediate appeal was made by Mr and Mrs P to the Court of Appeal; it was rejected.[31]

In 2011, Baker J, in *Re T (a child) (surrogacy: residence order)*,[32] stressed the considerable risks attached to surrogacy arrangements, particularly when entered into on an informal basis and without any professional advice. The surrogate mother had met the intended parents over the internet. She already had twins aged 5 living with her, and was estranged from their father. She agreed to be impregnated with Mr W's sperm and hand over the baby at birth but changed her mind during the pregnancy.

Both the mother and Mr and Mrs W had exercised a somewhat economic approach to the truth in their relations with each other and with the court. The mother had adopted a false persona and used it in her e-mail correspondence with Mr and Mrs W to find out what they would do when they learned of her change of mind. She had also altered e-mails, which she had received from Mr and Mrs W, and presented them as evidence to the court of their behaviour. Baker J felt that her conduct called into question whether she could be trusted as a mother. He was also concerned about her heavy use of the internet and her sobriquet for a chat room which was 'Thongs, G-Strings, French Knickers, IT'S ALL GUD'. He felt that she was exposing herself to dangerous influences via the internet which could affect the children if she were not more restrained.

Baker J's concerns with respect to Mr and Mrs W centred on their relationship with a woman well known to the police who was a prostitute, with seven children in care. They had met her through the internet. She had stayed with Mr and Mrs W when pregnant with her sixth child. Baker J suggested that it was irresponsible of Mr and Mrs W to invite the woman into their home, with

---

[31] *P (A Child)* [2007] EWCA Civ 1053.
[32] [2011] All ER (D) 171 (Jan).

no apparent awareness of the potential risks involved. There were suggestions that Mr and Mrs W were contemplating using the woman as a surrogate mother. Baker J also found that Mr and Mrs W had lied about their previous experiences in their search for a surrogate mother, and about incidences of domestic violence between them. He thought that the couple demonstrated a startling lack of insight with respect to a young baby's needs, and the difficulties that might arise if T, still being breastfed and who had bonded with the surrogate mother, were to be transferred immediately, as they had requested, into their care.

Baker J distinguished the circumstances in *Re T* from those of *Re P*. He found that the surrogate mother had not set out with the deliberate intention of hoodwinking Mr W into providing her with a baby. She had acted in good faith. In his view:

> ' . . . the natural process of carrying and giving birth to a baby creates an attachment which may be so strong that the surrogate mother finds herself unable to give up the child . . . To remove her from her mother's care would cause a measure of harm. It is the mother who, I find, is better able to meet T's needs, in particular her emotional needs.'

However, it was not the end of the story for Mr and Mrs W, as they were given interim visiting contact with T, an arrangement which would be monitored by social workers. There would be a later hearing to decide T's long-term future.

(b)   Neither the surrogate mother nor the intended parents wish to keep the child

Where neither the surrogate mother nor the intended parents wish to keep the child, the child will become available for adoption and those deemed to be the legal parents of the child (see above Part IV(a)) will have to give their consent, unless the court is satisfied that their consent should be dispensed with.[33]

In 2000, an English woman agreed with an Italian man and his Portuguese wife, who lived in France, to become a surrogate mother for them. Donor sperm, obtained from an American sperm bank based in Copenhagen, and donor eggs, from an English woman, were used to create the embryos which were implanted by a Greek doctor in Athens – a truly international affair. However, a problem arose, as the foetuses turned out to be twin girls and not the boys which the intended parents had hoped for. They asked the surrogate mother to have an abortion and she refused. She did not, however, want to keep the children for herself and began the search for alternative parents. A lesbian couple in California put in a bid for the children via a surrogacy agency there. The twin girls were eventually born in hospital in California at a cost to the surrogate of $25,000 which the couple refused to reimburse. They subsequently adopted the babies. Professor Robert Winston, an English fertility expert,

---

[33]   See Adoption Act 2002, Chapter 3.

described the affair as an illustration of the worst aspects of surrogacy; the babies were treated as commodities rather than human beings.[34]

(c) The intended parents are domiciled outside the jurisdiction

In *Re G (Surrogacy: Foreign Domicile)*,[35] the intended parents, Mr and Mrs G, were domiciled in Turkey. They approached COTS and were introduced to a surrogate mother, Mrs J, who was separated from her husband, Mr J. Conception took place in Mrs J's home using Mr G's sperm. A baby girl, M, was born and she was handed over to Mr and Mrs G. They applied for a parental order. Two matters concerned the court, first, parental consent, and second, the intended parents' domicile. Mrs J's estranged husband was based in Spain and had failed to provide any information to the court about his attitude to the surrogacy. Mrs J's account was that Mr J had been aware of her general intention to act as a surrogate mother and had not objected but he was not aware of the actual surrogacy procedure that led to M's conception. The court took a wide approach to the issue of consent and declared that, in the absence of any communication from Mr J, he had not consented to his wife's insemination. He could not therefore be M's legal father and his consent to the grant of the parental order was not required.

There was a further problem in that Mr and Mrs G had not realised that they could not apply for a parental order because applicants must be domiciled in the jurisdiction. Their application was doomed. They successfully applied for an order under the Children Act 1989 which would give them parental responsibility and would terminate Mrs J's parental rights. The order would allow them to return to Turkey and adopt the child there.[36]

McFarlane J expressed the view, in *Re G*, that lessons must be learned from 'this cautionary tale' which had cost the taxpayer £35,000, and had delayed any permanent arrangement being made for M for 9 months after her birth. He laid down guidelines for future surrogacy arrangements:

- non-commercial surrogacy arrangements for intended parents domiciled outside of the jurisdiction should be discouraged because they cannot apply for a parental order under the HFEA 1990 (now see HFEA 2008). The arrangements have huge financial implications for public services if the child has to be adopted by the intended parents abroad. The child will have British nationality resulting from the surrogate's British nationality

---

[34] See *BioNews* 057, 8 May 2000 available at www.bionews.org.uk (accessed May 2011).
[35] [2007] EWHC 2814.
[36] See Adoption and Children Act 2002, s 84 which grants parental responsibility to proposed adoptive parents who intend to adopt outside of the jurisdiction. In order to qualify, applicants for a s 84 order must be neither domiciled nor habitually resident in England and Wales and the child must have had her home with the applicants during the preceding 10 weeks. Mr and Mrs G's circumstances plainly met those requirements at the time that they issued their application under s 84.

and a full enquiry will have to be made by social workers before the child
can leave the jurisdiction for adoption;

- agencies, such as COTS, should familiarise themselves with the law;

- applications for parental orders involving international elements should
  be dealt with by one of the specialist courts dealing with intercountry
  adoption or the High Court;

- courts have a duty to ensure that all of the qualifying conditions for the
  grant of parental orders must be met when the case involves an
  international element. There was evidence that the courts had not been
  taking a strict approach towards the need for applicants to meet the
  requirements and that parental orders had been incorrectly granted;[37] and

- where a married woman is estranged from her husband, all reasonable
  attempts should be made to establish that he did not consent to the
  surrogacy arrangement.

(d)   Overseas surrogacy for intended parents domiciled within the jurisdiction

Many would-be parents resort to using commercial overseas agencies because
they have difficulties in finding a surrogate mother in the jurisdiction. India, in
particular, has become an important centre of international outsourcing of
surrogacy for intended parents. Many of these are ethnic Asians, domiciled in
the jurisdiction, who would prefer to have a surrogate mother of Asian
ethnicity. The cost of surrogacy in India is regarded as low in the Western
context, around £2,500 plus medical costs. There has been substantial debate
about Indian surrogacy mainly relating to exploitation of surrogate mothers
and the lack of regulation of the practice.[38] Dr Naina Patel, who runs a
well-known reproduction clinic in Gujerat, does not accept that surrogate
mothers are exploited although she does acknowledge that surrogacy is
minimally regulated in India. She maintains that Western outsourcing of
surrogacy is a positive service for both infertile couples and surrogate mothers.
Her view is that the latter are well looked after during pregnancy. They are
housed in dormitories attached to the clinic where they are given expert medical
supervision, and receive a good diet, to ensure the birth of a healthy child. The
women earn more than the equivalent of ten times the salary of a rural Indian
which will transform their lives, and allow them to buy a house or educate their
own children. Dr Patel demands that intended parents provide their own sperm

---

[37]   The social worker from COTS maintained that COTS had been involved in at least 20 cases
where parental orders had been granted to intended parents domiciled outside of the
jurisdiction.

[38]   Amelia Gentleman 'India Nurtures Business of Surrogate Motherhood' *New York Times,* 10
March 2008; Anand Kumar 'Ethical Aspects of Assisted Reproduction – an Indian viewpoint'
(2007) 14(1) *Reproductive BioMedicine Online* 140–142.

and eggs to create the embryo, so the children born are not biologically related to the surrogate mother. She recruits only women who already have their own children because she believes that they are less likely to become emotionally attached to their surrogate babies on birth. Dr Patel maintains that she always ensures that the women are willing to become surrogate mothers and not being pressured to do so by their families for economic reasons.

Dr Mohanlal Swarankar, chairman of the Mahatma Gandhi Institute of Medical Sciences in Jaipur, and one of the leading fertility experts in India, does not share Dr Patel's view. He sees commercial surrogacy as exploitative and would like to see it outlawed. He argues that many of the women have to lie to their families and friends, and pretend that they are studying, or have jobs, away from home to avoid the shame attached to surrogacy. He is also concerned that it is impossible to tell whether the women are freely offering their services; the money they receive may be forcibly taken from them by those who have pressurised them into surrogacy. He believes that the women will be socially stigmatised, and may experience difficulties in their marital relationships. In a conservative society, carrying a child for another man, who is a stranger, is not to be publicised. It is viewed as not far removed from adultery.

At the other end of the spectrum, many English intended parents, particularly gay couples, have sought surrogate mothers in the US where commercial surrogacy in most states is unregulated. Thus, people may engage in surrogacy arrangements without fear of legal redress but the courts will not necessarily enforce the surrogacy agreement if the surrogate mother changes her mind. Tony and Barrie Drewitt-Barlow, gay civil partners living in England, have acquired five children by way of surrogacy in the US. They have used donor eggs and their sperm to create embryos which were implanted into a US-based surrogate mother. They have now opened the British Surrogacy Centre with an office in California to coordinate and match up surrogates, donors and parents from both America and the UK.[39]

Although it may be easier to find surrogate mothers overseas, many intended parents have experienced difficulties when they try to return to the jurisdiction with a child born by way of surrogacy overseas. Two major interrelated problems face them, first, the issue of commercial payments to the surrogate mother which, although legal in the overseas surrogate mother's country, remain illegal in England. Secondly, the intended parents confront the complexities, and at times, the irrationality, of the immigration law which is frequently at odds with the law of the child's birth. They may be forced to find devious and different ways around the immigration laws to bring the child into the country[40] and apply for a parental order.

---

[39] See www.britishsurrogacycentre.com. It is rather strange that the agency in itself is not illegal as it is not charging intended parents a fee but it is advising parents to go to the US knowing full well that they will have to pay a fee there to the surrogate mother which will be illegal in England.

[40] Some intended parents have brought children into the country on a passport of the child's

In *X and Y (Foreign Surrogacy)*,[41] Hedley J aptly described the path to parenthood for an English husband and wife, who were applying for a parental order for twins born in the Ukraine after a surrogacy agreement with a Ukrainian married woman, as:

> '. . . less a journey along a primrose path, more a trek through a thorn forest. The court shares their hope that their experiences may alert others to the difficulties inherent in this journey.'

The intended parents had agreed with a married Ukrainian woman that she would be implanted with embryos created from the intended father's sperm and anonymously donated eggs. In the Ukraine, surrogacy agreements are legally enforceable, and on the birth of the child, the surrogate mother loses all her parental rights and duties. The intended parents are registered on the child's birth certificate and acquire all parental rights and duties. The child has no rights of residence in, or citizenship of, the Ukraine. The state has minimal responsibility for such a child other than to house him or her in one of its orphanages as a basic act of humanity.

The surrogate mother duly gave birth to twins in the Ukraine and handed them over to the intended parents. Under English law, the intended parents had, of course, no parental rights over the children until they acquired them either by the grant of a parental order under the HFEA 1990 (see now HFEA 2008) or an order under the Children Act 1989 or the Adoption Act 2002. The Ukrainian mother and her husband, who had consented to the surrogacy, remained the twins' legal parents. Hedley J highlighted the fact that the combined effect of Ukrainian and English law resulted in the twins being 'marooned stateless and parentless whilst the applicants could neither remain in the Ukraine nor bring the children home'. In the end, the intended father succeeded in satisfying the UK immigration authorities by way of DNA tests, processed in the jurisdiction, that he was the biological father of both children. The twins were then given discretionary leave to enter the jurisdiction with the intended parents 'outside the rules'.[42] This would allow the intended parents to apply for a parental order.

Hedley J commented that:

> 'It requires little imagination to appreciate, even for a professional couple as resourceful and competent as these applicants, the stress and anxiety involved let

---

country of birth after applying for a UK tourist visa. On arrival in the jurisdiction, they have then applied for UK citizenship for the child. This does not resolve the issue of parental rights with respect to the child.

41 [2008] EWHC 3030 (Fam).

42 The UK Border Agency has issued guidance for an application to be made 'outside the Rules'. It states: 'If either of the commissioning couple has a genetic connection with the child, entry outside the Rules at the discretion of the Secretary of State may be possible, but such entry clearance will only be granted on condition that a Section 30 Parental Order is applied for within 6 months of birth and where evidence suggests that such an order is likely to be granted . . .'.

alone the expense of prolonged accommodation in the Ukraine (at comparable cost to England), the obtaining of expert legal advice, both English and Ukrainian, the cost of testing and immigration negotiations and so forth – all this in the context of first-time parenting. It was as well in this case that there was no pressing need for medical treatment. It may be worth adding that the grant of a parental order does not of itself confer citizenship although the evidence suggests that it is very unlikely to be denied if sought.'

Hedley J also acknowledged that, in these overseas surrogate birth cases, the time taken to obtain the necessary paperwork to enable the children to legally enter the jurisdiction could mean that the parents would find themselves outside the strict 6-month post-birth limit for applications for parental orders.

At the hearing for the parental order, the intended parents had fulfilled all the conditions except one; there remained the outstanding question of their payments to the surrogate mother. She had received €235 per month during pregnancy, and had been given an additional €25,000 after the birth of the twins. This latter sum was dependent on the completion of the Ukrainian legalities and her consent to the grant of the English parental order. The payments were legal in the Ukraine but there was no doubt that these sums significantly exceeded 'expenses reasonably incurred' as permitted under the SSA 1985. The surrogate mother intended to use some of the money to put down a deposit for the purchase of a flat. Hedley J accepted that the law allowed him to authorise the illegal payments retrospectively but there was no guidance in the Act on the basis for any such approval. He found it difficult to see any other reason for authorisation than the welfare of the child for whom the parental order was sought.

Hedley J found the process of authorisation most uncomfortable and explained:

'What the court is required to do is to balance two competing and potentially irreconcilably conflicting concepts. Parliament is clearly entitled to legislate against commercial surrogacy and is clearly entitled to expect that the courts should implement that policy consideration in its decisions. Yet it is also recognised that as the full rigour of that policy consideration will bear on one wholly unequipped to comprehend it let alone deal with its consequences (ie the child concerned) that rigour must be mitigated by the application of a consideration of that child's welfare. That approach is both humane and intellectually coherent. The difficulty is that it is almost impossible to imagine a set of circumstances in which by the time the case comes to court, the welfare of any child (particularly a foreign child) would not be gravely compromised (at the very least) by a refusal to make an order . . . If public policy is truly to be upheld, it would need to be enforced at a much earlier stage than the final hearing of a s 30 application.[43] In relation to adoption this has been substantially addressed by rules surrounding the bringing of the child into the country and by the provisions of the Adoption with a Foreign Element Regulations 2005. The point of admission to this country is in some ways the final opportunity in reality to

---

[43] Now see HFEA 2008, s 54.

prevent the effective implementation of a commercial surrogacy agreement. It is, of course, not for the court to suggest how (or even whether) action should be taken, I merely feel constrained to point out the problem.'

He proceeded to ask whether the intended parents were acting in good faith and without 'moral taint' in their dealings with the surrogate mother, and whether they had been involved in any attempt to defraud the authorities. He found that they were acting in good faith and had not taken advantage of the surrogate mother. The monies paid were not so disproportionate to 'expenses reasonably incurred' that to authorise them and grant the parental order would be an unacceptable affront to public policy. In his judgment, the ascertainment of what amounts to 'expenses reasonably incurred' is a question of fact in each case. The welfare of the twins and their need for a stable family life necessitated the grant of the order. Hedley J suggested that these complex international surrogacy cases should be dealt with by the High Court. He reserved his final comments for Parliament:

'In the Parliamentary debates surrounding human fertilisation and embryology this year, the government indicated that it was minded to review the law and regulation of surrogacy. It is no part of the court's function to express views on that save perhaps to observe that some of the issues thrown up in this case may highlight the wisdom of holding such a review. In any event, part of the purpose of adjourning this case into open court was to illustrate the sort of difficulties that currently can and do appear. This relates to the obvious difficulties of nationality, control of the commercial element, the rules of consent and the question of legal parentage. Less obviously, but importantly, is the fact that the present law (at least as understood by this court) might encourage the less scrupulous to take advantage of the more vulnerable, unmarried surrogate mothers and to be less than frank in the arrangements that surround foreign surrogacy arrangements. Whether surrogacy should be examined in isolation from other contentious issues surrounding the inception or creation of life (let alone the fraught questions of end of life) is not for this court to say beyond the observation that these issues merit the widest public debate even if the ultimate conclusion be that they continue to be finally resolved on a case-by-case basis by judicial decision.'

In *L (A Minor)*,[44] the English intended parents had also acted illegally when they agreed with an American woman to pay her beyond her reasonable expenses to act as a surrogate mother for them. The agreement was legal in Illinois, USA. By the time the intended parents' application for a parental order reached the court, the HFEA 2008 was in force. Hedley J highlighted the fact that the new Act emphasised that the welfare of the child should be the court's paramount consideration and not merely its first consideration as in HFEA 1990, s 30 applications.[45] It followed therefore that he had little choice other than to authorise retrospectively the unreasonable payments to the surrogate mother. He maintained that:

---

[44]   [2010] EWHC 3146.
[45]   The significant change in the new Act, other than the enlargement of the scope of applicants, relates to the welfare test. The effect of the 2010 Regulations (SI 2010/986) is to import into s 54 applications the provisions of s 1 of the Adoption and Children Act 2002. In fact in *Re X*

' . . . it will only be in the clearest case of the abuse of public policy that the court will be able to withhold an order if otherwise welfare considerations support the making of an order. This underlines the High Court's earlier observations that, if it is desired to control commercial surrogacy arrangements, those controls need to operate before the court process is initiated ie at the border or even before.'

It is difficult to see how Hedley J's views could be put into practice. Once a child has been born as a consequence of an overseas commercial surrogacy agreement, and is handed over to the intended parents, he or she would inevitably suffer harm if denied entry into the jurisdiction. The intended parents are unlikely to have rights of residence in the country of the child's birth, and if they were forced to leave the child behind, he or she would become a legal orphan. Whilst it might, in principle, be possible to impose fines on those who break the law, or even remove the child and place him or her for adoption, the welfare of the child would undoubtedly be affected.

In *Re K (Minors) (Foreign Surrogacy)*,[46] Hedley J yet again was forced to draw attention to the immigration problems which stem from overseas surrogacy agreements. An English couple had agreed with a married woman, who lived in India, that she would be implanted with embryos created from anonymous donor eggs and the intended father's sperm. The woman gave birth to twins in India. The intended parents applied for a parental order but required entry clearance to bring the children into the jurisdiction before their application could be considered. The court was asked to indicate whether it was likely that their application for a parental order would be granted to conform with the UK Border Agency's guidance known as 'The Inter-Country Surrogacy and the Immigration Rules'. Paragraph 41 states:

'If either of the commissioning couple has a genetic connection with the child, entry outside the Rules at the discretion of the Secretary of State may be possible, but such entry clearance will only be granted on condition that a . . . Parental Order is applied for within 6 months of birth and where evidence suggests that such an order is likely to be granted . . .'

Hedley J felt considerable disquiet about indicating the likelihood of a parental order being granted and declined to do so. He explained that:

'In the first place I am not presently satisfied that I currently have jurisdiction over these children. Secondly, there remain both outstanding welfare enquiries and an invitation to the Court to exercise its jurisdiction under Section 30(7) to approve certain payments under the agreement. Thirdly the court must be careful not to usurp functions which specifically belong to the executive. And fourthly the giving of advisory opinions (as opposed to Declarations establishing rights or the lawfulness of an action) are alien to the traditional practice of the court. On the other hand it is difficult not to be sympathetic to the actual difficulties faced by

---

and Y (n 41 above) the court had adopted in its welfare consideration the perspective of the 2002 Act. What has changed, however, is that welfare is no longer merely the court's first consideration but becomes its paramount consideration.

[46]   [2010] EWHC 1180.

these applicants . . . it is necessary that the court acts correctly and not simply out of sympathy . . . If and when the children are in the country (and only then) can the court proceed further with this application.'

Hedley J accepted that his decision had serious consequences for future applicants who might find that the 6-month time limit for applications for parental orders had elapsed before they could enter the country.

The intended parents in *Re K* found themselves in a bizarre, and impossible, Alice in Wonderland world, forced to remain in limbo and apart from their children. Their only hope was that Hedley J's obiter comment that they appeared to have fulfilled most of the necessary conditions would be found by the Entry Clearance Office to be sufficiently helpful to allow the children's entry into the jurisdiction.

VI   CONCLUSION

Surrogacy has changed dramatically since the first legislation to control it was enacted in 1985. It no longer involves a small group of people who engage in home insemination but rather an ever-increasing number of intended parents seeking various forms of highly technological reproduction in licensed clinics in the jurisdiction and in clinics overseas. It is unrealistic to imagine that this can be achieved by non-commercial transactions for the majority of would-be parents and surrogate mothers.

The decisions discussed in this *Survey* demonstrate the need for an urgent overhaul of the law relating to surrogacy. It is ludicrous to have a law based on a half-hearted disapproval of surrogacy, a law which permits the practice in a way which does not serve the interests of the parties involved. Uncertainty prevails, and children's lives are put on hold as two sets of potential carers fight about their future. Procreation by way of surrogacy appears to be the legal poor relation of children's law. It is such a poor relation that it has not been seen worthy of serious legislation judging from Parliament's minimalist efforts to date. The recent amendments to the original legislation, which are contained in the HFEA 2008, alongside the 2010 Regulations,[47] have not addressed any of the problematic issues facing the participants in surrogacy arrangements. One is led to conclude that the government and its predecessors have all put their heads in the sand, with the hope that the problem will go away.

This approach is short-sighted; surrogacy, and particularly, overseas surrogacy, is growing rapidly. Commercial surrogacy, although forbidden by law, is retrospectively authorised by the courts on a regular basis. The lack of serious regulation sits rather uneasily with the strict regulation of both domestic and international adoption in the jurisdiction. Commercial adoption in any form is not permitted, and any prospective adoptive parent who attempted to engage in

---

[47]   Above n 45.

it would soon find that adoption was no longer open to them.[48] All prospective adoptive parents must also go through an elaborate vetting process.

Because surrogacy is possible does not mean that it should not be regulated. There are ethical decisions to be made about its desirability,[49] and what forms of surrogacy, if any should be permitted. A number of ethical issues need to be addressed prior to any further decisions about its regulation. The HFEA, or its replacement body, would seem to be the appropriate body to reconsider the practice of surrogacy and suggest a realistic way forward. It is only then that legislation can be formulated. Some of the important questions which require consideration are:

- What forms of surrogacy should be permitted? Should familial surrogacy, or surrogacy undertaken by friends, where no payment is involved be regarded differently from surrogacy involving reasonable payments to the surrogate mother?

- Should all insemination take place in licensed clinics?

- Should there be a vetting procedure by social services of both surrogate mothers and intended parents in advance of any surrogacy agreement? If so what sanctions should there be for going ahead with an agreement without obtaining approval?

- Should the retrospective authorisation of payments deemed to be unreasonable be repealed?

- What sanctions should be exercised against parents who flout the commercial surrogacy rule? Would sanctions include fines or the draconian removal of the child for adoption by a third party?

- Should the absolute right of a surrogate mother to veto a parental order be reconsidered? In any application for such an order, should the court decide, on the basis of the paramountcy principle, the possibility of adoption of the child by a third party?

- Should overseas surrogacy be banned? If so, what sanctions should there be for intended parents commissioning overseas surrogacy? If it is not to be banned, what concern should there be about exploitation of women in underdeveloped countries? And how should the Immigration Rules be modified to allow children to be brought into the jurisdiction?

---

[48] *Re C (A Minor) (Adoption Application)* [1992] 1 FCR 337.
[49] See Susan Golombok, Clare Murray, Vasanti Jadva, Fiona MacCallum and Emma Lycett 'Families Created Through Surrogacy Arrangements: Parent–Child Relationships in the 1st Year of Life' (2004) 40(3) *Developmental Psychology American Psychological Association* 400, which gives a positive view of surrogacy.

- Should surrogacy agencies be permitted to exist and if so how should they be regulated? Should they be brought under the umbrella of the HFEA, or its replacement body or under local authority children's departments?

- Why should single parents be unable to obtain a parental order?

Natalie Gamble and Louisa Ghevaert, lawyers practising in the surrogacy field have stated in a compelling way that:[50]

> 'We need a better and more planned approach to surrogacy. Of course, there are difficult and sensitive issues to be handled in creating new law. Surrogacy arrangements are among the most ethically and humanly complex in assisted reproduction, with three or even four adults involved throughout the process of conception, pregnancy and birth, and possibly third party gamete donors as well. The respective interests, protection and independence from exploitation of all these adults and, most importantly, the resulting child, need to be adequately balanced and protected by the law.'

---

[50] *BioNews* 532, 2 November 2009: available at www.bionews.org.uk (accessed May 2011).

France

REVIEW OF FAMILY LAW IN 2010

Centre de droit de la famille (Université Jean Moulin, Lyon)[*]

Résumé

Dans cette chronique du droit de la famille pour l'année 2010, les auteurs abordent plusieurs sujets. Au cours de la dernière décennie, la question de l'ouverture du mariage aux personnes de même sexe a fait l'objet en France de grands débats. Le droit français ne reconnaît pas le mariage entre personnes de même sexe. Il est probable que le droit européen n'obligera pas les États à légiférer en la matière. En revanche, pour ce qui est de la reconnaissance en France de mariages homosexuels qui ont été valablement célébrés à l'étranger, l'appartenance de la France à l'Union européenne pourrait bien avoir de lourdes conséquences. Ce texte examine également la question du rapprochement des statuts conjugaux, l'homoparenté, l'adoption par un couple homosexuel, les évolutions de la justice familiale, l'allègement des procédures de divorce, les problèmes actuels reliés aux conséquences du divorce, ainsi que la question de la gestation pour autrui. Certains ont pu tenter de contourner la prohibition française de la gestation pour autrui en se rendant dans un État autorisant le recours aux mères porteuses afin d'y faire établir un lien de filiation avec l'enfant avec l'espoir de faire ensuite reconnaître son statut en France.

I THE QUESTION OF SAME-SEX MARRIAGE

Over the last decade, same-sex marriage has been a controversial topic in France. Currently, French law does not allow couples of the same sex to marry. Even if the law did not specifically exclude it, the Civil Code can be used in support of this position.[1] This argument was applied by the *Cour de Cassation* (Supreme Court) on 13 March 2007 after a French civil officer had conducted a marriage ceremony for two men in 2004, despite opposition from the Minister for Public Affairs. The court said that 'according to French law, marriage is the union between a man and a woman'. The case has been appealed to the

---

[*] This chapter was written under the supervision of Professor Hugues Fulchiron, Director of the Centre de droit de la famille, by Benoît de Boysson, Amélie Panet, Christine Bidaut-Garon, Renaud Daubricourt, Younes Bernand, Stessy Têtard and Aurélien Molière, researchers at the Centre de droit de la famille.

[1] Compare arts 75, 108, 144, 197 and those prohibiting incest.

European Court of Human Rights (ECtHR);[2] but France should be able to avoid an adverse judgment if the ECtHR remains consistent with its judgment in *Schalk*.[3]

Thanks to recent constitutional reform, every citizen has had the right since 1 March 2010 to contest the constitutionality of a law, which helps to uphold the rights and liberties guaranteed by the Constitution. The supporters of homosexual marriage have taken the opportunity to refer art 144 and 75, last paragraph of the Civil Code, to the *Conseil Constitutionnel* (Constitutional Council). In its decision on 28 January 2011,[4] the *Conseil Constitutionnel* affirmed that restricting marriage to people of the opposite sex does not compromise the liberty of same-sex couples, whether they live together or have entered a *Pacs* (similar to a registered civil partnership). They also held that the constitutionally guaranteed right to family life does not imply a right for same-sex couples to marry. Having recalled that 'the principle of equality does not forbid the legislator from using different legal forms for different types of relationship, provided that in each case the difference in treatment that results is in proportion to the purpose of the law', the court, as it had said some weeks earlier in relation to adoption by a homosexual couple,[5] decided not to substitute its own opinion for that of the legislator on the question of whether the difference in circumstances justifies a difference in treatment. They sent the legislation back to Parliament in order to decide the question applying the court's dicta on proportionality. This decision is an appropriate one for the legislator to make: justice may compel them to change the definition of marriage but this is a political choice rather than an obligation for the courts. The French position corresponds anyway to that of the ECtHR.

(a)   The ECtHR and same-sex marriage

The ECtHR has (finally!) released a statement on the refusal to allow same-sex couples to marry, in its judgment *Schalk et Kopf v Austriche* of 24 June 2010. Evoking a 'large area of discretion for political, economic or social policies', the Court limited its jurisdiction on this issue of discrimination. It decided that neither Art 12 of the European Convention on Human Rights (ECHR) nor Arts 8 and 14 together have the effect of obliging states to open marriage to same-sex couples. It recognised, however, that, when such a couple's relationship is stable, they have a right to respect for their family life. The judgment is important for the Charter of Fundamental Rights, which accompanied the introduction of the Lisbon Treaty, now at the heart of the European Union. The Charter does not address the issue of sexuality. Article 9 provides:

---

2   *Chapin et Charpentier v France*, App no 40183/07, 27 October 2009.
3   *Shalk and Kopf v Austria*, App no 30141/04, 24 June 2010.
4   Decision no 2010–92, QPC.
5   See Part III.

'The right to marry and the right to found a family shall be guaranteed in accordance with the national laws governing the exercise of these rights.' The EU member states retain, therefore, a certain amount of freedom: as the Presidium of the Convention on the Charter of Fundamental Rights of the European Union had affirmed, 'this article does not require marriage to be extended to couples of the same sex.'

The European Court of Justice (ECJ) seems loyal to a traditional concept of marriage: it affirmed in a judgment on 31 May 2001[6] that 'the term marriage . . . designates a union between two people of the opposite sex'. Since then several member states have opened up marriage to homosexuals (Netherlands in 2001, Belgium in 2003, Spain in 2005, Sweden in 2009, and Portugal and Slovenia in 2010). However, it is unlikely that EU law will oblige states to legislate domestically in favour of same-sex marriage. On the other hand, on the issue of the recognition in France of same-sex marriages validly celebrated overseas, EU membership could have important implications for France.

(b)   The recognition in France of same-sex marriages validly celebrated overseas.

The French administration seems rather favourable to the recognition in France of same-sex marriages validly celebrated overseas. In 2008, the French tax department allowed two Dutch couples to fill out a tax declaration, proof that these relationships are easily assimilated with marriage. The issue of the recognition of a same-sex marriage validly celebrated overseas has not yet come before the French courts, but it is possible to speculate what impact the ECJ jurisprudence will have. The judgments of *Garcia Avello* in 2003 and *Grunkin Paul* in 2008 emphasise the tendency of the ECJ to promote freedom of movement of EU citizens, sometimes to the detriment of the coherence of the private international law systems of its member states. The ideal of European citizenship requires freedom of movement throughout the EU, and it is not unlikely that a similar argument will lead the French courts to recognise marriages between people of the same-sex validly celebrated within the EU. Although marriage raises fundamental issues in society, the ECJ has shown itself to be especially bold concerning the prerogatives which have not been transferred from member states to the EU.[7] The freedoms and benefits which the EU guarantees its citizens are fundamental rights that take priority over the views of the states and forces them to modify their legislation even if this means that it would be contrary at a purely domestic level to their public order.

---

6   *Allemagne and Royaume de Suède v Conseil de l'Union Européenne*, aff. jointes C-122/99 P et C-125/99 P (*Kingdom of Sweden v Council of the European Union*, joined cases C-122/99 and C-125/99 P).

7   Notably in the case *Rottman* of March 2010, where the Court declared itself competent to control the motives in withdrawing German nationality from an individual, despite this being a sovereign prerogative of the states, because that ought to be one of the incidences of European citizenship.

II THE CONVERGING OF DIFFERENT KINDS OF CONJUGAL STATUS

Since the law of 15 November 1999,[8] France has allowed heterosexual couples to choose between three forms of legally recognised relationships: concubinage (the equivalent of the common law de facto relationship), the civil pact of solidarity (Pacs) and marriage. Same-sex couples may only choose from the first two. However, for couples concerned about legalising their relationship, the consequences are becoming less important, because the reconciliation between the different couple laws is so great.

The first type of union, concubinage, in principle only describes a set of facts rather than implying important rights or particular protection. The legislator gave a legal definition of concubinage in 1999,[9] but the definition did not match the nature of concubinage at all. However, concubinage seems to be benefiting from the spontaneous development of a type of *droit commun du couple*. The legislator's practice consists of referring to *la vie de couple* (a phrase not distinguishing between concubinage, Pacs and marriage) with the aim that each of the three legal forms of relationship will be treated alike. Several examples highlight this process.

With regards to domestic violence, the law of 12 September 2005[10] had already reinforced the rights of the *procureur de la République* (public prosecutor) where the defendant commits an offence against a cohabitant, civil partner or spouse. The law of 4 April 2006[11] generalised this approach to the family unit within the criminal law by making the fact that the victim is the defendant's partner an aggravating circumstance for a crime or offence, whatever the legal form of the couple's relationship. The law of 9 July 2010[12] integrated this approach into the civil law. It created a special provision in the Civil Code devoted to 'measures protecting victims of violence', which through arts 515–519 applies indiscriminately to 'violence between the couple'.

Another example of the idea of a *droit commun de couple* is the law of 12 May 2009[13] which entrusts jurisdiction to the same Family Court judge whatever legal form the couple's relationship takes. The law of 5 March 2007[14] allows the partner of someone who has a mental or physical disability to request the judge

---

[8] Law no 99–104 relating to the civil pact of solidarity, *Official Journal of the French Republic* (JORF) 15 November 1999, www.legifrance.gouv.fr.
[9] Ibid.
[10] Law no 2005–1549 in relation to the treatment of recidivism of criminal offences, JORF 13 December 2005, www.legifrance.gouv.fr.
[11] Law no 2006–399 reinforcing the prevention and suppression of violence between the couple or committed against minors, JORF 5 April 2006, www.legifrance.guv.fr.
[12] Law no 2010–769 relating to violence specifically against women, violence between the couple and incidences against children, JORF 10 July 2010, www.legifrance.gouv.fr.
[13] Law no 2009–526 on the simplification and clarification of the law and procedural relief, JORF 13 May 2009, www.legifrance.gouv.fr.
[14] Law no 2007–308 reforming the legal protection of adults, JORF 7 March 2007, www.legifrance.gouv.fr.

to declare that the vulnerable person[20] requires assistance in making their decisions. There are three possible ways of doing this: *tutelle* (which removes all decision-making power from the vulnerable person), *curatell* (in which the person is allowed to do some things him or herself) and *sauvegarde de justice* (in which the person is allowed to do most of his or her own transactions). The decision-making power should usually be given to the vulnerable person's partner as a matter of priority.

Finally, concubinage relationships are not usually taken into account for tax purposes. There is an exception however when it comes to the *solidarité sur la fortune* tax,[15] although this is not really an advantage. This tax applies when the taxpayer's assets reach a value of €790,000. The tax department adds the assets of each partner to determine whether the tax applies.

The second status, Pacs, took a step closer to marriage with the law of 23 June 2006.[16] It brought Pacs so much closer to marriage that some scholars talk about the 'matrimonialisation' of Pacs. Pacs are seen as similar to marriage because they must be notified on the state register. There is also a right of succession if one partner dies.[17] The similarity in treatment is also seen in the way tax is applied: although the tax department once distinguished between married couples and non-married couples, the dichotomy is now between those who have formalised their relationship (through marriage and Pacs) or those who have not (concubinage).

Those who have formalised their relationship through Pacs can take advantage of benefits of the tax regimes which apply to married couples. First, regarding income tax, couples no longer need to wait until the third year of their union before they can benefit from the ability to be taxed together as a couple.[18] Secondly, regarding succession, the same tax regime applies to Pacs and marriage. A 2005 law removed the earlier 2-year requirement. The TEPA law of 21 August 2007[19] completed the assimilation process from Pacs to marriage in regard to succession. Today they benefit from identical abatements and tariffs concerning inter vivos transactions and a complete exemption in relation to succession matters.

Numerous other advantages have been explicitly extended to Pacs partners which were previously reserved for married couples. The law of 1 July 2010 reformed the area of consumer credit[20] by aligning joint and several liability law for the debts of partners with those of married couples: each partner is held jointly liable for the debts taken on by the other partner for daily expenditure,

---

[15] ISF – Art 885 E of the General Tax Code, www.legifrance.gouv.fr.
[16] Law no 2006–728 reforming the law of succession and gifts, JORF 24 June 2006, www.legifrance.gouv.fr.
[17] Articles 515-3-1, 515–6 and 763 of the Civil Code, www.legifrance.gouv.fr.
[18] Law no 2004–1484 of 30 December 2004 on the finances for 2005, JORF 31 December 2004, www.legifrance.gouv.fr.
[19] Law no 2007–1223 on work, employment and purchase power, JORF 22 August 2007, www.legifrance.gouv.fr.
[20] Law no 2010–737 reforming consumer credit law, JORF 2 July 2010, www.legifrance.gouv.fr.

unless they are unreasonable or arise from a hire-purchase or a loan (unless these are obtained for reasonable daily expenditure).[21] Therefore, even if the debt has been incurred by only one partner, creditors may enforce its entire payment against the other partner.

The attraction of the matrimonial model explains the trend to develop the Pacs more closely in line with marriage. One current parliamentary debate concerns the possibility of extending the *pension de réversion* to unmarried couples. This *pension de réversion* corresponds to a social security payment to the surviving partner or a proportion of the retirement pension of the deceased partner. Currently this pension (provided by the social security system) is only available to married partners. A certain number of writers and statements of the law tend to generalise what appears like a real advantage for married people.

The third status, marriage, has several aspects that mask its uniqueness. It is discussed in two contexts: the frequency of divorce, recently facilitated by the amendments of 26 May 2004,[22] and secondly, the evolution of the law of filiation, aligning 'natural' and 'legitimate' births.[23] Elsewhere, whether the adoption provisions are consistent with art 365 of the French Civil Code has recently been considered by the *Cour de Cassation au Conseil Constitutionnel*.[24] It flows from this provision that, outside of marriage, the adoption of the partner's child deprives the partner of their parental authority. The court ruled on 6 October 2010 that 'the difference in the situations of married and unmarried couples justifies, in the interests of the child, the differences of treatment in the adoption process'. Above all it considered that it was not right 'to substitute its view for that of the legislature on the consequences to be drawn from the special situation where children are brought up by two persons of the same sex'. The court therefore sent the law back to the legislature to reconsider the issue whether couples of the same sex can adopt.[25]

III   SAME-SEX PARENTS

The *Cour de Cassation* had refused, on 23 February 2007, to sanction the adoption by a woman of her partner's child. The rationale was that, because of art 365 of the Civil Code,[26] the adoption would transfer the rights of parental authority to the adoptive parent, which would effectively deprive the biological mother of her rights.

---

21   Civil Code, art 220 for spouses and art 515–4 for partners, www.legifrance.gouv.fr.
22   Law no 2004–439 on divorce, JORF 27 May 2004, www.legifrance.gouv.fr.
23   Ordinance no 2005–759 of 4 July 2005 reforming filiation, JORF 6 July 2005, and law no 2009–61 of 16 January 2009 ratifying the ordinance of 4 July 2005 reforming filiation and modifying or repealing various provisions relating to filiation, JORF 18 January 2009, www.legifrance.gouv.fr.
24   Decision no 2010–39 QPC of 6 October 2010, www.conseil-constitutionnel.fr.
25   Cf in the same sense, the decision of the *Conseil Constitutionnel* on marriage between persons of the same sex, above Part I.
26   Article 365 of the Civil Code: 'An adopter is, with regard to the adoptee, alone invested with all the rights of parental authority, including that of consenting to the marriage of the adoptee,

A similar issue has recently been examined by the ECtHR in its decision on 31 August 2010 in *Gas et Dubois v France*. Without making a final judgment, the ECtHR declared admissible the petition of a woman whose application to adopt her lesbian partner's child had been refused. Counsel argued that the rejection of the adoption application by France, again authorised by art 365 of the Civil Code, discriminates against the rights of homosexuals to private and family life, in violation of both Arts 8 and 14 of the ECHR. The case will be worth following.

For homosexuals who wish to adopt alone and not as a couple, French law does not in principle oppose this parental goal: since 1966 single (ie unmarried) people have been able to adopt, but only one such order has been made. The French administrative practice very often fails to give effect to such policies: to adopt in France requires an administrative agreement, which is particularly difficult to obtain for homosexuals. The ECtHR in its ruling in *EB v France* of 23 January 2008 condemned France for discrimination based on sexual orientation. Even if the European jurisprudence seems to be pushing France to comply with its EU obligations regarding homosexuals, dismissing the argument about the absence of a father figure, it is likely that French authorities will continue to put up some resistance.

On the other hand, France has been flexible when deciding whether to recognise adoption orders made validly in a foreign country. In a ruling on 8 July 2010, the *Cour de Cassation* arranged the transcription on the state register of an American adoption order in favour of a homosexual couple. An American woman had conceived a child through artificial insemination; her partner, of French nationality, had asked and obtained from the superior court of Delkab (Georgia) an adoption order in her favour. The American decision envisaged a sharing of parental authority between the biological mother and the adoptive mother, and the rectification of the birth certificate describing the French adopter as 'parent', and the biological mother as mother. The adoptive mother petitioned the *TGI de Paris* and then the *Cour d'Appel de Paris* for the execution of the American judgment. The petition was refused because according to art 365[27] adopting the child vests all the parental authority in the adoptive parent: therefore the biological mother would be deprived of all her parental rights, which would be against the interests of the child, embarrassing France internationally. The *Cour de Cassation* overturned the decision: since the American decision envisaged sharing parental authority between the mother and the adoptive parent, it was unlikely to embarrass France or compromise the child's interests.

---

unless she or he is the spouse of the father or of the mother of the adoptee; in that event, the adopter has parental authority concurrently with his or her spouse, who retains its exercise alone, subject to a joint declaration with the adopter before the chief clerk of the tribunal de grande instance for the purpose of an exercise in common of that authority.'

[27] Which, according to the lower court judges, regulates the effects of adoption in relation to parental authority in France.

The creation of a same-sex family in France is therefore still excluded, but orders which have been made overseas may be recognised.

IV   DEBATES ABOUT SURROGACY

Some people have tried to bypass the French prohibition on surrogacy by entering into a surrogacy agreement in a foreign state where they are recognised as the legal parent, and then returning to France hoping to have the parentage recognised.

The Supreme Court of California, in a judgment on 14 July 2000, had conferred on a French couple, Mr and Mrs Menesson, the legal status of parents for two children conceived through surrogacy. In 2002 the children's births were put on the register in Nantes, until, at the request of the public Ministry, the registration was removed. On appeal, the *Cour d'Appel de Paris* ruled that the action of the Ministry was improper. Furthermore, in an obiter dictum, the court affirmed that 'not transcribing births would be contrary to the best interests of the children, who, under French law, would be deprived of the benefits obtained through legal recognition of their filiation, including the relationship with their biological father'. The *Cour de Cassation*, on 17 December 2008, overturned the *Cour d'Appel's* judgment and declared that the actions of the official were proper. The *Cour d'Appel*, differently constituted, was required to make its decision again.

Applying the *Cour de Cassation's* judgment, the *Cour d'Appel* declared, in a ruling on 18 March 2010, that the Californian judgment 'by indirectly validating a surrogacy agreement had compromised the French conception of the international public order'. The public order argument is not new, but the judgment gives it an international dimension: in order to maintain consistency with the decision to forbid the practice of surrogacy in France, it is necessary to override concerns about the international public order in relation to recognising a surrogacy agreement validly entered into overseas.

When discussing the interests of the child, which it advanced as a compelling argument in a 2007 decision, the *Cour d'Appel de Paris* made a volte face by effectively suppressing this principle as found in international conventions:

> ' . . . the best interests of the child would still be upheld, despite the very real difficulties presented by this situation, by validating the process a posteriori through French legislation. For now, the absence of registration does not deprive the two children of their American citizenship and does not prevent them from enforcing their rights as children of M and Mme Menesson under Californian law.'

Therefore, the *Cour d'Appel* explicitly admitted the creation of a rather awkward situation: legal parentage exists on the American register and the children may take advantage of it, but there was no obligation to register their parentage in France. In the end, the interests of the children, who would probably want to see the link to their parents recognised on French soil, meant little.

This is the latest episode to date in the 'judicial soap opera' of the Menesson twins. An appeal to the *Cour de Cassation* has not been ruled out, but it is likely that the *Cour Régulatrice* might consider the matter not worth pursuing. However, if it were to maintain its position, the ECtHR could also be successfully appealed to. In the important decision of *Wagner* delivered on 28 June 2007, the ECtHR condemned Luxembourg for refusing to recognise a Peruvian adoption in favour of a single woman, because Luxembourg did not allow single people to adopt. Basing itself on the right to respect for family life existing de facto, the ECtHR held that the superior interests of the child took priority and that it was necessary to register the adoption in full, thus taking account of the social reality of the situation and providing legal protection to family life, whatever form it took.

The situation of the Menesson twins is not strictly identical but it is in fact certain that the twins have lived as this French couple's children for the last 10 years. Their social status is well established, and arguably the best interests of the child as analysed by the ECtHR requires France to recognise and register the Californian adoption.

V NEW FAMILY COURT PROCEDURES

The evolution of family law is directly linked to the way the family unit has itself changed: the increase of divorce and separation, the increase in custody rights disputes, the increase of non-marital relationships, Pacs and concubinage. This all reflects changes in the concept of what a family is.

Created in 1975 to administer the divorce laws, the *juge de aux affaires matrimoniales* (JAM) became in 1993 the *juge aux affaires familiales* (JAF) with jurisdiction extending to custody disputes, whether or not the child is legitimate. Despite controversy over non-marital relationships on 12 May 2009[28] a new law extending the jurisdiction for these types of families was passed. Therefore the *juge aux affaires familiales* is now the *juge de toutes les 'familles'* (the judge of all kinds of families). The uniform treatment of all the different forms of family is ongoing.

One objective which is met by widening the jurisdiction of this court is to reduce the length of the process and to make lawsuits more efficient. The tightening of the budget (including for the Department of Justice) and the explosion in the number of lawsuits were additional justifications for this process as well as for the 'dejudiciarisation' of family law. Law in general and

---

[28] Entitled, a little misleadingly, law no 2009–526 on the simplification and clarification of the law and procedural relief, JORF 13 May 2009, www.legifrance.gouv.fr.

family law in particular seem to be thought of as a straightforward application of administrative rules rather than nuanced decision making focused on resolving family disputes.

Towards a simplification of divorce procedures?

The 2004 reforms have substantially modified divorce procedures. The legislator introduced common procedures for all types of divorce disputes with the goal of simplification and harmonisation. In order to lighten the divorce by mutual consent procedures, the law was changed so that, instead of two appearances, the parties must now only come before a judge once. Some, like the psychologist Irène Théry, believe that the legislator has not gone far enough in freeing up the divorce procedures. Instead, they are in favour of a divorce procedure without the involvement of a judge. Others consider that the law of 26 May 2004[29] has diluted marriage so that it is no longer distinguishable from other legal statuses.

A Bill recently placed before the Senate dealing with these issues will no doubt find support with law reformers like Irène Théry, but will stir up a little more opposition among conservatives. This Bill, which anticipates a new simplification of divorce by mutual consent, is consistent with the recommendations of the Guinshard commission.[30] It envisages modifying art 250 of the Civil Code in order to exempt childless couples from automatically being required to appear in front of a JAF. Nevertheless they will still have to meet the following two requirements: the consent of each party, and the assurance that the interests of each person is sufficiently preserved. If these conditions are fulfilled, the judge will make an order approving the agreement and pronouncing the divorce. If the conditions are not met, the judge has the right to require the couple to appear.

The Bill may seem attractive because it allows spouses to divorce more cheaply, as well as unblocking the courts. Nevertheless, there are some concerns which must be addressed when attempting to simplify divorce by mutual consent procedures. In general, French law, and family law especially, is increasingly being reformed in response to political pressure. The laws are based more and more on the immediate positive effect that can be gained for society without consideration for the consequences. This Bill, by its mutual consent procedure, marks a new retreat from the role of the judge in divorce without sufficiently weighing up the consequences, which may be disastrous.

Very often, divorce by 'mutual consent' is, in reality, wanted by one party and accepted by the other. Divorce without an appearance in front of a judge may be harmful for a spouse who has passively accepted divorce and the agreement that accompanies it. The problem is very serious because, legally, there is an

---

29   Above n 22.
30   'L'ambition raisonnée d'une justice apaisée', Report for the Ministry of Justice, 2008, www.uja.fr/attachment/96144.

indivisible link between the agreement recognised by the judge and the pronouncement of the divorce, making it very difficult to challenge either. The link between the two makes both very difficult to challenge. An appearance in front of a judge gives the vulnerable partner the best possible protection of their rights.

VI CONTEMPORARY PROBLEMS WITH THE CONSEQUENCES OF DIVORCE

Just like the cycle of the seasons, French divorce legislation seems to keep returning to the same starting point. This metaphor is particularly true of divorce, a sensitive subject which concerns social realities and the evolution of public morality, but one which is also used by politicians to appeal to the public. It should be handled with the greatest care.

Outside the 1975 divorce law reforms, the abandonment of periodic maintenance payments (*la pension alimentaire*) – intended to support the living costs of the recipient and to reflect the fault of the payor – is consistent with the aim of non-acrimonious divorce and reduction of its effects. The legislator replaced this with a mechanism more focused on compensation: *prestation compensatoire* (compensatory benefit) designed to compensate as much as possible for the economic hardship caused by divorce.[31] In principle, this benefit should be one single capital payment, which can be revised. Those who favoured the old system point to the way the tax system disadvantages these types of payments. The judges have for a long time disappointed the legislator by making most of the benefit orders in the form of allowances, and then opening up the possibility of revising them. This resistance has driven Parliament to forcefully reaffirm on two different occasions[32] the principles that registration of the compensatory benefit is final and that it is in the form of a capital payment. The legislator's intention seems to have been achieved: today, benefits are typically in the form of capital.

Two phenomena should be highlighted. On the one hand, statistics from the Ministry of Justice, such as surveys carried out by the Law Centre in Lyon, show, when making divorce agreements, a number of couples stay loyal to the idea of a periodic allowance. On the other hand, the figures reveal a very low number of *prestations compensatoires*: these appear in only two out of ten divorces. It may be important to see the consequence of the trivialisation of divorce, now simply a risk of marriage. Female emancipation and the realisation of the legal equality of the sexes have also driven this trend: in 1975 working women were the exception, which made economic support for divorced women necessary; today the number of employed women and men are coming together. This has meant that the *prestation compensatoire* no longer

---

[31]   Article 270 of the Civil Code.
[32]   Under the law of 30 June 2000, devoted to the *prestation compensatoire*, then during the divorce reform of the law of 26 May 2004.

reflects contemporary reality. Rather than pretending to compensate for the economic hardship created by divorce, without ever succeeding, would it not be better to put in place a system of capital payments intended to help the recipient partner to restart his or her life?

Germany

COURTS STRENGTHENING EQUALITY AND NEW WAYS IN CROSS-BORDER MATRIMONIAL PROPERTY QUESTIONS

Nina Dethloff and Alexandra Maschwitz[*]

Résumé

En 2010, des décisions d'importance nationale ont été rendues en matière d'égalité entre les hommes et les femmes dans le domaine de la filiation et en matière d'égalité entre les partenaires enregistrés et les époux. Les réformes successives du droit de la famille visent essentiellement à réaliser les changements exigés par la cour européenne des droits de l'homme ainsi que par la cour fédérale constitutionnelle d'Allemagne. D'une part, la situation des pères fait l'objet d'une attention particulière de la part des tribunaux depuis un certain temps déjà. Même si les droits des pères non mariés et des pères biologiques, dont la paternité n'est pas légalement établie, ont été de plus en plus reconnus par des décisions de principe et des réformes législatives, il reste que d'importantes différences continuent d'exister entre les mères et les pères. D'où de récents jugements de la cour européenne droits de l'homme et de la cour fédérale constitutionnelle en rapport avec la question de la responsabilité parentale des parents non mariés et des droits d'accès des pères biologiques. La question d'égalité était également au coeur de plusieurs décisions concernant la différence de traitement entre les partenaires enregistrés et les époux. Les décisions-phare de la cour constitution- nelle démontrent bien qu'il existe actuellement une tendance à réduire ces différences. Par ailleurs, la coopération juridique entre la France et l'Allemagne a permis de mettre en place un nouveau mécanisme pour les couples transfrontaliers en matière de propriété matrimoniale: un régime matrimonial commun a été créé permettant à ces couples de choisir leur régime sur une base contractuelle.

I   INTRODUCTION

The year 2010 has been one of landmark rulings favouring equality between the sexes with regard to parentage as well as equality between registered partners and spouses. Ongoing family law reforms mainly serve to implement the changes that the European Court of Human Rights (ECtHR) and the

---

[*]   Prof Dr Nina Dethloff, LLM, is Director of the Institute for German, European and International Family Law at Rheinische Friedrich-Wilhelms-Universität Bonn.
Alexandra Maschwitz, Academic Assistant at the Institute for German, European and International Family Law at Rheinische Friedrich-Wilhelms-Universität Bonn.

German Federal Constitutional Court (*Bundesverfassungsgericht* – BVerfG) required. On the one hand, the position of fathers has been at the centre of attention of the courts for quite some time now.[1] Even though the rights of unmarried fathers and biological fathers, whose parentage has not been legally recognised, were continually strengthened through several noteworthy rulings and law reforms, marked differences between the rights of mothers and fathers respectively still exist. Hence, recent judgments of the ECtHR and the German Federal Constitutional Court dealt with parental responsibility for unmarried parents (Part II(a)) and access rights for biological fathers (Part II(b)). Equality was further at the heart of several rulings with regard to the treatment of registered partners as compared to spouses. The milestone judgments of the German Federal Constitutional Court show a clear trend to narrow the gap between registered partnerships and marriage (Part III). Furthermore, legal co-operation between France and Germany created a new option for cross-border couples with regard to matrimonial property: a common matrimonial property regime was set up to allow spouses to choose a marital property regime on a contractual basis (Part IV).

II STRENGTHENING THE RIGHTS OF FATHERS

(a) Unmarried parents

Two landmark decisions in 2009 and 2010 strengthened the position of unmarried fathers. Both, the ECtHR and the German Federal Constitutional Court, had to decide on complaints of unmarried fathers who were trying to gain at least shared parental responsibility.

Hitherto, the legal situation was as follows: according to s 1626a of the German Civil Code (*Bürgerliches Gesetzbuch* – BGB), if the parents are not married to each other at the time of the child's birth, the mother as a rule has sole parental responsibility. The parents of an out-of-wedlock child do, however, have the option to both issue declarations of parental responsibility, which, if effective, result in the bestowal of joint responsibility upon both parents.[2] As both parents have to issue a respective declaration, the father cannot obtain joint parental responsibility unless the mother agrees. A similar approach concerns situations, in which the parents are living apart where the mother has parental custody: an application to the court in order to transfer parental custody to the father alone or in part requires the consent of the mother.[3]

---

[1] Cf Dethloff 'Redefining the Position of Fathers in German Family Law' in A Bainham (ed) *The International Survey of Family Law* (Jordan Publishing Limited, 2005) pp 253–266.

[2] German Civil Code, s 1626a(1).

[3] Ibid. Additionally, under s 1666 of the German Civil Code the parental responsibility can be transferred to the father, if the child's well-being is threatened by negligence on the mother's part.

As a result, not only did unmarried fathers not receive joint parental responsibility upon the birth of the child, but what is more they could not obtain (joint) parental responsibility later on, unless the mother consented to the transfer of parental custody. According to the ECtHR the general exclusion of a judicial review of the attribution of sole custody to the mother of a child born out of wedlock discriminates (Arts 14 and 8 of the Convention on the Protection of Fundamental Rights and Freedoms – ECHR) unmarried fathers from unmarried mothers as well as from divorced fathers.[4] The Court stated in *Zaunegger v Germany* that, while the legitimate aim of the German regulation was to protect children born out of wedlock by determining their legal representative immediately upon birth and avoiding disputes between the parents on matters of the exercise of the parental responsibility at the child's expense, the Court did not find it necessary to exclude unmarried fathers as a rule from a court decision on the allocation of parental responsibility taken in the best interest of the child.[5] Potential physical and/or social strains through a judicial inquiry are no counter-argument either, as these may also exist in cases where the court has to decide on the allocation of parental responsibility after a divorce or in cases following a prior declaration of joint responsibility.[6]

A good half year later the Federal Constitutional Court had to decide in a similar case:[7] an unmarried father had tried unsuccessfully to apply for at least joint parental responsibility when the mother announced that she was moving with her son to another part of Germany. The German courts rejected his complaint on the basis of the German Civil Code, which as mentioned above does not include a right of the father to apply for (joint) parental responsibility. The Federal Constitutional Court acknowledged the decision of the ECtHR in *Zaunegger v Germany* and found s 1626a(1) no 1 and s 1672(1) of the German Civil Code to be in breach of art 6(2) of the German Basic Law (*Grundgesetz* – German Constitution). Until the legislator amends the unconstitutional norms, they have to be read as allowing the courts to decide upon the allocation of the parental responsibility even in cases where the solely responsible mother does not agree to a transfer of parental responsibility.[8] The best interest of the child serves as a yardstick.[9]

So far two reform proposals have been made: the German Women Lawyers Association as well as the Ministry of Justice suggested joint parental responsibility on request of the father as long as the mother does not object within a certain period of time; in the case of an objection a court should decide based on the best interest of the child.[10] Alternatively, the Bavarian

---

[4] ECtHR, *Zaunegger v Germany* App no 22028/04, 3 December 2009.
[5] Ibid, para 52 et seq.
[6] Ibid, para 61.
[7] *Bundesverfassungsgericht* (Federal Constitutional Court – BVerfG), 21 July 2010 NJW (*Neue Juristische Wochenschrift*) 2010, 3008.
[8] BVerfG, 21 July 2010 NJW 2010, 3008 at 3015 (paras 75, 76).
[9] Ibid, para 75.
[10] German Women Lawyers Association, Press release, 13 September 2010, available at www.djb.de/Kom/K2/pm10-24_Sorgerecht/; for the Ministry of Justice see http://beck-online.beck.de/Default.aspx?typ=reference&y=300&Z=becklink&N=1008808.

Ministry of Justice recommended keeping the option of joint parental responsibility based on mutual declarations, but added the right to appeal to a court for a ruling based on the best interests of the child, where the mother refuses to make the necessary declaration.[11] The first alternative seems preferable since it takes into consideration that in Germany the situation of children born out of wedlock still varies considerably. Granting the 'interested' father equal rights without a formal court proceeding while at the same time allowing the mother to object and request a judicial review strikes a fair balance between the competing rights and allows for solutions in the best interest of the child.

(b) Biological fathers

Another recent decision of the ECtHR deals with the situation of biological fathers whose parentage has not been legally recognised. In the decision *Anayo v Germany* the ECtHR stated that in denying the biological father access rights to his child, German courts failed to consider the child's best interest and violated the father's rights under Art 8 of the ECHR.[12]

Contact rights of a biological father can be established, in principle, in two different ways. First, the biological father can acknowledge his paternity and thus gain access rights as a legal parent.[13] However, in cases where a presumption of paternity applies for the mother's husband and a social and family relationship between the child and the legal father exists, the paternity presumption cannot be challenged and thus an acknowledgement of paternity is not possible.[14] Secondly, the biological father could have access rights as a 'third party' under s 1685(2) sentence 1 of the German Civil Code. Access rights for third parties exist only where the third party is regarded as a 'close person', requiring a social and family relationship with the child concerned.[15] Thus, if the mother did not want the biological father to be a part of the child's life, she could easily deny him any contact with the child thus preventing the establishment of a social and family relationship with the child and consequently the obtaining of access rights. Likewise, until now, according to German case–law, biological but not legal fathers and their children have built a family within the meaning of art 6(1) of the German Basic Law only if a social and family relationship between them already existed;[16] access rights could thus not be based on a constitutional foundation either.

---

[11]   Bavarian Ministry of Justice, Press release no 3/2011, 10 January 2011, available at www.justiz.bayern.de/ministerium/presse/archiv/2011/detail/3.php.

[12]   ECtHR, *Anayo v Germany* App no 20578/07, 21 December 2010.

[13]   German Civil Code, s 1592 no 2 (acknowledgment of paternity) or s 1592 no 3 (judicial declaration of paternity) and s 1684 para 1 (access rights of parents).

[14]   German Civil Code, s 1600(2).

[15]   German Civil Code, s 1685(2).

[16]   Cf BVerfG 9 April 2003, FamRZ *(Zeitschrift für das gesamte Familienrecht)* (2003), 816; *Bundesgerichtshof* (Federal Court of Justice – BGH) 9 February 2005, NJW-RR (2005), 729; BVerfG 20 September 2006, FamRZ (2006), 1661.

In *Anayo v Germany* the biological father did not a have a social and family relationship with his children, as the mother had ended her relationship with him before the birth of their twins and had returned to her husband, who in turn is the legal father. Solely because the legal parents refused his requests, the biological father could not establish any contact with his children. The ECtHR stated that an intended family life might – exceptionally – fall within the ambit of Art 8 of the ECHR where the fact that family life had not been established was not attributable to the applicant.[17] Even assuming that his relations with his children fell short of 'family life' they concerned an important part of the biological father's identity and thus his 'private life' for the purpose of Art 8 of the ECHR.[18]

In accordance with the – later overruled – family court of first instance, the ECtHR stressed the importance of the assessment of the child's interest in relation to access rights of the biological father. The Court acknowledged the legitimate aim of German family law which is to give existing family ties precedence over the relationship between a biological father and a child. However, the Court required that this aim must be fairly balanced with the competing rights under Art 8 of the ECHR not only of the legal parents and the child, but also of the biological father and other individuals concerned, for example the other existing children of the legal parents. The reasons stated by the German court were not sufficient for the purposes of Art 8(2) of the ECHR and thus the interference was not necessary in order to obtain the legitimate objectives.[19]

Again the general exclusion of a judicial petition for contact rights – decided on the basis of the best interests of the child – was found to be in violation of the father's human rights. The Federal Ministry of Justice announced an examination of the German rules on access rights for biological fathers. Whereas it seems right that family life as protected by Art 8 of the ECHR can encompass the ties of a biological father and his child in a situation where they have not yet had a chance to develop a relationship, and therefore competing rights must be balanced, contact may ultimately be granted only if it is in the child's best interest. In cases where the mother (as well as the legal father) strictly opposes any contact with the biological father, as was the case here, more often than not contact will probably not be in the child's best interest. There may, however, be cases where the opposite holds true. In any event, if biological fathers are generally to be granted the right to petition for contact where this is in the child's best interest, as the legislator will now have to do, this will serve as a signal that mothers may no longer decide upon granting access on their whim.

---

[17] ECtHR, *Anayo v Germany* App no 20578/07, 21 December 2010, para 60.
[18] Ibid, para 62.
[19] Ibid, para 72.

III ENHANCING THE EQUALITY OF REGISTERED PARTNERS AND SPOUSES: TAXES AND PENSION RIGHTS

Whereas in most family law respects registered partners[20] enjoy the same rights and obligations as spouses, in matters relating to public law, particularly tax law, and labour law (regarding remuneration and pension rights) equality seemed a long way off. Even though as early as 2002 the Federal Constitutional Court had confirmed that the institution of the registered partnership for same-sex partners, providing for substantially the same rights and obligations as for spouses, does not violate the constitutional protection of marriage in art 6(1)of the German Basic Law, this was not interpreted as implying a general prohibition to distinguish registered partnerships from marriage.[21] In contrast, it was predominantly assumed that art 6(1) of the Basic Law allowed (or even required) preferential treatment in favour of marriage, thus preventing registered partners from invoking the equality principle of art 3(1) of the Basic Law.[22]

In 2008 the European Court of Justice (ECJ) was presented with the question of whether discrimination within the meaning of Art 2 of the Council Directive 2000/78 existed when after the death of his registered partner the surviving partner does not receive a survivor's benefit equivalent to that granted to a surviving spouse. In *Tadao Maruko v Versorgungsanstalt der deutschen Bühnen*[23] the ECJ ruled that (1) survivor's benefits under a compulsory occupational pensions scheme form a part of the remuneration and as such fall within the scope of the Council Directive 2000/78 and that (2) where, under national law, a registered partnership places persons of same sex in a situation comparable to that of spouses as far as survivor's benefits are concerned the state is obliged to respect the equality principle.[24] Different treatment of registered partners as compared to spouses amounts to direct discrimination based on sexual orientation.[25]

---

[20] Registered Partnership Act 2001 (*Lebenspartnerschaftsgesetz* – LPartG). For more details see Dethloff 'The Registered Partnership Act of 2001' in A Bainham (ed) *The International Survey of Family Law* (Jordan Publishing Limited, 2002) pp 171–180.

[21] BVerfG, NJW (2002), 2543, 2548; and the interpretation thereof in BVerfG 20 September 2007, NJW (2008), 209 at 211 as well as the *Bundesverwaltungsgericht* (Federal Administrative Court – BVerwG), 15 November 2007, NJW (2008), 868, 869.

[22] BVerfG 20 September 2007, NJW 2008, 209 at 211; differing from Dethloff *Familienrecht* (Munich, 29th edn, 2009) p 243 et seq as well as Bruns 'Die Maruko-Entscheidung im Spannungsfeld zwischen europäischer und nationaler Auslegung' NJW (2008), 1929 at 1930.

[23] European Court of Justice (ECJ), C-267/06, *Tadao Maruko v Versorgungsanstalt der deutschen Bühnen*, NJW (2008), 1649.

[24] ECJ, C-267/06, *Tadao Maruko v Versorgungsanstalt der deutschen Bühnen*, NJW (2008), 1649 at 1653 (para 58 et seq); the German courts had hitherto argued that the Council Directive 2000/78 establishing a general framework for equal treatment in employment and occupation was not applicable, as marital status was left out in recital 22 of the Directive.

[25] ECJ, C-267/06, *Tadao Maruko v Versorgungsanstalt der deutschen Bühnen*, NJW (2008), 1649 at 1653 (para 72).

Approximately one year later a comparable case arose before the Federal Constitutional Court:[26] a constitutional complaint related to the unequal treatment of marriage and registered partnerships with regard to survivor's pensions under an occupational pension scheme for employees in the civil service according to the Rules of the Supplementary Pensions Agency for Federal and Länder Employees (*Versorgungsanstalt des Bundes und der Länder* – VBL). The Federal Constitutional Court seized the chance and clearly stated that (1) unequal treatment between registered partners and spouses must pass the requirements set up by art 3(1) of the Basic Law, (2) unequal treatment based on sexual orientation is comparable to the criteria mentioned in art 3(3) sentence 2 of the Basic Law (such as sex, birth, race, etc) and a differentiation must therefore pass strict scrutiny whether sufficiently weighty reasons exist, and (3) a mere reference to the constitutional protection of marriage under art 6(1) of the Basic Law does not suffice as a justification. Concerning the survivor's pensions no differences between registered partners and spouses could be identified: with regard to the granting of remuneration no differences between married and 'registered' employees exist and the maintenance obligations between partners and spouses are almost similar. Furthermore, a differentiation could not be justified by the fact that married couples typically have a different pension requirement due to the bringing up of children. The Federal Constitutional Court emphasised that the protection of marriage under art 6(1) of the Basic Law is not based on the idea that every marriage has children and that the traditional role model (breadwinner marriage) is no longer reality and thus cannot serve as the yardstick for assigning survivor's benefits. As a result the Federal Constitutional Court decided that the challenged court rulings violate the complainant's fundamental right to equal treatment under art 3(1) of the Basic Law. The Federal Court of Justice acknowledged this decision a few months later and stated that as of 1 January 2005[27] registered partners are entitled to survivor's benefits and a funeral allowance according to s 38(1) and s 85 sentence 1 of the Rules of the Supplementary Pensions Agency for Federal and Länder Employees (VBLS) respectively.[28] Similarly, the Federal Labour Court stated that the foreign country allowance pursuant to s 55(2) of the Federal Civil Service Remuneration Act (*Bundesbesoldungsgesetz* – BBesG), which is attributed to married couples only, discriminates against registered partnerships.[29]

In July 2010 the Federal Constitutional Court extended its reasoning from remuneration matters to inheritance and tax law issues.[30] Two 'widowed' registered partners had complained that the taxation of their inheritance discriminated against them on the grounds of their sexual orientation.

---

[26] BVerfG 7 July 2009, NJW (2010), 1439.

[27] The date corresponds to the entry into force of the *Gesetz zur Überarbeitung des Lebenspartnerschaftsrechts* of 15 December 2004 (Law on the Revision of the Registered Partnership Act), which further equated registered partnerships with marriages.

[28] *Bundesgerichtshof* (Federal Court of Justice – BGH) 11 June 2010, VersR *(Versicherungsrecht-Rechtsprechung)* (2010), 1208; cf also BGH 7 July 2010, FamRZ (2010), 1545 (survivor's benefits pursuant to s 38 of the VBLS).

[29] *Bundesarbeitsgericht* (Federal Labour Court – BAG) 18 March 2010, FamRZ (2010), 1333.

[30] BVerfG 21 July 2010, FamRZ (2010), 1525.

Pursuant to s 15 et seq of the Gift and Inheritance Tax Act (in the version dated 20 December 1996 from the 1997 Annual Tax Reform Act) registered partners were significantly more burdened than spouses under inheritance tax law. Not only were they classified as 'other recipients' and placed in Tax Class III (with tax rates ranging between 17 and 50%) as compared to spouses who are subject to the most beneficial Tax Class I (with tax rates ranging between 7 and 30%), but also their personal exemption amounted only to a fraction ($\frac{1}{60}$) of the personal exemption for spouses and the exemption for retirement benefits did not apply to them at all. While the exemptions were amended in 2008, the classification remained intact. Again the Federal Constitutional Court tested whether the unequal treatment of registered partners as compared to spouses was justified under art 3(1) of the Basic Law. It reiterated that art 6(1) of the Basic Law does not suffice as a justification and that a strict standard must be applied; other sufficiently weighty reasons were not provided either.[31] The legislator reacted promptly and equated registered partnerships as far as inheritance tax law is concerned with spouses; the amendments through the Annual Tax Reform Act (8 December 2010) take retrospective effect as of 1 August 2001, the entry into force date of the Registered Partnership Act.

Whereas these decisions imply that equal treatment is required in all areas of public and labour law, differences in family law are yet largely unchallenged. Remaining differences concern the formalities of the celebration of a registered partnership and the rules pertaining to its dissolution[32] as well as, in particular, rights concerning adoption and assisted reproductive technology. The gradual equation of registered partnerships and marriage did not happen undisputedly, but meanwhile scholars and the public in general increasingly welcome this development. Concerning the initially highly controversial issue of adoption by gays and lesbians, a study initiated by the Federal Ministry of Justice concluded that children with two fathers or two mothers respectively suffer no detriment in the development of their personality, their development at school and their occupational development; furthermore, the majority of the children claimed that they had so far experienced no social discrimination.[33] Consequently, the well-being of children and their best interest can no longer be used to justify the unequal treatment of registered partners, who may not jointly adopt a child, and spouses, who may do so.[34] On the contrary, it may well be in the best interest of children if an existing social parent-child

---

[31] BVerfG 21 July 2010, FamRZ (2010), 1525 at 1526 (para 75).

[32] Whereas in most federal states (*Länder*) partners like spouses register their partnership at the civil registry office (*Standesamt*), e g in Bavaria they can alternatively register their partnership at a notary. Additionally, while the dissolution of marriage differs between divorce and annulment (*Aufhebung*) – in case an impediment to marriage exists – the dissolution of a registered partnership is called annulment (*Aufhebung*) in either case and mirrors divorce.

[33] Rupp (ed) *Die Lebenssituation von Kindern in gleichgeschlechtlichen Partnerschaften* (Cologne, 2009). An English summary is available at the homepage of the Federal Ministry of Justice, www.bmj.de/SharedDocs/Downloads/EN/The_living_conditions_of_children_in_same_sex_civil_partnerships.pdf?__blob=publicationFile (accessed 31 May 2011).

[34] So far s 9 of the Registered Partnership Act limits the adoption rights of registered partners to a stepchild adoption; the joint adoption of a not blood-related child is not possible, only one partner can adopt the child (s 1741(2) sentence 1 of the German Civil Code).

relationship could be legally protected through an adoption, for example where a child has already been adopted by one of the partners, which is currently possible, or has lived for a significant period of time with his gay foster parents and there is no prospect of return to his or her biological family.[35] Recently a reform proposal has been made;[36] however, the chances of it being passed by the German Parliament (*Bundestag*) seem to be rather low.[37]

IV THE FRANCO-GERMANIC OPTIONAL MATRIMONIAL PROPERTY REGIME OF THE COMMUNITY OF ACCRUED GAINS

When France and Germany signed the agreement on 4 February 2010 an additional optional matrimonial property regime was created, which provides uniform rules for both countries.[38] In Germany a draft Act for the transformation of the agreement has been presented,[39] so that the agreement can soon take effect. The agreement on the common optional property regime of a community of accrued gains combines elements from French and German matrimonial property law. It is a novelty as for the first time in Europe uniform substantive family law will apply in two states.

Spouses, whose matrimonial property regime due to (national)[40] choice of law rules is regulated by French or German law, may opt for the new Franco-Germanic community of accrued gains.[41] As an optional matrimonial property regime spouses must enter a matrimonial agreement before or during the marriage in order to choose the new regime.[42] The basic structures of the

---

[35] Dethloff 'Assistierte Reproduktion und rechtliche Elternschaft in gleichgeschlechtlichen Partnerschaften – Ein rechtsvergleichender Überblick' in Funcke and Thorn (eds) *Die gleichgeschlechtliche Lebensgemeinschaft mit Kindern – Interdisziplinäre Perspektiven* (Bielefeld: Transcript-Verlag, 2010) pp 161 et seq.

[36] Draft Act on the Amendment of the Registered Partnership Act and other Laws Regarding Adoption Rights (*Entwurf eines Gesetzes zur Ergänzung des Lebenspartnerschaftsgesetzes und anderer Gesetze im Bereich des Adoptionsrechts*), Parliament Printed Papers (BT-Drs) 17/1429.

[37] In 2009 the Higher Regional Court (*Oberlandesgericht* – OLG) Hamm, 1 December 2009, NJW (2010), 2065 denied a woman the right to adopt the adoptive child of her registered partner based on current law in Germany. Against this judgment a constitutional complaint is pending before the Federal Constitutional Court (1 BvR 3247/09). For details see Henkel 'Fällt nun auch das "Fremdkindadoptionsverbot"?' NJW (2010), 259 et seq.

[38] For more information see Dethloff 'Der neue deutsch-französische Güterstand. Wegbereiter für eine Angleichung des Familienrechts?' forthcoming; Simler 'Le nouveau regime matrimonial optionnel franco-allemand de participation aux acquêts' (2010) 5 *Droit de la famille* étude 8 as well as Fötschl 'The COMPR of Germany and France: Epoch-Making in the Unification of Law' (2010) 4 *European Review of Private Law* 881–889.

[39] *Referentenentwurf des Bundesministeriums der Justiz* of 14 September 2010 (Draft Act of the Federal Ministry of Justice).

[40] Cf however the Green Paper on Conflict of Laws in Matters Concerning Matrimonial Property Regimes, Including the Question of Jurisdiction and Mutual Recognition, Com (2006) 400 final.

[41] Agreement on the Optional Matrimonial Property Regime of a Community of Accrued Gains, art 1.

[42] Ibid, art 3(2).

Franco-Germanic community of accrued gains are taken from the German default regime of community of accrued gains (*Zugewinngemeinschaft*) as well as from the French contractual regime of community of accrued gains (*participation aux acquêts*). The main idea is property division during marriage and a monetary compensation at the termination of the property regime (through divorce, change of property regime or the death of a spouse). The property regime is complemented by rules on the acquisition and disposition of common household goods or the family home. While dispositions of household goods or the family home generally require the approval of the other spouse, contracts concerning the running of the household or the needs of any children can be concluded by each spouse.[43] As long as the contract does not contain an obligation that is obviously inadequate with regard to the living standards of the couple, the spouses are joint debtors.[44] Even though the property regime in itself is unchangeable, some rules especially concerning the compensation claim may be altered.[45]

The bilateral agreement – for the time being – is open for access to all member states of the European Union, which may thereby introduce the additional marital property regime.[46] It remains to be seen whether the agreement serves as a starting point for optional harmonisation of substantive family law.[47] Apart from its potential for becoming a multilateral agreement it could also be supplemented by another contractual property regime, for example a community of property, or even a more encompassing optional regime of a European Marriage.[48] Future endeavours should draw upon the extensive comparative research, in particular, of the Commission on European Family Law, which is currently working on the formulation of Principles for Property Relations between Spouses.[49]

V   PROSPECTS

Besides the aforementioned ongoing law reforms several other areas will be revised in the coming year. Equality for children born out of wedlock shall be extended to cover all children even those born before 1 July 1949, who have

---

[43]   Ibid, arts 5 and 6.
[44]   Ibid, art 6.
[45]   Ibid, art 3(3) and Chapter V.
[46]   Ibid, art 21.
[47]   Cf Dethloff 'Der neue deutsch-französische Güterstand. Wegbereiter für eine Angleichung des Familienrechts?' forthcoming.
[48]   Dethloff 'Die Europäische Ehe' (2006) StAZ *(Das Standesamt)*, 253–260.
[49]   Boele-Woelki, Braat, Curry-Sumner (eds) *European Family Law in Action*, Volume IV: Property Relations Between Spouses (Antwerp: Intersentia, 2009); for already established principles see Boele-Woelki, Ferrand, González Beilfuss, Jänterä-Jareborg, Lowe, Martiny, Pintens (eds) *Principles of European Family Law Regarding Divorce and Maintenance Between Former Spouses* (Antwerp: Intersentia, 2004); Boele-Woelki, Ferrand, González Beilfuss, Jänterä-Jareborg, Lowe, Martiny, Pintens (eds), *Principles of European Family Law Regarding Parental Responsibilities* (Antwerp: Intersentia, 2007).

until now been discriminated against with regard to inheritance rights.[50] In the transformation of the Directive 2008/52 of the European Parliament and of the Council of 21 May 2008 on certain aspects of mediation in civil and commercial matters a new Act on Mediation will be implemented and is likely to include mediation in family matters as well.[51] Furthermore, the law on guardians and custodians will be revised again.[52] A Federal Act on the Protection of Children shall create new and improve existing public services for the protection of children.

---

[50] Cf the Draft Act of the Federal Government: *Entwurf eines Zweiten Gesetzes zur erbrechtlichen Gleichstellung nichtehelicher Kinder* (4 November 2010, BT-Drs 17/3305).

[51] Cf the Draft Act of the Federal Government: *Gesetz zur Förderung der Mediation und anderer Verfahren der außergerichtlichen Konfliktbeilegung* (12 January 2011).

[52] Cf the Draft Act of the Federal Government: *Entwurf eines Gesetzes zur Änderung des Vormundschafts- und Betreuungsrechts* (4 November 2010, BT-Drs 17/3617).

Hungary

HOW COHABITANTS AND REGISTERED PARTNERS CAN OR CANNOT BE A CHILD'S LEGAL PARENTS IN HUNGARY WITH A SPECIAL VIEW TO THE 'PATER EST' PRINCIPLE FOR COHABITANTS

Dr Orsolya Szeibert*

Résumé

Pendant la dernière décennie plusieurs modifications essentielles ont affecté le droit hongrois de la famille, notamment sur le droit des couples non-mariés. Bien que les époux puissent être les parents communs d'un enfant par plusieurs manières, les mêmes règles juridiques ne sont pas applicables ou le sont moins facilement pour partenaires et ne sont pas possible pour les partenaires enregistrés (qui peuvent être de même sexe). Cette intervention traite des difficultés que rencontrent deux concubins ou partenaires enregistrés pour acquérir ou non le statut de père et mère de l'enfant commun. Cette question a encore émergé à propos des couples qui vivent sous le même toit et qui ont le désir d'avoir un enfant en commun reconnu par le droit. Cette contribution analyse la manière dont les concubins et partenaires enregistrés peuvent être parents d'un enfant commun, dans quelle mesure cela est possible, ainsi que le contexte théorique qui apparait alors. Aussi, de nombreuses tentatives de réformes du droit ont été initiées.

I   INTRODUCTION

In the last decade some essential modifications have affected Hungarian family law, primarily the law of non-marital partnerships. New Acts and new decisions of the Constitutional Court followed each other in a pretty short time period. New institutions had been created and later diminished, which has resulted in a confusing story of codification of non-marital partnerships, including the legal consequences. Several ideas had been based on distinguishing the personal consequences of partnerships from marriage and later a lot of ideas were eliminated. At the same time the recodification of the Hungarian Civil Code is

*   PhD, Assistant Professor, Department of Civil Law, Law Faculty, Eötvös Loránd University, Budapest, Hungary.

taking place and, as the Family Law Book is going to be part of the new Civil Code, it affects the adjudication of non-marital partnerships.

Although spouses can be common parents of a child in several ways, the same legal solutions are not or not so easily available for cohabitants and not available for registered partners. The issue we are dealing with is how two cohabitants or registered partners can or cannot acquire paternal and maternal status with respect to a common child. This question has emerged again and again as cohabiting couples have a human desire to have their common child legally recognised.

This contribution analyses how cohabitants and registered partners can be parents of a common child, if at all, and the theoretical background is shown. Also legal attempts at law reform are introduced.

(a) Partnerships

There are three forms of partnership in Hungary in 2011, namely marriage, cohabitation and registered partnership.[1] Marriage as a traditional and primarily supported institution is regulated in the Family Act in a broad way.[2] The brief rules on cohabitation are contained in the Civil Code.[3] Actually, cohabitation is not as such an issue for family law at all.

Registered partnership was introduced into Hungarian law in 2009 and regulated partly in a special, independent Act and partly in the Civil Code, the Family Act and other legal sources.[4] Nevertheless, the main rules are in the special Act. The Act of 2009, namely the Act No XXIX 2009 on Registered Partnership and the Modification of Legal Rules in Connection with Registered Partnership and the Facilitation of the Proof of Cohabitation, has introduced a new opportunity especially for cohabitants. They can request the registration of their statement of cohabitation in the Register of Cohabitants' Statements. This registration does not alter the legal characteristics of cohabitation, especially its de facto character. Inclusion in the Register of Cohabitants' Statements does not create a new type of partnership but it does have some meaning. Its importance has partly remained and partly been eliminated in the field of the presumption of paternity.

Only a man and a woman can marry and only two same-sex persons above 18 can enter into a registered partnership. Two different-sex persons and two

---

1   Orsolya Szeibert 'Cohabitation, Registered Partnership and their Financial Consequences in Hungary' in Bill Atkin (ed) *The International Survey of Family Law* (Jordan Publishing Limited, 2009) pp 205–206. That article introduces and studies the forms of marital and non-marital partnerships.

2   Family Act, ss 2–33 concerning marriage, marital bond and property issues.

3   Civil Code, ss 578/G(1)-(2), 685/A and 685(b).

4   Act No XXIX 2009, ss 1–4. Several paragraphs of the Family Act and the Civil Code have been modified. Act No XLV 2008 on Notarial Non-litigious Proceedings also contains some regulations in connection with the termination of registered partnerships.

same-sex persons can both live in cohabitation and both different-sex cohabitants and same-sex cohabitants can request the registration of their statement of cohabitation.

(b)   Legal changes and the codification process

The Family Act is dated from 1952 and, although it has been modified several times, the regulations on marriage are essentially and principally the same. Cohabitation was introduced into the Civil Code in 1977. The definition of cohabitation was modified at first in 1996, when the gate of cohabitation was opened to same-sex partners, and secondly in 2009, when the legal definition was completed with some new elements. The first Act on registered partners was accepted in 2007 and it was repealed in 2008. The registered partnership as a brand new institution entered into force in July 2009.

The codification of the Civil Code began in 1998 and resulted in the acceptance of the Civil Code in autumn 2009. Nevertheless, this code, with Act No CXX 2009 in the Civil Code, never entered into force and in spring 2011 the development of a new Civil Code is moving ahead, of course with attention to the accepted and repealed version.

(c)   Spouses and children

Spouses can become parents of a common child by several means. These solutions have been enacted gradually during the last decade and have not been modified principally since then. In Hungary there are some established, and both legally and socially accepted, ways of having a common child.

The spouses can be the genetic parents of a child who was conceived through sexual intercourse. According to Hungarian law the woman who gave birth to the child is his or her mother. The father who is the mother's husband will be the legal father by the operation of law.[5] The Hungarian Family Act regulates several paternal presumptions. First, there is the so-called primary presumption which automatically emerges and creates legal fatherhood in the man who was the mother's husband in the period between the conception of the child and his or her birth, even for a short time.

Secondly, they can be genetic parents of their child by assisted conception techniques. These methods are regulated in Act No CLIV 1997 on Public Health. Artificial insemination and in vitro fertilisation, happening without any donation of either egg or sperm, provide the blood relationship between the parents and their child even if there is a heath indication which excludes the possibility of having a healthy common child through sexual intercourse.

---

[5]   Family Act, s 35(1).

Thirdly, this Act makes the medically assisted reproduction process involving sperm or egg donation also available for spouses. The spouses' common written statement is necessary for each assisted conception technique. This common statement is essential for the father's presumption of paternity.[6]

Lastly, spouses can adopt a common child.[7] They have two possibilities, as they can adopt a child who does not belong to the family or one of them can adopt the partner's child even if that child is this spouse's adopted child. Of course, the status of the child's other parent should be 'empty'. If this other parent waives his or her parental rights, all relatives of this parent lose their contact rights with the child. If this other parent has died, his or her relatives, especially the grandparents, reserve their contact rights with the child. Even a single person can adopt a child who does not belong to the family but according to the Governmental Decree No 147 1997 on the Public Guardianship Authority and Proceedings in Child Welfare and Guardianship Cases married couples are given priority over single persons in such cases.

The parent's rights and obligations depend on whether they have maternal or parental status with respect to the child. The status of the mother is not debated, as in Hungary there is no surrogacy at all. (I should remark that some rules about surrogacy had been introduced into the aforementioned Public Health Act but those were repealed before coming into force.) If the spouses acquire parental status in relation to a common child, their legal position and legal relationship towards the child are wholly independent of the legal presumption of paternity. In the case of an adopted child the child automatically receives the status of a blood-related child.[8]

II COHABITANTS

Cohabitation has been regulated in brief in the Civil Code, namely Act No IV 1959, since 1977. One provision provides the definition of cohabitation. This definition has been modified twice since its enactment, once in 1966 and once 2 years ago, in 2009. According to this definition unmarried partners are two persons (either different-sex or same-sex persons) who live together, without entering into a marriage or a registered partnership, in a common household, in an emotional fellowship and economic partnership (community of life). They cannot be related to each other in direct line, cannot be siblings or half-siblings and neither of them can live at the same time in a marital community of life, a community of life in a registered partnership or in cohabitation with a third person. The Civil Code contains a rule about their property relations.[9]

---

6   Ibid, s 36(d).
7   Ibid, ss 47 and 51(2).
8   Ibid, s 51(1).
9   Concerning the legal status of cohabitants and the judicial practice in detail in English, see Orsolya Szeibert-Erdős 'Unmarried Partnerships in Hungary' in Katharina Boele-Woelki (ed) *Common Core and Better Law in European Family Law* (Intersentia, 2005) pp 313–330.

(a) Different-sex cohabitants and children

(i) Maternal and paternal status in a genetic family with a special view to the 'pater est' principle

(1) If the cohabitants have a common child and the mother became pregnant through sexual intercourse, according to the principle *mater semper est* the mother is the one who gave birth to the child. The father can fill the paternal status through recognition of the child.[10] According to the Family Act the man can recognise the child if no other man has to be considered as the legal father by operation of law and he is at least 16 years older than the child. The recognition has to be done personally and also the consent of the mother is needed. If the child's legal representative is not the mother, this person has to give his or her consent to the recognition and so does the child, if he or she is over 14.

The recognition procedure is not complicated but in reality some problems can occur. If the mother has a marital bond with another man, her husband has paternal status automatically. In these cases it takes longer for the biological father to become the legal father. Sometimes cohabitation has already ended at time of birth and the mother refuses to give her consent to the ex-cohabitant's recognition in spite of the fact that he is the genetic father. The mother's consent cannot be substituted by the guardianship authority, except when the mother has died or she is absent for a long time. The father can apply to the court[11] but if another man recognises the child as his own, the civil procedure finishes.

(2) Until the end of 2009 recognition and a judicial order were the only possible ways of becoming the legal father in an informal cohabitation and now, in 2011, they are also the only means. In 2010, actually from the 1 January 2010 until 31 December 2010, the father living in cohabitation could become the legal father by operation of law.[12] The *pater est* principle in the case of cohabitants was not as strong as the *pater est quem nuptiae demonstrant* principle in the case of married partners. Nevertheless, gaining paternal status was much easier with respect to children born in that one-year period.

The possibility was introduced by Act No XXIX 2009 on Registered Partnership and the Modification of Legal Rules in Connection with Registered Partnership and the Facilitation of the Proof of Cohabitation. As mentioned above, the Act created the Register of Cohabitants' Statements. The registration of the statement of cohabitation has a declaratory character and is important in cases when two people dispute whether they lived in cohabitation or not. It mostly occurs in judicial proceedings in connection with one cohabitant's property claim. Although this declaratory character principally

---

[10] Family Act, ss 36(a) and 37.
[11] Ibid, ss 36(c) and 38.
[12] Ibid, s 35(4)–(5).

does not alter the legal features of cohabitation, the legislator linked one important legal consequence to the registration of the statement of cohabitation.

According to the Act (which modified the family rules) if the mother had no marital bond in the period from the conception until the birth of child, even for a short time, the man with whom the mother lived from the conception until the birth of the child, even for a short time, in cohabitation proved by the Register of Cohabitants' Statements had to be regarded as the legal father of the child. This rule could not apply if the mother lived in the period from the conception until the birth of the child in more than one cohabitation according to the Register of Cohabitants' Statements. However, these rules have already been repealed. The rule of the Family Act was modified in late 2010. This modification introduced a new rule into the Family Act according to which:

- if the child was born in the period between 1 January 2010 and 31 December 2010; and

- the mother did not live in a marital bond in the period between the conception and the birth of the child; and

- the mother lived in cohabitation, registered in the Cohabitants' Statements; and

- no more than one cohabitation of the mother in the period between the conception and the birth of the child was registered in the Register of Cohabitants' Statements,
  that cohabiting man has to be regarded as the legal father of the child.[13]

The Family Act contains the regulation according to which recognition, judicial decision or medically assisted reproduction result in paternal presumption only if the mother was not married and did not live in cohabitation, registered in the Register of Cohabitants' Statements, in the abovementioned period. Although the *pater est* principle seems to be a general rule for such cohabitants, it is not true except for the year 2010.

I have to add that registration was popular in that year and the elimination of the special paternal presumption for cohabitants was motivated by the administrative burdens which the new presumption had caused. Unfortunately, it had only one year to function.

(ii) Maternal and paternal status in the case of medically assisted reproduction

The Public Health Act makes it possible for different-sex cohabitants to take part in the medically assisted reproduction process. Either artificial

---

[13] Ibid, s 112.

insemination or in vitro fertilisation without egg or sperm donation is available for different-sex cohabitants, which results in a genetic family. Besides, assisted reproduction techniques which involve sperm or egg donation can also serve the purpose of founding a family with common child.

The requirements are mostly the same as in the case of married couples. Nevertheless, there are some special extra conditions for cohabitants. The Act is from the late 1990s and it was not modified in 2009, so no registration in the Register of Cohabitants' Statements is required for taking part in medically assisted reproduction. Special preconditions are that neither of the cohabitant can live in a marriage with another person and the cohabitants have to give a declaration of cohabitation in a deed.

The cohabitants' common written statement is necessary for each assisted conception technique. This common statement is essential for the father's paternal presumption which emerges according to the Family Act. The Family Act specifies that the man who took part with the mother in medically assisted reproduction is to be regarded as the legal father if the birth of the child was a consequence of the reproduction process.[14]

(iii) Adoption

Cohabitants cannot adopt a common child. It means that neither of them can adopt the partner's adopted or blood-related child and they cannot adopt jointly a child not belonging to the family. As single persons can adopt, it is possible for somebody living in cohabitation to adopt a child alone. Cohabitation – even if it is in the Register of Cohabitants' Statements – does not create a personal status. Nevertheless, the circumstances of the adoptive parent are scrutinised by the guardianship authority, so some importance is given to the fact that the adoptive parent lives in common household with someone else.

The partner of the adoptive parent with whom he or she lives together in cohabitation is not obliged to be heard during the procedure for adoption and his or her consent is not needed. This is contrary to the legal rules concerning an adoptive person who adopts a child alone in spite of the fact that she or he is married. In this second case the other partner has to be heard by the guardianship authority and also his or her consent is needed except where there is no matrimonial community (common life) between them.

In the course of the codification of the Civil Code, which began more than 12 years ago, the idea of permitting the cohabitants to adopt each other's child or a child not belonging to the family emerged. Act No CXX 2009 in the Civil Code, which never entered into force, let the cohabitant adopt the partner's child. Preconditions of the adoption in the case of cohabitant partner would have been the following alongside the general conditions: the adopted child

---

[14] Ibid, s 36(d).

would have been only the child of the partner; the partner would have had to consent; and they would have to have been caring for the child jointly and permanently before the adoption. In early 2011 an attempt to let different-sex cohabitants adopt each other's child, if they registered their statement in the Register of Cohabitants' Statements, was once more initiated. At the time of finishing this contribution, in April 2011, cohabitants cannot adopt a child as a common child even if they are different-sex partners.

(b) Same-sex cohabitants and children

Same-sex cohabitants cannot acquire parental status of a common child. They cannot take part in a medically assisted reproduction process according to the Public Health Act. They cannot do that as partners and, even if one of the lesbian partners takes part in the reproduction process and becomes the mother of the child, the other woman cannot obtain any parental status. Act CXX 2009 would have permitted not only different-sex cohabitants but also same-sex cohabitants to adopt each other's child. This idea has not yet re-emerged.

A man or a woman living in cohabitation with his or her same-sex partner is not excluded from adoption as a single person. Although cohabitation does not alter personal status, the guardianship authority is obliged to scrutinise the personal circumstances. We do not know what would be the guardianship authority's attitude towards this adoptive parent. There are a lot of couples in Hungary eager to adopt a child and, as mentioned before, couples are given priority over single adoptive parents.

III REGISTERED PARTNERS AND CHILDREN

Registered partnership would have been open to both same-sex and different-sex partners according to the 2007 Act which never entered into force.[15] This Act introduced an institution resembling marriage. The property consequences of marriage and that of registered partnership would have been just the same. Some personal consequences, including adoption, would not have been permitted for registered partners irrespective of whether they were different-sex or same-sex partners. One distinction would have been introduced between different-sex registered partners and same-sex registered partners, as the rules of paternal legal status would have worked automatically – by the operation of law – in the case of a man and a woman just as in the case of married couples.

---

[15] On same-sex partners in Hungary and the 2007 Act on Registered Partnership, see (in English) Orsolya Szeibert-Erdős 'Same-Sex Partners in Hungary. Cohabitation and Registered Partnership' (2008) 2 *Utrecht Law Review* 212–221. On the 2007 Act on Registered Partnership, see (in German) Emilia Weiss 'Gesetz über die registrierte Partnerschaft in Ungarn' (2008) 18 FamRZ 1724–1725.

A registered partnership can be established only by two same-sex partners according to the effective rules. Act XXIX 2009[16] definitely specifies that they cannot adopt a child jointly and cannot take part in medically assisted reproduction processes. The new Civil Code would not alter that situation, as it would confirm that the regulations on paternal presumption, adoption and medically assisted reproduction are not to be applied to registered partners.

IV   COHABITING PARTNERS' PARENTAL STATUS: RIGHTS AND OBLIGATIONS OF THE PARENT'S PARTNER

In the case of unmarried partnerships only different-sex cohabiting partners can obtain maternal and paternal status of a common child. They can be the genetic parents and can take part in medically assisted reproduction processes. If they are the legal parents, they get the same parental rights and obligations which a married couple has. Cohabiting partners are in the same position as spouses in connection with their child regardless of how the man became the child's legal father.

Same-sex cohabitants and registered partners cannot have a common child, but it can occur in each partnership – marriage, cohabitation, registered partnership – that the partners care for the child of one partner together. If the spouses bring up the father's or the mother's child in a common household, the step-parent's position is factually quite strong, but legally is rather weak. No parental responsibility can be delegated to him or her or shared with the step-parent even temporarily. Nevertheless, the Family Act obliges the step-parent to maintain the minor if this child was taken into the common household with the consent of the parent's spouse. This child maintenance of course does not affect the obligation of the blood-related parents. Regardless of the contact rights which the step-parent as the parent's spouse has, there is no other declared right or obligation on the side of the step-parent.

The Family Act does not mention cohabitants with the consequence that the parent's cohabitant is not to be legally regarded as step-parent. He or she will not have either any parental rights and obligations or the obligation to support the parent's child. Although a registered partner is also not a step-parent, the fact that a registered partner maintains the child of either of them has some meaning. Registered partnership terminates by death and can be terminated not only by the court but also by a public notary. One case when they cannot choose termination by public notary is when they have a child whom they are jointly obliged to maintain. The registered partner cannot be regarded as a step-parent according to the Family Act, but his or her role bears some importance according to the legislator.

---

[16]   Emilia Weiss 'Neues zur Regelung der registrierten Partnerschaft in Ungarn' (2009) 18 FamRZ 1566–1567.

V CONCLUSION

The three stages of partnerships are clearly distinguished upon the broad, the narrow possibility and impossibility of becoming legal parents of a common child. Spouses are wholly supported by the civil law. Different-sex cohabitants cannot adopt each other's child and cannot adopt jointly a child not belonging to the family, but they can obtain parental status of a common child. Biological and legal parentage does not coincide in every case but this is true for the spouses' child, as well. Although the *pater est* principle has already been terminated for cohabitants, this unfortunate elimination does not alter the fact that the man living in cohabitation can get the same parental responsibilities which a husband has if he fulfils the conditions of recognition and recognises the child.

The fact that the Register of Cohabitant's Statements does not play any role in determining parental status or adoption rights does not favour cohabitants but it is in harmony with the declarative character of this kind of registration. Either of the cohabitants can give a unilateral statement that his or her cohabitation does not exist. The public notary is obliged to register this statement and inform the other party about it.

Neither same-sex cohabitants nor registered partners can become legal parents of a common child. This attitude does not seem to change as the Constitutional Court gave two judgments on registered partnership.[17] The first decision was handed down in 2008, the second in 2010. Both decisions confirmed that marriage can exist only between a man and a woman and registered partnership has to be reserved for same-sex partners. The standpoint of the Constitutional Court is also definite about cohabitation, as this institution is regarded as a partnership which has to be regulated not on the same legal level as marriage (and registered partnership).

---

[17] Decisions of the Constitutional Court No 154/2008 (XII 17) and 32/2010 (III 25).

India

CUSTOM AS AN IMPORTANT SOURCE OF HINDU LAW: ITS USAGE IN INTERNATIONAL FAMILY MIGRATION

*Anil Malhotra and Ranjit Malhotra**

Résumé

La coutume est une source juridique importante en droit hindou et elle est reconnue en tant que telle par la Loi sur le mariage hindou de 1955. La jurisprudence est abondante sur le sujet. La Cour suprême de l'Inde, de même que plusieurs Hautes Cours de justice à travers le pays, ont constamment rappelé leur position qui est bien ancrée à cet égard, tant dans le domaine du mariage que de celui du divorce. L'objectif du présent texte est d'assurer que les personnes impliquées dans de tels mariages ou divorces, puissent bénéficier d'une approche qui soit respectueuse de la coutume, particulièrement dans le contexte de la migration internationale. Il arrive que certaines autorités diplomatiques indiennes, ne reconnaissent pas les mariages et les divorces coutumiers. La connaissance approfondie du droit familial interne est donc cruciale ici.

I INTRODUCTION

As practitioners in the area of private international law, when dealing with major embassies and high commissions in New Delhi on behalf of intending settlement applicants in the context of family migration, it is essential for foreign immigration and family law lawyers to understand the legal position in India as to family law issues. These issues include the statutory recognition of customary marriages and divorces and the registration of marriages under the provisions of the Hindu Marriage Act, 1955 (HMA 1955) as applicable to non-resident Indians staying abroad. This is the main thrust of this chapter. Due to local variations and the recognition of customs under Indian law, immigration law at the Indian end has a very different complexion. These differences are critical to foreign immigration lawyers preparing immigration applications, at the initial stages of lodging the family reunion applications and of course in the event of any litigation before immigration adjudicators and tribunals.

---

*   Anil Malhotra LLM (London), Advocate, Chandigarh; Ranjit Malhotra, LLM (London) Advocate, Chandigarh.

Apart from statutory recognition by HMA 1955, this chapter also traces the case-law on the subject of customary marriages and divorces. The case-law analysis is in chronological order from 1969 with reference to some very old decisions of the Privy Council to 2010 taking into account the important relevant judgments. The judgments quoted are of the Supreme Court of India and various High Courts in the country, especially the Punjab and Haryana High Court, within whose jurisdiction the bulk of the population of Punjabi origin resides, as well as the neighbouring states. Customary Karewa marriages are popular among certain agricultural sects in rural parts of Punjab. Also, it is manifest from the case-law analysis that customary marriages including the custom of Karewa marriages, which are defined below, have not been overruled, modified or diluted in any form at all.

It is pertinent to mention that Karewa marriage is just one of the many forms of customary marriages, but as a matter of fact customary marriages in India vary within different communities and regionally as well. Karewa marriage was defined way back by Sir WH Rattigan, before the partition of India took place, as follows:[1]

> 'A "Karewa" marriage with the brother or some other male relative of the deceased husband requires no religious ceremonies, and confers all the rights of a valid marriage.'

The relevant case-law analysis on customary marriages and customary divorces in this chapter is to drive home the point that custom traditionally is an important source of Hindu law, and that continues to be the position.

II   FAMILY IMMIGRATION ISSUES

(a)   Indian marriages: registration of marriages – law and custom

Both formally registered and customary marriages are recognised under the laws of India. Visa officers have full information about the state of origin of the applicants. They are quite up to date on issues like land value, monies earned from cultivation per acre, Indian customs, etc. In Hindu marriage cases they view the *Saptapadi* photographs with a jeweller's focus. *Saptapadi* is the

---

[1]   WH Rattigan *A Digest of Customary Law* (Allahabad: University Book Agency, 15th edn, revised by Prakash Aggarawala, with a foreword by Dr Bakshi Tek Chand, 1989) para 75 of ch 5. For further details see pp 525–555. The first edition of this book was published in the year 1880, and further six editions of this book were brought about by the author himself, the last of his original work having been published in 1901. This has been followed by revised editions. The introduction at p 1 of this book reads as follows: 'A Digest of Civil Law for The Punjab Chiefly Based On The Customary Law. Preliminary: Custom in this Province is the first rule of decision in all questions regarding succession, special property of females, betrothal, marriage, divorce, dower, adoption, guardianship, minority, bastardy, family relations, wills, legacies, gifts, partitions, any religious usage or institution, alluvion and diluvion.'

taking of seven steps by the bridegroom and the bride jointly before the sacred fire. The marriage becomes complete and binding when the seventh step is taken.

At the major embassies and high commissions in New Delhi including the office of the Canadian consulate at Chandigarh, the capital of the state of Punjab, most visa officers will be aware that in certain areas in the state of Punjab especially in Jalandhar and Hoshiarpur Districts, which are famous for outbound family migration, fake marriages are performed with all the pomp and show without the religious ceremonies actually taking place at all. This is to facilitate migration through the family route.

A typical case is where the British Asian boy or girl is from the Midlands in the UK or a spouse from Maryland in the USA or from areas having dense Indian population in Canada, who is being married to a spouse from the state of Punjab. And the parents, being wary of the outcome of the spouse application, insist on a contingent arrangement. In such a situation, a fake marriage certificate is submitted to the immigration authorities. In an attempt to safeguard the interests of their children, the parents fall prey to bad advice. It is sad to mention that dubious travel agents and unqualified local consultants thrive on this non-resident clientele.

Under s 8 of the HMA 1955, the principal law governing Hindu marriages, registration of marriages is not compulsory. This is primarily because Hindu marriages and most marriages in India have always been performed in public with wide publicity. Section 8(2) provides that any state government may make rules for the compulsory registration of Hindu marriages. Furthermore, s 8(5) specifically expresses that failure to register a Hindu marriage does not affect its validity. Even where compulsory registration of marriage is laid down under the rules, non-registration does not affect the validity of the marriage, but merely entails a nominal fine. Moreover, mere registration of a marriage under s 8 will not ipso facto make the marriage valid.

In light of the prevailing law in India, registration of marriages in this region by non-resident Indians is only undertaken to satisfy the immigration authorities. It is not very difficult to obtain fake marriage certificates in the abovementioned areas of Punjab. Such false practices have a direct bearing on genuine applicants. Even their documentation and circumstances leading to the marriage are viewed cautiously.

Customary marriages are also performed in limited situations where one of the spouses is resident abroad. Generally, it is the husband who is resident abroad.

III CUSTOM AS AN IMPORTANT SOURCE OF HINDU LAW

The HMA 1955 is an Act of the Parliament of India to amend and codify the law relating to marriage among Hindus. At the outset, it is important to mention that s 5 of the HMA 1955, which deals with the conditions for a valid Hindu marriage, also by virtue of s 5(iv), allows marriage within the prohibited relationship degrees as and when permitted by the custom or usage governing the parties to the marriage, as is generally the situation in customary marriages. It is also important to mention that s 29 recognises customary marriages before the enactment of the HMA 1955 while simultaneously recognising customary divorces even after the enactment of the HMA 1955. To make matters explicitly clear customary divorces, subject to conditions of compliance, are clearly recognised under the provisions of s 29 of the HMA 1955. Customary marriages within the prohibited degrees of relationship are specifically recognised by virtue of s 5(iv) of the HMA 1955 after the legislation came into force, on 18 May 1955, and this continues to be the position to date.

It is important to consider the other relevant provisions of the HMA 1955. The relevant sections relating to the territorial jurisdiction and the extraterritorial application are defined in s 1 of the HMA 1955. The application of the said central legislation is defined in s 2, while the definition clause is contained in s 3. The conditions for a valid marriage are stipulated in s 5 and registration of marriages under the legislation is provided in s 8. The savings clause has explicit recognition in s 29.

The relevant sections of the HMA 1955 with regard to the scope of the present chapter are reproduced below.

'1. Short title and extent.

(1) This Act may be called the Hindu Marriage Act, 1955.

(2) It extends to the whole of India except the State of Jammu and Kashmir, and applies also to Hindus domiciled in the territories to which this Act extends who are outside the said territories.

2. Application of Act.

(1) This Act applies –

(a) to any person who is a Hindu by religion in any of its forms or developments, including a Virashaiva, a Lingayat or a follower of the Brahmo, Prarthana or Arya Samaj,

(b) to any person who is a Buddhist, Jaina or Sikh by religion, and

(c) to any other person domiciled in the territories to which this Act extends who is not a Muslim, Christian, Parsi or Jew by religion, unless it is proved that any such person would not have been governed by the Hindu law or by any custom or usage as part of that law in respect of any of the matters dealt with herein if this Act had not been passed.

Explanation.–The following persons are Hindus, Buddhists, Jainas or Sikhs by religion, as the case may be:–

(a) any child, legitimate or illegitimate, both of whose parents are Hindus, Buddhists, Jainas or Sikhs by religion;

(b) any child, legitimate or illegitimate, one of whose parents is a Hindu, Buddhist, Jaina or Sikh by religion and who is brought up as a member of the tribe, community, group or family to which such parent belongs or belonged; and

(c) any person who is a convert or re-convert to the Hindu, Buddhist, Jaina or Sikh religion.

(2) Notwithstanding anything contained in sub-section (1), nothing contained in this Act shall apply to the members of any Scheduled tribe within the meaning of clause (25) of article 366 of the Constitution unless the Central Government, by notification in the Official Gazette, otherwise directs.

(3) The expression "Hindu" in any portion of this Act shall be construed as if it included a person who, though not a Hindu by religion, is, nevertheless, a person to whom this Act applies by virtue of the provisions contained in this section.

3. Definitions.

In this Act, unless the context otherwise requires,–

(a) the expressions "custom" and "usage" signify any rule which, having been continuously and uniformly observed for a long time, has obtained the force of law among Hindus in any local area, tribe, community, group or family: Provided that the rule is certain and not unreasonable or opposed to public policy; and
Provided further that in the case of a rule applicable only to a family it has not been discontinued by the family;

(b) "district court" means, in any area for which there is a city civil court, that court, and in any other area the principal civil court of original jurisdiction, and includes any other civil court which may be specified by the State Government, by notification in the Official Gazette, as having jurisdiction in respect of the matters dealt with in this Act;

(c) "full blood" and "half blood"–two persons are said to be related to each other by full blood when they are descended from a common ancestor by the same wife and by half blood when they are descended from a common ancestor but by different wives;

(d) "uterine blood"– two persons are said to be related to each other by uterine blood when they are descended from a common ancestress but by different husbands;

Explanation.–In clauses (c) and (d), "ancestor" includes the father and "ancestress" the mother;

(e) "prescribed" means prescribed by rules made under this Act;

(f)
(i)   "sapinda relationship" with reference to any person extends as far as
       the third generation (inclusive) in the line of ascent through the
       mother, and the fifth (inclusive) in the line of ascent through the father,
       the line being traced upwards in each case from the person concerned,
       who is to be counted as the first generation;
(ii)   two persons are said to be "sapindas" of each other if one is a lineal
       ascendant of the other within the limits of sapinda relationship, or if
       they have a common lineal ascendant who is within the limits of
       sapinda relationship with reference to each of them;
(g)   "degrees of prohibited relationship"–two persons are said to be within the
       "degrees of prohibited relationship"–
(i)   if one is a lineal ascendant of the other; or
(ii)   if one was the wife or husband of a lineal ascendant or descendant of
       the other; or
(iii) if one was the wife of the brother or of the father's or mother's brother
       or of the grandfather's or grandmother's brother of the other; or
(iv)   if the two are brother and sister, uncle and niece, aunt and nephew, or
       children of brother and sister or of two brothers or of two sisters;

Explanation.–For the purposes of clauses (f) and (g), relationship includes–

(i)   relationship by half or uterine blood as well as by full blood;
(ii)   illegitimate blood relationship as well as legitimate;
(iii) relationship by adoption as well as by blood; and all terms of
       relationship in those clauses shall be construed accordingly.'

It is important to mention that a definition similar to s 3(a) of the HMA 1955
is also found in s 3(a) of the Hindu Adoptions and Maintenance Act 1956
(HAMA 1956).

Section 5 of the HMA 1955 prescribes the valid conditions for a Hindu
marriage, which are stated below. It will be noticed that s 5(iv) explicitly
recognises customary marriages.

'5. Conditions for a Hindu marriage.

A marriage may be solemnised between any two Hindus, if the following
conditions are fulfilled, namely:–

(i)   neither party has a spouse living at the time of the marriage;
(ii)   at the time of the marriage, neither party–
       (a)   is incapable of giving a valid consent to it in consequence of
             unsoundness of mind; or
       (b)   though capable of giving a valid consent, has been suffering from
             mental disorder of such a kind or to such an extent as to be unfit for
             marriage and the procreation of children; or
       (c)   has been subject to recurrent attacks of insanity;
(iii) the bridegroom has completed the age of twenty one years and the bride the
       age of eighteen years at the time of the marriage;

(iv) the parties are not within the degrees of prohibited relationship unless the custom or usage governing each of them permits of a marriage between the two;

(v) the parties are not sapindas of each other, unless the custom or usage governing each of them permits of a marriage between the two.'

Clearly, it will be noticed that s 5(iv) statutorily permits marriage between the degrees of prohibited relationship on the basis of custom or usage.

Section 8 of the HMA 1955 provides for registration of marriages, and even validly performed customary marriages can be registered under s 8 of the HMA 1955 which reads as follows:

'8. Registration of Hindu marriages.

(1) For the purpose of facilitating the proof of Hindu marriages, the State Government may make rules providing that the parties to any such marriage may have the particulars relating to their marriage entered in such manner and subject to such conditions as may be prescribed in a Hindu Marriage Register kept for the purpose.

(2) Notwithstanding anything contained in sub-section (1), the State Government may, if it is of opinion that it is necessary or expedient so to do, provide that the entering of the particulars referred to in sub-section (1) shall be compulsory in the State or in any part thereof, whether in all cases or in such cases as may be specified, and where any such direction has been issued, any person contravening any rule made in this behalf shall be punishable with fine which may extend to twenty-five rupees.

(3) All rules made under this section shall be laid before the State Legislature, as soon as may be, after they are made.

(4) The Hindu Marriage Register shall at all reasonable times be open for inspection, and shall be admissible as evidence of the statements therein contained and certified extracts therefrom shall, on application, be given by the Registrar on payment to him of the prescribed fee.

(5) Notwithstanding anything contained in this section, the validity of any Hindu marriage shall in no way be affected by the omission to make the entry.'

Section 29 of the HMA 1955 gives statutory recognition to customary divorce and the same is stated below for ease of reference.

'29. Savings.

(1) A marriage solemnised between Hindus before the commencement of this Act, which is otherwise valid, shall not be deemed to be invalid or ever to have been invalid by reason only of the fact that the parties thereto belonged to the same gotra or pravara or belonged to different religions, castes or sub-divisions of the same caste.

(2) Nothing contained in this Act shall be deemed to affect any right recognised by custom or conferred by any special enactment to obtain the dissolution of a Hindu marriage, whether solemnised before or after the commencement of this Act.

(3) Nothing contained in this Act shall affect any proceeding under any law for the time being in force for declaring any marriage to be null and void or for annulling or dissolving any marriage or for judicial separation pending at the commencement of this Act, and any such proceeding may be continued and determined as if this Act had not been passed.

(4) Nothing contained in this Act shall be deemed to affect the provisions contained in the Special Marriage Act, 1954 (43 of 1954) with respect to marriages between Hindus solemnised under that Act, whether before or after the commencement of this Act.'

IV   ESSENTIALS OF A VALID CUSTOM

It is important to refer to the essential ingredients of a valid custom, which essentially require that the custom should be ancient, certain, reasonable and not opposed to public policy. In 1969, in *Rabindra Nath Dutta v The State*[2] the Calcutta High Court laid down that the provisions of the HMA 1955 do not provide for any particular kind or form of ceremonies to be observed in a Hindu marriage. The judgment reads as follows:[3]

'20. The Hindu Marriage Act does not lay down any special or particular kind or form of ceremonies to be compulsorily observed in all Hindu marriages. In fact, the form of marriage, prescribed by the Sastras, is subject to modifications by custom or usage. But the expression "Customary Ceremonies" cannot be taken to mean that "Sastric Ceremonies" have been totally ignored. The expression "Customary Rites and Ceremonies" naturally means such sastric ceremonies, which the caste or community to which the party belong is customarily following. Customary rites and ceremonies to be accepted must be shown that such custom as an essence of marriage ceremony had been followed definitely from ancient times and that the members of the Caste, Community or Sub-Caste had recognised such ceremonies as obligatory. Once it is proved by evidence what ceremonies had been followed as customary rites, it is no longer left to the will of the Caste, Community or Sub-Caste to alter them as the essence of custom is that on account of its definiteness it had been recognised and adopted by the caste or community with certainty and without any variation.'

The Supreme Court of India in the case of *Harihar Prasad Singh and Others v Balmiki Prasad Singh and Others*[4] held that the specific family custom pleaded in a particular case should be proved. The initial onus lies on the plaintiffs to prove the special custom. It must be proved that the custom has been acted

---

[2]   All India Reporter (AIR) 1969 Calcutta 55.
[3]   Ibid, para 20, p 58.
[4]   AIR 1975 SC 733.

upon in practice for such a long period and with such invariability as to show that it has by common consent been submitted to as the established governing rule of the particular family.

V TRADITIONAL REASONS AND OBJECTIVES BEHIND CUSTOMARY MARRIAGES

The *Chadar* ceremony (the second marriage which is one of the forms of Karewa marriage), is a brief marriage ceremony which is basically handing over the bride to the bridegroom. This custom of low-key marriages is uniformly followed within the Jatts and certain sections of the Sikh community and is an established ongoing practice of Karewa marriages within the Sikh community. There is no dispute as to the validity of such a custom.

This customary wedding ceremony is generally a small low-key ceremony. Given the circumstances of such a wedding, no celebrations are held at all. No guests are invited nor are any pictures taken at all. These Karewa marriages, generally as per custom, are usually performed in such a low-key manner. Following the tenets of the Sikh religion, no actual wedding ceremony is performed in a Sikh temple, unlike a wedding ceremony in normal circumstances. The main reason for following such a practice is that it is a remarriage of a widow, quite often within the immediate family itself.

Traditionally, one of the prime objectives of such a customary marriage is the rehabilitation of the widow within the family fold, and to retain the land holding within the family fold. Since, Karewa marriages emanate from the state of Punjab, which is known for its flourishing agriculture, the size of the land holdings have added significance for the family name. Land holdings in the state of Punjab are considered to be the pride of the family and more valuable than the family silver.

VI ADDITIONAL MODES OF PROVING VALID CUSTOMARY MARRIAGES: CREDIBLE EVIDENCE BY WAY OF AFFIDAVITS AND EXPERT LEGAL REPORTS

Evidence as to the usage and continuance of customary marriages and practices can be put forward in the shape of affidavits, to demonstrate the genuineness of the same to the satisfaction of the immigration authorities when they doubt the existence and usage of such customary practices. The claim may additionally be supported by expert reports from lawyers of repute, in the event of any post-refusal appeal proceedings or in any litigation in any foreign court or tribunal.

Such affidavits should be tendered by the aggrieved beneficiary applicant wife, and made by the *Sarpanch* (the elected village headman including several respectable elderly people from the village from different walks of life). There should be at least eight to ten such affidavits couched in very specific terms as to the applicability, specific practice, usage and continuity of the custom within the community.

The Supreme Court in *Harihar Prasad*[5] has traced the history of the usage of the family customs, also placing reliance on some of the very early decisions of the Privy Council:

> '6. Now on whom does the burden rest and what is the scope of the evidence that is admissible? The earliest decision on the question regarding proof of custom in variance of the general law is found in *Ramalakshmi Ammal v Shivanatha Perumal* (1872) 14 Moo. Ind. App. 570 at p 585 (PC) to the effect:
>
> > "It is of the essence of special usages modifying the ordinary law of succession that they should be ancient and invariable; and it is further essential that they should be established to be so by clear and unambiguous evidence. It is only by means of such evidence that the Courts can be assured of their existence, and that they possess the conditions of antiquity and certainty on which alone their legal title to recognition depends."'

This passage was quoted by this court with the approval in its decision in *Pushpavathi Vijayaram v P Visweswar*[6] and this court went on further to observe:

> 'In dealing with the family custom, the same principle will have to be applied, though, of course, in the case of a family custom, instances in support of the custom may not be as many or as frequent as in the case of customs pertaining to a territory or to the community or to the character of any estate. In dealing with family customs, the consensus of opinion amongst the members of the family, the traditional belief entertained by them and acted upon by them, their statements, and their conduct would all be relevant and it is only where the relevant evidence of such a character appears to the Court to be sufficient that a specific family custom pleaded in a particular case would be held to be proved, *Abdul Hussein Khan v Bibi Sona*, (45 Ind. App.10= AIR 1917 PC 181).'

The observations of the Supreme Court of India back in 1964 in *Pushpavathi Vijayaram v P Visweswar*, were subsequently reiterated in *Harihar Prasad* in 1975. Obviously, affidavits of local village people should state that the customary marriage of the applicant was on the basis of family custom, consensus of the applicant wife and also the family and the community and they acted accordingly upon the traditional belief entertained by them.

It should not be the case at all that the usage of the custom of Karewa marriage, other forms of customary marriages or divorces by either of the spouses with their consent and the support of the family has sprung up overnight, possibly to circumvent immigration rules. The pleaded custom

---

5   Ibid, para 6, p 737.
6   AIR 1964 SC 118.

should be supported by affidavits of respectable community members and there should exist no such infirmity in the pleadings made by them.

VII CUSTOMARY DISSOLUTION OF MARRIAGES, UNDER HMA 1955, S 29(2)

Customary dissolution of marriages is permitted under s 29(2) of the HMA 1955. There is a direct judgment of the Jammu and Kashmir High Court in *Smt Rano Devi v Rishi Kumar*.[7] The interpretation of s 29(2) of the HMA 1955 in crystal clear terms reads as follows:

> 'It clearly states that marriage may be dissolved in accordance with a custom governing the parties, or under any other law providing for the same. This sub section is couched in a stronger language and says that notwithstanding anything contained in the Act, including Sections 4 and 13, a Hindu marriage may be dissolved even under the customary law of the parties, by adopting a mode different from the one provided under the Act. This is what has happened here also. Instead of approaching the District Court in a petition under Section 13, the parties, by mutual agreement, dissolved their marriage by executing a deed of divorce, a mode permissible under the customs followed by them. The trial Court was, therefore, right in dismissing the appellant's petition on the ground that since the marriage between the parties already stood dissolved through a customary divorce, no decree for the restitution of conjugal rights could be passed in her favour.'

There is a custom among the Sikh Jats of Amritsar, by which a husband can dissolve a marriage out of court, preferably by written instrument, which of course is saved by s 29(2) of the HMA 1955. Thus, a second marriage after such a customary divorce was held not to be void. This was held in the case of *Balwinder Singh v Gurpal Kaur*[8] which has elucidated the position of customary divorces in very eloquent terms as follows:

> '20. The upshot of the whole discussion, therefore is that there is ample oral as well as other evidence on record to warrant the conclusion that there does exist a custom amongst Sikh Jats of District Amritsar under which a marriage can be dissolved out of court preferably through a written instrument. The very fact that dissolution of marriage amongst Sikh Jats of that district has been taking place even after the enactment of the Act is in itself a strong proof of its recognition by the community concerned. It would show that despite the relief of dissolution of marriage by divorce being available under the Act people still prefer to resort to customary law rather than seek redress in a court of law under the Act. So, the mere fact that the appellant has not furnished any old instance would not undermine the evidentiary value of the instances cited by various witnesses in Court; rather they tend to establish beyond doubt that such a custom is firmly rooted and is still prevalent despite the remedy of divorce being available under statutory law. Hence, I hold accordingly.'

---

[7]   AIR 1981 Jammu and Kashmir 2, para 6, p 4.
[8]   AIR 1985 Delhi 14, para 20.

Quite often, there are refusal letters by the embassy authorities in instances of Karewa marriages or other forms of valid customary marriages. That such an assertion in the case of a valid customary marriage that the beneficiary has married her former brother-in-law, which of course is not legally sustainable also in light of the law laid down in *Parkash Chander v Smt Parmeshwari*.[9] The most relevant paragraph relating to the interpretation of Karewa marriages reads as follows:

> '12. The next question of definite importance which arises in this case is whether during the lifetime of Ishwar Singh who was very much present in the village, any Karewa marriage could be legally entered into between the respondent and the appellant, or had it in fact been so taken place. There is no doubt whatsoever in my mind that in the presence of Ishwar Singh, who was very much alive in the village, no valid marriage could take place between the parties. Such a marriage would be void in the face of the provisions of Section 5 (1) of the Act wherein it is laid down that a marriage may be solemnised between any two Hindus if neither party has a spouse living at the time of the marriage. It has been held by the Supreme Court in *Mohd. Ikram Hussain v. Stat of Uttar Pradesh,* All India Reporter 1964 Supreme Court 1625, that in view of provisions of Sections 5 and 11 of the Act, such a marriage would be null and void. In para 74 of the Digest of Customary Law by Sir W.H. Rattigan (13th edition), it has been laid down that until the former marriage is validly set aside, a woman cannot marry a second husband in the lifetime of her first husband.'

VIII   THE WIFE SHOULD NOT HAVE A LIVING SPOUSE FOR A VALID KAREWA MARRIAGE

It is very important that for a Karewa marriage to be valid the wife should have no living spouse at the time she solemnised her subsequent Karewa marriage.

In the abovementioned case of *Parkash Chander* (1987), the Karewa marriage was held to be invalid because the original husband of the wife was subsequently found not to be dead. He was found to be alive after a certain period of time. Meanwhile, the wife had entered into a Karewa marriage with her brother-in-law. In this particular case, the wife pleaded the custom raising the presumption that, since her first husband had not been heard of for 7–8 years he was presumed to be dead. This contention was rejected outright on the ground that the alleged custom was contrary to s 108 of the Indian Evidence Act, 1872. The Punjab and Haryana High Court tersely held as follows:[10]

> '20. . . . In the instant case what the respondent had pleaded was that since Ishwar Singh, her husband, had not been heard of and his whereabouts were not known for a period of 7–8 years, she entered into a Karewa marriage with the appellant. Therefore, it is not necessary to probe into the facets of the issue whether there is a custom prevalent in the community of the parties which permits dissolution of marriage on the ground that either party had been mentally insane, had become

---

9   AIR 1987 Punjab and Haryana 37, para 12, p 42.
10   Ibid, para 20, p 46.

impotent or was incapable of performing the duties of husband/wife. The only aspect that needs examination and determination is whether a divorce is permissible in the community of the parties under custom where one of the spouses is unheard of or his whereabouts are not known. Before examination of this aspect of the issue, it has to be kept in mind that a custom to be valid must not contravene any express provision of the law. It should not be against public policy nor it should be contrary to justice, equity and good conscience and it should be ancient, certain and invariable. These ingredients of a valid custom are laid down in para 1 of Rattigan's digest of Customary Law ibid . . .'

In the event of refusal of a settlement visa for a wife to join her husband overseas in the case of a valid customary marriage, support can very much be drawn by the beneficiary wife from these observations of the Punjab and Haryana High Court. This is to the effect that the custom of Karewa marriage pleaded by the beneficiary wife is very much valid, does not contravene any express provision of law and nor is it against public policy.

Under the provisions of the HMA 1955 both parties to the marriage are at full liberty to solemnise their marriage by way of customary rites and ceremonies generally prevalent in their community. However, such ceremonies and rites should essentially fulfil the essential ingredients of a custom, as already stated above. But, if *Saptapadi* (taking of seven steps around the holy fire) and invocation before the sacred fire are made, the marriage is validly solemnised under the Shastric law.

IX CUSTOMARY MARRIAGES WILL NOT BE RECOGNISED IN THE ABSENCE OF COGENT RELIABLE PROOF

In a customary marriage case where there is no proof of custom nor is a customary marriage pleaded, such a customary marriage will not be recognised. In this particular regard, it is important to note the observations of the Kerala High Court in *Chakki v Ayyappan*:[11]

'10. The appellant cannot succeed only by a showing that in other marriages of the community there were exchange of rings and pooja and thali etc. Those can be accepted as requirements of customary marriage only if they are proved to be sufficiently ancient and definite and that members of the community recognise them as obligatory. It should also be shown that those formalities were unalterable. As we indicated earlier, there are no pleadings, much less any proof of an ancient, definite and unalterable custom in this regard.'

By way of clarification, in this case, the marriage was held to be valid on the basis of the performance of the statutory essential requirement of a Hindu marriage, ie invocation before the sacred fire, and *Saptapadi* (taking seven steps by the groom and bride jointly before the sacred fire).

---

[11]   AIR 1989 Kerala 89, para 10, p 92.

X KAREWA MARRIAGES GENERALLY PREDOMINANT IN AGRICULTURAL TRIBES OF PUNJABI ORIGIN

In *Garja Singh and another v Surjit Kaur and another*,[12] it was held that a marriage will be valid only if the ceremony through which it is solemnised is sanctioned by the religion of either party as a customary ceremony. Therefore, merely going through some ceremonies like distribution of *Gur* and *Shakkar* (sugar) with the intention that the parties be taken to have been married will not make them the customary ceremonies prescribed by law or sanctioned by custom. Even in the general customary law in Punjab as applicable to the predominantly agricultural tribes, the Karewa marriage with the brother or some male relative of the deceased husband requires no religious ceremonies and confers all the rights of a valid marriage. However, the bride in this case had no connection whatsoever with the deceased, alleged to be her husband prior to the execution of the 'Karewa Nama'. The marriage with a stranger has to be performed in accordance with the customary rights or ceremonies as prescribed by law. There was no allegation, much less proof, as to what were the customary ceremonies performed for solemnising the marriage between the deceased and the defendant claiming a share in the estate of the deceased, as his widow. This is also one of the judgments which categorically notices that such Karewa marriages are generally predominant in agricultural tribes of Punjabi origin.

XI CUSTOM SHOULD BE PROVED IN THE FOLLOWING TERMS

Furthermore, the Punjab and Haryana High Court in *Asha Rani v Gulshan Kumar*[13] has elaborated on the way in which custom should be proved:

> '10. A custom must be proved to be ancient, certain and reasonable if it is to be recognised and acted upon by Courts of Law. The specific family custom pleaded in a particular case should be proved by the party pleading it. It must be proved that the custom has been acted upon in practice for such a long period and with such invariability, as to show that it has, by common consent, been submitted to as the established governing rule of the particular family. Custom no doubt can be proved by oral evidence of witnesses acquainted with custom, instances and general pronouncements. Section 29 (2) of the Act does not disturb the position which a customary divorce occupied before the enactment of the Act.'

As stated above customary marriage and divorce, qua the aggrieved beneficiary applicant, can additionally be proved by key credible witnesses from the community and possibly community leaders as well, in the shape of affidavits.

---

[12] AIR 1991 Punjab and Haryana 177.
[13] AIR 1995 Punjab and Haryana 287, para 10, p 289.

XII NOT NECESSARY FOR PARTIES TO OBTAIN DIVORCE FROM COURT, ON GROUND ALREADY RECOGNISED BY CUSTOM

In *Rita Rani v Ramesh Kumar*[14] it was held that, if there is a local custom by which marriage can be dissolved either by brotherhood or by executing an agreement, such a customary dissolution of marriage is saved by s 29(2) of the HMA 1955. And more importantly the parties are not required to obtain a decree of divorce through a court, after such a customary divorce has been effected. The Punjab and Haryana High Court held as follows:[15]

> '7. Relying on *Balwinder Singh v Smt. Gurpal Kaur*, AIR 1985 Delhi 14: [1985(1) All India Hindu Law Reporter 442 (Delhi)], *Smt. Sudarshan Kaur v Major Manmohan Singh Bhatt*, AIR 1978 Punjab and Haryana 115; A Digest of Customary Law by Sir W.H. Rattigan (Fourteenth Edition) page 470; and Hindu Law by Mula 16th edition page 745, he contended that from the pleadings and sole testimony of Ramesh Kumar, it is evident that in the cast of the parties, there is customary mode of marriage and customary mode of dissolution of marriage also. Therefore, Ramesh Kumar himself dissolved his earlier marriage with Rita Rani under this customary mode ie dissolution of marriage by "biradari". He stressed that under Section 29(2) of the Act, it is not necessary for parties in any such case to go to Court to obtain divorce on ground recognised by custom. It is not the case of Ramesh Kumar that this customary mode of dissolution of marriage is either against the public policy or is not upheld by Courts.'

The ruling in this case is of immense significance. It has been categorically held by the Punjab and Haryana High Court at Chandigarh in this case that it is not necessary for the parties to go to court on the ground that such a divorce is recognised by custom. Likewise, it is argued by analogy that it is not mandatory for the parties to the marriage as in the present case to go to court for validation of their customary marriage. Generally, there is an assertion in the refusal letters in settlement cases by the embassy authorities to the effect 'also please provide a court order stating that this relationship is allowed'. Clearly, in light of the settled position of law as stated above, the assertion of a court declaration by the embassy authorities to the effect that the relationship is permitted by law is not a sustainable action.

XIII COURTS CAN TAKE JUDICIAL NOTICE OF GENERAL CUSTOMS

The Punjab and Haryana High Court in *Ranbir Kaur alias Harjit Kaur v Gurnam Singh*,[16] held that the courts can take judicial notice of general customs. The court elaborated that the term 'general custom' is used in the sense that it has, by repeated recognition by courts over a period of time,

---

[14] 1995 (2) *Hindu Law Reporter* 338 (Punjab and Haryana).
[15] Ibid, para 7, p 339.
[16] 1996 (2) *Hindu Law Reporter* 71.

become entitled to judicial notice. This judgment crystallises the law on judicial
notice of general customs by consolidating the earlier case-law as follows:[17]

> '8. Whoever sets up a custom must prove the same. Sometimes the custom is
> recognised by Courts and it passes into the law of land. This question was
> considered by the Supreme Court in the case of *Ujagar Singh v Mst. Jeo*, AIR
> 1959 SC 1041. In paragraph 14 it was held:
>
>> 14. It therefore appears to us that the ordinary rule is that all customs,
>> general or otherwise, have to be proved. Under S.57 of the Evidence Act
>> however nothing need to be proved of which courts can take judicial notice.
>> Therefore, it is said that if there is a custom of which the courts can take
>> judicial notice, it need not be proved. How the circumstances in which the
>> courts can take judicial notice, it need not be proved. How the circumstances
>> in which the courts can take judicial notice of a custom were stated by
>> Lord Dunedin in *Raja Ram Rao v Raja of Pittapur*, 45 Ind App 148 at pp
>> 154, 155: (AIR 1918 PC 81 at P.83), in the following words, "When a custom
>> or usage, whether in regard to a tenure or a contract or a family right, is
>> repeatedly brought to the notice of the Courts of a country, the Courts may
>> hold that custom or usage to be introduced into the law without necessity of
>> proof in each individual case." When a custom has been so recognised by the
>> courts, it passes into the law of the land and the proof of it then becomes
>> unnecessary under S.57 (1) of the Evidence Act. It appears to us that in the
>> courts in the Punjab the expression "general custom" has really been used in
>> this sense, namely, that a custom has by repeated recognition by courts,
>> become entitled to judicial notice as was said in *Bawa Singh v Mt. Taro*, AIR
>> 1951 Punjab 239; and *Sukhwant Kaur v Balwant Singh*, AIR 1951 Punjab
>> 242.'

The judgment specifically highlights the importance of general custom. This
term is used in the sense that the same by repeated recognition by the courts has
become entitled to judicial notice.

Thus, it can be stated that the onus of proving and establishing a custom would
lie on the party who claims its benefit. As already stated before, from the
catalogue of evidence in the shape of affidavits furnished by the beneficiary
applicant, other members of the family, as also by respectable people from the
community, the practice of customary marriages and divorces can be proved
successfully. Whether the same is acceptable for judicial notice or it is to be
proven separately would depend on the facts and circumstances of each case. It
is clear that, in the northern Indian state of Punjab, customary divorce and
customary widow remarriage is an acceptable customary practice in some local
communities.[18]

---

[17] Ibid, para 8, p 74.
[18] For further details see Sir WH Rattigan *A Digest of Customary Law (in Punjab)*, 1880, and
      reprinted subsequently by other authors, which discusses in great detail customary law
      practices prevalent in Punjab in all walks of life (above n 1). In the most recent edition (1995),
      chapter V specifically reports and discusses known prevalent customary practices of marriage
      and divorce in different classes and communities in Punjab.

The scheme and object of the HMA 1955 are not to override any such custom which recognises divorce, and explicit recognition is given to the same by the saving clause contained in s 29(2). It is not necessary for parties in any such case to go to court to obtain divorce on the grounds that it is already recognised by custom. The custom, as elaborated above must be a valid custom. Section 29(2) saves customary divorce but the party relying on a custom needs to prove the existence of such custom and also that it is ancient, certain, reasonable and not opposed to public policy. In *Mariammal v Padmanabhan*,[19] the Madras High Court overruled the finding of the trial court that there cannot be customary divorce after the coming into force of the HMA 1955. It held that divorce was recognised by custom even before the Act, and after the Act courts also uphold the custom if not opposed to public policy.

From the discussion and the case-law analysis on s 29 of the HMA 1955 it is manifest that the section specifically saves customs regarding marriage and divorce from the operation of the provisions of the HMA 1955 and they are legally recognised. In *Jasbir Singh v Inderjit Kaur*,[20] the husband sought annulment of his marriage on the ground that, at the time of marriage, his wife was already married. The wife's contention was that she had obtained a customary divorce from her previous husband and the petitioner was aware of this as he had seen the written deed of customary divorce; he was, therefore, estopped from taking the plea that the wife was already married and not divorced. The wife was a Jat Sikh from District Sangrur in Punjab. After going through the evidence, the court held that it was established that there is a custom among the Jat Sikhs of District Sangrur which permits divorce and the wife had obtained the divorce according to that custom. The validity of the custom being saved, it was not necessary for the parties to go to court to obtain divorce; it is open for the parties to dissolve the marriage out of court, in accordance with the custom. The court relied on, inter alia, *Gurdit Singh v Mst Angrez Kaur*[21] where the apex court held that there can be valid divorce where custom allows dissolution, and on dissolution of a marriage by custom, the party can enter into second marriage in the lifetime of the first divorced spouse. The husband's petition for annulment was consequently dismissed in *Jasbir Kaur* as, the wife having obtained customary divorce from her previous husband, the marriage with the petitioner was legal and valid. The Punjab and Haryana High Court held as follows:[22]

> '9. In AIR 1978 P&H 98 (supra) relied upon by the learned counsel for the appellant-husband, it has been held that a party relying upon a particular custom is called upon to allege and to prove that custom. It was further held that entries in a Riwaj-e-am, which pertain to a special custom applicable to a locality or a class of persons, should also be presumed to be correct unless rebutted . . .'

---

[19] AIR 2001 Mad 350.
[20] AIR 2003 Punjab & Haryana 317.
[21] AIR 1968 SC 142.
[22] *Jasbir Singh v Inderjit Kaur* AIR 2003 Punjab & Haryana 317, para 9 at p 319.

The court further held as follows:[23]

> '20. . . . In *Gurdit Singh v Mst. Angrez Kaur*, AIR 1968 SC 142, it was held by the
> Hon'ble Supreme Court that a custom exists among the Hindu Jats of the
> Jalandhar District which permits a valid divorce by a husband of his wife which
> dissolves the marriage. It was further held that on the dissolution of such a
> marriage the divorced wife can enter into a valid marriage with a second husband
> in the lifetime of the first husband. The law laid down by this Court in (1962) Punj
> LR 1179, was affirmed by the Hon'ble Supreme Court, in the said authority. In
> *Balwinder Singh v Smt. Gurpal Kaur*, 1985 Marriage Law Journal 414: (AIR 1985
> Delhi 14) it was held by the Delhi High Court that on a plain reading of
> Section 29(2) of the Hindu Marriage Act, it is manifest that a marriage may still
> be dissolved in accordance with a custom governing the parties or under any other
> law providing for the same. It was further held that the validity of any custom
> recognising the right to dissolve a marriage is expressly saved by this sub-section.
> It was further held that as a necessary corollary, it follows that it would not be
> necessary for the parties in any such case to go to Court to obtain divorce on
> grounds recognised by custom and it would be open to dissolve the marriage out
> of Court in accordance with such custom. It was further held that the net result
> will be that a Hindu marriage may now be dissolved under Section 13 of the
> Hindu Marriage Act or under any other special enactment or in accordance with
> any custom applicable to the parties. Reliance was also placed on the law laid
> down by Hon'ble Court, in *Gurdit Singh's* case (supra), in respect of the existence
> of such a custom in District Jalandhar. It was also held that the existence of such
> a custom permitting dissolution of marriage by divorce amongst Hindu Jats was
> also prevalent in District surrounding Jalandhar District, including Amritsar,
> Hoshiarpur and Ludhiana.
>
> 21. In view of the above, in my opinion, it can safely be held that there is a custom
> among Jat Sikhs of District Sangrur, permitting dissolution of marriage by
> divorce through writing executed by the parties in this regard and such a divorce
> would be recognised, in view of Section 29(2) of the Hindu Marriage Act and the
> law laid down by the Hon'ble Supreme Court and Delhi High Court, in the cases
> referred to above. I am further of the opinion, that the learned Additional District
> Judge had rightly found that the marriage between the petitioner and respondent
> could not be annulled under Section 11 of the Hindu Marriage Act, inasmuch as
> respondent had validly obtained a divorce from her previous husband Lachhman
> Singh, at the time when her marriage had taken place with the petitioner.
> Accordingly, I affirm the findings of the learned Additional District Judge in this
> regard.'

This ruling in *Jasbir Singh* laying in similar tenor to *Rita Rani*[24] is again of
immense significance. This is because it has been yet again categorically
reiterated by the Punjab and Haryana High Court at Chandigarh that it is not
necessary for the parties to go to court on the ground that such a divorce is
recognised by custom. Hence, if the denial letter by the embassy authorities in
the case of a valid Karewa marriage states to the effect 'also please provide a
court order stating that this relationship is allowed', clearly this would not be
legally sustainable according to the settled law, as elaborated above.

---

23 Ibid, paras 20 and 21, pp 323 and 324.
24 Above n 14.

XIV CUSTOMARY DISSOLUTION OF MARRIAGE DOES NOT REQUIRE VALIDATION FROM COURT – RECENT SUPREME COURT OF INDIA JUDGMENT

Much more recently, the Supreme Court of India in *Mahendra Nath Yadav v Sheela Devi*,[25] upheld the judgment of the Allahabad High Court stating that the High Court rightly held that dissolution of marriage through the panchayat (local elected village council at the grassroot level) according to custom cannot be a ground for granting divorce under s 13 of the HMA 1955. The facts of this case are as follows:[26]

'4. According to appellant, it was customary in the locality and in the community to which both parties belong to have a divorce through the Panchayat. Thus, the Panchayat was convened on 7-6-1997. The said Panchayat decided that the appellant should pay a sum of Rs. 30,000/- to the respondent's family. It was paid and a document was prepared which was duly signed by the parties. Thus, the marriage came to an end. In order to give legal effect to the said customary divorce, the appellant tried to persuade the respondent to get divorce from the Family Court under Section 13B of the 1955 Act, by consent. However, she did not agree. Thus the appellant approached the Family Court by filing Petition No. 370 of 1998 under Section 13 of the 1955 Act, seeking divorce on the ground of desertion and cruelty.

5. The respondent filed the counter-case ie Petition No. 57 of 1999 under Section 9 of the 1955 Act, for restitution of conjugal rights. The Family Court decreed the suit mainly on the ground that the marriage stood dissolved through Panchayat and dismissed the petition filed by the wife for restitution of conjugal rights vide order dated 15–09–2000. Being aggrieved, the respondent preferred appeals against both the orders before the High Court and the High Court has reversed the said order in both the cases. Hence this appeal.'

The reasoning clearly elucidated by the apex court in not interfering with the judgment of the High Court is as follows:[27]

'7.The High Court has rightly held that dissolution of marriage through Panchayat as per custom prevailing in that area and in that community permitted cannot be a ground for granting divorce under Section 13 of the 1955 Act. We fully agree with the said decision for the reason that in case the appellant wanted a decree on the basis of customary dissolution of marriage through Panchayat held on 7-6-1997, he would not have filed a petition under Section 13 of the 1955 Act. Filing this petition itself means that none of the parties was of the view that the divorce granted by the Panchayat was legal. In view of the above, we do not see any reason to interfere with the well-reasoned judgment of the High Court.'

---

[25] (2010) 9 SCC 484.
[26] Ibid, paras 4 and 5, pp 485–486.
[27] Ibid, para 7, p 486.

XV DIFFERENT TYPES OF CUSTOMS

The Supreme Court of India in an elaborate judgment handed down in 2007 has very clearly elucidated the three types of different customs in the case of *Smt Ass Kaur (Deceased) by LRs v Kartar Singh (Dead) by LRs and Ors.*[28] One of the key issues in this case was succession rights on the basis of Karewa marriage:

'10. Hindu law recognises three types of customs: local custom, class custom and family custom. The courts below have held that the parties were governed by Zimindara custom. Whether the said custom is a general custom, or a special custom or for that matter a family custom has not been stated. The customary law prevailing in the State of Punjab has received a statutory sanction by reason of the Punjab Laws Act, 1872, Sections 5 and 7 whereof read as under:

5. Decisions in certain cases to be according to Native law.– In questions regarding succession, special property of females, betrothal, marriage divorce, dower, adoption, guardianship, minority, bastardy, family relations, wills, legacies, gifts, partitions, or any religious usage or institution the rule of decision shall be –

(a) any custom applicable to the parties concerned, which is not contrary to justice, equity or good conscience, and has not been by this or any other enactment altered or abolished, and has not been declared to be void by any competent authority.

(b) the Muhammadan law, in cases where the parties are Muhammadans and the Hindu law, in cases where the parties are Hindus, except in so far as such law has been altered or abolished by legislative enactment, or is opposed to the provisions of this Act, or has been modified by any such customs as is above referred to.

7. Local customs and mercantile usages when valid.–All local customs and mercantile usages shall be regarded as valid, unless they are contrary to justice, equity or good conscience, or have, before the passing of this Act, been declared to be void by any competent authority.

11. Amongst the Sikh Jats of Punjab province, there exists a custom, where the widow marries her first husband's brother in the Karewa form, remarriage would not cause forfeiture of her own share.[29]

12. In respect of Jats belonging to Ferozepur district, it has been held that a widow who remarried her first husband's brother succeeds to a co-widow in preference to collaterals. But the widow's right only accrues on husband's death, and if it does not accrue then, it cannot accrue later by the death of subsequent heir. The fact, if the widow is a Karewa widow it would not affect her right in a suit the parties to which were the two widows of a Manhas Rajput resident in the Shakargarh Tehsil of Gurudaspur District, had that [sic] the plaintiff (upon whom under the

---

[28] *Judgments Today* 2007 (9) SC 118, paras 10–12, pp 121 and 122.
[29] See *Chunnilal v Mst Attar Kaur* AIR 1933 Lah 69.

circumstances the onus lay) had failed to prove a custom in her favour, excluding the defendant, who was a co-widow by a Karewa marriage, from succeeding to a share in the deceased husband's estate.[30] Even a woman who had contracted such marriage may not forfeit her life estate, if any, in her deceased husband's property despite the provisions of the Hindu widows Remarriage Act, 1856. However, the said principle would not apply where a remarriage is not with the brother of her deceased but with some other relative.'

Furthermore, the apex court in paras 17 to 19 of its judgment has reiterated the settled position of law that courts can take judicial notice of custom and as and when the custom has been recognised by the courts, the same need not be proved. Paragraphs 17 to 19 at pages 123 and 124 read as follows:

'17. We may, however, notice that customary law has been recorded in Rattigan's Digest of Customary Laws. The courts below have categorically held the law to be applicable in the instant case is the customary law having regard to the fact that the parties belonged to the community of Sidhu Jats.

18. In *R.B.S.S. Munnalal and Ors. v S.S. Rajkumar and Ors.* AIR 1962 SC 1493, this Court was considering the question as to whether a Jain widow could adopt a son to her husband without his express authority, being governed by the custom which had by long acceptance become part of the law applicable to them. Therein, it was observed:

... It is well-settled that where a custom is repeatedly brought to the notice of the Courts of a country, the courts may hold that custom introduced into the law without the necessity of proof in each individual case ...

19. The court can also take judicial notice of such customs in terms of Section 57 of the Evidence Act, 1872. As and when custom has repeatedly been recognised by the courts, the same need not be proved. Reference in regard to the Punjab 'general custom' may be made to *Ujagar Singh* (supra), and *Bawa v Taro* AIR 1951 Punjab 239.'

The law reiterated and the law laid down by the Supreme Court of India in *Smt Ass Kaur (Deceased)*, would clearly support the case of a beneficiary wife who is affected by the refusal of her settlement visa application. The apex court has yet again given clear-cut recognition to Karewa marriages, even in rights of succession. Furthermore, the observations in para 25 at pages 124 and 125 of the above judgment are also very important in a situation where a wife has performed a valid customary marriage:

'25. As statutory law did not exclude the applicability of the customary law, the principle that customary law would prevail over the statutory law would apply. It was so found by the courts below.'

The point to be conveyed is that, in the case of a valid customary marriage, the customary law would prevail over statutory law.

---

[30]   *Mst Dakho v Mst Gano* 22 PR 889.

Lastly, in relation to the present judgment, support is drawn from the observations in para 29 at page 125 of the *Smt Ass Kaur (deceased)* judgment which reads as follows:

'29. In *Daya Singh (dead) through L.Rs.* (supra), paragraph 23 of Rattigan's Digest of Customary Law of Punjab has been noticed. It was held:

It is on the basis of this Customary Law that the reversioners succeeded in the suit filed by them questioning the gift made by the respondents['] mother to her. There is no doubt that Rattigan's work is an authoritative one on the subject of Customary Law in Punjab. This Court in *Mahant Salig Ram vs. Musammat Maya Devi* said:

> The customary rights of succession of daughters as against the collaterals of the father with reference to ancestral and non-ancestral lands are stated in para 23 of Rattigan's Digest of Customary Law. It is categorically stated in sub-para (2) of that paragraph that the daughter succeeds to the self-acquired property of the father in preference to the collaterals even though they are within the fourth degree. Rattigan's work has been accepted by the Privy Council as a book of unquestioned authority in the Punjab. Indeed, the correctness of this para was not disputed before this Court in *Gopal Singh v Ujagar Singh.*'

The Andhra Pradesh High Court in 2008 has in relation to the constant usage of customary law has reiterated the relevant operative parts of earlier judgments of the Supreme Court of India and the Privy Council. This is in the case of *Atluri Brahmanandam v Anne Sai Bapuji*:[31]

'17. In *Gokal Chand v Parvin Kumari* AIR 1952 SC 231, Supreme Court laid down general principles, to be kept in view, in dealing with the question of customary law. Inter alia it is laid down that, "a custom in order to be binding must derive its force from the fact that by long usage it has obtained a force of law, but English rule that, 'a custom in order that it may be legal and binding, must have been used so long that the memory of man runneth not to the contrary' should not be strictly applied to Indian conditions. All that is necessary to prove is that the usage has been acted upon in practice for such a long period and with such invariability as to show that it has, by common consent, been submitted to as the established governing rule of a particular locality".

18. In *Raja of Pittapur* AIR 1918 PC 81, the Privy Council held as under:

> This proposition, it must be noted, does not negative the doctrine that there are members of the family entitled to maintenance in the case of an impartible zamindari. Just as the impartibility is the creature of custom, so custom may and does affirm a right to maintenance in certain members of the family. No attempt has been, as already stated, made by the plaintiff to prove any special custom in this zamindari. That by itself in the case of some claims would not be fatal. When a custom or usage, whether in regard to a tenure or a contract or a family right, is repeatedly brought to the notice of

---

[31]   2008 (2) *All India Hindu Law Reporter* 432, paras 17–20, p 437.

the Courts of a country, the Courts may hold that custom or usage to be introduced into the law without the necessity of proof in each individual case. It becomes in the end truly a matter of process and pleading.

19. In *Bai Sakar* AIR1937 Bombay 65, Supreme Court laid down as under:

> The fact that a particular custom has been judicially recognized establishes that the custom is reasonable and not opposed to public policy so that it will be upheld whenever it is proved. This is the legal aspect of custom: *Moult v Halliday* (1898) 1 QB 125. But, subject to what I shall presently state, judicial recognition of a custom in another suit leaves untouched the proof of the fact that the custom is applicable to the particular parties who are before the court.

20. In *Ujagar Singh* AIR 1959 SC 1041, while observing that every general custom relied on [by] a person must be clearly proved to exist, the Supreme Court ruled that if the Court takes judicial notice of such custom under Section 57 of Indian Evidence Act, 1872, no further proof is required. Keeping this in mind, the submission of learned Counsel for the appellant that the plaintiff did not plead and prove the existence of such custom is without any merit . . .'

Much more recently, the Punjab and Haryana High Court in *Rajinder Kaur v Kuldeep Singh*[32] refused to recognise a customary divorce in the absence of any evidence on record to prove that divorce through a *Panchyatnama* (written agreement executed before the local elected village council at the grassroots level), was actually permissible under any custom or usage prevalent in the society. In this particular case, the second marriage of the wife, without legally nullifying the earlier marriage, was held to be a nullity. The decree earlier passed by the trial court declaring the second marriage null and void on the petition of the husband was upheld by the High Court in no uncertain categorical terms.

Paragraph 11 at pages 207 and 208 of that judgment in this regard is most relevant and is reproduced hereunder:

> '11. As already observed above learned matrimonial court also found as a fact, that no evidence was led to establish that there was any custom or usage prevalent in the community of the appellant under which divorce through writing of panchayatnama was permissible. Hon'ble Supreme Court in the case of *M.M. Malhotra v Union of India and others* AIR 2006 SC 80, has laid down as under:–
>
>> "11. For appreciating the status of a Hindu woman marrying a Hindu male with a living spouse some of the provisions of the Hindu Marriage Act, 1955 (herein referred to as the 'Marriage Act') have to be examined. Section 11 of the Marriage Act declares such a marriage as null and void in the following terms:
>>
>> 11. 'Void marriage—Any marriage solemnised after the commencement of this Act shall be null and void and may, on a petition presented by either

---

[32]   2011 (1) *Haryana Law Reporter* 205.

party thereto against the other party, be so declared by a decree of nullity if
it contravenes any one of the conditions specified in clauses (i), (iv) and (v)
of Section 5.'"

Clause (i) of Section 5 lays down, for a lawful marriage, the necessary condition
that neither party should have a spouse living at the time of the marriage. A
marriage in contravention of this condition, therefore, is null and void. By reason
of the overriding effect of the Marriage Act as mentioned in Section 4, no aid can
be taken of the earlier Hindu law or any custom or usage as a part of that law
inconsistent with any provision of the Act. So far as Section 12 is concerned, it is
confined to other categories of marriages and is not applicable to one solemnised
in violation of Sections (i) of the Act. Sub-section (2) of Section 12 puts further
restrictions on such a right. The cases covered by this section are not void ab initio,
and unless all the conditions mentioned therein are fulfilled and the aggrieved
party exercises the right to avoid it, the same continues to be effective The
marriages covered by Section 11 are void ipso jure, that is, void from the very
inception, and have to be ignored as not existing in law at all if and when such a
question arises. Although the section permits a formal declaration to be made on
the presentation of a petition, it is not essential to obtain in advance such a formal
declaration from a court in a proceeding specifically commenced for the purpose.
The provisions of Section 16, which is quoted below, also throw light on this
aspect.

16. Legitimacy of children of void and voidable marriages:–

(1) Notwithstanding that a marriage is null and void under Section 11, any
child of such marriage who would have been legitimate if the marriage had
been valid, shall be legitimate, whether such child is born before or after the
commencement of Marriage Laws (Amendment) Act, 1976 (68 of 1976),
and whether or not a decree of nullity is granted in respect of that marriage
under this Act and whether or not the marriage is held to be void otherwise
than on a petition under this Act.

(2) Where a decree of nullity is granted in respect of a voidable marriage
under Section 12, any child begotten or conceived before the decree is made,
who would have been the legitimate child of the parties to the marriage if at
the date of the decree it had been dissolved instead of being annulled, shall
be deemed to be their legitimate child notwithstanding the decree of nullity.

(3) Nothing contained in sub-section (1) or sub-section (2) shall be
construed as conferring upon any child of a marriage which is null and void
or which is annulled by a decree of nullity under Section 12, any rights in or
to the property of any person, other than the parents, in any case where, but
for the passing of this Act, such child would have been incapable of
possessing or acquiring any such rights by reason of his not being the
legitimate child of his parents.

Sub-section (1), by using the words underlined above clearly implies that a: void
marriage can be held to be so without a prior formal declaration by a court in a
proceeding. While dealing with cases covered by Section 12, sub-section (2) refers
to a decree of nullity as an essential condition and sub section (3) prominently
brings out the basic difference in the character of void and voidable marriages as

covered respectively by Sections 11 and 12. It is also to be seen that while the legislature has considered it advisable to uphold the legitimacy of the paternity of a child born out of a void marriage, it has not extended a similar protection in respect of the mother of the child. The marriage of the appellant must, therefore, be treated as null and void from its very inception.

In view of the authoritative pronouncement of Hon'ble Supreme Court marriage between the parties was nullity, therefore, learned matrimonial court rightly allowed the petition and dissolved the marriage by way of a decree of nullity.'

The judgment above is significant for two reasons. First, the court tersely refused to recognise an invalid customary marriage. Secondly, the judgment explicitly lays down that no formal declaration from the court of competent jurisdiction is necessary in the case of void ipso jure marriages.

XVI CONCLUSION

Clearly, it emerges that custom is an important source of Hindu law, having due statutory recognition by virtue of the saving clauses under the provisions of the Hindu Marriage Act 1955. A huge amount of case-law is available on the subject.

There is a clear consistency of approach by the Supreme Court of India and various High Courts in different parts of the country in reiterating the earlier settled position of customary law with regard to marriage and divorce. The underlying aim of this chapter is to attempt to ensure that the principled approach in customary marriages and divorces, as applicable under the relevant provisions of the Hindu Marriage Act 1955, is duly availed of by the parties to such genuine customary marriages and divorces in limited situations, especially in the area of international family migration.

Sometimes, from practical experience it is noticed that parties who genuinely perform customary marriages and enter into customary divorces depending on the facts and circumstances of each case, intending to join their spouses resident abroad on the basis of family reunion, in the context of the present chapter, are not properly and professionally guided. This of course results in outright refusals, at the hands of the embassy authorities. The problem is compounded by the fact of lack of specialist knowledge on the part of visa and consular officers, obviously for which they cannot be blamed. Clearly, this is an avoidable situation. The fact of the matter is that such a gap needs to be plugged appropriately by proper paperwork substantially highlighting the statutory provisions and the settled position of law.

Lastly, as it will be noticed that knowledge of Indian family law also becomes essential for foreign immigration lawyers acting on the behalf of sponsors in appeal proceedings in the event of unsuccessful applications. Specialist domestic family law expertise is pivotal in customary marriages and divorces. The relevant provisions of Indian law in this regard will hopefully prevent foreign practitioners from unwarily walking into traps created by conflicts between local Indian laws and laws of their own jurisdiction.

Kazakhstan

MATRIMONIAL PROPERTY AND ITS CONTRACTUAL REGULATION IN KAZAKHSTAN

Mariya Baideldinova Dalpane[*]

Résumé

Le droit de la famille du Kazakstan montre encore et toujours d'importantes similitudes avec le droit des autres anciennes républiques soviétiques et cela s'explique par leur héritage soviétique commun. La communauté de biens y est le régime matrimonial légal. Le contrat de mariage peut cependant mettre en place tout autre régime qui s'appliquerait au patrimoine entier des époux ou à certains biens seulement. Le contrat de mariage peut régir tous les aspects des relations patrimoniales des époux mais non les questions d'ordre extra-patrimonial. Les ententes alimentaires ont pour objet de déterminer les modalités d'une éventuelle obligation alimentaire entre le créancier et le débiteur légaux. Même si le contrat de mariage et les ententes alimentaires sont considérés comme des instruments efficaces, leur utilisation reste marginale pour le moment. Toutefois, il semblerait qu'ils suscitent un intérêt croissant maintenant que les citoyens sont de plus en plus conscients de l'aspect juridique des choses et que le pays connaît une croissance de la prospérité.

I   INTRODUCTION

The Republic of Kazakhstan is a young independent state which appeared as such after the collapse of the Soviet Union. Upon the obtaining of its independence, Kazakhstan started to develop its own policies, international relations and legislation, without losing the previous tight connections with the former Soviet republics, particularly with the Russian Federation. These ties are reflected, alongside numerous bilateral and multilateral treaties, in the similarities in the legislation of the two countries. Indeed, the Law on Marriage and Family of Kazakhstan and the Family Code of the Russian Federation show only few minor differences. This allowed me to refer to both Kazakh and Russian doctrine when preparing this chapter.

---

[*]   Assistant Professor, School of Law, Kazakh Institute of Management, Economics and Strategic Research (KIMEP), Almaty, Kazakhstan.

The recent history of Kazakhstan left a mark on its legislation. The most important changes have been done, of course, in laws regarding economic matters. The planned economy has been changed to the market economy and this fact has necessarily been reflected in new laws. Some deep changes occurred also in other spheres of law, including family law. One of the most important changes in the family legislation of independent Kazakhstan was the introduction of the possibility for spouses to make marriage contracts. It is remarkable that before 1998 the only way to regulate property relations between spouses was the way provided for by the law. No marriage contracts were recognised as valid agreements and were thus illegal. The new law adopted in 1998 provided spouses with this new means of regulation of their property relations.[1]

II   LEGAL REGIME OF MATRIMONIAL PROPERTY

The matrimonial property regime, which is applied by default according to the family legislation of Kazakhstan, is the regime of limited community of property, namely the community of acquisitions. It is the same regime that the previous (soviet) family legislation provided for. According to this regime, all of the prematrimonial property remains the separate property of each spouse, while everything earned during the marriage becomes the subject of community; this happens regardless of the sums that were invested in the new property by each spouse and also regardless of who is indicated as the owner in the registration documents (if any). The spouse who bears the burden of the household and takes care of children[2] without bringing any factual income enjoys equal rights in the common property. The regime of community of property extends to things, money received as a salary, pension, scholarship, interests from investments, income from business, whether separately or commonly owned. Fruits and profits from a thing, according to the Civil Code of Kazakhstan, belong to the spouse who owns the thing that brings the fruits, unless regulated differently in a marriage contract.[3]

The legal regime of community does not extend to things of personal use of each spouse or to property or money received during the marriage by one of the spouses on a non-paid basis. Things of personal use include clothing, shoes, etc, which are used only by that spouse. Jewellery is not included in the category and is the subject of community along with other personal things of particular value. The legislation does not set out criteria to define a thing as one of particular value, so the judge considers each case depending on the economic situation of the couple and other peculiarities. Property received gratis during

---

[1]   In the article I consider the property relations between spouses, which do not involve third parties, namely children and other relatives. The term 'matrimonial property' applies to both separate and common property of the spouses.

[2]   According to the Labour Code of Kazakhstan, maternity leave is granted to one of the spouses upon the birth of a child, so there is no legal obstacle for a man to take care of children. In practice, however, such cases are very rare.

[3]   See below.

the marriage by one of the spouses includes, among others, gifts meant only for one of the spouses personally, an inheritance left to one of the spouses, lottery winnings of one of the spouses, restoration of health damages of one of the spouses, prizes, etc. Where a gift is given to both spouses, or the donor does not indicate the beneficiary, the gift becomes a common property of the spouses. Separate property of the spouses can become common if, during the marriage, the value of that property was increased at the common expense of both spouses or at the expense of the other spouse. Such expenses can take the form of monetary or property investments as well as the work of the spouse or spouses. The increase of the price of the property due to investments of third parties or due to circumstances that do not depend on the spouses (inflation, increase of prices for real estate, etc) does not result in transfer of the separate property into the community of the spouses.

Spouses possess, use and dispose freely of their common property. There is a presumption of each spouse's consent to dispose of the common property. The written consent is required in exceptional cases, provided for by the law (for example, regarding the disposal of immovable property).

(a)   Bearing the family expenses

The family legislation of Kazakhstan does not define expenses and does not contain any regulation for them. However, the legal regime of community of property presumes that, since the spouses have equal rights to the property, they have equal responsibility to pay for the expenses connected to this property. Any expenses that appear during the family life (among which are the expenses related to the children) must also be considered common. In my opinion, both spouses must have responsibility to maintain the property, which is separately owned by one spouse, but is used by both of them. Personal expenses must be borne by each spouse except in the case of spousal maintenance or care of a disabled spouse.[4]

(b)   Matrimonial debts

Debts of the spouses, which derive from the ownership of the common property, are shared. Since education and care of common children are a common duty of the spouses, the debts that might derive from it are also common. Debts that derive from the ownership of the separate property, as well as debts tightly connected with the person of debtor (debts relating to the restoration of one of the spouse's health, debts in money or things that were used for the personal needs of the spouse) are separate.

---

[4]   See below.

(c)   Common property division

The common property of the spouses can be divided upon divorce or during the marriage. Such division can be done by mutual consent by signing a marriage contract, or in the court. Under the division the shares of the spouses are usually equal. In the marriage contract, however, the spouses can deviate from this rule unless this puts one of them into a difficult financial situation. The court can also distribute shares differently from the common rule in order to protect the interests of minor children who remain with one of the spouses upon divorce.

(d)   Alimony obligations of spouses[5]

The spouses' alimony obligations are a part of their property relations. The Law on Marriage and Family of Kazakhstan provides for the general rules of alimony between spouses. The spouses are free to change these rules in a marriage contract or in an alimony agreement.

(i)   *Mutual maintenance of spouses*

The law obliges spouses to maintain each other. However, if one of the spouses refuses to maintain the other, the latter spouse does not always have the right to claim the maintenance in court. The Law on Marriage and Family provides for a list of cases, when the spouse can claim alimony from the other. In other words, according to the law, every spouse has the right to maintenance, but not every spouse can claim it in court.

Categories of spouses whose rights for maintenance are protected by the court are:

(1)   disabled spouse in need;

(2)   the wife during the whole period of pregnancy and 3 years after the birth of the child; and

(3)   spouse in need who takes care of a disabled child.

It is remarkable that the first and third cases consist of two components, both of which have to take place for the spouse to have a right to alimony from the other. Therefore, if, for instance, it is not proven that the disabled spouse needs maintenance, this spouse is not entitled to alimony. At the same time if the spouse is in need and cannot work due to reasons other than disability (unemployment, lack of education, care of minor children or elderly parents) again this spouse remains unprotected, according to the law.

---

[5]   In this chapter I consider only mutual alimony obligations between the spouses, which do not involve their alimony obligations towards third parties, such as children, parents and other relatives.

The alimony agreement, however, can establish other grounds for the spouses to claim alimony from the other.

For the spouse who has the right to alimony it is for the court to establish the amount of money to be paid, depending on the financial situation of each spouse and other circumstances that the court might regard as significant.

(ii)   *Alimony obligations of ex-spouses*

In some cases, the obligation of spouses to maintain each other lasts beyond the marriage. Even after the divorce, a disabled spouse in need (if this spouse has become disabled during the marriage) has a right to alimony from the ex-spouse. The pregnant ex-wife and ex-wife during the first 3 years after the birth of the common child has the same right, as well as the spouse who takes care of a common disabled child. If the grounds, which entitle the spouse to alimony, disappear (for instance, the pregnant ex-wife remarries), the obligation of the ex-spouse to pay alimony is eliminated as well.

The effects of the marriage contract between the spouses concerning alimony and the amount of such alimony can last after divorce.

III   CONTRACTUAL REGULATION OF MATRIMONIAL PROPERTY

Spouses are free to make any civil law contract with each other. However, specific family law contracts are the marriage contract, which can regulate any property relations between spouses, and the alimony agreement, which can regulate any alimony obligation.

(a)   Marriage contract

The legal regime of matrimonial property can be modified or completely substituted with another one in the marriage contract.

According to the Law on Marriage and Family,[6] the marriage contract is an agreement between persons who are entering into marriage or an agreement between spouses, which determines property rights and responsibilities of the spouses during the marriage and/or in the case of its dissolution. The marriage contract, as the definition indicates, can be prenuptial as well as post-nuptial. If it is stipulated before the marriage, it comes into force from the moment of the registration of the marriage. If the agreement is signed during the marriage, it takes effect from the moment of signing.

---

[6]   The Law on Marriage and Family is the main source of family law in Kazakhstan. Alongside it family law is regulated by norms contained in the Constitution, the Civil Code and other numerous Acts. The Law on Marriage in Family (No 321-I) was adopted in 1998.

(i)   Parties of the marriage contract

Generally, the capacity to contract in family law is regulated by the correspondent civil law norms,[7] however, with some peculiarities. The civil law rule states that a person, in order to be able to contract, must be not less than 18 years old and must be mentally sane. The age of a full capacity to contract can be reduced down to 16 in two cases: the reduction, under certain circumstances, of the age of entrance into marriage and the so-called emancipation of a minor. The decision on the reduction of the marriage age is made by the competent state body, which is called the Organ of Guardianship and Tutorship. The law does not specify the circumstances that are considered significant for the age reduction; however, in practice in most of the cases it is pregnancy of the minor bride. If the minor is allowed to get married before 18, he or she obtains full capacity to contract from the moment of the registration of the marriage.

The emancipation of a minor, according to the Civil Code, is a state of financial and economic independence of the child which was obtained due to the independent work of the child with a labour contract. A minor can apply to the Organ of Guardianship and Tutorship for emancipation from the age of 16. As soon as such an application is satisfied the minor receives full capacity to contract, namely he or she can stipulate any contract and enter into any kind of civil relations independently and without parents' consent. This, however, does not result in the minor's capacity to enter into marriage before the age of 18. If an emancipated minor wants to get married before attaining 18, he or she must obtain the permission of the Organ of Guardianship and Tutorship described above.

I am operating here with the term 'full capacity to contract' because under the legislation of Kazakhstan there is also a category of people with limited capacity to contract. Limited capacity to contract means that a person can participate in any kind of civil relations and sign any kind of civil contract, but only with the consent of parents, adopters or tutors [guardians]. The capacity to contract of a person can be limited by law or upon the corresponding court

---

[7]   In Kazakh doctrine (as well as in Russian and Ukrainian) there is a dispute about whether the norms of civil law can be applied to matters of family law. For more details see: M Antokolskaia Семейное право [*Family Law*] (Moscow: Юрист, 2nd edn, 2002); M Antokolskaia *Harmonization of Family Law in Europe: A Historical Perspective. A Tale of Two Millennia* (Antwerpen-Oxford, 2000); M Baideldinova Некоторые аспекты определения субъекта брачного договора и его правоспособности в законодательстве постсоветских государств [*Some aspects of defining of a party of marriage contract and its capacity to contract under the legislation of post soviet states*] (Almaty: Спектр, April 2009); M Baideldinova Семейное законодательство как отражение внутриэкономических и социальных преобразований в Казахстане и других постсоветских государствах в переходный период [*Family legislation as a mirror of political and economic changes in Kazakhstan and other post soviet states in a transition period*] (Almaty: Acts of the VII KIMEP International Research Conference, March 2010); B Gongalo and P Krashennikov Брачный договор. Комментарий семейного и гражданского законодательства [*Marriage contract. Comment to the family and civil legislation*] (Moscow: Statut, 3rd edn, 2006); L Maximovič Брачный договор в Российском праве [*Marriage contract in Russian law*] (Moscow: 'Os'-89', 2003) and others.

decision. Persons who are limited in their contract capacity by law are minors between the age of 14 and 18. They can autonomously dispose of their income and make day-to-day contracts, while for all other contracts the consent of parents (or adopters) is required. If such a minor has neither parents nor adopters, a tutor is appointed to guarantee the protection of the minor's interests. The court can limit an adult person's capacity to contract if this person has proven to be alcoholic or drug addicted, which puts the person's family into difficult economic conditions. The court's decision about the limitation of a person's capacity to contract also contains the appointment of a tutor for this person. Once this decision is made, the person requires the consent of the tutor to sign contracts, including a marriage contract.

(ii)   Content of the marriage contract

According to the legislation of Kazakhstan, the marriage contract can only regulate property relations, namely, the couple can use the marriage contract to change the legal regime of their marital property. The legal regime can be modified or substituted fully with a different one. The legislator establishes no limitations on the changes to the legal property regime. According to the laws of Kazakhstan, the spouses are free to establish any of the following regimes: absolute community of property, limited community of property, community of shares (absolute or limited) and absolute or limited separation of property.

The absolute community of property is a community of all the property of the spouses, regardless of which of them got the property and when.[8] The limited community of property presumes a limitation of community in time or in object. For example, the spouses can write in the marriage contract that the property becomes common after 5 years of marriage. This will be a time limitation of the community. The spouses can agree also, that, for instance, after 5 years of marriage only the movable property becomes common. This would be a limitation of the community by the object.

The spouses have the right to establish certain shares in the ownership of their property. These shares need not necessarily be equal. The spouses can determine who owns which part of which. They can extend this regime, as any other, to all their property, to a certain category of it or even for a single item. The marriage contract can concern the property of the spouses which they actually possess or the property which they may acquire in the future (regardless of whether they are sure about this acquisition or not). Such property can be detailed in the contract or can be indicated in general terms.

---

[8]   M Antokolskaia *Harmonization of Family Law in Europe: A Historical Perspective. A Tale of Two Millennia* (Antwerpen-Oxford, 2000); A Chloros, M Rheinstein and MA Glendon *International Encyclopedia of Comparative Law, Volume IV 'Persons and Family' (Martinus Nijhoff, 2007)* see ch 4 'Interspousal relations'; M Mukanova Брачный договор как способ регулирования отношений супругов [*Marriage contract as a mean of regulation of interspousal relation*]: Science Dissertation (Almaty, 2003).

The marriage contract may regulate maintenance issues as well. The alimony agreement (see below) also gives the spouses such a possibility. The alimony agreement, however, serves to determine the amount, frequency and modes of payment of the alimony, while the marriage contract can change the very grounds for payment. The law on marriage and family indicates, for example, that the incapable spouse in need has a right to maintenance. This means that, according to the law, the spouse, in order to have a right to alimony, has to satisfy both requirements: incapability and financial difficulties. In the marriage contract, spouses can agree that the existence of just one of the grounds is sufficient for maintenance. Spouses, however, can only broaden and not restrict the grounds for the rights to alimony. The law does not specify the meaning of the term 'in need'. Usually it is the judge who determines it. In the marriage contract, however, the spouses can agree on the precise income level that they would consider as financial difficulty. The spouses, then, can change completely the meaning of maintenance in the marriage contract. It can be not only the protection of the vulnerable spouse, as the law provides for, but also maintenance as compensation (for example, in the case of divorce by unilateral initiative)[9] or maintenance as a means to incentivise certain behaviour.

Thus, the spouses have very wide freedom in choosing a new regime for their property through a marriage contract. This freedom, however, is limited by art 40(3) of the Law on Marriage and Family, which states:

> 'The marriage contract cannot limit the legal capacity or the capacity to contract of the spouses and their right to the court's protection of their rights; it cannot regulate either personal non-property relations between the spouses or their rights and obligations towards children; it cannot limit the right to maintenance of the incapable spouse in need; it cannot contain other conditions which put one of the spouses into extremely unfavourable conditions or contradict the fundamentals of family legislation.'

The law does not specify what exactly is meant by 'extremely unfavourable conditions'. This gives the possibility – and, actually, the obligation – to the judge to intervene and to decide on modifications, amendments or voidance of the contract as a whole or of some parts of it.

(iii) Modifications, amendments and dissolution of marriage contract

The marriage contract is stipulated in written form with compulsory notarial certification. The marriage contract which changes the legal regime of the immovable property of the spouses must be registered according to art 118 of the Civil Code of the Republic of Kazakhstan. The spouses can change or amend the marriage contract any time by mutual agreement. All amendments must be made in the same form as the contract itself: written form with notarial certification.

---

9   L Maximovic Брачный договор в российском праве [*Marriage contract in the law of Russia*](Moscow, '03–89', 2003) p 95.

A marriage contract terminates at the moment of the termination of marriage except those norms which the marriage contract provides for the time after the marriage is terminated. A marriage contract can be also terminated after an agreed period of time or after a certain event. Unilateral modification or dissolution of marriage contract is impossible. The few exceptions of the rule are described in the Civil Code for civil law contracts and can be applied to marriage contracts. Among them are significant violations of the contract by the other party, bankruptcy of the party who had payment obligations, impossibility of fulfilling contractual obligations for reasons which do not depend on the party and changes of the legislation on which the contract is based (Law on Marriage and Family).

By the unilateral claim of one of the spouses the court can recognise the marriage contract as invalid if it puts the spouse into, significantly unfavourable conditions. It is up to the judge to decide which conditions count as significantly unfavourable.

(iv) *Guarantees for creditors*

Creditors must be informed about the existence and the content of the marriage contract. If the marriage contract is signed or amended after the credit was given, the creditors receive the right to claim cancellation of amendments and even dissolution of the marriage contract. However, in order to use this right, the creditor must prove in court that the stipulation of the marriage contract (its amendments or modifications) significantly change the conditions for the creditor. Significant change in this case means that, if the conditions were such at the moment of giving the credit, the credit would have never been given.

(b) Alimony agreement

The alimony agreement between spouses serves to determine the amount, modes and frequency of payment of alimony. Unlike the marriage contract, the alimony agreement is not used to change the grounds of alimony.

(i) *Parties of the alimony agreement*

The alimony agreement is signed between the person who has the obligation to pay the alimony and the person entitled to this alimony. In the case of incapacity to contract of one of the parties, the agreement is signed by his or her legal representative. In this way, the agreement, according to which the father has to pay alimony for the minor child, is signed by the father – on one side, and the child – on the other. But since the minor child does not have the capacity to contract, it will be signed by the child's legal representative, who, in most of such cases, is the child's mother.

The incapacity to contract of the party who must pay the alimony usually means mental insanity of the person. Mental disease which results in the loss of capacity to contract means also the loss of labour capacity. A labour incapable person may receive an exemption from the payment of alimony through the corresponding court's decision, if he or she had no other income than salary. If such an exemption is not given, the alimony agreement has to be signed by the legal representative of the incapable alimony payer. If the legal representatives of both parties is the same person, an ad hoc representative is appointed for the incapable alimony payer.

(ii) Content of the alimony agreement

In contrast to the marriage contract, the aim of the alimony agreement is not to change the grounds for payment of the alimony, but, as mentioned above, to determine details of payments: frequency, amount, currency, etc. Such an agreement is obligatory for the alimony payer and has the same juridical power as a corresponding court's decision. The parties to the agreement can decide that the amount of alimony is calculated as a certain percentage of the payer's wage or a fixed sum of money; they can decide how often this sum has to be paid and, finally, they can decide that the alimony payer does not pay money at all, but provides for some property – for ownership or usage by the receiver of the alimony.

(iii) Modifications, amendments and dissolution of alimony agreement

The alimony agreement is a civil law contract, so it fully obeys the rules of the Civil Code, including the rules on modifications, amendments and dissolution of contract – by mutual consent of the parties or unilaterally.

The alimony agreement can be modified or dissolved by mutual consent of the parties at any time. The modification and the dissolution of the agreement must be made in the same form as the agreement itself, which is written form with notarial certification.

The unilateral modification, dissolution or refusal to fulfil the agreement are prohibited, unless there are grounds for an exception, as provided for in the Civil Code. Such grounds, as well as those of unilateral modification and dissolution of a marriage contract, are: impossibility of the spouse to fulfil the obligations due to bankruptcy or other reasons which do not depend on the alimony payer and relevant changes to the legislation which regulates the alimony agreement (Law on Marriage and Family and Civil Code). Moreover, the alimony agreement can be unilaterally modified or dissolved in court by the alimony payer in case of 'significantly changed financial or family status' and if mutual consent is not reached. The judge decides which changes must be regarded as significant and, taking into account all relevant interests of the parties, whether the alimony agreement must be modified or dissolved.

IV PROPERTY RELATIONS IN UNMARRIED COUPLES

Marriage, according to the legislation of Kazakhstan, is an officially registered union between a man and a woman. The union of people, who live together without registering the marriage with the competent state body, is not recognised by the state and does not have any legal consequences, either property or non-property. Religious marriages, that is, those celebrated in front of religious authorities but not registered with the secular authorities, also have no legal effects. The presence or absence of common children has no influence on the validity of the union.

In such unions, property relations are regulated by the Civil Code in the part dedicated to simple partnership. The property acquired in such unions is common shared property, which means that all things acquired by the couple belong to them in parts proportionate to their investments in each thing.

If the common property of an unregistered couple is to be divided, it is the couple's responsibility to provide proof of the amount of investments made in common property. If such proof is missing and there is no mutual consent by the couple on the property rights to a particular thing, the judge makes a corresponding decision, based on common sense.

Couples whose union is not officially registered do not have the right to make a marriage contract having legal effects. They can, however, make any other kind of contract in which they regulate their property rights in accordance with the Civil Code of Kazakhstan.

V CONCLUSION

The family legislation of Kazakhstan keeps showing strong analogies with the family legislation of the other former soviet countries, that can be explained mainly by the common soviet heritage.

Community of property is the legal regime of the property of the spouses which functions by default in the absence of a marriage contract. The marriage contract can replace the legal property regime with any other and apply it to all the property of the spouses or for just a certain part of it. This contract can regulate any other property relations of the spouses. It cannot regulate any personal non-property relations.

The alimony agreement serves to determine the modality of payment of the alimony. It is made between the person who has the obligation by law to pay the alimony and the person who has right to receive it.

Although good instruments to regulate property relations between spouses, neither marriage contracts nor alimony agreements are widespread in Kazakhstan. There appears, however, to be a growing interest in these contracts that is related to an increasing legal consciousness of the people in the sphere of family law and to the rising well-being and prosperity of the country.

The Netherlands

NATIONAL AND INTERNATIONAL SURROGACY: AN ODYSSEY

*Ian Curry-Sumner and Machteld Vonk**

Résumé

En 2010, les trois concepts-clés du droit de la famille, le pouvoir discrétionnaire, le statut et l'argent, ont été à l'avant-scène en Nouvelle-Zélande. Les décisions concernant les enfants cachent inévitablement des jugements de valeurs, ce qui introduit un élément de hasard dans le processus décisionnel. Du statut dépend l'autorité et les pouvoirs. Historiquement, le droit de la famille réserve ceux-ci aux seules personnes expressément reconnues par l'État. Cette discrimination, qui est au cœur du droit de la famille, doit être questionnée sans relâche. Quant à l'argent, il est le nerf de la guerre dans le contentieux familial. Les fortunés peuvent engager des avocats qui mèneront la bataille jusqu'à la victoire. Les autres n'auront souvent d'autre choix que de signer des ententes moins avantageuses que ce que prévoit la loi elle-même. La jurisprudence récenteen matière de déménagement du parent gardien, d'adoption et d'obligation alimentaire éclaire ces trois concepts.

I SETTING OUT UPON THE JOURNEY

In recent years both the Central Authority for International Adoption and the Dutch Children Protection Board have been made aware of a number of cases concerning commercial surrogacy and the unlawful placement of foreign children in the Netherlands. Many of these cases have also received broad media attention. A number of Belgian cases have attracted particular attention in the Netherlands. The Dutch government operates a very restrictive policy with respect to commercial surrogacy. Incidents in recent years have led to numerous parliamentary questions being raised in the Second Chamber of the Dutch Parliament. The Minister of Justice has responded to the Dutch Parliament by commissioning research to be conducted into the nature and scope of the problems related to commercial surrogacy and the unlawful placement of children. The aim hereby is to ensure that more clarity can be gleaned as to what actually occurs in the countries where the possibilities are

---

* Ian Curry-Sumner, Senior University Lecturer and Researcher, UCERF, Molengraaff Institute for Private Law, Utrecht University. This contribution was made partly possible by the Innovation Research Grant of the Dutch Scientific Organisation (NWO).
Machteld Vonk, University Lecturer and Researcher, UCERF, Molengraaff Institute for Private Law, Utrecht University.

greater than in the Netherlands, as well as providing information with regards to the Dutch response upon the return of the commissioning parents to the Netherlands.

From April 2010 until January 2011, researchers of the Utrecht Centre for European Research into Family Law (UCERF) at the Molengraaff Institute for Private Law of Utrecht University conducted the research commissioned by the Minister of Justice.[1] The resulting report was published on 2 March 2011.[2] The report contains an in-depth study of Dutch criminal and civil law on the consequences of surrogacy and a detailed analysis of the way Dutch Private International Law does and could regard international surrogacy. Furthermore, it contains reports from four jurisdictions that allow surrogacy, namely California (USA), India, Greece and Ukraine, and eight reports from European countries that are faced with the same problems as the Netherlands, namely Belgium, England, Germany, France, Norway, Poland, Spain and Sweden. In these country reports, answers are provided as to whether specific rules exist regulating surrogacy and which measures have been adopted to ensure the enforcement of those rules.

In legal literature a distinction is drawn between different types of surrogacy. High-technological surrogacy makes use of IVF, in which a reproductive expert must always be involved. This form of surrogacy offers commissioning parents the possibility to conceive a child that is genetically related to both commissioning parents. This is not, however, a requirement. Alongside high-technological surrogacy, low-technological surrogacy is also possible. In this case the surrogate is always genetically related to the child. The commissioning father may or may not be genetically related, depending upon whether the couple has used his sperm or that of a donor. In low-technological surrogacy the egg will be fertilised by means of artificial insemination. Furthermore, parties may also be involved in a surrogacy arrangement, despite the fact that the child was conceived by natural means or self-insemination. In this final scenario the child could be genetically related to the surrogate and her husband. Another important distinction concerns the difference between altruistic and commercial surrogacy. In general, it would appear difficult to draw a distinct line between these two forms of surrogacy arrangements. In both cases, financial payments will be made. However, the financial payments in commercial surrogacy arrangements are often (if not always) concerned with profit, whereas in altruistic surrogacies the main object is to help another couple have a child.

---

[1]   The research team consisted of Professor Katharina Boele-Woelki (chair of the research group), Ian Curry-Sumner, Wendy Schrama and Machteld Vonk.

[2]   This contribution is for a large part based on that report: K Boele-Woelki, I Curry-Sumner, W Schrama and M Vonk *Draagmoederschap en illegale opneming van kinderen* (The Hague: WODC 2011).

II FIRST STOP: SURROGACY IN THE NETHERLANDS

(a) Dutch attitude

The Netherlands does not look very favourably upon surrogacy arrangements.[3] Although altruistic surrogacy is allowed under certain very strict conditions, Dutch law has no special procedure geared towards transferring parental rights and duties from the surrogate mother (and her husband) to the intentional parents.[4] After the introduction of IVF in the Netherlands in the late 1970s, discussion arose as to whether or not surrogacy should be allowed. On the whole, the answer to this question was negative, which resulted in the criminalisation of mediation by means of a professional practice or company and the publication of supply and demand requests concerned surrogacy arrangements.[5] It has become clear from subsequent parliamentary debates[6] that it is not the intention of the applicable provisions in the Dutch Criminal Code[7] to convict doctors co-operating with surrogacy, but to avoid the situation where women offer themselves as surrogate mothers for payment as this might lead to a form of trade in children.

IVF surrogacy is very strictly regulated in the Netherlands. In 1989 the Ministry of Health, Welfare and Sport determined in its IVF regulation statement that surrogacy in combination with IVF was not allowed. However, after active lobbying by interest groups[8] combined with the fact that the passing of time had proven that there appeared to be less interest than expected in IVF surrogacy, the IVF regulation statement issued in 1997[9] allowed for surrogacy in combination with IVF under very strict conditions. When this regulation statement was discussed in Parliament, the minister stated no special regulations for the transfer of full parental rights from the surrogate mother to the intentional parents were envisioned.[10]

Moreover, the IVF regulation statement determines that IVF in combination with surrogacy must take place in accordance with the guidelines on

---

[3]   H Roscam Abbing 'Enige gezondheidsrechtelijke aspecten van het draagmoederschap' in K Boele and M Oderkerk *De (on)geoorloofdheid van het draagmoederschap in rechtsvergelijkend perspectief* (Antwerpen: Intersentia, 1999) p 26.

[4]   K Boele-Woelki and M Oderkerk (eds) *De (on)geoorloofdheid van het draagmoederschap in rechtsvergelijkend perspectief* [*The permissibility and unpermissibility of surrogacy in comparative perspective*] (Antwerp: Intersentia 1999) pp 25–44; P Vlaardingerbroek 'Mens en maatschappij: Draagmoederschap: een gecompli-ceerde constructie' (2003) 52 *Ars Aequi* 171–178.

[5]   Act of 16 September 1993, Stb 486.

[6]   *Dutch Second Chamber* 1996–1997, 25 000-XVI, No 62, p 14.

[7]   Articles 151(b) and 151(c), 225, 236, 278, 279 and 442a of the Dutch Criminal Code.

[8]   SM Dermout *De eerste logeerpartij: Hoogtechnologisch draagmoederschap in Nederland* [*The first sleep-over: High-technology surrogacy in The Netherlands*] (Groningen: Groningen University, 2001) pp 13–17.

[9]   *Planningsbesluit in-vitrofertilisatie* (Staatscourant 1998/95) pp 14–18.

[10]   *Dutch Second Chamber* 1996–1997, 25 000-XVI, No 62, p 13.

high-technological surrogacy[11] of the Dutch Society for Obstetrics and Gynaecology. These guidelines require IVF clinics to draw up their own protocol regarding IVF surrogacy. This protocol must at least ensure that the following conditions are met: there must be medical grounds for the procedure (specified in the regulation statement); the surrogate mother must have one or more living children whom she gestated and gave birth to without complications;[12] there must be adequate information provision to the surrogate mother and the intended parents; and preceding the treatment the responsible doctor must draw up a statement to the effect that the above conditions have been met and that he considers the treatment to be justified.[13]

In the late 1990s a pilot was started to study whether or not surrogacy should be allowed as a means to help a certain group of infertile couples to have a child of their own.[14] This pilot ran until mid 2004 and only allowed for surrogacy with the intentional parents' own genetic material.[15] The intentional parents had to bring their own surrogate mother. In order to be admitted to the surrogacy programme, couples had to pass a medical, psychological and legal screening procedure. In the course of this pilot 200 couples were admitted to the initial screening procedure. Of the 105 couples that passed the initial screening, 58 couples stopped before the medical screening or did not pass the medical screening. The 47 couples that passed the medical screening subsequently attended a psychological interview. In the end 35 couples were given legal advice and entered the IVF surrogacy program. Twenty-four women completed the IVF treatment cycle. As a result of this pilot 16 children were born to 13 women. The other 11 women who completed a full IVF cycle did not achieve ongoing pregnancies. No problems were reported with the acceptance of the babies in the intentional families or with giving up the baby after birth. The intake centre that was established as a result of this pilot was forced to close in July 2004, since no Dutch IVF clinic was willing at that point to participate in gestational surrogacy.[16] However, in April 2006 one of the

---

[11]   *Hoogtechnologisch draagmoederschap* Richtlijn Nederlandse Vereniging voor Obstetrie en Gynaecologie, No 18 January 1999, available at www.nvog.nl/ (accessed 30 January 2011).

[12]   The guidelines also state that the surrogate mother must consider her own family to be complete, probably in order to minimise the risk that she decides to keep the child for herself.

[13]   *Dutch Second Chamber* 25 000-XVI, No 51, p 2.

[14]   The results of this trial are described in SM Dermout *De eerste logeerpartij: Hoogtechnologisch draagmoederschap in Nederland* [*The first sleep-over: High-technology surrogacy in the Netherlands*] (Groningen: Groningen University 2001).

[15]   Dermout, Van der Wiel, Heintz, Jansen and Ankum 'Non-commercial surrogacy: an account of patient management in the First Dutch Centre for IVF Surrogacy, from 1997 to 2004' (2010) 25(2) *Human Reproduction* 443–449.

[16]   See www.draagmoederschap.nl (accessed 30 January 2011). The initiator of the trial states, in a letter posted on the website referred to, that in the past 15 years she strove to make IVF surrogacy acceptable to the public, the media, the insurance companies, the Dutch Society of Obstetrics and Gynaecology and the medical profession in general. She and others managed to do all that, however 'the internal obstacles in the Academic Hospitals themselves, the ethics commissions and/or the board of directors are elusive, in particular because they do not send a reasoned rejection, just a message without any further comments that the hospital has decided not to offer IVF surrogacy services. It is impossible to discover their real reasons'.

Dutch licensed IVF clinics announced that it will make gestational surrogacy services available to married couples (VUMC, 6 April 2006).[17]

From case-law and interviews with lawyers and professionals from the Dutch Child Protection Board, it is clear that other forms of surrogacy also occur in the Netherlands. In all these cases that do not involve IVF, the surrogate mother is the genetic and biological mother of the child, this means that she provides the egg and gives birth to the child. Regarding the sperm used to conceive the child, there are a number of possibilities: this may be provided by the surrogate's partner, the intentional father or a known or unknown donor. As long as there is no commercial element and the couples involved abide by the rules set out below for the transfer of a child to another family than the birth family, the couples do not breach Dutch law.[18] However, this does not mean that they will succeed in bringing the legal situation in line with the social situation.

(b) Transfer of parenthood and parental responsibility

The transfer of full parental rights in surrogacy arrangements will not occur against the will of any of the parties involved. This means that the surrogate mother has no legal duty to hand over the child, nor are the intentional parents under a legal duty to accept the child. This also applies where a contract has been drawn up in which the parties have agreed on the placement of the child in the family of the intentional parents. If the child is not yet 6 months old the intentional parents may take the child into their home only with the consent of the Child Protection Board.[19]

Under Dutch law, the woman who gives birth to the child is the child's legal mother, whether or not she is also the child's genetic mother.[20] This is a mandatory statutory provision from which parties cannot deviate.[21] Whether the child born to the surrogate mother will automatically have a legal father depends on the surrogate's marital status.[22] It will be obvious that the surrogate mother's marital status is of great relevance where the transfer of parental rights to the intentional parents is concerned. The marital status of the intentional parents may also play a role where the transfer of parental status is concerned.[23] In the discussion below the starting point will be the placement of the child in the family of the intentional parents. This means that there is still

---

[17] See also the letter of 15 May 2006 to the Second Chamber by the then Secretary of State on this issue (vws0600778).

[18] Using an unknown donor whose origin cannot be traced is contrary to Dutch law. However, this will not necessarily lead to problems with the transfer of parental rights. See, for instance, Rb Roermond, 24 November 2010, *LJN* BO4992.

[19] DCC, art 1:241(3) and Foster Children Act (*Pleegkinderenwet*), art 1.

[20] DCC, art 1:198.

[21] Rb Den Haag, 11 December 2007, *LJN* BB9844.

[22] DCC, art 1:199.

[23] However, as is clear from the policy guidelines of the surrogacy centre established at the VUMC, only married intentional parents at present have access to gestational surrogacy services.

agreement between the surrogate mother and the intentional parents that the child will grow up with the intentional parents. Where relevant the genetic connection between child and intentional parents will be discussed. The schedule below shows the possibilities for the transfer of parental rights. First of all the situation will be discussed where the surrogate mother is married and subsequently where she is unmarried.

(i)   Surrogate mother is married: the child has two legal parents at birth

The surrogate mother will be the child's legal mother and if she is married her husband will be the child's legal father;[24] both will have parental responsibility over the child by operation of law.[25] In the very unlikely situation that the surrogate mother's husband did not consent to the conception of the child, he may challenge his paternity.[26] This means that, unless the surrogate father was completely unaware of the fact that his wife was acting as a surrogate for another couple, he is highly unlikely to succeed. In most surrogacy arrangements the surrogate's husband will play a role. In cases of surrogacy in combination with IVF, the requirements are such that the surrogate mother's husband's consent is required.[27] In a recent case the paternity of the surrogate's husband was challenged in the name of the child through an ad hoc guardian (*bijzonder curator*). The child may challenge the paternity of any non-biological father and is not bound by the consent of adults or their marital status.

All this means is that full parental status can only be transferred to the intentional parents through joint adoption. However, before the child can be adopted by the intentional parents, the surrogate parent(s) will first have to be divested of their parental responsibility.[28] Divestment of parental responsibility is a measure of child protection used in cases where parents are unable or unfit to look after their child.[29] Parents cannot apply to the court to be divested. Only the Child Care and Protection Board and the Public Prosecution Service can apply to the court to have parents divested of their responsibility.[30] In the late 1990s there was discussion in Parliament about whether parents themselves should not be given a right to apply for divestment, but the Minister of Justice at that time was against such a measure as it would introduce a possibility for parents to relinquish their parental rights.

---

[24]   DCC, art 1:198 (mother) and art 1:199(a) (father).

[25]   DCC, art 1:251(1).

[26]   DCC, art 1:200(3).

[27]   *Richtlijn hoogtechnologisch draagmoederschap* [*Guidelines high technology surrogacy*], NVOG 1998, para 3.3. VUMC treatment protocol: 'If the surrogate mother has a partner, the partner has to give his written agreement to the surrogate mother's decision to carry a surrogate pregnancy', see www.vumc.nl/communicatie/folders/folders/IVF/Hoog-technologisch%20draagmoederschap%20.pdf (accessed 30 January 2011).

[28]   DCC, arts 1:1228 (1)(g) and 1:266.

[29]   LE Kalkman-Bogerd 'Ontheffing en draagmoederschap' (1998) 9 *Tijdschrift voor Familie- en Jeugdrecht* 198–202.

[30]   DCC, art 1:267.

Flowchart: Transfer of parental rights

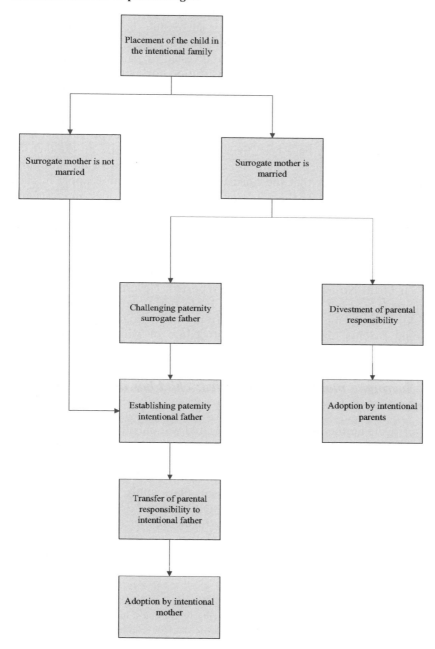

The outcome of a divestment procedure is uncertain as the Dutch Supreme Court has not yet had the opportunity to decide on divestment in the context of surrogacy.[31] However, decisions by various Courts of Appeal allow for the

---

[31] The Dutch Supreme Court did, however, judge in a case unrelated to surrogacy that parents

divestment of the surrogate parents on the ground that they are unable or unfit to care for this particular child since they did not intend to have it for themselves.[32] If the divestment procedure is successful, the intentional parents may be attributed with joint guardianship, which is very similar to parental responsibility. Normally, when parents are divested of parental responsibility, guardianship will be attributed to an institution for family guardianship.[33] However, in the surrogacy cases that have been published, guardianship was attributed to the intentional parents if the court considered this to be the best possible solution for the child concerned. If the intentional parents have taken care of the child together for a year they may file for an adoption order with the court, provided they have been living together for 3 years on the day the adoption request is filed. There is no special post-surrogacy adoption procedure, which means that the normal criteria for adoption apply in such cases. These criteria require the adoption to be in the child's best interests and state that adoption cannot take place if the child's parents object. Only in a very limited number of circumstances may a court disregard parental objections.[34] The court may for instance disregard parental objection if the child has not lived with the parents since birth. In the earlier mentioned IVF surrogacy pilot all the children were adopted by the intentional parents a year after their birth. No legal problems were reported. Nevertheless, in particular where parents have not involved the Child Protection Board before the birth of the child, transferring parental rights from the surrogate parents to the intentional parents may be a lengthy procedure of which the outcome is uncertain.

(ii) Surrogate mother is not married: child has one legal parent at birth

If the surrogate mother is not married, the child will only have one legal parent by operation of law: the surrogate mother. She will also be the only holder of parental responsibility. The intentional father may recognise the child with the surrogate mother's consent. Once the intentional father has acquired the status of legal parent through recognition, he may apply for sole parental responsibility, to the exclusion of the surrogate mother.[35] The intentional father can only file such an application if the surrogate mother is the sole holder of parental responsibility.[36] The intentional mother may subsequently adopt the child after she has been taking care of that child with the intentional father for a year and all the other criteria for adoption have been met.

---

may be unable or unfit to take care of a specific child (HR 29 June 1984 *NJ* 1984/767). This judgment has been used by Courts of Appeal to justify divestment in surrogacy cases.

32 Hof Amsterdam, 19 February 1998, *NJ Kort* 1998/32 and Hof 's Gravenhage, 21 August 1998, *NJ* 1998, 865.

33 DCC, art 1:275.

34 DCC, art 1:228(2).

35 DCC, art 1:253c.

36 Dutch law is ambivalent on this point, an in-depth discussion of this issue can be found in MJ Vonk *Children and their parents: A comparative study of the legal position of children with regard to their intentional and biological parents in English and Dutch law* (Antwerp-Oxford: Intersentia, 2007) ch 6 on partially genetic primary families.

It is unclear whether the unmarried intentional mother will be attributed with parental responsibility by operation of law through partner adoption. If one follows the system of the law regarding parental responsibility, joint parental responsibility does not come about by operation of the law for cohabiting couples as a result of adoption. However, in particular in the case of joint adoption it would be rather awkward to attribute parental responsibility to only one of the adoptive parents, while the other can only obtain it through registration in the parental responsibility register (as is normally the case for cohabiting parents). In the case of partner-adoption it might be more defensible not to attribute parental responsibility to the adopting partner by operation of law, although it might well be contrary to the adopter's expectations.[37]

(iii) Surrogate mother has entered into a registered partnership: child has one legal parent at birth, but both registered partners have parental responsibility

In the Netherlands, different-sex and same-sex couples have the opportunity to enter into a registered partnership. The legal consequences of such a partnership are almost the same as those of a marriage. However, an important difference between registered partnership and marriage concerns the legal status of children. If the surrogate mother has entered into a registered partnership, her registered partner will not be a legal parent, but he or she will have parental responsibility unless the child was recognised by a third party before the birth.[38] So if the intentional father recognises the child before birth the transfer of parenthood and parental responsibility will follow along the lines described for the unmarried surrogate mother. However, if the recognition takes place after birth, the surrogate mother's registered partner will have parental responsibility. This may complicate the transfer of parental responsibility to the intentional father as the partner's parental responsibility will need to be terminated.

III SECOND STOP: SURROGACY IN CALIFORNIA[39]

Dutch case-law shows that Dutch couples, and male same-sex couples in particular, travel to California to enter into surrogacy arrangements. Commercial surrogacy is allowed in California, though there may be limits to what is considered to be reasonable payment to the surrogate mother. Both same-sex and different-sex couples can make use of the services offered by a

---

[37] J Kok 'Gezamenlijk gezag en voorkinderen' (2006) *Tijdschrift voor Familie- en Jeugdrecht* 209 who refers to JE Doek *Losbladige personen- en familierecht (Titel 14, aant 2A bij art 1:251 DCC)* (Deventer: Kluwer, 2006).

[38] DCC, art 1:253sa.

[39] In this section use has been made of material provided by Jessica Dorsey LLM for the Californian report in the Report on surrogacy for the Dutch Ministry of Justice: K Boele-Woelki, I Curry-Sumner, W Schrama and M Vonk *Draagmoederschap en illegale opneming van kinderen* (The Hague: WODC 2011).

number of surrogacy agencies in California. A Dutch couple entering into a surrogacy arrangement in California can become the legal parents of the child born to the surrogate mother under Californian law. The first step is to have both the surrogate mother (and her husband if she is married) and the intentional parents agree on the terms of a surrogacy contract. Such a contract will generally contain provisions dealing with custody of the child(ren), parental relationships, financial compensation to the gestational mother, insurance arrangements, medical issues, evaluations (physical and psychological) of all parties and considerations about selective reduction in the case of multiple foetuses.[40]

The next step is to file a petition to the court with affidavits of support from all parties, attorneys and doctors involved, to obtain a Judgment of Parentage. This Judgment of Parentage terminates any rights presumed by the surrogate (and her husband, in the case she is married), establishes the intended parent or parents as the legal parents, and directs the local vital records office on how to fill out the birth certificate. In California, any intended couple (same-sex, different-sex, married or unmarried – regardless of whether there is a biological connection to the child or not) can obtain parental rights, but the manner in how they do so will vary, depending on the circumstances. Below follows a very brief overview of some of the possibilities.

Where a surrogate mother gives birth to a child for another couple or person, the only way the intended parents can be listed immediately on the birth certificate is if they have a Judgment of Parentage. After the child is born, the hospital will send the birth certificate with the names of the intended parents (as per Judgment of Parentage) to the California State Department of Vital Records. The intended parents will also need the birth certificate to obtain a passport for the child, if they want to travel back to the Netherlands.[41] Another possibility is to have the surrogate mother and the intended father listed on the child's birth certificate. The other intentional parents can become a legal parent at a later stage through adoption.

For gay or lesbian couples as intended parents, the Judgment of Parentage should stipulate that both names go on the birth certificate, one as 'father' and one as 'mother'. Subsequently, the couple should have the birth certificate reissued (also allowed for in the Judgment of Parentage) with the word 'parent' before each name. This leads to an amended birth certificate. Without a Judgment of Parentage, the surrogate (and her husband, in case she is married) will be listed as the natural parent(s) of the child on the birth certificate.[42] This

---

40 Center for Surrogate Parenting, Inc at www.creatingfamilies.com/IP/IP_Info.aspx?Type=47 (accessed 15 September 2010).
41 Since the child is born in the United States it will obtain an American passport (8 USC (United States Code), s 1401).
42 Thomas M Pinkerton et al, National Fertility Law Clinic *Parentage, Adoption and Child Custody*, found at www.nationalfertilitylaw.com/acrobatfiles/parentage-adoption-custody.pdf (2006) (accessed 15 September 2010).

means that the intended parents will have to go through the adoption procedure to become the legal parents of the child.

This means that, upon returning to the Netherlands with their baby, the couple may be in the possession of a birth certificate with both their names listed as the child's parents (as an amended or original birth certificate with a Judgment of Parentage), they may return with a birth certificate that lists the surrogate mother and the intended father on the birth certificate (an original birth certificate), or they may return with an adoption order in one or both of their names (judicial adoption order).

IV COMING HOME: DUTCH PRIVATE INTERNATIONAL LAW

(a) Introduction

The question arises: what happens when a Dutch couple returns to the Netherlands with a child conceived through surrogacy? At this stage a distinction should be made based upon the legal procedure that has taken place abroad. Although the scenario utilised in this contribution focuses on the judicial determination of parentage coupled with the subsequent issuance of an amended birth certificate, there are jurisdictions and situations in which surrogacy arrangements ultimately lead to the issuance of a judicial adoption order. Accordingly, the applicable private international law rules can and often will be very different. Nonetheless, the rules applicable to these different procedures will not all be dealt with in this contribution. This section will follow the vast majority of surrogacy cases entering into the Netherlands, namely on the basis of the alleged creation of legal familial ties, ie parentage.

(b) Variety of possible procedures

(i) *Initial contact with Dutch authorities abroad*

The diversity of the situations in which surrogacy arrangements come to light negates the possibility of dealing with all cases in depth in this report. However, it is possible to illustrate the variety of routes along which surrogacy cases can surface with the Dutch authorities. One possibility is that the case first arises outside the Netherlands at the Dutch consulate. Roughly speaking these cases can be divided into three main categories.

(1) Passport application: the Dutch commissioning parents may wish to apply for a Dutch passport. In this scenario, the Dutch commissioning parents will argue that the relationship of parentage established abroad has resulted in the child acquiring Dutch nationality. Although such a request must be submitted to the Dutch consulate or embassy abroad, it is ultimately the Dutch Ministry of Foreign Affairs in The Hague that is

competent to issue the passport. The application of the Dutch rules on private international law is, however, executed in the first instance by the consulate registrar abroad.

(2)   Residence permit: Dutch commissioning parents may also wish to apply for a provisional permission to remain in The Netherlands (the so-called *machtiging tot voorlopig verblijf, MVV*). This is, however, only necessary if the child possesses the nationality of a country with an MVV-obligation.[43] The United States is not one of these countries, and so these requests are not received with regards to children with American citizenship (ie all children born on US soil).

(3)   Short stay visa: Dutch commissioning parents may also wish to request a short stay visa. This visa is also known as a tourist visa and is only issued via the Dutch Immigration and Naturalisation Service (*Immigratie en Naturalisatie Dienst* (IND)).

In short, the Immigration and Naturalisation Service or the consular registrar will always be the first authority to assess any request made by Dutch commissioning parents abroad, irrespective of whether this request concerns an issue related to nationality or immigration. The relevant statutory rules applied by the various civil servants in these cases are always the same, namely:

- Private International Law (Parentage) Act (*Wet Conflictenrecht Afstamming* (Wca));

- Private International Law (Adoption) Act (*Wet Conflictenrecht Adoptie* (Wcad)); and

- Placement of Foreign Children for Adoption Act (*Wet Opneming van Buitenlandse Kinderen ter Adoptie* (Wobka))

(ii)   Initial contact with authorities in the Netherlands

Alongside the procedures that may be started abroad, there are also situations in which a surrogacy arrangement may surface after the Dutch commissioning parents have returned to The Netherlands, without prior contact with Dutch consular services abroad. In these situations, initial contact is with the Registrar of Births, Deaths, Marriages and Registered Partnerships ('the Registrar') in a municipality in the Netherlands. This can happen in the following situations:

---

[43]   On the basis of §4.1.1, Part B, Chapter 1 of the Aliens Circular 2000 (*Vreemdelingencirculaire 2000*) an application for the issuance of a residence permit will not be rejected on the basis of art 17(1) of the Aliens Act (*Vreemdelingenwet*) due to the absence of an MVV, if the child has the nationality of one of the following countries: Australia, Canada, Japan, Liechtenstein, New Zealand, Vatican City, the US and South Korea. (This is also the case for citizens of the European Union and the Schengen-area.)

- If the child possesses the nationality of a country that does not have an MVV-obligation (eg the United States) and has obtained valid travel documentation from that country (eg a passport),[44] the child may enter the Netherlands without prior contact with Dutch authorities abroad.

- The commissioning parents may also arrive in the Netherlands from a country within the Schengen-area.[45] This can, for example, happen when a Greek-Dutch couple travel to Greece and conceive a child through the legally available surrogacy possibilities there.[46] According to Greek law, the commissioning parents would be the legal parents of the child, whereby the child would obtain Greek nationality. Accordingly, the commissioning parents would be permitted to travel with the child without an MVV. Furthermore, the commissioning parents would be able to travel freely within the Schengen-area without prior consultation with the Dutch consulate.

(iii) Summary

According to the given circumstances, the question whether the commissioning parents have become legal parents of a child conceived by means of a surrogacy arrangement can present itself in a variety of different settings. Furthermore, the request made by the commissioning parents can also arise with respect to an application for a Dutch passport,[47] the registration of a foreign birth certificate[48] or the determination of child maintenance.[49] On the basis of research into the law of California, Greece, India and Ukraine,[50] it is clear that commissioning parents involved in a surrogacy arrangement in one of these jurisdictions can return to the Netherlands with a variety of different documents, for example an original birth certificate, an amended birth certificate, a judicial decision, an administration decree or an adoption order. Nevertheless, despite the variety of situations, legal questions and documents, the same Dutch rules will apply in all cases. Due to space restrictions, in this contribution attention will only be paid to the situation in which the commissioning parents return to the Netherlands and allege that they are

---

[44] The US utilises the ius soli principle, meaning that all children born on American soil acquire American citizenship: 8 USC, s 1401.

[45] These countries are also exempt from the obligation to obtain an MVV. Aliens Circular 2000, §4.1.1, Part B, Chapter 1 in combination with §2.2, Section B, Chapter 10.

[46] K Boele-Woelki, I Curry-Sumner, W Schrama and M Vonk *Draagmoederschap en illegale opneming van kinderen* (The Hague: WODC 2011) pp 137–143.

[47] For example, HR (Supreme Court) 27 May 2005 *LJN*: AS5109 en HR 28 April 2006, *LJN*: AU9237.

[48] For example Rb 's-Gravenhage 21 June 2010, *LJN* BN1330.

[49] K Saarloos *European private international law on legal parentage? Thoughts on a European instrument implementing the principle of mutual recognition in legal parentage* (Océ: Maastricht 2010) p 210.

[50] K Boele-Woelki, I Curry-Sumner, W Schrama and M Vonk *Draagmoederschap en illegale opneming van kinderen* (The Hague: WODC 2011) pp 91–162.

already the legal parents of the child as a result of the rules of parentage. This contribution will therefore not deal with the situation in which the parents have adopted their child abroad.

As has already been explained in Part III, it is generally the case that commissioning parents who have utilised procedures in California will possess a judicial determination of parentage (so-called Judgment of Parentage), as well as an amended or original birth certificate. If the commissioning parents allege that parentage has already been established abroad or wish to have this parentage established in the Netherlands, two different routes need to be distinguished depending upon whether the parentage has been established abroad by virtue of a legal fact (eg birth) or legal act (eg recognition) (both issues discussed in Part IV(c)) or in a judicial decision (Part IV(d)). In the following sections the rules regarding these different situations will be dealt with, in order to explain how Dutch law currently deals with parentage that has been established abroad in surrogacy cases.

(c) Confirmation of alleged parentage: legal acts or facts

(i) General criteria

Due to the lack of specific private international law rules in cases of surrogacy, reference must be made to the general rules laid down in the Private International Law (Parentage) Act (Wca). Article 10 of the Wca stipulates the conditions that must be satisfied in order to recognise a foreign legal act or fact in the Netherlands. Before dealing with the criteria themselves, it is important to appreciate that two different situations fall within the purview of this provision, namely legal facts (*rechtsfeiten*) and legal acts (*rechtshandelingen*).

First, as already described above, Dutch commissioning parents can return to the Netherlands with a birth certificate according to which they are the legal parents of the child. The birth certificate would appear to provide prima facie evidence of legal parentage. In California the birth certificate may refer to an underlying judicial decision, namely the Judgment of Parentage, but this is not always the case. The question is whether this 'legal fact' that has been recorded on the birth certificate can be recognised in the Netherlands according to the criteria laid down in art 10 of the Wca. The birth certificate in this sense is to be regarded as confirmation of a legal fact. The second scenario that falls within the ambit of this provision is that of the legal act. An example is the recognition of the child by a man. The recognition also ultimately leads to the acquisition of a formal confirmation of the act that has taken place. In the Netherlands, for example, recognition by the father of a child leads to the acquisition of a deed or certificate of recognition.

The criteria that apply in both situations are that the deed or certificate must:

- have been issued by a competent authority;

- have been issued abroad;

- be laid down in a legal document;

- have been made in accordance with local law; and

- not be contrary to Dutch public policy.

The majority of these conditions do not raise specific issues within the context of surrogacy, with the exception of two aspects in particular, namely that the deed or certificate must have been issued 'in accordance with local law' (Part IV(c)(ii)) and that recognition of the deed must not be contrary to Dutch public policy (Part IV(c)(iv)).

(ii) 'In accordance with local law'

A Dutch civil servant confronted with the question of whether a foreign deed can be recognised in the Netherlands will first need to determine whether the legal familial ties have been created in accordance with foreign law. With respect to this question, it would appear that the civil servant must determine whether the legal facts have been registered in accordance with the rules applicable in the jurisdiction in which the legal fact has been registered. Generally speaking, the civil servant is to assume that this is the case, and only when the civil servant has 'sufficient doubt' that this is not the case can the Dutch civil servant request further supplementary evidence to support the claims made in the foreign deed.[51] With respect to the criterion of 'sufficient doubt', it is important that two questions be answered separately. First, what circumstances can give rise to 'sufficient doubt'? Secondly, what steps need to be taken once the civil servant has established that he or she has sufficient doubt?

With respect to the first question, one must refer to the general starting point in relation to the recognition of foreign deeds, namely that the Dutch civil servant should display trust when confronted with foreign documents. The civil servant can only determine that he or she has 'sufficient doubt' on the basis of objective indications to the contrary. It is also necessary to know in relation to what the Dutch civil servant may have 'sufficient doubt'. The sufficient doubt in this context must relate to the correct application of the rules applicable in the jurisdiction in which the deed or certificate was issued. Accordingly, a distinction must be made between jurisdictions in which surrogacy is permitted and jurisdictions that do not permit surrogacy.

If a jurisdiction permits surrogacy arrangements, and furthermore also permits commissioning parents to be registered on the original birth certificate, then a birth certificate upon which Dutch commissioning parents have been registered

---

[51] Vonken *Personen- en Familierecht. Het internationale afstammingsrecht* (Deventer: Kluwer, 2009), art 10 of the Wca, note 1, p 2173.

as the legal parents has been issued in compliance with the applicable rules of the jurisdiction issuing the deed. In Ukraine, for example, it is permitted for a birth certificate to be issued to commissioning parents, as long as one of the parents is genetically related to the child.[52] In this situation, the civil servant must determine whether he or she has doubt that the deed or certificate has been issued contrary to the proper observance of this rule. The fact that the civil servant thinks that the persons registered on the birth certificate have used a surrogate is not sufficient grounds (with regard to this condition) to refuse recognition of the birth certificate. This may, however, nonetheless provide sufficient grounds for non-recognition with respect to the application of the public policy exception.[53]

If, however, the foreign jurisdiction does not permit surrogacy, and the civil servant has sufficient objective indications that the commissioning parents have used a surrogate, then the civil servant may take the necessary steps to discover whether the deed has been drawn up in accordance with the locally applicable rules. The question arises, however: when can the civil servant state that he has sufficient objective indications to believe that the local law has not been observed? This question can best be answered using a number of illustrations. If, for example, two white Caucasian commissioning parents wish to register their child in a Dutch municipality and the child is not Caucasian but instead from a different ethnic origin, then the civil servant will have sufficient objective indications to doubt that the local rules have been followed.

Once the civil servant has determined that he has sufficient doubt to question whether the local rules have been applied correctly, the next question is which steps can the civil servant then take? The normal procedure will be for the civil servant to request supporting documentation. According to Ukrainian law, for example, the registration of the child in the registers of the local municipality requires a certificate in which the genetic relationship of the child is determined with respect to at least one parent. This certificate does not, however, state that use has been made of a surrogate. The commissioning parents will generally also be in possession of a surrogacy contract wherein all the agreements between the commissioning parents and surrogate parents are laid down. Should the commissioning parents not possess such a contract (or refuse to hand it over), it would seem very difficult on this ground to determine that the parents have used a surrogacy arrangement. Nonetheless, this does not exclude the possibility of non-recognition on grounds of public policy.

(iii)   Grounds for refusal

Despite satisfying the abovementioned criteria, a foreign legal act or legal fact can also be denied recognition.[54] With respect to the non-recognition of foreign legal acts and facts, the public policy exception is the most important exception

---

[52]   K Boele-Woelki, I Curry-Sumner, W Schrama and M Vonk *Draagmoederschap en illegale opneming van kinderen* (The Hague: WODC 2011) p 159.
[53]   See further Part IV(c)(iii).
[54]   Wca, art 10(1).

and will form the basis of this section. The aim of the public policy exception is to block the application of foreign law and the recognition of legal facts and acts concluded abroad, if the application or recognition would lead to a situation contrary to the fundamental principles and values of the Dutch legal system.[55] Article 10(2) of the Wca lists three specific cases which will always be deemed contrary to Dutch public policy. These situations will be dealt with first (Part IV(c)(iv)) prior to an analysis of the general grounds for non-recognition on public policy grounds (Part IV(c)(v)).

(iv) Specific public policy grounds

In art 10(2) of the Wca three specific situations are listed in which a foreign legal act or legal fact will be regarded as contrary to Dutch public policy, namely:

(a) if the recognition is made by a Dutch national who, according to Dutch law, would not have been entitled to recognise the child;

(b) if, where the consent of the mother or the child is concerned, the legal requirements applicable pursuant to art 4(4) of the Wca were not complied with; or

(c) if the instrument manifestly relates to a sham transaction.

It would appear that the latter two conditions have not provided any real problems with respect to surrogacy arrangements. The first condition has, however, raised a number of problems that will be discussed here further. If a Dutch man recognises a child abroad, yet according to Dutch law he would not have been permitted to recognise the child, then the foreign recognition will not be recognised in the Netherlands. The aim behind this non-recognition clause is that otherwise Dutch fathers would easily be able to circumvent the adoption legislation by recognising children abroad. The conditions for recognition can be found in art 1:204 of the Dutch Civil Code (DCC). The condition listed in art 1:204(1)(e) of the DCC is of crucial importance in the context of surrogacy. This provision determines that a recognition will be regarded as null and void if it made:[56]

> ' . . . by a man who is married at the time of the recognition to another woman unless the district court has prima facie held that there is or has been a bond between the man and the mother which may, to a sufficient degree, be regarded as sufficiently equivalent to a marriage, or that there is a close personal relationship between the man and the child.'

---

[55] L Strikwerda *Inleiding tot het Nederlands Internationaal Privaatrecht* (Deventer: Kluwer, 2008) p 53.

[56] Translation provided by H Warendorf, R Thomas and I Curry-Sumner *Civil Code of The Netherlands* (Deventer: Kluwer 2009) p 75.

Prior to discussing the intricacies of these exceptions, it is first important to explore the extent of the prohibition itself. The Court of Appeal Amsterdam has, for example, determined that the prohibition does not apply if the man is involved in a registered partnership with another woman,[57] whilst the District Court Arnhem has applied this prohibition in a case when a man was married to another man.[58] Furthermore, the prohibition does not apply to a non-Dutch man, who is permitted according to the law of his nationality to recognise a child of another woman.[59]

With respect to the exceptions to this prohibition, two separate questions must be posed, namely:

(1)   When are the conditions for the exceptions satisfied in an international context?

(2)   Does prior permission need to be requested from the district court in order to satisfy the exception provided for in art 1:204(1)(e) of the DCC?

In answering the first question, reference can be made to the decision of the Supreme Court on the 27 May 2005. This case was discussed extensively in the 2006 Survey.[60] As stated in the 2006 Survey, the case revolved around a child born in 2001 in Turkey. The Dutch father had provided a notarial instrument in 2001 in which he had stated that he was the biological father of the child. A problem arose because at the time the father was married to another woman (and had been since 1973). The Dutch Supreme Court held that the mandatory nature of the public policy exception must lead to the conclusion that the man was not competent to recognise this child. The Supreme Court referred to a number of facts and circumstances that were relevant in determining whether a married man is competent to recognise a child, namely 'the man's evidenced interest and commitment to the child both before as well as after the birth. Furthermore, more is required than simple contact during a limited period of time'.[61] The District Court Assen has, moreover, determined that no close personal relationship can exist between an unborn child and the man, since this relationship can only develop after the child is born.[62]

With respect to the second question, the Dutch Supreme Court has also provided clear directions in 2006. In this case, the central question was whether the recognition in Vietnam by a Dutch national could be recognised in the Netherlands. The child was born to an unmarried Vietnamese mother and recognised by a Dutch national who was married to another woman at the

---

57   Hof Amsterdam 18 August 2002, *LJN* BG2522.
58   Rb Arnhem, 26 April 2008, *LJN* BI3495.
59   HR (Supreme Court) 28 April 1986, *NJ* 1987, 926.
60   I Sumner and C Forder 'The Dutch Family Law Chronicles: Continued Parenthood notwithstanding divorce' in A Bainham (ed) *International Survey of Family Law 2006 Edition* (Jordan Publishing Ltd, 2006) pp 264–265.
61   Hof Den Haag, 27 May 2009, *LJN* BI1434. See also MJ Vonk 'Een, twee of drie ouders?' (2003) *Tijdschrift voor Familie- en Jeugdrecht* 122–128 at 124–125.
62   Rb Assen 15 June 2006, *LJN* AY7247.

time. According to the district court the man satisfied the requirement of art 1:204(1)(e) of the DCC and therefore the Vietnamese recognition could be recognised in the Netherlands. However, the man had not requested prior permission from the district court as required by art 1:204(1)(e) of the DCC. The Supreme Court held that this was not required, as long as the man could prove that he substantively satisfied the necessary requirements.[63] On 30 November 2007, the Supreme Court provided even more clarity in explaining that the relationship between the man and the child can be evidenced on the basis of the agreements and circumstances surrounding the case.[64]

The two abovementioned questions raise particular problems with respect to surrogacy cases. If the commissioning father satisfies the substantive criterion of a 'close personal relationship' with the child, then it is possible to recognise the child in the country of origin, regardless of whether or not he is married to another woman. Since it is also not required that the man who recognises the child be the biological father, this route would appear to be a rather 'simplified' one, should adoption prove to be too difficult, too expensive, or procedurally impossible.

(v)   General public policy grounds

Alongside these specific public policy grounds, art 10(1) of the Wca provides for a general public policy exception. The question arises whether international surrogacy arrangements will fall foul of this exception. In discussing this topic a number of different scenarios must be distinguished. Due to space restrictions, only one of those scenarios will be discussed here, namely whether the lack of a birth mother on the birth certificate should lead to non-recognition.

Two cases have dealt with the issue of a birth certificate upon which no mother is listed. The first case concerned three Dutch persons, two men (in a relationship) and a woman, who acted as the surrogate. The surrogate did not wish to have any role in the child's life, but knew that if she gave birth in the Netherlands she would be regarded as the child's legal mother. As a result, they decided that she should give birth in France, since anonymous birth is possible according to French law. After the birth, they returned to the Netherlands, with a French birth certificate, upon which only the biological father was listed. The Dutch registrar refused to register the birth certificate stating that this was contrary to Dutch public policy. The District Court of The Hague agreed with the registrar, basing their conclusion on Art 7 of the UNCRC (United Nations Convention on the Rights of the Child). On the basis of this provision, every child has a right to know his or her parents and be raised by them. The district court held that in recognising the birth certificate, upon which no details were provided with regards the mother, the identity of the mother would in this way be withheld from the child. As such:

---

[63]   HR 28 April 2006, *LJN* AU9237.
[64]   HR 30 November 2007, *RvdW* 2007, 1023.

' . . . the child should be granted the choice to be able at a later age to give form to his or her identity. In doing so, he or she needs, as far as possible, full access to details of his or her parentage. Registration of the French birth certificate therefore contravenes Dutch public policy.'

In another unpublished decision of the District Court of The Hague, the judge decided that a birth certificate from the United States upon which two men were registered as the parents also contravened Dutch public policy. It was held that the mater certa semper est rule is of fundamental public policy and therefore a birth certificate with two men could not be recognised in the Netherlands.

(d)   Confirmation of alleged parentage: judicial decisions

(i)   General criteria

In a similar vein to art 10 of the Wca, art 9 lays down the specific conditions according to which a foreign judicial decision with regard to legal parentage can be recognised in the Netherlands. The conditions with respect to an enforceable decision, jurisdiction of the foreign judge, and adherence with the rules of a fair trial do not appear to have presented any particular problems for Dutch judges and civil servants with respect to the specific complexities in surrogacy cases. These conditions will therefore not be discussed here.

(ii)   Competence of the civil servant

If the Dutch civil servant is unsure whether a foreign judicial decision should be recognised, he or she is obliged to request the advice of the Advice Committee for Issues relating to Civil Status and Nationality (*Commissie van Advies voor de Zaken betreffende de Burgerlijke Staat en de Nationaliteit*).[65] The civil servant must request this advice at the moment that he or she has 'sufficient doubt' that the judicial decision does not meet the required criteria laid down in Dutch law. There are, however, no cases with respect to when the civil servant may assume that he or she has 'sufficient doubt'.[66]

(iii)   Public policy

If the recognition of the foreign judicial decision would be contrary to Dutch public policy, then the decision will not be recognised. As already stated in Part III according to the law of California parties can request the judge to determine parentage prior to the birth of the child. In a recent unpublished decision of the District Court of The Hague, the court was confronted with such a case. Parentage between the applicants and two children had been determined by the Superior Court of California prior to the birth of the children. The Californian court also ordered that the civil servant draw up the

---

65   Article 1:29c of the BW (Dutch Civil Code).
66   It is suggested that the same criteria and reasoning would apply here as are applicable with
     regards the recognition of foreign legal facts and legal acts.

birth certificate accordingly upon the birth of the children. The District Court of The Hague refused to recognise and register the birth certificates in the relevant registers in the Netherlands. The District Court argued:

> 'The judicial decision from the Superior Court of California of 15th April 2008 cannot be recognised since this is contrary to Dutch public policy, bearing in mind the aforementioned fundamental rule of family law (mater certa semper est) and the fact that the judicial decision was ordered without the legal mother first being determined.'[67]

Question marks can, however, be placed with respect to this line of reasoning. The determination of paternity is not always dependent upon the prior determination of maternity. Especially when considering that the applicant in the case was also the biological father of the children, why is the recognition of a decision with regard to the determination of paternity of the biological father contrary to Dutch public policy? Furthermore, according to Californian law all parties must have provided consent prior to the issuance of a judicial determination of parentage.[68] If the biological mother had already been consulted and provided consent to the Judgment of Parentage, why is the recognition of such a decision contrary to Dutch public policy? In addition, arguments and reasoning are absolutely essential.

(e)   Summary

This section of the chapter has hopefully illustrated the complex nature of the recognition of foreign birth certificates and judicial decisions regarding parentage. The current private international law rules in the field of parentage have not been designed to deal with the complex issues that present themselves in surrogacy cases. Specific recognition rules need to be designed that show deference to the complexity of the cases, as well as the diversity of the relevant factors.

V   CONCLUSION

It is plausible that the strict rules applicable in substantive Dutch law with respect to surrogacy cases lead many couples to search for alternatives abroad. Although the causal link between the one and the other cannot be proven without empirical research into the motivation of couples embarking upon surrogacy arrangements abroad, the link is certainly more than plausible.

If this is the case, a number of questions arise. First, should the Dutch substantive rules regarding access to high technology surrogacy be amended so as to abate the increasing flow of couples seeking solace abroad? If the Dutch

---

[67]   Authors' own translation.
[68]   K Boele-Woelki, I Curry-Sumner, W Schrama and M Vonk *Draagmoederschap en illegale opneming van kinderen* (The Hague: WODC 2011) p 134.

government properly regulates access to high-technology and low-technology surrogacy, as well as providing a civil law method enabling the transfer of parental rights from the surrogate parents to the commissioning parents, perhaps fewer couples would need to seek the assistance of foreign medical partners. In this sense, inspiration could certainly be sought from the recently amended English legislation that has now been operational for more than 20 years. The parental order provides for a secure and certain process through which the rights of all parties involved in the process are taken into account, yet the whole process is governed by the best interests of the child.

Secondly, if the Dutch government does not intend to address the issues surrounding access to high-technology cases within the Netherlands, questions will increasingly need to be asked with regards the escalating number of international cases. When is surrogacy against Dutch public policy? In answering this question, it is of the utmost importance that one does not generalise. Distinctions need to be drawn between different cases depending upon the genetic relationship between the commissioning parents and the child. The protection offered by the UNCRC should protect the child in two senses, namely the right to know one's biological heritage, as well as the right to know that one was conceived as a result of surrogacy. In taking these two principles as a starting point, it is difficult to see the justification for refusing to recognise a birth certificate drawn up abroad upon which the genetically related commissioning parents are listed as the legal parents, despite the fact that the child was conceived through surrogacy. It is difficult to see how the recognition could be against Dutch public policy in a case where the identity of the surrogate mother is easily traceable, for example in Ukraine. Since the child has access to information regarding his or her status (ie as a child conceived through surrogacy), as well as his or her biological parents (ie the commissioning parents), it is difficult to see how the lack of a reference on the birth certificate should lead to non-recognition.

The answer may, and perhaps should, be very different if neither the commissioning parents nor the surrogate parents are genetically related the child. In this case, the question should be raised what makes this case any different to adoption? It would appear that the only difference is that in a surrogacy case agreements and arrangements are made prior to the birth of a child, whereas adoption involves the transfer of parental rights of a child who has already been born and is in need of a familial home. In our opinion, the single fact that commissioning parents have made arrangements prior to the birth should not mean that adoption legislation can be circumvented. Although this will no doubt raise problems in practical terms (eg how can the state conduct a home study if the child has already been conceived? If a negative advice is to be given from the local Child Protection Board, what happens to the child who has been conceived?), these difficult questions need to be raised and should not be shied away from simply because of the difficult answers that they may lead to.

New Zealand

DISCRETION, STATUS AND MONEY: THE ESSENCE OF FAMILY LAW IN NEW ZEALAND

Mark Henaghan[*]

Résumé

En 2010, les trois concepts-clés du droit de la famille, le pouvoir discrétionnaire, le statut et l'argent, ont été à l'avant-scène en Nouvelle-Zélande. Les décisions concernant les enfants cachent inévitablement des jugements de valeurs, ce qui introduit un élément de hasard dans le processus décisionnel. Du statut dépend l'autorité et les pouvoirs. Historiquement, le droit de la famille réserve ceux-ci aux seules personnes expressément reconnues par l'État. Cette discrimination, qui est au cœur du droit de la famille, doit être questionnée sans relâche. Quant à l'argent, il est le nerf de la guerre dans le contentieux familial. Les fortunés peuvent engager des avocats qui mèneront la bataille jusqu'à la victoire. Les autres n'auront souvent d'autre choix que de signer des ententes moins avantageuses que ce que prévoit la loi elle-même. La jurisprudence récenteen matière de déménagement du parent gardien, d'adoption et d'obligation alimentaire éclaire ces trois concepts.

I INTRODUCTION

The big three of family law, discretion, status and money were prominent in New Zealand family law in 2010. The use of discretion is widespread. Decisions about children inevitably obscure choices of value beneath the surface, bringing an element of randomness to decision making. Status is about who has authority and power and who does not. Historically family law has given authority and power to those who are approved by the state and withheld it from others. This discrimination is at the heart of family law and needs constantly to be challenged and scrutinised. Money is the bottom line in family law disputes. Those who have money can afford to pay lawyers to draw out and win their cases, those without it often have to settle for less than the law would otherwise entitle them to. This summary will illustrate how these three concepts were played out in New Zealand family law in 2010.

---

* Professor and Dean of Law, University of Otago, Dunedin, New Zealand. I would like to thank my research assistant Ruth Ballantyne LLB, BA(Hons) for her invaluable contribution.

II DISCRETION

In 1984, John Eekelaar said:[1]

> 'Family law has too long suffered from the myth that, as every case is different, their resolution must be left to the discretion of individual judges. Matters of principle are confronted at every turn. It is time we faced up to them.'

So-called 'relocation cases' are a major issue in the New Zealand Family Court. They are decided on a discretionary basis and as the following analysis of the leading case shows, different points of principles are seized upon by different judges on essentially the same facts.

The leading New Zealand relocation case is *Kacem v Bashir*.[2] The basic facts revolve around the question of where two young Muslim girls (aged 7½ and nearly 6 at the time of the Supreme Court hearing) should live. The mother wanted to relocate to Australia with the two children to be close to her family, and to lessen the conflict between the father and herself. However, the father wanted the children to remain living in New Zealand. At first glance it sounds like a fairly typical relocation case. However, over the past 2 years this lengthy litigation has progressed through New Zealand's entire court hierarchy and its unusual facts have 'given rise to [serious] differences of judicial opinion'.[3] The father, a Muslim who had fled from Algeria with his wife and child, lived in a detention centre for refugees in Australia. The mother, who is of Lebanese descent and grew up in Australia, met the father while visiting the detention centre and she helped the father and his wife and child escape the detention centre and come to New Zealand. The mother became the father's 'second wife' in New Zealand and had two daughters with him.

The Supreme Court finally decided the case in September 2010 and held that the children are to remain living in New Zealand.[4] The case's journey through the courts shows different aspects of discretion being emphasised at different times.

(a) The Family Court decision

In the Family Court,[5] Judge de Jong refused the mother's relocation application. Judge de Jong considered that the reasons against a move to Australia outweighed those favouring a move. He found that:[6]

---

[1] John Eekelaar 'Trust the Judges: How Far Should Family Law Go?' (1984) 47 *Modern Law Review* 593 at 597.
[2] *Kacem v Bashir* [2010] NZSC 112, [2010] NZFLR 884.
[3] Ibid, at [16].
[4] Ibid, at [1].
[5] *B v K* FC Auckland FAM-2006–004–1761, 5 September 2008.
[6] Ibid, at [48].

'Although the Australian proposal may result in continuity and stability in the children's care it is most unlikely to promote ongoing parental consultation and co-operation, or strengthen relationships between the children and paternal family in a way which allows both families to be a part of the children's lives in a real and significant way.'

Judge de Jong was concerned that the proposed relocation would result in less frequent face-to-face contact than the young children were currently used to, and that the father's legal status prevented him from visiting the children in Australia.[7] Judge de Jong also found it relevant that the mother had already moved on several occasions, disrupting her children, and thus Judge de Jong raised concerns about the mother's level of insight and ability to provide stability for the children in the future.[8] Judge de Jong also believed that if both parents remained in New Zealand they would be able to participate in counselling programmes together.[9]

Ultimately, Judge de Jong held that 'it is in the children's interest and welfare for them to live in New Zealand where both parents are able to care for and participate in their daily lives'.[10]

(b)   The High Court decision

The mother appealed this decision to the High Court[11] where Courtney J reversed the Family Court's decision and allowed the mother to relocate to Australia with the two children. In making this decision she recognised that relocation would limit the children's face-to-face relationship with their father. However, Courtney J emphasised the serious conflict between the two parents and how this has affected, and will affect, the children in the future if they remain in New Zealand. Courtney J held:[12]

'I have reached the conclusion that remaining in New Zealand carries an unacceptable risk of damage to the children as a result of the conflict between their parents. In my judgment moving to Australia ultimately carries less risk because the girls' attitude to their father and relationship with him are more likely to remain positive than if they remain in New Zealand and are exposed to the ongoing and damaging conflict between their parents. I accept that there will be disruption and a sense of loss, especially for [the oldest child]. But if there is provision made for regular contact and visits with [the father], the long term prospects for both children are better if they are living in a secure extended family environment free of conflict than growing up amid the kind of destructive conflict to which they are now exposed.'

---

7   Ibid, at [49].
8   Ibid.
9   Ibid.
10   Ibid, at [50].
11   *K v B* (2009) 27 FRNZ 417 (HC).
12   Ibid, at [54].

(c)   The Court of Appeal decision

The father was granted leave to appeal and appealed the High Court's decision to the Court of Appeal.[13] The appeal revolved around the approach to be adopted on an appeal from the Family Court, the application of the principles enshrined in s 5 of the Care of Children Act 2004, the role of parental conflict, and whether Courtney J had given appropriate weight to all relevant factors in reaching her decision.[14] Ultimately, the Court of Appeal allowed the appeal and found that it was in the children's best interests to remain living in New Zealand.

This decision was assisted by an updated psychological report about the children (that the High Court had not had) which said that the 'long-running litigation posed increased risk to the children's well-being', but that there was 'some indication that the parents were doing better in sheltering their children from the conflict between them'.[15] The psychological report also said 'It was in the interests of both children that they maintain meaningful relationships with both parents'[16] and that the children had settled well into the shared parenting regime.[17]

In reaching their decision, Glazebrook, O'Regan and Arnold JJ accepted that the ongoing conflict between the parents could affect the children adversely and that the mother was likely to face some difficulties from having to remain in New Zealand without the immediate support of her family.[18] However, the court pointed out that if the children were to relocate to Australia, this would significantly reduce their relationship with their father.[19]

Ultimately, the Court of Appeal held that the factors favouring relocation were outweighed by factors against relocation. The court states:[20]

> 'In the present case, in part because of the length of the litigation, the girls have been the subject of shared parenting arrangements that appear to be working for them, and have become settled at school. Given the desirability of preserving continuity for the children and the importance of strong child/parent relationships, we do not think the risks associated with parental conflict, or the risk that the mother might become isolated to the extent that it affects her ability to be a good parent, are sufficient to justify disturbing what has become a good, working solution for the children . . . In these circumstances, we consider that it is in the best interests of the girls that they remain in New Zealand.'

---

13   *Bashir v Kacem* [2010] NZCA 96, [2010] NZFLR 865.
14   Ibid, at [26].
15   Ibid, at [44].
16   Ibid.
17   Ibid, at [62].
18   Ibid.
19   Ibid.
20   Ibid, at [66] and [67].

(d)   The Supreme Court decision

The mother was granted leave to appeal this decision to the Supreme Court.[21] The mother argued that the Court of Appeal erred in holding there was some weighting or priority in favour of the principles contained in s 5(b) and (e) of the Care of Children Act 2004. Ultimately, the Supreme Court unanimously dismissed the appeal, which means the children remain living in New Zealand.

Elias CJ held that the Court of Appeal did not misinterpret or misapply the principles contained in s 5 of the Care of Children Act 2004 and said:[22]

> 'I do not think the Court of Appeal was in error in pointing to the emphasis in s 5(b) on the relationship of the child to both parents . . . Section 5(e) imposes a check on the general theme contained in s 5 of the value to the child of family contact by insisting (both as a stand-alone value and in relation to family members specifically) that "the child's safety must be protected and, in particular, he or she must be protected from all forms of violence."'

William Young J agreed that the appeal should be dismissed, but like Elias CJ did 'not accept that the Court of Appeal made the error which has been attributed to it' by the majority.[23] William Young J considered the legislature has given s 5(e) of the Care of Children Act 2004 greater emphasis than other s 5 principles because of the use of the word 'must'.[24] As far as s 5(b) of the Care of Children Act 2004 is concerned, William Young J held:[25]

> ' . . . the legislature, by the use of the words "in particular", has emphasised the significance of parent/child relationships where no similar statutory emphasis is given to the other family or kin relationships referred to within s 5(b). So in that sense there is a weighting which is internal to s 5(b), albeit that the s 5(b) principle has no greater legal weight than any of the other s 5 principles.'

Blanchard, Tipping and McGrath JJ took a different approach and concluded that the Court of Appeal did err in their interpretation of s 5 of the Care of Children Act 2004, but held that the error was not material. The majority held that none of the principles contained in s 5 of the Care of Children Act 2004 have any greater weight than any of the other principles contained in s 5, but rather that 'individual principles may have a greater or lesser significance in the decision-making process, depending on the circumstances of individual cases'.[26]

---

21   *Kacem v Bashir* [2010] NZSC 112, [2010] NZFLR 884.
22   Ibid, at [7].
23   Ibid, at [46].
24   Ibid, at [47].
25   Ibid.
26   Ibid, at [19].

(e)   No 'a priori' presumptions

There is a significant difference between the majority and the minority decisions of the Supreme Court regarding the interpretation of s 5 of the Care of Children Act 2004. The majority of the Supreme Court was concerned that any indication of 'weighting' or 'priority' of principles by the Court of Appeal in s 5 could create a starting point in cases of 'some presumption against relocation on account of principle 5(b)'.[27] The Supreme Court unanimously agreed that, when the Court of Appeal applied the principles in s 5 to the facts, there was no indication of a statutory presumption against relocation, nor any indication that one principle had greater weight than any other. The 'case-specific nature of the inquiry' was emphasised by the Supreme Court with the welfare of the 'particular child' in 'their particular circumstances' as the key focus.[28]

This is consistent with the previous Court of Appeal relocation cases *Stadniczenko v Stadniczenko*[29] and *D v S*[30] which were decided under the Guardianship Act 1968. These cases held that the preferable approach in relocation decisions was to weigh and balance factors relevant to the particular circumstances, before deciding what was best for the particular child,[31] and to have no a priori assumptions.[32]

(f)   Principles and factors that may be taken into account

Judges must emphasise the welfare of the particular child in the circumstances before them and then work through the principles contained in ss 4 and 5 of the Care of Children Act 2004 as well as the s 6 children's views principles and then show their relevance to the particular case. A court is not limited to the principles contained in ss 4, 5 and 6 of the Care of Children Act 2004. In *Kacem v Bashir*[33] the Supreme Court states: 'Section 4(6) makes it clear that the s 5 principles are not exhaustive of the matters that may be relevant to the welfare and best interests of the child or children involved'.[34] For example the psychological stress felt by the mother in *Bashir v Kacem*,[35] who was isolated from her family, was seen as relevant to the well-being of the children. The mother's stress was taken into account by the Court of Appeal, despite not being a principle under s 5 of the Care of Children Act 2004.

Another factor that is not directly mentioned in s 5 of the Care of Children Act 2004 is the conflict between parents, and the impact such conflict may have

---

27   Ibid, at [29].
28   Ibid, at [18].
29   *Stadniczenko v Stadniczenko* [1995] NZFLR 493.
30   *D v S* [2002] NZFLR 116.
31   *Stadniczenko v Stadniczenko* [1995] NZFLR 493, at 500.
32   *D v S* [2002] NZFLR 116 at [33].
33   *Kacem v Bashir* [2010] NZSC 112, [2010] NZFLR 884.
34   Ibid, at [18].
35   *Bashir v Kacem* [2010] NZCA 96, [2010] NZFLR 865, at [62].

on children. This was considered by the Court of Appeal in *Bashir v Kacem*, but not given much weight because the court believed it would reduce over time and they accepted the view of the psychologist in the updated report that the 'parents are making greater efforts to shelter their daughters from exposure to their hostility for one another'.[36] The Court of Appeal in *Stadniczenko v Stadniczenko* regarded the reasons for the move and the distances involved as further important considerations in relocation cases.[37]

Whilst the Court of Appeal in *D v S* recognised that 'freedom of movement is an important value in a mobile community',[38] the Court of Appeal in *Bashir v Kacem* said that 'the primary consideration is the best interests of the children – a parent's freedom of movement is relevant only within that overall context'.[39]

Once a court has considered all the non-exhaustive principles and other factors that are relevant to a particular child, then weight and priority can be given to the principles and factors that will best achieve the welfare of the particular child.

In *Kacem v Bashir* Tipping J said:[40]

> 'At the highest level of generality the competition in a relocation case is likely to be between declining the application for relocation because the children's interest are best served by promoting stability, continuity and the preservation of certain relationships, as against allowing it on the ground that the interests of the children are thereby better served.'

In *Kacem v Bashir* Elias CJ points out that s 5 of the Care of Children Act 2004 places emphasis on the 'value to the child of the parental relationship' and considers that the 'importance of the child-parent relationship is also to be seen throughout the Act'.[41] Elias CJ explicitly draws attention to: s 5(a) of the Act, which places primary responsibility on parents and guardians for the child's care, development, and upbringing; s 5(b) of the Act, which refers to continuity of relationships with the child's wider family but places particular emphasis on a continuing relationship with both parents; s 5(c) of the Act, which encourages the child's care to be facilitated by co-operation between parents and guardians exercising day-to-day care; s 5(d) of the Act, which places value on preserving and strengthening family relationships; and s 5(f) of the Act, which says that a child's identity should be preserved and strengthened (if the parental connection is seen as important to the child's identity); which are all relevant to a child's relationship with a parent.

---

[36]   Ibid.
[37]   *Stadniczenko v Stadniczenko* [1995] NZFLR 493, at 500.
[38]   *D v S* [2002] NZFLR 116 at [30].
[39]   *Bashir v Kacem* [2010] NZCA 96, [2010] NZFLR 865, at [62].
[40]   *Kacem v Bashir* [2010] NZSC 112, [2010] NZFLR 884, at [23].
[41]   Ibid, at [7]. Elias CJ refers to ss 3(2)(a), 16 and 17 of the Care of Children Act 2004.

Tipping J reiterates that, if a situation appears to be working for a child, it will be a factor the court will take into account. Tipping J states:[42]

> 'If, on an examination of the particular facts of a relocation case, it is found that the present arrangements for the children are settled and working well, that factor will obviously carry weight in the evaluative exercise.'

(g)   The crucial facts in *Kacem v Bashir*

That is in fact what happened in the Court of Appeal in *Bashir v Kacem*. The court gave weight to the children having a close relationship with their father (as shown by the updated psychological report) and therefore concluded that relocation could have a significantly detrimental effect on the children's development. The benefit of a closer relationship with the mother's family in Australia if relocation was allowed was outweighed by an emphasis on the children's relationship with their father. The fact that the father would be unable to visit the children if they relocated to Australia, because he had left that country illegally, added weight to his request to keep the children in New Zealand. The parents had shared the care of the two young girls for 38 months by the time of the Court of Appeal hearing. The children (based on the updated psychological report) were said to have 'settled well into the shared parenting regime'.[43]

Whilst there is no express presumption against relocation in the Care of Children Act 2004, where there is a significant relationship with both parents, in an environment that is working well for the children, the parent who wants to relocate will have to provide significant countervailing factors. As Elias CJ said in the Supreme Court *Kacem v Bashir* decision:[44]

> 'Change that would disrupt settled arrangements and important relationships prompts justification by other considerations if the paramount consideration of the welfare and best interests of the child is to be fulfilled.'

(h)   The child's safety must be protected

The primary check on the theme in s 5 of maintaining, strengthening and continuing relationships and care arrangements is s 5(e) of the Care of Children Act 2004, which insists, 'the child's safety must be protected and, in particular, he or she must be protected from all forms of violence'. Elias CJ said, 's 5(e) *must* be fulfilled and so may displace other principles in a particular context'.[45] Tipping J said that if s 5(e) 'is engaged it is likely to have decisive weight, not because of any presumptive legal weighting, but because of the

---

42   *Kacem v Bashir* [2010] NZSC 112, [2010] NZFLR 884, at [24].
43   *Bashir v Kacem* [2010] NZCA 96, [2010] NZFLR 865, at [62].
44   *Kacem v Bashir* [2010] NZSC 112, [2010] NZFLR 884, at [9].
45   Ibid, at [8].

crucial factual importance of protecting the safety of children when compared with the objectives at which the other principles are aimed'.[46]

The Court of Appeal in *Bashir v Kacem* held there were no concerns for the 'physical safety' of the children, nor was there any concern about 'physical abuse being directed at them'.[47] Psychological effects the children may suffer from observing conflict between their parents were not seen as a safety issue under s 5(e) of the Care of Children Act 2004 by the Court of Appeal.[48] The court did discuss the ongoing conflict between the parents as having the capacity 'to affect the girls adversely' as a general consideration.[49] There is no reason why parental conflict cannot be discussed as a safety issue because safety should not be restricted to physical and psychological abuse.

This is supported by the Domestic Violence Act 1995 which defines the psychological abuse of a child as causing or allowing the child to hear the physical, sexual or psychological abuse of a person with whom the child has a domestic relationship or putting the child, or allowing the child to be put, at real risk of seeing or hearing the abuse occurring.[50]

Where there is conflict between parents, as there was in *Bashir v Kacem*, there will inevitably be psychological abuse that the children will see or hear (or be at risk of seeing or hearing). The updated psychological report given to the Court of Appeal stated that the parents were 'making greater efforts to shelter their daughters from exposure to their hostility for one another'.[51] However, this does not remove the risk of psychological consequences for the girls. Section 5(e) requires safety to be considered. By putting the risk of psychological consequences for children in conflicted families under s 5(e) it is likely to be considered more carefully.

In the psychological report given to the Family Court in *SCS v GMS*,[52] conflict between parents that did not abate was described as 'bordering upon psychological violence' which 'impacts developmentally on secure relationships between children and parents'.[53] In this case, Judge Annis Somerville held that the high level of parental conflict had affected the children, and this was a significant reason as to why she allowed the mother to relocate to England. Judge Annis Somerville states:[54]

> 'The boys have not been protected from the psychological violence that has been perpetrated by the parents. The parental conflict is affecting the children . . . The parents' parenting styles also appear to be impacting on the children, however the

---

46 Ibid, at [19].
47 *Bashir v Kacem* [2010] NZCA 96, [2010] NZFLR 865, at [62].
48 Ibid.
49 Ibid.
50 Domestic Violence Act 1995, ss 3(3)(a) and (b).
51 *Bashir v Kacem* [2010] NZCA 96, [2010] NZFLR 865, at [62].
52 *SCS v GMS* FC Tauranga FAM-2003–070–0000473, 30 April 2010.
53 Ibid, at [197] and [198].
54 Ibid, at [265] and [268].

major factor is the conflict. Having the children in New Zealand under a shared parenting plan has not worked. Having the children under the guardianship of the Court with an arrangement whereby the mother has the children during the week and the father at the weekend has also not worked. The psychological safety of the children is dependent upon the parents having the assistance necessary to enable the children to develop satisfactorily.'

The mother's 'real stress as a result of feeling isolated' in *Bashir v Kacem* could also be a potential safety issue for the children if it affects the mother's ability to look after the children.[55] The Court of Appeal considers 'that the mother will be able to overcome any personal difficulties which she faces so as to facilitate her daughters' best interests'.[56]

In *RMB v ARZB*[57] the mother's medically diagnosed depression caused by being forced to remain in New Zealand was described by Judge Coyle as a significant factor and given considerable weight in the Family Court because the child's 'best interests are inextricably linked into his mother being psychologically well'.[58] The mother in *Kacem v Bashir* had not reached a sufficient level of stress or depression for the court to give significant weight to this factor.

(i) Children's views

Because the appeal to the Supreme Court in *Kacem v Bashir* focused on the interpretation and application of ss 4 and 5 of the Care of Children Act 2004, there was no analysis of whether or not the children's views had been considered in compliance with s 6, which requires the children's views to ascertained, taken account of and then given the appropriate weight. According to Court of Appeal, the (then) 6-year-old child in *Bashir v Kacem* 'expressed a clear wish to reside in Australia' and the younger 5-year-old child appeared to be 'fairly positive about relocation to Sydney'.[59] The Court of Appeal did not take account of the children's views, dismissing them based on the children's 'cognitive and emotional maturity' and 'limited ability to project into the future'.[60]

The words 'age and maturity' are *not* in s 6 of the Care of Children Act 2004. Children's views should not be dismissed on that basis. The section requires that children's views be taken account of. That means the courts need to show how children's views fit within all the other factors that need to be considered. The children's perspectives in *Bashir v Kacem* were consistent with the mother's

---

55   *Bashir v Kacem* [2010] NZCA 96, [2010] NZFLR 865, at [62].
56   Ibid.
57   *RMB v ARZB* FC Dunedin FAM-2010–017–000023, 2 November 2010. In this case, the mother was given permission to relocate with the child from New Zealand to England where she and the father were originally from.
58   Ibid, at [109].
59   *Bashir v Kacem* [2010] NZCA 96, [2010] NZFLR 865, at [45].
60   Ibid.

feelings of isolation from her family in Australia. When deciding the weight to be given to the children's views in *Bashir v Kacem*, the Court of Appeal needed to consider the girls' views alongside other factors such as the importance of the girls' relationship with their father, rather than merely dismissing their views as 'immature'. It is not possible to do justice to the best interests principle if the children whom the dispute is about are not listened to, nor their views taken account of.

(j) The role of appellate courts in relocation cases

The Supreme Court in *Kacem v Bashir* commented on the role that appellate courts play. On a 'general appeal' the 'appellate court has the responsibility of considering the merits of the case afresh'.[61] The appellate court is not required to be 'uninfluenced' by the reasoning of the court below.[62] The appellate court is free to take the previous reasoning into account, or ignore it, according to how the appellate court sees the matter. The fact that leave was required to appeal from the High Court to the Court of Appeal did not stop the appeal being a general appeal.[63] Because the Court of Appeal had power to rehear the whole or any part of the evidence, and to receive further evidence under s 145(2) of the Care of Children Act 2004, these powers were seen as a 'classic indicator' of a general right of appeal.[64] As the Supreme Court said, relocation cases involve assessments of fact and degree and entail value judgments. These matters do not remove such cases from being matters of general appeal, where the appeal court can substitute its opinion on matters of fact and degree and use its own value judgment to decide the appeal.

This approach is supported by the Supreme Court decision *Austin, Nichols & Co Inc v Stichting Lodestar*.[65] Elias CJ, in delivering the judgment of the Supreme Court in *Austin, Nichols & Co Inc v Stichting Lodestar*, states:[66]

> 'Those exercising general rights of appeal are entitled to judgment in accordance with the opinion of the appellate court, even where that opinion is an assessment of fact and degree and entails a value judgment. If the appellate court's opinion is different from the conclusion of the tribunal appealed from, then the decision under appeal is wrong in the only sense that matters, even if it was a conclusion on which minds might reasonably differ. In such circumstances it is an error for the High Court to defer to the lower Court's assessment of the acceptability and weight to be accorded to the evidence, rather than forming its own opinion.'

A general appeal is distinguished from an appeal against a decision made in the exercise of a discretion where the criteria for appeals are stricter. In that kind of appeal the criteria are '(1) error of law or principle; (2) taking account of

---

[61] *Kacem v Bashir* [2010] NZSC 112, [2010] NZFLR 884, at [31].
[62] Ibid.
[63] Ibid, at [33]. As according to s 145(1) of the Care of Children Act 2004.
[64] Ibid, at [33].
[65] *Austin, Nichols & Co Inc v Stichting Lodestar* [2007] NZSC 103, [2008] 2 NZLR 141.
[66] Ibid, at [16].

irrelevant considerations; (3) failing to take account of a relevant
consideration; or (4) the decision is plainly wrong'.[67] An example of exercising
a discretion given by the Supreme Court is the decision whether to rehear the
evidence or receive further evidence under s 145(2) of the Care of Children
Act 2004.[68]

(k)   The problem with discretion

Thus, in New Zealand family law we have a broad discretion, based on a
non-exhaustive list of principles, where judges give weight to the principles and
other relevant factors depending on how they see the particular facts. For
example in *Kacem v Bashir* if the mother had grown more distressed with being
required to remain in New Zealand, and the father had been able to visit the
children in Australia, the likely outcome would have been quite different. It was
very virtuous of the mother to make adjustments for the children's sake, but, if
she had not been able to cope, then paradoxically, she may well have had a
stronger case to return with the children to Australia. The updated
psychological report given to the Court of Appeal was crucial and carried
significant weight.

Relocation cases change quite dramatically over time. Relocation research,
funded by the New Zealand Law Foundation, shows that 'a relocation
"dispute" is not a discreet, one-time only event, but is instead illustrative of an
ongoing process of family post-separation transition(s)'.[69]

The open-ended nature of both the deciding factors and the opportunity for an
appellate court to decide the case according to its particular values mean that
relocation cases will continue to be costly affairs both for the litigants and,
most importantly, the children involved. First-rate legal advice, which reality
tests clients as to the strengths and weaknesses of their case, whether it is for or
against relocation, is essential, but difficult given the lack of direction from the
legislature. The most lawyers can do is to discuss with their clients the range of
potential factors that are likely to be relevant to their case and then help their
client decide whether it is really worth taking a case all the way through the
courts.

The parties in *Kacem v Bashir* are likely to be exhausted by the emotionally
difficult and lengthy litigation that has occurred over several years. Both parties
have also had to live with constant uncertainty about the ultimate result, which
must have been extremely unsettling. Hopefully the children have now adjusted
to their circumstances and have been able to get on with their lives.

---

[67]   *Kacem v Bashir* [2010] NZSC 112, [2010] NZFLR 884, at [32].
[68]   Ibid, at [33].
[69]   Nicola Taylor, Megan Gollop and Mark Henaghan 'Relocation Following Parental Separation
        in New Zealand: Complexity and Diversity' (2010) IFL 97 at 102.

While relocation cases are fought in the name of the best interests of the child, they are often not about the children's best interests at all. Many relocation cases are about parents who are simply unable to agree on arrangements for their children after the parents' relationship has come to an end. It is hard not to conclude that decisions in relocation cases are more about the best interests of the parents, rather than the children.

(l)   Discretion trends

Trends in New Zealand relocation decisions oscillate depending on which aspects of principle are emphasised under the court's discretion. Sometimes it is the well-being of the primary parent, and in more recent times it has been the emphasis on shared care.

Up until the late 1990s, New Zealand judges followed the English case *Poel v Poel*,[70] which meant that 62% of applicants for relocation were successful.[71] This success rate trended downwards as the idea of shared care emerged in the New Zealand Family Court.[72]

The New Zealand Care of Children Act 2004 was a response in part to pressure on the government of the day to provide a rule of equal time once parents separated. The Care of Children Act 2004 did not go that far, but it did implement principles, which emphasised the joint responsibility, co-operation and consultation of both parents, and continuity of arrangements and relationships, particularly the relationship with both parents.[73] The Principal Family Court Judge, Peter Boshier, wrote an article that indicated that as 'parenting orders include this principle as a fundamental constituent, it may become more difficult for a parent to convince the Court that it is in the welfare of the child to be removed from the parameters of the order'.[74] The result was that in 2005 only 21% of applications for relocation within New Zealand were allowed, and just 38% of international relocation applications were granted.[75]

In the first High Court relocation case under the Care of Children Act 2004, *Brown v Argyll*,[76] Priestley J made it clear he did not agree with Judge Boshier

---

[70]   *Poel v Poel* [1970] 1 WLR 1469 at 1471.

[71]   Mark Henaghan and Bill Atkin *Family Law Policy in New Zealand* (LexisNexis New Zealand Ltd, 3rd edn, 2007) p 329. This figure includes relocation within New Zealand. If the parents cannot agree, then because both parents have equal rights to decide where the child lives, whether they are primary caregivers or not, the court decides.

[72]   Ibid.

[73]   Care of Children Act 2004, s 5.

[74]   Peter Boshier ' Relocation Cases: An International View From the Bench' (2005) 5 NZFLJ 77 at 82. To be fair to Judge Boshier, he also states at p 80: 'It is not an absolute that the new Act will introduce a major change to the law of relocation as it exists. There are also factors that point towards the current approach being largely retained.'

[75]   Mark Henaghan 'Going, Going ... Gone – To Relocate or Not to Relocate, That is the Question' (conference paper for New Zealand Family Law Conference, Auckland, 2009) at p 14.

[76]   *Brown v Argyll* [2006] NZFLR 705.

that the new Act made relocation more difficult.[77] This led to an increase in the number of allowed relocations as illustrated by the fact that in 2006 up to 48% of relocation applications were allowed within New Zealand, and 61% of overseas relocation cases were successful.[78] The trend for relocations within New Zealand dropped to 43 and 42% in 2007 and 2008, with the corresponding successful overseas relocations being 56% in 2007 and 71% in 2008.[79] In 2009, the number of successful relocations, both overseas and within New Zealand changed. Just 32% of applications to relocate overseas were successful, but within New Zealand relocation applications were successful 60% of the time.[80]

In March 2010, the New Zealand Court of Appeal decision *Bashir v Kacem*[81] was released. The decision emphasised the 'desirability of preserving continuity for the children and the importance of strong child/parent relationships', in a factual situation where there were shared parenting arrangements in place that appeared to be working.[82] In 2010, the 2009 trend was reversed, and 42% of the overseas relocation applications were successful, compared to just 22% of relocation applications within New Zealand being allowed.[83] The trends reflect the facts of individual cases, but also show that adopting a mindset for or against relocation can make a significant difference in how a particular case is decided.

III   STATUS

In June 2010, a full High Court bench of Wild and Simon France JJ held in *Re Application by AMM and KJO to adopt a child*[84] that a heterosexual de facto couple can adopt a child under the Adoption Act 1955. The wording of the 1955 Act states that 'two spouses jointly' can adopt a child together. There is no doubt at that time 'spouses' meant a married couple. The word 'de facto' did not exist in legal language. It was called 'living in sin'.

The facts in *Re Application by AMM and KJO to adopt a child*[85] are somewhat unusual. The couple concerned had been 'in a settled de facto relationship for nearly ten years'.[86] When the relationship began, the mother ('AM') had a young child whom she had conceived with the assistance of an unknown sperm donor. Her de facto partner ('KO') had parented her child for the last 10 years

---

77 Ibid, at [58] and [59].
78 Mark Henaghan, 'Going, Going ... Gone – To Relocate or Not to Relocate, That is the Question' (conference paper for New Zealand Family Law Conference, Auckland, 2009) at p 14.
79 Ibid.
80 Ibid.
81 *Bashir v Kacem* [2010] NZCA 96, [2010] NZFLR 865.
82 Ibid, at [66].
83 This is based on a recent analysis of 30 relocation cases decided in New Zealand across the Family Court, High Court, Court of Appeal and Supreme Court.
84 *Re Application by AMM and KJO to adopt a child* [2010] NZFLR 629 (HC).
85 Ibid.
86 Ibid, at [1].

and now the couple wanted KO to be able to adopt the child as his own. Despite the fact that AM was in fact the biological and legal mother of the child, the couple had to apply jointly to adopt the child in order for KO to become the legal father of the child. If KO made an adoption application on his own:[87]

> ' . . . the effect would be to terminate AM's status as mother, because that is what adoption does. It kills off any existing parental status in favour of the new parents. So even though AM is already [the child's] mother, she needs to make a joint application with KO.'

The issue was whether the courts or Parliament should change the meaning of 'spouse' in the legislation. The Attorney-General was given representation as intervening and conceded that the law as it stands discriminates against de facto couples like AM and KO, but that it was for Parliament to provide a remedy, not the courts.

Section 6 of the New Zealand Bill of Rights Act empowers a court where an enactment 'can be given a meaning that is consistent with the rights and freedoms contained' in the Bill of Rights to prefer that meaning. The key word is 'can'; Parliament is still supreme in New Zealand, and the courts do not have the authority to override the clear intent of Parliament. Parliament can pass legislation that places limits on protected rights and freedoms. In 1955, when the Adoption Act was passed, the rights and freedoms of de facto couples were not contemplated.

The High Court held that:[88]

> 'We conclude that a meaning more consistent with the right to freedom from discrimination can be found. It is to interpret "spouses" as including de facto couples of the opposite sex. Although not the meaning that was intended at the time of enactment, it is a meaning that is consistent with the purposes of the Act, is not a strained meaning of "spouse", and is workable within the other parts of the Act. It will have quite limited consequences beyond the area of adoption.'

Despite the fact that the term 'spouse' could not possibly have been intended to include de facto partners in 1955 when the Adoption Act was passed, the court felt that it was not too much of a strain to include heterosexual de facto partners in the term spouse. The court ultimately held that:[89]

> 'Even though it is plainly arguable that Parliament wishes to correct the discrimination on its own timeframe, we have come to the view that our task is to alleviate the discrimination now to the extent possible.'

The court specifically limits this decision to heterosexual de facto couples, which in itself contradicts the court's position, because this further

---

[87] Ibid, at [2].
[88] Ibid, at [50].
[89] Ibid, at [72].

discriminates against same-sex de facto couples. The reason why the Adoption Act 1955 has not been amended by Parliament is because politicians are afraid to address the issue of same-sex couples adopting as couples. There is nothing in New Zealand to stop a homosexual person individually adopting a child, as was the case in *Re T*.[90] However, same-sex couples adopting children is much more controversial, and many politicians do not wish to confront the issue. By not confronting the issue of same-sex couples adopting children, discrimination becomes entrenched. While the High Court appeared to be interpreting the law in a non-discriminatory way by allowing heterosexual de facto couples to adopt, this will inevitably delay reform to the Adoption Act 1955, and further entrench discrimination against same-sex couples adopting children.

In *Quilter v Attorney-General*[91] the New Zealand Court of Appeal was faced with an application by same-sex couples to be able to be married under the Marriage Act 1955. The Marriage Act 1955 uses terms such as 'husband' and 'wife', and therefore, like the Adoption Act 1995, is very clearly based on the idea of marriage being between members of the opposite sex. The Court of Appeal unanimously said in *Quilter v Attorney-General*[92] they could not use the Bill of Rights Act 1990 discrimination provisions to replace what was the clear intent of Parliament.

The High Court in *Re Application by AMM and KJO to adopt a child*[93] said that that case could be distinguished because it involved 'broad social policy issues', and adoption was seen as a 'discrete area'.[94] The only difference is that numbers of people using the Adoption Act 1955 are much greater than those wishing to marry. But in both cases the court was faced with the clear intent of 1955 legislation, and in one it chose to uphold the will of Parliament, and in the other it chose to override it.

Whilst one can sympathise with the need to progress the law of adoption, it should be done through the democratic process, and not through the courts on a piecemeal basis. Such a piecemeal approach merely further isolates same-sex couples from Adoption Act 1955 status, despite same-sex couples being recognised in virtually every other statute including the Property (Relationships) Act 1976, the Family Proceedings Act 1980, the Domestic Protection Act 1982, the Domestic Violence Act 1995 and the Care of Children Act 2004.[95]

---

[90] *Re T* [2008] NZFLR 185.
[91] *Quilter v Attorney-General* [1998] NZFLR 196 (CA).
[92] Ibid.
[93] *Re Application by AMM and KJO to adopt a child* [2010] NZFLR 629 (HC).
[94] Ibid, at [40] and [41].
[95] For a more detailed analysis of *Re Application by AMM and KJO to adopt a child* see Nathan Crombie and Bill Atkin 'New Meaning for Historic Term: De Factos as "Spouses" in New High Court Ruling' (2010) 6 NZFLJ 313.

IV   MONEY

(a)   *C v G*

In *C v G*[96] the Court of Appeal refused to include legal costs as part of a spousal maintenance award. The primary reason given by the court was that maintenance is designed to assist with ongoing costs. The court held that legal costs are 'more properly regarded as a one-off debt'.[97] However, there is nothing in the spousal maintenance provisions that requires that maintenance awards only cover ongoing costs. For example, parties who have to re-establish a home for themselves can gain maintenance to buy new furniture and household items. New furniture could also be regarded as a one-off debt. As Courtney J states in *B v B*:[98]

> 'The expenses incurred in resolving the legal issues between the parties are a natural consequence of the separation, as much as the need for the party leaving the matrimonial home to purchase new furniture.'

More importantly, legal costs by their very nature are not one-off costs; rather, they are usually ongoing as people work their way through the legal process. The Court of Appeal went on to say that it was more appropriate to deal with any disparity, in terms of the party's ability to pay their legal costs, by a traditional award of costs at the end of the proceedings.[99] The problem with this justification is that there is no guarantee that costs will be awarded; costs in this sense are not based on need as maintenance is; rather, they are based on whether one party had a legitimate case or not.

The Court of Appeal also seemed worried that there could be two costs claims, one for maintenance (including an applicant's legal expenses) and one for traditional costs. This is easily addressed because maintenance and costs serve different purposes. Maintenance grows out of the reasonable needs that a party has, which they are unable to meet themselves. Legal expenses represent a reasonable need to be able to fund a legitimate claim. Traditional costs arise because one party may have unfairly or inappropriately prolonged or delayed a case. A court would also have the ability to take into account legal costs paid as part of any maintenance order when deciding whether to award traditional costs, and on what basis, at the end of the proceedings. It is thus unlikely that an applicant would be allowed to double dip.

The Court of Appeal was also concerned that an award of maintenance for legal costs presupposes an outcome.[100] However, this is incorrect. No one can guarantee the outcome of any case. Maintenance for legal expenses is not outcome-based; it is paid so the applicant has the opportunity to make a claim

---

96   *C v G* [2010] NZCA 128, [2010] NZFLR 497.
97   Ibid, at [52].
98   *B v B* [2008] NZFLR 789, at [17].
99   *C v G* [2010] NZCA 128, [2010] NZFLR 497, at [52].
100 Ibid.

based on professional legal advice and representation. The full cost of legal representation is often not fully met by a traditional costs award by the court. If we take away legal costs as a reasonable need, then it simply means that many applicants with limited financial resources will be unable to legitimately make a claim. This totally undermines the wide basis for maintenance, which revolves around the applicant's reasonable needs. If the ability to make a legal claim to what you are entitled to is not a reasonable need, then what is a reasonable need? As Holman J in *A v A*[101] explains, legal costs can be an applicant's crucial reasonable need. He states:[102]

> ' . . . the costs of the suit itself . . . are, after the provision of a roof over her head and food in her mouth, the wife's most urgent and pressing need and expense. She could manage without holidays, though I have made some provision for them. She could no doubt manage for a while without buying new clothes. She could manage without her manicures, pedicures and yoga and keep fit classes . . . But she simply cannot make any progress with the dominating issue in her life if she cannot pay her lawyers.'

(b)   Interim maintenance

In *C v G*,[103] the decision concerned the appropriate quantum for a final maintenance order. The case was not based upon interim maintenance. Thus, it is possible to distinguish the judgment in relation to interim maintenance on the basis that the legislative provisions give the court an extremely wide jurisdiction to award interim maintenance. Section 82(1) of the Family Proceedings Act 1980 states that:

> 'Where an application for a maintenance order or for the variation, extension, suspension, or discharge of a maintenance order has been filed, any District Court Judge may make an order directing the respondent to pay such periodical sum as the District Court Judge thinks reasonable towards the future maintenance of the respondent's spouse, civil union partner, or de facto partner until the final determination of the proceedings or until the order sooner ceases to be in force.'

There is some authority to support the claim that legal expenses can properly be included as part of an interim maintenance order. Courtney J discussed legal expenses and interim maintenance in *B v B* and said:[104]

> 'Whether legal and accounting costs may, as a matter of law, be included in an interim maintenance order under s 82 does not appear to have been the subject of judicial consideration . . . I do not see any reason that legal and accounting expenses should not be viewed in the same way as any other expenses that might form the basis for an application for interim maintenance. In particular I do not accept that they should be treated as costs in the cause to be determined at the conclusion of the proceeding.'

---

[101]   *A v A (Maintenance Pending Suit: Provision for Legal Fees)* [2001] 1 FLR 377.
[102]   Ibid, at 382.
[103]   *C v G* [2010] NZCA 128, [2010] NZFLR 497.
[104]   *B v B* [2008] NZFLR 789, at [15] and [16].

The principle contained in *B v B* has since been considered by several cases. In *G v R*,[105] Judge Russell was concerned that to award an applicant their total legal expenses as interim maintenance may mean an applicant will not consider the costs involved in bringing litigation as carefully. Judge Russell said:[106]

> '[31] . . . While *it is clear that wider legal costs can be considered as part of an interim spousal maintenance claim*, care needs to be taken to ensure no duplication occurs between the legal expenses claimed by the wife and other Court ordered costs the wife may receive.
>
> [32] I also do not consider it appropriate that there should be a full recovery of legal costs on a solicitor/client basis. To do so would give the wife the ability to fund a legal campaign against the husband at no cost to herself. In my view this is not desirable because parties to any dispute or litigation should be required to have some regard to the costs they are likely to incur when making decisions with their legal/accounting advisors about how to resolve or have determined the matters in dispute.
>
> [33] *I consider it is appropriate that a reasonable contribution towards the wife's wider legal costs unrelated to these proceedings and the pending costs claim should be incorporated as part of the interim spousal maintenance award*. She will need to meet the balance of her legal costs from the capital assets which are available to her.' (emphasis added)

Judge Russell accepted the general principle contained in *B v B* and allowed some of the wife's legal costs to be incorporated into the interim spousal maintenance award. However, in *G v R*, Judge Russell provided some limits because he did not allow all of the wife's legal expenses to be paid for as part of interim maintenance. In *K v K*,[107] Heath J discussed *B v B* and stated:[108]

> 'In *B v B* . . . Courtney J held that spousal maintenance could be used to ensure one party to the marriage had adequate ability to meet legal and accounting costs in relation to the inevitable relationship property disputes that would arise.'

Heath J did not overturn the principle as such and stated that the wife, though not awarded specific moneys to meet anticipated legal and accounting fees, would be able to use the interim maintenance she was awarded to pay for such costs.[109] In *Lintott v Rands*,[110] Judge de Jong considered himself bound by the decision in *B v B* that found 'that legal and expert costs can be taken into account when assessing maintenance expenses'.[111] However, Judge de Jong did note that *B v B* is under appeal.[112]

---

[105] *G v R* FC Nelson FAM-2008–042–728, 17 December 2008.
[106] Ibid, at [31] to [33].
[107] *K v K* HC Auckland CIV-2009–404–4421, 20 November 2009.
[108] Ibid, at [27].
[109] Ibid, at [30].
[110] *Lintott v Rands* FC Auckland FAM-2007–004–1465, 30 September 2008.
[111] Ibid, at [41].
[112] Ibid. I am currently unable to find a decision that appeals *B v B* [2008] NZFLR 789.

There is currently nothing to limit the court from awarding interim maintenance based on the legitimate needs for legal costs to mount a claim. Using interim maintenance to assist with legal costs in this way is in keeping with the rationale behind spousal maintenance. The rationale of maintenance is to allow people to get back onto their feet so that they can meet their own needs after a relationship ends. One of the best ways to do this is for former partners to be able to get legal and expert advice to assist in claiming their entitlements at the end of their relationship. This enables former partners to meet their own needs more quickly. To cut off the ability to use maintenance as a means of funding legal claims is to undermine the whole policy behind the maintenance provisions.

V CONCLUSION

Family law is inherently personal law, which impacts very deeply on individual lives. Broad judicial discretion leaves individuals at the mercy of the judge on the day. This creates an atmosphere of uncertainty, and encourages people to litigate their way through the New Zealand court hierarchy, until they get a judge who looks at the facts of their case the way the person wants them to. Certainty and finality would be better enhanced by reducing judicial discretion and providing more definite guidelines for family law situations. This would also enable people to order their affairs accordingly and move on with their lives more quickly.[113]

Decisions about status leave some people out, while other people are brought into the fold. This is clearly illustrated by *Re Application by AMM and KJO to adopt a child*,[114] which gives heterosexual de facto couples the legal status to adopt, but expressly excludes same-sex couples from adopting children. Such discrimination is not based on the well-being of society, or on the worth of those who are included, or left out, but rather on historic notions of how families should be organised. Those in minority families, such as same-sex couples, struggle the hardest to be recognised in New Zealand family law. There should no place for such discrimination in New Zealand. There is no evidence that same-sex couples are not able to bring up children successfully.

Money to fight for redress is essential for those who want to challenge and have upheld their legal entitlements. Without such money, family law can be unfair and unbalanced because people simply cannot enforce their legal rights. In *C v G*,[115] the Court of Appeal refusing to allow claims for legal costs as part of spousal maintenance, has subjected non-earning or low earning spouses to accepting their financial lot, rather than mounting a legal challenge to obtain what they are legally entitled to. Without money to fight for one's legal

---

[113] For an attempt to set out more detailed guidelines in relocation decisions see Mark Henaghan 'Relocation Cases – The Rhetoric and the Reality of a Child's Best Interests: A View From the Bottom of the World' (2011) *Child and Family Law Quarterly* (UK) vol 23, no 2.

[114] *Re Application by AMM and KJO to adopt a child* [2010] NZFLR 629 (HC).

[115] *C v G* [2010] NZCA 128, [2010] NZFLR 497.

entitlements, hiring a lawyer can be impossible, and this ultimately inhibits people from even passing the first hurdle, let alone achieving justice.

Norway

EQUAL PARENTHOOD: RECENT REFORMS IN CHILD CUSTODY CASES

*Tone Sverdrup**

Résumé

En Norvège, le droit de l'enfant est devenu, comme dans plusieurs pays, un domaine névralgique donnant lieu à une importante activité législative. Dans le courant des trois dernières années, le Children Act a, en effet, connu des changements majeurs qui reflètent les nouvelles conceptions sociales en la matière de même que les plus récentes connaissances en psychologie et les avancées biotechnologiques. En 2008, les couples de femmes, qu'elles soient mariées ou non, obtiennent la possibilité d'accéder au statut de co-mères et elles se voient accorder le même accès à la reproduction médicalement assistée que les couples hétérosexuels. Quant à la réforme de 2010, elle s'inscrit sous le signe du principe d'égalité entre les parents. Les nouvelles dispositions portent sur la résidence alternée, le déménagement d'un parent à l'intérieur du pays, le droit d'accès et la violence à l'égard des enfants. Ces nouveautés font l'objet d'une analyse dans la deuxième partie de ce texte. Les procédures en matière de garde ont fait l'objet d'une réforme en 2003. La troisième partie de ce texte fait état de la mise en oeuvre de celle-ci. Le principe d'égalité est solidement ancré dans la tradition juridique norvégienne, ce qui favorise considérablement son application dans le domaine de la parentalité. Le droit de l'enfant est devenu un enjeu important des politiques d'égalité entre hommes et femmes et il reste plusieurs questions à régler à ce sujet. Quoi qu'il en soit, il existe en Norvège une conscience réelle du danger d'une juridicisation excessive de la vie privée et du fait que les enfants subissent des dommages lorsqu'ils sont au centre de conflits parentaux. C'est la raison pour laquelle la Norvège consacrera dans les prochaines années d'importants efforts en vue de développer le droit procédural et le droit substantiel dans le sens d'une meilleure prévention des conflits.

I   INTRODUCTION

As in many other countries, child law in Norway has become a key policy area with frequent legislative amendments. Over the past 3 years, significant changes to the Children Act reflect revised social conceptions and new psychological knowledge, as well as biotechnological achievements. In 2008, female spouses and cohabitants were given the status of co-mothers in the Children Act and were given the same access to medically assisted reproduction as different-sex

---

*   Professor, Department of Private Law, University of Oslo.

couples.[1] These amendments to the law were presented by John Asland and Peter Hambro in the 2009 edition of *The International Survey of Family Law*.[2] In 2010, the Children Act was amended again, under the keyword 'equal parenthood'. The new enactments concerned alternating residence, relocation inside the country, right to access and the use of violence in the upbringing of children. These changes will be discussed in Part II of this chapter. The legal procedure in custody cases was reformed in 2003, and the implementation of these changes has since been assessed: see Part III of the chapter.

II CHILD LAW REFORM 2010

'Equal parenthood' has become the keyword denoting an important political objective of recent child law reforms.[3] Among others, fathers' participation in child care is promoted by granting them more rights under this label. But confusion reigns as to what equal parenthood entails. A Child Law Commission stated in 2008 that in the vast majority of cases, the greatest possible contact with both parents would be in the child's best interest.[4] The Commission has been accused of not seeing the difference between quantity and quality – it is not the 'greatest', but the 'best' overall parental contact that is in line with the child's best interest and with legal doctrine.[5] On the other hand, the Commission maintains that in the specific case, gender equality may still indirectly have a decisive importance, due to the fact that 'the same amount of contact' with both parents often will be in the child's best interests.[6] The debate is symptomatic of the difficulties that arise when the interests of the child and gender equality are combined in a single consideration.

(a) Alternating residence

As parental responsibilities are normally shared even if the parents move apart, the majority of intra-family disputes concern the child's residence after

---

[1]   Biotechnology Act 2003, ss 2–2 and 2–3, Children Act 1981, ss 3 and 4. English version of the Children Act 1981, last amended by the Act of 9 April 2010, can be found at www.regjeringen.no/en/dep/bld/Documents/Laws-and-rules/Laws.html?id=334 (accessed 22 February 2011).

[2]   J Asland and P Hambro 'New Developments and Expansion of Relationships Covered by Norwegian Law' in B Atkin (ed) *The International Survey of Family Law* (Jordan Publishing Limited, 2009) pp 378–384. A comprehensive Marriage Act covering both different-sex and same-sex couples, was enacted in 2008; cf the Marriage Act 1991, s 1.The Act gives same-sex couples the right to enter into marriage on the same basis as heterosexuals. An amendment to the Adoption Act 1986 made accommodation for same-sex couples to gain the ability to apply for adoption as well.

[3]   Child Law Commission 2008, NOU 2008: 9, *Med barnet i fokus*, p 15. Norwegian version at www.regjeringen.no/pages/2067864/PDFS/NOU200820080009000DDDPDFS.pdf (accessed 1 June 2011).

[4]   NOU 2008: 9, pp 40, 61–62 and 63.

[5]   See T Haugli 'Er barnet i fokus?' (2008) 6 *Tidsskrift for familierett, arverett og barnevernrettslige spørsmål* 156–172 at 157–158. See also L Smith and P Lødrup *Barn og foreldre* (Oslo: Gyldendal Akademisk, 7th edn, 2006) pp 164–165.

[6]   NOU 2008: 9, p 29.

relationship breakdown. The parents may agree that the child shall live permanently either with one of them or with both of them, and contrary to the situation in many other countries, the agreement between the parents is not subject to any public scrutiny. If an agreement is not reached, the dispute will be settled by the courts. Decisions in all custody cases 'shall first and foremost' have regard for the best interests of the child. Regard should be paid to ensuring that the child is not subjected to violence or in any other way treated in such a manner as to impair or endanger his or her physical or mental health.[7] When deciding the child's permanent residence, there are no further statutory guidelines.[8]

As in other countries, a long-standing argument has taken place in Norway as to whether the court ought to rule that the child should reside on an alternate basis with the parents if the parents do not agree on such an arrangement. Up until 2010, the Norwegian courts could not rule that residence should be divided between the parents against the will of one or both of the parents. In 1996 the Ministry of Children and Equality found it inappropriate to create such a general rule which 'took greater account of distributive justice between the parents and thereby impaired the best interest of the child'.[9] The political atmosphere, however, gradually changed in Norway as in many other countries, and a compromise was adopted in 2010.[10] As a main rule, the court must decide that the child shall live permanently with one of the parents, but when 'special reasons so indicate', the court may order an alternating residence for the child even without the parents' agreement.[11] The reason why alternating residence may be imposed only in exceptional cases is the high level of conflict that normally exists in cases that come before the courts. It is therefore unlikely that shared custody will work in practice.[12] According to the preparatory works, certain minimum conditions must be met in order for alternating residence to be imposed against the will of the parents: the parents must live in geographic proximity to each other; the child must be able to maintain contact with friends and pursue leisure activities from both homes; the parents must be able to co-operate well in relation to the child and not have a high level of conflict; and

---

[7]   Children Act 1981, s 48, cf s 36.

[8]   Case-law assigns particular importance to certain factors, such as the child's emotional attachment and the parents' personal qualities, the regard for stability, the risk associated with a change of environment and the regard for the best possible overall parental contact, see IL Backer *Barneloven. Kommentarutgave* (Oslo: Universitetsforlaget, 2nd edn, 2008), pp 337–349.

[9]   Ot prp nr 56 (1996–1997), (Proposition to the Odelsting), p 261 (electronic version).

[10] Preparatory works are Ot prp nr 104 (2008–2009), ch 8 and the Child Law Commission 2008, NOU 2008: 9, ch 10.

[11] Children Act 1981, s 36, second paragraph. The majority of the members in the Child Law Commission had proposed this provision of alternating residence as well, and referred among others to CEFL's (Commission on European Family Law) Principles on parental responsibilities, Principle 3:20, cf K Boele-Woelki et al *Principles of European Family Law Regarding Parental Responsibilities* (Antwerp: Intersentia, 2007) p 130.

[12] Ot prp nr 104 (2008–2009), p 53 and p 72.

the child must feel comfortable with such an arrangement. Imposition of alternating residence is not regarded as reasonably appropriate for children under the age of 7.[13]

(b) Notification of change of residence

At present, disputes related to specific issues concerning the upbringing of the child cannot be resolved by the legal system. The legislators have sought to reduce the number of such conflicts after relationship breakdown by allowing the parent with whom the child lives to make decisions concerning important aspects of the child's care.[14] One of these aspects is the place in the country where the child shall live, and this provision is perceived as discriminatory by many, especially fathers' groups. The reason is that the right of access can be made illusory when a child is moved across great distances inside Norway. After a heated debate, however, the provision was upheld in 2010. It was believed that the resident parent is in the best position to make judgments on whether relocation is an appropriate or necessary decision.[15] An obligation to notify change of residence was adopted instead. If one of the parents wishes to move, and an agreement or decision has been made regarding access, the parent who wants to change residence shall notify the other parent 6 weeks prior to the move at the latest.[16] The rationale behind this notification rule is that it would encourage parents to agree upon a new arrangement, possibly with the help of mediation. Moreover, a 6-week's notice would give the other parent the opportunity to demand a new (interim) decision as to the parent with whom the child should live permanently if he or she believed that relocation was not the child's best interest. The duty to give notice cannot be sanctioned. However, if the other parent demands a new decision regarding the child's permanent residence, failure to notify could be a factor counted to the disadvantage of the resident parent.[17]

(c) Amendments relating to the right of access

The parents are free to make contact arrangements, and such agreements are not subject to any scrutiny by the authorities. The parents shall, however, agree on the right of access based on what they believe to be in the best interests of the child.[18] If an agreement is not reached, the dispute will be settled by the court. When 'ordinary right of access' is agreed or determined without any further explanation or specification, the legislator provides a legal definition.[19] This definition was extended in 2010: 'Ordinary right of access' entitles the parent to spend one afternoon a week with an overnight stay, every other

---

[13] Ot prp nr 104 (2008–2009), pp 72–73.
[14] Children Act 1981, s 37.
[15] Ot prp nr 104 (2008–2009), p 43.
[16] Children Act 1981, s 42, first paragraph.
[17] Ot prp nr 104 (2008–2009), p 45.
[18] Children Act 1981, s 43, first paragraph.
[19] Children Act 1981, s 43, second paragraph.

weekend, a total of 3 weeks of the summer holiday and alternate autumn, Christmas, winter and Easter holidays with the child. (Earlier, the definition read: one afternoon a week, every other weekend, two weeks of the summer holiday, and alternate Christmas and Easter holidays.) It is worth noting that the judge is not bound by this definition when he or she determines the extent of access – the definition applies only if the parents have agreed on 'ordinary right of access'.[20]

Traditionally, children have had little right to access to persons other than parents (for example, grandparents, step-parents, siblings or other relatives). Persons other than the parents may only under certain limited conditions be given a right of access, and such contact may be granted only on condition that the parent has been denied contact or that the parent is deceased.[21] Similarly, no person other than the legal father or mother can obtain parental responsibility, except in the event of the death of a parent and in cases where the child is neglected.[22] Bio-scientific developments, however, have made current the thought of a more differentiated concept of parenthood and parental responsibility, where different people have the status of biological/ genetic, social and legal parents, and where various legal consequences are attached to the different roles. This idea of a more differentiated concept of parenthood was rejected by the Commission on Paternity 2009,[23] but one can see the germ of such a development in the recent amendment of the Adoption Act, where visitation rights for biological parents were established after their child has been adopted in child welfare cases.[24]

Similar access rights for persons who lose paternity in legal proceedings have been proposed, but have not yet been enacted in the Children Act. At present, a man who claims to be the biological father of a child born in marriage may at any time bring an action before the courts relating to paternity. No time-limits exist for the entitlement to institute such legal proceedings.[25] The fact that a

---

[20] Children Act 1981, s 43, second paragraph. In deciding access rights, the statute provides a checklist: importance shall be attached, among other things, to ensuring the best possible overall parental contact, to the age of the child, the degree to which the child is attached to the local neighbourhood, the distance that must be travelled between the parents and the child's interests in all other respects. The decision on the parents' right to access can be enforced by means of a coercive fine, c f Children Act 1981, s 65.

[21] Children Act 1981, s 45. When one or both of the parents are deceased, relatives of the child or persons who are close to the child may request the court to establish whether or not they have right of access to the child, and the extent of such contact. In cases where a right of access of a parent has been denied by the court, the parent in question may request that the court determine whether his or her parents shall have a right of contact with the child. Such contact by grandparents may be granted only on condition that the person who has been denied contact is not allowed to be with the child.

[22] Children Act 1981, s 38 and Child Welfare Act 1992, s 4–20.

[23] NOU 2009: 5, ch 3.9.

[24] Child Welfare Act 1992, s 4–20a (enacted 4 June 2010).

[25] The Children Act 1981, s 6. This provision was the result of law reforms in 1997 and 2002, see P Lødrup 'Challenges to an Established Paternity – Radical Changes in Norwegian Law' in A Bainham (ed) *The International Survey of Family Law* (Jordan Publishing Limited, 2003), pp 353–362.

third party can intrude in this way on an existing family unit and disturb the harmony of an established family relationship has been criticised and found not to be in the best interest of the child. On this background, the Commission on Paternity 2009 proposed reintroduction of time-limits for the parties' entitlement to institute legal proceedings,[26] and proposed that a father deprived of paternity by a court judgment, should be given an opportunity to claim the right of access to the child.[27] The Commission further proposed a new provision giving the child a right to know the identity of his or her biological father without this entailing a change of legal paternity.[28]

Contact rights for pretended parents who are denied adoption in surrogacy cases have also been proposed. As regards maternity, the law expressly states that the woman who gives birth to a child is the child's legal mother. Surrogacy is not permitted in Norway, and an agreement to give birth to a child for another woman is not binding.[29] The Commission on Paternity 2009 maintains that it 'does *not* find it correct to adapt Norwegian statutory provisions concerning parenthood in order to enable residents of Norway to more easily make use of facilities available abroad that are not permitted in Norway'.[30] Thus, if a couple residing in Norway enters into an agreement with a surrogate mother in a foreign country, there is a chance that the parenthood will not be recognised and the child will become stateless. In any case, the transfer of maternity to the non-biological mother is only possible by means of adoption. Surrogacy cases involve difficult and delicate moral and legal issues, and there are no easy answers.[31] However, for the time being, it may appear that surrogate children find themselves in a situation similar to that of illegitimate children during the previous century: Because society has disregard for the way they are conceived, they must bear the burden of society's lack of legal recognition of their family ties.[32] Even if the biological father gains legal recognition, the consequence of this provision is that the child runs the risk of losing the opportunity to live with its social (and genetic) mother. This could be the outcome if the mother did not apply for adoption when returning to Norway, but instead pretended to be the mother, and the couple later divorce. If the legal father then refuses to consent to the mother's adoption, he will remain the only legal parent. Thus the question of parental responsibility and residence will not be decided on the basis of the best interest of the child. On this background the Commission on Paternity 2009 proposed that the mother shall be given an

---

26   NOU 2009: 5, ch 14.
27   NOU 2009: 5, ch 14.7.
28   NOU 2009: 5, chs 14.2 and 14.3, cf pp 139 and 146.
29   Children Act 1981, s 2, cf J Asland 'Norvège' in F Monéger (ed) *Gestation pour autrui – Surrogate motherhood*, Colloque vol 14/International academy of comparative law (Société de législation comparée, 2011) pp 198–200.
30   NOU 2009: 5, ch 1.2, cf pp 101–102.
31   See 'Rapport fra en interdepartemental arbeidsgruppe om håndtering av surrogatisaker' (Report from an Interministerial Working Group on Surrogacy, 28 June 2010) pp 35–40. Norwegian version available at www.regjeringen.no/en/dep/bld/pressesenter/pressemeldinger/2010/anbefaler-a-frarade-bruk-av-surrogatmodr.html?id=610404 (accessed 6 February 2011).
32   See A Singer 'Den moderna reproduktionstekniken – en utmaning för familjerätten' (2008) 6 *Tidsskrift for familierett, arverett og barnevernrettslige spørsmål* 95–106 at 106.

opportunity to institute legal proceedings in order to determine her right of access to the child in such cases.[33] The Commission also proposed a wider access to adoption of stepchildren, but according to the Commission the consent of the legal parent should always remain a prerequisite.[34]

(d) Clarification of the prohibition against the use of violence in the upbringing of children

The law has little to offer when it comes to ensuring children optimal parenting in the family. The Children Act states that parental responsibility shall be exercised on the basis of the child's interests and needs,[35] but only in cases where the child is neglected will the state take action, pursuant to the Child Welfare Act. However, on the issue of physical and psychological punishment of children, both legislators and judges have been active. In 1972, after much political debate, the right of parents to punish children physically was rescinded in Norway. In 1987 punishment of children was expressly prohibited in s 30 of the Children Act, which states: 'The child must not be subjected to violence or in any other way be treated so as to harm or endanger his or her mental or physical health.' Violation of this provision was punishable under penal law, which was illustrated by a Supreme Court decision in 1990, where a father was convicted after having reprimanded his son once by pinching his lip. The father was irritated that his son of 1¾ years had bitten his hand, and the pinch resulted in cuts in the boy's lip. The Supreme Court held that such behaviour was unacceptable and the incident was viewed as a regular violation of the Penal Code 1902, s 228 (assault).[36] However, a Supreme Court decision in 2005 created uncertainty in the interpretation of the provisions. In this case the stepfather was convicted, but the presiding justice held that a 'light smack' in the course of child-rearing should not be punishable (obiter dictum).[37] The government, however, wanted to make it clear that the right of parents to use physical and psychological punishment had been fully eliminated in Norway and the Children Act was therefore amended in 2010. In order to remove all discussion about the interpretation of its provisions, Parliament voted in favour of an addition to the original wording in s 30: 'This shall also apply when violence is carried out in connection with upbringing of the child. Use of violence and frightening or annoying behaviour or other inconsiderate conduct towards the child is prohibited.' Violation is punishable under penal law.[38]

---

[33] NOU 2009: 5, ch 14.7.4.
[34] NOU 2009: 5, pp 94–102.
[35] Children Act 1981, s 30.
[36] Rt 1990 (Supreme Court Reports) p 1155.
[37] Rt 2005 p 1567.
[38] For example the Penal Code 1902, ss 223, 228, 246, 247 and 390a.

III THE LEGAL PROCEDURE REFORM 2003 AND HOW IT WORKED OUT

The legal procedure in custody cases (parental responsibilities, residence and access rights) was reformed in 2003.[39] The aim was to bring more professional expertise into the court at an earlier stage in the process in order to achieve a more targeted process and more durable agreements through the use of alternative dispute resolution models and the use of court-appointed experts in a more flexible manner.[40] The basic assumption has always been that it is in the child's interests that an agreement on custody matters is reached between the parents and that an agreement will provide a better basis for future co-operation between the parents than a court order.[41] One idea behind the reform was that the combination of the solemnity of the court and the assistance of professionals – judges, lawyers and experts – would facilitate the process of finding a solution. The process should thereby be redirected away from biased conflict and more towards the child's needs and the parents' shared experiences in coping with parenting.

After the procedural reform in 2003, experts could attend the preparatory meetings and assist in mediation between the parents both in and out of court.[42] The judges were obliged at every stage of the case to consider whether it was possible to reach a settlement between the parties and make arrangements for this.[43] The court could give the parties the opportunity to try out an interim agreement for a specified period of time, and could also appoint an expert to advise the parents during the trial period.[44] The costs of these initiatives are covered to a certain extent by the state.[45]

The Ministry of Children and Equality wanted to assess the implementation of these changes, and a report from psychologist Katrin Koch was delivered in 2008.[46] The reform has proven successful in several respects. The use of experts

---

[39] Children Act 1981, ss 59–61. The new procedural provisions came into force 1 April 2004.
[40] Ot prp no 29 (2002–2003), chap 1.
[41] On this background, compulsory mediation in the effort to reach an agreement was introduced in Norway 20 years ago, in 1991.Today, married and cohabiting parents with children under 16 years of age who move apart or are considering legal proceedings can be provided up to 7 hours of free mediation, including one compulsory hour, cf the Marriage Act 1991, s 26, the Children Act 1981, s 51. In order to make mediation more flexible and channel resources to the cases where parents could benefit from mediation, the compulsory part of the mediation was reduced in 2007 to one hour (previously 3) while the voluntary part was extended, cf the Mediation Regulation ss 8 and 13. About €1.7m were allocated for payments to mediators in 2007, cf Norway's Fourth Report to the UN Child Committee on the Rights of the Child – 2008, para 195, English version on www.regjeringen.no/en/dep/bld/tema/barn_og_ungdom/fns_barnekonvensjon/norges-rapporter-til-fns-komite-for-barn.html?id=415461 (accessed 4 February 2011).
[42] Children Act 1981, s 61.
[43] Children Act 1981, s 59.
[44] Children Act 1981, s 61, first paragraph, no 7.
[45] Children Act 1981, s 61, second paragraph.
[46] K Koch 'Evaluering av saksbehandlingsreglene for domstolene i barneloven – saker om foreldreansvar, fast bosted og samvær' Report (2008), (An assessment of the legal procedure

increased significantly from about 30% in 2002, to 75% in 2005. One third of all cases that were brought forward went to trial, while the rest were resolved through the new alternative dispute resolution model introduced by the reform. Of the cases brought before the court in 2002, about 65% ended in an in-court settlement – in 2005, after the reform, this number rose to 78%. However, of the cases in 2005 that went as far as to the main hearing, about half were settled and this was the same percentage as before the reform. The main advantage of the reform seemed to be the possibility of introducing interim solutions and professional support in focusing on the child's interests and needs.

The reform was considered by judges, lawyers and experts to be positive; however, certain negative aspects emerged as well. The reform entailed lengthy proceedings and the risk of undue pressure as well as concealment of important information. Even though some cases were less time-consuming than before the implementation of the new rules, the average use of time had not been reduced. The reduction of conflict seemed to be relatively slight and agreed settlements were complied with to a somewhat lesser degree in 2005 than in 2002.

About 1.1 million children are living with their parents in Norway.[47] About 75% of them live with both parents,[48] while 21% live with their mother and 4% with their father.[49] Even though a minority of all child custody cases are brought before the court, the numbers are increasing. In 2007 around 2,200 child custody cases were brought before the district courts (first instance in Norway), which accounted for 17% of all the incoming civil cases to the district courts.[50] Between 2001 and 2006, the number of custody cases increased by about 50%, and a substantial part of this increase could be related to the introduction of the procedural law reform.[51] Even though many disputes are settled in court, these settlements have not proven to be any more durable than the settlements under the previous system. Time-consuming court cases and parents returning to the court to have their cases heard a second or a third time are commonplace. Furthermore, the mixing of roles is problematic – the role of mediator prior to the case and then the role of expert witness in the legal proceedings are difficult to reconcile.

---

reform with summary in English), at www.regjeringen.no/en/dep/bld/dok/rapporter_planer/rapporter/2008/evaluering-av-saksbehandlingsreglene-for.html?id=503721 (accessed 4 February 2011).

[47] Official numbers 2010 from 'Statistics Norway', cf www.ssb.no/english/subjects/02/01/20/barn_en (accessed May 2011).

[48] 57% with married parents and 18% with cohabiting parents.

[49] See www.ssb.no/english/subjects/02/01/20/barn_en (accessed May 2011).

[50] St meld nr 26 (2008–2009) Om offentleg rettshjelp (Report to the Storting on public legal assistance), ch 11.1 (estimated number).

[51] K Koch 'Evaluering av saksbehandlingsreglene for domstolene i barneloven – saker om foreldreansvar, fast bosted og samvær' Report (2008), (An assessment of the legal procedure reform with summary in English), at www.regjeringen.no/en/dep/bld/dok/rapporter_planer/rapporter/2008/evaluering-av-saksbehandlingsreglene-for.html?id=503721 (accessed 4 February 2011).

In three quarters of the child custody cases, at least one of the parties received free legal aid, and more than 60% of government expenditure on legal aid was spent on child custody cases.[52] The question has been raised as to whether it is in the child's best interest that the government covers the costs when the parents present the case for a second hearing, often with negligible modifications of the original decision.[53] Moreover, the current regulations might seem unfair to the parents who fall outside the scheme. New regulations with less harsh threshold effects have therefore been proposed.[54]

IV CONCLUDING REMARKS

Equality has a strong footing in Norwegian legal heritage, and the objective of 'equal parenthood' has a favourable wind behind it. Child law has become an important arena for gender policy, and the final word has not yet been spoken in this respect. However, there is also significant awareness of the dangers of 'juridification' of private life, and the fact that children are harmed by being subjected to conflicts between the parents. Efforts to develop both procedural and substantive provisions that could prevent and ease conflict will therefore be given high priority in Norway in the years to come.

---

[52] Numbers are for 2007; cf St meld 26 (2008–2009) Om offentleg rettshjelp (Report to the Storting on public legal assistance), ch 11.4.1 and ch 11.1.

[53] Access to the court is fairly good in child custody cases. The state covers the costs of mediators and of certain experts. In addition the scheme of free legal aid would help many parents with low incomes and little capital (apart from capital tied up in the family home). People with low income will receive free legal advice and have their lawyer's expenses and court costs covered. The upper income threshold is €30,750 per year for a single person to qualify for free legal aid, cf Legal Aid Act 1980, cf Legal Aid Regulation, FOR-2005–12–12–1443 s 1–1. However, there are still financial risks involved in litigation, since the court is empowered to order the losing party to pay the other's legal costs, and these expenses are normally not covered by the legal aid scheme.

[54] St meld nr 26 (2008–2009), ch 11.4.2.

Samoa

ADOPTION AND 'VAE TAMA' IN SAMOA

*Jennifer Corrin and Lalotoa Mulitalo**

Résumé

Les tensions entre le droit coutumier et le droit étatique sont particulièrement nombreuses dans le domaine du droit de la famille, en raison de l'influence qu'exercent la coutume et la culture sur celui-ci. À partir de l'exemple de l'adoption aux Samoa, cet exposé s'intéresse aux conséquences du pluralisme juridique sur le droit familial de la région du Pacifique. Après avoir brossé à grands traits le tableau de la culture et du droit des Samoa, le texte traite de l'adoption coutumière ainsi que des dispositions légales en matière d'adoption, celles qui existaient avant la récente réforme législative et celles qui prévalent aujourd'hui. L'auteur analyse également la jurisprudence en la matière. Il discute des questions que suscite le régime actuel avant de conclure par quelques propositions de réforme.

I INTRODUCTION

Like many other former colonies, Samoa has in place a complex system of legal pluralism. Since independence, customary law is formally recognised as a general source of law,[1] with a place in the hierarchy of state laws. However, legislation rarely makes any concessions for customary law. Law reform in Samoa and other Pacific island countries has, at least until quite recently, tended to rely on overseas models, without taking account of local culture and practices. Any consultation has tended to be based on an agenda developed from the basis of transplanted ideas and precedents.

The tension between customary law and state law is often particularly acute in the area of family law, where the influence of custom and culture is strong. One area of family law which has, until quite recently, received very little attention in the Pacific is adoption. Most adoptions in Samoa take place within the extended family according to customary law and practice. However, there are still a considerable number of formal adoptions; in 2000 about 70 children were

---

* Jennifer Corrin is Director of the Centre for International, Public and Comparative Law and Associate Professor in the TC Beirne School of Law at the University of Queensland.
Lalotoa Mulitalo is former Parliamentary Counsel of Samoa and a PhD student at the University of Queensland.

[1] See Constitution of the Independent State of Western Samoa 1960 ('Constitution of Samoa 1960'), arts 111 and 114.

adopted by overseas adopters.[2] Between 2000 and 2005 there were about 76 overseas adoptions.[3] By 2010, whilst the number of formal adoptions had risen to 651, only one was an overseas adoption.

In spite of the critical importance of providing strong safeguards for all concerned, many countries in the region have relied on introduced legislation or enacted provisions based on foreign legislation. Such legislation has not always provided the necessary protection nor has it always served to accommodate local values or practices and in many cases it is incompatible with the local values and practices. In 2005, the unfortunate death of a child awaiting adoption by overseas adopters focused attention on the formal adoption regime in Samoa and provided a tragic example of the perils of failure to have a rigorous adoption process in place to govern this regime.[4] It also demonstrates the inadequacy of a Western legal transplant imposed on Samoa in 1961[5] to deal with the issues relating to formal adoptions and adoption agencies (which are themselves quite alien to Samoa), arising some 50 years later.

This chapter looks at the consequences of the lack of coherence in Pacific family law in the context of adoption in Samoa. Commencing with a brief outline of Samoa's cultural and legal background, it looks at customary adoption. It then analyses the statutory provisions for adoption both before and after the recent amendments to the law and considers the relevant case-law. The issues arising from the current regime are discussed and some suggestions for reform are put forward.

II CULTURAL CONTEXT

Samoa, known formerly as Western Samoa,[6] has a population of about 182,000 and lies about half way between Hawaii and New Zealand.[7] Samoa has been inhabited by Polynesian people since before 1000 BC.[8] Before European contact, community rules were pronounced orally by traditional leaders of individual groups, influenced largely by the community's response to the environment. Communities operated autonomously and conducted their affairs independently. They engaged in warfare with other groups in order to assume control of land and exert their authority. In 1881, Malietoa, urged on by foreign influences, whose interests were served by having a single, central government authority, proclaimed himself as paramount chief and king of

---

[2] XIII Parliament of Samoa, Interpretation of Debates, Session V, vol 1, 772.

[3] Pound Pup Legacy cites this as the figure revealed by District Court records: 'A Brief Outline of Customary Child Adoption Practices in Samoa', 21 September 2005, available at http://poundpuplegacy.org/node/30038 (accessed 15 March 2011).

[4] Samoa (Constitution Amendment) Act (No 2) 1997.

[5] Infants Ordinance 1961.

[6] Samoa (Constitution Amendment) Act (No 2) 1997.

[7] It consists of two main islands, Savai'i and Upolu, as well as seven small islets. It has a land area of 2,934 sq km and a population of approximately 214,000.

[8] George Turner *Samoa: a Hundred Years Ago and Long Before* (Institute of Pacific Studies, University of the South Pacific (reprint), 1884).

Samoa.[9] King Malietoa issued laws that applied throughout the whole country.[10] However, individual, village-based communities, of which there are about 330, are still strong. Each village is made up of several *aiga*. The meaning of the term *aiga* is well explained by Te'o:[11]

> '[T]he term Aiga as used in the Samoan sense includes not only the immediate family, father, mother and children, but also the whole union of families of a clan and even those who although not related are yet subject to the family control.'

Village communities are divided into 11 traditional districts,[12] ranging in size from a few *aiga* to much larger groups. Within each village, the *aiga* wields power in proportion to the size of the family group. At the head of each *aiga* is the *matai* who has authority over all its affairs. Village societies are governed by a complex code of social rules. Each village has a *fono* (council) made up of the *matai* (chiefly head), as representatives of their *aiga*. The *fono* is responsible for governing village affairs but the church is a strong influence in the village and is the focus of social life.[13]

The Samoan concept of family is very different from the Western understanding of the term. In the Samoan setting, family is the institution that shapes and determines a person's future. The family into which they are born determines their status and duties in the village, as well as the extent of entitlement to customary land.[14] One of the many unique features of a Samoan family is that a person born to a Samoan mother or Samoan parents is automatically entitled to some customary land and family property. There is a Samoan saying '*O oe ma lou aiga*' which translates to 'you and your family', meaning that whatever a person does reflects on their whole family. If a person excels, this enhances the reputation of their family; if they go astray, it is not only they who are disgraced but their whole family. The whole family also pays the penalty for the person's wrongdoings. Having no family is unknown in Samoa and the term 'orphan' is just as foreign.

The national government has superimposed legislative authority on village governments, with a view to building bridges between national and traditional sectors. The village *fono* has been endorsed by legislation, although this step has arguably had some negative consequences.[15] Further, each village is

---

9   Jennifer Corrin and Don Paterson *Introduction to South Pacific Law* (3rd edn, Palgrave MacMillan, 2011) in press.

10 *Sia'aga v OF Nelson Properties Ltd* (unreported, Court of Appeal, Samoa, Baragwanath, Slicer, Fisher JJA, 19 September 2008) accessible via www.paclii.org at [2008] WSCA 14.

11 Tuvale Te'o 'The Constitution of the Samoan Family' available at www.nzetc.org/tm/scholarly/tei-TuvAcco-t1-body1-d26.html (accessed 23 February 2011).

12 Since independence, Samoa has been divided into 41 territorial constituencies for election purposes: Constitution of Samoa, art 44. The boundaries are set out in the Territorial Constituencies Act 1963.

13 About 47% of the population belongs to the Congregational Christian Church of Samoa, while the Roman Catholic and Methodist Churches each account for 20% of the population.

14 About 80% of the land is customary.

15 See further, Stephanie Lawson *Tradition Versus Democracy in the South Pacific: Fiji, Tonga and Western Samoa* (Cambridge: Cambridge University Press, 1996); Jennifer Corrin Care 'A

required to nominate a *Sui o le Nuu*,[16] who is then appointed by the Minister to carry out certain duties under the Internal Affairs Act.[17] The *Sui o le Nuu* is required to assist the government to implement its policies in the village and to complete local and national projects. More particularly, they are under a duty to promote harmony in their village; encourage the maintenance of law and order; carry out economically viable development projects, which are also culturally and environmentally sensitive; encourage village cleanliness and beautification; and assist government officials to conduct surveys, research and debt collection.[18] Since 2004, Government Women Representatives, known as *Sui o le Malo*, have also been appointed under the Internal Affairs Act. The *Sui o le Malo* comprises of women representatives from each village and is the women's equivalent of the *Sui o le Nuu*. Like the *Sui o le Nuu*, the *Sui o le Malo* are the mediators between government and village programmes and policy level action. Both the *Sui o le Nuu* and *Sui o le Malo* represent the village on national committees. The welfare of children in the village is one of the general concerns of the *Sui o le Nuu* and *Sui o le Malo*.

III   SAMOA'S LEGAL SYSTEM

(a)   Historical development and sources of law

In 1989, the British, Germans and Americans signed the Final Act of the Conference of the Affairs of Samoa, which, subject to the assent of King Malietoa, which was given on 19 April 1890, established a Land Commission, a Supreme Court and the office of Chief Justice in Samoa, with responsibilities including the settlement of all land disputes. In 1900, Samoa became a German colony. In 1914, after the outbreak of World War I, New Zealand assumed control of Samoa. This arrangement was continued after the Second World War, when New Zealand was authorised to administer Samoa as a United Nations trust territory. The foreigners brought with them their own laws and dispute resolution mechanisms and enacted 'colonial' laws to deal with local matters. Decrees were made by the German Governor between 1900 and 1914. These were substantially repealed by the Samoa Constitution Order 1920 (NZ), which applied the common law of England to Samoa.[19] However, custom was retained as the law governing rights to customary titles and land[20] and the validity of marriages prior to 1921.[21]

In 1962, Samoa became the first Pacific Island country to gain independence. Samoa retained its pluralistic legal system, with customary law operating

---

Green Stick or a Fresh Stick: Locating Customary Penalties in the Post-Colonial Era' (2006) 6(1) *Oxford University Commonwealth Law Journal* 27.

16   The Internal Affairs Amendment Act 2010 amended the term *Pulenuu* to *Sui o le Nuu*. The definition and duties remain the same.
17   Internal Affairs Act (Samoa) 1995, s 14.
18   Internal Affairs Act (Samoa) 1995, s 15.
19   See also the Samoa Act 1921 (NZ).
20   Samoa Act 1921 (NZ), s 278 and Samoan Land and Titles Ordinance 1934, s 37.
21   Samoa Act 1921 (NZ), s 372.

alongside state law.[22] State law consists of the Constitution; Ordinances made by the Administrator and later by the High Commissioner prior to independence ('colonial legislation');[23] and legislation enacted by Parliament or made under delegated authority after independence. State law also includes common law made by the Samoan courts.[24] In addition to these locally made laws, English legislation in force in Samoa at independence in 1962[25] and some specific New Zealand Acts continued to apply after independence but, with a few exceptions, these have since been repealed.[26] English common law and equity remains in force if not excluded by any other law and so far as applicable to the circumstances of Samoa.[27]

Unfortunately, the precise relationship between the different sources of law, both local and foreign, is not always clear.[28] Whilst the Constitution states that it is the supreme law[29] and appears to suggest that legislation is next in importance, a hierarchical approach does not reflect the importance that society gives to customary law. Nor is the relationship between customary law and common law and equity straightforward.[30] The Constitution states that, unless otherwise provided or demanded by the context, the law includes common law and equity to the extent it is 'not excluded by any other law in force in Samoa, and any custom or usage which has acquired the force of law in Samoa or any part thereof under the provisions of any Act or under a judgment of a Court of competent jurisdiction'. This suggests that, once custom has acquired the force of law, it will be applied in preference to common law and equity. However, the provision also suggests that custom will not be recognised by law unless and until incorporated in legislation or declared to be law by a court.[31] No indication is given of the criteria to be applied by a

---

[22] See Constitution of Samoa 1960, arts 2, 100, 111 and 114.

[23] During the period of German Administration Proclamations were made by the Governor. Germany renounced rights in respect of Samoa by the Treaty of Peace 1919. Regulations were made by the Military Administrator of Samoa until 1920 when the Council of the League of Nations mandated power to administer Samoa to New Zealand.

[24] See further, Jennifer Corrin Care *Civil Procedure and Courts in the South Pacific* (Cavendish, 2005) pp 32, 37–38.

[25] Constitution of Samoa 1960, art 114.

[26] By 1977, only one British Act of Parliament (the Wills Act 1837 (UK)), and three New Zealand Acts of Parliament (Bankruptcy Act 1908; Companies Act 1955; and Property Law Act 1952), and ss 360, 362 and 367 of Samoa Act 1921, were stated to be in force: see notes to *Reprint of Statutes Act 1972* in Revised Statutes of Samoa 1977. Wills Act 1837 (UK) and Companies Act 1955 (NZ) have since been repealed: Wills Act 1975 (Samoa); Companies Act 2001 (Samoa), s 352.

[27] Constitution of Samoa 1960, art 111(1); Samoa Act 1921 (NZ), s 349 (1).

[28] Jennifer Corrin and Don Paterson *Introduction to South Pacific Law* (3rd edn, Palgrave MacMillan, 2011) in press, chapters 2 and 3.

[29] Constitution of Samoa 1960, art 2(1).

[30] Jennifer Corrin and Don Paterson, *Introduction to South Pacific Law* (3rd edn, Palgrave MacMillan, 2011) in press.

[31] See further, Jennifer Corrin and Don Paterson *Introduction to South Pacific Law* (3rd edn, Palgrave MacMillan, 2011) in press, chaps 2 and 3.

court in deciding whether to recognise a custom as law. The limited case-law on this point appears to suggest that a custom will not be applied if it is contrary to common law notions of justice.[32]

(b)   The state family law regime

The state legal system includes a number of statutes governing family matters.[33] Legislation governing marriage, divorce and financial provision includes the Marriage Ordinance 1961; the Divorce and Matrimonial Causes Ordinance 1961; and the Maintenance and Affiliation Act 1961. This legislation, dating from just before independence, is foreign to the local setting and had become very outdated. In response to the need for reform, the Divorce and Matrimonial Causes Amendment Act 2010 and the Maintenance and Affiliation Amendment Act 2010 introduced significant changes. Whilst these reforms constitute a significant improvement, the legislation still does not constitute a coherent regime; nor does it take account of local culture.

Common law and equity also form an important part of family law, particularly in relation to matrimonial property.[34] As mentioned earlier, customary law is particularly strong in relation to family matters. This gives rise to tensions between customary and state laws, which are exacerbated by the lack of clarity concerning the interrelationship between the two, which is discussed above.

(c)   Adoption law

(i)   Customary adoption law

Customary 'adoption' has always been a common occurrence in Samoa. However, such adoption is very different from the Western notion of adoption. In fact, it is so different that it has to be questioned whether it is appropriate to use the term adoption at all. It is difficult to equate 'adoption' in the Western sense to 'customary adoption' given the substantive differences in the rationale that supports it and the spirit in which it takes place. Certainly, where the state process involves an application by strangers to become adoptive parents of a child, severing relationships with all blood relations, there is no Samoan equivalent. Where a child is given into the care of another under custom, this does not sever the ties with the biological parents. It is taken for granted that the child remains the child of the biological parents and may even return to the care of the biological parents at a future date. Customary adoption is underpinned by cultural structures. One of the prime influences shaping customary adoption is the concept of *aiga*, which, as discussed above, differs

---

32   *Mose v Mosame* [1930–49] WSLR 140. See also Jennifer Corrin and Don Paterson *Introduction to South Pacific Law* (3rd edn, Palgrave MacMillan, 2011) in press, ch 3.

33   Marriage Act 1961 (Samoa); Marriage Ordinance 1961 (Samoa); Maintenance and Affiliation Act 1967 (Samoa); and Divorce and Matrimonial Causes Ordinance 1961 (Samoa).

34   Jennifer Corrin and Don Paterson *Introduction to South Pacific Law* (3rd edn, Palgrave MacMillan, 2011) in press, ch 7.

considerably from the Western notion of family. Generally, customary adoption is a transparent process, with no secrecy attached and the ties with the natural parents are not severed. As Brown notes in the context of Melanesia:[35]

'A crucial distinction between the customary and western adoption paradigms is that the former is a private inter-family arrangement whereas an integral characteristic of the latter is the public element inherent in its subjection to state control. This is manifested by the necessity for a judicial order of approval and the essential involvement of social caseworker investigation . . . The principle in non-customary systems that adoptions severs the biological family and creates a new family has no real imperative in custom where the dominant motives are to maintain family links, assist childless kinfolk or invest a successor.'

The Samoan term for a child not raised by the biological parents is *tama fai*, which literally translated means 'child made', and the process is called *vae tama* which translates to 'separating the child'. In the Samoan setting, reference to *tama fai* is commonly understood to mean that the child's parents are not the biological parents of the child, but are related to the natural mother or father of the child. It is also understood that there are *aiga* reasons for this arrangement. Historically, it has been said that Samoans resorted to adoption as part of ceremonial exchange; to replenish human resources, usually in the event of failure to produce heirs; or to lay a claim to a higher noble title.[36] Nowadays, the main reasons for adoption include the fact that a couple cannot bear children; or to give an unmarried sister or brother a child to call their own. A *vae tama* often takes place where one or both natural parents have a large number of children, in contrast with the adopting relative, who has few or none.

Until recently, the process of obtaining a *tama fai* was informal. Arrangements were made between the members of the nuclear or extended family. There was no reference to the introduced law and no written formalities; it was understood that the child would remain the child of the biological parents, and a member of the extended family as a whole.[37] Until recently, these arrangements were common within families and there was no concern about issues of identity of the child. The validity of such arrangements was rarely, if ever, contested. Rather, they fitted in with the everyday lives of Samoans and the fabric of their society. In the early Samoa, there is no child without a family, and no person without a family.

In Samoa today adopters are still predominantly relatives of the child's mother or father. Adoption by foreigners is much less common. For example, in 2010,

---

[35]   K Brown *Reconciling Customary Law and Received Law in Melanesia: the Post-Independence Experience in Solomon Islands and Vanuatu* (Darwin: Charles Darwin University Press, 2005) pp 142–143.

[36]   Unasa L F Vaá 'Samoan Custom and Human Rights: An Indigenous View' (2009) 40 VUWLR 237, 241.

[37]   'A Brief Outline of Customary Child Adoption Practices in Samoa' available at http://poundpuplegacy.org/node/30038 (accessed 15 march 2011).

out of a total of 651 adoptions only one was an overseas adoption.[38] However, with the move away from subsistence living towards a cash economy and with increased mobility there has been a change in community priorities. There has been an emphasis on formal education and tertiary studies, which are more readily accessible overseas, and on cash income, which has motivated the search for overseas work with higher salaries. The lack of international recognition of customary adoption means that formal adoption is required if adopted children are to travel overseas, for example, to New Zealand, to be cared for by overseas *aiga*.[39]

(ii)   State adoption law

Prior to colonisation adoption in the Western sense was unknown. Customary 'adoption' was governed solely by customary law. This continued to be the position during the colonial era, until 1931, when the General Laws Ordinance was passed. However, whilst there was no local legislation on point before that time, 'the law of England as existing on the fourteenth day of January eighteen hundred and forty' was stated to be in force,[40] in addition to certain named Acts of the New Zealand Parliament.[41] No New Zealand Acts relating to adoption were named, so the only question is whether there was an English adoption Act prior to 14 January 1840, which applied in Samoa. Any such legislation would have to be assessed for conformity with the proviso on the application of English legislation, which provided, amongst other things, that such legislation would only apply if applicable to the circumstances of Samoa.[42] In fact, there was no English statute on adoption prior to 1840, the first such Act being the Adoption of Children Act 1926. Accordingly, it is not necessary to consider the question of applicability.

In 1931, s 25 of the General Laws Ordinance 1931 was introduced to govern adoption. That section provided that on an application to what was then High Court (now the Supreme Court) by any person of good repute, an order of adoption of a child could be made in his or her favour.

In 1961, shortly before independence, the relevant sections of the General Laws Ordinance were repealed by the Infants Ordinance.[43] Part II, which governs adoption, is based on the New Zealand Adoption Act 1955.[44] In relation to potential applicants or the relationship between the applicants and an infant, the Ordinance takes no account of local culture; nor does it make any mention of the common practice of interfamilial adoption. It empowers the court,

---

[38] Obtained upon request from the Ministry of Justice and Courts Administration January 2011.
[39] *Devoe v Attorney-General* (unreported, Court of Appeal, Samoa, Vaai J, 14 September 2007), accessible via www.paclii.org at [2007] WSCA 5.
[40] Samoa Act 1921 (NZ), s 349(1).
[41] Samoa Act 1921 (NZ), s 351.
[42] Samoa Act 1921 (NZ), s 349(1).
[43] 1961, Sch.
[44] *Re Application for Adoption by Solomona* (unreported, District Court, Samoa, Vaai J, 1 January 1999), accessible via www.paclii.org at [1999] WSDC 1.

which is defined to mean the District Court,[45] to make an adoption order in respect of an infant, which is defined to mean a person under 21.[46] Application may be made by any person (whether domiciled in Western Samoa or not).[47] Orders may be made in favour of individuals[48] or jointly in favour of spouses,[49] and it is specifically provided that the mother or father of the infant might apply together with their spouse.[50]

Before making an adoption order the court must be satisfied that:

(a) the applicant is of good repute and a fit and proper person to have the care and custody of the infant and has 'sufficient ability to bring up, maintain, and educate the infant';[51]

(b) the welfare and interests of the infant will be promoted by the adoption;

(c) if the infant is over the age of 12 years, he or she consents to the adoption; and

(d) any parents living at the date of the hearing of the application (or if both parents were dead any legal guardian of the infant) consent to the order of adoption.

However, the court may dispense with the consent of a person who is permanently absent from Samoa, incapable of giving consent, or is for any reason unfit to have the custody or control of the infant or, in the case of a parent, has deserted the infant.[52]

Infants are defined in the Ordinance as meaning any person under the age of 21 years,[53] so, although this is not specified as a requirement, the court must also be satisfied that the adoptee is under 21. There is no requirement that the adoptee be resident or domiciled in Samoa. This question was discussed in *Re Solomona*,[54] where the District Court held that it had no jurisdiction to make an adoption order in relation to a child who was not domiciled in Samoa at the time of the application for adoption. However, this decision was reversed on appeal.[55]

---

45 Infants Ordinance 1961, s 2, as amended by the District Courts Amendment Act 1992/3.
46 Infants Ordinance 1961, s 2.
47 Infants Ordinance 1961, s 7.
48 Infants Ordinance 1961, s 7(4).
49 Infants Ordinance 1961, s 7(2).
50 Infants Ordinance 1961, s 7(3).
51 Infants Ordinance 1961, s 8(a).
52 Infants Ordinance 1961, s 8, Proviso.
53 Infants Ordinance 1961, s 2.
54 Unreported, District Court, Apia, Vaai J, 1 January 1999, available via www.paclii.org at [1999] WSDC 1.
55 *Re S and M* (unreported, Supreme Court, Samoa, Sapolu CJ, 16 June 2000), available via www.paclii.org at [2000] WSSC 42.

The Act prohibits giving or receiving any payment or reward in respect of an adoption, except with the consent of the court.[56] The consequences of breach of this provision are not stated but, presumably, the court would refuse to make an order if it became aware of any such payment or reward. This is discussed further under the issues section below in Part IV(f).

The Act goes on to state the consequences of an adoption order, which has the effect of:

(a) conferring the name of the adopting parent on the adopted infant with such proper or Christian name as the court might fix;

(b) deeming the infant to be born in lawful wedlock of the adopting parent;

(c) conferring on the infant all legal and equitable liabilities, rights, benefits, privileges and consequences of the natural relation of parent and child;[57]

(d) deeming the adopting parent to be the parent of the adopted infant and to be subject to all liabilities affecting such infant as if he or she were their natural child born during their marriage;[58] and

(e) terminating all the rights and legal responsibilities and incidents existing between the infant and his or her natural parents except the right of the infant to inherit property as heir or next of kin of the natural parents directly or by right of representation.[59]

This last provision, which is contained in s 10(2), has been interpreted by the Samoan courts to apply only to legitimate children.[60]

The Act also makes it clear that adoption will not:

(a) confer any right, title, or interest in property which would devolve on the issue of the adopting parent by virtue of any instrument made prior to the date of the adoption order, unless the instrument expressly states this; nor

(b) confer a right to any property expressly limited to the heirs of the body of the adopting parent nor property from the lineal or collateral relatives of that parent by right of representation; nor

---

[56] Infants Ordinance 1961, s 9.
[57] Infants Ordinance 1961, s 9.
[58] Infants Ordinance 1961, s 10(2).
[59] Infants Ordinance 1961, s 10(2).
[60] *Stowers v Stowers* (unreported, Supreme Court, Samoa, Sapolu CJ, 14 June 2010) accessible via www.paclii.org at [2010] WSSC 30.

(c)   confer a right to any property vested or to become vested in any child of a marriage of the adopting parent in the case of the intestacy of such child or other than a right devolved directly through such adopting parent.[61]

The Act also provides for the adoption order to be varied or discharged on such terms and conditions as it thinks fit.[62] The effect of this is that, subject to any court order to the contrary, the infant and its natural parents are deemed to be restored to the same position as they were in immediately before the adoption order was made. This is subject to a provision that discharge of the order does not affect anything done while the order was in force.[63] The District Court was called on to decide whether it had jurisdiction to discharge an order of adoption relating to an adoptee who was over 21. The court answered this question in the affirmative.[64]

Part II of the Infants Ordinance was amended in 2005 to make special provision for overseas adoptions and, in particular, to govern the establishment of overseas adoption agencies in Samoa. This move followed the scandal created by the death of the child awaiting adoption in the care of an unauthorised overseas adoption agency in Apia.[65] The adoption agency was one of two established without approval in Apia and was the only one operated by an expatriate. This American agency, Focus on Children, negotiated with a relatively small number of Samoan parents for their children to be adopted by overseas adopters. The agency carried out the process of adoption under the Act and made the handover arrangements.

The 2005 amendments left all the existing provisions referred to above intact, but the amending Act inserted two new sections in Part II. It also inserted definitions of 'adoption agency', 'citizen' and 'overseas adoption'. The first new provision, s 7A, provides that a court may not make an adoption order in favour of adopters who are not citizens of Samoa,[66] until it has received a certificate from the Attorney-General certifying that there:

'(a)   is no one suitable in Samoa who is willing and able to provide for the care, support and welfare of the child in question; and
(b)   are no other suitable arrangements which can be made for the care, support and welfare of the child in Samoa.'

The new section also requires all persons involved with the child and the overseas adoption, 'including but not limited to any parent, guardian, relative, carer or teacher of the infant, any adopting parent applicant, and any solicitor,

---

61   Infants Ordinance 1961, s 10(1).
62   Infants Ordinance 1961, s 11(1).
63   Infants Ordinance 1961, s 11(2).
64   *Re Utumapu* (unreported, District Court, Apia, Nelson DCJ, 30 November 2004) available via www.paclii.org at [2004] WSDC 6.
65   Infants (Adoption) Amendment Act 2005. See further TVNZ 'Death Prompts Samoan Adoption Change' 27 June 2005 available at http://tvnz.co.nz/view/page/411424/594334 (accessed 10 November 2010).
66   'Overseas adoption' is defined by the amended s 2.

medical practitioner, nurse social worker or other health care professional' to provide such information and assistance as the Attorney-General may require to discharge his duty to carry out the certification exercise. A penalty is imposed for failure to do so.[67]

Due to the communal nature of the *aiga* in the Samoan society, s 7A effectively prevents Samoan children from being adopted by foreigners. The section does not extend to Samoan citizens living overseas, who will still be able to adopt. In practice, the amendment results in familial adoption being the only practical adoption process in Samoa.

Section 9A deals with regulation of adoption agencies. It prohibits the operation of an adoption agency without the prior written authorisation of the Attorney-General.[68] Such authorisation may be provided if the Attorney-General is satisfied that the applicant is suitably qualified and experienced; is a fit and proper person; and has complied, or will comply with the Adoption Agency Code of Conduct (the Code of Conduct). Provision for the Code of Conduct is made in s 9A(4), which empowers the Head of State, acting on the advice of Cabinet, who in turn must consult with and take into account any advice from the Court and the Attorney-General, to establish a code to regulate the actions and conduct of adoption agencies. A code has been drafted, but is yet to be finalised. The Attorney-General may revoke his or her authorisation at any time if of the opinion that the conditions on which it was granted are no longer being met.[69] Section 9A also puts a duty on any adoption agency and any person acting on behalf of that agency to comply with any Code of Conduct. Failure to do so is an offence punishable by a fine of up to 1000 penalty units or imprisonment of up to 2 years, or both.[70] The specification of penalties in ss 7A and 9A is in contrast to s 9, which prohibits payment in consideration of adoption but, as mentioned above, fails to state a penalty for this.

The 2005 Act was accompanied by the Infants (Adoption) Regulations 2006, which came into force on 17 July 2006. The regulations lay down the procedure for applying to be recognised as an adoption agency[71] and for obtaining the Attorney-General's certificate of approval.[72] In both cases, the duty to administer the process is conferred on the Chief Executive Officer of the Ministry of Justice and Courts Administration.[73] The regulations also contain the prescribed forms for both applications, which must be completed as statutory declarations.[74] If the Attorney-General considers that further

---

[67]   Section 7A(4). The penalty is 10 penalty units.
[68]   Section 9A(1).
[69]   Section 9A(4).
[70]   Section 9A(5).
[71]   Infants (Adoption) Regulations 2006, regs 5 and 6.
[72]   Infants (Adoption) Regulations 2006, regs 5 and 6.
[73]   Infants (Adoption) Regulations 2006, Parts 2 and 3.
[74]   Infants (Adoption) Regulations 2006, Schs 1 and 2.

investigation is warranted, he or she may appoint any person as an investigator including a social worker, psychologist, medical practitioner, or police officer.[75]

With regard to common law and equity, this is not relevant to the creation of an adoptive relationship, which is a creature of statute. The common law provides no means of extinguishing the rights of natural parents.[76] However, it is relevant to the interpretation of adoption legislation and insofar as it sheds any light on the court's approach to the exercise of any discretion under the legislation. The limited case-law on this point is referred to in the relevant parts of this chapter.

IV ISSUES CONCERNING ADOPTION

As is common in pluralistic societies, there are areas in which introduced laws and concepts do not fit in well. One of the reasons is that an introduced law may not be compatible with customary practices of an indigenous society, particularly if the law is not supported by the local infrastructure. For Samoa, it must adhere to legal formal adoption if it is to keep up with the changing global environment.

(a) Absence of a Code of Conduct

As mentioned above, s 9A(4) requires the Head of State, acting on the advice of Cabinet to establish an Adoption Agency Code of Conduct (Code of Conduct) to facilitate the proper regulation of adoption agencies. To date this has not been accomplished, although a draft is under consideration. Although the requirement for the Head of State to establish a Code of Conduct is phrased in permissive, rather than mandatory terms, compliance with the Code of Conduct is one of the matters that the Attorney-General must be satisfied of in order to issue an authorisation to an adoption agency. Further, the regulations require an applicant for such authorisation to certify that he or she has 'read, understood and is committed to abide by the Code of Conduct'.[77] In the light of these requirements, it is arguable that the lack of a code renders the amended scheme unworkable.

In practice, the Attorney-General has issued authorisation to certain Samoan law firms to act on behalf of overseas adopters. The two unauthorised adoption agencies, whose activities led to the 2005 Amendments, have ceased to operate. It appears there has been no attempt to apply for authorisation to act and operate as an adoption agency, other than from local law firms, and this probably explains the lack of pressure for finalisation of the Code.

---

[75] Infants (Adoption) Regulations 2006, reg 6 and note to Regulations.

[76] JJ Jackson (ed) *Rayden's Law and Practice in Divorce and Family Matters in All Courts* (Butterworths, 10th edn, 1979) para 1138; *Brooks v Blunt* [1923] 1 KB 257.

[77] Infants (Adoption) Regulations 2006, Sch 1, [F].

(b)   Attorney-General

As outlined above, the task of considering requests to act as an adoption
agency has been given to the Attorney-General. He or she is also charged with
assessing whether a certificate for overseas adoption should be granted. The
Attorney-General is appointed by the Head of State, acting on the advice of
the Prime Minister, from persons qualified to be a judge of the Supreme Court
of Samoa.[78] His or her constitutional role is to advise the government 'on legal
matters' and 'to institute, conduct or discontinue any proceedings for an
offence' at his or her discretion,[79] and 'has a right of audience in', and takes
'precedence over any other person appearing before, any Court or tribunal'.
The assessment role allocated by the Act is an unusual one for the most senior
legal officer or officers acting under him or her.[80] The Attorney-General and
the other lawyers in the office are highly trained in legal matters rather than the
social work skills required to assess the information that is to be provided
under the regulations. However, as the office is almost entirely staffed by local
lawyers, they do have the local and cultural knowledge to make the relevant
decisions, such as, for example, as to suitability of arrangements 'for the care,
support and welfare of the infant'.[81]

(c)   Lack of consultation

Another criticism of the 2005 amendments is the lack of consultation with the
community. Many people were unaware of the changes and had not been asked
their opinion on them at any time. The regulations require the applicant for a
certificate for overseas adoption to provide information about any suitable
arrangement available in Samoa for the care, support and welfare of the
adoptee. One source from which information is to be obtained is the *Sui o le
Nuu*[82] of the village where the infant resided at the time of the request, and
another suggested source is the *Sui o le Malo* in the village. However, there
appears to have been no formal consultation with either of these groups before
the changes were made. This lack of consultation has left them uninformed;
many of them do not even know that these laws exist. Nor have these
government-endorsed, village officers been given any information about the
laws since they were passed or training to assist them in carrying out the task of
providing this information. A number of factors impact on the ability to carry
out an effective consultation programme in South Pacific countries, which may
be outside the control of the responsible agency or sponsoring Ministry. These
include international and political pressure, the urgency of law reform and the
high cost of consultation. Cost is a particular impediment in Samoa, given the
customary protocols that precede and conclude a single consultation. However,

---

[78]   Constitution of Samoa 1960, art 41.
[79]   Constitution of Samoa 1960, art 41.
[80]   The Attorney-General may delegate his duties: Constitution of Samoa 1960, art 41(4).
[81]   Infants Ordinance 1961, s 7A.
[82]   Appointed under the Internal Affairs Act 1995, s 14.

even if consultation is not comprehensive, some effort must be made to obtain opinions, particularly in the case of family law.

(d) Failure to take account of local culture

Stemming partly from this lack of consultation is a further criticism, which is the failure of the legislation to take into account local culture on adoption. As discussed above, there is a strong distinction between the customary and Western adoption paradigms. The amendments make some attempt to take cultural practices into account by including the *Sui o le Nuu* and *Sui o le Malo* in the overseas adoption process. However, formal adoption still proceeds on the basis of the Western approach of severing the ties between child and natural parents, as opposed to the customary approach which is more akin to fostering.

(e) Difficulties with recognition of customary adoptions

As discussed above, the position of customary law in the state system is not entirely clear. It seems that custom will not be recognised by law unless and until incorporated in legislation or declared to be law by a court.[83] There is currently no express recognition. However, there is some indication that the Samoan courts do accept their validity. In *Re the Estate of Tu'i*,[84] for example, it seems to have been accepted that customary adoptions were valid, although the point was not directly in issue. More recently, in *Devoe v Attorney-General*,[85] the court had to consider the status of a child adopted under custom in an application to correct the Register of Births Deaths and Marriages. In the absence of 'researched arguments', the court was not prepared to make a ruling on whether customary adoptions were recognised by state law in Samoa or under the laws of Germany or New Zealand, which formerly applied, but it seems to have been accepted that the child, born in 1876, had been adopted by custom. Further, the court went on to state that although adoptions may not be registered under any enactment, it does not necessarily follow they are not recognised by law.[86] The Court of Appeal[87] has since ruled that, whilst His Honour was correct to adjourn the matter for it to be argued fully, together with the claims to the estate of the adoptive father, Papalii Folau, he should not have done so on an indefinite basis. The court referred the matter back to the Supreme Court for directions to be made to have both matters determined together including decisions on the following questions:

[83] See further, Jennifer Corrin and Don Paterson *Introduction to South Pacific Law* (3rd edn, Palgrave MacMillan, 2011) in press, chs 2 and 3.

[84] Unreported, Supreme Court, Samoa, Bisson J, 4 September 1996, accessible via www.paclii.org at [1996] WSSC 1.

[85] Unreported, Supreme Court, Samoa, Vaai J, 2 March 2007, accessible via www.paclii.org at [2007] WSSC 13.

[86] Citing *Estate of Tui v Faumui Su'e* (unreported, Supreme Court, Samoa, 4 September 1996) and *Samoan Public Trustee v Collins* (1960–1969) WSLR 52.

[87] Unreported, Court of Appeal, Samoa, Baragwanath, Salmon, and Paterson JJ, 14 September 2007, accessible via www.paclii.org at [2007] WSCA 5.

- Which legal system governs the validity and effect of the adoption, customary law, Samoan law, German colonial law, New Zealand colonial law or statute law?

- If the adoption was under customary law, is the adoption capable of being registered under the Births and Deaths Registration Ordinance 1961?

- Does the Birth Deaths and Marriage Registration Act 2002 affect the position?

- Is an adoptee entitled to share in the distribution of the estate of the adopting parent under customary law?[88]

At the time of writing, this case has yet to be heard, but it has far-reaching potential for the law on customary adoption in Samoa.

In other countries of the South Pacific, difficulties have arisen in gaining official recognition of their customary adoptions in overseas countries. For example, in *R v Takabea*,[89] the High Court of Solomon Islands refused to recognise an adoption which had taken place under customary law in Kiribati. Similar issues arise in relation to an adoption under Samoan custom, although the issue does not yet appear to have come before the courts. In *Devoe v Attorney-General*,[90] the question arose whether customary adoptions in Samoa were recognised under the laws of Germany and New Zealand, when those countries administered Samoa. However, Vaai J was not prepared to decide the matter. As discussed above, the Court of Appeal has since referred the matter back to the Supreme Court to consider this question after hearing argument on this point.[91]

There have been particular issues where the potential adopters are not indigenous,[92] issues which exist even within the boundaries of the country where the custom prevails. In most countries of the region, including Samoa, it is unclear whether a foreigner may adopt a child by custom. In Papua New Guinea, the courts have held that he or she may not, at least, unless the adopter is part 'of a traditional community, that is, if by custom he [or she] were seen as being part of their culture group'.[93] However, by analogy with cases on customary marriage,[94] Solomon Islands might be prepared to recognise such an

---

88   Unreported, Court of Appeal, Samoa, Baragwanath, Salmon, and Paterson JJ, 14 September 2007, accessible via www.paclii.org at [2007] WSCA 5.
89   *R v Takabea* [1993] SBHC 81.
90   Unreported, Supreme Court, Samoa, Vaai J, 2 March 2007, accessible via www.paclii.org at [2007] WSSC 13.
91   Unreported, Court of Appeal, Samoa, Baragwanath, Salmon, and Paterson JJ, 14 September 2007, accessible via www.paclii.org at [2007] WSCA 5.
92   *Elijah v Doery* [1984] PGNC 16.
93   *Elijah v Doery* [1984] PGNC 16, 17.
94   See, eg, *Rebatai v Chow* [2002] 4 LRC 226. See further, J Corrin and K Brown 'Marit Long Kastom: Marriage in Solomon Islands' (2004) 18 *International Journal of Law, Policy and the Family* 52.

adoption. Given that customary adoption in Samoa is interfamilial it would appear that a foreigner could not normally adopt in custom. However, this prohibition might be relaxed if he or she had been accepted as a member of the *aiga*. It will be interesting to see whether this question is answered by the court in deciding the case of *Devoe v Attorney-General*,[95] referred to above, and the related claims to the estate of the adoptive father, Papalii Folau, which are all to be determined at the same time.

(f) Uncertainty regarding payment and reward

Another issue that arises from the legislation is the application of the prohibition of payment or reward in consideration of adoption. Section 9 of the Act states, 'it shall not be lawful for any person to give or receive or agree to give or receive any payment or reward in consideration of the making of arrangements for an adoption or proposed adoption'. The only exception, which is contained in the introductory proviso, is where leave has been given by the court. The adoption agencies operating in Apia before the changes to the law would obviously be making some charge for their services. During the second reading debate on the 2005 amendments it was certainly asserted that payment was made to and by the agencies.[96] The question then arises whether the court gave leave for this or not. As the adoption agencies existing prior to 2005 were unauthorised, the answer must be no. Further uncertainty is instilled by the regulations. Schedule 1, para E, requires an applicant for adoption agency status to state whether he or she 'proposes to seek any reward or benefit for themselves as a result of operating an adoption agency' and, if so, to provide details. Schedule 2, para B5 requires an applicant for the Attorney-General's certificate for overseas adoption to provide information as to whether any payments have been made or requested by any party and, if so, to provide details. No mention is made in either Schedule to a court order and this seems to suggest that such payments may be permissible in some circumstances, even without such an order. The only approved agencies at the current time are law firms, which would no doubt be charging legal fees. Such fees would fall within a literal reading of the term 'payment or reward in consideration of the making of arrangements for an adoption'. In practice, it seems that legal fees are being distinguished from payment or reward relating only to the placement of the child.

V SUGGESTIONS FOR REFORM

One possibility for reform would be to confer formal recognition on customary adoptions. A precedent for making statutory provision for customary adoption exists in another part of the South Pacific. In Papua New Guinea, Part VI of the Adoption of Children Act, chapter 275, was originally enacted as the

---

[95] Unreported, Court of Appeal, Samoa, Baragwanath, Salmon, and Paterson JJ, 14 September 2007, accessible via www.paclii.org at [2007] WSCA 5.

[96] XIII Parliament of Samoa, Interpretation of Debates, Session V, vol 1, 773, 774, 778.

Adoption of Children (Customary Adoptions) Act 1969. The Adoption of Children (Customary Adoption) Bill 1969 was introduced in response to the Adoption Ordinance 1969, which provided for adoption in accordance with the Western paradigm, resulting in a complete change of status whereby the adopted child acquired the same rights as a naturally born child of the adopters. The Adoption of Children (Customary Adoptions) Act was enacted to give legal recognition to the customary adoption practices of Papua New Guinea. Adoption by custom in Papua New Guinea, as in Samoa, involves the practice of assuming responsibility for other people's children. The consequences of this depend on a number of factors. As stated by the mover of the Adoption of Children (Customary Adoptions) Bill in 1969:[97]

> ' . . . it is common for people to care for children other than their own, sometimes forever. In some places the child returns to his or her natural parents when of marriageable age, in other places this does not happen. In most places both adopting parents and the natural parents make arrangements acceptable to both regarding land rights, marriage gifts, the length of time for the adoption, and even to the choice of a wife or husband.'

Such flexible arrangements also exist in Samoa, although marriage gifts and choice of spouse are not normally brought into the discussion.

The Papua New Guinea Act provides that, where a child is being or has been brought up, maintained and educated by an individual or by spouses jointly as their own child under a customary adoption, the child is deemed to have been adopted in custom.[98] Such adoption takes effect in accordance with the applicable custom, including any conditions as to the period of the adoption, rights of access and return and property rights or obligations.[99] In order to combat the problems of recognition that might arise from lack of formality, the Act also provides that a Local Court may grant a certificate that the adoption has been made and as to the relevant conditions.[100] The legislative authority and court's endorsement provide the basis for the issue of a passport and other formal documents in Papua New Guinea and there is no reason to suggest that these would not be accepted by overseas countries. Introduction of a similar provision in Samoa would solve the problem facing adopters who wish to take their child overseas, who are faced with no alternative other than to go through the formal adoption process, which results, at least in theory, in a complete change of status for the child. In Australia, the idea of formally recognising Aboriginal customary adoptions has been dismissed on the grounds that they cannot be equated with Western style adoptions.[101] However, the discussion did not extend to recognition in the state system of 'adoption' arrangements on a customary basis, as has been done in Papua New Guinea.

---

[97] Cited in *Elijah v Doery* (unreported, National Court, Papua New Guinea, Woods J, 2 November 1984) available via www.paclii.org at [1984] PGNC 16, 17.
[98] Adoption of Children Act 1968, s 53(1).
[99] Adoption of Children Act 1968, s 53(2).
[100] Adoption of Children Act 1968, s 54(1).
[101] ALRC *Recognition of Aboriginal Customary Laws*, Report 31, 1986, para 386.

Another, less comprehensive change might be to limit the formal recognition of customary adoptions to proceedings relating to Samoan land or chiefly titles. These issues are dealt with in the Land and Titles Court.[102] The status of a child and whether or not a *tama fai* was intended to inherit land or a title is obviously of prime concern. Whilst a detailed discussion of the Land and Titles Court and the issues surrounding it are outside the scope of this chapter, arguably this is the most suitable forum for questions relating to customary adoptions to be determined.

On the eve of reaching 50 years of independence in 2012, Samoa finds itself faced with more issues highlighting the incompatibility of pre-independence legal transplants with the customary structures in the family law area: the crucial area that defines a Samoan and Samoan identity. The existing formal family law regime in Samoa is still Western-oriented as can be seen from its origins, ie family laws are pre-independence laws transplanted directly from the statute books of New Zealand.[103] Rather than making piecemeal amendments to each piece of legislation to respond to issues as they arise,[104] to celebrate Samoa's coming of age and ability to make laws more relevant and appropriate for its own people, a full reform on all laws relating to 'family' to take account of *aiga* is recommended, to allow for a holistic approach to a family law regime that is Samoa oriented.[105] More piecemeal amendments will create more confusion than resolutions. A proper well planned framework will prevent overlapping and repetitious statutory duties and powers, particularly where different family legislation is administered by separate Government Ministries. For the public, it will be easier to understand a new but well set up Samoan framework springing from within society than to try and understand several ordinances created in and based on a foreign environment. The current Samoa Law Reform Commission project on the 'Protection of Children' looking at this area with a view to proposing new legislation and the current Family Protection Draft Bill could well be included in this reform. In saying this, law reform that takes account of both the Western systems and the customary systems is no small challenge for any Pacific island. Indeed this is one of the biggest challenges for law reform in the South Pacific as strong traditionally based societies come to accept that being independent means also being governed by Parliament-made laws. However, if laws are to work for society, law reform in this area as in all areas, must take account of both customary and

---

[102] See further, Jennifer Corrin 'Resolving Land Disputes in Samoa' in Theo Levantis, Marjorie Sullivan, Peter O'Connor, John Munro and Steven Wawrzonek (eds) *Making Land Work* (Canberra: AusAID, 2008) p 199.

[103] Marriage Ordinance 1961; Divorce and Matrimonial Causes Ordinance 1961; Maintenance and Affiliation Act 1961; Property Law Act 1952; Wills Act 1975; Administration Act 1975; and Births Deaths and Marriages Registration Act 2002.

[104] For example, Infants Ordinance Amendment Act 2005; Divorce and Matrimonial Causes Amendment Act 2010; Maintenance and Affiliation Amendment Act 2010; and Births Deaths and Marriages Registration Act 2002 which repealed Births and Deaths Registration Ordinance 1961.

[105] Other recent Acts with relevance to the family are Young Offenders Act 2007 and Education Act 2009.

Western systems. If there is to be a marriage of the two systems, and if the best of both worlds is to be adopted, there must be some sacrifices.

VI CONCLUSION

The traditional family structure in Samoa has particular consequences for adoption in Samoa, where a child's status and cultural inheritance, including property rights and *matai* title are determined at birth. Whilst this culture endures, there is a need to retain the *tama fai*, as formal adoption in the Western sense does not serve the same purpose. Although there is general understanding of the legislative scheme for formal adoptions in Samoa, there is a tendency to resort to this only for legal reasons, such as the issue of birth certificates, the issue of a passport, or to meet overseas legal requirements. Where there is no dispute within the local community on *tama fai* and *vae tama*, the common tendency is to ignore the formal adoption process and to avoid the substantial costs involved. As disputes regarding the interfamilial practice of *tama fai* are rare in the local community, to date there has been little pressure on the formal legal sector to recognise customary adoptions. However, this may change in the near future, due to changes in society, such as the move towards a cash economy and individual property holding, and an increase in overseas work and education. Disputes between *tama fai* and biological children have already come before the courts and others are bound to follow. All these factors make an increase in formal adoption applications inevitable if no alternative is provided.

In spite of the critical importance of achieving the fine balance of providing strong safeguards for natural parents and their children, whilst also protecting prospective adopters, the current adoption regime in Samoa has not achieved this aim. The amendments to the Infants Ordinance in 2005 have introduced badly needed protection against unscrupulous agencies and ill-considered overseas adoptions. However, they have not bridged the divide between formal and customary adoptions. Whilst there is evidence that Samoans are moving away from informal adoptions, this appears to be motivated by the need to enter into an arrangement which will be recognised overseas, rather than by an acceptance that the Western adoption paradigm is appropriate in Samoa. The 2005 amendments also highlight the need for consultation, and by this is meant not merely a presentation based on a predetermined agenda, but a more open discussion of a full range of options and with reference to local culture and aspirations.[106] Without the input and acquiescence of the population, reforms run the risk of being divorced from local culture and norms.

Education is also a vital part of any successful law reform initiative. If members of society are uninformed about laws or do not understand or accept them,

---

[106] See further, Katy LeRoy *Constitutional Renewal in Solomon Islands: Public Participation in Theory and Practice* (Melbourne: Centre for Comparative Constitutional Studies, University of Melbourne, 2008).

they are likely to ignore them in favour of customary laws and practices. This may be all very well if their co-operation is not required to make the state scheme work. However, that is not the case here, where, for example, the proper investigation of a proposed overseas adoption requires information to be provided by the *Sui o le Nuu* and the *Sui o le Malo*. Structures, such as the village *fono*, *Sui o le Nuu* and the *Sui o le Malo* could be used to disseminate information and provide training in village communities.

The Law Reform Commission Act 2008, which established a Samoa Law Reform Commission[107] in Samoa, states that one of the purposes of the Act is to allow 'the development of the laws of Samoa in order to promote Samoan custom and traditions'.[108] If this mandate is to be given meaning then reform of the law in Samoa must look beyond Western paradigms. In this respect it may well be that, as illustrated by the Adoption of Children (Customary Adoptions) Act 1969, South Pacific countries where custom and tradition are still strong provide more appropriate inspiration for reform than other more foreign regimes.

On the eve of the fiftieth anniversary of independence, which will be reached in 2012, Samoa is faced with a further example of the incompatibility of pre-independence legal transplants with customary structures. Family law is a crucial area for Samoan identity. The historical evolution of the current family law regime from pre-independence laws transplanted directly from the statute books of New Zealand[109] has resulted in its Western orientation. To celebrate Samoa's coming of age, perhaps now is the time to demonstrate Samoa's ability to make laws more relevant and appropriate to its own people. Rather than making piecemeal amendments to each statute in response to issues as they arise,[110] a comprehensive reform programme including all 'family' law and taking account of *aiga* might be considered. This would allow a holistic approach to be taken to law reform, a family law regime that is Samoa oriented.[111] A proper well-planned framework might avoid some of the confusion which has arisen from piecemeal amendments, which create overlapping and repetitious statutory duties and powers, particularly where different family legislation is administered by separate Government Ministries. For the public, a new Samoan framework springing from within society would be easier to understand than a patchwork of Ordinances created in and based on a foreign paradigm. The current Samoa Law Reform Commission project,

---

[107] Law Reform Commission Act 2008, s 5.
[108] Law Reform Commission Act 2008, s 4.
[109] Marriage Ordinance 1961; Infants Ordinance 1961; Divorce and Matrimonial Causes Ordinance 1961; Maintenance and Affiliation Act 1967; Property Law Act 1952; Wills Act 1975; Administration Act 1975 (an Act to regulate the administration of the estates of deceased persons); Births Deaths and Marriages Registration Act 2002.
[110] For example, Infants Ordinance Amendment Act 2005, Divorce and Matrimonial Causes Amendment Act 2010; Maintenance and Affiliation Amendment Act 2010; Births Deaths and Marriages Registration Act 2002 which repealed Births and Deaths Registration Ordinance 1961.
[111] See n 105 above.

the 'Protection of Children', is working on proposals for new legislation in this area and the current Family Protection Draft Bill could be included in such a reform strategy.

As strong traditionally based societies in the South Pacific, such as Samoa, move towards acceptance that independence means being governed by state law as well as customary law, accommodating legal pluralism is one of their biggest challenges. However, if Samoa is to have the best of both worlds, with both systems working together, the law reform process in the area of family law, as in all others, must take into account both customary and Western legal paradigms.

Scotland

'THE EASING OF CERTAIN LEGAL DIFFICULTIES': LIMITED LEGAL RECOGNITION OF COHABITATION UNDER SCOTS LAW

Elaine E Sutherland[*]

Résumé

Jusqu'à une époque récente, la loi écossaise ne définissait pas de manière précise le statut des concubins. Ce n'est qu'une loi de 2006 qui prévoir des règles particulières applicables aux couples de concubins et précise le régime applicable au droit de propriété pendant la vie commune des intéressés, sur la répartition des biens en cas de séparation ou de décès de l'un des membres du couple. La loi de 2006 ne confère pas aux concubins le statut reconnu aux personnes mariées ou des partenaires légalement reconnus. La loi a pour objectif essentiel de régler certaines difficultés propres au concubinage et de corriger des situations jugées injustes. Après cinq ans d'application de la Loi de 2006, il est possible de tirer des enseignements de son application au regard de son interprétation jurisprudentielle. Cet examen met en exergue la nécessité de réformer la loi de 2006 sur le statut des concubins et impose et de réfléchir, d'une manière plus générale, sur les objectifs que devraient poursuivre les normes gouvernant le statut de personnes cohabitant.

I INTRODUCTION

Until recently, Scots law paid scant attention to non-marital cohabitation, having long since given up the business of policing the consensual sexual relations and living arrangements of sufficiently-unrelated adults.[1] A small number of statutes provided some assistance to cohabitants on specific issues.[2] By and large, however, cohabitants were left to make their own arrangements.

---

[*] Professor of Child and Family Law, Stirling Law School, University of Stirling, Scotland, (elaine.sutherland@stir.ac.uk), and Professor of Law, Lewis and Clark Law School, Portland, Oregon (es@lclark.edu).
[1] Both underage sex and incest remain of concern to the criminal law. See, the Sexual Offences (Scotland) Act 2009, ss 18-41 and the Criminal Law (Consolidation) (Scotland) Act 1995, s 1, respectively.
[2] For example, the Matrimonial Homes (Family Protection) (Scotland) Act 1981, s 13, provided remedies to different-sex cohabitants, primarily in the context of domestic abuse. These remedies were only extended to different-sex cohabitants in 2006.

Widespread misconceptions about the legal consequences of cohabitation,[3] combined with the climate of optimism that accompanies a new relationship, meant that many cohabitants failed to make such arrangements and it was only when the relationship broke down that they found themselves resorting to general legal principles in the hope of resolving disputes.[4] In addition, the law was of little or no assistance to a surviving cohabitant whose partner had died as a result of natural causes[5] or third party negligence.[6]

Thus, the stage was set to consider the case for greater legal recognition of cohabitation and the debate, in Scotland, played out – and continues to play out – along lines similar to those found elsewhere. Since whole forests have been sacrificed to that debate, the familiar arguments need be explored in outline only here. Supporters of ascribing greater legal consequences to cohabitation point to the need to take a functionalist approach to family relationships. They argue that the legal problems of cohabitants frequently mirror those of married couples since the parties will often have developed similar patterns of joint endeavour, sacrifice and dependence in the interests of the relationship. That being the case, there is as much need for the legal system to provide for efficient resolution of disputes and to protect the ignorant and the vulnerable in either case. Opponents argue for the need to respect autonomy, allowing individuals a choice between different kinds of relationships with different consequences. Some view the suggestion that according greater legal recognition to cohabitation undermines marriage as a benefit to be embraced with enthusiasm, while others see it as cataclysmic threat.

These considerations were reflected by the Scottish Law Commission in 1992, when it stated the goals of its modest recommendations for reform. It believed that the law:[7]

> ' . . . should neither undermine marriage, nor undermine the freedom of those who have deliberately opted out of marriage . . . [and] . . . should be confined to the easing of certain legal difficulties and the remedying of certain situations which are widely perceived as being harsh and unfair.'

Like so many other Scottish law reform proposals of that time, neither the time nor the political will was found at Westminster to implement them.[8] In the

---

[3]   See, L Nicholson *Improving Family Law in Scotland: Analysis of Written Consultation Responses* (Scottish Executive Social Research, 2004), para.5.6 and table 8, available at www.scotland.gov.uk/Publications/2004/10/20057/44653 (accessed June 2011).

[4]   See, eg, *Shilliday v Smith* 1998 SC 725; *Satchwell v McIntosh* 2006 SLT (Sh Ct) 117; *McKenzie v Nutter* 2007 SLT (Sh Ct) 17.

[5]   Cohabitants had none of the automatic succession rights of spouses or civil partners. See, below n 162 and accompanying text.

[6]   While the Damages (Scotland) Act 1976, allowing for recovery of damages on the death of a loved one, was extended to different-sex cohabitants in 1981, same-sex cohabitants were not included until 2006. For an illustration of the pre-2006 problem, see, *Telfer v Kellock* 2004 SLT 1290.

[7]   *Report on Family Law* (Scot Law Com No 135, 1992) para 16.1.

[8]   See, EE Sutherland, KE Goodall, GFM Little and FP Davidson (eds) *Law Making and the Scottish Parliament: The Early Years* (Edinburgh University Press, 2011) ch 1.

meantime, social attitudes and the law were moving on. Civil partnership, the marriage equivalent for same-sex couples, became available in 2005,[9] informal cohabitation was becoming more common[10] and more socially acceptable[11] and a greater percentage of children born in Scotland started life with unmarried parents.[12] Increasingly, cohabitation was attracting greater legal consequences in other jurisdictions.[13]

Finally, post-Devolution and after further consultation,[14] the (then) Scottish Executive decided to implement most of the Scottish Law Commission's recommendations. Again, it stressed that the purpose of the reform was:[15]

' . . . to provide a clearer statutory basis for recognising when a relationship is a cohabiting relationship; and a set of principles and basic rights to protect vulnerable people either on the breakdown of a relationship, or when a partner dies. The Scottish Ministers do not intend to create a new legal status for cohabitants. *It is not the intention that marriage-equivalent legal rights should accrue to cohabiting couples, nor is it the intention to undermine the freedom of those who have deliberately opted out of marriage or of civil partnership.*'

Thus, the policy decision was taken to ascribe greater legal consequences to cohabitation than had been the case hitherto at the same time as retaining the distinction between cohabitation, on the one hand, and marriage and civil partnership, on the other. That approach involves, 'drawing the line' somewhere between the two and is fraught with problems, since it will mean the legal regime established will deal well with a cohabitant in situation X, but poorly with another in situation Y. In any event, the Family Law (Scotland) Act 2006

---

9   Civil Partnership Act 2004, in force, 5 December 2005.

10   In the 2001 Census, 326,868 people described themselves as cohabiting and cohabiting couple families doubled in relative terms from 1991 (3.5%) to 2001 (6.9%): *The Registrar General's 2001 Census Report to the Scottish Parliament* (General Register Office for Scotland, 2003), SE/2003/6, available at www.gro-scotland.gov.uk/files1/stats/rg_report_parliament.pdf (accessed June 2011).

11   66% of those responding to the Scottish Social Attitudes Survey in 2000 saw no problem with couples living together rather than marrying: *Scottish Social Attitudes Survey, 2000* (National Centre for Social Research, 2002).

12   It was not until 2008 that the proportion of non-marital births exceeded 50% of all births, but that reflected a general trend since the figures for 1988 and 1998 were 25.4% and 38.9%, respectively. See, *Scotland's Population 2008: The Registrar General's Annual Review of Demographic Trends* (General Register Office for Scotland, 2009) p 25 available at www.gro-scotland.gov.uk/statistics/at-a-glance/annrev/2008/index.html (accessed June 2011).

13   For developments in Canada, see, N Bala 'Controversy Over Couples in Canada: The Evolution of Marriage and Other Adult Independent Relationships' (2003) 29 Queen's LJ 41. In New Zealand, see, B Atkin 'The rights of married and unmarried couples in New Zealand – radical new laws on property and succession' (2003) 15(2) CFLQ 173. In the US, see American Law Institute *Principles of the Law of Family Dissolution: Analysis and Recommendation* (LexisNexis, 2002).

14   *Parents and Children: The Scottish Executive's proposals for improving Scottish Family Law* (Scottish Executive, 2000) and *Family Matters: Improving Family Law in Scotland* (Scottish Executive, 2004).

15   *The Family Law (Scotland) Bill: Policy Memorandum* (Scottish Executive, 2005) para 65 (emphasis added), available at www.scottish.parliament.uk/business/bills/36-familyLaw/b36s2-introd-pm.pdf (accessed June 2011).

created presumptions of joint ownership of certain money and property during the cohabitation, provided for limited redress on relationship breakdown and allowed the survivor to apply to a court for an award in the event of a partner's death. Cohabitants may avoid these legal consequences by agreement or, in the case of inheritance, by making a will.

There can be no doubt, then, that the Scottish legislation is far more limited in scope than that in a number of other jurisdictions. Nonetheless, it effected a significant change in the legal position of cohabitants. At the time of writing, the provisions of the 2006 Act have been operating for a little under 5 years and a small, but significant, body of case-law has been reported. In addition, a study, analysing the views of 97 family law practitioners has been published.[16] The purpose of this chapter is to examine how well the legislation is working in the context of its limited goals, always bearing in mind that these goals themselves may warrant re-examination.

II DEFINING COHABITANTS

One objection sometimes raised to attaching legal consequences to cohabitation stems from the difficulty of defining the relationships that are to be included. Unlike marriage and civil partnership, the starting date of cohabitation is not marked by an easily-verifiable record in an official register. Similarly, there is no court decree marking the end of cohabitation. In short, it does not come in a neat package. Then there is the variable nature of the relationship itself. As a general rule, couples are either married or they are not and, by and large, the same holds true for civil partnership.[17] They can live apart for work or other reasons or share their time between two homes and they are still married or civilly enpartnered. In the absence of a formal relationship, when are couples 'cohabiting' and when are they engaged in some other kind of relationship, like a casual liaison, 'living apart together'[18] and so forth?

The 2006 Act provides that two people are cohabitants if they 'are (or were) living together as if they were' husband and wife or civil partners[19] and offers further statutory guidance in the form of a non-exclusive list of relevant factors.[20] The relevant factors are the length of time the parties lived together, the nature of the relationship and the nature and extent of any subsisting

---

[16] F Wasoff, J Miles and E Mordaunt *Legal Practitioners' Perspectives on the Cohabitation Provisions of the Family Law (Scotland) Act 2006* (Centre for Research on Families and Relationships, 2010) (hereinafter, *Practitioners' Perspectives*), available at www.crfr.ac.uk/ researchprojects/rp_cohabitation.html (accessed June 2011). The respondents to the study were almost all solicitors, rather than advocates; 19 participated in follow-up telephone interviews.

[17] Of course there are cases where a marriage will be regarded as valid in one jurisdiction but not in another and there is greater scope for civil or registered partnerships to suffer from inconsistent recognition.

[18] See, I Levin 'Living Apart Together: A New Family Form' (2004) 52(2) *Current Sociology* 223.

[19] Family Law (Scotland) Act 2006, s 25(1).

[20] Ibid, s 25(2).

financial arrangements. Unlike the systems operating in many other jurisdictions, there is no reference to a minimum period of time before cohabitation will be presumed, nor is there any reference to the couple having children.

The reported cases to date on financial provision have involved cohabitation of between 5 and 30 years.[21] However, in one of the few succession cases under the Act, a period of 2 years and 8 months was accepted by the court as sufficient, albeit the survivor failed to secure an award.[22] In all three of the cases where the pursuer was awarded something in respect of her own losses during the cohabitation, children were present, but the absence of children need not be fatal to establishing cohabitation. Thus far, interpreting the statutory definition has been largely unproblematic.[23] Of course, it is not known how often a prospective applicant/pursuer has been advised not to proceed on the basis that the characteristics of the relationship were such that it simply did not qualify as 'cohabitation' for the purposes of the 2006 Act.[24]

III   CONSEQUENCES DURING THE CURRENCY OF THE RELATIONSHIP

The 2006 Act created a rebuttable presumption that qualifying cohabitants have equal shares in household goods and money and property derived from a housekeeping allowance.[25] That these provisions have not given rise to litigation is no surprise and, indeed, there are no reported decisions under the, much older, parallel provisions under the Family Law (Scotland) Act 1985, applying to spouses and civil partners.[26] While a relationship is going well, people give little thought to the ownership of household goods and savings, with disputes surfacing in the context of relationship breakdown and the provisions may be of assistance at that time.

---

[21]   In a very recent unreported case, where the parties lived together for 2 years and 2 months, the court had no difficulty in accepting they had been cohabiting for the purpose of the Act, albeit no award was made to the pursuer: *Mitchell v Gibson*, 14 February 2011, Sheriff Principal, Tayside Central and Fife.

[22]   *Savage v Purches* 2009 SLT (Sh Ct) 36.

[23]   The first reported case under the cohabitation provisions of the 2006 Act, *Chebotareva v King's Executrix* 2008 Fam LR 66, concerned succession and was disposed of on the basis that the deceased had not been domiciled in Scotland at the time of his death. Thus, whether the parties were cohabiting was of no relevance. This may explain the court's rather loose treatment of that issue, where it noted, at [19], that 'they had been in a relationship for a substantial number of years'. With respect, that alone would not be enough to establish cohabitation under s 25. In *Fairley v Fairley* 2008 Fam LR 112, the dispute related to whether the parties were cohabiting when the 2006 Act came into force on 4 May 2006, it being agreed that they had been cohabitants at an earlier stage.

[24]   *Practitioners' Perspectives*, n 16 above, pp 50-54, gives some idea of cases presenting to practitioners.

[25]   2006 Act, ss 26 and 27. Property acquired by gift or succession from a third party is excluded. 'Household goods' does not include money, securities, motor vehicles or domestic animals.

[26]   1985 Act, ss 25 and 26.

For completeness, it is worth noting that, while spouses and civil partners owe each other an alimentary obligation during the currency of the relationship,[27] the 2006 Act created no parallel support obligation for cohabitants. This is consistent with the Scottish Law Commission's recommendations and is simply an example of 'drawing the line' once the decision has been taken that cohabitation will have more limited legal consequences than do marriage and civil partnership.

IV FINANCIAL PROVISION ON RELATIONSHIP BREAKDOWN

For the first time, in Scotland, the 2006 Act sought to provide parting cohabitants with a mechanism for obtaining a measure of financial redress. While this advance should not be underestimated, the goal was never to put cohabitants on a par with spouses and civil partners who have the benefit of a comprehensive scheme under the Family Law (Scotland) Act 1985. That statute created what is, essentially, a community property system, deferred until relationship breakdown, empowering the court to make a wide range of orders dealing with division of money, pensions and other property and with ongoing financial support.[28] Crucially, the 1985 Act provides clear principles to guide the court in determining which orders are appropriate and when. These principles seek to achieve fair (prima facie, equal) sharing of most property acquired during the marriage or civil partnership and to reflect the economic advantages and disadvantages, as well as economic and non-economic contributions and sacrifices, of the parties during the relationship. While the goal is to enable each party to move on with his or her life, unencumbered by the other, the system accommodates circumstances where instalment payments or continuing support, or both, are justified by the criteria in the Act. While the 1985 Act went through a process of interpretation early in its life, on the whole, judges, practitioners and academics regard the system it provides as effective[29] and, indeed, it has been eyed with admiration from abroad.[30] In short, it provides a clear, flexible and principled approach to disputes and is designed to encourage the parties to reach agreement, rather than dissipate resources on costly litigation.

Section 28 of the Family Law (Scotland) Act 2006, empowering the court to make financial provision for a former cohabitant when the relationship has ended other than by death, has less comprehensive ambitions and, consequently, is of much more limited scope. Unlike the 1985 Act, it is not designed to effect the division of property acquired during the cohabitation.

---

27 Ibid, s 1(1)(a)-(bb).
28 For details of the system, see, EE Sutherland *Child and Family Law* (W Green, 2nd edn, 2008) at paras 16-017–16-186.
29 For a discussion of reactions to the system and, in particular, criticisms of it by the respected Scottish Law Lord, Lord Hope, see, Sutherland, ibid, paras 16-181–16-182.
30 See, eg, *Charman v Charman* [2007] 1 FLR 1246 at [107], where Sir Mark Potter noted the 'clarity and certainty' of the Scottish system.

Thus, a host of orders available to the court in the context of divorce and civil partnership dissolution, like those effecting property transfer, pension-sharing or pension-splitting, are simply absent in respect of former cohabitants. Whereas the 1985 Act established a scheme premised on entitlement, that entitlement being triggered by marriage or civil partnership, the 2006 Act opens the door for an award to be made but only where the applicant makes a case justifying the award on the basis of limited criteria.

It may be stating the obvious to note that a dispute falls to be determined under one regime or the other. Either the parties are spouses or civil partners and their claims are resolved using the 1985 Act, or they are former cohabitants and the 2006 Act applies to them. There is no scope – nor should there be – for arguing, as did one pursuer/applicant, that she warranted some kind of elevated status because she had been engaged to be married to her partner and, thus, had acquired quasi-spousal expectations.[31]

(a)   The orders the court may make and the criteria

A qualifying former cohabitant may apply to the court for any or all of three different orders, each with a distinct purpose.

- The first, a s 28(2)(a) order, is for the payment of a capital sum. In considering an application for such an award, the court is directed to reach its decision 'having regard to' whether the defender has derived economic advantage from the pursuer's contributions and whether the applicant/pursuer has suffered economic disadvantage in the interests of the defender or a relevant child.[32] In assessing the defender's economic advantage the court must have regard to the offsetting effect of any disadvantage suffered by the defender in the interests of the pursuer or a relevant child.[33] Similarly, in assessing the pursuer's economic disadvantage, the court is directed to offset against it any economic advantage the pursuer has derived from the defender's contributions.[34] Nowhere in the Act is there any explicit statement of what the court is supposed to do with the results of this process or of its ultimate goal and there has been no shortage of judicial complaint over the lack of guidance. However, as the Inner House of the Court of Session confirmed in *Gow v Grant*,[35] the first appeal to be heard under the 2006 Act, the court should effect a balancing exercise between net advantages and disadvantages. Redress

---

[31]   *Selkirk v Chisholm* 2011 Fam LR 56 at [124]. In *Windram, Applicant* 2009 Fam LR 157, at [14], while the sheriff observed that had the deceased 'not died suddenly it is likely that the deceased and the pursuer would have married', this was one of many considerations of which the court was entitled to take account under s 29(3)(d).

[32]   2006 Act, s 28(2).

[33]   2006 Act, s 28(5).

[34]   2006 Act, s 28(6).

[35]   22 March 2011, available at www.scotcourts.gov.uk/opinions/2011CSIH25.html (accessed June 2011); 2011 Fam LR forthcoming, at [3].

here may be made only by ordering the payment of a capital sum and the court may specify when payment is to be made[36] and order payment by instalments.[37]

'Economic advantage' 'includes gains in capital, income or earning capacity' and economic disadvantage is the flip side of that.[38] 'Contribution' is defined as including 'indirect and non-financial contributions (and, in particular, any such contribution made by looking after the relevant child or any house in which they cohabited)'.[39] A 'relevant child' is one who is under the age of 16 and includes not only the couple's child (whether by birth, adoption or through assisted reproductive technology), but also a child 'accepted by the cohabitants as a child of the family'.[40]

- The second, a s 28(2)(b) order, has a clear purpose since it requires:

> ' ... the defender to pay such amount as may be specified in the order in respect of any economic burden of caring, after the end of the cohabitation, for a child of whom the cohabitants are the parents.'[41]

Since only 'child of whom the cohabitants are the parents' is included, there is no scope to provide for the future childcare costs of an 'accepted' child. Again, a child is 'a person under 16 years of age'.[42] In making an award here, the court may order payment of a capital sum, again specifying when payment is to be made[43] and making the award payable by instalments.[44] While there is scope for debate on the point, since the statutory language is untidy, practitioners and courts appear to be proceeding on the basis that true periodic payments are not permissible.

- The third, a s 28(2)(c) order, allows the court to make 'such interim award as it thinks fit'.[45]

The prospect of receiving an award is subject to a general and serious limitation since any application under s 28 must 'be made not later than one year after the day on which the cohabitants cease to cohabit'[46] and the court has no discretion to extend the time period, something recommended by the Scottish Law Commission. Clearly, the intention of the legislators was to allow the parties to draw a line under their relationship and move on with their lives. However, practitioners have expressed concern that the time-limit may impede

---

[36] 2006 Act, s 28(7)(a).
[37] 2006 Act, s 28(7)(b).
[38] 2006 Act, s 28(9).
[39] 2006 Act, s 28(9).
[40] 2006 Act, s 28(10).
[41] 2006 Act, s 28(2)(b).
[42] 2006 Act, s 28(9).
[43] 2006 Act, s 28(7)(a).
[44] 2006 Act, s 28(7)(b).
[45] 2006 Act, s 28(2)(c).
[46] 2006 Act, s 28(8).

the process of negotiation and result in a rush to litigation for fear of an action becoming time barred.[47] The courts are familiar with grappling with just when the parties ceased to cohabit since it can be important in the context of financial provisions on divorce,[48] and it has given them little trouble in the cohabitation context to date.[49]

While it is competent for an applicant to seek redress in either the Court of Session or the sheriff court,[50] it was always anticipated that these actions would be largely the province of the sheriff court. This has proved to be the case since only two of the s 28 cases to date began in the Court of Session.

(b) Applying s 28(2)(a): advantages, disadvantages and contributions

The judiciary did not find s 28(2)(a) particularly user friendly, contrasting it unfavourably with the parallel provision of the 1985 Act. In addition, there was judicial frustration over the lack of detailed financial information provided to the court in a number of the early cases. However, the judges were consistently clear that they had far greater discretion under the 2006 Act than they had under the 1985 Act, entitling them to take a 'broad axe'[51] and the, rather more familiar, 'broad brush'[52] approach under the former. In *Gow v Grant*,[53] the Inner House may have been seeking to discourage this latitude when it warned that 'a court must have regard to the precise wording' of the statute.[54] In one respect, the judges were operating within their comfort zone since the credibility and reliability of the parties and their witnesses often played a significant part in decisions. For solicitors, identifying advantages and disadvantages, combined with the width of the court's discretion, caused concern.[55]

Much judicial energy went into exploring how to approach the task of interpreting the 2006 Act and practitioners' hearts sank when the first two substantive decisions[56] under s 28(2)(a) took diametrically opposite views on

---

47   *Practitioners' Perspectives*, n 16 above, p 126.
48   *Banks v Banks* 2005 Fam LR 116; *Bain v Bain* 2008 Fam LR 81.
49   *Fairley v Fairley* 2008 Fam LR 112; *Lawley v Sutton*, Sheriffdom of Grampian, Highlands and Islands at Wick, 18 March 2010; 2010 WL 1368703.
50   Family Law (Scotland) Act 2006, s 28(9).
51   *M v S* 2008 SLT 871, at [305] and [319].
52   *M v S* 2008 SLT 871, at [210]; *Gow v Grant* 2010 Fam LR 21, at [45] and [62]; *Selkirk v Chisholm*, Court reference number A15/08, 25 November 2010, Sheriffdom of Lothian and Borders at Duns, unreported, but available at 2010 WL 4810772 at [99].
53   22 March 2011, available at www.scotcourts.gov.uk/opinions/2011CSIH25.html (accessed June 2011); 2011 Fam LR forthcoming.
54   At [4].
55   *Practitioners' Perspectives*, n 16 above, pp 130–134.
56   Which gets the glory of being the first substantive case to address s 28 proper is a matter of debate. Lord Matthews had been 'informed by counsel for the pursuer that this is the first time that the financial provisions of the 2006 Act have been judicially considered': at [252]. Depending on the time it took the respective judges to deliver their decisions, this may or may

whether the parallel provisions of the 1985 Act was relevant to that process. In *M v S*,[57] Lord Matthews had no doubt that they were, while, in *Jamieson v Rodhouse*,[58] Sheriff Hogg was equally firm that they were not. That issue was put beyond doubt, at least for the time being,[59] when the Inner House handed down its opinion in the appeal *Gow v Grant*.[60] It stated, quite unequivocally, that 'sections 8-10 of the 1985 Act have no bearing on the construction of section 28'.[61] While their Lordships justified their position on the basis of the radically different purposes of the two statutory schemes, there is the danger that they have deprived future courts of useful guidance on interpreting terms, like 'economic disadvantage', that are defined similarly in both statutes.[62]

(i) The 'four questions'

The Inner House, in *Gow v Grant*,[63] may have been crystal clear on how *not* to interpret the 2006 Act, but it offered disappointingly little detailed guidance on how the process *should* be carried out. While the court acknowledged that the cases to date had taken 'varying and contradictory approaches' to the task, it took the view that it was unnecessary for it 'to express any general view of the construction of section 28'.[64] This is all the more surprising because, insofar as a consistent picture had begun to emerge from the lower courts, a number of the sheriffs attributed the Damascus moment to the very decision of the lower court in *Gow v Grant*[65] that their Lordships were reversing. The only real guidance offered by the Inner House lies in its reference to 'compensation for an imbalance of economic advantage and disadvantage'[66] and its injunction that is, that 'a court must have regard to the precise wording' of s 28 and, later, that it 'should be applied in accordance with its precise terms'.[67]

Uncertainty does not help practitioners advising clients, nor does it create climate of predictability that is the bedrock of negotiated settlements. While it

---

not be the case. The decision in *M v S* was handed down on 2 September 2008, but the judgment in *Jamieson v Rodhouse* 2009 Fam LR 34, was delivered over a month earlier, on 1 August 2008.

[57] 2008 SLT 871, at [271]–[272].

[58] 2009 Fam LR 34, at [51].

[59] It has been suggested that the decision may be the subject of a further appeal to the Supreme Court, which replaced the House of Lords as the final domestic court of appeal in civil matters, in August 2009.

[60] 22 March 2011, available at www.scotcourts.gov.uk/opinions/2011CSIH25.html (accessed June 2011); 2011 Fam LR forthcoming.

[61] At [3].

[62] With respect, it is submitted that the more nuanced view of Sheriff Miller in *Lindsay v Murphy* 2010 Fam LR 156, at [58], represents a preferable approach.

[63] 22 March 2011, available at www.scotcourts.gov.uk/opinions/2011CSIH25.html (accessed June 2011); 2011 Fam LR forthcoming.

[64] At [3].

[65] 2010 Fam LR 21, cited in *Lindsay v Murphy* 2010 Fam LR 156 and *Selkirk v Chisholm* Court 2011 Fam LR 56. In truth, the seeds of this approach can be found in *F v D* 2009 Fam LR 111 at [54]–[60].

[66] At [4], an unfortunate choice of terminology to which we will return below, at nn 114–116 below and accompanying text.

[67] At [4].

is wholly proper that judges should work these things out for themselves, there is no escaping the fact that a precise application of the statutory language – and one that was consistent, in general terms, with their Lordships' view – had been articulated at an early stage in academic commentaries on the Act.[68]

In considering an application under s 28(2)(a), the court should address the following four questions:

- Has the defender derived economic advantage from contributions made by the applicant?[69]

- To what extent, if any, has the economic advantage derived by the defender from the applicant's contributions been offset by any economic disadvantage suffered by the defender in the interests of (i) the applicant, or (ii) any relevant child?[70]

- Has the applicant suffered economic disadvantage in the interests of (i) the defender, or (ii) any relevant child?[71]

- To what extent, if any, has the economic disadvantage suffered by the applicant in the interests of (i) the defender, or (ii) any relevant child, been offset by any economic advantage the applicant has derived from the defender's contributions?[72]

Despite the lack of express direction, it is submitted that the court should then seek to effect a balancing of advantages and disadvantages and, by and large, that is what the courts have done.

At the time of writing, only seven cases addressing the real substance of s 28 have been reported,[73] all involving female applicant/pursuers and male defenders.[74] Three of the seven resulted in awards to the applicant, albeit one award was very small. In each of the three, an order was made in respect of future childcare costs as well, with every application for such an award being

---

[68] See, eg, K McK Norrie *The Family Law (Scotland) Act 2006: Text and Commentary* (Dundee University Press, 2006) pp 66–69 and Sutherland *Child and Family Law*, n 28 above, paras 16-205–16-210.

[69] 2006 Act, s 28(3)(a).

[70] 2006 Act, s 28(5).

[71] 2006 Act, s 28(3)(b).

[72] 2006 Act, s 28(6).

[73] Two other cases under s 28(2)(a) dealt with jurisdictional or procedural matters. See, *Fairley v Fairley* 2008 Fam LR 112 and *Lawley v Sutton*, Sheriffdom of Grampian, Highlands and Islands at Wick, 18 March 2010, 2010 WL 1368703.

[74] Lest the reader be tempted to conclude that parting same-sex cohabitants resolve any disputes without resort to litigation, it is worth noting the decision in *Souter v McAuley* 2010 SLT (Sh Ct) 121, where the defender was successful in securing the transfer of a joint tenancy into his sole name under the Matrimonial Homes (Family Protection) (Scotland) Act 1981, s 18, a statute whose protection was only extended to same-sex cohabitants by the Family Law (Scotland) Act 2006.

successful. To put it another way, childcare did not feature in the cases where the applicant received no award, although, as we shall see, that is not the sole explanation for these decisions.

Since securing an award under s 28(2)(a) requires the pursuer/applicant to justify the claim, that claim being tested by the court in terms of the 'four questions', it is instructive to analyse the reported decisions to date within the framework of these hurdles at which any application may fall. Of course, each case turns on its own peculiar facts and some fall at more than one hurdle, rather getting in the way of the neat composition so beloved of academics.

Has the defender has derived economic advantage from contributions made by the applicant?

Fundamental to a successful claim is demonstrating that the defender gained some economic advantage. If there is no advantage, then there is nothing against which to balance any disadvantage sustained by the applicant/ pursuer.[75] That point is illustrated most clearly, perhaps, in *Cameron v Leal*[76] (the case of the written-off car), an action that was, it is submitted, misconceived from the outset. While the facts of the case might provide a good basis for an action in a delict (*anglicé* tort), the court concluded, quite correctly, that the 2006 Act did not provide a remedy.

Esther Cameron and Stuart Leal had been cohabiting for some time when Stuart, having consumed an unspecified quantity of alcohol, wrote off Esther's car. In the circumstances, the insurance company declined to reimburse Esther and the couple took out a joint loan, secured on their home, to meet the outstanding loan payments due in respect of the car. Esther then took out a fresh loan to purchase a BMW, with instalments being paid out of couple's joint bank account. After the couple separated, she could no longer afford to service that loan and she returned the BMW to the seller, attracting a stiff financial penalty. She paid the penalty with money she borrowed from her father, that loan remaining outstanding. Esther sought an award of a capital sum of £16,500, reflecting half of the joint loan taken out to meet the payments on the written-off car (£12,500) and half of the penalty occasioned by the return of the BMW (£4,000). Noting that Stuart had gained no economic advantage but, rather, that both parties had suffered a loss, Sheriff Harris concluded, quite correctly, that:

> 'What is sought by the pursuer is compensation from the defender for a wrong on his part which resulted in loss to her ... the [2006] Act does not provide a mechanism for so doing.'[77]

---

[75] While little economic advantage accrued to the defender in *M v S* 2008 SLT 871, the case is discussed at nn 96–103 below and accompanying text, in terms of the pursuer/claimant's economic disadvantage.

[76] 2010 SLT (Sh Ct) 164; 2010 Fam LR 82.

[77] 2010 SLT (Sh Ct) 164 at [10]. He noted further that the parties had agreed on how to deal with the loss occasioned by the destruction of the first car: at [11].

However, it is not enough that the defender should have garnered some economic advantage, since that advantage must be derived 'from contributions made by the applicant'.[78] It follows, then, that what qualifies as such a contribution will be of crucial importance.

A narrow view of what was a relevant contribution featured in *Jamieson v Rodhouse*[79] (the case of 'good fortune of property price appreciation'), one of the early cases under the 2006 Act. Janet Jamieson and John Rodhouse had lived together for some 30 years and, while they were both in paid employment for much of that time, they adopted the older, traditional model of housekeeping. Janet took care of the housework, did a little decorating, paid for food, clothing for herself and her son by a previous relationship and bought small household items. Meanwhile, John paid the mortgage and other larger costs associated with the various homes in which they lived over the years, each of these homes being in his name. When they parted company, Janet sought a capital sum of £50,000 under s 28(2)(a) of the 2006 Act.

Like so many others in the early cases, the sheriff was frustrated by the dearth of hard financial evidence presented to the court. This paucity of information may have been due, in part, to Janet's ignorance of certain financial details, but it was exacerbated by John's, quite deliberate, prevarication in the witness box.[80] Why the pursuer's solicitor had not sought specification of documents, inviting the court to order mortgage and bank statements, tax returns and the like to be produced, is as much of a mystery to the present author as it was to the sheriff.[81]

Reviewing how the couple had lived during their time together, the court concluded that, while John had gained some economic advantage from Janet's contribution in providing housekeeping services, it was unable to put an economic value on them. This is a troubling observation. The 2006 Act defines contributions as including 'indirect and non-financial contributions' and 'in particular, any such contribution made by looking after . . . the house' in which the couple cohabited.[82] Was the sheriff saying that Janet might have fared better had some attempt been made to put a notional valuation on these contributions? Prudent solicitors would be wise to heed the warning.

For Janet, the real problem was the court's conclusion that the free capital in the home resulted, not from contributions she had made, but from 'the good fortune of property price appreciation'.[83] Former cohabitants do not benefit from such windfalls, since s 28 is simply not designed to effect the

---

[78] 2006 Act, s 28(3)(a).

[79] 2009 Fam LR 34.

[80] As the sheriff put it, at [36], 'I did not find the defender's evidence at all credible. He was vague, unable to answer a straight question and at pains to try and confuse. I did not accept that he could not produce details of his pension, bank statements and mortgage payments.'

[81] At [36].

[82] 2006 Act, s 28(9).

[83] At [48].

all-encompassing, end-of-relationship reckoning available to spouses and civil partners on the parting of the ways. Nonetheless, if, as the court accepted, John had derived economic advantage from Janet's contributions – and a monetary value had been attributed to them – then it is difficult to see how the court could have avoided the conclusion that some aspect of John's economic advantage derived from Janet's contributions.

However, in all likelihood, such a conclusion would have made no difference to the outcome of the case. When the court turned to the third question under s 28(2)(a), it found that Janet had not suffered economic disadvantage in the interests of either John or the child, being able to work at the only job for which she was qualified.[84] Furthermore, there was the matter of John having paid for the roof over the heads of Janet and her child, Kevin, whom John had accepted as a member of his family. Thus, even if Janet had sustained economic disadvantage, it was offset by having a home provided for her. In short, Janet's claim fell at multiple hurdles.

The most recent reported decision under the 2006 Act, *Selkirk v Chisholm*[85] (the case of the 'old fashioned relationship'), again reflects a narrow view of relevant contributions. Mary Selkirk and Robert Chisholm became engaged to be married in 1998 and moved into the house Robert bought the following year. Title to the home was taken in his name alone and he paid the mortgage. The 9-year, child-free cohabitation ended on 6 March 2008, when Mary returned home to find the locks had been changed. By that time, the free equity in the house was £25,300. Mary sought an award under s 28(2)(a) of the 2006 Act.

Mary was employed throughout most of the cohabitation, albeit her earnings were modest, and she left the relationship with no discernable assets. Meanwhile, Robert established his own successful business, financing it from an inheritance and the proceeds of remortgaging the home. The couple organised their lives in a way that Mary described as 'very old fashioned',[86] with her taking care of cleaning, laundry and indoor tasks and Robert cutting the grass and doing exterior jobs. Each party seems to have harboured suspicions that the other was having an affair, but the court found no evidence to support these suspicions. In any event, infidelity would have been irrelevant to the matter before the court.[87]

---

[84]   The court had observed earlier, at [21], that: 'She was unskilled before coming to cohabit and had not required to work as she had been supported by her then husband.' Of course, this was a common pattern, at least in middle class families, in Scotland, in the mid-twentieth century.

[85]   2011 Fam LR 56.

[86]   Pursuer's Evidence at [11].

[87]   Unlike the Family Law (Scotland) Act 1985, s 11(7), which makes clear that the conduct of the parties is irrelevant, save in very limited circumstances, the 2006 Act makes no mention of conduct. However, since there is no (even notional) obligation of sexual fidelity attaching to cohabitation, it is inconceivable that a court would regard it as relevant. Conduct adversely affecting resources may be another matter and one which has yet to be raised before the court under the 2006 Act.

Turning to the first of the 'four questions' to be answered in assessing a claim under this part of the Act, Sheriff Hammond was satisfied that Robert's economic position has been enhanced during the cohabitation since he now owned a house in which there was substantial free equity and a successful business. However, the sheriff attributed the increased equity in the house as being 'due solely to market forces'[88] and the success of the business as representing 'the fruits of defender's labour, together with investment which he was able to make from the funds he inherited and the proceeds of the re-mortgage of the house'.[89]

The sheriff found no evidence of Mary making an economic contribution to this advantageous position, beyond paying for the monthly food shopping. In terms of her non-economic contributions, he concluded that she had 'exaggerated her involvement' in the business, her role amounting to little more than answering the telephone occasionally and passing on the odd message. While he found that household tasks were shared between the parties, he did accept that Mary's share 'would have been greater, given the long hours worked by the defender', but went on to observe that he could not see 'that this contribution can be said to have led to any gain in the defender's capital, income and earning capacity'.[90] With respect, this is a curious conclusion. If the business flourished, in part, because of the time and effort Robert put into it, was his doing so not facilitated by Mary taking a disproportionate share of the domestic burden? This would seem to be precisely what the Scottish Parliament had in mind when it defined 'contributions' as it did but, yet again, a member of the judiciary was unwilling to accept domestic labour as the right sort of contribution.

As in *Jamieson v Rodhouse*, a more comprehensive approach to contributions might have made no difference at the end of the day, since the court went on to conclude that Mary had suffered no economic disadvantage. It was not prepared to accept that paying a share of the bills (and there was doubt that Mary had done so) amounted to economic disadvantage since she would have had to pay bills had she lived alone. In reality, Mary's loss amounted to nothing more than her perception that, because the parties were engaged to be married, she had expectations – now disappointed – of sharing in Robert's financial gains. The sheriff concluded, quite correctly, that what she was really seeking was a remedy akin to that of a spouse under the 1985 Act. Such a remedy was simply not available under the 2006 Act. In any event, even if she had established economic loss, the sheriff noted that it would have been offset by Robert's contributions in terms of providing her with a home and paying the bill in respect of it.

A broader approach to what constitutes a contribution has been adopted in other cases. In both *M v S*[91] and *F v D*,[92] the court recognised childcare and

---

88   At [118].
89   At [113].
90   At [105].
91   2008 SLT 871, discussed below at nn 96–103 and accompanying text.

home-making as contributions, suggesting the courts may find it easier to accord such recognition when children are present. That theory is supported by the decision in *Lindsay v Murphy*,[93] albeit the contributions there ranged widely and were somewhat case-specific.

To what extent, if any, has the economic advantage derived by the defender from the applicant's contributions been offset by any economic disadvantage suffered by the defender in the interests of (i) the applicant, or (ii) any relevant child?

Even if the pursuer/applicant can demonstrate that the defender sustained economic advantage as a result of her contributions, her case may still fall if the defender can show the requisite offsetting economic disadvantage. To date, defenders have had no success in doing so. In *Gow v Grant*,[94] the defender had attempted to argue that his business loan to the pursuer's adult child by a previous relationship represented offsetting economic disadvantage to him. Quite correctly, the sheriff dismissed that claim since the loan was not done 'in the interests of' Jessamine or, indeed, a relevant child. The Inner House did not comment on that aspect of the case.

It will become apparent that what can be characterised as one party's contribution might, in some circumstances, also be classified as economic disadvantage that party has sustained. As we shall see in *F v D*,[95] the defender tried to argue that he had contributed to the pursuer by supporting her and their child. Equally, that might have been presented as economic disadvantage sustained by him, but it was not.

Has the applicant suffered economic disadvantage in the interests of (i) the defender, or (ii) any relevant child?

Having vaulted the hurdle of establishing that the defender derived economic advantage from the pursuer's contributions, the pursuer/applicant must then demonstrate that he or she has suffered economic disadvantage – and not simply any disadvantage, but disadvantage suffered in the interests of the defender or any relevant child. The pursuer's disadvantage is as essential a part of the balancing exercise to be carried out by the court as is the defender's economic advantage.

That point is illustrated in *M v S*[96] (the case of leaving the court in the dark). S moved into M's flat, in 1998. Initially, both parties worked full time but M, a legal secretary, secured part-time employment with the same employer when she became pregnant with the couple's first child and, apart from periods of maternity leave, worked part time thereafter. A second child was born to the

---

[92]   2009 Fam LR 111, discussed below at nn 104–107 and accompanying text.
[93]   2010 Fam LR 156, discussed below at nn 124–130 and accompanying text.
[94]   2010 Fam LR 21, at [53]. In any event, the loan had been repaid with interest and was in the nature of an investment.
[95]   2009 Fam LR 111, discussed below at nn 104–107 and accompanying text.
[96]   2008 SLT 871.

couple. M had been a member of the firm's pension scheme, but stopped contributing after she ceased full-time employment. There had been discussions about her employer funding her training as a paralegal, but she did not pursue this career-enhancing option after her first pregnancy. S continued to work full time, began a training course and contributed to household bills, becoming the breadwinner and paying the mortgage and other bills when M ceased or reduced her employment. Loans were obtained to finance the expansion of M's flat through the purchase and remodelling of the property on the floor below in order to provide a three-bedroomed home that suited the family's needs rather better than the original one-bedroomed flat.

After the couple separated in 2006, M was left with the (now enlarged) home she had owned when the cohabitation began, albeit the property was now burdened with a larger mortgage. S left the relationship with no heritable (*anglicé* real) property and had to make fresh arrangements to buy a home. Both children lived with M, whose father provided considerable assistance with childcare, and had regular contact with S, who lived nearby. It was in this context that M sought an order for £50,000, under section 28(2)(a), and for £20,000 under section 28(2)(b).

Given the fact that this case was an early one, the Lord Ordinary did not apply a strict 'four questions' analysis, although addressing the substance of these questions was inherent in his approach. That S had derived economic advantage by the contributions of M was demonstrated by the fact that he had been able to continue and develop his career for 8 years and had improved his earning capacity, while M looked after the home and their children.

M's claim that she had suffered economic disadvantage had three distinct elements: her past loss of earnings, resulting from her moving to part-time work; her loss of pension entitlement; and her loss of opportunity to advance her career by training as a paralegal. The court found ample evidence to support the first two heads, while the third was, necessarily, a little more speculative. In addition, it had to be remembered that S had paid household bills and the mortgage, becoming the main breadwinner after the first child was born.[97]

Having found a certain balancing of advantages, disadvantages and contributions, thus far, perhaps the most telling feature of the case was the overall position of the parties at the end of the relationship. M had a bigger home, albeit one burdened by a larger mortgage than the original flat, while S had 'no discernable assets'.[98] Lord Matthews made clear that he viewed the dearth of evidence about the current value of that home as a 'serious omission'.[99] It had been M's choice 'to leave the court in the dark as to the

---

[97] At [292]–[299]. The court refused to accept counsel for the pursuer's characterisation of these contributions as 'merely alimentary': at [294]–[295].

[98] At [310].

[99] At [216]. S, who represented himself, had not sought valuation.

value of this substantial asset'[100] and, as a result, his Lordship was 'unable to say whether she had been disadvantaged by the cohabitation'.[101] As a result, the court made only the very small award of £1,460.31 under s 28(2)(a) in respect of the very subsidiary matter of balancing the value of the parties' endowment policies and the outstanding liability for overpaid tax credits[102] – far less than the £50,000 M had sought. On the more general claim in respect of lost wages, pension and opportunities, M was awarded nothing, those losses being balanced, in a general sense, by what she had gained. M fared rather better in respect of her claim for future childcare costs under s 28(2)(b) to which we shall return presently.[103] While *M v S* illustrates the importance of providing hard evidence when claiming disadvantage, it may be that M's failure to provide this evidence was because, in truth, she had sustained little or no overall disadvantage.

A somewhat inconsistent approach to proof of economic disadvantage was taken by the court in *F v D*,[104] (the case of the now-unemployed father). F already had a child, N, when she went to live with D in 2002. Initially, she was a student, later working part time. A child, K, was born to the couple. F continued in part-time employment after the separation and claimed that her childcare responsibilities prevented her from attending courses and advancing her career. D was 36 years old and had been employed full time throughout the cohabitation, his earnings increasing from £20,000 to £26,000. He stopped working after the separation and was in receipt of state benefits.

During the cohabitation, both parties contributed to household costs, with D paying for more than F, and F being primarily responsible for childcare and housekeeping. In 2003, D purchased a flat for £50,000 in his sole name, the purchase being financed by a mortgage of £47,000 and loans from F's father and D's parents of £1,500 each. It was sold after the separation, leaving net proceeds of about £28,000, much of which D used to pay off debts he had accumulated. He had paid very little to support the child, K. F sought awards under both s 28(2)(a) and (b).

The sheriff was satisfied that D had derived economic advantage from F's contributions, both in terms of his capital gain and in respect of childcare and household duties. Rather more tangentially, he viewed D's opportunity to borrow £1,500 from F's father as part of the picture of contributions, presumably on the basis that the father only lent the money because D was living with his daughter. However, he echoed the frustration of earlier judges over the lack of concrete evidence presented to him in respect of crucial information. While he accepted that F might have earned more had she not been restricted to part-time employment by her childcare responsibilities, the court was presented with no evidence of how her career might have developed.

---

[100] At [312].
[101] At [314].
[102] At [316]-[318].
[103] See, below nn 140-144 and 158 and accompanying text.
[104] 2009 Fam LR 111, also known as *Falconer v Dodds*.

Nor had he been presented with credible evidence of any economic disadvantage D had suffered in the interests of F or the child, K, this paucity of evidence being exacerbated by the fact that D was not 'a frank and trustworthy witness'.[105]

Where Sheriff Henry parted company with his fellows was over what he felt able to do with this partial picture since he took 'a broad approach' and awarded F £6,000 under s 28(2)(a).[106] A further award was made in respect of childcare costs and we shall return to it presently. It is tempting to suggest that, as in *M v S*,[107] the sheriff was letting the consequences of a failure to furnish the court with evidence lie at the door of the party responsible for the omission. But that is hardly what he did since both parties had failed to provide concrete evidence, F, in terms of her lost opportunities, and D, in respect of his alleged disadvantage. Perhaps the distinction is that D's action was seen as a product of his dishonesty, while F's may have amounted to no more than poor preparation. Such distinctions can be important in the exercise of discretion by a court faced with an untrustworthy defender – and one who seemed to be shirking his parental obligations to boot.

So much for the pursuer demonstrating economic disadvantage, but what of the need to show that this was sustained 'in the interests of the defender' or a relevant child? That element was to prove crucial to the Inner House when it heard the first appeal to reach it under the 2006 Act, in *Gow v Grant*[108] (the not 'in the first flush of youth' case). Jessamine Gow and Angus Grant became engaged to be married 2002 and began cohabiting in Angus' home the following year, parting company in 2008. Each had been married before, had grown-up children and, as Sheriff Mackie, who heard the case at first instance, put it candidly, if somewhat uncharitably, 'neither party was in the first flush of youth'.[109]

Jessamine was employed for most of the cohabitation, albeit she gave up work for about 2 years at Angus' request. She owned a flat, which she sold with his encouragement, receiving a net sum of £50,000. She used the money to pay off her debts, make a loan to her son for his business and to meet the couple's general living expenses. She also contributed £1,500 more than Angus to the purchase of a timeshare in Madeira. Angus took voluntary severance from his lecturing post, receiving payment totalling £46,000, and continued to work part time. During the cohabitation, Angus spent about £5,500 per year on household bills. Detailed evidence of the parties' financial dealings was provided, leading the sheriff to conclude that they had 'lived beyond their

---

[105] At [53].
[106] At [60].
[107] 2008 SLT 871, discussed above at nn 96–103 and accompanying text.
[108] 2011 Fam LR 50.
[109] 2010 Fam LR 21, at [46].

means'[110] and the Inner House to note that they had 'enjoyed a relatively extravagant lifestyle'.[111] Jessamine sought a payment of a capital sum under s 28(2)(a).

Both the sheriff and the Inner House approached their task – quite correctly, it is submitted – by distinguishing the goals of the 2006 Act, in dealing with parting cohabitants, from those of the 1985 Act, designed for spouses and civil partners. As the Inner House put it, echoing a similar observation from the sheriff,[112] while the 1985 Act 'established a scheme for . . . the fair distribution of matrimonial property acquired . . . during the subsistence of the marriage [or civil partnership]', the 2006 Act 'is not concerned with distribution of property'.[113]

Where both courts took a most regrettable turn was in describing an award to a former cohabitant as being 'in the nature of compensation'.[114] As Sheriff Miller had observed, in *Lindsay v Murphy*,[115] the term 'compensation' is 'pre-loaded with too many other shades of meaning in law to be of assistance here'.[116] The present author is prepared to put it in more forthright terms. To characterise a payment under s 28(2)(a) as 'compensation' is simply erroneous, since the term implies payment to make up for one party's loss, there being no need for the other party to have gained anything. As we have seen, an essential element of the test for an award is that the defender must have gained economic advantage.

However, the crucial issue on which the courts differed was whether the economic loss suffered by Jessamine had been sustained in Angus' interests. She had sold her home for £50,000 and it would have been worth in the order of £88,000 by the time the parties ceased cohabiting. Thus, she had lost £38,000. Since the sale had occurred with Angus' encouragement 'and in the interests of furthering their relationship',[117] the sheriff concluded that she had suffered economic disadvantage in Angus' interests and awarded her £38,000 in respect of it. The Inner House was simply not prepared to characterise the sale in this way, noting that:[118]

> 'The fact that the sale was encouraged by the defender is . . . insufficient to draw the inference that the transaction was in his interests. Likewise, the fact that the

---

[110] At [66].
[111] Inner House decision of 22 March 2011, above n 108 at [10].
[112] She had noted that the 2006 Act did not seek 'to achieve a fair division of parties' assets' but, rather, its goal was to review each party's contributions and effect redress of 'any net economic disadvantage': 2010 Fam LR 21, at [42].
[113] Inner House decision of 22 March 2011, above n 108 at [3].
[114] Inner House, ibid, at [3]; the sheriff at 2010 Fam LR 21, at [46].
[115] 2010 Fam LR 156 discussed below at nn 124-130 and accompanying text.
[116] 2010 Fam LR 156 at [62].
[117] Ibid, at [56].
[118] Inner House decision of 22 March 2011, above n 108 at [9].

sale was intended to further the parties' relationship is insufficient to justify the conclusion that it was in the defender's interests; those two matters appear to us to be conceptually quite distinct.'

Indeed, it noted that the sale had been in Jessamine's interests insofar as it enabled her to pay off some existing debts and make a loan to her son to help with his business.[119] Thus, Jessamine's economic loss did not qualify as the kind of economic disadvantage contemplated by the 2006 Act and the sheriff's award was overturned.

In addition, the sheriff had taken no account of Angus' economic contributions, in paying bills in respect of the home, and non-financial contributions, like the preparation of meals, viewing them as insufficient to offset Jessamine's economic disadvantage in respect of her contribution to the parties' joint living expenses and the timeshare purchase.[120] Again, the Inner House took a different view. It put Jessamine's contributions 'in the context of the parties' general finances and . . . [the fact that] the defender paid somewhat more towards joint expenses than the pursuer did'[121] and overturned the remaining £1,500 of the sheriff's award as well. Yet another parting cohabitant left the court empty handed.

To what extent, if any, has the economic disadvantage suffered by the applicant in the interests of (i) the defender, or (ii) any relevant child, been offset by any economic advantage the applicant has derived from the defender's contributions?

That the pursuer sustained economic disadvantage will not be sufficient to guarantee an award since any such disadvantage must be offset against any advantage derived from the defender's contributions.

As we saw in *Jamieson v Rodhouse*[122] (the case of 'good fortune of property price appreciation') and *Selkirk v Chisholm*[123] (the case of the 'old fashioned relationship'), the pursuer/applicants' claims failed, in part, due to the courts' rather narrow approach to what amounted to relevant contributions. However, even if the relevant contributions had been found to be present, success would still have eluded them because they could not demonstrate the requisite economic disadvantage. Janet Jamieson worked at the only job for which she was qualified, bought food and small household items, while Mary Selkirk did little more than pay for groceries. Even if an element of economic disadvantage had been present in either case, each woman had been provided with a roof over her head, and the effect of offsetting meant that neither could be said to be worse off than if she had been supporting herself alone.

---

[119] Ibid.
[120] The sheriff had also disregarded the fact that Jessamine remaining in Angus' home rent-free for some 18 months after the cohabitation ceased since it did not occur during the cohabitation. The Inner House did not address this point and it is discussed below at nn 193-197 and accompanying text.
[121] Inner House decision of 22 March 2011, above n 108 at [9]–[10].
[122] 2009 Fam LR 34.
[123] 2011 Fam LR 56.

(ii)   The final calculation

Assuming the pursuer/applicant has vaulted the hurdles outlined above, the court will then assess the quantum of the award to be made. How one court approached its task is illustrated by *Lindsay v Murphy*[124] (the 'Beckhams of Hawick' case),[125] the facts of which are somewhat singular and would have infuriated those on the political right in Scotland, had they received greater publicity.

Angela Lindsay and George Murphy cohabited from 2001 until 2007 and had three children together. Prior to the birth of their first child, Angela had worked as a financial controller, earning an annual salary in the region of £20,000, but ceased work, primarily to care for the children. Since the separation, she had returned to part-time work, earning £130 net per week. George had been diagnosed with depression and continued to be in receipt of state benefits. Throughout the cohabitation, neither George nor Angela was in employment and the family relied wholly on state benefits.

Despite that, the parties had become co-proprietors of a home, valued at £350,000. How they came to own such a valuable asset was the subject of much of the evidence in the case, but the tale of good fortune can be summarised as follows. In 2003, Angela purchased a plot of land, located in the town of Hawick, from George's brother for £6,000 and the court accepted that she would not have secured such a favourable deal but for her relationship with George. Thereafter, she expended considerable drive and energy obtaining planning permission to build a house on the land, engaging an architect and organising the construction project. George contributed to the process by arranging for building work to be carried out by trades people at less than commercial rates in the context of what the court described as 'a community where much business was done through the exchange of favours'[126] and in assisting with the work. Funding for the project came from the proceeds of the sale of a flat (£57,300) which Angela had co-owned with her mother and on which George had carried out improvements valued at £5,000. Further funding, in the form of gifts totalling £35,500, came from Angela's mother.

After the parties parted, Angela moved out of the house with the children and obtained rented accommodation. George continued to live in, and to maintain, the house. In November 2008, having taken separate and independent legal advice, they signed a minute of agreement to the effect that the property would be sold as soon as was reasonably practicable. By the time of the case, the property had not been sold. It was in this context that Angela sought division

---

[124] 2010 Fam LR 156.

[125] The sheriff found evidence of the pursuer's 'hubristic self-exaggeration', at [70], when the pursuer referred to the parties being described as 'the Beckhams of Hawick'. Sadly, this little gem is omitted from the report, but can be found in the transcript at 2010 WL 2832909 at www.scotcourts.gov.uk/opinions/AJ298_07.html (accessed 14 June 2011), the unreported ref is Court ref no AJ298/07.

[126] At [74].

and sale of the home;[127] an award of a capital sum of £312,000, under s 28(2)(a), and a further capital sum of £100,000, under s 28(2)(b). George counterclaimed for a capital award of £300,000.

Before answering the 'four questions', Sheriff Miller quantified the various contributions of the parties. Again, he had plentiful evidence with which to work and assessed Angela's financial contribution at £84,500 and that from Angus at £5,000. He viewed the increased value of the land (£74,000) as being 'attributable in equal measure to the non-financial contributions' of the parties and their roles – Angus' relationship with Angela as the motivation for his brother to sell her the land and Angela's obtaining of planning permission – as being 'mutually interdependent'.[128] If one might be permitted a little quibble with the learned sheriff here, while the 'but for' nature of Angus' contribution is clear, it is arguably rather too passive to be described as a 'contribution'. Nor does mutual interdependence necessarily imply that the contributions were to be quantified equally. Similarly, and arguably with greater justification, the sheriff found that each of the parties had contributed equally to the substantial saving (£136,500) on the cost construction – Angela, by organising and planning the project, and Angus, in securing the services of trades people at reduced cost by calling in favours owed by friends and assisting in the work himself.

Applying this to the 'four questions', the sheriff concluded that Angus had derived economic advantage to the tune of £39,750, there being no offsetting disadvantage to him. Angela's claim that she suffered economic disadvantage comprised two elements – her lost employment opportunities and her greater contribution to the value of the house. On the first element, the sheriff found there to be no disadvantage. While he was prepared to credit her with a strong work ethic, he noted that, since 2004 and childcare aside, her energies had been focused largely on the house-building project: something for which she had derived significant capital. In addition, her potential earnings were highly speculative and he preferred Angus' evidence on his willingness to care for the children should Angela have chosen to return to the workplace. Turning to the second element, Angela's economic disadvantage in terms of her greater contribution to the value of the house, the sheriff looked at what she had suffered in overall terms, concluding that this amounted to £14,750, being the amount by which the value of her contributions to the property exceeded the value of her one-half share of it. Given the interdependent nature of the parties' contributions, he felt that any offsetting there had already been taken into account.

It was at this point that Sheriff Miller interpreted his discretion under the Act as permission to 'be fair to both parties', something he regarded as quite permissible since the statute simply required him to 'have regard to' the various

---

[127] The court dismissed this crave fairly quickly on the basis that there had been no breach of the agreement, fairly concluded: at [55].

[128] At [82].

factors.[129] In his view, weighing Angus economic advantage (£39,750) against Angela's economic disadvantage (£14,750) would not do that, nor would focusing attention solely on the extent to which Angela's contributions exceed the value of her half share in the property, since that would deny her the benefit of her share in the increase in value of the property (£14,750). Rather, it would be 'fairer to see the property as a joint venture to which the parties made unequal contributions' and to award Angela a capital payment of £39,750.[130] So, having analysed the statute, identified the steps to be taken and applied them to the facts, it all came down to 'fairness' at the end of the day. A separate award was made in respect of future childcare, the subject to which we now turn.

(c)   The future economic burden of childcare: s 28(2)(b)

The courts have clearly found it very much easier to deal with awards under s 28(2)(b), designed to cover the future economic burden of childcare, albeit, again, they were not slow to highlight some flaws in this part of the legislation. Certainly, pursuers are faring much better in claims under this provision, meeting with success in all three cases decided to date. That may be, in part, because the concept of parents supporting their children is more familiar and universally accepted. In addition, it was easier for pursuer/applicants to furnish the courts with solid evidence of the cost of substitute care. Where the courts seem to be doing little, however, is in addressing the carer's lost employment opportunities occasioned by the fact that she (and, so far, it has always been a 'she') will have extensive childcare responsibilities.

It will be remembered that, due to the child support rules in place at the time dealing with the matter, this provision was not a part of the Scottish Law Commission's original recommendations and, thus, did not benefit from its process of considered reflection. As we shall see, s 28(2)(b) has some problematic features, largely amenable to remedy by judicious statutory amendment. It is worth bearing in mind that any sum awarded under s 28(2)(b) is most unlikely to be all that the defender will pay in respect of a child since child maintenance[131] and aliment[132] fall to be calculated separately and paid in addition to any award under this head.

(i)   The criteria

In assessing an application under s 28(2)(b), the court is directed to have regard to two of the criteria for an award under s 28(2)(a): namely, any economic advantage the defender has derived from the applicant's contributions and any economic disadvantage sustained by the pursuer in the interests of the defender

---

[129] At [89].
[130] Ibid.
[131] Child Support Act 1991, as (very extensively) amended. See further, Sutherland *Child and Family Law*, n 28 above, paras 8-024–8-079.
[132] Family Law (Scotland) Act 1985, s 1(1). See further, Sutherland, *Child and Family Law*, n 28 above, paras 8-080–8-102.

or a relevant child. However, this time, there is no requirement to engage in the offsetting exercises, encapsulated in subsections 5 and 6. Unlike s 28(2)(a), where there is express reference to payment of 'a capital sum', s 28(2)(b) refers to the order requiring 'the defender to pay such amount' as is specified and there is further provision permitting the court to stipulate when payment is to be made and to make the award payable by instalments.[133] Practitioners and the judges are reading this as meaning that *only* a capital sum may be awarded and ruling out the possibility of truly periodic payments.

Unlike s 28(2)(a), this provision has a clearer purpose, insofar as any award is directed at 'any economic burden' of caring for the couple's child after the cohabitation ends. The parallel provision of the 1985 Act requires that burden to be 'shared fairly' between the parties[134] and, while the 2006 Act imposes no such requirement, it is difficult to see what else the court might think itself supposed to do but to effect some equitable sharing of the economic burden of childcare. Nor does the 2006 Act provide the neat checklist of factors to be taken into account in making an award, found in the 1985 Act.[135] Indeed, as Sheriff Miller observed in *Lindsay v Murphy*,[136] 'the factors to which the court is to have regard [under the 2006 Act] are expressed, rather curiously, solely in the past tense'.[137]

(ii) Only the couple's child

An application under s 28(2)(b) can be made only in respect of the care of a child of whom the former 'cohabitants are the parents' and not to an 'accepted' child. In this respect (but not others), it replicates the parallel provision in the 1985 Act, applying to spouses and civil partners.[138] The bumper sticker may proclaim, 'A puppy is for life, not just for Christmas', but Scottish de facto and de jure step-parents have more limited responsibilities.

For cohabitants, a peculiarity of the provision is that the trigger for an award under s 28(2)(b) involves having regard to past advantages and disadvantages, including disadvantage sustained in the interests of a 'relevant child', that term including an 'accepted' child. Furthermore, one can acquire the obligation to aliment (but not to pay child maintenance in respect of) a child by accepting him or her into one's family.[139] One assumes that law teachers are already busy drafting fiendish examination problems incorporating these curiosities.

---

[133] 2006 Act, s 28(7)(b) and (c). The statutory language is untidy and there is certainly scope to argue that periodic payments may be competent under s 28(2)(b).

[134] Family Law (Scotland) Act 1985, s 9(1)(c).

[135] Ibid, s 11(3).

[136] 2010 Fam LR 156.

[137] At [66].

[138] Family Law (Scotland) Act 1985, s 9(1)(c).

[139] Ibid, s 1(1)(d).

(iii)   Economic burden

In *M v S*[140] (the case of leaving the court in the dark), it will be remembered that M left the relationship with a larger home where she lived with the parties' two children. S had regular contact with them and they stayed with him overnight twice each week. Hitherto, substantial amounts of childcare had been undertaken by M's father, 'a very caring grandfather who had not sought payment for his assistance'[141] and this was likely to continue as long as the grandfather's health permitted. Since the 2006 Act talks in terms of the *economic* burden of childcare, Lord Matthews felt that he had to leave out of account 'some notional economic burden that was never borne',[142] albeit he acknowledged that this might reflect 'a flaw in the legislation'.[143] With respect, it is submitted that he had to do no such thing. While other terms used in s 28 are defined, 'economic burden' is not. Given the speculative nature of the exercise in which the court was engaged and the 'broad axe' approach it was taking, it would have been quite possible to attach a notional figure to the grandfather's contribution and factor it into the overall calculation. That seems particularly appropriate in the case of services supplied by a 66-year-old man with some health concerns. This problem could be resolved for the future by minor amendment to the statute, defining economic burden more fully.

Then there was the issue of S having indicated that he would be willing to play a greater role in childcare. Quite correctly, the Lord Ordinary regarded the issue of contact as one to be resolved on the basis of the best interests of the children.[144] Since that matter was not before the court, he took no further account of it. The same issue arose in *Lindsay v Murphy*[145] (the 'Beckhams of Hawick' case), where separate proceedings were under way in respect of contact, and Sheriff Miller took much the same approach. Of course, these cases highlight the benefits of having all the issues in respect of relationship breakdown resolved in a single set of proceeding before the same judge, but that is a debate for another day.

(iv)   A duty to minimise loss?

Rather curiously, in *M v S*, the Lord Ordinary addressed the issue of the pursuer/applicant's duty to minimise her loss in the context of a situation where the cost of childcare might outweigh the carer-parent's earnings from employment.[146] While he concluded that there was no duty to minimise loss, the fact that the matter was raised at all is troubling. Are women – and it will usually be women – to be denied the opportunities associated with participation in the workforce because the only job they might be able to get, at least initially, is poorly paid?

---

[140] 2008 SLT 871.
[141] At [323].
[142] Ibid.
[143] At [324].
[144] At [226].
[145] 2010 Fam LR 156.
[146] 2008 SLT 871, at [320]–[321].

(v)   Are the defender's resources relevant?

Unlike the parallel provision in the 1985 Act,[147] the 2006 Act makes no express reference to taking account of the resources of the parties in making an award in respect of future childcare. At first glance, the failure to mention resources in the more limited context of the 2006 Act seems unimportant, since it might be assumed that a court would not make an award where it was wholly unrealistic for the defender to pay the sum involved.

Certainly, that was the view of the Lord Ordinary, in *M v S*, where he observed that, 'it might be that courts will be slow to make an award which will plainly be unenforceable'.[148] However, that was not the approach taken by Sheriff Hendry in *F v D*[149] (the case of the now-unemployed father). Refusing the request that payment of any capital sum awarded be deferred or made subject to instalment payments, he pointed out that, unlike the 1985 Act, the 2006 Act did not require him to take account of the parties' resources.[150] In any event, he noted that there was no evidence that the defender's circumstances would change in the foreseeable future. Of course, it must be remembered that what looks increasingly like an aberrant decision was taken in the context of a defender who the sheriff believed had given up his job in order 'to evade paying anything to the pursuer'.[151] Contrasting the context in which these decisions were made, Sheriff Miller, in *Lindsay v Murphy*,[152] was unwilling 'to take a hard and fast position on this issue',[153] preferring to let the decision be driven by the circumstances of the instant case.

(vi)   Awards not subject to future variation

The Lord Ordinary's observation, in *M v S*,[154] that s 28(2)(b) 'requires the court to indulge in certain speculation as to the future',[155] seems baffling insofar as it states the obvious. However, his, very legitimate, concern stemmed from the fact that this speculation took place without the possibility, present in the systems for assessment of child maintenance and aliment, of an award being varied at a future date, should circumstances change.[156] The real source of the problem is that, by and large, capital awards are not subject to future variation, while awards of periodic payments can be varied on showing a change of circumstances. Both types of awards are possible in respect of future children care under the 1985 Act.[157] While there is scope for debate on the point, since the statutory language is untidy, the courts are proceeding on the basis that

---

[147] Family Law (Scotland) Act 1985, s 11(3)(g).
[148] 2008 SLT 871, at [261].
[149] 2009 Fam LR 111.
[150] At [63].
[151] At [53].
[152] 2010 Fam LR 156.
[153] At [67].
[154] 2008 SLT 871.
[155] At [319].
[156] At [319] and earlier, at [262].
[157] Indeed, this very problem was addressed, in the context of the 1985 Act, in *Munro v Munro*

only the former are available under the 2006 Act. Of course, a court may order instalment payments of a capital award under the 2006 Act, but it remains a capital award and, as such, not subject to variation. Yet again, a statutory amendment, making express provision for variable, periodic payments under the 2006 Act, would address this problem very easily.

(vii)   Calculating the award

In calculating the quantum of the award to be made, the judges engaged in number-crunching exercises, albeit, they were conscious that what they were doing was not an exact science. They based their calculations on evidence provided by pursuer/applicants of the cost of items like school uniforms and outings, breakfast and after-school clubs and the like. They then applied what they regarded as suitable multipliers to the sums arrived at, sometimes adjusting down to take account of times when the child would be cared for by the pursuer, older siblings or other relatives or spending time with friends.

In *M v S*, the Lord Ordinary carried out this exercise in respect of the two children and simply split the resulting total between the parties, ordering S to pay £13,000 in specified instalments.[158] While acknowledged that the 6-year-old boy, in *F v D*, would be a 'child' for another 10 years, the sheriff applied a multiplier of seven to the total sum he calculated as appropriate to accommodate 'the unpredictable aspects of life' and awarded £3,000.[159] In *Lindsay v Murphy*, the sheriff took the view that 'The children will be highly unusual indeed if they will consent to be sent to a day-care facility right up to the age of 16',[160] calculated care costs up to each child's 12th birthday, discounted these by 25% to allow for holidays, family input and time with friends and came up with a grand total of £8,320 in respect of the three children.

(viii)   What is missing here?

All three of the mothers in the cases to date were working part time. Yet in none of these cases was there any discussion of an award in respect of her economic loss occasioned by the fact that these mothers would, in all probability, have to limit their career development because of future childcare responsibilities. In *Lindsay v Murphy*, Sheriff Miller acknowledged that the defender was 'deriving economic advantage in that the pursuer is taking the lion's share of responsibility for the parties' children',[161] but that was in the context of finding the test for an award under s 28(2)(b) satisfied and related to past losses. There was no mention of the ongoing economic impact this

---

2006 Fam LR 50, where payment of a capital sum was deferred until the young woman involved reached 18 to allow for the fact that she might (again) change her mind about which parent she wished to live with.

[158]   2008 SLT 871 at [352].

[159]   2009 Fam LR 111 at [61].

[160]   2010 Fam LR 156 at [91]

[161]   2010 Fam LR 156 at [90].

responsibility would have on the pursuer. Granted, the point does not appear to have been put to the court in any of the cases and, such is the nature of the adversarial system, that it is not the judge's responsibility to make the argument. However, since fresh economic loss will accrue over the years to come, if the pursuer continues to bear a disproportionate share of the childcare burden, it is part of the economic cost of childcare. This is clearly an aspect of any claim deserving of attention from savvy solicitors in the future.

V   SUCCESSION

If Scots law did little to help parting cohabitants in the past, it did absolutely nothing for the survivor where the other cohabitant died. In the absence of a will-making provision for the surviving partner, he or she was treated like a stranger as far as sharing in the deceased partner's estate was concerned. In contrast, spouses and civil partners have substantial automatic succession rights, known as prior rights and legal rights – rights regarded as so fundamental that they cannot be displaced by a will.[162] Of course, there the argument can be made that, had the deceased wanted to provide for a cohabitant, he or she could have done so by making a will. But, whether due to inertia or a reluctance to face the reality of one's own demise, many people fail to execute a will.

Again, since it never intended to place cohabitants in the same position as spouses and civil partners, the Scottish Law Commission's recommendation for reform of the law was less generous to them.[163] The legislation enacted is less generous still.[164] To date, only three cases have been reported under s 29 of the 2006 Act so it may be too soon to draw general conclusions about its efficacy.

(a)   When s 29 applies

A surviving cohabitant[165] who was cohabiting with the deceased immediately before his or her death may apply to the court, within 6 months of the death, for an award, provided that the deceased died domiciled in Scotland.[166] The court has no discretion to extend that period of time. An award may be made from the deceased's 'net intestate estate', being such of the estate as is not

---

[162]   Succession (Scotland) Act 1964, ss 8 and 9. See further Sutherland, *Child and Family Law*, n 28 above, paras 16-218–16-248. For the wisdom of executing a fresh will on separation, see *Price v Baxter* 2009 Fam LR 138.

[163]   *Report on Family Law*, (Scot Law Com No 135, 1992) para 16.1, available at www.scotlawcom.gov.uk/publications/reports/1990-1999/ (accessed June 2011) paras 16.24–16.37.

[164]   The Commission would have allowed the court discretion to extend the very short time-limit and defined 'net estate' much more widely. For more detailed discussion of the Commission's proposals and the provision, see Sutherland, *Child and Family Law*, n 28 above, paras 16-249–16-262.

[165]   As defined in the 2006 Act, s 25, discussed above at nn 20–25 above and accompanying text.

[166]   2006 Act, s 29.

subject to a will, minus debts, taxes and the prior and (most of) the legal rights of any surviving spouse or civil partner.[167] Thus, priority is given to a spouse or civil partner,[168] but not to children, who also have automatic inheritance rights.

It was rather disappointing that the first case reported under s 29 fell at the jurisdiction hurdle. In *Chebotareva v King's Executrix*,[169] a whole host of factors, including the fact that the deceased was born and died in London and retained property there in which he lived and at which he was registered to vote, led the court to conclude that he 'had never changed his domicile and retained his domicile of origin which was England'.[170] That being the case, s 29 simply did not apply.

(b)   The orders and the criteria

Any award is at the discretion of the court and may not exceed what the surviving cohabitant would have received had he or she been a spouse or civil partner.[171] It may take the form of any or all of the following: an order for the payment of a capital sum; an order transferring specified heritable or moveable property to the survivor and such interim order as the court think fit.[172] In exercising its discretion, the court must have regard to: the size and nature of the deceased's net intestate estate; any benefit received (or to be received) by the survivor on, or in consequence of, the deceased's death and from somewhere other than the deceased's net estate; the nature and extent of any other rights against, or claims on, the deceased's net estate; any other matters the court considers appropriate.[173] Notably absent from the checklist is any express reference to the length and nature of the cohabitation but, as we shall see, that has not precluded courts from considering them under the feneral heading of 'other matters'.

In *Savage v Purches*,[174] the first reported case under the 2006 Act to feature a same-sex relationship, James Savage and Graham Voysey had cohabited for some 2 years and 8 months until Graham's death at the age of 44. He died intestate and was survived by a half-sister, the defender, Sandra Purches. While the sheriff found that James and Graham had been cohabiting at the time of Graham's death, he observed that James 'exuded a sense of self entitlement'[175] throughout the proceedings and noted 'a distinct whiff of avarice about the

---

[167] 2006 Act, s 29(10).

[168] This is not so in respect of the spouse's claim to legal rights from the 'free estate', but that aspect of succession law need not detain us here.

[169] 2008 Fam LR 66, also reported as *Chebotareva v Khandro (King's Executrix)* 2008 GWD 12-231. Dorje Khandro was not only the deceased's executrix, she was also his sister and, as is common in such cases, had a pecuniary interest in its outcome.

[170] 2008 Fam LR 66 at [17].

[171] 2006 Act, s 29(4).

[172] 2006 Act, s 29(2).

[173] 2006 Act, s 29(3).

[174] 2009 SLT (Sh Ct) 36; 2009 Fam LR 6.

[175] At [4].

whole action raised by the pursuer'.[176] As directed by the Act, the court took account of the fact that James had already received £120,000 from Graham's pension fund, being one half of a death benefit from the deceased's pension scheme (the other half going to Sandra) and an annual pension of about £9,500 (estimated as having a replacement value of £298,900) from Graham's employers. The court also took account of the short duration of the cohabitation, the higher standard of living James had enjoyed during that time[177] and Graham's failure to execute a will in James' favour, something he had done in respect of a previous cohabitant. In the event, the court refused to award James anything at all.

A rather more sympathetic applicant fared better in *Windram, Applicant*,[178] albeit her success came at the price of encroaching substantially on her children's inheritance. Mandy Windram and William Somers Giacopazzi had lived together for 24 years until William's death at the age of 46. They had two children, aged 15 and 12, and their lives together were based on Mandy being the homemaker, while William was the breadwinner. Under the law on intestate succession, the children stood to inherit his whole estate, worth in the region of £300,000 and including the family home, which was in William's name and on which there was an outstanding mortgage, its contents and other assets. While Mandy received some £25,000 from William's pension fund, this, combined with modest part-time earnings, was not enough to enable her to provide a home for the family. A curator ad litem was appointed to represent the children's interests.

Seeking to 'strike a fair balance'[179] between the interests of Mandy and those of the children, Sheriff Scott ordered the home and its contents to be transferred to Mandy, along with £34,000 to enable her to pay off the mortgage and to meet maintenance and other costs associated with the home, leaving the children with some £70,000 each. In reaching her decision, the sheriff considered the following 'other factors' to be relevant: the couple's lengthy 'stable close relationship',[180] their plans to marry that were defeated by William's sudden death, Mandy's past dependency due to her role as a 'full time mother and housewife', her care of William throughout his final illness and her continuing obligations to their children.[181]

---

[176] At [5].
[177] The court, at [3] and [5], made rather a lot of Graham's generosity to James and only time will tell if a similar approach will be taken by a future court faced with a man being equally generous to a female cohabitant.
[178] 2009 Fam LR 157.
[179] At [13].
[180] At [3].
[181] At [14].

VI CONCLUSIONS

It will be remembered that the 2006 Act did not seek to equate cohabitation with marriage and civil partnership but, rather, was aimed at 'the easing of certain legal difficulties and the remedying of certain situations which are widely perceived as being harsh and unfair'.[182] Has it achieved this modest goal?

There is no doubt that many of the judges were frustrated by the fact that the provisions of the 2006 Act lacked a clear statement of purpose and some questioned the limited goals of the legislation. Time and again, they contrasted s 28 unfavourably with the 1985 Act's crisp principles and fuller guidance. Practitioners echoed these concerns and were troubled by the width of the court's discretion that resulted. While these criticisms have some validity, it is worth remembering that most statutes take a little time to bed down and the early days of the 1985 Act were not without debate. In *Gow v Grant*,[183] the Inner House was given the opportunity to provide guidance that was missing from the statutory provisions, thus assisting future courts on applying it. Sadly, the court did not grasp that opportunity with any real enthusiasm. On occasion, the courts were simply not given enough information with which to work in applying the 2006 Act and sometimes the party responsible paid the price for deceit or prevarication. But there is no escaping the fact that responsibility for the dearth of information sometimes lay at the door of the solicitor who prepared the case. It is tempting to suggest that this may be a result of overworked solicitors operating within the constraints of a legal aid system that fails to reward them adequately for the time required to prepare a case. However, solicitors clearly heeded the warnings from the bench and, in later cases, at least some of which involved legal aid, the court was furnished with much more detailed information.[184]

For couples whose relationship has not worked out, it seems there is less than a 50-50 chance of securing an award under s 28(2)(a). Simply cohabiting while a partner accumulates assets will, by itself, be of no assistance to an applicant,[185] but that reflects the fact that s 28(2)(a) was never designed to create a property-sharing regime akin to that available to spouses and civil partners on relationship breakdown. In establishing economic advantage and disadvantage, what the court accepts as a contribution is crucial. Supplying capital for a project passes muster most easily,[186] but simply paying a share of the bills may not.[187] Non-economic contributions that open the door to the accumulation of

---

[182] *Report on Family Law* (Scot Law Com No 135, 1992), para 16.1, available at www.scotlawcom.gov.uk/publications/reports/1990-1999 (accessed June 2011) para 16.1.
[183] *Gow v Grant*, above nn 108–121.
[184] *Gow v Grant*, above nn 108–121, *Lindsay v Murphy*, above nn 124–130 and *Selkirk v Chisholm*, nn 85–90 above.
[185] *Jamieson v Rodhouse*, nn 79–84 above and *Selkirk v Chisholm*, nn 85–90 above.
[186] *Lindsay v Murphy*, above nn 124–130.
[187] *Selkirk v Chisholm*, above nn 85–90.

wealth, like facilitating a loan[188] or managing a project,[189] again, gain recognition. The greatest inconsistency arises in respect of housekeeping duties, since they gain credit in some cases[190] but not in others.[191] The problem here lies not in the legislation, which defines contributions quite clearly, but in judicial attitudes. The courts have found s 28(2)(b), dealing with awards in respect of the economic burden of future childcare to be easier to apply, albeit some fine tuning of the legislation may be warranted. On the basis of the few inheritance cases to date, the courts appear to be finding that s 29 and, in particular, the device of 'other factors', offers sufficient flexibility to enable them to tailor-make solutions to fit the instant case.

Nonetheless, there is scope for amendment of the legislation itself. The time-limits for raising the action – one year for financial provision cases and 6 months for succession cases – are arguably too short, resulting in a rush to litigation when the parties might have been able to negotiate a settlement, had they been given more time.

The parameters of the time frame for calculating advantages, disadvantages and contributions might benefit from being stated expressly. As we saw in *Gow v Grant*,[192] the sheriff took no account of the defender's contribution in providing a home for his former partner after the cohabitation ceased since the parties were no longer cohabitants and, thus, s 28 no longer applied to them.[193] In effect, the end of the cohabitation acted as a portcullis, slamming down to render future actions irrelevant. It might reflect the whole picture better if contributions benefitted from greater latitude. What of the other end of the time frame and advantages and disadvantages sustained in anticipation of cohabitation? Take, for example, the pursuer who, encouraged by the defender, sold her home or gave up a good job in order to move across the country to live with him (or her). Does the loss occasioned fall to be disregarded because the action predates the cohabitation and so, by definition, the parties were not cohabiting at the time? Certainly, spouses have been able to recoup their losses in similar circumstances,[194] but the 1985 Act makes express reference to advantage and disadvantage that occurred 'whether before or during the marriage'.[195] Perhaps the answer here lies in amending the definitions in the 2006 Act to reflect similar breadth – and to do so before the courts have to struggle with the issue, running the risk of inconsistent decisions.[196]

---

[188] *F v D* 2009, nn 104-107 above and *Gow v Grant*, nn 108–122 above.

[189] *Lindsay v Murphy*, above nn 124–130.

[190] *F v D* 2009, above nn 104–107.

[191] *Jamieson v Rodhouse*, nn 79–84 above, *Gow v Grant*, nn 108–121 above and *Selkirk v Chisholm*, nn 85–90 above.

[192] See above nn 108–111.

[193] The Inner House made no reference to that aspect of the case, neither endorsing nor disapproving the sheriff's approach.

[194] *Dougan v Dougan* 1998 SLT (Sh Ct) 2. It must be admitted that the courts have not been wholly consistent in respect of future benefits under the 1985 Act, see also *Cahill v Cahill* 1998 SLT (Sh Ct) 96.

[195] Family Law (Scotland) Act 1985, s 9(2).

[196] In *Mitchell v Gibson*, 14 February 2011, Sheriff Principal, Tayside Central and Fife, a recent

The 1985 Act again provides a model for other useful amendments to the 2006 Act in other respects and the latter could be amended usefully to state expressly whether a party's conduct is relevant and whether resources should be taken into account in making an award. The fact that an award under s 28(2)(b), in respect of future childcare, cannot be varied subsequently is inexorably tied to the prevailing view that the legislation limits any award to a capital sum and thought might be given to introducing the option of periodic payments that could be varied on showing a change of circumstances. Both the 1985 Act and s 28(2)(b) of the 2006 Act might benefit from amendment, clarifying what constitutes the 'economic burden' of childcare and, in particular, making it clear that the carer's loss of earnings is part of the picture. More fundamentally, the policy question of who bears the future cost of caring for an 'accepted child' is ripe for re-examination, possibly as part of a more wide-ranging review of what it means to be a step-parent.

It is over a quarter of a century since the Scottish Law Commission examined the legal consequences of cohabitation and much has changed in that time. Same-sex couples now have the option of entering a civil partnership in Scotland, and many jurisdictions around the world have placed cohabitants on a par with couples who have formalised their relationships. Most of the modest reforms proposed by the Commission have been implemented and, while some flaws in the legislation could be addressed by statutory amendment, there is a more fundamental question to address. Do these modest reforms provide for adequate legal recognition of cohabitation, a form of relationship that has increased in both popularity and social acceptability over the intervening years? Certainly, some of the judges have expressed doubt on that score.[197] In short, it is time to refer the matter back to the Commission with a direction to undertake a comprehensive review of the legal consequences of cohabitation.

---

unreported case, the pursuer had given up rented accommodation in order to cohabit with the defender, but the court did not address the questions of time frame, dismissing her claim on other grounds.

[197] See, eg, *M v S*, above nn 96–103 per Lord Matthews at [260]: 'It is not clear to me why some greater concession to a concept of community property was not included in the 2006 Act ... but there it is.'

Serbia

INHERITANCE RIGHTS OF A SURVIVING SPOUSE UNDER SERBIAN LAW

*Olga Cvejić Jančić**

Résumé

L'auteur analyse la situation successorale du conjoint survivant relevant du premier ou du second ordre d'héritiers. Des différences existent entre les règles successorales à proprement parler et les autres dispositions. Elles portent notamment sur la déchéance du droit d'hériter du de cujus ou sur les hypothèses dans lesquelles la part successorale peut être réduite ou augmentée. Les règles varient aussi quant à la possibilité qui s'offre au conjoint survivant de conserver des biens particuliers appartenant à la succession, quitte à en payer le prix aux autres héritiers. Cette étude aborde également la situation successorale du conjoint lorsqu'il est héritier testamentaire protégé.

I PRE-WAR LAW

Inheritance law, as well as the complete legal system in Serbian society, has been significantly changed in the period after the Second World War (WWII), compared to the pre-war period. Before WWII, inheritance law, governed by the Serbian Civil Code (1844),[1] was based on the patriarchal concept of family and dominant legal status of a man to the detriment of a woman. This concept actually means that daughters or other female offspring could not inherit if there were male offspring, who were favoured. It was similar with the inheritance rights of a wife, who could only retain the lifetime usufruct (jointure) after the death of her husband. Such differences in the inheritance rights of female and male heirs were abolished after WWII when they obtained equal inheritance status.

---

*   Professor, University of Singidunum, Faculty of European Legal and Political Studies, Department of Private Law, Novi Sad, Serbia, e-mail: olgacvejic@gmail.com.
[1]   Serbia was one of the rare countries in Europe at that time that enacted the Civil Code. The first and most famous Civil Code in Europe was enacted in 1804 in France under the name of the Napoleonic Code. The second one was the General Civil Code (Allgemeines Bürgerliches Gesetzbuch) enacted in Austria in 1811. The Serbian Civil Code (enacted in 1844) was brought under the significant influence of the Austrian General Civil Code: see more in D Nikolić *Uvod u sistem gradjanskog prava* (*Introduction in the system of Civil Law*) (Novi Sad, 2005) pp 158–160.

II   THE CONSTITUTIONAL BASES OF INHERITANCE

Nowadays, inheritance is governed by the Serbian Constitution (2006)[2] and the Inheritance Act (1995),[3] while the Serbian Civil Code (SCC) (1844) was abolished after WWII. The most important constitutional principles of inheritance law are the principle of prohibition against discrimination based on sex, the principle of guarantee of the right to inheritance and the principle of equalisation of a child born out of wedlock with a child born in wedlock.

(a)   The principle of prohibition against discrimination based on sex

The principle of prohibition against discrimination based on sex (art 21(3) of the Constitution) is a very important one for the legal status of a woman in the field of inheritance. Thanks to that principle, introduced by the first post-war constitution (1946) and remaining until now, a woman acquired the right to inheritance on equal bases as a man. That means that a wife has a right to inherit from her husband (and vice versa) and daughters or other female offspring have the same rights to inherit from their parents and relatives as the male heirs. That was a very revolutionary principle because before WWII under the SCC a wife could not inherit from her husband (and vice versa),[4] and daughters and women generally could not inherit until there were male heirs. A widow could, after the death of her husband, inherit only a right to maintenance[5] and usufruct of the husband's property (jointure)[6] which lasted until her death or remarriage.

(b)   The principle of guarantee of the right to inheritance

Our Constitution provides that the 'right to inheritance shall be guaranteed in accordance with the law', and that the '[r]ight to inheritance may not be denied or restricted for failing to observe public duties'.[7] This provision is perhaps not so interesting today, because nobody denies the right to transfer property of a decedent to his or her heirs, either by the law or by a will, and in some legislation even under a contract of inheritance. However, in the communist regimes those rights have been questioned, because the inheritance of family property was considered as a means of transferring social inequality in general.

---

[2]   The Constitution, which is now in force, was adopted on 30 September 2006, the Official Herald of Republic of Serbia, No 83/2006.

[3]   The Inheritance Act of Serbia, published in the Official Herald No 46/1995 and 101/2003.

[4]   Bearing in mind that women usually did not work outside the household and did not have valuable property, the question of inheritance rights of a surviving husband was also meaningless.

[5]   SCC, para 412.

[6]   SCC, para 413.

[7]   Serbian Constitution, art 59.

(c)   The principle of equalisation of a child born out of wedlock with a child born in wedlock[8]

Under the SCC, children born out of wedlock had no inheritance rights. They were deemed illegitimate children and did not have any rights to inherit from their parents and other relatives, except upon their express will.[9] However, when the parents after the child's illegitimate birth concluded a lawful marriage and therefore the child was legitimised, he or she could acquire the full inheritance rights like a child born in wedlock.[10]

After WWII a child born out of wedlock had a right to inherit the property of the parents (a father and a mother), as well as the property of the relatives of his or her mother. A child born out of wedlock had a right to inherit the property of the relatives of his or her father only if paternity was established by the recognition of the father and not by a court's decision. This legal situation lasted from 1974 until the Constitution, which abolished any differences between the legal status of a child born in wedlock and a child born out of wedlock. Both of them have full inheritance rights towards their parents and all their relatives.

III   THE INHERITANCE RIGHTS OF A SPOUSE[11]

Under the Serbian Inheritance Act there are two legal bases for inheritance. It is possible to inherit on the basis of the statute (intestate succession) and on the basis of a testament (will). An inheritance contract is not a legal ground for inheritance since the end of WWII. Before the war, an inheritance contract was the third ground for inheritance,[12] but, as is emphasised in the legal literature, it was not clear enough whether this inheritance contract could have been concluded only between spouses or between all persons.[13] The pre-war Serbian Civil Code was under the significant influence of the General Civil Code of Austria, which in arts 602 and 1249 prescribes that an inheritance contract could be concluded only between spouses (later, from 1817 it was also allowed

---

8   Serbian Constitution, art 64(4).
9   SCC, art 409(2) which reads: 'children born out of wedlock, as illegitimate, cannot have a legal right to inherit from their father's or mother's property, except according to their express will'.
10   SCC, art 409(1).
11   The community of life of two persons who did not conclude a marriage (cohabitants) does not produce any inheritance rights, irrespective of whether they are of different or same sex. However, between them there are great differences in their legal status. While heterosexual cohabitants enjoy the same rights as spouses regarding *marital rights and obligations* (such as mutual maintenance, property regime, right to adopt a child, right to the treatment of infertility by medical assisted reproduction, right to cohabitation) if their community of life lasted a longer time and there are no impediments for conclusion of the lawful marriage, same-sex cohabitants are discriminated against and do not enjoy any mutual rights.
12   SCC, art 394.
13   See B Blagojević and O Antić *Nasledno pravo* (Beograd, 1991) g str363 i 364 [*Inheritance Law* (Belgrade, 1991) pp 363–364].

between fiancés).[14] However, in the SCC this was not specified and therefore art 394 of the SCC was very confusing.

A testament is a stronger ground for inheritance than the statute, which means that the property of a decedent (defunct, deceased) will be distributed in accordance with the Inheritance Act only if the decedent died intestate, if his or her testament is null and void, if due to other reasons a testament cannot be administered (a testamentary heir refuses to accept his or her share, dies before a testator without offspring and so on) or if a testator did not dispose of the entire property by a testament. As a matter of fact, a testator can leave his or her property to any natural person or legal entity. Nevertheless, a testator is completely free to dispose of the 'free' part of the property, but not with the whole property. A so-called 'protected (reserved) part of inheritance' belongs to so-called 'protected (necessary) heirs'. The provisions which regulate the protected succession are compulsory (imperative) and if a testator does not comply with them, the necessary heirs have a right to ask the court to reduce the estate in order to compensate the reserved share of the protected heirs.[15]

However, in most European countries, ie in the continental part of Europe, as well as in Serbia, a testament is not very common in practice. People have great confidence in the inheritance law regulations, because they believe they would have disposed of their property in the same way if they had composed a will.

Intestate succession is organised according to inheritance orders. A closer inheritance order includes closer relatives as heirs, while further inheritance orders include further relatives. A surviving spouse may inherit in the first or in the second inheritance order, which depends on the circumstances I am going to explain in detail later in Part IV.

In the first inheritance order are included the children of the decedent (born in wedlock, out of wedlock and adopted children) and their descendants per stirpes, as well as a surviving spouse.[16] A surviving spouse and children divide the inheritance equally and should receive equal shares, while the descendants of a child who could not inherit, divide the inheritance in parts. They inherit on the basis of the principle of representation, meaning that the share of their ancestor will belong to them in equal parts.[17] For example, if a decedent has a surviving spouse and three children, all of them will receive one-quarter of the property (succession). If one child passed away before a decedent, that child's quarter will be distributed to his or her children (grandchildren of a decedent) in equal shares, and so on. The principle of representation may be applied in

---

[14]   Ibid.
[15]   Inheritance Act, arts 58–60.
[16]   Inheritance Act, art 9(1).
[17]   Inheritance Act, art 10.

the first inheritance order without any restrictions, until there are descendants of the heir who cannot[18] or do not want to inherit.

Besides the principle of representation, the second governing principle of intestate succession is the principle of 'increment of inheritance share'. This principle means that, if an heir who died before the decedent has not left offspring or cannot or does not want to inherit, his or her portion will be distributed to other heirs of the same order, because the principle of representation cannot be applied. For example, if a decedent has a spouse and three children, and one of the children who died before the decedent does not have any offspring, his or her share will be distributed to the spouse and two other children in three equal shares. So, the spouse and children will receive one-third of the inheritance, instead of one-quarter.

In distinction to the principle of representation, the principle of increment is not unlimited. Thus, if a spouse remains the only heir in the first order of inheritance,[19] according to the principle of increment the spouse would inherit the entire property of the decedent. But, this is not allowed under the Serbian Inheritance Act. In such a case, a spouse will not receive the entire inheritance, but will now belong to the second order of inheritance. In the second order, a spouse has a privileged position with respect to the other heirs, and will receive one-half of the inheritance. The second part of the inheritance will be distributed to the parents of a decedent in equal share, meaning that a mother will receive one-quarter and a father of the decedent the other quarter. If the parents or one of them passed away before a decedent, their portion will be distributed to their offspring (to siblings and half-brothers/sisters of a decedent and their offspring, per stirpes).

If a spouse remains the sole heir in the second order, he or she will receive the entire inheritance, because there are no more exceptions to the principle of increment and all the shares of other heirs from the second order will belong to a surviving spouse.[20] On the other hand, if a spouse does not survive a decedent, or cannot or does not want to inherit, the entire inheritance will be divided between the parents of a decedent in equal parts – one-half will belong to the father and the second half to the mother.[21]

When the surviving spouse loses the right to inherit

The Inheritance Act provides for situations when a surviving spouse will lose the right to inherit from a decedent although their marriage legally exists at the moment of death. That will happen in the following situations:[22]

---

[18] An heir cannot inherit, for example, if he or she passed away before a decedent, was unworthy to inherit or is penalised with other inheritance sanctions, such as exclusion from inheritance rights or deprivation of reserved share.

[19] It will be the case if a decedent had no offspring or they cannot or do not want to inherit.

[20] Inheritance Act, art 15.

[21] Inheritance Act, art 12(3).

[22] See art 22 of the Inheritance Act.

(1) *If a decedent during his or her life has initiated divorce proceedings and after death the court established that there were grounds for divorce.* As a matter of fact, the marriage ends with the death of one spouse and the court cannot dissolve a marriage that has already been ended by the death of one spouse, because dead people cannot divorce.[23] However, the Family Act allows the heirs of a deceased spouse to continue already initiated divorce proceedings in order to determine that there were grounds for divorce.[24] This way they will eliminate a surviving spouse from the possibility of inheriting from the decedent. It should be emphasised that the continuation of the court proceedings may be requested by the heirs of a plaintiff as well as the heirs of a defendant, since both of them have an interest in a surviving spouse not receiving any part of the decedent's property.

(2) *If the marriage has been annulled after the death of a decedent, for reasons that were known to a surviving spouse,* in other words, if a surviving spouse was unconscionable at the time of entering the marriage. That means that he or she had known that there were causes for the annulment of the marriage and despite that agreed to enter into the marriage. Unlike the previous case (under (1)), if the marriage is null and void the court proceedings may be initiated even after the death of one spouse, because in such cases no deadline for annulment is prescribed. If the court annuls the marriage, a surviving spouse will not be able to acquire inheritance rights after the death of the decedent. On the other hand, the heirs of a decedent may continue the court proceedings, if the action for annulment was brought before the court during the decedent's life but before the end of the proceedings the decedent dies.[25]

---

[23] O Antić and Z Balinovac *Komentar zakona o nasledjivanju* (Beograd, 1996) g str 151 [*Commentary of the Inheritance Act* (Belgrade, 1996) p 151].

[24] Family Act, art 220(2) and (3). It should be emphasised that a continuation of the court proceedings may be requested by both the heirs of the plaintiff as well as the heirs of a defendant spouse. This is an innovation introduced for the first time in our law by the Family Act in 2005, until the Family Act had entered into force, a continuation of the court proceedings in matrimonial disputes could only be requested by the heirs of a plaintiff and not by the heirs of a defendant. However, this was completely wrong because from 1980 in our family law fault as the basis for divorce no longer had any influence on the right to ask for a divorce, as it was before that. This means that before 1980 it could never happen that a spouse who was solely to blame for divorce initiated divorce proceedings and had the status of a plaintiff. After 1980 it was possible and therefore both the heirs of the plaintiff as well as the heirs of the defendant were justifiably entitled to continue matrimonial disputes in order to prove that there were grounds for the cessation of the marriage. See more in O Cvejić Jančić *Porodično pravo* Knjiga I 'Bračno pravo' (Novi Sad, 2001) str 186–187 [*Family Law*, vol I, 'Marital Law' (Novi Sad, 2001) pp 186–187].

[25] The circle of persons entitled to initiate court proceedings for the annulment of a marriage that is null and void is wider than that entitled to initiate divorce proceedings or proceedings to annul a voidable marriage. Spouses, persons having a legal interest in the annulment of the marriage and the public prosecutor are entitled to initiate the annulment of a null and void marriage. The right to sue cannot be lost due to the passage of time (art 212 of the Family Act). The right to initiate divorce proceedings pertains only to spouses, while in the case of a voidable marriage the right to sue pertains to spouses and to the parents of an underage spouse until that spouse reaches majority.

(3) *If the common life of the spouses had permanently ceased before the death of the decedent,* due to the fault of the surviving spouse or due to their agreement that they do not want to live together any more. Since the marriage has no meaning for them, ie their marriage became only 'an empty shell' without marital substance, it is justified that the surviving spouse cannot inherit from the decedent. The fault for the break-up of the common marital life has an important role for the recognition of the right to inherit. If a surviving spouse is to blame for separation, he or she will not be entitled to inherit from the deceased. The same rule is applicable if both of them agree that it is better for them to live separately and independently. However, if the decedent due to his or her behaviour contributed to the break-up of the common life, the surviving spouse will retain the full right to inherit.

This solution is completely reasonable, since the community of life of the spouses is a substantial condition for a valid marriage and, if the marriage is entered in order to achieve other goals, then the marriage is null and void and is called 'a fictive marriage'. The Inheritance Act equalises the community of life broken up without the fault of the surviving spouse or based on their agreement with the 'fictive marriage', as regards inheritance. The only difference is that the substantial condition for a valid marriage, ie the community of life, disappears later during the marriage, while, from the beginning (ab initio), that condition does not exist when the marriage is fictive.

IV   DEVIATIONS FROM THE REGULAR RULES OF STATUTORY (INTESTATE) INHERITANCE

In the situations provided for by the Inheritance Act there are possibilities to deviate from the regular rules of inheritance. The Inheritance Act provides for two kinds of deviations. The first one refers to the reduction of the inheritance share of a spouse, while the second one refers to the augmentation of the inheritance share.

(a)   The reduction of the inheritance share

The reduction of the inheritance share of a spouse may occur when a spouse inherits in the first and second order of succession.

(b)   A spouse as an heir of the first order of inheritance

The legal conditions for the possibility of the reduction of the inheritance share of a surviving spouse in the first order of succession are as follows:[26]

---

[26]   Inheritance Act, art 9(3).

(1) that a decedent has a child whose other parent is not a surviving spouse, which means that the decedent has a child from a previous marriage or a child born out of wedlock. At least one of the previously mentioned children must be alive after the death of the decedent. If there are no surviving children but only their offspring, the regular rules will be applicable;

(2) that the separate property of a surviving spouse is greater than his or her inheritance share that the survivor would inherit according to the ordinary rules, ie if the succession would have been divided in equal shares;

(3) that the court, after considering all the circumstances, appraised that it is justified. For example, if all the decedent's children are older persons with good financial standing, the court can assess that there is no need to increase their inheritance share at the expense of the inheritance share of the spouse because it would not be justified.[27]

Otherwise, if all three mentioned conditions are met, then each child may get a greater part than a spouse. The children's shares may be augmented until they get twice as much as the spouse. The court shall, taking into account the individual circumstances of each case, decide how much the reduction of the inheritance share of a spouse and the augmentation of the share of the children should be. If one of the children is underage, the court can decide on the reduction of the share of a spouse ex officio, without any requests.[28] If all children are of full age, the court cannot reduce the inheritance share of a surviving spouse and increase the inheritance share of children without the request of an entitled heir. Although this is not explicitly regulated by the Inheritance Act, this results from the Constitution, which provides for a child to enjoy special protection, in accordance with the law.[29] Therefore, the court shall ex officio take care of the special protection of the rights of a child in any court proceedings, implying that a child is every person younger than 18 years.

(c) A spouse as an heir of the second order of inheritance

If a spouse inherits with the parents of a decedent, his or her inheritance share may be reduced under two different circumstances.

First, when a spouse is invited to inherit with the heirs of the second order of succession and the decedent's inherited property is greater than a half of his or her separate property. In this case, the heirs of the second order may, within one year from the decedent's death, require the reduction of the spouse's

---

27   O Antić and Z Balinovac, above n 23, p 132.
28   O Antić *Nasledno pravo* (Beograd, 2007) str 124 [*Inheritance Law* (Belgrade, 2007) p 124]. Contrary to this opinion, Prof Svorcan thinks that the court may not ex officio reduce the inheritance share of a surviving spouse without the request of the child. See further, S Svorcan *Nasledno pravo* (Kragujevac, 2006) str 151 [*Inheritance law* (Kragujevac, 2006) p 151].
29   Article 66(1) of the Constitution.

inheritance to a quarter of the inheritance, if the community of life between a decedent and the surviving spouse did not last a long time.[30] This also means that they do not have common children, because in that case a spouse would inherit as a heir of the first order. The purpose of this provision is to prevent the transition of the property, which was perhaps created by generations of ancestors of the decedent before his or her death, to the surviving spouse, especially because their marriage lasted a short time and they did not have common children. In deciding on the scope of the reduction of the spouse's inheritance, the probate court estimates the value of the inherited assets and the duration of cohabitation of the decedent and the surviving spouse. The increased share will be assigned only to an heir who requested it. However, a spouse is entitled to choose whether to inherit a part of the property in kind up to one-quarter or to accept a lifetime usufruct on half of the property. As long as the court does not decide the claim of other heirs, a spouse can make a choice between a greater part in the lifetime usufruct and a smaller part in the ownership of property in kind. If a spouse dies before making a statement on the choice, his or her heirs can only inherit the property in kind.

Secondly, when a spouse is invited to inherit with the decedent's parents, who are very poor and do not have the necessary means for existence, the decedent's parents may, within one year of the decedent's death, request a lifetime usufruct on the whole or a part of the property inherited by a spouse.[31] When the value of the inheritance is so small that its division can lead the decedent's parents into poverty, they can request that they inherit the entire inheritance. In deciding on the request of the decedent's parents, the court shall take into account the financial status and working capacity of the parents, of the surviving spouse and the offspring of the parent who cannot or does not want to inherit, the duration of cohabitation of the decedent and the spouse and the value of the inheritance. This case is different from the previous one, not only in that the inheritance share of the surviving spouse may be reduced, but also because the survivor may lose the whole inheritance in favour of the decedent's parents.

As I have already mentioned, the Inheritance Act also provides for the possibility of augmenting the inheritance share of a surviving spouse. This may occur if a surviving spouse is so poor that he or she cannot provide the necessary means for living. In this situation, a surviving spouse, who will inherit with the heirs of the second order of succession, may, within one year from the death of a decedent, request the right to a lifetime usufruct on the whole or a part of the property inherited by the other heirs of the second order of succession.[32] Similarly to the previous situation, when the parents of a decedent are very poor and the value of the inheritance is so small that its division can lead them into poverty, in this situation the surviving spouse may request not only to get the ususfruct on the entire inheritance but to inherit the entire inheritance in kind. In deciding on the request of the surviving spouse, the

---

[30] Inheritance Act, art 26.
[31] Inheritance Act, art 31.
[32] Inheritance Act, art 23.

court shall take into account the duration of cohabitation of the decedent and the spouse, the value of the property, the working ability of the surviving spouse and other heirs, and the value of the inheritance.

The augmentation of the inheritance share of the surviving spouse can happen only within the second order of inheritance and never in the first order, when a surviving spouse will inherit with the decedent's children and other offspring.

V THE LEGAL INHERITANCE REGIME FOR HOUSEHOLD ITEMS

The Inheritance Act prescribes a two-fold regime for household items, depending on their value. If the household items are not significantly valuable, they will not be included in the inheritance and then a special regime is provided, and vice versa.

A surviving spouse is included in the circle of privileged persons who may hold on to items of the common household, which are excluded from inheritance. Thus, the items of the common household which are not of a great value (furniture, bedding, cutlery, etc) and are used in the everyday life of the descendants, the spouse of the decedent and his or her parents, are not included in the inheritance. These items become a common property of these persons who lived with the decedent in the same household, no matter whether they are the heirs in the particular case.[33] The above-mentioned members of the common household of a decedent continue to use these houshold items, as they used them during the decedent's life.

On the other hand, household items which have a greater value and yet serve the everyday needs of a spouse and other heirs who were living in the same household as the decedent cannot be exempt from the inheritance because they are included in the property suitable for inheritance. However, a surviving spouse and other heirs who were living together in the same household may instead request that these household items belong to them in place of their inheritance share. If the value of these items exceeds the value of the inheritance share, the heir who inherited them must pay the difference to the other heirs, within a period determined by the court as appropriate according to the particular circumstances.[34]

---

[33] For example, if a grandchild of the decedent has lived in the decedent's household because his or her parents are employed abroad, the grandchild will not be an heir, since his or her parents are alive and they will inherit, but the child will be a holder of the right to use the said household items together with the other members of the decedent's household (art 1(3) of the Inheritance Act).

[34] Inheritance Act, art 234.

VI A SPOUSE AS A TESTAMENTARY HEIR

A testator may leave the available part of the inheritance to any person including his or her spouse, intestate heir or other, unrelated person. This is not debatable. However, the question is what happens if a testator became incapable of reasoning after he had written a will leaving property or a part of it to the surviving spouse. For example, before the death of the testator the marriage may end in divorce, the surviving spouse may commit adultery or other circumstances may happen under which the testator would have changed the will written before becoming incapable of reasoning.

In principle, the loss of ability for reasoning after a testament was written does not affect its validity. However, if the circumstances, which were the decisive cause for the testator to write the testament, have been significantly changed, the court may only exceptionally, upon the request of any interested party, repeal certain provisions or the entire testament. Given that it would be unjustified for the surviving spouse, as well as any other testamentary heir, to inherit from the decedent in situations when some significant changes relevant for the testator's bequest have occured, the testament can be revoked. Any interested person (usually they would be legal heirs) may request the revocation of the testament within 3 years from the date of its promulgation.[35]

The second case when the inheritance rights of the surviving spouse can be questioned is when divorce occurred after the drafting of a testament by which the testator left the entire or a part of the property to a former spouse. Since the testament is a revocable act, it would normally be expected that the testator, after the divorce, would revoke the testamentary disposition in favour of the former spouse. The testator can do that by deleting certain provisions of the testament, by the destruction of the testament, by writing a new will, by the disposal of a part of the property that was bequeathed to the spouse, etc.

What is the situation if the testator did not do so? Theoretically, the question is whether the court should recognise the right of the surviving spouse to inherit the former spouse's share (based on the testament), because the former spouse's marriage was terminated before the death of the testator, meaning that at the same time the effects of the testament regarding a former spouse should also be terminated. The Inheritance Act does not provide that divorce (or annulment) may have any consequences on the testamentary inheritance between the spouses. There are also opinions that the same rules which regulate the loss of inheritance rights of the surviving spouse in terms of statutory inheritance should be applied to testamentary inheritance.

However, in the opinion of some authors, a dissolution of marriage after the testator had written the testament in favour of the former spouse does not result in automatic loss of testamentary rights in relation to the former spouse, because this is not a matter of statutory but voluntary, testamentary

---

[35] Inheritance Act, art 80.

inheritance, which the testator can always change.[36] The same view has been expressed in our case-law.[37] There are also the opposite points of view, which emphasise that the testament should be interpreted according to the real intentions of the testator. When the real intention of the testator cannot be determined, the testament should be interpreted in a manner that is more favourable to the legal heirs or in favour of those to whom some obligations were imposed.[38] Hence, when it is not clear enough whether the intention of the testator was to leave the estate to the former spouse despite the divorce (or the annulment of marriage), the court has to summon witnesses in order to establish the real intention of the testator.[39] If we accept this opinion, then the principle of the revocability of the testament remains blurred and disputable, especially if the testator, before death, has not been prevented from revoking it.

VII A SPOUSE AS A PROTECTED (NECESSARY) HEIR

As already mentioned, the testator is not completely free to dispose of his or her estate by will because one part of it has to be left to the closest relatives and the surviving spouse. The part of the inheritance which the testator cannot dispose of post mortem is called the protected share or the necessary portion and the heirs whom the protected shares favour are called the protected heirs or the necessary heirs. In the first inheritance order, the protected heirs are all offspring of the decedent and the surviving spouse. Their protected share is always one-half of the statutory share, ie one-half of the estate they would inherit if there is no testament. In the second order the surviving spouse has a privileged position since his or her protected share is also one-half of the statutory share, while the other protected heirs have a smaller share. Besides, the circle of the other protected heirs in the second order is much narrower than the circle of statutory heirs and includes the parents of the decedent and his or her siblings, half-brothers and half-sisters, but not their offspring. Except for the parents, other heirs of the second inheritance order (brothers, sisters, half-brothers and half-sisters) can be the protected heirs only if they meet the statutory requirements. These supplementary requirements are that a brother or a sister are incapable of working and do not have enough money for their livelihood. Their protected share amounts to one-third of the statutory share.

If there are no more surviving heirs in the second inheritance order, except a spouse, he or she may receive one-half of the entire inheritance on behalf of the protected share, since the protected share of the surviving spouse is one-half of his or her statutory share, irrespective of the inheritance order in which the spouse will inherit.

---

[36] See O Cvejić Jančić *Porodično pravo* (Novi Sad, 2009) str 201-202 [*Family Law* (Novi Sad, 2009) pp 201-202].

[37] The decision of the Supreme Court of Serbia, No Gž 915/1964, taken from B Blagojevic and O Antic, above n 13, p 307.

[38] Inheritance Act, art 135.

[39] O Antic, above n 28, pp 261-262.

The protected share may be affected by testamentary dispositions or by gifts which the testator made during his or her life. In such cases, a protected heir may submit a claim to the court for the recognition of the right to the protected share. The legal nature of the protected share under Serbian law is, in principle, in the form of monetary compensation. Only exceptionally may a protected heir request the reduction of testamentary dispositions or the return of the gifts in order to satisfy the necessary shares in kind instead of the reception of monetary compensation.[40] The deadline in which the request must be submitted to the court is 3 years from the promulgation of the will if the protected share was affected by the will or 3 years from the death of the testator if the protected share was affected by gifts.[41]

VIII   CONCLUDING REMARKS

We may say that the inheritance status of the surviving spouse under Serbian law is very favourable, especially in comparison with the inheritance rights before WWII. Before the war the surviving spouse could only receive the usufruct, which lasted until death or remarriage. The surviving spouse could never receive a part of the inheritance by way of ownership.

Under modern Serbian law, the surviving spouse may inherit as the heir of the first and the second inheritance orders. In the first order, the spouse has equal status with the children of the decedent and will receive the same share as each child. In the second order, the surviving spouse has a privileged status because his or her share is one-half of the inheritance, while other heirs (the parents of the decedent) will divide the second half.

In some cases the inheritnace share of the surviving spouse may be reduced or augmented, under conditions prescribed by the law. The surviving spouse is also the protected heir and may, in respect of that protected share, receive one-half of the statutory share. Cohabitants, irrespective of whether they are of different or the same sex, do not have any inheritance rights.

---

[40]   Upon the request of the protected heirs, the court may decide that they receive part of the estate which is a part of the inheritance instead of monetary compensation, or the testator may decide in the will that the protected heir should receive a real part of inheritance.

[41]   Inheritance Act, arts 58–59.

South Korea

THE ADOPTION SYSTEM OF KOREA AND ITS PROBLEMS

Youmee Kim[*]

Résumé

Le système coréen connaît trois formes d'adoption: l'adoption commune et l'adoption plénière sous le Code civil et l'adoption dans le cadre d'une législation particulière qui fait la promotion de l'adoption et qui en encadre la procédure (ci-après la Loi sur l'adoption). L'adoption commune se réalise par une entente entre l'adopté et l'adoptant. On considère généralement que cette forme d'adoption ne sert pas véritablement l'intérêt de l'enfant car ses effets sont limités. De plus, elle vise également l'adoption d'adultes. L'adopté ne peut prendre le nom de l'adoptant et l'accès au registre de l'adoption demeure ouvert. À la suite de pressions, le gouvernement créa l'adoption plénière en 2005. Cette réforme est entrée en vigueur le 1er janvier 2008. Par contre, l'adoption prévue dans la législation particulière est plus simple puisqu'elle ne nécessite pas d'autorisation judiciaire. Le problème avec ces trois types d'adoption est que le droit de l'enfant d'être entendu n'y est pas garanti et que l'intervention judiciaire est lacunaire. L'adoption commune ne devrait être possible que sur permission du tribunal de la famille, comme c'est le cas pour l'adoption plénière. De la même manière, un tel contrôle devrait être requis dans le cas des adoptions anonymes réalisées dans le cadre de la loi spéciale. Par ailleurs, en cas d'annulation d'une adoption plénière, le retour de l'enfant dans sa famille biologique ne devrait être possible que sur décision judiciaire. Le droit de l'enfant d'être entendu et l'intervention judiciaire devraient toujours faire partie du processus d'adoption car il s'agit de principes fondamentaux visant à garantir la protection de l'intérêt de l'enfant.

I   INTRODUCTION

Generally speaking, adoption systems around the world have changed from 'adoption for adults' to 'adoption for children'. The system of adoption in Korea has a similar history, but it is regarded as still not placing enough emphasis on the interests of the child.

It is difficult to say anything about the exact origin of adoption in Korea but from the Koryo Dynasty, adoption began to be regulated by law.[1] In those days,

---

[*]   Professor of Law, Department of Law, University of Ulsan, Korea.

[1]   AD 918–1392. Byungho Park *Legal History of Korea* (Korea National Open University Press, 1990) p 151.

the main purpose of adoption was the succession of family lineage and family property although adoption was possible for an abandoned child. Adoption in Korea is still characterised by these purposes and there have been many criticisms of this. In spite of some reformation, problems remain.

The adoption system of Korea consists of common adoption in the Korean Civil Code (KCC), full adoption in the KCC and the adoption in the Act on Special Cases Concerning the Promotion and Procedure of Adoption (ASPPA).

Common adoption is established by agreement between an adoptee and an adopter. It is regarded as an easy method compared with other forms of adoption because the requisites of common adoption are less constricted and it can be dissolved by agreement or by the court. But it is also regarded as 'not achieving the goal of the best interests of the child' because of its incomplete effect and provision for adult adoption.

Before 2008, an adoptee under common adoption could not take the adopter's family name although he or she became the child of the adopter in law. However, the registration of adoption was made possible, so most adopters in Korea registered the adoptee as their natural child. The Supreme Court of Korea accepted this as an adoption registration under certain conditions. However, many Koreans wanted adoptees to be able to have the same family name as their adopter and for the adoptee's relationship with his natural relatives to be extinguished. In 2005, the government finally created the full adoption system, which took effect on 1 January 2008. But the full adoption system is also regarded as 'not achieving the goal of the best interests of the child'.

ASPPA is a special law in the KCC. Adoption under ASPPA is more restricted, and its effect differs slightly from common adoption. In most cases, this system is used as an easy method of adoption because the permission of court is not necessary under this system.

The Ministry of Justice of Korea announced the reform of the system of adoption on 26 September 2010, and the committee for the reform of adoption is now working in Korea.

II COMMON ADOPTION UNDER THE KCC

(a) Requisites

(i) Agreement

There must be an agreement between two parties, an adoptee and an adopter. If there is no agreement, the adoption is a nullity.[2] If the adoptee is under the age

---

[2]   KCC, art 883(1).

of 15, the parent of the adoptee (or the person who has the right to represent the child) assents to the adoption on his behalf.[3] The guardian must give his assent to the adoption after obtaining the permission of the Family Court.[4]

(ii)   Requisites of an adoptee

The adoptee must be younger than the adopter. The adoptee must not be an ascendant of the adopter.[5] An adult can be an adoptee. Except for these two factors, there is no restriction on the qualifications of an adoptee.

(iii)   Requisites of an adopter

Any person who wants to be an adopter must have attained majority.[6] It does not matter whether the adopter is married or not and whether he has children or not.

(iv)   Consent

If the adoptee has not attained majority and he has neither parents nor any lineal ascendants, he must obtain the consent of his guardian, with the permission of the Family Court.[7] Even if the adoptee has attained majority, he should obtain the consent of his parents. And if such consent cannot be obtained from the parents due to death or another cause, the consent of other lineal ascendants, if any, should be obtained. In the case of an incompetent person, he may adopt a child or may be adopted upon the consent of his guardian.[8] When a person who has a spouse adopts a child, he should do it jointly with the spouse. When a person who has a spouse is adopted, he should obtain the consent of the other party.[9]

(v)   Registration

Adoption becomes effective when it is reported under the Act on the Registration, etc of Family Relationship (ARFR).[10] In the case of the registration of common adoption, adoption and the name of the natural parent are not concealed.

---

[3]   KCC, art 869.
[4]   KCC, art 869.
[5]   KCC, art 877.
[6]   KCC, art 866.
[7]   KCC, art 871.
[8]   KCC, art 873.
[9]   KCC, art 874.
[10]   KCC, art 878.

(b) Effect

(i) Incomplete effect

At the date of registration of adoption, the adoptee becomes the legal child of the adopter. The adoptee and the adopter have the duty and right of support and inheritance from each other. On the other hand, the relationship between an adoptee and his natural parents is not terminated. So the adoptee and his natural parents have the duty and right of support and inheritance. The adoptee is not completely cut off from his original family. Although the adoptee has two pairs of parents, the adopter's parental responsibility takes precedence over that of the natural parents.

(ii) The problem of family name and 'Bon'

In Korea, family names and 'Bon'[11] represent a sense of belonging. Generally, the family name represents the paternal bloodline.[12] Before 2008, the adoptee of a common adoption could not take the family name and Bon of the adopter. In such a case, the adoptee may not feel a sense of belonging after being adopted, and the difference between the adopter and adoptee's names makes the adoption obvious to outsiders. This can be emotionally harmful to an adoptee, especially to an adolescent adoptee. Most adopters in Korea register the adoptee as their natural child to avoid this situation. This false registration is illegal,[13] but the Supreme Court of Korea have accepted it as the registration of adoption under certain conditions.[14] From 2008, the adoptee can take the same family name as the adopter according to KCC, art 781(6).

(c) Dissolution of adoption

Common adoption can be dissolved by an agreement between the two parties, or by a decision of the Family Court. The adoptee whose adoption is dissolved returns to his natural family, and parental responsibility for the minor belongs once again to the natural parents. The effect of dissolution of adoption is not retroactive. But a marriage may not be allowed between a couple who were within the sixth degree of relationship of the adopter's blood relatives or within the fourth degree of relationship of the adopter's in-laws.[15]

---

[11] 'Bon' means the name of the place of the ancestor's birth or origin.
[12] From 2008, a child can take his mother's family name and Bon if the parent agreed to it at the marriage registration.
[13] KCC, art 228.
[14] Korean Supreme Court Decision 77Da492, delivered on 26 July 1977.
[15] KCC, art 809(3).

(d) Remaining problems

(i) *The necessity for permission of the Family Court*

Common adoption is established by an agreement. There is no intervention of the Family Court in the process of adoption except in the case in which a guardian's consent is required. But there is the possibility that the adoptee's parents consent or give assent to a minor's adoption for their own benefit, rather than in the minor's interest. In this situation, the minor adoptee could become a beggar or be exploited[16] or exposed to human traffic. Apart from the abandonment of the care of a child, neither the government nor the court intervenes in the process of adoption.[17] Therefore permission from the Family Court should accompany the consent of the parent to minor's adoption.[18] It is also right to demand such permission on the dissolution of the adoption of minors.[19]

(ii) *The consent of minor adoptees especially under the age of 15*

In common adoption, the adoptee of 15 years or over can agree with the adopter although he should obtain his parent's consent. But in the case of an adoptee under the age of 15, he does not have the opportunity to express his opinion about the adoption, because in that case, only the assent of the adoptee's parent is required. Even if the adoptee is under the age of 15, his opinion on the process of adoption[20] (including the process of dissolution of adoption)[21] should be considered in proportion to his age and maturity.

III ADOPTION UNDER THE ASPPA[22]

(a) Requisites

The ASPPA is a special law in the KCC. There are restrictions on the qualifications of an adoptee and an adopter in ASPPA, and the process of adoption in ASPPA is different from the process in the KCC.

---

16 So-called 'slave adoption': *The Korean Times*, 22 August 2001.
17 Sohye Hyun *Direction for the Advancement of Adoption Law* (Report of Korean Ministry of Justice, 2009) p 72.
18 Sohye Hyun, ibid p 72; Junghee Kwon 'Child Welfare and Adoption Law in Korea' (1997) 11 *Korean Journal of Family Law* 690; Junghee Kwon, 'A Study on the Consolidation of Adoption Law – Review of the Draft Legislation on Full Adoption' (2002) 16-1 *Korean Journal of family Law* 255.
19 Jinsu Yune, 'The Convention on the Rights of Children and Korean Family Law' (2005) 8 *Journal of International Human Rights* 34; Sangyong Kim 'The Problem and Solution of Adoption Law' (2009) 632 *Bubjo* 65.
20 Youmee Kim 'A Study on the Laws Relating to the Realization of Children's Rights' (1996) 10 *Korean Journal of Family Law* 419.
21 Sohye Hyun, above n 17, p 87.
22 ASPPA deals with international adoption too, but in this chapter only domestic adoption is discussed.

(i)   Requisites of an adoptee[23]

Only a child who is under the age of 18 and needs to be protected can be an adoptee.[24] Moreover, they must meet the requirements of art 4 of ASPPA. There are three ways of meeting these requirements. The first is where a person is deserted by a protector and for whose protection the Mayor/Do governor or the head of the Si/Gun/Gu makes a request to the assistance facilities prescribed by the Basic Livelihood Security Act, because it is impossible to confirm who is the person liable for the adoptee's support. Secondly, this article applies to children of a person who has been declared to have forfeited parental responsibility by the court, and for whose protection the Mayor/Do governor or the head of the Si/Gun/Gu has made a request to the assistance facilities. The third category is those persons whose parents (other lineal ascendants if the parents are unable to give the consent due to death or for other reasons) or whose guardian consents to the adoption, and whom the assistance facilities or an adoption organisation are requested to protect. Most adoptees in the last category are the children of unmarried mothers.[25]

(ii)   Requisites of an adopter

To be adopters, they should possess enough property to support the adopted child; they must observe the adopted child's freedom of religion, and have the ability to bring up and educate him as a member of society; they should live in perfect harmony with members of the family, and should not have any noticeable mental or physical impediment likely to affect the support of the adopted child; they should be eligible to be adoptive parents under the law of their domicile if they are not nationals of the Republic of Korea; they should meet such requirements as determined by the Ordinance of the Ministry of Health, Welfare and Family Affairs for the sake of the welfare of the child to be adopted. The adoptive parents should not force the adopted child to engage in any inferior occupations or other occupations which might infringe upon the child's human rights.[26] Those who are eligible to be an adopter should be aged 25 or over, and the age gap between the adopter and the adoptee should be under 60 years.[27] When the Family Investigation Agency accepts the suitability of the adopter's environment for bringing up the adoptee, the adopter need not satisfy these age requirements.[28]

---

[23]   ASPPA, art 4.
[24]   The term 'children requiring protection' means those who have no protector or are separated from a protector, or those whose protector is unsuitable for rearing children or incapable of rearing them, because the protector abuses them. Child Welfare Act, art 2(2).
[25]   Sohye Hyun 'The Problems of the Korean Anonymous Adoption System and Their Solutions' (2010) 50 *The Korean Journal of Civil Law* 555.
[26]   ASPPA, art 5.
[27]   Enforcement Decree of ASPPA, art 2.
[28]   Enforcement Decree of ASPPA, art 2.

(iii) *Consent*

ASPPA does not provide for an agreement between the parties as clearly as KCC, art 883.[29] It only provides for consent. Under an ASPPA adoption, the consent of the adoptee's parents should be obtained, and if his parents are dead or unable to consent for other reasons, the consent of other lineal ascendants should be obtained. If it is impossible to find his parents or other lineal ascendants, the consent of his guardian should be obtained. But in the case of an adoptee whose parents (other lineal ascendants if the parents are unable to give consent due to death or for other reasons) or guardian consents to the adoption, and whom the helping agencies or an adoption organisation are requested to protect, the consent to an adoption made at the time of the request for protection may be substituted for the consent to another adoption.[30]

Unlike adoption under the KCC, the guardian may give consent to adoption without the permission of the Family Court. This may be because the adoptee under ASPPA is usually a child in residential accommodation, whose guardian is the head of the residence, and there is less possibility of the head of the residence abusing his power to consent to the adoption, compared with other guardians.[31] If the adoptee is over 15 years of age, the consent of the person to be adopted should be obtained in addition to the consent of the parents, etc.

(iv) *Registration*

Adoption under ASPPA takes effect by making a report under the provisions of ARFR.

(b) Effect

Like adoption under the KCC, the adoptee and the adopter have the duty and right of support or inheritance. The adoptee has legal kinship with the adopter's blood relatives. The relationship between the adoptee and his natural parents is not extinguished. If the adopter wishes, the adoptee may take the adopter's family name.[32]

(c) Dissolution

The provisions concerning the dissolution of adoption in the KCC are applied to adoption in ASPPA.[33] But there is a restriction on the period in which litigation may be filed for the revocation of adoption. If the adoptee is

---

[29] There are competing claims in Korea whether adoption in ASPPA is a contract or not.
[30] ASPPA, art 6(1).
[31] Sohye Hyun 'The Problems of the Korean Anonymous Adoption System and Their Solutions', above n 25, p 557.
[32] ASPPA, art 8.
[33] ASPPA, art 26.

abducted or kidnapped, or the adoption is made by fraud or duress, this restriction on the period does not apply.[34]

(d) Remaining problems

(i) The possibility of anonymous adoption

In the case of an adoptee whose parents (or other lineal ascendants, if the parents are unable to give consent due to death or for other reasons) or whose guardian consents to the adoption, and whom the assistance facilities or an adoption organisation is requested to protect, the consent to adoption made at the time of the request for protection may be substituted for the consent to another adoption.[35] This consent may be a comprehensive consent because the consent was made under circumstances in which the adopter had not yet been determined. This prior consent for the quick progress of adoption has the risk of harming not only the right of the parent to participate in the process of adoption but also the welfare of the adoptee.[36]

The consent of parents etc should be made at the time of determining the adopter. When it is difficult to obtain the consent of the parents, etc at that time, there should be an exemption from the consent of the parents, etc.[37] Recently, there has been an assertion that there should be permission from the Family Court on an adoption under ASPPA.[38]

(ii) Consent of the adoptee under the age of 15

According to art 6(2) of ASPPA, an adoptee who is 15 years old or over must consent to the adoption in addition to the consent of the parents. Even if a child is under the age of 15, he may be mature enough to understand the meaning of adoption. To protect the children's right to express a view, the practice of requiring the adoptee's consent only once a fixed age is reached should be abolished, and the necessity of a minor adoptee's consent should be handed over to the Family Court.

IV   FULL ADOPTION UNDER THE KCC

Full adoption means adoption that makes the adoptee the natural child of the adopter for legal purposes. The relationship between the adoptee and his

---

[34]   ASPPA, art 9(1)(2).
[35]   ASSPPA, art 4(2) and art 6.
[36]   Sohye Hyun 'The Problems of the Korean Anonymous Adoption System and Their Solutions', above n 25, p 581.
[37]   Ibid, p 590.
[38]   Ibid, p 588.

natural parents is extinguished, and dissolution is much more difficult than that under the KCC or ASPPA.[39] The adoptee is registered as the natural child of the adopter.

(a) Requisites

(i) Requisites of an adoptee

An adoptee must be under the age of 15. This restriction stems from the idea that the younger the adoptee is, the easier it is to create a relationship between the adoptee and the adopter akin to that of biological parent and child.

(ii) Requisites of an adopter

The adoption should be made jointly by a husband and wife who have been married for 3 years or more. However, where a person seeks full adoption of his or her spouse's child, they only need to have been married for a year or more.[40] A couple belonging to a de facto marriage cannot obtain full adoption. The 3-year requirement comes from the idea that the 3 years of married life will ensure a stable environment for the adoptee.[41] In order to give the adoptee an opportunity to grow up in a sound family, adoption should be made jointly by the husband and wife.[42]

(iii) Consent of adoptee's natural parents

The opinion of the adoptee's natural parents should be considered because full adoption terminates the relationship between the adoptee and the natural parents. As the natural parents of the adoptee have the right of consent, it does not matter whether they have parental responsibility or the right of bringing up the child. But if such consent cannot be obtained due to the termination of parental responsibility, death of the parents or any other reasons, the requirement of consent is exempted.[43]

(iv) Assent of legal guardian

Assent should be obtained from the child's legal guardian.[44] When the natural parents are the legal guardians of the adoptee, they can give consent as parents at the same time as they assent to adoption as guardians.[45] If there is a legal

---

[39] Byungho Park and Youmee Kim *Family Law* (UOU Press, 2009) p 234.
[40] KCC, art 908–2(1)1.
[41] Soonhan Kwon *Family Law* (Fides, 2009) p 236.
[42] Rainer Frank 'Full Adoption (Adoption, Family and Welfare of Child)' (Sourcebook of a lecture at the Korean Legal Aid Center for Family Relations, 2002) p 15.
[43] KCC, art 908–3(1)3.
[44] KCC, arts 908–2(1)4 and 869.
[45] The consent of parents means the consent to the termination of the natural relationship, while the assent of a legal guardian means that they are parties in the adoption contract. Whasook Lee *Commentary and Assessment of Family Law Reformed in 2005* (Sechang Press, 2005) p 91.

guardian due to the death of the parents or any other reasons, assent of the legal guardian should be obtained after obtaining permission from the Family Court.

(v)   Request to the Family Court and permission of the Family Court

Any person who intends to obtain full adoption of a child should make a request to the Family Court after meeting the above requirements (adoptee, adopter, consent, assent).[46] The Family Court may reject the request if it concludes that full adoption is not appropriate for the welfare of the adoptee, considering the situation of the child's upbringing, the motives for full adoption, the competence of the prospective adoptive parents for bringing up the child and other circumstances.[47]

The Family Court must hear from some of the people who are associated with the adoption before granting its permission: the person who intends to be an adopter, the natural parents of the child to be adopted, or a legal guardian of the child to be adopted, or any person who is not the child's parent but has parental responsibility for the child to be adopted, or a legal guardian of the parents of the child to be adopted.[48] If the Family Court cannot hear from the natural parents of the child to be adopted due to death or any other reasons, it should hear from the closest lineal ascendant of the child to be adopted.[49]

(b)   Effect

(i)   Extinction of the relationship between an adoptee and an adoptee's natural parents

The pre-existing relationships of the adopted child before full adoption are terminated when a full adoption is ordered by the Family Court. But when a husband or a wife has obtained full adoption of the spouse's child as his or hers independently, the relationship of the child with the spouse and the spouse's relatives is not extinguished.[50] The relationship to be extinguished is not the blood relationship but the legal relationship, so consanguineous marriage is still not permitted.[51]

---

[46]   KCC, art 908–2(1).

[47]   KCC, art 908–2(2).

[48]   Enforcement Rule of Family Litigation Act, art 62–3(1).

[49]   Enforcement Rule of Family Litigation Act, art 62–3(2).

[50]   For example, if a husband adopts his wife's child, the relationship between the child and his natural father and his relatives is extinguished, but the relationship between the child and his natural mother and her relatives is not extinguished.

[51]   KCC, art 809(1). A marriage is not allowed between blood relatives (including the blood relatives of an adoptee before full adoption) within the eighth degree of relationship.

(ii)   Legitimation of an adoptee

The child adopted through full adoption is deemed to be born during the marriage of the adoptive parents. The adopter has parental responsibility over the adoptee. The adoptee and the adopter have the mutual duty and right of support or inheritance. The adoptee takes the adopter's family name unless the adopter agreed that their children would take the mother's family name.[52] It would be possible to change the adoptee's given name, too.[53]

(iii)   The characteristics of registration of full adoption

The child adopted through full adoption is registered as a child born during the marriage of the adoptive parents. The registration of the adoption and the names of the adoptee's natural parents are not accessible to the public.[54] An adoptee who has reached the age of marriage and wants to avoid consanguineous marriage can have access to the registration. And the registration is also accessible when there is written request from an investigative agency, or a request from the court to investigate a fact, or in other cases prescribed by the Rule of Supreme Court.[55]

(c)   Dissolution of full adoption

Because the adoptee is deemed to be born during the marriage of the adopter, there should be no dissolution of full adoption. The KCC provides that the articles on the dissolution of common adoption do not apply to the dissolution of full adoption.[56] On the other hand, the KCC provides special reasons for the dissolution of full adoption. It is possible to dissolve a full adoption where the adopter has abused or deserted the adoptee or has severely impaired the welfare of the adoptee and where it is impossible to maintain the relation of the full adoption due to any immoral conduct committed against the adopter by the adoptee.[57]

Full adoption is dissolved only by the decision of the Family Court. The Family Court may reject the request for dissolution if it concludes that dissolution is not in the interests of the adoptee, considering the situation of the child's upbringing, the motives for dissolution, the competence of the adopter for bringing up the child, and other circumstances.[58] Dissolution extinguishes the legal relationship between the adoptee and the adopter, and the relationship between the adoptee and his natural parents revives.

---

[52]   In Korea a child takes his father's family name if there is no agreement on the child's taking his mother's family name. KCC, art 781(1).

[53]   Kyungae Cho 'For the Improvement of the Full Adoption System (Based on Case Research)' (2008) 22(3) *Korean Journal of Family Law* 330; Soonhan Kwon, above n 41, p 239.

[54]   In common adoption, registrations are opened.

[55]   ARFR, art 14(2).

[56]   KCC, arts 908–5(2), 898 and 905.

[57]   KCC, art 908–5(1).

[58]   KCC, arts 908–6 and 908–2(2).

(d) Remaining problems

(i) Age of an adoptee

The government's original draft provided for the age limit of an adoptee to be set at 7 because the child's social life begins at school age in Korea. But during the deliberations this was changed to 15. This could cause some problems. If a widow remarries it will be impossible for the second husband to take full adoption of the wife's child if the child is over 15 years old. For example, if the widow had two children, one is under 15(A) and the other is over 15(B), there could be common adoption for B and full adoption for A. As said previously, A and B could take the same family name as their stepfather, but the registration of B cannot be concealed. Therefore it will be public knowledge that B was adopted. This could injure B's sense of kinship with either A or his stepfather. In the interests of the adoptee, it should not be necessary to limit the age of an adoptee.[59]

(ii) Consent of natural parents

The opinion of the adoptee's biological parents should be considered because full adoption terminates their relationship. But there should also be a limitation placed on the weight given to the opinion of biological parents of an adoptee in the interests of the adoptee. For example, when a natural father who abuses his child but does not have his parental responsibility terminated by the court does not consent to the adoption,[60] it would not promote the welfare of the adoptee to say that there should not be full adoption without the father's consent. There should be avenues for obtaining full adoption without the biological parent's consent if, contrary to the welfare of the adoptee, the natural parent does not consent.[61] For example, the decision of the Family Court could be substituted for the consent of natural parents.[62]

(iii) Hearing of the adoptee under the age of 15

The persons to be heard by the Family Court in the process of full adoption are: the person who intends to be an adopter, the natural parents of the adoptee, a legal guardian of the adoptee, any person who is not his parent but has parental responsibility for the child to be adopted or a legal guardian of the parent of the child to be adopted.[63] If the Family Court cannot hear the

---

59 Kyungae Cho, above n 53, at 314; Whasook Lee, above n 45, p 91; Jinsu Yune *Source Book of Public Hearing on the Revision of Civil Law* (Legislation and Judiciary Committee of National Assembly, 2002) p 22. There is another claim that to raise the age of the adoptee could be an obstacle to the psychological stability of the relationship between the adoptee and the adopter. Bonghee Han 'What is Full Adoption?' (2006) 8 *Mediation of Family Affairs* 183.

60 Whasook Lee, above n 45, p 90.

61 Kyungae Cho, above n 53, at 318; Whasook Lee, above n 45, p 91; Seungwoo Lee 'A Study on the Full Adoption' (2007) 19(2) *SungKyunKwan Law Review* (The Institute of Legal Studies of SungKyunKwan University) 182.

62 Jusu Kim and Sangyong Kim *Family Law and Inheritance Law* (Bubmunsa, 9th edn, 2008) p 349.

63 Enforcement Rule of Family Litigation Act, art 62–3(1).

natural parents of the child to be adopted due to death or any other reasons, it should hear the closest lineal ascendant of the child to be adopted.[64] The Enforcement Rule of Family Litigation Act does not include the child to be adopted as a person to be heard by the court. Full adoption impacts greatly on the adoptee; it terminates the relationship between the adoptee and his natural parents and changes the family name he has used, etc. Even if the child to be adopted under the age of 15 has not attained the capacity of an adult, taking his opinion into consideration would promote the adoptee's welfare.

(iv)   Dissolution for the adopter

Any immoral conduct which the adoptee has committed against the adopter can be a cause of dissolution of full adoption. This means that, although in a full adoption the adoptee is 'deemed' to be a child born during the marriage of the adopter, the adoptee is placed in a different position from the parents' biological children. The adoptee's position as a natural child is compromised. Taking account of the welfare of the child, dissolution for these causes should be strictly limited. The Family Court should reject a request of dissolution of a full adoption if the dissolution is contrary to the welfare of the adoptee.

(v)   The intervention of the Family Court in the dissolution of full adoption

If full adoption is annulled or dissolved, the adoptive relationship is terminated and the biological relationship is re-established.[65] This means that the dissolved adoptee returns to his natural parents. If the natural parents are not qualified to be good parents, the automatic return to the natural parents would be against the interests of the child. The natural parents may have consented to the adoption because they are incapable of bringing up the child or their parental responsibility had been terminated, and so on. The automatic return to these natural parents could result in not only harm to the welfare of the child but also a lack of care for the child. To avoid these situations, the Family Court should appoint a guardian for the 'dissolved' adoptee. This means that the Family Court should intervene in the process of the dissolution of a full adoption as in the process of the establishment of full adoption.

V   CONCLUSION

There are problems common to all three methods of adoption: lack of 'protection of the child's right to express views' and lack of 'intervention by the court' in the adoption process.

As the hearing from and the consent of an adoptee under the age of 15 are not part of the adoption process, the child's right to express his views is not fully

---

[64]   Enforcement Rule of Family Litigation Act, art 62–3(2).
[65]   KCC, art 908–7(1).

protected. An adoptee under the age of 15 must have an opportunity to understand the meaning of adoption and to express freely his opinion about the adoption.

Because common adoption is made by the agreement of two parties, there is potential for a child to be adopted for the benefit of the adults involved (adopters or the parents of adoptee), rather than that of the child. For the minor adoptee's interests, the Family Court should be involved as in the case of full adoption.

In relation to adoption under ASPPA, there could be an anonymous adoption according to art 6. As anonymous adoption can be not only an invasion of the parent's right to participate in the process of adoption but also a threat to the minor adoptee's interests, permission should be required from the Family Court for anonymous adoption.

In the case of dissolution of a full adoption, the adoptee returns to his natural parents, etc. The adoptee's parents may not be able to care for the returned child, so the automatic return to the natural parents may be against the minor adoptee's interests. Therefore, in the dissolution of a full adoption, there should be oversight from the Family Court.

It would be not excessive to demand the protection of the child's right to express his opinion and the intervention of the Family Court in the adoption process, for these are important factors in protecting the interests of a child.

Switzerland

TEN YEARS DIVORCE REFORM IN SWITZERLAND

*Ingeborg Schwenzer**

Résumé

Depuis les années 1970, la législation familiale suisse a été progressivement modifiée. La première étape fut relative aux règles sur l'adoption d'enfants en 1973, suivie des règles générales sur le droit des enfants en 1978 et de la loi sur le mariage en 1988. Le 1er janvier 2000, la nouvelle réglementation sur le divorce est entrée en vigueur après des préparatifs qui ont duré plus de 20 ans. Depuis lors, plusieurs modifications du droit de la famille dans le Code Civil suisse, ainsi que d'autres lois touchant à la famille, ont été entreprises et davantage sont en cours et devrait entrer en vigueur dans un avenir plus ou moins proche. Après avoir donné quelques éléments factuels sur le divorce suisse et la statistique familiale, ce chapitre donnera un bref aperçu de l'évolution de la loi sur le divorce au cours des dix dernières années depuis l'entrée en vigueur de la réforme.

I INTRODUCTION

Since the 1970s, Swiss family law has been amended step by step. The first step was the rules on adoption of children in 1973,[1] followed by the general rules on the law of children in 1978[2] and the rules on the law in marriages in 1988.[3] On

---

* Professor, Dr LLM, Basel, Switzerland, LLM. I am deeply indebted to my research assistant Adam Herzfeld, MLaw, for his help in preparing this chapter.
  The following abbreviations are used in this article:
  BFS (Bundesamt für Statistik) – Statistics of the Swiss Federal Statistical Office; SR (Systematische Sammlung des Bundesrechts) – Swiss Classified Compilation of Federal Legislation; BGer (Schweizerisches Bundesgericht) – Swiss Federal Supreme Court; BGE (Entscheidungen des Bundesgerichts) – Decisions of the Swiss Federal Supreme Court.
[1] Articles 264–269 of the Swiss Civil Code of 10 December 1907 (Schweizerisches Zivilgesetzbuch (ZGB)), SR 210, cited as CC; cf Message of the Federal Council of 12 May 1971 on amendments to the CC (adoption and art 321) [Botschaft über die Änderung des Zivilgesetzbuches (Adoption und Art 321 ZGB)], Bundesblatt 1971 I 1200 et seq.
[2] CC, arts 252–327; cf Message of the Federal Council of 5 June 1974 on amendments to the CC (child law) [Botschaft über die Änderung des Zivilgesetzbuches (Kindesverhältnis)], Bundesblatt 1974 II 1 et seq.
[3] CC, arts 159–251; cf Message of the Federal Council of 11 July 1979 on amendments to the CC (marriage law, marriage property law and inheritance law) [Botschaft über die Änderung des Zivilgesetzbuches (Wirkungen der Ehe im allgemeinen, Ehegüterrecht und Erbrecht)], Bundesblatt 1979 II 1, 191 et seq.

1 January 2000 the new rules on divorce law[4] entered into force after preparations that had taken more than 20 years. Since then further amendments to the family law provisions of the Swiss Civil Code (CC) as well as to other statutes relating to family law have been undertaken[5] and still more are pending and expected to come into force in the far or near future.[6] After giving some factual background on Swiss divorce and family statistics, this chapter will give a short overview of the development of the law on divorce during the last 10 years since the coming into force of the reform.

II FACTUAL BACKGROUND

Since 2005, the divorce rate in Switzerland has been around 50%.[7] In urban areas it can even be expected that two out of three marriages will end in divorce. In international comparison Switzerland thus is among the countries with the highest divorce rate. An even higher divorce rate may be found in Belgium, Denmark, Spain[8] and some of the US states. Switzerland has now even outrun many of the Scandinavian countries[9] which for decades were

---

4   CC, arts 111–149; cf Message of the Federal Council of 15 November 1995 on amendments to the CC (divorce law) [Botschaft über die Änderung des Schweizerischen Zivilgesetzbuches (Personenstand, Eheschliessung, Scheidung, Kindesrecht, Verwandtenunterstützungspflicht, Heimstätten, Vormundschaft und Ehevermittlung)], Bundesblatt 1996 I 1 et seq, cited as Msg Divorce.

5   Law on Registered Partnerships of 18 June 2004 [Partnerschaftsgesetz (PartG)], SR 211.231; Rules on protection against domestic violence: especially CC, art 28b (particularly para 2), art 123 No 2 Op 3 and 4, art 126(2), 180(2) Criminal Code of 21 December 1937 [Strafgesetzbuch (StGB)], SR 311.

6   Swiss Code on Civil Procedure of 19 December 2008 [Schweizerische Zivilprozessordnung (ZPO)], Amtliche Sammlung des Bundesrechts 2010 1739, cited as CCPr, entered into force on 1 January 2011; cf Message of the Federal Council of 28 June 2006 on the CCPr [Botschaft zur Schweizerischen Zivilprozessordnung], Bundesblatt 2006 7221 et seq, cited as Msg CCPr; Amendments of 19 December 2008 to the CC (adult protection, law of persons and child law) [Schweizerisches Zivilgesetzbuch (Erwachsenenschutz, Personenrecht und Kindesrecht)], Bundesblatt 2009 141 et seq, cited as Draft Tutelage, will enter into force probably in 2013; Draft of 2010 Day Care Ordinance [Vorentwurf Kinderbetreuungsverordnung (KiBeV)], www.bj.admin.ch/content/dam/data/gesellschaft/gesetzgebung/kinderbetreuung/entw2-d.pdf (accessed 20 September 2010); Consultation Draft CC (pension splitting in case of divorce) of December 2009 [Vernehmlassungsvorlage Schweizerisches Zivilgesetzbuch (Vorsorgeausgleich bei Scheidung)], www.bj.admin.ch/content/dam/data/gesellschaft/gesetzgebung/vorsorgeausgleich/entw-d.pdf (accessed 20 September 2010), cited as Draft Pension Splitting; Draft CC (parental custody) of January 2009 [Vorentwurf Schweizerisches Zivilgesetzbuch (Elterliche Sorge)], www.admin.ch/ch/d/gg/pc/documents/1661/Vorlage_ZGB.pdf (accessed 20 September 2010), cited as Draft Custody; Draft Adoption Ordinance [Vorentwurf Adoptionsverordnung (AdoV)], www.bj.admin.ch/content/dam/data/gesellschaft/gesetzgebung/kinderbetreuung/entw-adov-d.pdf (accessed 20 September 2010); Rapport and draft on legal actions against forced marriage [Gesetzliche Massnahmen gegen Zwangsheiraten, Bericht mit Vorentwurf], www.ejpd.admin.ch/content/dam/data/gesellschaft/gesetzgebung/zwangsheirat/vn-ber-d.pdf (accessed 20 September 2010).

7   BFS, www.bfs.admin.ch/bfs/portal/en/index/themen/01/06/blank/key/06/03.html (accessed 20 September 2010).

8   Statistisches Jahrbuch der Schweiz 2010, Zürich 2010, p 492 (T 21.3.3).

9   Ibid, p 493 (T 21.3.3).

known as being especially divorce prone. In many cases minor children are affected by the divorce of their parents, in 2009 all in all 13,789 children.[10]

On the other hand the marriage rate is on the decline and the number of births out of wedlock is steadily increasing. Although with 18% in 2009 the figure of children born out of wedlock is still very low in international comparison, it is remarkable that since 1990 this figure has indeed tripled.[11]

In Switzerland it is still the family and primarily mothers who have to look after their children. In 2008 only 3.7 day nurseries were available for 1,000 children.[12] With these figures Switzerland ranks last on the international scale. In contrast, in Denmark third-party childcare reaches 73%, in the Netherlands 45% and in Sweden 44%.[13] Many countries report having childcare facilities for up to 95% of children between 3 years and first grade.

The employment situation mirrors the lack of childcare facilities on the one hand and traditional role perception between men and women on the other hand. In 2009, in families with children, 89% of the fathers were full-time employed but only 15% of the mothers. Part-time employment can be found with 7% of the fathers and 61% of the mothers. Of the fathers, 4% were not gainfully employed, and 24% of the mothers. In families with children under the age of 6 this figure rises to 31%. Among single mothers 32% were working full time, 60% part time and 8.5% were not gainfully employed at all.[14] It does not come as a great surprise that in 2000, 90% of all single parents with children under the age of 16 were women.[15]

III GROUNDS FOR DIVORCE

Since 2000 the Swiss Civil Code in essence distinguishes between two kinds of divorce: divorce by mutual consent (CC, art 111, 112) and divorce without the consent of one of the spouses. The latter can be decreed either after a certain period of factual separation (CC, art 114) or because the upholding of the marriage appears to be unacceptable for the claimant (CC, art 115).

---

[10] BFS, www.bfs.admin.ch/bfs/portal/en/index/themen/01/06/blank/key/06/06.html (accessed 20 September 2010).

[11] BFS, www.bfs.admin.ch/bfs/portal/en/index/themen/01/06/blank/key/02/03.html (accessed 20 September 2010).

[12] BFS, www.bfs.admin.ch/bfs/portal/en/index/themen/20/05/blank/key/Vereinbarkeit/06.html (accessed 20 September 2010).

[13] Eurostat, http://epp.eurostat.ec.europa.eu/cache/ITY_PUBLIC/3–05122008-AP/EN/3–05122008-AP-EN.PDF (accessed 20 September 2010).

[14] BFS, www.bfs.admin.ch/bfs/portal/en/index/themen/20/05/blank/key/Vereinbarkeit/01.html (accessed 20 September 2010).

[15] BFS, www.bfs.admin.ch/bfs/portal/de/index/regionen/thematische_karten/gleichstellungsatlas/familien_und_haushaltsformen/allein_erziehende_muetter.html (accessed 20 September 2010).

Although under the old law most couples already agreed on divorce itself,[16] divorce by mutual consent was established as a ground for divorce only by the reform of divorce law.[17] However, in order to safeguard the institutional character of marriage the legislature intended to put up certain hurdles against hasty divorces.[18] According to art 111(1) of the CC the spouses have to appear before the judge who hears the parties individually as well as together. The judge has to make sure that both parties agree on the divorce as well as on the divorce settlement. Furthermore the judge must be convinced that the settlement can be approved. According to art 111(2) of the CC in the 2000 version the parties had to reconfirm their willingness to divorce as well as the settlement in writing after 2 months. This reflection period was looked upon critically from the very beginning, especially in cases where the parties had been separated for a longer period of time before they initiated divorce proceedings.[19] In a survey among judges and practitioners 73% voted against the reflection period.[20] Accordingly, as of 1 February 2010 this reflection period was abolished by the legislator,[21] which is but another step towards further facilitating divorce.

In cases of unilateral divorce, too, the legislator originally intended to build up a high threshold. After intensive discussions in Parliament unilateral divorce was made available only after 4 years of having lived separately (CC, art 114 in the 2000 version); otherwise severe facts had to be alleged to convince the judge that holding up the marriage could no longer be forced upon the claimant (CC, art 115). After the divorce reform entered into force, it did not come as a great surprise that the 4-year separation period was just too long for persons wanting to divorce. Thus, many spouses tried to circumvent the 4-year separation period by relying on art 115 of the CC instead. However, the Swiss Federal Supreme Court interpreted art 115 of the CC rather strictly and rarely conceded circumstances that led to a situation of hardship for the claimant.[22] It was only shortly after the divorce reform came into force that there was a parliamentary initiative to considerably shorten the period necessary for unilateral divorce.[23] Since 2004 only 2 years of separation are required before a unilateral divorce

---

[16] Sutter and Freiburghaus *Kommentar zum neuen Scheidungsrecht* (Zürich: Schulthess Juristische Medien, 1999) Vorbemerkungen zu arts 111–118 N 2, 3.

[17] Ibid, N 6.

[18] Ibid, N 5.

[19] Report of the commission for legal questions on the parliamentary initiative 'Mandatory reflection period and Art. 111 CC' [Obligatorische Bedenkfrist und Artikel 111 ZGB – Bericht der Kommission für Rechtsfragen des Nationalrates], Bundesblatt 2008 1959, 1966; Neue Zürcher Zeitung of 27 December 2000, p 10.

[20] Report of the Federal Office of Justice on a survey with judges, lawyers and mediators about the rules on divorce, May 2005 [Bericht über die Umfrage zum Scheidungsrecht bei Richter/innen und Anwält/innen sowie Mediatoren/Mediatorinnen], www.ejpd.admin.ch/content/dam/data/pressemitteilung/2005/pm_2005_07_01/ber-scheidungsumfrage-d.pdf (accessed 20 September 2010), p 7.

[21] CC, art 111.

[22] Steck 'Die Praxisentwicklung zu den Scheidungsgründe' *Die Praxis des Familienrechts* (FamPra.ch) 2004, 206, 215 et seq; cf, eg, BGer, 14 September 2000, 5C.85/2000, E.4 – *Die Praxis des Familienrechts* (FamPra.ch) 2001, 354, 355 et seq.

[23] Parliamentary Initiative of Nabholz of 20 March 2001 for shortening the separation period for

can be asked for.[24] The consequences of this change have been striking; whereas in 2001 out of a total of 15,778 divorces 494 cases were based on art 114 of the CC and 310 on art 115 of the CC, in 2008 out of 19,613 divorces 1,420 cases were based on art 114 of the CC and only 93 on art 115 of the CC.[25]

IV CONSEQUENCES OF DIVORCE

(a) Pension splitting

One of the central aims of the divorce reform has been the implementation of pension splitting in arts 122–124 of the CC.[26] The central principle is laid down in art 122(1) of the CC according to which all pension claims acquired during the marriage must be shared equally. There is no hardship or escape clause; thus it does not matter whether one of the spouses suffered any marriage related detriments in relation to his or her pension claims. Freedom of contract is not acknowledged in this field; in the divorce settlement a party may waive the right to pension splitting only if there is alternative sufficient provision for old age and disablement (CC, art 123(1)). Likewise even the court may exclude pension splitting only if it finds that pension splitting would be greatly inequitable having regard to the respective economic situation of the spouses after property division (CC, art 123(2)). Claims to pensions cannot be split once one of the parties is already drawing retirement or disablement benefits. In this case splitting is replaced by paying an equitable amount of money (CC, art 124).

Despite the prominent role given to pension splitting in divorce reform empirical studies have shown that in many cases where typically wives were entitled to pension splitting they waived this right and the respective settlement found the approval of the court.[27] In 50% of all cases no pension splitting takes place.[28] Thus pension splitting in many instances does not lead to the results envisaged by the legislator.

As regards pension splitting, a further legislative reform[29] is already pending at the moment aiming at more flexibility for divorce settlements and better protection of the entitled spouse in cases where the other spouse is already drawing benefits.

---

uniliteral divorce [Parlamentarische Initiative (01.408) Nabholz Lili: Trennungsfrist bei Scheidung bei Klage eines Ehegatten], *Amtliches Bulletin Nationalrat* 2003, 2129.

[24] CC, arts 114, 115.

[25] Steck and Gloor 'Rückblick auf 10 Jahre neues Scheidungsrecht' *Die Praxis des Familienrechts* (FamPra.ch) 2010, 1, 7.

[26] Msg Divorce (above n 4), Bundesblatt 1996 I 1, 2, 30 et seq.

[27] Baumann and Lauterburg 'Teilen? Teilen!' *Die Praxis des Familienrechts* (FamPra.ch) 2003, 745, 757 et seq; Baumann and Lauterburg in: Schwenzer (ed) *Fam Kommentar Scheidung* (Bern: Stampfli Verlag, 2005), cited as FamKomm, Vorbemerkungen zu arts 122–124 N 82–87.

[28] Isabelle Egli *Die Eigenversorgungskapazität des unterhaltsberechtigten Ehegatten nach Scheidung* (Bern: Stampfli Verlag, 2007) p 133 et seq.

[29] Draft Pension Splitting (above n 6).

(b) Spousal support

As in many legal systems spousal support is one of the most debated issues in Swiss divorce law. It was a real achievement of the reform of divorce law that it abandoned the concept of fault-based spousal support. However, the legislator did not succeed in introducing a clear and convincing concept of spousal support. There was much talk about the individual responsibility of each spouse after divorce, but also about post-divorce solidarity[30] and compensation of marital detriments.[31] The Swiss Civil Code in art 125 itself as it has been introduced in 2000 and is still in force, gives only a small guideline to make spousal support predictable. Article 125(1) of the CC states the principle that spousal support may be asked for only if it is not reasonable for this spouse to cover his or her own support alone. This principle is often referred to as the 'clean break' principle,[32] used in many legal systems in order to restrict spousal support. Article 125(2) of the CC contains a more or less haphazard list[33] of criteria to be considered when deciding whether spousal support has to be granted at all, and, if yes, for which amount and for how long. Finally, art 125(3) of the CC emphasises that spousal support that is otherwise due may be excluded in cases that could be labelled an abuse of right.

During the first years after the divorce reform came into force, the Swiss Supreme Court more or less continued along the lines of reasoning it had already pursued before the reform. In assessing spousal support practitioners were used to the following method:[34] in a first step the minimum needed for both spouses including the children has to be established, in the second step the possible relevant incomes are compared to the needs, and finally in the third step any surplus funds are equally divided between the spouses. However, if the divorced couple has children, sometimes a different formula has been suggested, since the children, too, should adequately participate in the surplus.[35] In 2007 however, the Swiss Supreme Court found this method of calculation to be inappropriate for the situation of the spouses after divorce because of the clean-break principle. It therefore rejected equal participation in the surplus, since, according to the court, the post-divorce earnings of the woman would suffice to establish the same living standard as during the time of marriage.[36] This decision was heavily criticised by the legal community.[37] This

---

[30] Cf, eg, Msg Divorce (above n 4), Bundesblatt 1996 I 1, 31, 44, 114.

[31] Ibid, pp 45, 114.

[32] Ibid, p 44; Votum Raggenbass, Amtliches Bulletin Nationalrat 1997, 2698.

[33] Vetterli 'Unterhaltsrecht quo vadis?' *Die Praxis des Familienrechts* (FamPra.ch) 2010, 362, 363.

[34] Schwenzer, FamKomm (above n 27), art 125 N 75 et seq.

[35] Schwenzer, FamKomm (above n 27), art 125 N 78; cf, eg, BGE 126 III 8, 9, E.3c; BGer, 6 June 2003, 5P.102/2003, E.3.2, suggesting a quote of two-thirds for the parent who looks after the children.

[36] BGE 134 III 145, 146 et seq E.4. – *Die Praxis des Familienrechts* (FamPra.ch) 2008, 392, 394 et seq.

[37] Aeschlimann 'Urteilsanmerkung' *Die Praxis des Familienrechts* (FamPra.ch) 2008, 295 et seq; Spycher '"Vereinfachte" Berechnung des nachehelichen Unterhalts oder das Kind mit dem Bade ausgeschüttet?' *Zeitschrift des bernischen Juristenvereins* 2008, 514 et seq; Hausheer 'Die privatrechtliche Rechtsprechung des Bundesgerichts 2007' *Zeitschrift des bernischen*

in turn prompted the Swiss Supreme Court to immediately withdraw its statement,[38] albeit only half-heartedly. It now stated[39] that, although spousal support should not lead to a financial continuation of the marriage, a division of the surplus might still be appropriate when dealing with long traditional marriages in the average range of income. Since then the Swiss Supreme Court emphasised[40] that no standard method of calculation should be favoured: instead it heavily relies on the discretion of the court in assessing spousal support.

Another field of long debate in Switzerland has been how to deal with cases of deficit, ie where the respective incomes of the spouses do not suffice to cover the minimum needs of the two post-divorce families.[41] Already under the old law the Swiss Supreme Court[42] ruled that any deficit should be borne by the claimant spouse which in practice is the wife. In contrast, the minimum needed by the earning spouse, in practice the husband, should be left untouched. The main reasons given for this position are that otherwise the wage earner would be discouraged from working and that the administrative costs doubled if both spouses had to seek welfare.[43] Thus it is the wife only who has to apply for welfare.[44] This in turn means that the welfare authorities may have a recourse claim to the wife's relatives for the full deficit covered by welfare. Likewise, if the wife herself earns more than the minimum at a later stage she – and only she, not the husband – must pay back what she received under the welfare scheme. All these arguments have already been brought forward under the old law[45] but the legislator could not be convinced to provide for equal participation in the deficit. A parliamentary proposition in this respect was explicitly rejected.[46] Thus it did not come as a great surprise that during the first years after the coming into force of the reform the Swiss Supreme Court adhered to this position. However, in 2006 the Swiss Supreme Court[47] seemed to signal that it would be willing to reconsider this hotly debated issue. The case involved a wife who during the time of separation had received welfare payments in the amount of CHF 81,000 – while looking after the 5-year-old child of the marriage. She wanted to have declared that in case of recourse by the welfare authorities the husband would have to share the costs equally. The Swiss Supreme Court rejected this request but indicated that one might

---

Juristenvereins 2008, 553, 568 et seq; Vetterli 'Zur Bemessung des nachehelichen Unterhalts – ein Klärungsversuch' *Aktuelle Juristische Praxis* 2009, 575 et seq.

[38] BGE 134 III 577 – *Die Praxis des Familienrechts* (FamPra.ch) 2009, 203 et seq.

[39] Ibid, E.3, p 204.

[40] BGer, 21 December 2008, 5A_384/2008, E.4.2.3 – *Die Praxis des Familienrechts* (FamPra.ch) 2009, 190, 195.

[41] Schwenzer, FamKomm (above n 27), art 125 N 31–34 with further references.

[42] BGE 121 III 301, 302 et seq E.5b; BGE 121 I 97, 99 et seq E.3; BGE 123 III 1, 3 et seq E.3.; BGE 126 III 353, 356 E.1a/aa; BGE 127 III 68, 70 et seq E.2c.

[43] BGE 121 III 301, 303 et seq E.5b.

[44] Sutter/Freiburghaus (above n 16), art 125 N 64.

[45] Ibid.

[46] *Amtliches Bulletin Nationalrat* 1998, 1187 et seq.

[47] BGer, 14 December 2006, 5C.77/2006 – *Die Praxis des Familienrechts* (FamPra.ch) 2007, 391 et seq.

consider 'deficit sharing' in the future.[48] The long-awaited decision[49] then was handed down in 2008. To the great disappointment of many in the legal community, however, the court retained its previous rationale. It is now up to the legislator again to finally solve the issue and it is expected to do so in the near future.[50]

Another important aspect of spousal support is just emerging: the special role of spousal support for the parent who is taking care of the children after the divorce.[51] In art 125(2) No 6 of the CC the necessity to take care of children is just one among eight different criteria to be taken into account upon the assessment of spousal support. There are no special rules applying to this kind of spousal support. That means that just as in any other case of spousal support it may be excluded if deemed to be unconscionable. It can be reduced as soon as the caretaking spouse is earning any money or when she or he remarries or even lives in a meaningful non-marital relationship, which is presumed after it has lasted for 5 years.

As regards the age of children when the care-giving spouse can be expected to seek employment and thus be responsible for her or his own support, the Swiss Supreme Court has been constantly applying the so-called 10/16-rule.[52][53] That means the care-giving spouse is expected to take up part-time employment as soon as the youngest child has reached the age of 10; once the youngest child has reached the age of 16 working full-time is expected. However, trial courts regularly fall well below this threshold.[54]

All in all, probably like in many countries of the world, in Switzerland spousal support is more and more losing acceptance. A field study revealed that in more than 70% of all divorces no spousal support was agreed upon by the parties nor ordered by the court.[55] Where employment rates among women are very high this mirrors the decline of marriage as a lifelong institution in support of women. Where however, as in Switzerland, gender role models persist in wide parts of society and childcare facilities are still frowned upon and,

---

48   Ibid, E.4 – *Die Praxis des Familienrechts* (FamPra.ch) 2007, 391, 395.
49   BGE 135 III 66 – *Die Praxis des Familienrechts* (FamPra.ch) 2009, 145 et seq.
50   Schöbi 'Unterhaltsrecht quo vadis?' *Die Praxis des Familienrechts* (FamPra.ch) 2010, 362, 376; a parliamentary Initiative of Thanei for equal treatment in case of deficit [Parlamentarische Initiative (07.473) Thanei Anita: Gleichbehandlung in Mankofällen] was rejected in May 2009, *Amtliches Bulletin Nationalrat* 2009, 931 et seq. However, in September 2009 the Federal Council recommended the approval of a motion which was submitted in June 2009 by the same National Councillor with the same purpose [Motion Thanei Anita (09.3519): Gleichbehandlung in Mankofällen], *Amtliches Bulletin Nationalrat* 2009, 1802.
51   Cf Schwenzer and Egli 'Betreuungsunterhalt – Gretchenfrage des Unterhaltsrechts' *Die Praxis des Familienrechts* (FamPra.ch) 2010, 18 et seq; Rumo-Jungo 'Betreuungsunterhalt bei getrennt lebenden nicht verheirateten Eltern – ein Denkanstoss, recht' *Zeitschrift für juristische Weiterbildung und Praxis* 2008, 27 et seq.
52   BGE 115 II 6, 9 et seq E.C3c.
53   Schwenzer, FamKomm (above n 27), art 125 N 59.
54   Freivogel 'Unterhaltsrecht quo vadis?' *Die Praxis des Familienrechts* (FamPra.ch) 2010, 365, 366.
55   Egli (above n 28) p 154.

consequently are rather scarce, this necessarily leads to many divorced women, especially with minor children, falling below the poverty line. In 2008 from the totality of households in Switzerland 3.6% were on welfare. Among single-parent households, however, the number of welfare recipients lies at 16.4%.[56]

(c)   Parental responsibility

Although on a comparative level the term 'parental responsibility' is being increasingly used, Swiss law still favours the term 'parental care'.

It was not until the divorce reform of 2000 that joint parental custody after divorce was formally allowed in Switzerland.[57] However, whereas in many countries joint custody nowadays has become the rule, in Switzerland the threshold is still very high. In art 133(1) of the CC the starting point is very clear when stating that the court assigns parental custody to one of the parents and makes provision for visitation rights and child support. It is rather seen as an exception that – by court decree – parents may keep joint custody after divorce.[58] Article 133(3) of the CC allows for joint custody if the parents have agreed on their relative shares in caretaking and child support and if the court finds that joint custody is in the best interests of the child. During the first year after the divorce reform came into force joint custody was decreed for only 14.7% of the children.[59] Soon however, the number started to increase. By 2009 it has reached 39.4%[60] which is still very low compared to international experience. In 2009, sole custody, which is still the rule, was given to mothers for 92.6% and to fathers for 7.4% of the children.[61]

In the field of joint custody, too, further legislative reform is pending. According to a 2009 draft bill[62] joint custody after divorce will become the rule.[63] This principle will also apply in case of non-married parents once the father has acknowledged fatherhood.[64] For the time being it cannot be predicted when this amendment will come into force. But finally, the law of custody in Switzerland will then be in line with what has been achieved in other countries since the 1980s.[65]

---

[56]   BFS,   www.bfs.admin.ch/bfs/portal/en/index/themen/13/22/press.Document.130367.pdf (accessed 20 September 2010).
[57]   Cf arts 156, 297(3) of the CC in the version before 2000.
[58]   Wirz and Egli, FamKomm (above n 27), Vorbemerkungen zu art 133/134 N 10.
[59]   BFS,   www.bfs.admin.ch/bfs/portal/de/index/themen/01/06/blank/data/03.Document.67609.xls (accessed 20 September 2010).
[60]   Ibid.
[61]   Ibid.
[62]   Draft Custody (above n 6).
[63]   Article 133(1) of the Draft Custody (above n 6).
[64]   Article 298(1) of the Draft Custody (above n 6).
[65]   Cf National reports on questions 15, 16, 20 in Boele-Woelki, Braat and Curry-Summer (eds) *European Family Law in Action*, Volume III: Parental Responsibilities (Antwerp: Intersentia, 2005) pp 265–297, 339–344.

(d)   Child's right to be heard

According to art 144(2) of the CC the court itself or via a third person has to hear the child. This provision is envisaged as implementing Art 12(2) of the UN Convention on the Rights of the Child. The Swiss Supreme Court has ruled[66] that as soon as the child has reached the age of 6 years it should in principle be heard. Although this threshold is still rather high in comparison to other countries[67] where children already at age 3 or 4 are heard by the court it is not even accomplished in practice. Judges are very reluctant to hear children and obviously have difficulties in acknowledging the child's right to be heard.[68]

To an even lesser extent courts order the separate representation of the child which according to art 146 of the CC should be considered especially in cases where the parents cannot agree on custody after divorce.[69]

V   DIVORCE PROCEEDINGS

Still in 2010 in Switzerland there exist 27 different statutes on civil procedure, 26 in the 26 different cantons and one for the Swiss Federal Supreme Court. To guarantee a minimum of uniformity the federal legislator set up certain benchmarks in the (substantive) family law provisions in the Swiss Civil Code. By an amendment[70] to the Swiss Constitution in 1999 that entered into force on 1 January 2007 the Federation now has the power to legislate for procedural law. The new Federal Code of Civil Procedure (CCPr)[71] entered into force on 1 January 2011. Divorce proceedings are comprehensively dealt with in arts 274–294 of the CCPr. These provisions are supplemented by arts 297–301 of the CCPr that contain special rules for procedures involving children such as the child's right to be heard, etc. In essence, the new procedural rules correspond to the former procedural rules laid down in the Swiss Civil Code[72] which are going to be replaced.[73]

Unfortunately, again the time seemed not to be ripe to establish specialised family courts in Switzerland. Although nowadays more than 50% of all cases in civil law matters tried before the judge of first instance are family law matters

---

[66]   BGE 131 III 553 – *Die Praxis des Familienrechts* (FamPra.ch) 2005, 958 et seq.
[67]   Cf the comparison with Germany in Sutter and Freiburghaus (above n 16), art 144 N 35.
[68]   Simoni, Büchler and Baumgarten 'Interviews mit den Richterinnen und Richtern' in Büchler and Simoni (eds) *Kinder und Scheidung: Der Einfluss der Rechtspraxis auf familiale Übergänge* (Zürich: Ruegger, 2009) pp 107, 115.
[69]   Schreiner and Schweighauser 'Die Vertretung von Kindern in zivilrechtlichen Verfahren' *Die Praxis des Familienrechts* (FamPra.ch) 2002, 524, 525.
[70]   Article 122(1) of the Federal Constitution of 18 April 1999 in the 2007 version [Bundesverfassung der Schweizerischen Eidgenossenschaft (BV)], SR 101; cf Message of the Federal Council of 20 November 1996 on a new Federal Constitution [Botschaft über eine neue Bundesverfassung], Bundesblatt 1997 I 1 et seq.
[71]   Above n 6.
[72]   CC, arts 135–149.
[73]   Msg CCPr (above n 6), Bundesblatt 2006 7221, 7359.

and despite numerous requests from scholars and practitioners alike[74] the cantons were strongly opposed to changing their court structure. This is all the more unfortunate as the reform of child protection and tutelage will order the setup of specialised interdisciplinary authorities and courts.[75] This leads to somewhat absurd results; in the case of children whose parents are not married child protection measures have to be dealt with by the specialised authority; if, however, the same question comes up within divorce proceedings concerning a child of married parents a non-specialised court – usually a sole judge – will have jurisdiction. The lack of specialised family courts will become even more obvious as more and more lawyers are specialising in family law by passing a special one-year training with interdisciplinary elements.

Although it was not possible in 2000 to make it mandatory for the cantons to introduce the possibility of mediation in divorce proceedings,[76] out of court mediation since then has flourished on a private basis in Switzerland. Many lawyers as well as judges have undergone intensive training in mediation. The Federal Code of Civil Procedure acknowledges these positive movements and for the first time establishes certain rules on mediation (CCPr, arts 213–218, 297(2)). In particular, it clarifies the relationship between mediation and court proceedings. Special importance is attached to mediation in cases of international child abduction. There, mediation is explicitly provided for in order to accomplish the voluntary return of the child or an amicable settlement of the case.[77] The parties involved therefore shall be induced in a proper way to engage in mediation.[78]

VI SUMMARY

The divorce reform that in 2000 entered into force in Switzerland certainly was not revolutionary. In many parts it followed the lines of what many countries had already enacted in the 1970s and 1980s. Family law reform in Switzerland is and will be a difficult business. As the matters to be dealt with are emotional and highly political there is always the danger that very conservative parts of society are able to raise the quorum to force a referendum. Thus a whole statute may be endangered and years of political compromises and preparation may be

---

[74] Schwenzer 'Braucht die Schweiz Familiengerichte' in Vetterli (ed) *Auf dem Weg zum Familiengericht* (Bern: Stampfl, 2004) p 89 et seq; Aeschlimann *Familiengerichtsbarkeit im internationalen Vergleich* (Bern: Verlag, 2009) p 133 et seq.

[75] Eg Art 440 of the Draft Tutelage (above n 6), Bundesblatt 2009 141, 164.

[76] Article 122(2) of the Federal Constitution in the version of 18 April 2000, *Amtliche Sammlung des Bundesrechts* 1999 2556.

[77] Article 3(1) of the Statute on International Child Abduction of 21 December 2007 [Bundesgesetz über internationale Kindesentführung und die Haager Übereinkommen zum Schutz von Kindern und Erwachsenen (BG-KKE)], SR 211.222.32, cited as SICA, in force since 1 July 2009; cf Message of the Federal Council on the SICA [Botschaft zur Umsetzung der Übereinkommen über internationale Kindesentführung sowie zur Genehmigung und Umsetzung der Haager Übereinkommen über den Schutz von Kindern und Erwachsenen], Bundesblatt 2007 2595.

[78] SICA, arts 4(2), 8(1) (above n 77).

lost. In the case of the divorce reform it was mostly the splitting of pensions that was desperately needed to come into force as soon as possible.

This explains why many questions – such as the reflection period and the separation period in case of unilateral divorce – were decided in a rather cautious and conservative manner. That they no longer conformed to modern views of family law is clearly shown by their being amended anew within a very short period of time after coming into force. The same applies to the question of joint custody after divorce and for non-married parents, which will be tackled soon.

All in all Swiss family law still remains rather status-orientated. This holds true for example not only for questions of spousal/partner support but also as concerns questions of parentage. It will probably take some more decades until marital and non-marital children will be put truly on equal footing in Swiss family law.

United States

CONSTITUTIONAL RIGHTS OF PARENTS AND CHILDREN IN CHILD PROTECTIVE AND JUVENILE DELINQUENCY INVESTIGATIONS

*Barbara Bennett Woodhouse**

Résumé

L'article proposé s'intéresse à l'équilibre à rechercher entre, d'une part, la légitimité d'investiguer dans le cadre de la protection de l'enfance lorsque des violences sont alléguées et, d'autre part, le droit à la vie privée et le principe d'autonomie familiale, lesquels ont une valeur constitutionnelle. Cette contribution envisage également les droits des membres de la famille dans le contexte de délinquance juvénile, c'est à dire lorsque l'enfant est l'auteur présumé d'un crime et non pas la victime. L'affaire *Camreta v Greene* est en outre particulièrement étudiée. La Cour suprême y a été interrogée sur le point de savoir si l'audition dans une école d'un enfant – simplement potentiellement victime de violences – par un enquêteur des services de protection de l'enfance accompagné d'un agent de police, sans avoir obtenu de mandat judiciaire ou d'autorisation parentale, constitue une violation du 4ème Amendement interdisant les fouilles et emprises injustifiées. Le délibéré est encore attendu mais les plaidoiries des parties et les mémoires abondants des intervenants volontaires illustrent d'ores et déjà la difficulté de concilier les valeurs de protection de l'enfance, de sécurité publique et d'autonomie familiale.

Dans une décision rendue le 26 Mars 2011, la Cour a déclaré la cause sans objet, laissant ainsi ouverte la question controversée du 4e Amendement.

I INTRODUCTION

This chapter will discuss contemporary issues in the United States implicating the constitutional rights of parents and children in child protective and juvenile justice proceedings. In many countries, children below a certain age are considered in need of protection and treatment regardless of whether they are the victims of child abuse or the perpetrators of a bad act. However, in the US, even very young perpetrators are often separated from their families and

---

* LQC Lamar Chair in Law, Co-director Barton Child Law and Policy Clinic, Emory University, Atlanta, Georgia.

sentenced to long periods of confinement in juvenile detention centres. In many cases, they are tried as adults and imprisoned with adults. Thus, the legal systems for protecting children and for prosecuting children both significantly impact the rights of child and parent to personal liberty and family integrity.

This chapter will trace the development of constitutional doctrines involving the fundamental rights of parents and children to be free from state intrusion in their family and personal privacy. It will describe the special legal system developed to handle protection of children who are suspected victims of abuse (the child protection system) and the systems for control of children who are suspected perpetrators of delinquent or criminal acts (the delinquency and criminal justice systems).[1] After discussing these systems' evolution and their similarities and differences, the chapter will then utilise the issues presented in *Camreta v Greene* and *Alford v Greene*, to explore the constitutional rights of parents and children during child abuse investigations conducted on school grounds. Children spend the majority of their waking hours in school. Schools become entangled in both the child protection and delinquency systems when children are victims or perpetrators of unlawful acts. In both the protection context and the delinquency context, there is a very real danger of the state infringing the rights of parents and children and there are also important child protection and public safety interests at stake.[2]

In US constitutional law, the Supreme Court must balance these individual and state interests in order to define the contours of parents' and children's rights and the boundaries of state intervention. Because the Constitution requires a live case or controversy, issues of constitutional law are litigated by individuals and thus cases focus on a fact-specific claim. To avoid the pitfalls of a narrow adversarial focus, interested non-parties such as NGOs and non-party governmental entities and legal or scientific scholars may provide information to the court through amicus curiae or friend of the court briefs designed to alert the justices to systemic issues that the parties may overlook. At the time of writing, the court has not yet ruled on the issues in *Greene* and it is likely, as explained below in Part III and at the end of the chapter, that the justices will find a way to avoid deciding the *Greene* cases on the merits. This chapter will

---

[1]   In this chapter, the term child protection system refers to the public systems for dealing with parental abuse and neglect. Delinquency refers to conduct that would not be a crime if committed by an adult, e g status offences such as running away and skipping school, as well as to conduct that would be a crime if committed by an adult (battery, theft, etc) but is handled instead as a civil matter in the juvenile justice system when committed by someone under the age of 18 or, in many states, under the age of 16. The term criminal justice system refers to the system for prosecuting and punishing crimes.

[2]   The docket numbers for the *Camreta* and *Alford* cases, which were consolidated for argument, are 09–1454 and 09–1478, respectively. The American Bar Association provides access to the texts of Supreme Court merits briefs, amicus briefs in these and other cases at www.americanbar.org/publications/preview_home/alphabetical.html. Transcripts of oral arguments are available on the Supreme Court's website at www.supremecourt.gov/oral_arguments/argument_transcripts.aspx (accessed June 2011).

examine the lower court opinions and briefs in the *Greene* cases and will also explore the more comprehensive background addressed in amicus briefs submitted in these cases.

II US CONSTITUTIONAL LAW AND FAMILY RIGHTS WITHIN THE CHILD PROTECTIVE AND JUVENILE JUSTICE SYSTEM

(a) The role of the Constitution in allocating authority and defining rights

The United States Constitution generally allocates responsibility for family law, juvenile law and child protection to the courts and legislatures of the 50 states. In the last century, as knowledge about the harmful effects of child abuse accumulated, states enacted child protection laws. By 1967, every state in the United States had enacted reporting laws and laws protecting children from abuse and neglect. The United States Congress, in Washington DC, while it is limited in its powers to enact substantive child protection and criminal laws, has the authority to pass laws providing funding for child welfare programmes enacted by states. In 1974, Congress enacted the Child Abuse Prevention and Treatment Act (CAPTA), which conditioned receipt of federal funds on compliance with certain standards. Amendments to CAPTA and other federal laws, which include the 1984 Adoption Assistance and Child Welfare Act (AACWA), the 1996 Adoption and Safe Families Act (ASFA) and the 2008 Fostering Connections to Success and Increasing Adoption Act (FCSIAA), have encouraged a certain measure of uniformity in these state child protective systems. These federal laws also allow substantial latitude to states to tailor policies to their own local needs and priorities.[3]

Of course, neither the states nor the federal government may enact laws that infringe fundamental rights. But the contours of such rights remain unclear in the United States. The United States has not ratified the United Nations Convention on the Rights of the Child (CRC) and has been wary of other global human rights instruments. Nor does the US recognise the authority of its regional human rights body, the Organization of American States, to bind US courts and legislatures.[4] While states parties to the European Convention on Human Rights look to decisions of the European Court of Human Rights for guidance,[5] courts in the US look to the Constitution of the United States to

---

[3] See Douglas E Abrams and Sarah H Ramsey *Children and the Law: Doctrine, Policy and Practice* (West, 4th edn, 2010) pp 284–287 and figure 4 for discussions of the history and functioning of the US child protective system.

[4] Barbara Bennett Woodhouse and Brooke Hardy 'Advocating for Children's Rights in a Lawless Nation: Articulating Rights for Foster Children' in Martha Fineman and Karen Worthington (eds) *What is Right for Children? The Competing Paradigms of Religion and Human Rights* (Ashgate, 2009).

[5] The text of the European Convention and information about the European Court of Human Rights are available at the Court's web page at www.echr.coe.int/ECHR/homepage_en.

determine when laws infringe the fundamental rights of parents and children. Unlike many modern constitutions and human rights charters, the US Constitution, drafted in 1789, makes no mention of the family or of the rights of children and parents. Instead, the job of interpreting the Constitution's broad principles in specific application to cases involving parents and children has fallen to the courts, with the United States Supreme Court having the last word.[6]

(b) Development of rights in child protection and juvenile delinquency contexts

Over the past century, the Supreme Court has handed down a number of important opinions with significant implications for the balancing of individual rights of family members and states' interests in public safety and child protection. For example, the court recognises that parents have a fundamental right to direct the upbringing of their children, but has held that the state may interfere with parents' autonomy if it is necessary to protect the child from harm. States may prohibit child labour, require vaccinations and enact mandatory schooling laws but rights of parents must be taken into account even in these contexts. Drawing a proper balance between the interest of the state in protection of the child and the interests of the parent in family privacy and autonomy has not been easy. Although the court does not always apply these precise words in it opinions, generally, a law or practice that infringes on parental rights must be given 'strict scrutiny' and examined to see if it is 'narrowly tailored to achieve compelling state interests'.[7] Children's rights are rarely mentioned in US legal decisions, but instead are framed as children's 'best interests'. It is important to note that, while states have the authority to enact and implement child protection laws, they have no constitutional obligation to do so. The Supreme Court has explicitly rejected the notion that children who are not currently in state custody have a constitutional right to protection from harm at the hands of their parents.[8]

Government may also displace parental authority and intervene in the family when parents are unable to control their children or when children pose a danger to themselves or others. Police may arrest and detain minors who disobey adult authority, commit status offences such as skipping school or running away or engage in delinquent acts – conduct that would be a crime if done by an adult. Since the early twentieth century, cases involving youths who committed such acts generally have been handled in special juvenile courts. Rather than being tried by a jury and found 'guilty' of a crime, youths were 'adjudicated delinquent' by a juvenile court judge. Reformers insisted that

---

6   Barbara Bennett Woodhouse 'Constitutional Interpretation and the Reconstitution of the Family in the United States and South Africa' in John Eekelaar and Thandabantu Nhlapo (eds) *The Changing Family: Family Forms and Family Law* (Hart Publishing, 1998).

7   See, eg, *Meyer v Nebraska*, 262 US 390 (1923); *Pierce v Society of Sisters*, 268 US 510 (1925); *Prince v Massachusetts*, 321 US 158 (1944); *Wisconsin v Yoder*, 406 US 205 (1972); *Troxel v Granville*, 530 US 57 (2000).

8   *DeShaney v Winnebago County*, 489 US 189 (1989).

children who were adjudicated delinquent be detained in youth facilities that embraced a rehabilitative and educational approach rather than being incarcerated in adult penal facilities.[9] Although delinquency proceedings, like child protection cases, are not technically criminal in nature, the Supreme Court has held that these proceedings trigger some of the same constitutional protections as criminal investigations of adults. The US Constitution in its Bill of Rights imposes specific limitations on investigations and trials of persons accused of crimes. The Fourth Amendment protects individuals from unreasonable searches and seizures; the Fifth Amendment provides protections against self-incrimination and rights to legal representation. Beginning with *In re Gault*, the court has interpreted the due process clause of the Fourteenth Amendment, which applies to civil as well as criminal cases, as extending to children in delinquency proceedings many of the constitutional protections afforded to adult defendants in criminal proceedings.[10] For example, minors in juvenile courts have the right to a lawyer and the right to remain silent. Unlike adults, suspects in juvenile courts do not have a right to trial by a jury or the right to post bail to avoid pretrial detention.[11]

(c)   US children in state custody: disparate numbers and disparate impact

The sheer numbers of children in state custody, either in foster care or in the justice system, has forced a re-examination of the impact of these systems on family rights. Both of these systems have a disparate impact on minority race children in the US. In 2007, the families of 1.86 million American children were investigated for suspected abuse. There were 720,000 or one in every hundred children identified by states as abused or neglected.[12] In 2008, at any point in time there were approximately 463,000 children in foster care in the US. Black children in the US are more likely to enter foster care than white children. While black children make up 19% of the US child population they make up 37% of the foster care population.[13]

While it is difficult to trace the precise reasons for these disparities, both poverty and discrimination are believed to play a role. High rates of removal of children from their families have a profound effect on low income American

---

[9]   See Abrams and Ramsey, above n 3, pp 953–966, 970–976, for a discussion of the history of status offences and development of separate juvenile justice system. See Thomas Grisso and Robert G Schwartz (eds) *Youth on Trial: A Developmental Perspective on Juvenile Justice* (Chicago University Press, 2003) for a social science perspective on the current system.

[10]   *In re Gault*, 387 US 1 (1967).

[11]   *McKeiver v Pennsylvania*, 403 US 528 (1971) (no right to trial by jury); *Schall v Martin*, 467 US 253 (1984) (upholding pretrial detention).

[12]   Christina Paxon and Ron Haskins 'Introduction to the Issues' in *Prevention of Child Maltreatment*, vol 19, no 2, Future of Children (Fall 2009), available at http://futureofchildren. org/futureofchildren/publications/journals/journal_details/index.xml?journalid=71 (accessed June 2011).

[13]   Fred Wulczyn and Bridget Lery *Racial Disparities in Foster Care Admissions* (Chapin Hall, 2007) available at www.chapinhall.org/sites/default/files/old_reports/399.pdf (accessed June 2011).

families generally and black families in particular. Despite the strong doctrines of parental autonomy and state non-interference identified by the Supreme Court, each year hundreds of thousands of children are removed from the custody of their parents and placed in protective custody with foster families or in state institutions. Under federal guidelines, if parents are unable to remedy the situations that brought their children into state care, states are expected to initiate a termination of parental rights (TPR) to permanently end the children's relationships with their families of origin and free them for adoption. Many gain new families through adoption but approximately 20,000 'legal orphans' turn 18 each year and graduate from the child protective system without any family to provide support and guidance.[14]

High volumes of detentions of youth and large racial disparities in arrest and detention rates are also evident in the US juvenile justice system. In 2007, for example, there were 1,928,200 arrests of children aged 10–17 and 148,600 children were placed in detention facilities. Although minority children made up less than 25% (7,494,000 of a total population of 33,328,000) of children aged 10–17, minorities were arrested at a far higher rate than whites (1,294,500 whites and 633,700 minorities). Of 148,600 cases resulting in confinement in a secure facility, whites represented 85,000 and minorities 63,600.[15]

In addition, the bright lines between juvenile and adult systems that were developed by nineteenth-century reformers were erased in the last decades of the twentieth century and the first decade of the twenty-first century. During those decades, the pendulum of popular opinion swung away from rehabilitation towards systems that treat juveniles as if they were adults.[16] All of the states have enacted laws allowing children to be tried as adults, in adult courts. These laws, often referred to as transfer laws, allow the prosecutor or judge to transfer the child from juvenile court to adult court, or allow the prosecutor to file initially in an adult court, if a juvenile of a certain age has committed a specific level of crime.[17] While some states have established a minimum age below which a child may not be deemed responsible for criminal acts, in more than half the states there is no minimum age below which a child cannot be prosecuted as an adult.[18] In 2008, an 8 year old in Montana who was afraid of being spanked was charged with first degree murder for shooting his father. In 2001, a 12 year old in Florida was charged as an adult with felony murder and sentenced to life in prison without parole for crushing a 6 year old

---

[14] The term 'legal orphan' was coined by Martin Guggenheim 'The Effects of Recent Trends to Accelerate the Termination of Parental Rights of Children in Foster Care – An Empirical Analysis in Two States' (1995) 29 FAM LQ 121.

[15] *National Disproportionality Minority Contact Databook*, 2007 case processing summary, available on the US government's Office of Juvenile Justice and Delinquency Prevention website at www.ojjdp.gov (accessed June 2011).

[16] See Laurence Steinberg and Robert G Schwartz 'Developmental Psychology Goes to Court' in *Youth on Trial*, n 9 above, pp 9–32.

[17] Howard Snyder and Melissa Sickmund *Juvenile Victims and Offenders: 2006 National Report* p 110, available at http://eric.ed.gov/PDFS/ED495786.pdf (accessed June 2011).

[18] Michele Deitch et al *From Time Out to Hard Time: Young Children in the Adult Criminal Justice System* (University of Texas, 2009).

during play.[19] The physical lines of separation between children and adults were also routinely breached. In 2009, over 10,000 children were held on any given day in adult jails and prisons.[20]

In most states, although the age of majority is 18, children tried as juveniles may be detained until 21. Children tried as adults may be subjected to the same lengthy jail terms as adults, up to and including life in prison. Unlike the vast majority of nations, until recently the United States allowed the execution of individuals whose crimes had been committed when they were under the age of 18. In *Roper v Simmons*, the Supreme Court held that this practice was 'cruel and unusual punishment' prohibited by the Eighth Amendment to the Constitution.[21] In 2010, the Court addressed, in *Graham v Florida*, the question of whether sentencing a defendant to life in prison without possibility of parole for an act committed before the age of 18 is also a violation of the Eighth Amendment. The Court invalidated as unconstitutional the imposition of a sentence of life in prison without possibility of parole for crimes in which no victim died.[22] Under the *Graham* decision, states may still sentence prisoners to life without parole for cases involving homicide even if the juvenile was not the actual killer.

While cases involving life without parole attract international attention, they are the most extreme examples of a larger phenomenon – zero tolerance policies towards children who break laws or violate school rules. Critics in the US have coined the phrase 'The School-to-Prison Pipeline' to describe how easily a child who breaks a school rule or gets into a fight at school may find himself charged as a delinquent and imprisoned in a juvenile detention facility.[23]

The borders between the schoolhouse and the courthouse are extremely permeable. In response to high profile school shootings such as Columbine and Jonesboro, and as part of the No Child Left Behind Act, Congress has provided funds to schools to station a police officer referred to as 'School Resource Officer' (SRO) on site in the school buildings.[24] The roles of these police officers in protecting children and enforcing school rules often shade over into pursuing accusations of criminal acts by children. For example, a

---

[19] See Debra Cassens Weiss '8 Year Old Boy Charged with Murder; Prosecutors May Seek to Try Him as Adult' (10 November 2008) *ABA Journal*; Barbara Bennett Woodhouse *Hidden in Plain Sight: The Tragedy of Children's Rights from Ben Franklin to Lionel Tate* (Princeton University Press, 2008) (discussing the case of 12 year old Lionel Tate).

[20] Todd D Minton *Prison and Jail Inmates at Midyear 2009* (US Department of Justice, Bureau of Justice Statistics, June 2010).

[21] *Roper v Simmons*, 543 US 551 (2005).

[22] *Graham v Florida*, 560 US (2010).

[23] American Civil Liberties Union *The School to Prison Pipeline* at www.aclu.org/racial-justice/school-prison-pipeline; *Federal Policy, ESEA Reauthorization and the School-to-Prison Pipeline* (joint position paper of the Advancement Project, Education Law Center, Juvenile Law Center, NAACP Legal Defense Fund, National Center for Fair and Open Testing, and Forum for Education and Democracy, March 2011).

[24] James E Ryan 'The Perverse Incentives of the No Child Left Behind Act' (2004) 79 NYUL Rev 932.

child who has a temper tantrum and hits a teacher or kicks a door can be charged with destruction of government property or assault on a school official and hauled into court. Two children fighting in the hall can both be charged with assault, adjudicated delinquent and placed in jail or under probation. If they violate probation, they will be confined in juvenile facilities. Many of these juveniles end up in prison as adults.

This background information on the US juvenile justice and child protective systems illustrates the importance of the rights of parents and children during investigations of suspected cases of abuse or delinquency. Investigations in both settings can lead to severe deprivations of liberty and lengthy and even permanent separation of children from their parents.

III *CAMRETA V GREENE* AND *ALFORD V GREENE*: APPLYING THE CONSTITUTION TO CHILD ABUSE INVESTIGATIONS

(a) The background facts of the *Greene* case

The cases of *Camreta v Greene* and *Alford v Greene*, which were consolidated for argument before the US Supreme Court, illustrate the difficulty of balancing state interests, children's rights and parents' rights. They also illustrate how the relations between parent, child and state may differ in investigating allegations that the child is a victim of parental abuse and in investigating allegations that a child has committed a delinquent act. The *Greene* case began in the State of Oregon, with a report that Nimrod Greene had sexually molested a young boy.[25] A report that a child has been molested by someone outside the family triggers a criminal investigation aimed at finding and arresting the perpetrator. The parents who reported that Nimrod Greene had molested their son also reported that Sarah Greene, Nimrod Greene's wife and mother of his two young daughters, had told them she did not like the fact that Nimrod made his 5-year-old and 9-year-old daughters sleep in the bed with him when he was intoxicated and did not like the sexual way he touched his daughters when they sat on his lap. The parents reported that Nimrod himself had told them that Sarah had accused him of sexually molesting his daughters. This sort of report of possible parental abuse, in addition to triggering a criminal investigation, triggers a civil child protective investigation aimed at assuring the safety of a child who may be at risk in his or her own home.

Acting on information provided by police that Mr Greene may have been molesting his own daughters, an investigator for the child protective agency, accompanied by a police officer, went to the school attended by the older

---

[25] The facts are taken from the appeals court opinion in *Greene v Camreta*, 588 F 3d 1011 (9th Circuit 2009) and from submissions to the Supreme Court available on the internet, see above n 2.

(9-year-old) daughter to interview her. It is common practice in many states for investigations to be conducted by a multidisciplinary team composed of a police officer and a social worker and/or medical professional. The interview took place in a closed room and accounts differed as to how long it lasted and whether the investigator's questions influenced the child's responses. Mr Camreta, the child protection investigator, concluded that the child's statements about how and where her father touched her indicated she may have been molested and decided to pursue further investigation. But when the team went to the Greenes' home, they denied there was any problem and claimed their daughter had been coerced into making statements that falsely suggested she was being molested and she had now recanted. Over the mother's objections, but with judicial approval, the child and her younger sister were evaluated at a local child protective clinic specialising in evaluations of suspected victims of child sexual abuse. The examination was inconclusive. The girls were taken into protective custody and placed in foster care and Mr Greene was charged with the crime of sexual molestation of the boy and of his own daughters.

The jury could not reach a verdict on his guilt. This is referred to as a 'hung jury'. In most criminal cases, the jury must be unanimous in order to convict the defendant, but a new jury may be impanelled and the case may be retried if the first jury fails to reach a conclusion. In order to avoid a new trial, Mr Greene entered a plea maintaining his innocence but admitting that the State of Oregon had sufficient evidence to convict him of the case involving the neighbour child. In exchange, the State Court dismissed the charges involving his daughters.

(b)   The Greenes' civil rights claim goes to the Supreme Court

The story did not end there. Mrs Greene, on her own behalf and that of her daughter, SG, brought a civil rights law suit in federal court against the investigator and the police officer claiming they had violated her constitutional rights and those of her daughter. She argued that the interview conducted at the child's school was an unlawful 'seizure' of the child in violation of the Fourth Amendment of the US Constitution. The Fourth Amendment guarantees the right of the people 'to be secure in their persons . . . against unreasonable searches and seizures' by 'government officials'. In general, searches and seizures require a warrant based on a judicial determination that there is 'probable cause' that a crime has been committed. However, the trial court held that an interview of a child at school falls under an exception to the warrant requirement and an interview may take place if the investigators have reasonable suspicion of child abuse.

Mrs Greene appealed the decision and the Court of Appeals for the Ninth Circuit rejected the trial court's reasoning. The Ninth Circuit commented that investigators must not treat the school setting as an exception to the Fourth Amendment requirement of obtaining a warrant or showing exigent circumstances before 'seizing' a child for an interview. Absent 'exigent circumstances' constituting a true emergency, the investigator must obtain a judicial warrant or obtain parental permission. However, the Ninth Circuit also concluded that the police officer and the child protection investigator were sheltered from civil liability by the doctrine of qualified immunity which protects officials acting in good faith. Thus, Mrs Greene and SG were not awarded money damages. Mr Camreta and Officer Alford, joined by the State of Oregon, petitioned the US Supreme Court to take jurisdiction of the case. Even though they had not been ordered to pay damages and were immune from liability, they argued that the Ninth Circuit's statements about the conduct of child protective investigations in schools established a precedent that would be detrimental to future child abuse investigations. The court granted certiorari and heard oral arguments on 1 March 2011. In addition to merits briefs by the parties, at least 28 amicus curiae briefs were filed by hundreds of different NGOs and professional or governmental entities.[26]

(c)   Reactions of the child advocacy and parental rights communities

The *Greene* case divided the community of advocates for children and parents along unusual lines and resulted in unusual alliances. Three different constituencies emerged with divergent perspectives: (1) the child protection perspective; (2) the juvenile defender perspective; and (3) the family rights perspective. The state officials and social workers in charge of investigations of child abuse believed the proper standard for an in-school interview of a child should have been whether there was reasonable suspicion that the child was a victim of abuse.[27] This standard had been used in several prior cases posing similar issues. It is also the constitutional standard approved by the Supreme Court when school officials question or search children suspected of violating school rules.[28] The standard for obtaining a judicial warrant is 'probable cause' – a higher standard than reasonable suspicion. The child protective agencies argued that probable cause that the suspect is guilty of a crime is difficult to prove without interviewing the victim, especially where the suspected conduct is sexual molestation. The child protection authorities claimed that asking parental permission in cases in which a parent was the suspect would be detrimental to the investigation and would allow parents to coach children on what to say and what not to say.

Forty states and many district attorneys, associations of school boards and other agencies charged with implementation of child protection laws made similar arguments.[29] They pointed out that, to be eligible for a grant under

---

26   The amicus briefs are available from the American Bar Association website under *Camreta v Greene* at www.americanbar.org/publications/preview_home/alphabetical.html (accessed June 2011).

27   See, eg, Brief of the National Association of Social Workers and the Oregon Chapter of the National Association of Social Workers as Amici Curiae in Support of Petitioners.

28   *New Jersey v TLO*, 469 US 325 (1985).

29   See, eg, Brief of the States of Alabama, Alaska, Arizona, California, Colorado, Delaware, District of Columbia, Florida, Georgia, Hawaii, Idaho, Illinois, Iowa, Kansas, Kentucky,

CAPTA, a state must submit a plan that includes an assurance that it has a child abuse programme in place that requires 'the cooperation of state law enforcement officials, courts of competent jurisdiction, and appropriate state agencies providing human services in the investigation, assessment, prosecution, and treatment of child abuse or neglect'.[30] The mere presence of a police officer, they argued, did not convert the interview of a victim into a law enforcement interrogation.

Other advocates for children, especially those who represent children in delinquency and school discipline cases, had a different perspective on the issue of in-school interviews.[31] They supported robust limitations on interviews of children in schools. They strenuously objected to the notion, advanced by the petitioners, that schools are different. One argument for the reasonable suspicion standard had been that being in school reduces the child's expectation of privacy and another argument was that schools stand in loco parents to children and should be free to question children much as parents might do. In the experience of these juvenile defenders, such in-school interviews could be used to coerce children suspected of crimes into waiving their constitutional rights to remain silent and to have a lawyer or a parent present during questioning. As the earlier discussion of the School-to-Prison Pipeline illustrates, they feared that any dilution of Fourth Amendment rights during in-school interviews in child protection investigations could have major spill-over effects in the context of juvenile justice proceedings.

Family rights advocates from both the liberal and conservative ends of the political spectrum filed briefs that argued that the questioning of a child without parental permission and in the absence of a judicial warrant infringed both parents' and children's rights to family autonomy. Advocates on the so-called 'liberal left' of the spectrum have long been concerned at the disparate impact on poor and minority families of aggressive child protective and delinquency investigations.[32] Advocates on the so-called 'conservative right,' while generally supportive of strict policies towards delinquent juveniles, believe that government investigations and seizures in connection with allegations of child abuse are too often groundless or based on bias against religious beliefs in corporal punishment. A number of groups have organised

---

Louisiana, Maine, Maryland, Michigan, Minnesota, Mississippi, Montana, Nebraska, Nevada, New Hampshire, New Jersey, New Mexico, North Dakota, Pennsylvania, Rhode Island, South Carolina, South Dakota, Tennessee, Texas, Utah, Vermont, Washington, West Virginia, Wisconsin, and Wyoming as Amici Curiae in Support of Petitioners; Amici Curiae Brief in Support of James Alford, Deputy Sheriff, Deshutes County, Oregon, by the Los Angeles County Attorney on Behalf of the Los Angeles County, The California District Attorneys' Association, the National District Attorneys' Association and the Arizona Prosecuting Attorney's Advisory Council.

[30] 42 USC § 5106a(b)(2)(A)(xi).
[31] See, eg, Brief for Legal Services for Children in Support of Respondents; Brief of the Legal Aid Society Juvenile Rights Practice in Support of Respondents; Brief for the Juvenile Law Center in Support of Respondents.
[32] See Martin Guggenheim *What's Wrong with Children's Rights* (Harvard University Press, 2005); Dorothy Roberts *Shattered Bonds: The Color of Child Welfare* (Basic Books, 2002).

around this threat to the traditional family and the authority of the parent in disciplining the child.[33] Some of the family rights amicus briefs analogised the in-school questioning of a possible victim with a seizure of parental property. Some argued that parents have a constitutional right to decide when and how their children will be allowed to discuss sensitive sexual topics and that even a brief questioning of the suspected child victim would infringe upon this parental right.[34]

As this discussion suggests, the list of briefs in support of Mrs Greene and SG included many strange bedfellows – the Family Research Council (a group focusing on protection of traditional family values), the Juvenile Law Center (an organisation advocating for recognition of children's rights) and the Rutherford Institute (a group advocating for a wide range of civil liberties and opposing the death penalty) all filed amicus briefs defending a strict application of the Fourth Amendment to child abuse investigations.[35]

Those arguing against the strict application of the Fourth Amendment often pointed out that differences exist between cases in which the child is a suspected victim or witness and cases in which the child is a suspected perpetrator.[36] They argued that school may be one of the few safe places in which a child can disclose that he or she has been the victim of parental abuse. Schools are legally obligated to report suspected abuse and to co-operate in investigations of abuse. In the view of these authorities, a brief initial interview conducted by a trained investigator in familiar surroundings and following professionally recognised best practices could be minimally intrusive and yet exceptionally valuable to an investigation of parental abuse of a child.

Several of the briefs focused very specifically on 'best practices' in investigations of child abuse. They argued that the touchstone of whether an interview of a suspected child victim of abuse is 'reasonable' should be its adherence to evidence-based methods designed to minimise trauma to the child while maximising accuracy of the information obtained. They marshalled scientific evidence of approaches that have been proved to enhance reliability and effectiveness of a child abuse investigation. Some of these champions of best practices were more critical than others of the methods used by Mr Camreta and Officer Alford. Especially problematic was the failure to video or audio tape the session. Without this widely accepted best practice meant that it was impossible to assess the validity of their version of the child's statements or to evaluate whether the child's recantation was credible. Clearly, a badly

---

33   See Brief Amicus Curiae of Eagle Forum Education and Legal Defense Fund, Inc in Support of Respondents.

34   See Brief for the New York University School of Law Family Defense Clinic, Columbia Law School Child Advocacy Clinic, the Bronx Defenders, the Brooklyn Family Defense Project and the Center for Family Representation, Inc, as Amici Curiae Supporting Respondents 12–14.

35   See Brief of the Family Research Council and the American Coalition for Fathers and Children in Support of Respondents; Brief for the Juvenile Law Center in Support of Respondents; Brief for the Rutherford Institute in Support of Respondents.

36   Brief for the Children's Advocacy Institute in Support of Neither Party; Brief for Cook County Public Guardian in Support of Neither Party and Suggesting Reversal.

executed initial interview can compromise the entire investigation. One argument made by parents' rights advocates, that parents have a right to be present during an interview, runs counter to the general consensus that it is essential to conduct the interview outside the presence of the parent.

As this author has discussed elsewhere, and many of the briefs highlighted, the situation is different when children are being questioned as suspects rather than as victims. Given the child's immaturity, parents play a unique role with respect to their children when the child is facing possible adjudication as a delinquent. They are also in a less conflicted position since they generally are not suspects themselves. Parents have a duty as well as a right to advise their children as well as a duty to protect them from harm. Parent, child and state all share a strong interest in assuring that parents are empowered to take part in the investigation, as parents are a crucial tool in delinquency prevention and rehabilitation. Seeking parental permission and allowing parents to be present during an in-school interview of a child suspect strikes a proper balance between the rights of parents and children and the maintenance of safe schools. Many states have enacted laws that require authorities to notify parents if their child is being interrogated or taken into custody under suspicion of a criminal or delinquent act. Many states require authorities to avoid questioning the child if the parent is not present.[37]

(d)   Oral argument at the Supreme Court: is there a case or controversy?

Greene may prove to be the beginning and not the end of the debate about questioning children in school. At oral argument, the Supreme Court justices showed a marked reluctance to address the case on its merits. To understand their reasoning it is necessary to know some procedural nuances of Article III of the US Constitution. Under the US Constitution, the federal courts are vested with jurisdiction over an enumerated range of 'cases' and 'controversies'. This has been interpreted as forbidding advisory opinions and requiring that there be a live 'case or controversy' in order for a federal court to rule on a case. Sometimes, by the time the case reaches the court, none of the parties has an actual stake in the outcome. In such situations, it will be deemed 'moot' and/or not 'justiciable' because it fails to present a live case or controversy. The framers of the Constitution wanted to make sure that both sides of a dispute would have strong incentives to argue aggressively for their positions.

At oral argument, the justices on both the political right and the political left grilled the advocates about whether there was truly a continuing case or controversy. Since Camreta and Alford, the defendants, in the civil rights case, were sheltered by qualified immunity, the Greenes had nothing to gain because they would receive no money even if they won on the Fourth Amendment issue.

---

[37] Steven M Reba, Randee J Waldman and Barbara Bennett Woodhouse "'I Want to Talk to my Mom": The Role of Parents in Police Interrogation of Juveniles' in Nancy Dowd (ed) *Justice for Kids: Keeping Kids Out of the Juvenile Justice System* (NYU Press, forthcoming 2011).

The Greenes' attorney countered that a ruling from the Supreme Court confirming that their rights had been violated would be a moral victory. When the lawyers for the State of Oregon and the lawyers for Officer Alford and Mr Camreta had their turn at the podium, the justices questioned them just as sharply about whether the defendants in the case had anything concrete to gain. The Ninth Circuit opinion finding immunity, which was not being challenged, already protected them from liability.

A decision in the case could issue at any time, and will undoubtedly issue by summer of 2011 (see note at the end of the chapter). Most court watchers believe that the Supreme Court will either dismiss *Greene* as improvidently granted or avoid addressing the merits of the Fourth Amendment issues through some other procedural move, such as vacating the part of the opinion dealing with the Fourth Amendment seizure of SG. If the Court takes this route, it will not be the first time it has stepped back from the brink of deciding a controversial case. Often, the Court allows constitutional issues to percolate in the state and lower federal courts before it weighs in with a definitive ruling. At present, there is a division among the federal circuits on the standard to be applied in such cases.[38] The law regarding in-school interviews of students suspected of violating rules and deciding when they cross the line into custodial interrogations requiring *Miranda* warnings and application of Fourth Amendment protections against unreasonable searches has also been in flux. In addition, there is a growing realisation that the movement towards zero tolerance and harsh approaches such as trying children as adults and incarcerating them with adults have been ineffective and actually counterproductive, leading to increased rates of recidivism. Consensus is emerging that too many young people are being tried as adults for non-violent crimes. A counter movement has gathered momentum across the states to repeal 'transfer' laws and to extend the jurisdiction of the juvenile courts to all persons under the age of 18.[39]

IV   BEST PRACTICES IN CHILD ABUSE INVESTIGATIONS

While the struggle for a proper balance is being waged at the level of constitutional doctrine, experts in child protection have been developing best practices for investigating allegations of child abuse. These procedures are especially important in investigating allegations of child sexual abuse. Rarely are there any witnesses to such acts, other than the child and the perpetrator. Often, sexual molestation which causes significant emotional harm leaves no detectable physical signs. Children are especially susceptible to leading questions and to the power of suggestion and they are also subjected to

---

[38] See *Tenenbaum v Williams*, 193 F 3d 581 (2nd Cir 1999) (prohibiting seizure of child at school without judicial order, parental consent or evidence of an emergency).

[39] Campaign for Youth Justice, State Trends: Legislative Victories from 2005 to 2010 Removing Children from the Adult Justice System, available at www.campaignforyouthjustice.org/key-research/national-reports.html (accessed June 2011).

pressure from parents or perpetrators to recant truthful statements. If not questioned in a victim sensitive manner, they may recant truthful statements or make false ones in order to be allowed to go home. Best practices, aimed at protecting children from traumatic and redundant interview situations and at assuring that information obtained is accurate and not the result of leading questions, could help mitigate the concerns of parents, children and the state.[40]

Careful training of interviewers to educate them about child development and cognition can minimise the use of leading or repeated questions that pressure children to say what they think the interviewer wants to hear. Audio and videotaping of interviews protects against coercive practices and also avoids the trauma of repeated interviews. If more in-depth investigation than a simple verbal interview is appropriate, it can be conducted at special multidisciplinary centres designed for evaluating allegations of child abuse. Called Child Advocacy Centers (CAC), these centres create safe places for children to be interviewed. Children are interviewed in a playroom furnished with toys and child-sized furniture by a single trained investigator and the interview is captured on videotape. Other interested parties can observe via closed circuit television and can speak with the investigator by phone and suggest follow-up questions for the investigator to ask. In this manner, all those involved can be sure what the child is trying to say without placing the child in an intimidating situation.

Practices that focus on avoiding unnecessary interviews, protecting children from trauma and assuring the validity and reliability of the information obtained may be the best means of protecting children from harm, while protecting the privacy rights of both children and parents. While a warrant has long been the gold standard for protecting adults from unreasonable searches and seizures, a child victim may be best protected by requirements focusing on the manner in which the interview itself is conducted. In the related context of the right of defendants to confront witnesses and fashioning rules that protect defendants without traumatising children, the Court has supported the use of technologies that did not exist at the time the Bill of Rights was drafted.[41]

In drawing this delicate balance, we should remember that innocent children are not always the victims – children who must be presumed innocent may be

---

[40] Among the many resources describing best practices are Hollida Wakefield 'Guidelines on Investigatory Interviews of Children: What is the Consensus in the Scientific Community?' (2006) 24 Am J Forensic Psych 3 available at www.ipt-forensics.com/library/ajfp1.htm (accessed June 2011); Theodore P Cross et al 'Child Forensic Interviewing in Children's Advocacy Centers: Empirical Data on a Practice Model' (2007) 31 *Child Abuse and Neglect* 1031; Lisa M Jones et al 'Criminal Investigations of Child Abuse: The Research Behind "Best Practices"' in *Trauma, Violence and Abuse* (Sage Publications, July 2005); US Dept of Justice, Office of Juvenile Justice and Delinquency Prevention *Forming a Multidisciplinary Team to Investigate Child Abuse* (2000) available at www.ncjrs.gov/html/ojjdp/portable_guides/forming/contents.html (accessed June 2011).

[41] *Maryland v Craig*, 497 US 836 (1990) (holding that the use of closed circuit television to enable children testifying in court to be in a different room from the alleged perpetrator does not violate the defendants rights under the confrontation clause of the Sixth Amendment).

suspects in a criminal investigation. Juvenile suspects should have a right to a lawyer and to have a parent present to protect them from coercive interrogation. While juvenile suspects facing the prospect of detention should have these rights during interrogation in a school setting, it does not necessarily follow that the Constitution requires the identical approach when the interview is of a suspected child abuse victim. Should child protective services have to show probable cause and obtain a judicial warrant (or obtain permission of a parent who may be the perpetrator of abuse or who may be protecting the perpetrator) before speaking with a suspected child victim? When the Supreme Court eventually decides this question, it is to be hoped that the justices will be influenced by multidisciplinary briefs detailing evidence-based best practices in both the child protection and juvenile justice settings and will be wary of establishing a sweeping rule in one setting that may have unintended consequences for children and families in another setting.

NOTE

On 26 May 2011, as this volume was going to press, the Supreme Court handed down an opinion in *Camreta v Greene* refusing to reach the substantive Fourth amendment issues because the case had become moot. Observing that SG had moved to a different state and would soon be an adult, the Court concluded that she lacked a sufficient stake in the outcome to assure a live case or controversy. However, Camreta and Alford continued to be affected since they were still involved in child protection in Oregon. The Supreme Court used its equitable powers to vacate the part of the 9th Circuit decision that had required a warrant or parental permission before interviewing a suspected victim in the school setting. As many court watchers had anticipated, the Supreme Court adroitly avoided becoming entangled in the controversy over in-school investigations of suspected child abuse, preferring to leave the issues to be further developed in the lower courts. While the decision is silent on the Fourth Amendment issues, the fact that the Court vacated the 9th Circuit opinion may signal some concern about applying the same high standards to interviews of suspected victims of abuse as apply to interrogations of suspected defendants. The decision, authored by Associate Justice Elena Kagan, with six other justices joining or concurring in her opinion, may be found on the Supreme Court of the United States web page at www.supremecourt.gov/opinions/10pdf/09-1454.pdf.